THE THERAPEUTIC RELATIONSHIP AND ITS IMPACT

A Study of Psychotnerapy with Schizophrenics

THE THERAPEUTIC RELATIONSHIP AND ITS IMPACT

A STUDY OF PSYCHOTHERAPY WITH SCHIZOPHRENICS

EDITED BY CARL R. ROGERS

WITH THE COLLABORATION OF
EUGENE T. GENDLIN
DONALD J. KIESLER
CHARLES B. TRUAX

GREENWOOD PRESS, PUBLISHERS
WESTPORT, CONNECTICUT

Library of Congress Cataloging in Publication Data

Rogers, Carl Ransom, 1902-
   The therapeutic relationship and its impact.

   Reprint of the ed. published by University of Wisconsin Press, Madison.
   Includes index.
   1. Schizophrenia. 2. Client-centered psychotherapy.
I. Gendlin, Eugene T. II. Title. [DNLM: 1. Physician--Patient relations. 2. Psychotherapy. 3. Schizophrenia--Therapy. WM203 T398 1967a]
RC514.R63 1976   616.8'982'06   76-14790
ISBN 0-8371-8358-8

Originally published in 1967 by the University of Wisconsin Press, Madison.

Reprinted with the permission of University of Wisconsin Press.

Reprinted in 1976 by Greenwood Press,
A division of Congressional Information Service, Inc.
88 Post Road West, Westport, Connecticut 06881

Library of Congress catalog card number 76-14790
ISBN 0-8371-8358-8

Printed in the United States of America

10 9 8 7 6 5 4 3

Contributors

Authors

Carl R. Rogers, Ph.D.*　　　　　Western Behavioral Sciences Institute, La Jolla, California

Eugene T. Gendlin, Ph.D.*　　　　Departments of Psychology and Philosophy, University of Chicago

Donald J. Kiesler, Ph.D.*　　　　Department of Psychology and University Counseling Service, University of Iowa

Charles B. Truax, Ph.D.*　　　　Department of Psychology and Rehabilitation Research and Training Center, University of Arkansas

Philippa L. Mathieu, Ph.D.*　　　Department of Counseling and Behavioral Studies, University of Wisconsin

Marjorie H. Klein, Ph.D.*　　　　Wisconsin Psychiatric Institute, University of Wisconsin

Contributing Authors

Byron L. Barrington, Ph.D.　　　University of Wisconsin Center, Wausau, Wisconsin

Vilma Ginzberg, M.S.*　　　　　Walworth County Counseling Center, Elkhorn, Wisconsin

Janet P. Moursund, Ph.D.*　　　　Michigan State University

Douglas Schoeninger, Ph.D.*　　　University of North Carolina

Norton Stoler, Ph.D.*　　　　　Dane County Mental Health Center, Madison, Wisconsin

T. M. Tomlinson, Ph.D.*   University of California, Los Angeles

Ferdinand van der Veen, Ph.D.*   University of Kansas, Lawrence, Kansas

Irene A. Waskow, Ph.D.   National Institute of Mental Health, Bethesda, Maryland

Commentators

Paul Bergman, Ph.D.†   National Institute of Mental Health, Bethesda, Maryland

O. Spurgeon English, M.D.   Department of Psychiatry, Temple University

William C. Lewis, M.D.   Department of Psychiatry, University of Wisconsin

Rollo May, Ph.D.   William Alanson White Institute, New York, New York

Julius Seeman, Ph.D.   George Peabody College, Nashville, Tennessee

Carl A. Whitaker, M.D.   Department of Psychiatry, University of Wisconsin (formerly of Atlanta Psychiatric Clinic, Atlanta, Georgia)

* Formerly member of the Psychotherapy Research Group, Wisconsin Psychiatric Institute, University of Wisconsin.
† Deceased.

Acknowledgments

The total number of individuals who worked on the program described in these pages comes to more than two hundred. They cannot all be named here, but grateful acknowledgment is made to all for the efforts they invested in the research.

Special mention must be made of the therapists who voluntarily, and without payment, contributed not only their time, but themselves, to the subtle and demanding encounter of working with hospitalized persons classed as schizophrenic. They also contributed hours of travel time, hours spent in dealing with recalcitrant recording machines, hours involved in working out effective arrangements with ward personnel. The whole program is indeed in their debt. Following are the names of the therapists who worked in the regular research design or in the "ward availability" project: Mrs. Helen DeBardeleben, Mr. Frank Farrelly, Dr. William Fey, Dr. Eugene T. Gendlin, Mrs. Vilma Ginzberg, Dr. Joe Hart, Dr. Philippa L. Mathieu, Dr. Janet P. Moursund, Dr. Allyn Roberts, Dr. Carl R. Rogers, Dr. Norton Stoler, Dr. Jack Teplinsky, Dr. Charles B. Truax, Dr. Ferdinand van der Veen, Dr. Albert Wellner.

The program was built on the cooperation of Mendota State Hospital —its administration, its research committee, and its staff physicians. We are particularly indebted to Dr. Walter Urben, Dr. Gilbert Tybring, Dr. Forrest Orr, Dr. Edward Petersen, Dr. Leigh Roberts, Dr. Bernard Bannon, Dr. A. Canfield, Dr. Anthony Coletti, Dr. Richard Thurrell, for their patient cooperation and help.

Dr. Robert Roessler invested a great deal of helpful and conscientious effort in interviewing all subjects in the research every three months. This work was completed by Dr. Rudolph Mathias. Their painstaking voluntary assistance is greatly appreciated.

Dr. Irene A. Waskow was very active in the initiation of the program. Later she served a most important function as critic of every research report, drawing upon her early knowledge of the design, and her research skill, with an objectivity which was aided by her being a thousand miles away.

Then there are those who were particularly involved in the research aspects—the psychometric testing, the development and use of rating scales, the collection, recording, analysis, and reporting of the data. Some of the most devoted and at times thankless efforts were contributed by these people. Outstanding in this group are Dr. Philippa L. Mathieu and Dr. Marjorie H. Klein, who carried a very heavy load, especially during the last years of the research. Others who made important contributions are Dr. Byron L. Barrington, Mr. Richard Boccini, Mrs. Sandra Boyes, Dr. Robert Carkhuff, Dr. Rosalind Dymond Cartwright, Miss Teresa de Lemos, Mrs. Emily Earley, Mr. Henry Ellis, Mrs. Shirley Epstein, Mrs. Roberta Farwell, Mr. Larry Feinberg, Miss Marilyn Geist, Mrs. Vilma Ginzberg, Dr. Joe Hart, Mr. David LeRoy, Dr. John Liccione, Mr. William Lydecker, Mrs. Martha Nelson, Miss Gail Palmer, Mr. Charles Richard, Miss Paula Rohrbaugh, Dr. Marshall Rosenberg, Dr. Douglas Schoeninger, Mr. Kenneth Simon, Mr. Jules Spotts, Mrs. Wendy Spotts, Dr. Norton Stoler, Dr. T. M. Tomlinson, Dr. Ferdinand van der Veen, Dr. Wesley Westman, Mr. Edward Williams.

The secretaries who have given loyally of their time and effort include Miss Sharon Bell, Miss Sue Berke, Miss Joyce Habich, Mrs. Rose Mary Jackson, Mrs. Eddye Lancelin, Mrs. Ruth Nielsen, Miss Frances Pape, Mrs. Carol Scott, Miss Carole Welker, Mrs. Phyllis Wetlaufer.

In addition to these individuals, we are deeply indebted to scores upon scores of raters, mostly graduate and undergraduate students, without whom the data of the research could not have been brought into being. This anonymous contribution is very gratefully acknowledged.

Another group which must remain anonymous is composed of the many patients in Mendota State Hospital who patiently or impatiently endured the research tasks we requested of them, some of them involved in a relationship with the therapists, all of them involved in teaching us about psychic disturbance, about psychotherapy, and about living. We do not forget them.

Finally, the sponsorship, encouragement, and financial assistance of the Wisconsin Psychiatric Institute, through its directors, Dr. Robert Roessler, and later Dr. Milton Miller, and its Executive Committee, provided the context in which the research was able to go forward.

The research would never have been possible without generous financial support from many sources. Our profound gratitude is extended to The Human Ecology Fund, the University of Wisconsin Research Committee, the Wisconsin Alumni Research Foundation, the Department of Psychology, University of Wisconsin, and the Wisconsin Psychiatric Institute, for funds which enabled us to get under way, for special grants at crucial points of need, for office and working space, and other facilitative efforts. To the National Science Foundation we extend appreciation for giving us help on the costs of computer use for data analysis. But for major and continuing financial assistance our gratitude goes to the Public Health Service for its research grant M 3496 from the National Institute of Mental Health.

To all of these mentioned, both the named and the anonymous contributors, goes the credit for the initiation, the arduous implementation, and the completion of this work.

CARL R. ROGERS, EDITOR

La Jolla, California
July, 1966

Contents

Introduction

Carl R. Rogers

I would like to tell the reader what is in this book, the elements which make it up, the context in which it may most profitably be read. But I feel baffled by the complexity of the task. As I consider the elements, the ingredients, out of which this book has grown, a helter-skelter array of unbidden images comes to mind. *What is this book?*

It is a grand research design, elegant and impeccable—it is also that design, less grand, more "peccable," as there were incorporated into it the disturbed, refractory, and apathetic individuals who were selected by the hand of fate (spelled "science") to be the human material for the study.

It is the experience of a dozen therapists—sincere, dedicated workers who, each in his own way, were trying to establish helpful contact with their clients. Their ways *were* different. One, Buddha-like, sits through thirty hours of silence with a woman patient before she begins to reveal herself. Another, in a second interview, says, "I won't listen to any more of that crap!"

It is the shut-in world—sometimes bizarre, sometimes perceptive, sometimes dull—of several dozen persons labeled schizophrenic, some of whom should also have been diagnosed as cases of chronic "hospitalitis."

It is columns of figures and *"t"* tests and the hum of the electric computer. It is the checking and rechecking of scores. It is analysis of variance and covariance. It is probabilities and trend tests.

It is *patience*—the plodding actions which by themselves seem so unimportant. It is the three hours spent in coaxing a patient to take an MMPI. It is days of poring over case histories to find two patients who "match." It is sitting with earphones clamped on your head, listening to segments of recorded interviews, and making dozens, even hundreds of ratings of these therapist-client interchanges.

It is the occasional high point—the deeply moving, sometimes frightening moment when two persons come together in an I–Thou relationship, when there is a deep encounter, when two very different worlds meet, when there is an *experience* of change.

It is the hard intellectual work of devising instruments to measure the intangible, constructing nets with which to capture the incredible subtleties of a fluid and changing relationship, or of an internal process of change, and to turn these subtleties into numbers and ranks and objectivity.

It is the lone researcher, working on the study he has carved out of the total enterprise—totting up columns, applying formulas, solving equations, extracting the significance from his assembled data.

It is the staff meetings—the searching, sometimes heated, attempts to understand the meaning of both the therapist's and client's behavior in the recorded interview being played. It is the disputatious sessions where arguments arise over the design of the research, or the next step to be taken, or the most unbiased way of handling the data, and the working out of these sharp human and scientific differences.

It is the many difficulties which beset the program. It is the staff crisis, where for a time the whole project seems doomed. It is the frightful moment in which much of the rated data disappears. It is the decision to recreate this data by rerating, with improved instruments, all of the interview segments, thus establishing a new research base on which our analyses and findings could be more solidly built. It is the achievement of this monumental task. It is the delicate and sensitive effort to assign credit fairly for work done by the many past and present members of the group. It is the challenging problem of making sense out of a vast array of separate studies and findings, confusing in their complexity. These are some of the images which come to mind.

There are other pictures, too numerous to mention. Comic moments, moments of real tragedy, moments of high enthusiasm, times of deep discouragement (which fortunately did not descend on all staff members at the same time), days of eager anticipation, when the first findings came in. There are these, and many, many others.

But these are fragments, moments, disconnected images. Let me try again, in a more logical and straightforward fashion, to tell you how this research came about.

At the University of Chicago my colleagues and I had gradually achieved a number of goals in the field of psychotherapy. We had developed a way of working in therapy which seemed effective with the wide range of individuals who came to us for help. We had conducted or stimulated a large number of empirical investigations in the field, the listing by Cartwright (1957) showing more than a hundred such studies. We had measured, objectively, some of the changes in personality and behavior which occur as outcomes of psychotherapy. A cluster of such studies in 1954 (Rogers and Dymond) focused particularly on the changes in the self-concept, in the personality as assessed by a projective test, and in the client's behavior as observed by friends. We had developed a theory of therapy and of interpersonal relationships (Rogers, 1951; 1959) which hypothesized that specific attitudinal elements in the relationship were the effective agents in producing change. A significant beginning had been made by several workers in testing and, in general, confirming the hypothesis. It seemed that we were on the track of the interpersonal qualities which promote constructive growth and change.

All of this was personally satisfying. Yet I began to have the feeling that I had, in a general way, made whatever contributions I was likely to make in that setting. We had at least opened up for more definitive study the field of psychotherapy with the clinic client who comes for assistance—the quality of relationship which helps, the kinds of changes which occur. I have gradually realized that I am essentially a "frontiersman," and while there remained enormous problems to be studied, analyzed, and resolved, I preferred to move into new areas.

The opportunity at the University of Wisconsin opened new vistas. Working in both the Departments of Psychology and Psychiatry, and later in the interdisciplinary Wisconsin Psychiatric Institute as well, I found readily available new fields of work. It seemed clearly possible to push in new directions. I had long wanted an opportunity to work with psychotic individuals who had been hospitalized. Would the hypotheses for which we had found empirical support in our work with maladjusted and disturbed individuals who had come for help, prove equally valid in work with those who reside in our state hospitals? I had also had the desire to test out these hypotheses with normal individuals. Would the kind of relationship which fostered constructive development in the disturbed person be of help to the normally functioning person, permitting him to grow beyond his present status into a richer kind of personal living? I felt that most of my clinical and research experience had been with an intermediate group—the neurotic, the maladjusted, the disturbed, the ambulatory or functioning psychotic, the individual with serious interpersonal problems. Now I wished to enlarge both my clinical and my research horizons to include the whole spectrum of individuals as they find ways of coping with and avoiding life—from the chronically hospitalized psychotic person at one extreme to the well-functioning normal person at the other. We had believed that the same kind of therapy or relationship would be effective with every sort of human being, no matter what his diagnostic label, no matter whether he was regarded as psychotic or non-psychotic. Would this prove to be true? I wanted to begin primarily with the psychotic, to explore this belief.

In order to fulfill this purpose I slowly began to make contact with a nucleus of persons who shared these interests. There were experienced individuals whose knowledge of psychotic individuals and their treatment far exceeded mine. There were therapists whose work, like my own, had been largely with the clinic client. There were graduate students with little experience but with rigorously trained minds. Many members of these groups became members of the Psychotherapy Research Group at the University of Wisconsin Psychiatric Institute. Others, while not directly affiliated with the Psychotherapy Research Group, have worked closely with it in cooperative efforts. Most of the members of this group will be found named in the list of authors or the Acknowledgments section of this book. It is this group which planned the research enterprise reported in this volume. It is this group which brought it into being through devoted effort. It is this group which has, cooperatively, written this book. So it is at this point of assembling the group that the story of this program ceases to be my own hope or wish and becomes the story of the plans, decisions, and actions of a group highly divergent in background, experience, and personality, but united in the desire to investigate the impact of a therapeutic approach upon hospitalized psychotic persons.

Though the many individuals who shared in this enterprise are named in a separate section, I would like to mention several whose leadership was especially significant in making the program what it is. Dr. Eugene T. Gendlin initiated the program, with all of the detailed arrangements which that implies, and has contributed a basic theoretical formulation upon which a number of our process measures have been built. Dr. Charles B. Truax organized the initial data collection and analysis. The ratings on which his studies were based mysteriously disappeared and have not been recovered. This unfortunate fact made Dr. Truax' preliminary reports unusable in this book. Dr. Donald J. Kiesler gave leadership to the rerating and re-analysis of all of the data, and has shown a high degree of determination, efficiency, and research competence in carrying through this task. The research sections of the present book represent the entirety of the final and definitive findings of the Wisconsin study.

Special mention is due to Dr. Philippa L. Mathieu, who gave time and effort without stint in helping Dr. Gendlin put the program in operation, and who was a key figure in the laborious task of conducting the rerating of all the interview material. Her devoted effort has been given to the project in many ways throughout its lifetime. Dr. Marjorie H. Klein's conscientious work in the rerating task, in the statistical analysis, and in the reporting of the research, also deserves special note. Dr. Norton Stoler gave so much effort to various aspects of the analysis of the data that he is listed as a contributor though his name does not appear on any of the chapters which were finally utilized in the book. Without the loyal labor of such individuals our early plans would have remained only a dream.

The manner in which our initial vision was organized into a program of research, the hypotheses we set out to test, the new measuring devices we developed, the vicissitudes of implementing our program, the findings which emerged—some confirming, some inconclusive, some negative— will be found in the pages which follow.

References

CARTWRIGHT, D. S. Annotated bibliography of research and theory construction in client-centered therapy. *J. counsel. Psychol. 4:*82–100, 1957.

ROGERS, C. R. *Client-Centered Therapy.* Boston: Houghton Mifflin, 1951.

ROGERS, C. R. A theory of therapy, personality, and interpersonal relationships as developed in the client-centered framework. In S. Koch (ed.), *Psychology: A Study of a Science,* Vol. III. New York: McGraw-Hill, 1959, pp. 184–256.

ROGERS, C. R., and DYMOND, ROSALIND F. (eds.). *Psychotherapy and Personality Change.* Chicago: University of Chicago Press, 1954.

PART I

The Plan, Its Implementation and Results:

An Overview

1. The Conceptual Context

The thinking of a great many psychologists and psychiatrists has contributed to the ideas formulated in this chapter. All of the initial staff of the Psychotherapy Research Group were involved in the early decisions described. The chapter was written by Eugene T. Gendlin and Carl R. Rogers.

The research program reported in this book is a study of the impact of a therapeutic relationship upon hospitalized schizophrenics and upon matched normal individuals. The general aim was to make an intensive study of the factors involved in the process of change in personality and behavior as it occurs in schizophrenic and normal individuals during a period of psychotherapy. What are the elements in the relationship which facilitate change? What is the process of change within the client? What are the types of change which occur? Can measurable indices be found which will enable us to be objective about (*a*) these facilitative elements in the relationship, (*b*) the characteristics of the therapeutic process in the client, and (*c*) the kinds of outcome change which occur? In large measure it has been possible to carry out these aims and to develop such measures, as will be evident in the chapters which follow.

The Background for the Study

Related Studies

Before describing the research itself, however, it may be well to try to place this program of investigation in a context of several related streams of investigative effort. As an attempt to advance knowledge in a certain field, where does this study stand in relation to other developing areas of knowledge?

There has been a great deal of study and research in the field of schizophrenia—its origin, its nature, its organic and psychological concomitants, and many other questions related to it. Although our investigation has to do primarily with schizophrenic individuals, our work does not spring from, nor is it closely linked with, this stream of effort. This is because it is basically a study of the therapeutic relationship rather than of schizophrenia. Hence references to this whole body of knowledge will be slight.

In the area of psychotherapy, research is new, having only been

3

carried on during approximately the past two decades. Prior to that time it had been thought that psychotherapy was so intimately involved with personal and subjective aspects of human behavior that it could not possibly be amenable to empirical measures. During the past twenty years, however, there have been numerous attempts to define and measure the variables involved in psychotherapy in such a way that the studies would be publicly replicable. The current program has built heavily on the research already completed in this area, though such research has been almost entirely with neurotic rather than psychotic individuals.

There have been many studies of psychotherapy in which personality and behavior have been measured before and after psychotherapy. These have demonstrated the possibility of measuring the outcomes of therapy. Although often contradictory and difficult to assess, there are actually many studies relevant to this issue, far too many to be listed separately. The volume by Mowrer (1953) presents, discusses, or has reference to, much of the major work up to 1952. The yearly chapters on psychotherapy in the *Annual Review of Psychology* from 1950 to the present testify to the many studies related to outcome which have been made. A 1954 volume (Rogers and Dymond) presents a cluster of outcome studies carried on within the client-centered orientation. There is even a very solid study of the outcomes of play therapy (Dorfman, 1958), and an ingenious comparative study of the outcomes of different types of group therapy with chronic alcoholics (Ends and Page, 1957). While it is certainly true that there are vast areas of ignorance regarding outcomes of therapy, there have been a sizeable number of studies in which the methodology is sophisticated, the controls adequate, and the findings carefully and realistically interpreted. Several of the authors of this volume have participated in such studies and this body of research has been one of the cornerstones on which we have built. These previous investigations have encountered many of the problems of research design, of controls, of measurement, which we also have met in the present program, and we have endeavored to profit from this earlier experience.

Another line of development in connection with the field of psychotherapy has been the attempt to specify the elements in any therapeutic relationship which make that relationship an agent of change. A series of hypotheses regarding "the necessary and sufficient conditions of therapeutic personality change" was advanced by Rogers in 1954 and these hypotheses were subsequently published (1957). The radical nature of these hypotheses consisted of the fact that certain attitudes experienced by the therapist in the relationship and perceived to at least a minimal degree by his client were posited as the *only* elements needed to bring about constructive change. Since that time, a number of investigations, but most notably those of Barrett-Lennard (1962), have tended to support these hypotheses with clinic clients who have presented themselves for help. The present program has had as one of its aims the further testing of these hypotheses by determining whether they also applied to relationships with hospitalized schizophrenics.

Another stream of research upon which the current program has been built is the increasing focus upon the process of psychotherapy. This trend is well documented in the report of the 1958 Conference on Research in Psychotherapy (Rubinstein and Parloff, 1959), in which it is clear that the major emphasis of many of those present had shifted from concern with the results of psychotherapy to a concern with the ongoing course of therapy, from "outcomes" to "process." This is a natural next stage of advance. From investigation of attributes before and after therapy, the focus has turned to a study of the events which themselves constitute psychotherapy, in an endeavor to identify and define the phenomenon of change itself. Consequently, alterations in interview behavior, in verbal expression, in autonomic function have all been subjects of study.

Turning more closely to the area of psychotherapy with schizophrenics, we find that there have been numerous descriptive reports of efforts to help hospitalized schizophrenics. There has been considerable evidence from these reports that talented, sensitive, and skillful people have been able to create a successful therapeutic climate in which change in schizophrenics appears to come about. Unfortunately, these reports have lacked research definition of exactly what has been done, and they have also been lacking in measurement of the results. Because of such deficiencies there has been a tendency for these gifted therapists to have less impact on their profession than they deserve.

There has been, however, some research on psychotherapy with schizophrenics and such work is very closely related to our own present program. The most noteworthy studies in this field are the pioneering investigations initiated by Whitehorn and Betz (1954, 1956), in which they attempted to relate different factors in the personality and therapeutic approach of a group of psychiatric residents to the improvement or lack of improvement of their schizophrenic patients. This study serves as a baseline for other research in the field, including ours. The program reported here has endeavored to go beyond it in its study of the crucial attitudinal aspects of the relationship in the interview, and in its focus upon the process of change rather more than on the gross aspects of outcome.

Some Early Decisions Regarding the Program

One of the decisions implicit in our thinking from the very first was that this was basic, not applied research. We wished to involve ourselves in a basic study of the qualities of human relationships which effected personality change. Eager as we were to be of help to the individuals with whom we worked, proof that we had aided these schizophrenics would not have been for us a fully satisfying outcome of the research. We wished to cut deeper, to find whether there are some invariant elements in those relationships which produce change—and we chose schizophrenics as the population on which to extend or modify the knowledge previously gained with clinic clients. Thus in a real sense the research has the nature of a laboratory study. One of the virtues of this is that to the extent that basic change-producing conditions can be defined and measured, it may become possible to devise modes of "mass production" of such conditions. In other words, a degree of generalization from the present study was one of our first concerns.

Perhaps it would be well to state here very briefly the basic research issue around which the whole program revolved. The chapters which follow are, of course, an explication of this issue and our findings regarding it. Putting it first in a scientific shorthand, it is an investigation to see whether X is always followed by Y, or whether X is in some other way invariably related to Y. More specifically, it is an investigation to see whether certain specified attitudinal conditions existing in the therapist or in the therapeutic relationship are an antecedent of, or are significantly related to, a specified process of therapeutic change in the client. It is part of an interest in an even broader hypothesis that certain "conditions" are invariably followed by a defined "process movement" in all human relationships, that X invariably leads to Y, and that the greater the degree of X, the greater the degree of Y—the greater the degree of these attitudes, the greater the degree of change. Thus we were primarily concerned with a question internal to the therapy interactions themselves: Would this process always occur to the extent that these therapist factors were present?

Another of our early decisions was to limit our work to those psychotics who had been diagnosed by the hospital staff as schizophrenic. We were and are quite aware of the shaky nature of many such diagnoses. We were not willing to commit ourselves to the concept of schizophrenia as a particular disease entity. The purpose was simply to measure the process and outcomes of psychotherapy in a segment of the population in which these had not heretofore been measured, namely, the "mentally ill." To limit ourselves to the group known as "schizophrenic" was simply a way of denoting one large and convenient subsection of the "mentally ill." Though we focused our attention on the schizophrenic group, we were quite aware that within this broad category there are wide and sometimes bewildering differences. We endeavored to obtain and to present enough of the test data so that any reader would be able to draw his own conclusions as to what extent any given definition of schizophrenia applied to our research population.

Another element of our plan was the inclusion of normal individuals as well as hospitalized psychotic persons in order to test our hypotheses more broadly. Much effort was expended in enlisting a group of "normals" who were matched in age, sex, and socio-educational level with our hospital group. To our surprise, the attempt to offer a therapeutic relationship to these adequately functioning individuals proved more difficult to implement than our program with psychotic persons. The story of why this was so, and our learnings from the attempt, will be found later in these pages.

In still another way we wished to enlarge the testing of our basic hypothesis. As stated, it is intended to apply to any helping relationship and not simply to client-centered therapy. It is our hypothesis that the attitudes being investigated are the effective agents of change, no matter what the orientation of the therapist. Consequently, it was our desire to include therapists of various persuasions in our study. Unfortunately— and this is itself a subject worthy of research—when therapists learned that the interviews were to be recorded and available to research workers for analysis, those whose approach was more interventive and interpretive tended to decline to participate. So the therapists who became a part of the study clustered in the direction of a client-centered orientation. Not all would have termed themselves client-centered, and one or two were quite sharply different in their therapeutic approach, but to a greater degree than we had wished, the participating therapists tended toward a client-centered way of working.

One very definite decision by the group was that the research should be rigorous in its methodology, meeting all the canons of scientific objectivity. Although we were told by a number of workers in the field that this was impossible, and were aware of the many barriers to objectivity in endeavoring to contain disturbed, uncooperative individuals in a rigorous design, this was nevertheless a fixed purpose in the group. In carrying it through, we consulted experts in research design, and planned our investigation in such a way as to provide adequate controls, and permit a sophisticated statistical analysis of our data. Thus we started with matched pairs of individuals, one of each pair chosen for therapy by the flip of a coin, the other remaining a control.

The interview segments chosen for analysis were randomly selected. Raters, assessing these segments for different qualities, worked "blind," without knowing whether the segment was from an early or late interview, or whether the case was regarded as successful or unsuccessful. All of this will be spelled out in the chapters devoted to the design and methods of the study. These items are mentioned here simply to underscore the determination of the group to produce findings—whether positive or negative—which could be accurately interpreted. The study was planned so that the source of any significant evidence of change could be discovered—whether related to the age or sex of the patient, the attitudes of the therapist, the passage of time, or the general treatment program of the hospital. We wished to be certain that we did not deceive or disappoint ourselves or others with findings which could be ambiguously interpreted.

There was one other commitment evident in the group from the first. It could scarcely be called a decision, since it was more of an assumption. The members of the group were committed to the goal of personal growth and health. It was our aim to facilitate the achievement of such a goal in the individuals with whom we worked. It would be a gross distortion to describe only the concern of the group with research and empirical method. As clinicians we invested ourselves in the effort to provide a relationship in which these schizophrenic persons might seek a more adequate process of coping and living. The research design was seen as the most favorable structure possible for the *assessment* of our efforts, but this was in no way intended to hamper our personal, clinical, experiential learnings as growing therapists. For all of us there was the clinical challenge of trying to make ourselves so meaningfully available to our schizophrenic clients that they could take psychological nourishment from the relationship and function more adequately as persons. For the majority of the therapists this was the first extensive work with hospitalized psychotics, so there was the added challenge of trying to discover, at a deep level, how we might relate to persons whose degree of disturbance, and/or whose chronic state, was a new experience for us.

Thus the program, in both its early and continuing stages, will best be thought of as proceeding along two major axes, or involving two major dimensions. One of these was the core of personal clinical effort, in which the aim was to relate, in whatever way might seem most fruitful, to the schizophrenic and the normal individuals who were selected for the study. This was a highly individual subjective learning experience, in which each person was trying to develop as a more effective therapist. It has been a difficult, sometimes baffling, often highly rewarding experience, not all of which can ever be communicated. The second axis or dimension of the program is the disciplined research effort. The aim in this respect was to define all terms operationally, to use only methods which would be publicly communicable and replicable, to use a design which would exclude, as far as possible, any subjective bias, any contaminating personal factor. Some members of the group were involved only as therapists. Others were involved only in the research dimension. But many of us experienced within ourselves the dynamic tension of the interplay between the two axes, being in one portion of our commitment as intuitive and subjective as it was within our capacity to be, and in another aspect of our commitment as hardheaded and tough-minded as it was within our power to be. To work with all of the sensitivity and personal responsiveness at one's command in therapy, and then to work with all the objectivity which scientific methodology makes possible in assessing the subtleties of that therapy, is not an easy tension to endure, but the experience is an invigorating one. It involves at one moment being open to all the possible levels of meaning in the hallucination this client is experiencing, and responding to this client with all of oneself—spontaneously, intuitively, skillfully. It involves at another moment being equally open to all of the possible ways in which subjective bias or personal desire might contaminate the collection or analysis of the data from such interviews, and selecting methods which will exclude any such bias. It involves at one moment a subjective faith in the spontaneously emerging potentialities of the person. At another moment it involves a faith in the methods of a rigorous science for getting closer to the factual truth. We have sometimes recognized jokingly that this has been indeed a "schizophrenic project" in its double commitment, but we believe this has been a healthy schizophrenia.

The Basic Concepts

As indicated earlier in this chapter, research in psychotherapy has been concerned with three major variables which are deemed to be important in any kind of change during psychotherapy. Listing them as problems, and putting them in the probable order of their occurrence, they are as follows:

1. What behaviors of the therapist are effective in initiating and maintaining change in the client or patient?
2. What behaviors of the client constitute the "process" of changing during psychotherapy?
3. What are the outcomes of this process?

In our research into the therapeutic relationship with schizophrenics and normals we were involved in all three of these issues. Some of the basic concepts which guided our work are described below.

Effective Therapist Behaviors

Our thinking in this area has been influenced by the developments in therapeutic thinking in general, but particularly by the evolution of client-centered therapy. The client-centered orientation was, at first, characterized by a rather specific technique or method: the therapist consistently responded by "reflecting" the client's feeling. This meant that the therapist avoided diagnosis and deductions about the client, or interpretations of hidden meanings the client did not intend. Instead, the therapist attempted always to state in his own words what he sensed to be the client's intended message, the client's perception of his feelings, situation, difficulties, and the like. In this effort the therapist tried to sense not merely what was on the surface but the deeply felt meaning which the client only haltingly approached in what he said. Such responding, when successful, meant that the client's own presently felt message was more deeply understood and responded to than he would have thought possible.

Gradually, the client-centered group noticed that the method was open to the pitfall of a rather wooden imitation, a sort of formula behind which a frightened or conflicted, or uninvolved, therapist could hide. The reflection formula of "You feel . . ." might look good on a transcript, but in action it could vary from a deep response to an artificial front. Seeman, Butler, Rogers, and others began to emphasize that not the technique but the personal attitude, involvement, and the genuineness of empathy constituted effective therapist behaviors. (Similar trends toward realness and personal involvement were being emphasized in other therapy orientations during the same period.)

As mentioned earlier, Rogers formulated three attitudinal conditions which he held were "the necessary and sufficient conditions of therapy" (1957). Regardless of what method or technique the therapist uses, regardless of the theoretical orientation he might hold, it was hypothesized that effective therapy would take place if the therapist fulfilled the following three "conditions": (*a*) The therapist responds as the real person he actually is in this relationship at this moment. He employs no artificial front and does not have to hide or fear his real reactions. This condition was termed "congruence" (congruence between the therapist's experiencing and his thoughts and behavior). (*b*) The therapist senses and expresses the client's felt meaning, catching what the client communicates as it seems to the client. This condition was termed "empathy." (*c*) The therapist experiences a warm and positive acceptance toward the client, a prizing of the client as a person whether the feelings and behaviors he is now exhibiting are regarded as valuable or as deplorable. This condition was termed "unconditional positive regard."

These three "attitudes," which are described much more fully in Chapter 6 on the therapeutic conditions antecedent to change, constitute one important cluster of variables which we have attempted to measure in this research. They are not, of course, as easy to measure as would be more clearly discernible verbal patterns such as interpretation, reflection, reassurance, suggestion. They were chosen as variables because theoretically they were deemed more significant than the simpler verbal patterns.

These "conditions" have certain novel aspects as research variables. In the first place they are intended to cut across the various schools of psychotherapy, and to apply to any type of psychotherapy. Since the various types of therapy appear to have a roughly similar incidence of success, it seems likely that the factors essential to success lie deeper than the different concepts and techniques of the various schools. The "conditions" are an attempt to define and measure these common underlying factors.

Secondly, the conditions pertain to underlying attitudes rather than to specific behaviors. Perhaps rather than the word "attitude" we should use some such term as "set." We are not talking of a transitory something which could be expressed in one act or sentence of the therapist, but of a continuing "set" which consistently infuses all the different behaviors in which the therapist may engage. The conditions as defined emphasize that it is not *what* one does, but *how* one does it. It is not the verbal meaning but the personal meaning which is decisive. The conditions refer not so much to easily observable behaviors (asking, telling, ordering, rephrasing, interpreting, persuading, arguing) as to kinds of interpersonal qualities (realness, understanding, prizing). Measurement of these conditions involves the defining of objective behavioral indices which are relevant to and indicative of subjective modes of personal response.

Thirdly, this concept of conditions is unusual in its omission of diagnostic and theoretical conceptual apparatus. For this reason the concept is often somewhat baffling to those for whom psychotherapy is primarily a cognitive venture, proceeding from a complicated theoretical structure. Though these attitudes of empathy, congruence, and unconditional positive regard are not easily acquired by the therapist, their learning is an experiential, rather than an intellectual matter. This has important implications.

There was one practical aspect of the use of such variables which we had not foreseen. Because they had to do with basic feelings of the therapist and not with his techniques, they imposed little or no restraint or self-consciousness upon the therapists in their dealing with their schizophrenic clients. Actually, as will be reported in more detail later, the therapists in our group found themselves trying out and developing many new and different modes of response behavior. The variety of specific behaviors among the therapists increased sharply. Even those therapists who were well aware of the therapist variables which would be studied felt very free to alter their mode of responding. If knowledge of these variables had any effect upon the therapist it was simply to focus more of his attention upon the feelings he was actually experiencing toward his client. The variables, because of their generality, remained applicable despite much variation in therapist behavior.

Client Behaviors Indicative of Ongoing Change

Turning now to the second major cluster of variables involved in our research, let us examine in a general way those elements of client behavior which seem to point to a process of change. The measurement of such behaviors is an important focus of the whole study.

On the basis of clinical observation, and after listening to many tape-recorded interviews, Rogers pointed out a number of behaviors which appeared to be characteristic of "movement" in therapy (1958). Gradually these behaviors have been incorporated into a theory of process, related to the theory of conditions described above. Briefly it may be said that as the client finds himself *prized,* in all the facets and aspects of himself which he is able to expose and express, he begins to prize himself, and to value his feelings and reactions. He commences to place more confidence in his own basic responses to situations. As the client finds himself *understood* by someone who seems to "stand in the client's place" in his understanding, he begins to take a more acceptantly understanding attitude toward his own reactions. He desires to know more of himself; he begins to regard the process of understanding his basic feelings as a worthwhile undertaking. As he recognizes the *realness* of the therapist, and the fact that the therapist is close to his own experiencing, able in the relationship to express and be his real feelings without fear, he (the client) is increasingly able to live in a closer relationship to *his* own experiencing, to what is going on within his own skin. He is able to express his feelings more accurately and with less fear. He discovers that his experiencing is a referent to which he may turn in guiding his behavior.

Thus, in response to the conditions the client has experienced in his relation to the therapist, he begins to show certain characteristic changes which will be spelled out in more detail in the chapters dealing with the measurement of process. He shows a change in the manner of his experiencing of his feelings, moving from a remoteness from what is going on in his organism to an ability to experience feelings and personal meanings with immediacy. He changes in the way in which he construes experience, from rigid constructs which are thought of as fixed facts to a recognition that he is the creator of these constructs and that they are best held tentatively and are subject to checking. He changes in his manner of relating to his problems, from viewing them as entirely outside himself to accepting his own contributions to his problems and the degree of his responsibility for them. He changes in his manner of relating to others, from avoiding any close or expressive relationships to living openly and freely in such relationships.

As we worked from these observations and this tentative theory, various instruments were devised to measure this process quality of the client's behavior: a global scale, measuring the multiple indicators of movement; a scale of experiencing, focusing on the remoteness or immediacy of the client's relationship to his inner experiencing; a scale of problem expression, focusing on his manner of relating to his problems; a scale of personal constructs, focusing on his manner of construing experience; a scale of relationships, assessing the quality of the client's relationship to others; a scale of intrapersonal exploration focusing on the depth of the inner search achieved by the client in the therapeutic hour. These will be presented or discussed in their appropriate place.

It should be noted that these variables having to do with client behavior have certain novel features. First, like the variables having to do with therapist behavior, they refer to *how* rather than *what*. It is not a matter of *what* the client talks about (whether job difficulties, sex life, childhood experience, life anxieties, power drives, etc.) but of the *manner* of his expressive behavior, the manner in which he is *relating* to whatever content he is expressing. It is possible, for example, for a client to talk about material which is supposedly "deep," such as early sex experience, in a manner which shows that he is very remote from the experiencing of any feeling regarding it, and does not own the experiences as his own.

It is clear that these variables of client behavior are applicable to any mode of psychotherapy. It is evident in this theory that though clients in the various orientations may differ in the content material they are led to discuss, their manner of relating to what they are experiencing is expected to change in the fashion described.

These variables are defined in terms of the manner in which experiencing functions during psychotherapy. The basic theory of experiencing as defined by Gendlin (1962) is fundamental to the whole conception. It is this which gives meaning to descriptions such as those of the client's movement in therapy. At the lower end of the continuum of process the client is "very remote from his experiencing and unable to draw upon it or symbolize its implicit meaning. There is little expression about self and that is about self as an object." At the upper end of the continuum "in the moments of movement which occur . . . there is a dissolving of personal constructs in a vivid experiencing of a feeling which runs counter to the constructs . . . . The self exits in the experiencing of feeling. At any given moment, the self *is* the experiencing." It is thus the experiential process in the client, rather than his concepts or words, which is central.

In spite of the above comments regarding the concept of process, it still may not be clear as to the way in which the process of therapy is different from the outcome or final result of therapy. A word may be in order about the use of the term "process." In the experiential flow of events in a series of therapeutic interviews, certain characteristic sequences have been noted clinically. These may be thought of as evidence of therapeutic movement, of process, of the changing which is going on. Since research can never study flow itself, process becomes defined operationally as those discriminable characteristic sequences which are hypothesized to be indicative of different degrees of ongoing changing. Thus the individual may become more expressive of self-related feelings now than he was a month ago, or communicate less of non-self material, and more of self-description. Though such indicators of process are related to outcome, they come from a different order of discourse, representing points in a sequential flow of process events, rather than end points such as cure, recovery, or social adjustment, which are terms relating to outcome.

The reason for the focus of this investigation upon process is that the rewards seem much greater insofar as fundamental increase of knowledge is concerned. If we can understand the nature of the complex process of personality change, we will know much more than simply that a given procedure reaches a pre-selected end point in a certain percentage of cases. The study of process promises to lead to an accurate description of those behaviors which in fact indicate that psychotherapy is going on in the client. Thus we can look forward to the time when we will be able to determine, with some degree of exactness, whether therapy is or is not occurring.

A final comment about this cluster of variables is that they seem to be close to what has been regarded in differing orientations as essential to therapeutic movement. It is generally recognized that psychotherapy is a highly subjective, experiential process. Alexander (1948) has called it "emotional learning." Freud (1936, 1959) pointed out that interpretations and their acceptance arc only the start. The "part of the work that effects the greatest changes in the patient" is "working through." Whitaker and Malone (1953) speak of a conversation of two unconsciousnesses, and they contrast this with "intellectual verbiage." The important contrast between "intellectualizing" and "defensive verbalizations," on the one hand, and "really being engaged in therapy," on the other hand, has long been recognized (Gendlin, 1964). In short, it is widely agreed that effective psychotherapy is, for the client, a deeply felt, concrete, emotional, experiential process, and that only through such an experience does change occur. The mere words or concepts can be sophisticated and correct, yet change does not occur through these alone. It is, therefore, of considerable significance to make the attempt to measure the observable behaviors in which the client engages when this experiential process occurs.

A Concept of Outcomes

In the initial planning of the research it was the aim to build our investigation almost entirely around the concepts of the "therapeutic conditions" in the relationship and the "process movement" in the client. By the time we were ready to draw up the actual research design, it was evident that it would be unwise to base the whole study on measures which were new—for the conditions measures had not been used on schizophrenics, and the process measures had been little used on any population. Consequently we felt the need to use some of the more generally acceptable criteria of outcome, even though we were well aware of their shortcomings. We needed such criteria in order to show what relationship existed, if any, between measures of the therapist factors and outcome, and between measures of the client's process and outcome. We also needed such outcome measures to communicate to the clinical worker who is more accustomed to thinking in terms of results rather than in terms of process.

As a consequence of this thinking, the research program made use of some of the more traditional diagnostic instruments, given at the start of therapy and at its conclusion. Initially we had hoped to be able to repeat these measures every six months during therapy in order to have measures of continuing change which would be directly comparable for every person in the study, but this aim proved impossibly ambitious, and could not be fully carried through. We were able, however, to obtain early and late or before and after measures for this purpose.

The tests which were used included, among others, the Rorschach, the

Thematic Apperception Test, the Minnesota Multiphasic Personality Inventory, a Q-sort for self-perception, the Wechsler Adult Intelligence Scale, and an anxiety measure compiled by Charles Truax.

There are difficulties involved in the use of these instruments as measures of change. First of all, in most instances they are designed to diagnose relatively permanent personality characteristics rather than characteristics of change. Thus Schactel, in a personal communication emphasizes that recovered schizophrenics and adequately functioning relatives of schizophrenics give Rorschach responses and patterns like those of schizophrenics. In other words, the test has tapped personality characteristics which seem not to change even when the person changes markedly in his social functioning. Similarly, the MMPI is made up in rather large measure of items phrased in the past tense such as "I have had very peculiar and strange experiences," and "I have had periods in which I carried on activities without knowing later what I had been doing." Once such statements are true for a person they would hardly be expected to change, even though the individual might have changed markedly in therapy. So although such instruments have often been used in studies of outcomes in therapy, they are actually decidedly deficient as measures of change.

Another difficulty is that for most of these tests there are various methods of analysis, and the choice of method is difficult. For example, in one research investigation two TAT experts analyzed "blind" the TAT tests given before and after therapy. Neither analyst knew which TAT came from a more successful case and which from a less successful. Using different modes of approach to the data, one analyst found the successful cases significantly improved, the other found them significantly regressed.

In an attempt to supplement such personality measures, ratings on hospital behavior were decided upon, to be obtained from hospital staff members. Such measures are also open to many serious criticisms, but at least they approached the issue of outcomes from a different perspective. Records were also kept of the length of hospitalization for each individual involved in the research.

The description of these deficiencies in the various types of instruments is sufficient to indicate why we did not wish to make such outcome measures the base of our study. Nonetheless we chose, for the reasons indicated earlier in this section, to make a broad approach to this problem. Our concept of outcome was an inclusive one, and measures of perception of personality change by a diagnostician, measures of personality change as self-perceived, measures of change in behavior and social adjustment, were all included. It was believed that these measures could be combined for a global indicator of degree of change, or could be used separately and related to various aspects of the measures of relationship and process. These measures are also helpful in assessing post-therapy behavior, being relatively free of the contamination of bias which is almost inevitable in the usual follow-up report of the individual's adjustment after therapy.

The Hypotheses

The central hypotheses of the study were formulated before the design was developed. These hypotheses were intended to explore the relationships between the three major concepts, outlined above, regarding therapy. They will be stated here briefly, and should be recognized as the heart and core of the research.

The First Hypothesis

It was hypothesized that *the greater the degree to which the conditions of therapy exist in the relationship, the greater will be the evidences of therapeutic process or movement in the client.*

This hypothesis builds on the concept that effective therapist behavior is constituted of the three attitudinal sets discussed earlier in this chapter —the realness, empathy, and unconditional positive regard of the therapist. The hypothesis states that a higher degree of these conditions— singly or in combination—will be antecedent to a higher degree of those client behaviors characteristic of movement in therapy.

The Second Hypothesis

This hypothesis was worded in different ways. Its first wording was: Given equivalent conditions of therapy, the therapeutic process or movement will be the same in the chronic schizophrenic, the acute schizophrenic, and the well-adjusted normal person. Somewhat later it was worded in a more practicable form: *The same variables of process movement will characterize the in-therapy behavior of more acute schizophrenics, more chronic schizophrenics, normals, and neurotics.*

It may surprise experienced therapists that we expected the process of therapy to be the same for these different groups, ranging from chronic schizophrenics to normals. Our essential interest in this hypothesis lay in the theoretical conviction that the process of constructive personality change would be basically similar no matter what the diagnosis or personality type of the individual involved. It was recognized that many therapists hold a sharply different view. For this reason it seemed important to test this conception.

In this connection, it must be emphasized, the prediction was that the *same variables* would show change, not that the change would be of the same amount, or would begin or end in the same place. It must also be emphasized that these variables are largely content-free and concern the *manner* in which experiencing functions in the individual. Thus the differences in what schizophrenics and neurotics say, how they approach therapy, what their difficulties are, need not be the same at all. For example, a neurotic may have a rigidly organized self-structure to which he pays a great deal of attention, and which he attempts to use as a guide to his behavior. He looks away from the felt process of his actual experiencing as it occurs within him. A disorganized psychotic, in contrast, may complain in bizarre and poetic terms that "I am not myself," that the person carrying his name is lost, and he may attribute what he thinks to evil-minded others who are sending him thoughts. Improvement—for each person but to quite different degrees—would involve, according to the prediction, an increase in his direct sense of felt experiencing and thereby a new sense of self as grounded, each moment, unfailingly, in this directly-felt experiencing. The assumption was that, basically, the process of therapy is this process of increasingly direct functioning of experiencing.

The hypothesis of the same process of therapy operating in these different populations, therefore, allows for a great many differences between them. Nevertheless the hypothesis implies that human nature, and the nature of personality change, is the same for schizophrenics as for others.

The Third Hypothesis

The third core hypothesis stated that *the process of therapy will occur to a significantly greater degree in a group of individuals to whom therapy has been offered than in a control group, paired and matched to the therapy group, to whom therapy has not been offered.*

This third hypothesis states that therapy makes a difference. It involved, of course, the process of selecting and matching two individuals, only one of whom, selected on a random basis, was taken into therapy. It raised the difficult question of how we were to measure the process of therapy in control cases. Our measures of process movement were based almost exclusively on tape recordings of interviews. Controls, by definition, received no therapy interviews. The problem was solved by giving all individuals (therapy and control cases) one interview every three months with one psychiatrist (the same interviewer for all patients and controls). This permitted the application of interview behavior measures to the controls in as comparable a way as possible. According to the third major hypothesis, these standard "sampling" interviews would show significantly more process movement for therapy cases than for controls.

A corollary drawn from the first and third hypothesis was implicit in our thinking, but not clearly formulated until the research was under- way. This hypothesis, III–A, was as follows: *Those individuals receiv- ing a higher degree of the conditions of therapy will exhibit a greater degree of the process of therapy than will those receiving a lower degree of therapeutic conditions, or those individuals constituting the paired and matched control group.*

The significance of this corollary is that it permits a comparison of individuals receiving more optimal therapeutic conditions with those receiving less optimal therapy or no individual therapy.

Three Additional Hypotheses

Implicit in these basic concepts were two other hypotheses, and a corollary hypothesis, which we did not formulate explicitly at the out- set. Looking back, it seems clear that we did not formulate them because we were determined that this would not be simply another study of outcomes in psychotherapy. We wished the focus to be upon the process concept. Yet these further hypotheses, which we have desig- nated as IV, IV–A, and V, were clearly implicit in the way in which we set up the program, and were investigated as the work developed.

The fourth hypothesis was that *evidences of positive outcome will be greater in the group of individuals to whom therapy has been offered than in a control group, paired and matched to the therapy group, to whom therapy has not been offered.* The rationale of this is obvious. Since we were hypothesizing that certain attitudinal sets in the therapist would bring about more process movement, such movement would be relatively meaningless if it were not also related to more constructive outcomes in the therapy. Clearly, these outcomes should be more marked in the group receiving therapy.

A more differentiated and powerful corollary of the fourth hypothesis, Hypothesis IV–A, was as follows: *The greater the degree to which the conditions of therapy exist in the relationship, the greater will be the evidences of constructive outcome.* In therapy or control individuals, those experiencing more of the conditions of therapy should show more improvement.

The fifth hypothesis stated that *the greater the evidences of process movement in the client in therapy, the greater will be the evidences of constructive outcome.* If process movement as measured by our instru- ments is indicative of change, this change should be reflected in the measures of final outcome.

Summary

It is hoped that this chapter will have clarified some of the fundamental purposes and concepts which were the cornerstones of this complex program of research. We committed ourselves to undertake a basic study of certain elements in the therapeutic relationship which were deemed, on the best theoretical formulation we could make, to be significant in initiating personality change. We determined to study these elements as they occurred in therapeutic interaction with hospitalized schizophrenics and with matched normal individuals. Our purpose was to investigate the correlation between the existence of these elements in the relationship, and the indicators of changingness in the client. Our hypothesis was that the indices of process movement or changingness would be positively related to the presence of these relationship elements. Our primary concern was to test whether the behaviors defined as the process of therapy in the client occurred to a greater extent when the defined therapist attitudes were at a high level. It was also implicit in our thinking that when the hypothesized conditions of therapy were markedly present in the relationship, not only would there be more evidence of a process of changing, but the outcome of the therapy would be more positive than in instances where the conditions of therapy were deficient, or where the individual had not been offered therapy. These orderly patterns would, we believed, be found not only in schizophrenics but in normals, and would be similar to the patterned process of change already studied in neurotic individuals. With this basic picture of the context of the research, we can now proceed to examine the specific design by which we hoped to test the various hypotheses.

References

ALEXANDER, F. *Fundamentals of Psychoanalysis.* New York: W. W. Norton, 1948.

BARRETT-LENNARD, G. T. Dimensions of therapist response as causal factors in therapeutic change. *Psychol. Monogr. 76,* No. 43 (Whole No. 562), 1962.

BETZ, B. J., and WHITEHORN, J. C. The relationship of the therapist to the outcome of therapy in schizophrenics. *Psychiat. res. Rep. 5:*89–117, 1956. See also title by these authors listed under Whitehorn.

CARTWRIGHT, D. S. Annotated bibliography of research and theory construction in client-centered therapy. *J. counsel. Psychol. 4:*82–100, 1957.

DORFMAN, E. Personality outcomes of client-centered child therapy. *Psychol. Monogr. 72,* No. 3 (Whole No. 456), 1958.

ENDS, E. J., and PAGE, C. W. A study of three types of group psychotherapy with hospitalized male inebriates. *Quart. J. Stud. Alcohol. 18*:263–277, 1957.

FREUD, S. Recollection, repetition, and working through. (1914) *Collected Papers,* Vol. II. New York: Basic Books, 1959, pp. 375–376.

FREUD, S. *The Problem of Anxiety.* (1926) New York: W. W. Norton, 1936.

GENDLIN, E. T. *Experiencing and the Creation of Meaning.* New York: The Free Press of Glencoe, 1962.

GENDLIN, E. T. A theory of personality change. In P. Worchel and D. Byrne (eds.), *Personality Change.* New York: John Wiley & Sons, 1964, pp. 100–148.

MOWRER, O. H. *Psychotherapy: Theory and Research.* New York: Ronald Press, 1953.

ROGERS, C. R. *Client-Centered Therapy.* Boston: Houghton Mifflin, 1951, chapter x.

ROGERS, C. R. The necessary and sufficient conditions of therapeutic personality change. *J. consult. Psychol. 21*:95–103, 1957.

ROGERS, C. R. A process conception of psychotherapy. *Amer. Psychologist 13*:142–149, 1958.

ROGERS, C. R. A theory of therapy, personality, and interpersonal relationships as developed in the client-centered framework. In S. Koch (ed.), *Psychology: A Study of a Science.* Vol. III, *Formulations of the Person in the Social Context.* New York: McGraw-Hill, 1959, pp. 184–256.

ROGERS, C. R., and DYMOND, ROSALIND F. (eds.). *Psychotherapy and Personality Change.* Chicago: University of Chicago Press, 1954.

RUBINSTEIN, E. A., and PARLOFF, M. B. (eds.). *Research in Psychotherapy,* Vol. I. Washington, D.C.: American Psychological Association, 1959.

WHITAKER, C., and MALONE, T. *Roots of Psychotherapy.* New York: Blakiston, 1953.

WHITEHORN, J. C., and BETZ, B. J. A study of psychotherapeutic relationships between physicians and schizophrenic patients. *Amer. J. Psychiat. 3*:321–331, 1954. See also title by these authors listed under Betz.

2. The Design of the Research

Many persons participated in planning the research. Special mention should be made of Eugene T. Gendlin, Philippa L. Mathieu, Charles B. Truax, Irene A. Waskow. Valuable assistance was obtained from David Grant, though he is not to be held responsible for the design which emerged. The chapter was written by Eugene T. Gendlin and Carl R. Rogers.

How can one determine empirically whether certain subtle qualities in a therapeutic relationship are associated with an equally subtle process of change in the personality and behavior of a hospitalized psychotic person? Even phrasing the question makes clear the difficulties with which we were faced. The staff of the project spent months in the endeavor to formulate a research design which would, so far as possible, give us the answer to our questions without involving bias or self-deception, and which would be as tight and rigorous as we could make it in the fluid world of clinical interaction. Much expert advice was sought and proved to be helpful. Gradually a design began to emerge, which was finally crystallized into a form to which we would hold during the period of the research. It is the purpose of this chapter to set forth some of the thinking by which we arrived at the final design, and to describe that design in its general form. The detailed implementation of the design, as we tackled different aspects of the problem, is left for the chapters in which those problems, and our findings in regard to them, are presented.

Choices and Decisions

The first choice we made has already been implied in the preceding chapter. It was our purpose to work with hospitalized psychotics in investigating some of our hypotheses regarding therapy, and we chose to limit our group to hospitalized schizophrenics. The basis of this decision was that we did not wish to include in one study all of the wide range of individuals found in state hospitals, which include the manic depressive, the epileptic, the brain-damaged, the alcoholic, the drug addict, the borderline mental defective, the senile, and other groups in their population. We therefore chose to limit ourselves to the largest and socially the most significant group found in such hospitals—the schizophrenics. This group was large enough and varied enough to permit a study which would keep us close to our aim of endeavoring to investigate the generality of our hypotheses regarding the process of therapy and its preconditions.

The Definition of "Schizophrenic"

But what is the definition of "schizophrenic"? Obviously there are many definitions and these definitions do not all agree. Workers in the field are in disagreement as to whether schizophrenia is an entity; also as to whether it is a disease. Fortunately for us we did not need to resolve these important issues in order to carry on our research, since the focus of our efforts was not schizophrenia as such, but the process of *therapy* in such a group. For our purposes it was important only that the group selected should be those individuals commonly regarded by professional workers as schizophrenic; and that the mode of selection should be such that no conscious or unconscious bias in regard to prognosis could enter in. Consequently we made the decision that our group would be limited to those individuals who had been diagnosed as schizophrenic by the staff of Mendota State Hospital, whose cooperation made the study possible.

In order to eliminate as many extraneous variables as possible, we chose to exclude from our population any diagnosed schizophrenic with concurrent conditions of organic central nervous system damage, mental deficiency, narcotic addiction, or major physical disability. We also excluded patients with a record of psychosurgery. Obviously our hope was to select individuals whose disturbance was relatively uncomplicated by additional physical and/or physiological disability.

For the same reason, we had initially hoped to choose subjects who had received no electroshock or insulin treatments. We found, however, that such individuals were extremely rare among the older and more chronic group in the hospital population, and that we would be introducing an unknown type of bias into our sample if we excluded all those who had had such treatment. Consequently we finally set the limit in this fashion. We would not select individuals who had had a course of more than 50 EST or IST. This eliminated those who had had very heavy exposure to these interventions, on the grounds that physiological damage might have occurred, and would thus cloud the factors we wished to study.

The Definition of "Acute" and "Chronic"

There was another choice which of necessity had to be made in regard to chronicity. The differences between the acute schizophrenic and the chronic individual on the back ward have been noted by clinician and researcher alike. We felt that our selection procedures might have a higher probability of selecting the more acute patient, since he would be less likely to have had extended shock treatment or psychosurgery. We did not wish our findings to be regarded as holding only for the acute or more promising patients. Actually, however, our hospital population contained nearly no acutes in the clinical sense we had intended this term, that is to say, very few individuals came to the hospital within a few days of the onset of disturbance. Nearly every patient residing in, or coming into, the hospital had first been treated elsewhere.[1] Such "acutes" might be new to this hospital, but were not "acute cases" in the sense we intended. We therefore arrived at a somewhat different classification: "more acute" vs. "more chronic," arbitrarily divided according to the length of the patient's total stay in hospitals. Under eight months was categorized as "more acute"; over eight months (with no maximum limit) as "more chronic." Our research included equal numbers of these "more acute" and "more chronic" patients, thus defined, giving us a reasonably representative sample of hospitalized schizophrenics. This also provided a dichotomy which might be helpful in interpreting our results, since the chronicity variable has often been regarded as prognostically significant.

The Choice of a Stratified Sample

Because we wished our findings to have significance for hospitalized schizophrenics in general, it was important to us that our sample be in some sense representative of that population. One way to achieve this is, of course, to take a purely random sample. With small numbers, however, a random sample may not prove to be a truly representative group. Consequently, we chose to use a stratified sample of the schizophrenics in the hospital. This means that in terms of predetermined characteristics we would have representatives of every category.

What should these characteristics be? We tried to choose, as bases of

1. Mendota State Hospital is essentially a referral hospital. Thus the incidence of the genuinely acute patient who is experiencing his first psychotic break is extremely low. At the other end of the continuum, the vegetative or very long-term chronic patient who has failed to respond to treatment is sent to the appropriate county hospital. These administrative arrangements have the effect of diminishing somewhat the numbers to be found at either end of the acute-chronic continuum. The hospital population consequently would appear to contain a lower proportion than some hospitals of those who are first experiencing breakdown, and those who have been hospitalized for many years.

stratification, elements which had been shown empirically to be related in some way to the process or the outcome of therapy. The elements on which we settled were sex, age, and socio-educational level. Some studies had found that younger clients were more likely to be successful in therapy than older ones. Another study found that females with male therapists more often succeed than males. The study by Hollingshead and Redlich (1958) indicated strikingly the effects of social class upon therapy. Therefore we wished to so plan our research as to include male and female, older and younger patients, and patients of lower and higher socio-educational levels, as well as to take into account the more-chronic, more-acute dichotomy previously mentioned.[2]

As to definitions of age and socio-educational level, we adopted simple criteria. From information gained from the Wisconsin Bureau of Statistics we calculated the median age of those whom we had defined as the more acute hospitalized schizophrenics, and the median age of the more chronic. These ages were 33 and 38 respectively. Consequently we wished to have half of our sample of the more acute cases below the age of 33 and half above. For the more chronic individuals the dividing line between younger and older was 38.

As to socio-educational level, our best information indicated that it would be wise to divide the group in the following way. Socio-educational status was defined as "lower" if the subject had less than a high school education, with occupation classed as unskilled, semi-skilled, or farmer. He was classed as "higher" if he had a high school education or beyond, with white-collar, skilled, or professional occupation.

These various definitions gave us the basis for selecting a stratified sample of the population of hospitalized schizophrenics. The importance of this procedure lay in the fact that this type of sample would be of great help in determining whether our findings were associated solely with the variable of therapy or with some other factor. Thus we hoped to be able to determine whether, in our population, the process of therapy was more marked in the chronic or in the more acute group (or in the group of normals to be described); whether change occurred primarily in a certain age group; or primarily in individuals of a certain socio-educational status; or primarily in relationship with certain individual therapists. We endeavored to build a design in which any findings, positive or negative, would be capable of meaningful interpretation.

2. With the wisdom of hindsight, we realize that motivation for help should probably have been another variable in our stratification, since this too has been judged to be related to therapeutic outcome. This factor was not, however, included in the design.

The Problem of Chemotherapy

Another important decision had to do with the problem of chemotherapy. The administration of tranquilizing drugs has become almost a standard procedure for the great majority of patients. Hence, unless provisions were made, our research patients were highly likely to be on tranquilizers. This would make the interpretation of any change in the individual more difficult. Another reason for being concerned about chemotherapy was that many of the drugs used tend to decrease the individual's experience of his emotions and his awareness of what troubles him, hence possibly impeding the process of psychotherapy. Such drugs may also have a tiring, dulling effect, with consequent loss of energy to invest in any relationship.

We therefore reached an agreement with the hospital that our research patients who were in therapy should not receive tranquilizing drugs, except in emergency situations when the ward physician might feel such medication necessary to control violent or difficult behavior. We hoped through this arrangement to have a better basis for interpreting our findings as being attributable to therapy and not to some chemical factor.

The Definition of "Normal"

Another group in which we were interested was that segment of the general population commonly described as "normal." An integral part of our hypothesizing had long been that the process of constructive personality change follows the same general pattern in everyone—schizophrenic, neurotic, and normal alike. By arranging our design so as to include people who were functioning well and evidenced no need for psychological or psychiatric assistance, we could accomplish two things: we could test whether or not their patterns of therapy behavior followed the schema which we felt represented the behaviors indicative of ongoing change, and we could also make direct comparisons between the "normal" and the schizophrenic groups.

The definition of "normal" which we chose has already been implied. For our purposes, "normals" are *any* individuals who are functioning adequately outside a hospital setting, with no external evidence of psychological malfunction and no expressed desire for help. While this definition may include many individuals who would be adjudged more or less disturbed on the basis of thorough examination, it also tends to foster minimal experimental bias on the part of the researcher involved in screening subjects.

Our normals were chosen from groups of volunteers obtained from church organizations, Grange chapters, and groups of employees. Although this sort of self-selection procedure inevitably carries with it a certain degree of restriction on subject type (e.g., those people volunteer who already have some interest in the area, and may well be qualitatively different from those who do not volunteer), this was held down by describing the project simply as a research study of personality. Thus the normals did not know, at the time they volunteered, that some of them would be offered psychotherapy. The normals selected for the study were chosen in terms of the same stratifying variables— age, sex, and socio-educational levels—as were used for the schizophrenic groups.

The Matter of Controls

In any research design, a variety of procedures are used to control for the effect of all other variables save those in which the experimenter is specifically interested at the time. Adequate controls in an investigation mean that the findings, whatever they are, may be logically and validly associated with the variables under experimental consideration. In this sense a number of the decisions already described in regard to the research constituted controls. If therapeutic change took place only in the normals and not in the schizophrenics, this would have given one meaning to our findings. If all of our younger patients improved and none of the older, this too would have constituted a control element in our research design. Thus, many of the choices which have just been described involved building adequate controls into our study.

The general rationale of this point of view may be illustrated in another way. A considerable amount of research has been completed on those individuals, largely neurotics, who come to an outpatient clinic or a counseling center for psychotherapy. The evidence gives some confirmation of the hypothesis that certain definable and measurable therapeutic conditions are associated with a definable and measurable process of psychotherapy. To learn whether these findings have to do with a stable phenomenon in all human beings, it is necessary to study the extreme groups: hospitalized psychotic individuals and normals. In this sense the study we were planning made both our psychotic and our normal subjects controls for the findings which came from the more heavily studied middle group, the neurotics. In other words, part of the purpose of the investigation was to determine whether the theory and hypotheses on which it was based were universally applicable or whether these were applicable only to the type of individuals who usually come voluntarily for psychotherapy.

In the same sense, the more acute and more chronic groups in our study were controls for each other. If the same principle was found to hold for both the chronics and the acutes, then the conditions of therapy, rather than the degree of acuteness of schizophrenia, would determine the occurrence of the therapeutic process.

Another meaning of the word "control" concerns the question, Are the effects which we term "process" and "outcome" really due to the relationship conditions which exist in the therapeutic hours or might they occur just as often spontaneously? To answer this question we had to have individuals who resembled the therapy clients as closely as possible and who lived under the same circumstances, the only difference being that they did not receive therapy. This required the selection of a control group which would fit the same categories of age, sex, socio-educational class, and chronicity as our therapy group. It was not too difficult to conceive of ways in which this much could be achieved, although it proved exceedingly difficult to carry out in practice.

But what would be the procedure whereby we could "control" for the factor of psychotherapy? If these individuals were to be taken to a room twice a week for some form of relationship other than therapy, this would permit us to measure the changes in them "without therapy," if one means by the word "therapy" certain exact behaviors of the interviewer during the therapy hour. Since our definition of "doing therapy" with someone is the providing of the essential attitudinal conditions which have been described, any "placebo" relationship situation resembling psychotherapy could in fact *be* psychotherapy to the extent that the basic attitudinal conditions prevailed.

To insure that no psychotherapy would occur in a relationship situation with the control patients, we would somehow have to insure that the interviewer was non-understanding, lacking in genuineness, and having little or no regard for the patient. Such a situation repeated twice weekly with emphasis on its importance would be almost certain to make the patients worse and would thus be a most unfair control group, biasing findings in advance in favor of the research—to say nothing of the moral issue involved.

It was consequently our conclusion that no relationship situation could be employed as a control for therapy. There remained the possibility of putting patients through the motions of going to a room and then being alone in it for an hour. This seemed to be an obviously different, poorer, and less desirable form of treatment, and again would have biased the research in favor of later differences between such a group and the therapy group.

Had we been working in the sort of hospital where most of the inmates get almost no attention, we would have had to adopt some procedure of giving at least some form of attention to our controls. But the hospital in which we worked has only some 800 to 900 patients and provides rather rich opportunities for nearly all of the patients, in the form of occupational therapy, recreational therapy, therapeutic community meetings, or group therapy sessions. Hence the therapy situation which we offered to our research subjects was as often an ill-fitting interruption in some activity as it was a form of attention which in itself could be thought to have therapeutic effects. The best control procedure, therefore, was to leave the control individuals to normal hospital procedure. The only exception to this was that the control individuals were to be tested in the same manner and at the same intervals as were the therapy clients, and that they were to be engaged in the "sampling interviews" which are described below.

This matter of a control for the therapy itself had its reverse aspects: If the hospital offered group therapy and various other therapeutic situations were not the controls really another group of therapy cases? This was indeed true and it made it less likely that we would find differences between our therapy group and a group of hospital patients who were being given everything that a progressive state hospital has to offer. This constituted both a challenge and a difficulty.

Thus it should be borne in mind, in considering the design of the research and in understanding the findings which have grown out of it, that our "no-therapy controls" often received group therapy, were frequently involved in therapeutic community meetings on the ward, and were the patients of an excellent staff whose proportion to the patients is about 55 treatment personnel for 800 to 900 patients. The difference, then, between the experimental and control groups was one of modern hospital treatment plus individual psychotherapy vs. modern hospital treatment only.

It was our judgment that if the measured conditions in the tape-recorded, twice-a-week therapy interviews were strong enough to account for a significant difference between the therapy group and the regular hospital group, then indeed we were dealing with a very potent factor.

Matching the Therapy and Control Individuals

It was important to our research that not only should there be control subjects receiving no individual therapy, but that these subjects should resemble the therapy subjects as much as possible. Obviously it was not feasible to match the subjects on all characteristics, but we wished to match them on the variables which we had already selected as significant, namely, age, sex, socio-educational status, and chronicity. Since past research indicated that these variables may have some effect on therapeutic prognosis, these would be significant variables on which to match the therapy and control cases. In addition, we felt that it was important to guard against the possibility that controls might be selected who were much more disturbed or much less disturbed than the therapy subjects. We therefore made two further decisions. We determined from the start to take subjects into the study by pairs. Only when we had two persons who were matched would we flip a coin between them and designate one as a therapy subject and the other as a control. Furthermore, feeling that any comparison of therapy subject with control subject would be meaningful only if the two persons of the pair were about equally disturbed at the beginning of the study, we searched for an instrument to assess the degree of disturbance. The only suitable measure which we found available was the Luborsky Health-Sickness Rating Scale (1962a, 1962b), which measures the degree of disturbance on a 0–100 scale, roughly from that of the completely vegetative individual in a chronic psychosis to the well-adjusted and well-functioning person in the community. We decided that the pairs of schizophrenics would be matched on this scale, though the scale itself needed to be refined to suit our purpose. The data on which we rated the degree of disturbance consisted of both historical information on the patient, gleaned from his records, and descriptive clinical information obtained in an interview with him. We felt that we now had selected the necessary methods and tools for making a satisfactory matching of our therapy and control individuals.

The Sampling Interview

One problem which plagued us in our early consideration of the research design was that many of the indices of therapeutic process could come only from the therapeutic interviews. Since the control individuals by definition would not be involved in individual therapy, we would have no comparable data from them on which to make the comparisons essential to some of our hypotheses.

At this point the group came up with an ingenious way of meeting the problem, a way which to the best of our knowledge has not been used before. We decided to ask one person, a competent and experienced clinician not otherwise associated with the research, to hold recorded interviews with every subject in the research, both therapy and control individuals, at three-month intervals. This clinician would be informed that these were not to be diagnostic interviews and should not include probing questions and the like. They were to be interviews in which he offered a receptive interest in the individual, his thoughts, feelings, and self-attitudes, and a willingness to receive and understand any communication which the patient might wish or be willing to make. The relationship which he offered was to be as similar from individual to individual as he could humanly make it. In this way he was to be a constant but very infrequent aspect of the individual's environment, and would be able to obtain a sampling of the personal expressiveness and mode of relating of which the individual was capable at any given time. Since he was to be relatively constant across all individuals in the study, direct comparisons could be made between the individuals receiving therapy and those who were controls. Recorded interviews would be available from both groups, giving us material on which we could use the same instruments of analysis.

Pre-Therapy and Post-Therapy Measurements

Although our major interest was in the process of change as it might be evident in the in-therapy behavior, we also decided to have a variety of data available in addition to the therapy interviews and the sampling interviews. These would permit the investigation of various types of change.

It was our decision that a number of instruments would be administered to the therapy and control subjects before the study began and at prescribed intervals thereafter. In addition, certain instruments were to be administered to the therapists at the same times. Behavior ratings on the therapy and control individuals were also to be filled out by hospital staff members.

The battery of instruments for the therapy and control subjects was to include the Minnesota Multiphasic Personality Inventory, the Rorschach, the Thematic Apperception Test (using only five cards, a modification suggested by Dr. William Henry), the Wechsler Adult Intelligence Scale, the Stroop Interference Test, a Q-sort of self items giving a picture of the individual's perception of his current self, a Truax Anxiety Scale developed prior to this study, and the Relationship Inventory, a questionnaire devised by Barrett-Lennard to measure the conditions of therapy as perceived by the individual. This last instrument the control subjects were asked to fill out in regard to "the person who has meant the most to you in your trouble." The therapy subjects were, of course, to fill it out in regard to their therapist.

The therapists were to be given the Relationship Inventory at the same intervals as their patients, in order to get their perceptions of the conditions in the relationship. They were also to be asked to fill out a rating scale as to the outcome of the therapy at the conclusion of their contacts.

The Wittenborn Psychiatric Rating Scales, devised to rate the behaviors of hospitalized psychotic individuals, were to be filled out by hospital staff for both the experimental and control patients, again at stated times.

This extensive battery of tests and other instruments to be given at intervals throughout the period of our contact with both therapy and control individuals was selected in order to provide us with analyzable data on the degree of change in the individual as measured by projective devices, by objectively scored tests, by the perceptions of the individual himself, and by the perceptions of ward personnel. It would also provide us with a measure of the relationship qualities in which we were interested, first as perceived by the client and second as perceived independently by his therapist.

The Therapists

Since our hypotheses had to do with the therapeutic relationship in general and not with any specific orientation to therapy, it was our hope that the therapists might represent widely divergent therapeutic orientations. For the reasons mentioned in Chapter 1, however, the eight therapists who volunteered to participate in this study, while varying considerably in their orientations and their ways of carrying on interviews, tended to cluster toward a client-centered point of view in therapy. The aim was also to include more experienced and less experienced therapists in our sample and in this we were successful.

It was a further aim that each therapist should take on a triad consisting of one more chronic schizophrenic, one more acute schizophrenic and one normal individual. The triad was to be selected so as to randomize the other factors involved in the study. Thus one therapist would work with a young chronic female of low socio-educational level, an older more acute female of high socio-educational level, and a young normal male of low socio-educational level. Each therapist would thus have a randomized triad with which to work.

The Research Design

The various decisions and choices made by the research group have been presented somewhat as they developed. Each of these decisions entered, of course, into our thinking about the research design. Different ways of carrying out the research were being formulated, modified, discarded, and re-formulated at the same time that the choices themselves were being considered, modified, and crystalized.

If the reader has a reasonably good grasp of the various definitions and basic choices made by the group, then the final design of the research can be presented rather simply.

1. Three groups of sixteen individuals each—a total of forty-eight individuals—were to be selected for the research. The first group was to be composed of more chronic schizophrenics, the second of more acute schizophrenics, and the third group of normals. These three groups were to be equivalent in sex, age, and socio-educational level.

2. The selection of individuals for the research was to proceed in pairs. Given the variables we had decided upon, we had twenty-four descriptive categories or cells such as the following: higher socio-educational status, young, female, chronic; lower socio-educational status, older, male, normal; higher socio-educational status, young, male, more acute. For each of these cells we were to select two matching subjects.

3. In the pairs of psychotic subjects there was to be one additional matching variable, that of degree of psychological disturbance. For each pair of psychotic individuals the degree of disturbance was to be within a five-point range on the Luborsky Health-Sickness Rating Scale.

4. Of the forty-eight individuals, twenty-four were to be selected for therapy. This was to be achieved by flipping a coin to determine the

Table 2.1—A graphic summary of the research design used in the study of psychotherapeutic change in schizophrenics and normals

THE CONTROL GROUP

Groups A, B, and C are equivalent in sex, age, and socio-educational status.

Group A (more chronic schizophrenics)	Group B (more acute schizophrenics)	Group C (normal persons)
MOL	MOL	MOL
MOH	MOH	MOH
MYL	MYL	MYL
MYH	MYH	MYH
FOL	FOL	FOL
FOH	FOH	FOH
FYL	FYL	FYL
FYH	FYH	FYH

Table 2.1, continued

THE THERAPY GROUP

This group was stratified in a fashion identical with the controls, and each individual was paired with the corresponding individual in the control group above. These pairs of individuals were matched for sex, age, and socio-educational status, and the schizophrenics were also matched for degree of psycho-social disturbance.

Group AT (more chronic schizophrenics)	Group BT (more acute schizophrenics)	Group CT (normal persons)
MOL	MOL	MOL
MOH	MOH	MOH
MYL	MYL	MYL
MYH	MYH	MYH
FOL	FOL	FOL
FOH	FOH	FOH
FYL	FYL	FYL
FYH	FYH	FYH

THE THERAPISTS

Each of the eight therapists carried on therapy with a diversified trio made up of one more chronic schizophrenic, one more acute schizophrenic, and one normal individual.

Therapist	More chronic schizophrenic	More acute schizophrenic	Normal
1	MYH	FYL	MOH
2	MYL	FYH	MOL
3	FOH	MOH	FYL
4	MOL	MYL	FOH
5	FYH	MOL	FOL
6	FYL	FOH	MYL
7	MOH	FOL	MYH
8	FOL	MYH	FYH

M = male, F = female; O = older, Y = younger (that is, above or below the median age of the group); H = higher socio-educational status, L = lower socio-educational status.

member of each pair to whom therapy was to be offered. The remaining individual was to serve as a control.

5. Each of eight therapists was to see a randomized triad for therapy—

one more chronic schizophrenic, one more acute schizophrenic, and one normal individual.

6. The battery of research instruments was to be administered at three- or six-month intervals, depending upon the particular test or instrument.

7. One interviewer would conduct sampling interviews with each of the forty-eight subjects early in the research and at three-month intervals thereafter.

Table 2.2—Design of the study

More chronic schizophrenic		More acute schizophrenic		Normal	
Therapy	Control	Therapy	Control	Therapy	Control
MOL	MOL	MOL	MOL	MOL	MOL
(T4)	—	(T5)	—	(T2)	—
MOH	MOH	MOH	MOH	MOH	MOH
(T7)	—	(T3)	—	(T1)	—
MYL	MYL	MYL	MYL	MYL	MYL
(T2)	—	(T4)	—	(T6)	—
MYH	MYH	MYH	MYH	MYH	MYH
(T1)	—	(T8)	—	(T7)	—
FOL	FOL	FOL	FOL	FOL	FOL
(T8)	—	(T7)	—	(T5)	—
FOH	FOH	FOH	FOH	FOH	FOH
(T3)	—	(T6)	—	(T4)	—
FYL	FYL	FYL	FYL	FYL	FYL
(T6)	—	(T1)	—	(T3)	—
FYH	FYH	FYH	FYH	FYH	FYH
(T5)	—	(T2)	—	(T8)	—

M = male, F = female; O = older, Y = younger (that is, above or below the median age of the group); H = higher socio-educational status, L = lower socio-educational status.

T1, T2, etc., refers to Therapist No. 1, Therapist No. 2, etc.

Further elements of the design

Every subject in the research was to be tested at the beginning of the program and at intervals thereafter, on the MMPI, Rorschach, TAT, Wechsler, Stroop, Truax Anxiety, and Q-sort of self items.

Both therapists and patients filled out Relationship Inventories after the fifth interview, and at intervals thereafter, assessing the relationship between them. Controls filled out these inventories for their relationship to the person they perceived as most helpful.

Every subject in the research was seen in a sampling interview three months after entering the program, and at three-month intervals thereafter.

Every subject in the research was rated as to his hospital behavior at three-month intervals, by ward personnel.

8. The data of the research would consist of the test batteries and the research instruments given at intervals throughout the research program, the recorded therapy interviews held with the experimental subjects, the sampling interviews held at three-month intervals throughout the program with every subject. Thus there would be available many measures of initial and later status for both experimentals and controls, providing indices of the extent of change throughout psychotherapy or an equivalent period. For both groups there would also be measures of the therapeutic or some other meaningful relationship. There would also be measures of the process of therapy as rated in the sampling interviews for both groups, and in the therapeutic interviews for the experimental group.

Since the design is complex it may be well to present it in slightly different form, in Table 2.2. The information as to matching and therapist assignment is similar to that presented in the previous table, but it is here set forth in a different manner, and Table 2.2 includes all the essential features of the design.

Summary

In this chapter, the basis of our research design and the design itself has been presented. There were many basic choices which had to be made before the design itself could be established. It was necessary to establish the definition of the groups with whom we intended to work, the size of those groups, the method of equating both groups and individual pairs, the tests to be included in the testing batteries, the assignment of the therapists, and the like. Out of all these considerations grew a research design which we believed would be sufficient to achieve two major aims. The first aim was to give an adequate test to the basic hypotheses of our study regarding the relationship conditions which were hypothesized as being followed by process movement and change in the individual schizophrenic or normal person. The second major aim was to make any findings, whether positive or negative, interpretable. Thus, we would be able to control for the variables of age, sex, socio-educational status, and degree of disturbance, in our study of the degree of change which occurred in the therapy subjects and controls in our group. The research which has been described has an unusual number of control features built into it in order that any findings would be interpretable.

We were now ready to place into the research design the very real and often uncooperative human subjects who would give it flesh and meaning.

References

HOLLINGSHEAD, A. B., and REDLICH, F. C. *Social Class and Mental Illness.* New York: John Wiley & Sons, 1958.

LUBORSKY, L. Clinicians' judgments of mental health. *Arch. gen. Psychiat.* 7:407–417, 1962*a*.

LUBORSKY, L. *Health-Sickness Rating Scale.* Topeka: Menninger Foundation, 1962*b*.

3. Putting the Design into Effect

The tremendously time-consuming burden of implementing the design was borne by the whole staff, but special commendation goes to Sandra Boyes, Eugene T. Gendlin, Vilma Ginzberg, Philippa L. Mathieu, Janet P. Moursund, Wendy Spotts, Charles B. Truax, and Irene A. Waskow, who were primarily responsible for the selection, matching, and testing of the groups. Robert Roessler gave freely of his time in conducting the sampling interviews.

The therapy was initiated and carried out by the following therapists whose devoted effort was the heart of the research: William Fey, Eugene T. Gendlin, Vilma Ginzberg, Joe Hart, Allyn Roberts, Carl R. Rogers, Jack Teplinsky, Charles B. Truax, Albert Wellner, with Emily Earley serving as co-therapist with one patient.

Therapists in the "ward-availability" project described at the end of the chapter included, in addition to several of the above, Helen DeBardeleben, Philippa L. Mathieu, and Ferdinand van der Veen.

This chapter was written by Eugene T. Gendlin, Janet P. Moursund, and Carl R. Rogers.

The People

In putting the research design into effect an enormous number of difficulties were encountered. In some instances the design had to be modified. The actual departures from the rigorous design were not very great, considering the many obstacles involved in working with a more or less chronic, hospitalized psychotic population. More often the implementation of the research design meant a considerable elaboration and thinking through of the exact meaning of the fundamental pattern which we had established. The following material endeavors to point up some of the changes and elaborations which were necessary in putting the design into operation with its all too human and often recalcitrant subjects.

The Problem of Matching

The task which seemed most difficult (and at times almost impossible) was that of matching individuals in groups and in pairs, a task definitely called for by the design. It seems useful to try to show in some detail the problems we encountered in this task, and the way in which we met them, to illustrate the conscientious effort invested in making the rigorous research design a reality. Other problems will be described much more briefly, but they often involved similarly elaborate considerations. There follows a rather comprehensive description of the difficulties encountered and the policies adopted in matching our subjects.

Sex.—It will be recalled from the design that we were concerned with two types of matching: equivalence between *groups,* so that the groups would have similar characteristics; matching between *pairs of individuals,* so that each subject in the research would have his individually matched control.

On the variable of sex there were four pairs of men and four pairs of women in each of the three groups: more chronic, more acute, and normal. This was the only matching criterion on which we had no great difficulty. On the basis of objective observation, consensually validated, we were able to distinguish males from females and to match males to males, females to females. As the research continued, we deeply wished that in matching the patients on the other dimensions we had equally clear-cut criteria!

Age.—Whether an individual was regarded as "older" or "younger" was determined by comparing him with the median age of the particular population group to which he belonged. The median age of chronic patients in Wisconsin state psychiatric hospitals—that is, those who had been hospitalized more than eight months—was 38. The median age of the more acute patients, those with a hospitalization record of less than eight months, was 33. We defined two patients as matched in age if they were less than nine years apart in age and fell in the same category of older or younger. Thus, if we had one chronic patient at age 41, he could be matched in age with another chronic patient of age 38 to 50. The second patient must, in other words, belong also to the older group and must not differ from the first patient by more than nine years.

In categorizing the normals we selected 35 as the dividing year between older and younger. This was as close as we could come to matching the normal group to *both* of the schizophrenic groups. In other respects the matching of pairs of normals followed the same rules as the matching of pairs in the other two groups.

In each of the three groups, the individuals were selected so that half were older, half younger.

Chronicity.—As has been indicated, the clinical determination of chronicity or acuteness of the schizophrenic condition is such a difficult and subjective task that for the purposes of research it was decided to use an operational, though admittedly somewhat arbitrary, definition of this dimension. Thus we defined a "more chronic" patient as one who had been hospitalized with a diagnosis of schizophrenia for a total of eight months or more in his lifetime; a "more acute" patient, as one who had been hospitalized with a diagnosis of schizophrenia for a total of less than eight months in his lifetime. Although the definition would be far from satisfactory from a clinical point of view, length of hospitalization has been regarded as influencing prognosis, and the definition thus makes sense from a research point of view. It did prove, however, to be inadequate for some of our "acute" patients. For example, we have used in the study, in some instances, a patient whose history suggested a schizophrenic process operant over a number of years but who had only recently been hospitalized with a schizophrenic diagnosis and was, therefore, classified in our study as "more acute." Whenever possible, we tried to select a matching patient who had shown the same type of earlier history.

One of the two groups of schizophrenics was composed of sixteen "more acute" individuals, the other of sixteen "more chronic" individuals.

Socio-educational status.—In applying our categories of higher and lower socio-educational status, a certain amount of judgment was involved on the part of the person doing the rating and matching. Sometimes it was clear enough. A person with high school training or more and in a skilled or professional occupation was easily classified as one of the higher group. Similarly the individual with less than high school education working in an unskilled occupation was easily classified as lower. In dealing with women patients it was somewhat more difficult. Here the judgment was sometimes necessarily based in part on the occupation and training of husband or father. Also, in considering men who were farmers, some account was taken of the nature of their farming enterprise, whether it represented a relatively skilled or an unskilled occupation. Again, in our matching we endeavored to match pairs who were not only within the same formal category but who seemed qualitatively similar in their socio-educational status.

It is to be noted that in our hospital population the group classified as "higher" socio-educational status was definitely not an upper-class group. A sociologist would probably term most of them middle or lower middle class in comparison with the general population. If at times we lapse into speaking of them as the "high" socio-educational group, it should be understood that this describes their status in the hospital population, not in the general population.

Degree of disturbance.—As has been indicated, we used the Luborsky Health-Sickness Rating Scale as the criterion for matching the degree of psycho-social disturbance of our subjects. We found, first of all, that most of our patients fell within the range of 15–30 on the scale, a very limited range.[1] Furthermore, the scale did not have enough specific criteria to differentiate helpfully within this range and thus to make the matching meaningful for our purposes. In the process of working out our preliminary matching procedures, Irene Waskow and Vilma Ginzberg modified and added to the Luborsky criteria until we had evolved a series of factors which seemed to be more satisfactory for evaluating the hospitalized schizophrenic population with which we were concerned. These criteria included many aspects of the patient's psychological structure and functioning. They utilized information obtained from the hospital records and from a brief interview with the patient. They combined objective data and clinical evaluations for the final global rating.

The ratings on which the matchings were based used four areas of judgment: (1) the subject's general behavior and manner of relating to others; (2) his disturbances of thought and distortions of reality; (3) his self-awareness, ego-strength, and psychological mechanisms; (4) his ability to function in the community. The complete outline on which the research worker who made the matchings based her judgment is contained in Appendix A: "The Form for Rating Degree of Disturbance."

While these criteria are appropriate for evaluating schizophrenic patients, they are also relatively independent of sub-categories of diagnosis (catatonic, hebephrenic, etc.), length of hospitalization, or duration of the psychosis. Thus they could be applied to more chronic or more acute patients, young or old, newly admitted or long hospitalized, high or low socio-educational status. They were also of help in evaluating the individuals in our normal population.

The staff member who was matching the pairs of patients did so on the basis of data from the hospital records, descriptions of the patients' behavior by physicians and ward personnel, and observations and impressions during a brief 20-to-30-minute interview with each patient. On the basis of this accumulated data, and using the criteria mentioned above, the rater made an overall judgment as to the degree of disturbance, classifying the patient at one of four points on a continuum from V (very disturbed) through Vm, vM, to M (moderate disturbance).

1. This should be compared with the assumption by the authors of the scale that the bulk of the general population falls between 60 and 85, and that patients who come for help to a psychiatric clinic such as the Menninger Clinic fall between 15 and 60 at the time they present themselves.

These judgments were roughly equivalent to scores of less than 15, 15 to 20, 20 to 25, and 25 to 30 on the Luborsky Scale. Both patients of a pair in any particular cell in the research design had the same rating.

Three examples of the notes and ratings made by the research worker are given below. The first is of a young woman.

This is the second hospital admission for this girl of 18. At the first admission she was shy, fearful, anxious, withdrawn, very flat in affect. She was hospitalized because she laughed and dressed in an inappropriate fashion and she was brought in by her parents. The second hospitalization was after some reckless driving in which there was an accident. Following this she tried to commit suicide. She has not been able to get along with her family or teachers or employer. She has had a violent temper. On the second hospital admission she has been hyperactive—noisy—though eager to help and please in a somewhat confused fashion. She has auditory hallucinations with sexual content. She is disturbed about sexual relations with relatives. She has a lack of judgment, is sometimes disoriented. She is assaultive at times toward other patients. Mood generally appropriate in interview, with some inappropriate laughter. No evidence of delusional thinking, though little insight, and judgment impaired. Seemingly long-time, withdrawn, schizophrenic personality. Disturbance rating, *Vm*.

The second is of a young man.

Age 24. Is paranoid. Seems disintegrated. Is puzzled. Can state a feeling but withdraws it quickly and becomes defensive. Relates to interviewer with suspicion. When he realized that he was revealing himself through his talking he remarked about that and then attacked the interviewer as "wanting to be rough on him." There are allusions to being punished electronically but he would not elaborate. He states that the hospital, the hospital superintendent, the interviewer, the Chamber of Commerce, all are working to hurt him. He seems confused, oriented with effort, hides his doubts with a "don't care" attitude. He says that he has been here before. He calls himself a bum and feels that maybe that's why people are after him. Disturbance rating, *Vm*.

The third is of an older man.

He is a pleasant person. Relates rather easily to the interviewer. Affect is generally appropriate. He has not worked for 12 years, though he has been hospitalized for only two of these years. His appreciation of reality seems definitely disturbed. His plans are unrealistic with no recognition of this fact. He has no insight into his condition. He is here because of physical ailments, according to his story, and shows much preoccupation with these. The hospital record indicates that in the past he has been classed as catatonic. Disturbance rating, *M*.

Whenever it was possible, the attempt was made to match subjects according to the sub-criteria involved in these ratings as well as in the overall degree of disturbance. For example, a patient experiencing hallucinations was matched with another experiencing hallucinations if the overall disturbance ratings were similar for both of them, and if the choice involved another non-hallucinating patient with the same overall disturbance rating.

Comments on the problem of matching.—Some of the procedures used in equating the groups and matching the pairs may seem somewhat crude. It may be helpful to state here the effect of the procedures described in this section. The overall result of our effort was that we were able to select pairs of individuals each of whom was in the same age range, of the same sex, with a comparable level of schooling and culture, with a similar diagnosis of schizophrenia, a comparable history of hospitalization for this psychosis, and a roughly comparable degree of current psychic disturbance. Considering the total variance in the general population, these pairs are very closely matched indeed; considering the total variance in individual personality and behavior, they are matched on only a small number of the possible dimensions.

As anyone knows who has tried to match on six factors, the problem of filling the desired cells becomes fantastically complex. We checked the records of all eight hundred patients in the hospital and checked immediately on every incoming patient, in our efforts to fill each cell. Even so, there was often long delay in finding a matched pair.

Selecting the Individual for Psychotherapy

Once a pair of patients was matched on all variables (sex, age, socio-educational status, degree of chronicity, degree of disturbance), a coin was tossed to determine which of the pair was to receive psychotherapy and which was to be the control. Ideally, one flip of the coin determined the fate of both subjects of the matched pair simultaneously. This occurred, however, in only ten of the sixteen pairs of schizophrenic subjects. The exceptions occurred primarily because of three obstacles: lack of suitable candidates for a cell of the design; passage of time, which turned a more acute patient into a more chronic one; hospital procedures such as discharge and transfer of patients. These factors necessitated some digressions from the rigorous practice of a single coin toss for each matched pair.

Lack of suitable candidates.—Some cells in the design were easier to fill than others. For example, patients of higher socio-educational status were difficult to find in our state hospital population probably because such patients tend to get help elsewhere. Also more chronic patients and older patients were often eliminated early in the screening because their hospital history indicated that they had exceeded our upper limits for shock therapy.

The time factor.—By the time a more acute patient had been discovered and interviewed by the rater, it was sometimes a matter of only weeks or days before he would pass the eight-month mark and cease to be operationally classifiable as more acute.

In the earlier stages of the research, such a patient, although unmatched for the moment, was subjected to the coin toss and put into the research as an experimental or control individual, the assumption being that soon the matched patient could be found who would then become the other subject of the pair in that particular cell. In some cases there was a long delay before the matched individual could be found.

After three such experiences, it was realized that the second member of the pair, though matched on all variables, did not have a 50–50 chance of being either an experimental or control. Thus, a more rigorous procedure was instituted for subsequent cells in which for any reason only one individual had been selected. Under the new procedure, the matching individual who was found for the cell had a coin tossed for him too so that he also had a 50–50 chance of being experimental or control. If the coin toss came out the same way as for the initial person in the cell, he was not entered into the study and we waited for another matching person whose fate in turn was determined by a toss of the coin until we did at last succeed in getting the opposite member of the pair, whether this was an experimental or a control. This was a time-consuming procedure, costly in patients, and in patience. We felt, however, that this elaborate procedure was necessitated in order to maintain the rigor of our design.

After several of these experiences, no individual was entered into the study singly. We waited until a matched pair had been selected and then tossed a coin to determine the fate of both subjects at once.

Administrative factors.—Occasionally it happened that a pair, after having been matched and discriminated as experimental and control, was broken up by circumstances beyond the control of the project group, usually by discharge of one of the individuals from the hospital or transfer to another hospital. This meant renewing the search to find another matching individual for the remaining subject, or finding an altogether new matching pair for the cell. Either alternative presented difficulties, not the least of which was the large amount of time involved.

It is no doubt clear by now that matching and entering a pair of subjects into our research design was often an incredibly difficult and nearly always a frustrating experience. The matchings, though they fitted our definitions, were not always qualitatively as close or as satisfactory as we would have liked. Considering the number of variables on which we were trying to match our subjects, however, it is believed that we filled the design with sets of matched pairs for which we do not need to apologize.

Having described at some length the elaborate operations involved in matching our subjects, we will present the remaining problems connected with the actuation of the design more briefly.

The Problem of Repeated Testing

One difficulty which we had not adequately foreseen in advance was the problem of retesting. It was our original plan to gather test data for both experimental and control individuals at three-month and six-month intervals—depending on the test involved—until termination of therapy for the experimental member of the matched pair. But what exactly is the meaning of the test, say a Rorschach, when it is being taken for the fourth time? And as for instructions, what kinds of instructions are necessary to give to a patient who is so familiar with the TAT that, as he says, he could take it without even looking at the pictures? We concluded that too frequent retesting would actually spoil the meaning of the test results and that our aim should be modified in this respect.

Another factor in this decision was the enormous difficulty in gaining the cooperation of the research subjects. In almost every instance they were inclined to be uncooperative in regard to taking tests, and in many instances the psychometrist had to spend hours and hours in order to get the minimum cooperation necessary for taking the test. Sometimes such tests as the MMPI had to be read aloud to the subject in order to get him to actually take the test. In seeing a patient repeatedly in order to give him tests, we often ran into scheduling difficulties natural in a treatment-oriented hospital. The patient went to occupational therapy or to the movies rather than taking the test, as arranged. These resistances and conflicts made it difficult to keep up with the testing schedule.

As matters turned out, we settled for a much more modest aim of having one pretest battery as complete as possible and at least one battery of tests late in therapy or at the end of therapy (and at the equivalent time for his matched control). We were in most instances able to achieve this goal.

In addition to the problems of repeated testing, and the difficulty in securing cooperation, there was naturally with this population the problem of comprehension. Many patients experienced difficulty in comprehending particular items. Others had trouble in understanding an entire instrument. Our psychometrists spent much time explaining or simplifying some aspects of the tests, endeavoring, however, to avoid biasing the patient's response.

Recording of Interviews

In some instances patients were dropped from the research because they were not willing to be recorded. This included patients who would not even come to the office for interviews but had to be contacted on the ward. Failure to record an occasional interview was not regarded as serious, but a persistent refusal to record meant that the patient had to be dropped from the research because we would have no adequate data to analyze. For the most part the patients' attitudes were clear cut. Either they paid no attention to the recording or they were openly and seriously opposed.

When individuals had to be dropped from the research, they were not, however, dropped from therapy. The therapist continued to work with the patient as long as possible. We have continued a clinical follow-up of these persons in order to see whether they represent a different kind of subject from those who continued in the research. At the present writing, nearly five years after the initiation of the research, one of our therapists is still working with a patient who had resolutely refused to be recorded. He has rejected and "signed off" with each of several therapists, but a therapist in the program is still continuing to see him and some progress has been made. Ironically, he has now given his permission for the interviews to be recorded. Thus, from the point of view of both our clinical responsibility and our research interest, we have maintained touch even with those who have of necessity been excluded from the research. This enables us to estimate, at least on a clinical basis, the type of selection which may be involved in the dropping of some individuals from the design.

Therapist Assignment

We were not always able to hold to the perfectly planned triad of cases for each therapist. Departures from this, however, were not great, and essentially the point was maintained that the therapists were assigned to three quite different individuals in the three major groups.

The Implementation of the Sampling Interviews

Like all the innovations in the research program, the sampling interview too involved its problems. We were fortunate in obtaining the help of Dr. Robert Roessler, at that time Chairman of the Department of Psychiatry and Director of the Psychiatric Institute at the University of

Wisconsin, for this important function. Appointments were set up so that he interviewed at three-month intervals, for a 20-to-30-minute period, every subject, normal or schizophrenic, therapy or control, in the research. The number of fruitless hours spent in waiting for individuals who did not appear can only be mentioned. Dr. Roessler was given no information in regard to the individual he was interviewing, so unless there was some mention of the therapist by the patient, he had no information as to whether he was interviewing an individual in therapy or a control. He had no other relationship to the research program and hence was essentially unbiased in his attitude.

In accordance with the design of the research, he tried to take as neutral an approach as possible with each interviewee, except that he showed a personal interest in the individual. In the initial contact it was decided that he would make approximately the following statement to the client, after the initial greeting was over, after the client had settled down, after the client understood that the interview was being recorded, and when it was clear that he was listening: "I would like to tell you why I wanted to talk with you. I am interested in the patients in this hospital, though I am not on the staff here." (For normal subjects, ". . . I am interested in the individuals in this research.") "I will plan to talk with you about every three months to see how you are getting along. I would like for you to tell me all that you are willing to tell me about yourself, and your situation, and how you feel about yourself and your situation. Anything you can tell me which will help me to know you better, I would like to hear." (Alternate form if necessary to repeat: "I would like to know about you and your situation as you see it, and the feelings you have about yourself and your situation.")

Beyond this statement of initial purpose, Dr. Roessler tried to respond to any client expression in an acceptant and non-threatening way, receiving and responding empathically to whatever depth of personal expression the individual was capable of achieving, or willing to communicate.

The Problem of Drug Therapy

In spite of the good intentions of the hospital administration, and the policy agreement which they had reached with the research group regarding the use of tranquilizers only in emergency situations, we were not able to avoid the use of drugs with some of the therapy patients. The situation was complex. Research subjects who were control patients received tranquilizing drugs, since it was part of the design that they would be a part of the normal hospital treatment program, and would receive group therapy, drugs, recreational therapy, etc., in whatever fashion and to whatever degree the hospital thought wise. The ward physicians often found it difficult, however, to withhold drugs from the therapy patients. The nurses and attendants were likely to request it when the patient was difficult or disturbed; the physician's whole set was toward giving anything which he thought might help. Hence to a greater extent than we wished, tranquilizers were administered to therapy subjects in the research. For some patients this was an occasional thing; for the more disturbed, drugs were sometimes felt to be necessary over fairly long periods; not infrequently, the research staff members were not informed when the agreement was breached; the turnover of staff physicians often meant that drugs were prescribed for a time by a physician who had no knowledge of the agreement. All in all, it must be said that the variable of therapy in the research was to some extent contaminated by the concurrent administration of drugs. This is unfortunate, but it should be recognized that it only makes more outstanding any of the positive findings of the research.

Perhaps a word of explanation is in order here. If the drugs produced some positive therapeutic effect, then it would be evident in the control individuals in any event. To the extent that the therapy cases received drugs, this should tend to wipe out any differences between the therapy and control groups. To the extent that the therapy group showed any positive changes over and above the changes in the controls, it is still clearly evident, in spite of their receiving a certain amount of chemotherapy, that such positive changes must be attributed to the variable of therapy.

The Design as Related to One Subject

To indicate something of what was involved in carrying through the design of the research, it may be helpful to present the procedures in the case of one therapy subject.

Miss FAS was originally selected for the research in the fall of 1958. Another subject was paired with her and the flip of the coin indicated that Miss FAS was to be offered therapy. She was entered in the research design in December 1958. Test data and research instruments were collected from her, her therapist, and the staff at three-month and six-month intervals. The results appear in Table 3.1. Sampling interviews were held every three months, although two such interviews were missed. At the time the table was constructed in 1961, she had completed four each of the Q-sort, WAIS, Rorschach, F Scale, Truax Anxiety Scale, and Stroop. She had taken five MMPI's, five TAT's, and six Relationship Inventories, and had participated in nine sampling interviews. The therapist had filled out seven Relationship Inventories

Table 3.1—Data collected during the case of Miss FAS

Source of data	Pre-therapy	Months of therapy									
		3rd	6th	9th	12th	15th	18th	21st	24th	27th	30th[a]
Three-month battery											
Sampling interview	X	X	X	X	X	X	X	—	—	X	X
Relationship Inventory (client)	—	X	X	—	X	—	X	X	—	X	—
Relationship Inventory (therapist)	—	X	X	X	X	X	—	X	—	X	—
Wittenborn Scales	X	X	X	—	X	X	—	X	—	—	X
Six-month battery											
Rorschach	X	—	—	—	X	—	X	—	—	—	X
TAT	X	—	X	—	X	—	X	—	—	—	X
Q-sort	X	—	X	—	—	—	X	—	—	—	X
Stroop	X	—	X	—	—	—	X	—	—	—	X
MMPI	X	—	X	—	X	—	X	—	—	—	X
Truax Anxiety	X	—	X	—	—	—	X	—	—	—	X
F Scale	X	—	X	—	—	—	X	—	—	—	X
WAIS	X	—	X	—	—	—	X	—	—	—	X
Therapy	—				Approximately two 30-to-50-minute interviews per week. Total, 238.						

[a] With Miss FAS the research concluded before the therapy concluded. The tests at the 30th month were used as the post-therapy measures.

and the ward personnel had returned seven Wittenborn Scales dealing with her ward behavior. This represents a total of 57 tests over a period of more than thirty months. During this time there were 238 tape-recorded therapy contacts with her. During this period Miss FAS was at times cooperative, more often indifferent, and rather frequently, aggressively hostile. In behavior she was at times under complete restraint, at other times in an open ward. There were periods of marked progress and periods of marked regression. She was tested and recorded at every stage of her changing behavior.

The Ratings

Obtaining Interview Samples for Rating

The recorded interviews both with the therapist and with the sampling interviewer were, it should be clear, of enormous importance to the research. It was on the basis of this interactional material that judgments of the attitudinal conditions in the relationship and judgments of the stage of process were to be made. We recognized in planning the research that this material would constitute some of our most important data.

In spite of this recognition it is doubtless fortunate that we could not fully foresee the enormous difficulties and the incredible amount of work which would be involved in carrying out these steps. It is a matter for some amusement that in the rather lengthy proposal which set up the whole design for the research, this aspect of it was mentioned in three brief sentences: "The data from the recorded interviews will be analyzed to test the general hypotheses mentioned. As a basis for testing our propositions regarding movement in therapy we will have various samplings of behavior gathered at different points in time. There will be the interview interactions between client and therapist; the interaction between the client and the sampling interviewer; the samplings of client behavior by means of objective and projective tests; the observations of his behavior." The way in which the research came to be carried out will be made more clear to the reader by specifying some of the elements involved in putting these three simple sentences, as they relate to interview material, into effect.

Earlier work by members of our group, particularly Hart, indicated that small samples of any given interview were sufficient to give a basis for judging its relationship and process qualities. The pilot studies indicated that one to three samples per interview, two to five minutes in length, would give an adequate basis for rating such characteristics. The number of samples to be taken from a given interview would depend on the refinement desired in the study. If it was a study of general trends, one sample was regarded as sufficient. For a study in which it was desired to test specific and detailed hypotheses, a larger number of samples was desirable. In practice, we used either one two-minute sample from the second half of the interview, or three four-minute segments, one from each third of the interview, depending on the type of study involved.

It is obvious that such samples must be picked in an unbiased fashion, precluding any prejudice on the part of the individual choosing the segments. What does this aim mean in practice? Perhaps the reader can best gain a knowledge of the precautions taken to insure objective and unbiased segmenting if we quote from the instructions to the worker who was to take the three four-minute segments from the therapy and sampling interviews for subsequent rating. A portion of these instructions, somewhat condensed, is as follows:

A. *Aim:* To obtain a unit approximately four minutes in length with two client and two therapist responses each long enough to express some meaning.
B. *Steps*
  1. Determine the approximate length of the interview and divide into thirds.
  2. Enter the first third of the interview at a point indicated by consulting a table of random numbers (if the first third of the interview is 15 minutes in length, this would mean consulting a list of random numbers from 1 to 11, thus leaving room for a four-minute sample even if entering at 11 minutes.)
  3. Beginning at the point of entry continue for four minutes. If the sample thus obtained contains two client and two therapist responses, each at least five words in length, it is complete.
  4. If a sample does not include two client and two therapist responses, continue listening until these are obtained. Reduce the periods of silence to 20 seconds each until the sample is no more than four minutes in length. Indicate each 30 seconds of silence by beeps on the recording. This sample is now complete.

Additional steps were listed trying to take account of every difficulty which the segment selector might encounter. In no case was it left to his subjective judgment to select a given segment. He followed the rules. In this manner, more than 3,000 segments were selected from our therapy and sampling interviews, each chosen in a prescribed and unbiased fashion from the recorded material.

These samples were edited for cues which might reveal the name of the therapist, or the length of time in therapy, or whether this was a sampling or therapy interview. Any such cues were deleted from the tape. Thus, the material to be presented to the raters was a brief sample, without any contextual basis, of human interaction between two individuals. It was possible from the content of the material to distinguish the therapist or interviewer from the interviewee. Otherwise there was nothing in the material which would indicate whether it was early or late in therapy, whether it was a control individual or a patient in therapy, whether this was a therapy interview or a sampling interview. It was a four-minute auditory snapshot of personal interaction, no more.

The Development of Rating Scales

What instruments were we to use on these carefully selected interview segments? It seemed clear that in spite of many deficiencies a rating scale, used by judges or raters competent in that scale, was the best current answer to our problem. No purely objective score, no word count, first-person-pronoun count, or other objective score could take the place of a trained human judgment as to whether a certain quality existed in the therapist or in the client. Thus one of the most significant aspects of our research program was the development of more and more refined rating scales for measuring the subtle qualities in which we were interested.

Scales were developed rather early for the judgment of empathy, unconditional positive regard, and congruence in the therapist. These initial scales were developed by Hart. By the time we were ready to make the final ratings on which the findings would be based, new scales had been developed for each of these qualities by Truax. Later a new scale for rating congruence was developed by Kiesler and re-ratings of the various segments were made. All of these scales were intended to be applied to the therapist responses in the interview segments.

Our other interest was in judging the process level achieved by the client at the moment the segment was recorded so that we could determine his level on what we conceptualized as a continuum of the process of therapy. Here there was a burgeoning of instruments. An overall scale for rating process, developed by Rogers and Rablen in 1958, spawned many others. Each of the scales developed after this point endeavored to be more specific as to the cues of in-therapy behavior on the part of the client which separately were helpful in defining each stage of the scale of process level. They also endeavored to be more explicit regarding the construct being rated so that it would be comprehensible and ratable by individuals with no particular training or experience in therapy. Among these scales were the Experiencing Scale (Gendlin) devised to assess the degree to which the individual was remote from or immediately in his experiencing; the Problem Expression Scale (van der Veen) to evaluate the manner in which the client related to his problems —whether denying his problems, feeling they existed at a distance, or accepting full and personal responsibility for his contribution to them; the Personal Constructs Scale (Tomlinson), an attempt to measure the degree of rigidity with which experience is construed; the Relationship Scale (Gendlin) assessing the relationship qualities or the ability to relate exhibited by the client.

Each of these scales is included in Appendix C: "Rating Scales for Therapeutic Process" in order that research workers may profit from our efforts. Each is described in more detail in the chapters discussing the findings based on these scales. The aim of this brief description is to indicate the extent of our effort to develop instruments which would measure reliably and satisfactorily those characteristics of the therapeutic relationship and those elements of the process of change in the client in which we were most deeply interested and around which our hypotheses were built.

The Raters and Their Work

Initially we thought it would be necessary to have individuals trained or experienced in therapy to rate the decidedly intangible qualities of the therapeutic relationship and the client process. During this initial period we experimented with our ratings on different segment lengths, using different scales and modifications thereof. Hundreds upon hundreds of such ratings were made, adding to our knowledge of the difficulties, providing helpful suggestions for revising the scales, giving us some notion of the degree of reliability which could be obtained, giving useful insights as to therapist errors, and the like. At this stage of the program the unremitting efforts of Emily Earley and Paula Rohrbaugh were of inestimable value to the research.

Two trends in our thinking developed out of this experience. If we were to use individuals who were knowledgeable in regard to therapy as our raters, this would greatly limit the number from which we could choose, and we recognized that the rating task would be an enormous one. We found that experienced therapists tended to rate on the basis of clinical judgment rather than on the definitions provided in the scale. Also, individuals who were close to this field tended to recognize the voices of some of the therapists or in some instances even voices of the clients. This would be a definitely biasing factor. Thus we became more and more unhappy with the thought of selecting as raters only individuals who had some training and experience in therapy.

At the same time, Charles Truax and other members of our research group were insisting that if the qualities we were rating were real and recognizable, they should be real and recognizable to any intelligent individual, not simply to those with experience of, or knowledge of, therapy. It was this insistence that led to the revision of all of our rating scales so they would be more specific, more closely related to behavioral cues, and less open to inference on the part of the rater.

To cut short what could be a lengthy story, we ended up by having all the ratings on which our major findings were based made by under-graduate students! Our rationale was this. For each of the constructs that we were rating, whether congruence, or level of experiencing, or relationship to problems, a specific definition was worked out, and equally specific observation terms were found for describing each level or stage. The rating scales were refined to a point where they referred to discriminable evidences in the therapists' or clients' expressions, as the case might be. Then we recruited students who were looking for work. Our only requirement was that they have a B average or better in their studies and be willing to commit themselves for a very considerable period of work. A small group of students was then assigned to be the rating group for a particular construct. The students were given a brief but intensive course of instruction in the meaning of this construct and the various observation aspects defining the levels of the scale which they were to use. They were instructed not to communicate with each other about the work they were doing until after their task was com-pleted. Thus as the program developed we had one group of student raters, quite naive in regard to psychotherapy, rating every segment for the degree of empathy which was evident in the therapist. We had another group of similarly naive students rating the immediacy of expe-riencing as evidenced in the client's expression. (In this case they were rating a construct of which it can be certain they had never heard until they came in for employment.) In a final re-rating of all of our segments, a fresh crop of student raters was trained to a suitable degree of interrater reliability before being permitted to listen to the segments involved in the research. Like many of the other aspects of this study, this procedure was time-consuming and costly. It had, however, many values. It meant that all of the construct ratings were completely independent, being done by different groups of judges who had no communication with each other. It meant that none of the ratings was biased by the rater's view of what therapists or psychotherapy ought to be, because every rater was decidedly naive in this respect. It meant that the methods employed could be transferred to another research setting, that the methods could indeed be replicated anywhere. It removed from our work more completely, we believe, than has ever been done in any psychotherapy research, any possible element of bias. It made it clear that whatever findings emerged would have a solidity heretofore unknown in this field.

While we tried out various modes of training, most often the individual rater spent a number of hours, sometimes as many as ten, in instruction in the construct he would be rating, and in the scale which he was to use. He listened to segments of interviews which had already been rated by others in order to get a feeling for the range of qualities which he would be assessing. He was able at this point to raise questions in order to clarify his own understanding of the construct and to get some feeling of confidence that he could rate the intangible qualities which were involved. He was at no time informed of the design of the research. Then he was assigned a recording machine and earphones and put to work. He was there simply to do the task for which he was hired —to rate some given number of interview segments in terms of the one quality for which he had been trained.

An odd sidelight on the research is that the work of the raters was, for visitors, a most impressive sight. To open the door to a sound-proofed, air-conditioned room in which up to a dozen young people were placed, each before his own recording machine, each with large foam-rubber-lined earphones clamped to his head, sitting in perfect silence, seemed a bit like science fiction. The research program is deeply indebted to the scores of raters, nameless so far as this research is concerned, who contributed their conscientious effort for the very small pay which is permitted to student workers by University policy. The more than 17,000 ratings which were made are in many respects the backbone of our findings. When it is recognized that each of these ratings was based upon listening carefully and intently to a brief existential fragment of interview interaction, that it was often necessary to play the segment over again several times to be certain of the quality which was being rated, then the depth of our indebtedness to these individuals may be recognized.

There is no doubt that one of the most important methodological aspects of the entire research has been the fact that we did carry out the plan of almost complete tape recordings of hundreds upon hundreds of psychotherapy hours, the randomized and painstaking methods of obtaining segments to be rated, and the development of refined rating methods approaching quantified objectivity on these intimate basic variables.

The Ward-Availability Project

Thus far the research has been spoken of as though it were composed entirely of one complex design. This is in large measure the case. Yet along with the so-called "main design," there gradually developed a secondary research project which enriched our learnings and findings, and which deserves a careful description. Since it definitely came into being as part of our reaction to the work of putting the "main design" into effect, its presentation has been put off until this point in our account of the research program.

In carrying out a carefully designed research, it is impossible to profit from one's learnings as one goes along, since one cannot change the research plan in midstream. During the five years of the program reported here, we learned much that could not be applied within the research we had already begun. Some of these learnings concerned the enormous difficulty of starting office psychotherapy with schizophrenic patients who are withdrawn, afraid, have never heard or thought of such a thing as psychotherapy, and refuse to meet, talk to, or engage in a relationship with, a psychotherapist.

A given therapist would go out to Mendota State Hospital (several miles from the center of Madison) twice a week to see a given patient. Not infrequently the patient would refuse to see him. The therapist might spend hours waiting in vain for his patient, or he might send for him through ward staff and then accept the reported refusal, or he might go to see the patient on the ward (if the patient hadn't purposely gone to the greenhouse or the laundry.) The therapist might force his presence on the patient, go to see him in the seclusion room (if the patient was confined there), or have him brought to the therapy office, more or less against his wishes, by ward aides. Every alternative was tried by one or another of the therapists. The patient might remain in the office for a few minutes and might then ask to leave. Many of our cases required weeks and months of this frustrating process before a relationship resembling the start of therapy began. This period was discouraging and demoralizing, partly because of the waste of therapist effort and time. It is difficult to give so much enthusiasm, good will, time, and involvement, and then to travel back again knowing that nothing has been accomplished except a few minutes of this slow and questionable wearing-down process. One is not even convinced that many rejections by the patient, if tolerated somehow, will eventually lead to a relationship.

After all, there is no opportunity for interaction when the therapist cannot maintain himself in the same physical space with the patient. All the therapist's skill, training, and personal involvement are useless. There is almost no opportunity for him to reach the patient.

The other side of this discouraging problem lay with the patient. Was it "therapeutic" or helpful for the patient to be forced? Was it a good opening for a deeply freeing human relationship if the patient was reduced to an object brought to a therapy office? Did the therapist help the patient by employing the hospital's coercive capacities to make the patient helpless? Was this an accurate way for the therapist to introduce himself to the patient?

The problem therefore was: How could a therapist maintain himself in the same space with a patient so that they might interact, and do so without coercion and without the waste of time involved in the few minutes of repeated rejection spread over many months?

One circumstance pointed to a possible answer for this problem. In going on the ward to see a patient who then rejected him, the therapist often spoke also with other patients. The research patient having refused and walked angrily away, it was at least somewhat satisfying for the therapist to speak with other patients who wished to talk with someone. In repeatedly going to the ward, the therapist came to know some of the patients, to speak with some and exchange glances with others. After some weeks and a good deal of interaction with many patients on the ward, the first therapist to whom this happened had a significant experience. His research patient said the first positive thing he had ever said: "I am glad you came to see me *too*."

It seemed that the research patient was considerably relieved by this ward procedure which showed him that he was not the only one who was (mysteriously) singled out for therapy. Also, the weeks just past had included more than the few moments in which the therapist attempted to talk with the patient and the patient rejected the therapist. During these weeks the research patient and the therapist had been in the same dayroom for many hours. The patient had observed the therapist. They had exchanged glances many times each hour. The therapist was there for the patient to approach, and although the patient did not do so, he spent entire hours (not just the few minutes) struggling around the question. Nor was the patient coerced. He could come closer and move away again. He could decide to relate with the therapist and then again change his mind, and then change it back again. The therapist had managed to maintain himself uncoercively in the same space with the patient, and had managed to interact with the patient for hours, not for minutes only. The therapist had even managed to show the observing patient some of his own attitudes and modes of working with people. And all this had come about accidentally.

The question naturally suggested itself: Could we design a situation to employ this mode of initiating psychotherapy? A ward of male chronic patients was chosen. Several mentally defective and several organically damaged patients were transferred out of the ward and other chronic patients brought in to replace them. Most of the patients were diagnosed "chronic schizophrenic" by the hospital, but patients with other diagnoses were also included. These were all long-term patients for whom "no release planning was contemplated."

We sought an arrangement which would allow not only speaking with patients on the ward but also the possibility of going with the patient into an office where tape recording was possible. We obtained an office *on* the ward, with its door open, to which patient and therapist could go.

The design aimed to initiate therapy with *all* the patients on the ward simultaneously rather than with only one patient at a time. Therefore, instead of assigning certain therapists to certain patients, we arranged for eight therapists to spend two hours weekly on the ward, speaking to any patients who wished, and exchanging a few words, glances, and invitations with those who did not. In this way all the patients on the ward could experience the *offer* of a relationship, and could either accept or reject this offer throughout a total of sixteen hours a week, spread over six days of the week. This was more than a puzzling verbal offer stated by a strange and threatening person for a few minutes. Rather, it was a concrete, observable, and experienced offer around which the patient could struggle, could think and feel.

Much of the time spent by the eight therapists was immediately pre-empted by two and soon by three patients who did want to come into the office to talk with someone. These three patients did not choose one among the eight therapists. They each spoke with all eight for as long as the therapists permitted. And at first the therapists were only too glad to permit it, since the open-ward situation was not easy for the therapist. Once in the office with a willing patient, the therapist was back in his element. It was not nearly as easy for the therapists to remain on the open ward, standing next to a silent patient, exchanging glances with another silent patient, initiating a conversation with a patient while four others listened suspiciously. Yet both inside and outside of the little office, the therapists managed to communicate enough of what they wished to do, and managed to develop enough tentative relationships, so that eventually all the patients entered into more or less consistent contact with one of the therapists in the office.

The way in which this occurred needs further description. For example, a therapist might speak briefly to a given patient twice a week. He might also stand next to a very withdrawn patient for a few minutes each time, perhaps saying a few words now and then through some minutes of silence. He might speak at more length to a third patient. He might then walk into the therapy office with one of the three motivated patients (who, as mentioned, spent as much time as they could with each of the therapists). In this manner, the therapist might come to feel that he had some degree of relationship with perhaps six or eight of the patients.

After a time the therapist would notice one or another of the patients waiting specifically for him. Upon entering at the ward door, the therapist would notice the patient at the other end of the long ward corridor. The patient was waiting at this therapist's regular time, twice a week. Perhaps by the time the therapist walked down the corridor to the dayroom the patient would seem to be engaged in looking at an old magazine and seem not to notice the therapist, yet at the next visit, there he was again, on the other end of the long corridor, waiting as the therapist entered the ward door. From such a stage of tentative relationship, not many weeks passed before therapist and patient would go together to the little office to spend twenty minutes or a half-hour in a much more therapy-like interaction.

Eventually, by far the greater part of therapist time was spent in actual therapeutic interaction (and tape recording) in the office. Even the time spent on the ward involved interacting positively with patients. In this way, without any wasted therapist time, twenty-one definitely "unmotivated" patients were given many hours during which to carry out the needed process through which such individuals can enter psychotherapy.

The Research Side of the Ward-Availability Project

An interesting aspect of this ward-availability procedure with eight therapists was that in many instances a given patient would see several therapists during the same period. Therapists could thus be compared with each other, as had never been possible before! Similarly, a given therapist saw numerous patients. Thus it was also possible to compare the same therapist in his interactions with different patients.

Though it could not be planned in advance, we did find later that of the twenty-four patients eleven saw four or more therapists, and eight of these patients saw four different therapists in such a way that a research analysis became possible.

Here was priceless data which we would not have dared to seek directly. A fantasy of all therapists is to wonder how another therapist would have dealt with this particular problem or this particular individual. Here we had data showing how Therapist A dealt with the patient on Monday; Therapist B on Tuesday; C on Wednesday, and so on. It enabled us eventually to throw some light on the extent to which the therapist influences the qualities of the relationship, and the extent to which the primary influence is that of the client.

For the hypothesis of our "main design" this was of major importance. We had predicted that the level of therapist attitudinal conditions would determine the degree of client improvement. But how were we going to decide whether the reverse was the case? Might it not be just as possible that those patients who (for reasons not yet fully understood) were already the improving ones enabled therapists to have these positive attitudes? One of several modes which could be adopted to deal with this problem was to examine each therapist with a number of patients. We could then see to what extent he was influenced by various patients, as compared with the extent to which he was consistently high or low with all patients. Similarly, we could examine a given patient's tape recordings with several therapists to see whether the patient managed to bring them all down (or up) to a similar level of attitudinal conditions, or whether (as we predicted) the different therapists were themselves the determinant of their attitudes so that therapists differ even with one and the same patient.

We found both effects, as will be indicated in later chapters, but by far the stronger factor seemed to be the therapist. The finding was that therapists are like themselves regardless of which patient they are with at the moment. Similarities among the different therapists of one patient were also found but constituted a weaker effect. The research made possible a quantitative measure of both effects.

In addition to these findings relevant to the "main design" research, we also have the following information for the five-month period of the project. There was at least one tape-recorded contact in the office with each of the twenty-four men. There were more than five interviews for sixteen of them. Of a total of 381 recorded interviews, 235, or 62 per cent, of the interviews were with the three men already mentioned as being "motivated" almost from the beginning. (It may be of interest that these three men were eventually discharged from the hospital and have not returned.) When the time spent with these three patients is subtracted, it seems that the initiating of therapy with twenty-one unmotivated men required an average of less than four hours per week. The judgment of the therapists was that perhaps ten or eleven of the twenty-four showed clearly perceptible improvement.

Eight patients settled into real therapy, each with one therapist, and continued it for up to two years. It eventually became natural for the therapists to meet these patients individually elsewhere than on the ward. The "cafeteria" nature of therapy offered by eight different therapists gradually ceased. The ward-availability project ended because of the pressures and time limitations existing for the therapists. The project's format, for our group of therapists at least, did not lend itself to *continuing* psychotherapy. The format seems to be successful for the initiating of psychotherapy with this type of client population.

In the context of the larger ongoing "main design," the ward-availability project not only afforded crucial additional data, but also gave the therapists a free-wheeling situation in which they could try themselves out with many more patients. There was a sharp need for this during the frustrating and difficult period when managing to see one's "design patient" even for a few minutes was an achievement, and when the exigencies of carrying out the research plan as predetermined weighed heavily on us.

4. The Human Side of the Research

This chapter is drawn from the experience of all the individuals who have in any way been associated with the reseach program. It has been brought together in written form by Carl R. Rogers.

To those of us who were involved in the program it seems quite impossible to understand the real significance of the research design or the meaning of the findings without having some feeling for the very human reactions which were involved in every aspect and phase of the research. It is not feasible to do justice to the highly individualized attitudes which were involved on the part of every participant, but this chapter endeavors to capture some of the more common reactions of the different individuals and groups related to the research.

The Experience of the Patient

The experience of the patient started with a contact on the ward with a stranger. He was informed that as a part of a study which was being carried on by some individuals at the University to learn more about how people might be helped in hospitals such as this, he would be asked to take certain tests and fill out certain forms and the like. He was asked if he would come to another room in order to undertake some of these tasks. Whether this explanation was given all at once or piecemeal, whether the patient resisted or whether he passively accompanied the stranger, there were many reactions of a feeling nature. One of the most frequent was, "Why have they picked me? Why do they want me? Why don't they pick someone else on the ward?" It was clear that being thus selected by "fate" often had a deep and sometimes frightening meaning.

Then came the arduous routine of testing. At first it might be interesting for the patient. At least it involved a contact with a new and friendly person. Yet, as the tasks continued and as they became both more difficult and more personal, the reaction often changed to one of resistance. The patient's self-esteem—often low at best—suffered in any real or imaginary failure on the tasks, and this tended to make the whole experience distasteful. The instrument which the patients liked least was the Relationship Inventory which they filled out either for the therapist with whom they were working or (in the case of the controls) for "the person who has meant most to me in my trouble." To evaluate a specific relationship, even by silently putting marks down on paper, seemed to be a threatening and difficult task which many disliked. Then, as the testing continued over months and even years, there was, even for the most cooperative, the double reaction of being glad to see the research worker again and at the same time the feeling, "Oh not again! Not all of those tests! I just took them a few months ago!" For some the reaction was much stronger. One woman came to hate the testing violently. She felt guinea-pigged, evaluated, psychologically undressed. Each test experience seemed like an operation—one she was not sure she would survive. It took the very best efforts not only of the psychometrist but in this case of the therapist as well, to persuade her to endure this "torture." This kind of response to the testing created real ethical problems for the research staff.

Then there were the interviews. On the first occasion, asked to accompany a new stranger to a room often distant from the ward, there were attitudes ranging from puzzlement to terror. Sometimes there was an immediate positive response, as in the patient who went back to the ward and told the attendant, "I think I have found somebody who really understands me." Much more often there was a questioning and reluctant feeling: "What am I supposed to do? What do you want me to talk about? Why do you want to see me? I didn't ask to see you." In some instances the patients refused at first to come into the room, refused to talk, were extremely frightened and wary.

Overriding all of the interview contacts was the settled conviction held by a great many of the patients, "Talking won't help." To the majority of the patients a word such as "psychotherapy" had no meaning. For the most part it seemed clear that they felt their lives had been hurt by talk rather than helped. They were concerned about the strange and probably dangerous motives involved in bringing them to this room with this doctor. They tended to be reluctant, suspicious, fearful, or cynical about this new relationship.

The therapist stressed the fact that he was not part of the hospital staff; that what was said in any contacts was confidential; and that even though the interviews were tape recorded no one from the hospital would be permitted to listen. The results of this explanation, so far as the patients were concerned, were partly positive and partly negative. Though a number of them accepted the assurances and became less fearful and suspicious, many of them began to raise the question, either in explicit or implicit ways, "But if you don't belong to the hospital, can you get me out of here?" When it was gradually realized that the therapist did not have an authoritative administrative relationship to his client, this often had, at least temporarily, a negative effect on the relationship: "What's the use of talking if you can't get me out of here?"

In spite of all the negative reactions, the fears and the scepticism, many and probably most of the individuals in therapy gradually came to feel, "Here is someone who does seem to be here, who seems to be here for me, who possibly cares, and with whom I do seem to feel more comfortable." Thus, increasingly, patients came to the interviews on their own volition and on their own responsibility. It seemed clear that in many instances they could not have given any articulate reasons for their continuing of the relationship, and yet they came.

The Experience of the Research Worker

The task of the research worker, especially in the early phases of the research, was indeed a frustrating one. It was difficult enough to find normal individuals who could be matched on three variables and who would be willing to undergo the various routines of the research itself. To find two schizophrenics in the hospital who matched on all four variables which were required—sex, age, socio-educational status, and degree of disturbance—was a time-consuming task, the magnitude of which can only be realized by someone who undertakes it. It meant poring over hundreds of hospital case histories, often a chaotic and contradictory accumulation of material over many years, in order to eliminate those who had at some earlier time had psychosurgery or an excessive number of EST. It meant painfully digging out the information which would enable a proper matching to be done. It meant contacting the individual patient in order to attempt to verify some of the information, and to gain a picture of his current behavior and disturbance. Then it meant the long-continuing search for another individual who matched. One of the stories of that period well illustrates the fantastic kinds of problems which were faced. After information concerning a particularly difficult and uncommunicative female patient had been collected, a match was sought for her. The research worker came back from the ward full of excitement saying: "They match—Mrs. X matches Mrs. Y. She won't talk to me either!"

There were other frustrations. After the long task of finding a pair of individuals who matched was completed, two days later one of them might be given a temporary dismissal from the hospital, thus making therapy impossible. Then, in order to fulfill the requirements of scientific rigor, the second individual of the pair had to be discarded and the search started all over again. The research members of our staff gathered information on all eight hundred hospital patients and selected, matched, and sometimes began to gather data on sixty-five patients, even though our actual design included only thirty-two schizophrenics.

Thus the simple statement that the design of our research is based on matched pairs conceals the year and more of conscientious and exceedingly frustrating effort to find individuals who were, in basic characteristics, somewhat equivalent.

Likewise, the statement that test batteries were administered at intervals to both our therapy cases and controls is misleadingly simple. It says nothing of the hours upon hours of time devoted by sometimes as many as three successive psychometrists, each trying in turn to win cooperation from a recalcitrant patient. It says nothing of the half-day which might be wasted in a carefully planned schedule of testing because two patients had been sent to watch the baseball game. It says nothing of the detailed effort to make sure that the different psychometrists who worked with the research (it was not possible to have one psychometrist carry the whole load) administered the tests in similar fashion. The unsung heroes of the research are those who did the basic work of matching the pairs in the first place and carrying out the heavy burden of psychometric testing throughout the program.

The Experience of the "Normals"

The individuals who made up our normal population usually heard of the research first in a group meeting at their church or Grange, or in a meeting of employees. They understood it to be a project of research in personality. They were told that the experience might or might not be useful to them but that it would aid the University in learning more about how to be of help to people. With this understanding, many people volunteered, and it is clear that their motives tended to be of the following type: "Sure, I'll help. It might be interesting. Besides, the University is a good place and has been of help to the people in the state, so I'll volunteer in order to be a part of the repayment of that debt."

Later the attitude of most of them tended to be, "What will these people ever do with all of these tests?" The cooperation they gave, however, was sometimes very loyal. The major problem was in scheduling appointments, at least with those who were selected by the flip of the coin as controls.

For those who were selected to come in for interviews, the reaction tended to be ambivalent. Some individuals were clearly rather fearful of interviews. Parents of some of the younger normals were resistant. Other members of the normal group were very friendly but kept contacts on a social, chitchat basis. Some seemed to be saying, "I don't want to reveal myself too deeply, even to this friendly stranger." Others implied, "I don't need to reveal myself. My life is going fairly smoothly." One woman opened up very freely in the initial interview, revealing many problems about which she was deeply concerned. Within a short time she decided not to continue the interviews at all. Her feeling was, "I know I have problems. If I ever want to do something about them I would like to come to talk with you. Right now, however, if I opened up these areas in myself and talked freely about things that are troubling me it would affect my husband, his career, our relationship, and many other aspects of my life. I choose not to do this and prefer to close these inner doors that I have opened."

As time continued, the element of distance—most of our normals lived some distance out of Madison—and the difficulties of scheduling appointments which did not conflict with work or other obligations came to have an overriding importance. Thus the farmer would feel, "I've got corn to harvest, cows to milk, I've had a hard day, I really cannot come in this evening." The weather of the Midwest also played its part. To make a 30-mile round trip in sleet and snow and rain in order to spend an hour talking with someone, when the contact had not been initially requested by the individual subject, seemed like a difficult burden.

Finally, the therapists were new to the task of relating to individuals who had not requested help. They were less expressive, less skilled in initiating a significant relationship than they later became. As therapists we failed to communicate to the normal subjects the possibilities which we had hoped they would discover in an expressive relationship.

As a consequence of these various elements, the interviews with the normals never exceeded twelve and thus were in no real way comparable with the continuing interviews held with the schizophrenic population. The failure to continue undoubtedly has something to do with the fact that our normals were of lower, or, at most, middle-class socio-educational status and that to some degree they shared the viewpoint of our hospital population that "Talking won't help." Though the therapists often learned a great deal from these contacts with normally functioning individuals, the data from the normals were not really comparable with the data from the schizophrenics and thus were relegated to a minor place in the research.

The Therapist and His Trials

The experience of most of the therapists on the project had been primarily with outpatient clients who came voluntarily for help. They were faced with many difficult problems in establishing a relationship with the hospitalized schizophrenics and likewise with the normals, both of the groups being composed of individuals who were not seeking help. The problems of the therapist and the solutions to these problems were manifold: sometimes pathetic, sometimes amusing. How is a male therapist to deal with a female research client who dashes into the women's washroom when she sees him coming? This is not the kind of problem which is covered in textbooks on therapy. What is the therapist to do with the client who remains absolutely mute? What about the ethical and technical problems involved in dealing with the client who does not want to see you? Do you have any right to impose your desire for a relationship on him? The ways our therapists found of working with these unmotivated clients will be described at greater length in Chapter 16.

Suffice it to say here that the therapists as a group gradually came to realize that the assortment of individuals with whom they were working —both schizophrenics and normals—were probably more unpromising as clients than any group which has ever been studied in psychotherapy research. Some therapists have worked with more disturbed individuals, but probably no therapists have ever worked with a group for whom the prognosis was so uniformly poor so far as therapy was concerned. The therapists came to realize that they were dealing with individuals who were unmotivated, often unreachable, largely without hope, lacking in any concept of therapy, and certainly lacking in any belief that a relationship could be helpful.

A therapist in the usual clinic or private practice setting is sought after, his help is desired, his client comes to him with the specific hope that he will prove to be a helpful and curative person. To be faced with the opposite of all these conditions constituted a troubling personal problem for our therapists. Their devotion and persistence in trying to meet the situation was an amazing chapter of the research. There were for all of them times of great discouragement. The following note by one of the therapists explaining his unwillingness to continue further with the ward-availability project, described in the preceding chapter, expresses some of the feelings experienced at one time or another by all of our therapists. He says: "The thing I have learned [in the ward-availability project] is that simply a supply of cooperative therapists such as ourselves will not suffice to clean out the back wards of state hospitals. I have been quietly horrified by the monolithic acceptance of the status quo I have seen among the patients here. I must have thought that *any* new thing appearing on the ward would be welcome, let alone this most precious and specific hope for a new life that we can offer them. To find the patient so indifferent to a chance to talk with someone really stuns me." This comment came from a therapist with many years of experience in dealing with outpatient clients. It illustrates well the magnitude of the problem which the therapists faced. To be consistently rejected, over and over, to be unable to do anything helpful, to see no progress over long periods of time, to see no sign in the patient that he has any understanding of the relationship, to desire very much to be in touch with this person and to be unable to get through— these added together constituted a devastating experience.

This is not to say that there were no highly rewarding moments. It is simply that the rewarding experiences were much fewer and were spaced at much longer intervals than would be true in dealing with outpatient clients. Thus there were moments of real sharing, dramatic experiences of change, developments in freedom of expression, clearly discernible alterations in behavior. These were the precious experiences which made it possible for the therapists to continue. Yet there is no doubt that for each therapist such experiences were interspersed with long periods of waiting, of silence, of lack of change, of seeming to be on a plateau. Thus the task of the therapists—and therapists by their very professional qualifications are sensitive individuals—was by any standard a most difficult one.

For some of the therapists there was an additional problem, that of powerlessness. It was consistent with our view of psychotherapy and a part of our agreement with the hospital that the therapists had no administrative authority or function in the hospital. Yet the carrying out of this policy created grave conflicts at times for the therapists. What does the therapist do when he feels that his patient has been kept in restraint for too long a period? How shall he behave when grounds privileges are consistently withheld from a patient who is struggling desperately toward independence? How can the therapist react when his patient behaves on the ward in a new, freer, and more independent fashion, and this behavior is perceived by the ward attendant simply as being troublesome? Any course of action seems unsatisfactory. To stand up for the patient or to fight for what are perceived as his rights is to intrude on the hospital administration in a way that will surely and naturally be resented. To stand by and watch a patient go down in his struggle for life is an even more crushing experience for the therapist. It is probable that most of the therapists came to the point where they felt that in any new program of research they would wish to be part of the hospital staff with some degree of authority and responsibility.

The Trials of the Hospital Staff

It is not an easy thing for the well-organized staff of a hospital with a long and honorable history to admit into its midst a group of research workers and research therapists. The problem is made more difficult by the fact that the incoming group has had much less experience in dealing with hospitalized patients than has the hospital staff. Nor is it made easier by the fact that the group comes from a university, with its connotation of intellectual search and intellectual interest, while the interest of the hospital staff is almost entirely practical and clinical in its nature.

In spite of these basic difficulties, the relationship of the hospital staff and the research group was marked by surprisingly few serious difficulties. Occasionally one of the research staff would, wittingly or unwittingly, usurp some of the authority which rightly lay with the hospital staff. This nearly always brought a quick and negative reaction. For the most part, however, the series of minor difficulties which naturally arose were the result of poor communication. The hospital administrators had a clear understanding of the program and gave it their thoroughgoing personal backing. In this respect, Dr. Gilbert Tybring was outstandingly helpful. But it was not easy for such understanding and acceptance of the project to filter down through all of the hospital staff. We were seeing patients in many different wards and cottages; there was turnover in the hospital staff as well as in the research staff; it was almost impossible for every hospital worker to have a clear picture of what the research was about.

Thus to many of the ward personnel, the purpose and function of the research staff was an ambiguous and mystifying thing. One kind of reaction was: "A person I have never seen before comes into the ward and wants to see Mr. X. I don't know who this stranger is nor why he wishes to see Mr. X nor what it is all about." There was naturally sometimes the feeling, "What are these people trying to find out? Are they in some way spying on us and what we do with our patients?" The restriction on the use of drugs was particularly hard for the ward personnel to understand. "Tranquilizers are of help to the patients and to us. Why should we be restricted from giving them?" Yet, to the great credit of both the hospital staff and the research staff, the most common reaction was, "I don't quite understand what these University people are trying to do but they seem to be serious in their intent to help. Since that is the case I will cooperate in any way I can."

The fact that one and later two of our therapists were members of the hospital staff undoubtedly made the relationship easier. Occasional open discussion meetings between the research committee of the hospital, or the hospital administrative staff, and the members of the research staff helped to keep the main channels of communications open. It is a tribute to both parties that during five years of this fundamentally difficult relationship no problems occurred which were not solved with relative ease.

The Experience of the Raters

For those raters who participated in the pilot aspects of the research and in the initial phases of our study, the rating of the interview segments on the various scales was in large measure a highly rewarding experience. Here were individuals with a knowledge of therapy ranging from modest to profound, engaged in the task of making the finest possible discriminations regarding therapeutic interaction. There is no doubt that this deepened their understanding of therapy and the therapeutic process. It seems possible that some of these raters have, because of their experience, developed a more discriminating and detailed understanding of the process of therapy as it relates to the therapist and to the client than anyone else in the profession. What they learned applying the rating scales was of the greatest value to the research staff in sharpening the scales and improving our understanding of the therapeutic interaction.

As to the therapeutically naive undergraduates who were employed to do the major ratings on the data, it can be said that their rating experience constituted a door into the internal workings of the person and in this respect was highly educational. In part, their small financial reward was balanced by the fact that their work gave them insights into human behavior which they might otherwise never have had.

In spite of these positive elements there were strong negative elements in the task of rating. To make a first judgment as to some subtle quality in an interview segment is a challenging task. The tenth such judgment may not only be challenging but may stimulate whole new lines of thought in the rater. The fiftieth rating involves for the rater a feeling of competence in his workmanship and ability to make fine discriminations. The three hundredth rating is a chore, pure and simple.

The Experience of the Data Analyst

From the point of view of those who were charged with the responsibility of analyzing the accumulated data, this research program was both frustrating and stimulating. On the one hand it was a program at the cutting edge of research, using new procedures, hopefully discovering new and significant knowledge. These were the rewards which raised the spirits of the data analyst while he worked at the calculator or fed the material into the digital computer made available to the project by the University.

The greatest frustration of the data analyst lay in the inevitable gaps in the data. There is no doubt that these staff people often longed for the definiteness of a research project in which every measurement called for by the design had been made, every bit of data had been gathered. In research involving dozens of staff people and half a hundred subjects, most of them psychotic, there could be no hope for perfection in the gathering of data. Consequently, the person analyzing the data was continually faced with problems such as these: "What shall I do about the problem created by the fact that Mr. Z refused absolutely to fill out the Relationship Inventory? What use shall I make of a test which is only partially completed? How will we handle the fact that there are no interview segments from interview 15 since the recorder broke down at that point? What shall I regard as the end of therapy when the patient has stopped his interviews and then two months later comes back for three more?" All of these questions demanded careful consideration and the answers to them were always matters of judgment rather than rule. It was only after these and many other compromising judgments were made regarding imperfect data that the staff member could proceed with the much more orderly and precise modes of analyzing the data which were available.

A Concluding Remark

It is hoped that this account of the various perspectives held by the widely different participants in the research will make clear the complexity of the human elements which entered into our research program. It can only be understood if it is recognized as a vast enterprise in which several hundred people were involved to varying degrees, at varying times, and with varying responsibilities or functions, drawn together into a meaningful pattern only by the overall design of the research and the determination of the staff. With this understanding of its human side, we can now proceed to look at some of the findings which emerged.

5. The Findings in Brief

Every one of the scores of individuals who worked on the research has contributed to this chapter. Carl R. Rogers wrote it.

In such a large and complex program of research, it is difficult to know how to present the findings. From a logical point of view it might seem best to take the reader through all of the massive detail of the study, and then to bring together the findings in a concluding chapter. From the psychological point of view, however, it appears preferable to present briefly, without any supporting documentation, the major significant results which have emerged from our studies. For a description of the way in which each of our findings was reached the reader should refer to the chapters following this one. In this chapter we present a general picture of the results which came from five years of effort, results which we believe will have meaning for the practice and theory of psychotherapy and for further research in the field.

A Theory of Psychotherapy Can Be Tested

The first finding of the study may seem to have only technical significance, but we believe that its importance goes far beyond its technical meaning. It was this: *It is possible to test a theory of therapeutic change by devising instruments to measure the conceptual elements of that theory.*

We were able to work out operational definitions of the constructs on which the study was based. In practice this means that we were able to develop both definitions and measuring instruments for the theoretical concepts having to do with the therapist's attitudes and behavior on the one hand, and with the in-therapy behavior of the client on the other. In regard to the therapist, well-defined scales were constructed to measure the degree to which he conveyed accurate empathy, and congruence, or genuineness. The rating scales for these qualities were developed to a point where they could be used with objectivity by unsophisticated workers who had had only a brief training in the particular concept. With this brief training these therapeutically naive individuals, working independently and without knowledge of the patients or the therapists, were able to make reliable ratings of these qualities, empathy and congruence. A reliable rating scale for measuring unconditional positive regard was not fully achieved. The ratings on this quality tended to be unreliable, and so had limited use in this study.

Another instrument for the measurement of therapist attitudes is the Relationship Inventory, suitable for measuring the perceptions of the relationship by the client or by the therapist himself. The reliability and presumptive validity of this scale in measuring empathy, congruence, positive regard, and unconditionality, had been established previously. Thus we had reliable measures of most of the elements of the therapeutic relationship regarded as theoretically important, and these measurements came from three different vantage points—that of the unbiased judge, that of the client or patient, and that of the therapist.

In terms of the client in-therapy behavior, we also made satisfactory progress in measuring comceptions basic to our theory. Here we were able to formulate clear and operational definitions and rating scales for the assessment of a number of highly intangible variables. The variable on which we concentrated the major part of our attention was the degree of immediacy of the client's experiencing—the degree to which he is "in" his experience or remote from it. Another way of describing this variable is that it is concerned with the degree to which the client is open to his feelings, able to own them, and to explore them in search of their personal meaning. A scale for measuring the manner of experiencing was developed and proved to be reliable. In addition to this scale, we developed rating scales to tap other dimensions of the therapeutic process: the degree of rigidity of personal constructs, the manner in which the person relates to his problems, the manner in which he construes his experience—whether rigidly or tentatively, and the quality of his relationships with others. Using these scales, naive raters, given a brief but intensive training, were able to make reliable judgments or measurements of these subtle types of client behavior in the interviews.

Another innovation which proved important in the testing of our theories was the use of brief samplings of the therapeutic interaction as a basis for making the ratings and judgments upon which our findings were based. Brief segments proved to be as satisfactory as longer ones for most purposes. The extent to which this opens up the field of psychotherapy for many types of investigation can hardly be exaggerated. Previously, investigators have tended to be overwhelmed by the mass of data involved in the recording of a long series of interviews. The method of taking brief random samplings from the interviews is a reasonable resolution of the problem of testing the many theories and hypotheses which are either explicit or implicit in the practice of all psychotherapy.

This first finding, that a theory of therapeutic change can be put to empirical test, may in some respects be our most important finding. Its significance lies in the fact that the field of psychotherapy is burgeoning with new theories as to the ways in which personality change comes about. Our experience, as expressed in these paragraphs, indicates that not only the theoretical views which stimulated *this* research but *any* theoretical view as to the way in which therapeutic change comes about can be put to empirical test. Acceptance of this conclusion should go a long way in bringing the field of psychotherapy out of the realm of dogma and opinion and argument into the realm of confirmed or confirmable fact. Psychotherapy may thus be able to make basic progress.

That such a testing of theory is in fact effective is indicated by the results of this research program. Some of our hypotheses were at least partially confirmed. Others were disproved. New evidence was unearthed which did not fit the theory from which we started. Thus a rethinking of the theoretical basis of our therapy became necessary and a more accurate (we believe) theoretical formulation has emerged from the program. This in our estimation is the way in which surer knowledge in the field of psychotherapy may advance.

Measurement of the Qualities of the Therapeutic Relationship

Our second cluster of findings had to do with the nature of the therapeutic relationships which were formed with our schizophrenic patients. One summary statement might be that *regardless of the degree of understanding, acceptance, and genuineness offered by the therapist, schizophrenic patients tended to perceive a relatively low level of these conditions as existing in the relationship, and only slowly over therapy did they perceive somewhat more of these therapist attitudes.*

Previous studies with neurotics, with therapists certainly no more competent than those in our group, have shown that neurotics perceive a relatively high level of these therapist attitudes in the relationship—a much higher level than perceived by our schizophrenics. Evidently the deeply disturbed psychotic is simply not able to perceive or report understanding, warmth, and genuineness to the same degree as the less disturbed person, even when these qualities may be objectively present in the relationship. Over the period of therapy, however, the schizophrenic patient comes to distinguish more sharply among the different therapist attitudes and also is able to perceive a higher level of these therapist conditions.

Another summary statement of findings in regard to the quality of the therapeutic relationship seems significant. *Neurotic clients appear to perceive primarily the understanding and genuineness of the therapist and thus it is natural that their central focus appears to be on self-exploration. Our schizophrenic patients on the other hand perceived primarily the levels of warm acceptance (positive regard) and genuineness. Their focus appeared to be on relationship-formation.*

Our therapists were sometimes baffled by the lack of self-exploration among our schizophrenic clients, since they had come to think of self-exploration as characteristic of most psychotherapy. The schizophrenic individual seems to be seeking a relationship he can trust, and it is the therapist's potential as a trustworthy, caring person which appears crucial to him. Hence, in terms of our measures, his perception of the congruence and positive regard of the therapist are central. Only later does empathic understanding become more important, and perceptible to a higher degree. This difference in the way neurotics and schizophrenics perceive the helping relationship has meaning for the therapist who would be of assistance to either group.

The different attitudinal elements of the therapeutic relationship appear to stabilize rather early in therapy and to remain at a rather consistent level throughout therapy. It was clear from our findings that while the attitudes of the therapist, as judged by raters, fluctuated considerably in the early interviews, by the eighth interview the relationship had a fairly stable quality which remained relatively constant. It is evident that the therapeutic relationship, at least in client-centered therapy, is not something which fluctuates from "very good" to "very poor" and back again. Instead, the therapeutic relationship, after some initial fluctuation, appears to remain much the same in its essential qualities throughout therapy. The therapist who is initially highly empathic is likely to remain so. The therapist who is initially lacking in congruence or genuineness is also likely to remain so. This stability is especially noteworthy in the perception of the relationship by both the patients and the therapists. The scores on the Relationship Inventory early in therapy correlated from .76 to .94 with the scores on the same instrument at termination. Evidently there was little shift in the perception of the attitudes exhibited by the therapist in the relationship.

The different elements of the therapeutic relationship which we attempted to measure evidently tap differing dimensions of the interaction, though these dimensions are positively related. At times during the research we wondered whether empathy, congruence, positive regard, unconditionality, might all somehow be simply different ways of assessing a relationship as either favorable or unfavorable. It is therefore important to recognize that though they tended to be positively correlated with one another, this positive correlation was not significantly high. Evidently our different measures were tapping discriminably different elements of the attitudes and behavior of the therapist in his interaction with his client.

Discrepancies Among the Vantage Points

Our attempt to measure the therapeutic relationship from three differing vantage points—the perception by the patient, the perception by the therapist, the rating by the unbiased judge—turned up an unexpected but highly consistent and rather startling finding. *In general, our unbiased raters and our schizophrenic patients tended to make similar evaluations of the therapeutic relationship; therapists, on the other hand, evaluated the relationship in ways so discrepant from the other two groups as to be negatively associated.*

The perceptions of the client and the rater were positively and often significantly related. This finding has considerable weight, considering the fact that the client was basing his assessment on his whole experience with the therapist, while the rater's evaluation rested on the hearing of very brief samplings of the interviews. Perception by the therapist and by the rater, on the other hand, were more often negatively than positively related and sometimes significantly so. And the perceptions of the therapeutic qualities by the client and therapist on the Relationship Inventory were so discrepant as to show a surprisingly consistent negative correlation. This last is even more striking when it is realized that the client and the therapist were both involved in the same relationship and were both using the same instrument to assess it. The therapist was apparently far more optimistic in his perception of the conditions he provided his client than was the client himself, and, more important, when he perceived himself as providing a high level of conditions, his client perceived him as providing low conditions, and vice versa.

It might be thought that the discrepancy between the therapist's perception and that of the *rater* was due to the fact that they were using different instruments. However, even when both used the same base of data, namely, the whole interview, and when both used the same instrument to assess the relationship, namely, the Relationship Inventory, the correlation between these assessments was still negative.

In contrast, the ratings by our naive judges of the degree of empathy exhibited by the therapist correlated significantly with the patient's perception of both the empathy and the congruence of the therapist, and with the patient's perception of the overall level of the therapeutic conditions. Likewise, the combined ratings of our judges on the different conditions correlated significantly with the overall perception by the patients, and with the patient's more specific perception of positive regard and congruence.

In general then, the patients and the raters perceived the therapist attitudes in similar fashion. When, however, they tended to see a therapist as low in empathy, the therapist's own perception of himself was likely to be that he was exhibiting a high degree of empathy. This is indeed a striking and unexpected contrast.

An explanation for this finding appeared when patients were divided into those with more and those with less successful outcomes, for a different picture emerged. *In the more successful cases, the patients and therapists tended to see the relationship in similar fashion with scores positively correlated.* In the less successful cases there was a sharply negative correlation between the perceptions of patients and therapists. Evidently in therapy which proves effective, patient and therapist share the same phenomenal world of the relationship, seeing its strengths and weaknesses in a similar way. In ineffective therapy the patient and the therapist, for whatever reason, are each living in an entirely different relationship-as-perceived. This provides much food for thought.

The fact of this general discrepancy in perceptions does not of course tell us which of these vantage points is more valid. Yet considering the fact that the therapist's rating of his own relationship tended to correlate negatively with the index of process in his client, and with the therapeutic outcome for his client, while the assessments by raters and patients tended to correlate positively with both process level and outcomes, the following statement may safely be made: *For the purposes of understanding and predicting the dynamics and outcomes of psychotherapy with schizophrenics, the assessment of the relationship by the therapist is less satisfactory and presumably less valid than the assessment by the patient or by an unbiased judge.*

It should be noted in passing that though this casts grave doubt on the therapist's ability to assess his own qualities and impact in the relationship, it has nothing to say in regard to the therapist's judgment of outcome, nor his judgment of the process movement which is being shown by his client. Other studies have indicated that the therapist's judgment of outcome holds up well in comparison with other objective indices.

There is another important point in regard to this complex of findings about the different vantage points. The theory with which we started stated that it was the patient's perception of the therapist's attitudes which was most crucial in predicting therapeutic movement and therapeutic outcome. This has been supported by the evidence. It is therefore most fortunate that the raters tended to see the relationship in ways similar to those of the patient, since many of our analyses were based on ratings by these judges. It appears clear that the unbiased judge tended to assess the qualities in the relationship in much the same fashion as the patient who was involved in it. This means that the judge's perception of the relationship, like that of the patient, was a good predictor of both process and outcome in therapy, definitely better than the therapist's perception of the relationship.

Measurement of Process Qualities

It has already been mentioned that several reliable indices of therapeutic process were developed. As will be evident from some of the later findings cited in this chapter, these measures seem to be tapping simultaneously two quite different aspects of therapy. We had hoped that they would be simple and unitary measures of stages of the therapeutic process. They have proven to be, first of all, primarily an index of involvement in change. Thus they tap or measure the behaviors of the person who is in process, the degree to which he is not static, his involvement in the ongoing, change-effecting process. We found that some of our therapy cases and some of our control cases were from the first more involved in change than were others. Secondarily, however, our process scales do measure the stage of changingness which the person has currently achieved. In this respect the scale shows increases in level throughout therapy. On the one hand there is the evidence of changingness as a quality of behavior, which is a good prognosticator of the likelihood of constructive change in personality and behavior. On the other hand there is also evidence of movement in therapy, which is evidence of the degree of change achieved.

Though more will be said later about the whole process concept and the ways in which it has been validated by this program of research, at least one aspect of our findings should be stated here. *Our schizophrenic patients exhibited, in general, a very low level of involvement in the process of change and were decidedly remote from their own experiencing. They also showed a very limited degree of movement on the instruments we devised for measuring stages of the therapeutic process.*

All things considered, this is not at all a surprising finding. These were for the most part patients who would be labeled chronic schizophrenics. Few if any were motivated for therapy. There was on their part little expectation of change. It is in accord with these facts, for example, that on the Experiencing Scale they tended to rate decidedly low, and that taken as a whole they showed relatively little change in the level of experiencing over the period of therapy. This was not true of all individuals or subgroups, but statements about this will be reserved until later in this chapter. For the present it is sufficient to point out that, as compared with a neurotic group for example, these were not individuals whose in-therapy behavior showed evidence of a high level of changing-ness nor were they individuals who showed a high degree of process movement over the period of therapy.

Outcomes in Therapy and Control Groups

From the point of view of the research group, the primary significance of the research lay in the possible relationship between the attitudinal set of the therapist and the process characteristics exhibited by the client in therapy. We have found, however, that most people want to know how the patients "came out," that is, what the findings were in regard to outcome before they can attend to the central findings of our study. Recognizing that this is a common attitude, let us first turn to the fourth hypothesis of the study and examine the prediction that those who had been offered therapy would show greater evidences of positive outcome than the matched control group.

One important finding in this respect is that on the various outcome scores, measures, and ratings, both the therapy group and the control group (the latter exposed to all the helping influences of a modern hospital) showed improvement on many of the indices. For both groups there was a reduction of schizophrenic behavior as measured by the MMPI. There was an overall reduction in psychopathology. When clinicians examined the pre- and post-batteries of psychological tests, they rated both groups as showing a small degree of improvement. Again, the observation of the hospital attendants as recorded on the Wittenborn Scales showed some small degree of improvement for both groups. Thus, one basic finding is that *both those patients who were exposed only to the general hospital program and those patients who in addition to the hospital program experienced individual psychotherapy showed some degree of small but definite improvement on various measurements of change.*

The point of greater interest of course is whether the therapy group as a whole showed more improvement than the control group. The find-ings in this respect can be briefly summarized as follows: *In many respects the therapy group taken as a whole showed no greater evidence of positive outcome than did the matched and paired control group. It had, however, a slightly better rate of release from the hospital, and this differential was maintained a year after the termination of therapy. The therapy group also showed a number of positive personality changes which were not evidenced by the control group. The differences be-tween the two groups, however, were not great.*

As indicated above, there was a tendency for the therapy group to have a more favorable release rate, and the comparison is especially favorable if the two groups are compared on the evidence from a full twelve months after the termination of therapy. Evidently those in the therapy group were more successful in maintaining themselves outside of the hospital.

The significant differences in personality change are evidenced in an independent study made of the Thematic Apperception Test records. The research worker had no knowledge of which tests were pre- or post-therapy, or which came from experimental individuals, which from controls, and which from normals. In general on this test the hospitalized therapy group showed definitely greater constructive personality changes than the hospitalized control group or the normal individuals who were a part of our study. For example, when summing up various indices of change on the TAT, the experimenter found that of the therapy group, ten showed definite improvement, one remained the same, one showed a decline in adjustment. This represented a statistically significant improvement. Of the control group, six were improved, one remained unchanged, and four showed negative change. The normal individuals showed a non-significant trend toward poorer adjustment between the pre- and post-test.

One of the sharpest changes shown by the therapy group was that their emotional distance from the experience they described in the TAT picture showed rather significant alteration from pre- to post-test. Evidently these therapy patients reduced their need to deny or emotionally distance themselves from their experience (a change paralleled on the Experiencing Scale, as we will show). The control group in the hospital, on the other hand, showed some tendency to become more defensive, more distant from the experience they were describing.

It is also of interest that the therapy group showed significant improvement in the appropriateness of their emotional expression where the control group showed a trend toward more extreme expression of emotions. The therapy group also gave evidence of improvement in their capacity to handle interpersonal relationships in a satisfying way. In this they were significantly different from the control group.

The investigator concluded that at the end of the period the therapy group were less vulnerable, psychologically, and more capable of facing themselves and their environment than were the control group.

Though these findings are of decided interest, and confirm the theory from which we started, it should be noted again that on many indices there was no significant difference between the therapy and the control groups.

In considering how small were the differences between the two groups, some words of qualification should be borne in mind. The members of the control group were receiving all the best treatment which a modern hospital could afford—occupational and recreational therapy, group meetings of an essentially therapeutic nature, in some instances group therapy. As to the therapy group, for a number of the patients who were particularly resistant to any helping relationship, the question might be raised whether they were actually in therapy at all. The basic question being answered by the research was whether the *offering* of approximately two hours of therapy per week over a period of from four months to two and one-half years would produce a *measurable* degree of change in the whole therapy group significantly over and above that which would occur as a result of the hospital program. Given the circumstances, it may seem somewhat surprising that any changes were measured in which the total therapy group showed discriminably more constructive change than did the control group.

Therapist Attitudes and Their Correlates

Therapist Attitudes and Process Movement

One of the central interests of the research program was the manner in which the attitudinal qualities of the therapist in the therapeutic relationship might relate to the evidence of changingness in his client.

We were interested in two questions. The first, dealt with in this section, was the degree of movement exhibited by the client or patient on the process scale as it related to the therapeutic conditions.

Our findings on this point were somewhat similar to what had been found in earlier studies of clinic clients. There is some perceptible change from early interviews to late on the process scale but by and large the process movement is very small in amount and complex in form. Our schizophrenic patients showed only a very mild degree of process movement, and this showed itself particularly in the slight but steady increase in the peak levels of experiencing evidenced on the Experiencing Scale. In general, the process movement in our schizophrenic group seemed fluctuating and complex. A U-shaped curve is suggested in which the experiencing level decreases for a time and then increases to somewhat beyond its original level.

The second finding was disappointing. *In general, there was no differential amount of process movement over therapy in our schizophrenic group as a function of different levels of therapist conditions.* In other words there seemed to be no significant relationship between the degree of therapist empathy, congruence, and acceptance, and the degree of process movement shown by the patient. This is in part, of course, explained by the fact that there was relatively little process movement in general.

Previous studies of neurotic clients have shown a slight trend toward a greater depth of experiencing in the second half of the therapeutic hour than in the first half. This was not so for our present group. *Our schizophrenic patients showed no greater degree of openness to experience in the second halves of the therapeutic interviews than in the first halves. With our normal individuals, who were not motivated for therapy, there was even a trend toward a more superficial level of experiencing in second halves of the therapeutic hours.* This finding in the normal individuals seems explainable on the basis of their tendency to execute a defensive retreat from therapeutic engagements.

Thus, in general our expectations and hypotheses in regard to a progression of stages of development in therapeutic movement throughout the process of therapy were not upheld in our work with these schizophrenic individuals.

Therapist Attitudes and Process Level in Therapy

The story was quite different when we examined the relationship between the therapist attitudes or conditions and the process *level* exhibited by our schizophrenic individuals. Here we found that *the deeper the level of the therapist's understanding and genuineness in his relationship with his patient, the more his patient was likely to exhibit a deeper level of self-experiencing and self-exploration at every point of therapy —initially, throughout therapy, and at termination.* As will be discussed later we cannot with any assurance attribute a causal relationship to this finding. It is nonetheless true that the patient's openness to his experience, his ownership of his feelings, was directly and positively related to the extent to which the attitudinal conditions of therapy were evident in the relationship.

In similar fashion it was found that *the more the patient perceived his therapist as congruent or genuine and the more the patient perceived all the conditions as present in the therapeutic relationship, the more likely he was to exhibit a high level on the process scale, indicating a greater degree of self-experiencing and self-exploration.*

The meaningfulness of these relationships is perhaps still further reinforced by the finding that *even on a moment-by-moment basis, the degree of accurate empathy exhibited by the therapist was associated with the immediacy of experiencing in the client, whether this experiencing was measured at its modal level or its peak level in the interview samples.*

The findings in this and in the preceding section brought about a rethinking of the meaning of our process measures. Perhaps they were not measures of a slowly changing type of client behavior indicative of slowly changing stages in therapy but were rather indices of client involvement in those in-therapy behaviors indicative of the process of change, an involvement which very often shows up in the beginning of the therapeutic relationship and does not greatly or significantly change over the course of therapy. There will be more discussion of this later in the chapter.

It may, however, be reasonably summarized that higher degrees of certain therapeutic attitudes, as judged by unbiased raters or as perceived by the patient himself, were definitely associated with greater evidences of process involvement or changingness in the client.

Therapist Attitudes and Patient Behavior Outside of Therapy

We naturally asked not only the question of whether the qualities of the therapeutic relationship affected the client's therapy behavior but also whether they affected his behavior in other situations. Given a qualitatively good therapeutic relationship, would the client behave differently in other relationships?

We had one specific measure of such behavior outside of the therapeutic hour. This was the behavior of our schizophrenic patients with a third person, the sampling interviewer. Here we found that *the higher the degree of the therapist's empathy and congruence in the therapeutic relationship, the higher the level of process involvement or immediacy of experiencing shown by the patient in the sampling interview.* In other words, the more satisfactory the relationship in therapy, the more likely it is that the client will show an openness to his own experience, less rigidity, more spontaneity, more capacity for communicating himself in his relationship with another person.

Though the above finding was based on raters' judgments, much the same statement could be made in regard to the patient's perception of the quality of the conditions in his therapeutic relationship. *The higher the patient's perception of these conditions in the therapeutic hour, the more likely that he would show a high level of openness to experience in his interview with a third person.*

Another way of summarizing some of our findings in this regard is that *the more empathic the therapist in his early interviews with the patient, the more warm and acceptant he was over the period of therapy, the more he was perceived by his patient as showing these attitudes, the greater was the probability that his patient would show a high level of openness to experience in his interviews with a third person, the sampling interviewer.*

When the therapy group was divided into those who received high conditions in the therapeutic relationship and those who received low conditions, a consistent and theoretically meaningful pattern became evident. In general it is possible to say that those patients whose therapeutic relationship was high in the therapeutic conditions exhibited a characteristic curve throughout the several sampling interviews. First there was a slight decline in their openness to experience, then a much higher and generally sustained level of openness in all of their later sampling interviews. The group which received low therapeutic conditions showed a curve of the same shape but continually declining in trend. The control group showed an initial rather sharp increase in openness to experience with the sampling interviewer but then a sharp decrease which continued downward throughout the course of the sampling interviews. *At the conclusion of the sampling interviews it would be accurate to say that the group showing the greatest openness to experience, the greatest spontaneity, the greatest capacity for communicating themselves, was composed of those who had been exposed to the highest level of therapeutic conditions. The next group was composed of those who had been exposed to lower therapeutic conditions, and the lowest group of all was composed of the control individuals who had received no specific individual psychotherapy.*

The Relationship of Therapist Attitudes and Patient Outcomes

We have shown that the attitudinal conditions of the therapeutic relationship are related to subtle qualities of changingness in the client and that these subtle qualities even show up in contacts with a third person. But is there evidence of changes in personality and in pathology? Were these schizophrenic individuals actually helped to become less schizophrenic and more normal?

Let us turn to this question by inquiring first about the relationship between therapeutic conditions and objective measures of personality change and outcome.

Perhaps one of the most important findings of the study was that *the group of patients receiving the highest level of accurate empathy in their therapeutic relationships showed the greatest reduction in schizophrenic pathology as measured by the subscale for schizophrenic tendencies of the Minnesota Multiphasic Personality Inventory.* This would seem to be a significant indication that the therapeutic relationships exhibiting an attitude hypothesized to be growth-promoting were also those in which our patients showed the sharpest recovery from their schizophrenic condition. This finding was strengthened by the further evidence that *those patients in relationships low in accurate empathy showed a slight increase in their schizophrenic pathology over the period of therapy.* This is a disturbing finding in that it would seem to mean that competent and conscientious therapists who have been unable to establish high levels of therapeutic attitudes in their relationship may actually worsen the condition of their schizophrenic patients. Consistent with these findings is the fact that *the controls who received no psychotherapy showed a slight reduction in schizophrenic pathology with results intermediate between the group which received a high degree of empathy and the group which received a low degree of empathy.*

By and large this was the picture for other changes in pathology measured by the MMPI. The other changes were consistent but not significant. In general the greater change was found in the group of patients who received a high level of empathy. There was no change or even negative change for those who received a low degree of empathy, and the controls tended to be intermediate between these groups.

When the criterion used was the hospitalization release rate, then the findings were somewhat mixed. Those patients who perceived their therapist as congruent and genuine showed a significantly better release picture than the other groups. However, the individuals in relationships rated low in empathy showed a more favorable release rate than either the high conditions group or the control group. Considering the many extraneous factors which can enter into hospital release, it is not certain how much significance should be attached to this finding, which is essentially contradictory.

When we turned to still another criterion of outcome—the global judgment of clinicians who had gone over all of the test materials without any knowledge of which individuals were therapy cases and which were controls—the trend of the findings was in line with our hypotheses. *Those patients who perceived a high degree of congruence in their relationship with their therapist were independently rated as showing the greatest degree of change. Those whose relationships were rated high in empathy ranked next. The control group followed, and those patients who were in relationships low in empathy and congruence showed no change or even regressive change.*

The above findings seem highly significant. In spite of the subtlety of the variables being measured, in spite of the crudity of the instruments used in measuring them, there appears to be substantial evidence that relationships rated high in a sensitively accurate empathic understanding and high in genuineness as perceived by the patient, were associated with favorable personality changes and reductions in various forms of pathology, particularly in schizophrenic pathology. Control individuals who had no individual psychotherapy but who were exposed to the constructive treatment program of the hospital likewise showed some positive change but to a lesser degree. On the other hand, those whose therapeutic relationships were deficient in the qualities mentioned had the poorest record of any of the groups, showing no change or even a worsening of the pathological state.

The Relationship of Process Indices to Outcome

One of the "far out" concerns of the research was to determine whether there was any relationship between the extremely subtle indices of the therapeutic process, gleaned from the interviews, and the hard-headed indices of social and personality outcomes. Would the manner in which the individual related to his own inner experiencing in the therapeutic hour bear any relationship to his ability to get out of the hospital, or to a reduction in his psychotic behaviors and attitudes? Our findings permit us to give a complex but definitely affirmative answer to this question.

Both in earlier studies with neurotic clients, and in this study of schizophrenic individuals, we found that *the process level exhibited by the client or patient was positively associated with many of the objective measures of outcome variables.* This trend is not completely clear-cut, but the association is definitely there. The individual who in his interview behavior showed more awareness of his inner feelings and reactions, more ownership of his own experiencing, more ability to use the meanings implicit in his experiencing as a basis for self-understanding and as a guide to his actions, was more likely to have a favorable outcome, as measured by a number of objective criteria. For example, those patients who showed the greatest decrease in schizophrenic pathology as measured by the MMPI, or showed decrease in other measures of pathology, or who were judged to have shown global improvement in adjustment by unbiased clinicians examining all the pre- and post-test data, showed a clearly higher process level on the Experiencing Scale.

There was also a relationship between the degree of therapeutic movement on the process scale, considered over the total period of therapy, and the favorableness of outcome.

The relationship was clearest when the schizophrenic individuals were divided, on the basis of objective indices of outcome, into a group of more successful and less successful cases. Though the finding was somewhat dependent on the criteria of outcome used for the division, it led us to conclude that *the more successful cases showed a definite positive change, over therapy, in their manner of experiencing.* When all four of our process scales were used, this was a clear-cut increase and we may say that *the more successful cases showed a degree of process*

movement sharply different from the less successful cases. In general,
*these less successful cases actually showed negative progress, moving
definitely lower on the process scale, becoming more remote from their
experience, showing less expression of, and less ownership of, their
feelings.*

How important is the relationship between process indices and outcome is shown by the data from the sampling interviews, the contacts
with a person outside the therapy relationship. It was found that *a
higher level of process in the patient in his contact with the sampling
interviewer, a higher degree of expressiveness of feelings, of self-exploration and self-awareness, was associated with a significant decrease in
schizophrenic pathology and symptoms, and with a better record of
remaining out of the hospital.*

Even more striking evidence of the significance of the process construct was that *in the control patients, who had had no individual
psychotherapy, a higher level of experiencing in the sampling interviews
was associated with a better hospital release rate, and with other evidences of favorable outcome.* It seems clear that our Experiencing Scale
(and our other process scales as well) were tapping behaviors associated
with personality and behavior change, whether these behaviors were
facilitated by planned therapy, or were due to other factors in the
patient's life.

All in all, then, the attempt to assess those behaviors which are
associated with the process of therapeutic change was rather markedly
successful, and the whole process construct received much support from
these findings. Through the original concept was modified by the findings, what emerged is very important for our knowledge of therapy. To
put it in the most global terms, we may say that *we were able, with
reasonable reliability, to assess in-therapy behaviors on the part of the
client which were evidences of engagement in the process of change in
personality and behavior. These evidences, exhibited early in therapy,
proved to be a good prognosis for successful outcome. During successful therapy the quality of these behaviors changed in theoretically significant ways, in the direction of greater closeness to feelings, greater
awareness of gut-level reactions, more use of these inner personal referents as bases for self-understanding and appropriate behavior.*

The Interaction of Patient and Therapist
in the Relationship

We come now to some very important new findings which were not
predicted. Before introducing them, let us look at the conceptual triangle which is created by the most clear-cut of our findings thus far.

It has been made clear that when certain attitudinal conditions exist in the therapeutic relationship, a higher index of process level is found in the client's behavior, both in and out of the therapy hours. Thus, to greatly simplify, conditions in the relationship are associated with process level in the patient. This is one side of our triangle.

The evidence is also clear that a high process level in the patient is associated with constructive change in personality and behavior. Process is correlated with outcomes. This is the second side.

Completing the triangle is the evidence that the attitudinal qualities of the relationship are associated with various types of constructive change in the patient. Conditions are correlated with outcomes.

This oversimplified schema helps to reveal the dilemma regarding causality. The viewpoint with which we began the research was that it was the therapist's offering of these attitudinal conditions (his experiencing and exhibiting of attitudes of empathy, congruence, and unconditional positive regard) which would *bring about* a therapeutic process in the patient, which would in turn *bring about* constructive change in the patient's personality and behavior. We cannot, from the findings, conclude positively that these causative hypotheses were proven.

When we examine the characteristics of those schizophrenic patients who were in relationships high in the attitudinal conditions, as compared with those who were in low conditions relationships, we find differences, some of them significant. Those in the high conditions group were more often male, of higher socio-educational status, tended to come from the more chronic rather than the more acute group, tended to have a higher verbal IQ, were less silent in the initial interviews, indicated (on the TAT) somewhat more desire for social contact, and showed less distance from their experience.

Some of these elements are puzzling. Why were the more chronic involved in relationships of better quality than the more acute? Why were men more often represented than women in the favorable relationships? Our therapists were nearly all men, and previous research seems to indicate that females respond better than males to male therapists. Why was age not a factor, the younger and older being evenly represented in both groups? Some explanations can be attempted, but these are perplexing questions, nonetheless.

The main thrust of these findings, however, appears clear. *The characteristics of the client or patient influenced the quality of the relationship which formed between himself and his therapist.* High levels of empathic understanding, genuineness, and warm acceptance in the therapist's behavior are more likely to be evident when he is dealing with a reasonably expressive individual with a socio-educational level closer to his own. The therapist's attitudes are clearly important, but the patient's characteristics appear to play a definite part in eliciting these qualities. High therapeutic conditions seem to be a product of interaction between the person of the therapist and the person of his client.

The Testing of the Hypotheses

Thus far it has seemed desirable to present the findings which have emerged from our research in their natural clusterings, without reference to the hypotheses from which we started. Let us now take up each hypothesis and indicate briefly the extent to which it was confirmed or disproved.

The first hypothesis was that the greater the degree to which the conditions of therapy existed in the relationship, the greater would be the evidences of therapeutic process or movement in the client. In general we found no evidence of a positive correlation between conditions and process movement, partly because such process movement was small in this schizophrenic group. This finding is similar to the most recent findings regarding neurotic clients as well.

Both the empathy of the therapist and his congruence or genuineness were definitely associated with the process *level* in the client. In so far as the hypothesis refers to those client behaviors characteristic of movement in therapy, then such behaviors were associated with therapist attitudes.

In general we would say that the hypothesis as stated was not confirmed. It could now be replaced by a statement of the association between therapist attitudes and client process *level*.

The second hypothesis was that the same variables of process movement would characterize the in-therapy behavior of more acute schizophrenics, more chronic schizophrenics, normals, and neurotics.

In so far as we were able to test this hypothesis, the evidence was generally confirmatory. The major change which emerged from our findings is that the schizophrenic initially focuses more on relationship formation than on self-exploration, and thus some of the most characteristic elements of process for the neurotic are not initially present for the schizophrenic. Indeed, such self-exploratory behavior may never occupy as prominent a position in the therapy of the schizophrenic as it does in the therapy of the neurotic.

The third hypothesis stated that the process of therapy would occur to a significantly greater degree in a group of individuals to whom therapy was offered than in a matched control group to whom therapy was not offered. The data for testing this hypothesis had of necessity to come from the sampling interviews. In general, it was not confirmed. There was little process movement in either group, and the difference in process level between groups in the sampling interviews was not significant.

The corollary hypothesis III–A was that those individuals receiving higher conditions of therapy would exhibit a greater degree of the process of therapy than those individuals receiving lower conditions or those in the control group. So far as process movement was concerned, this hypothesis was not confirmed. It was found, however, that the process *level* of the three groups was in line with the prediction; those exposed to higher conditions showed the highest process level in the sampling interviews, followed by those exposed to lower conditions. The lowest process level was shown by the members of the control group.

The fourth hypothesis made the prediction that evidences of positive outcome would be greater in those individuals receiving therapy than in a matched control group receiving no therapy. Here the research indicated that both groups showed positive change. The difference in outcomes between the groups was small, but both in personality changes and in record of hospital release, the experimental group had a more constructive showing than the control group. It could be said that the hypothesis was partially confirmed.

The corollary to the fourth hypothesis was that the greater the degree to which the conditions of therapy existed in the relationship, the greater would be the evidences of constructive outcome. The evidence definitely confirmed this hypothesis. An unexpected finding was that low conditions often brought about a worsening of the patient's condition.

The final hypothesis predicted that the greater the evidences of process movement in the client in therapy, the greater would be the evidences of constructive change. In so far as process *movement* is concerned, this hypothesis received only partial confirmation. What was found was equally significant, however—that there was a striking relationship between the process *level* in therapy, and various measures of outcome.

It should be evident from this quick review of the hypotheses from which we started that the value of this research program did not lie in the fact that our initial views and predictions were brilliantly or strikingly confirmed. Actually, many of the most impressive of our findings either went contrary to our expectations, or forced us to modify the theories from which we started, or turned up new facets of knowledge regarding therapy—elements which we had not in any way foreseen. In these respects it was a definitely fruitful program of investigation.

Summary

How may we draw together some of the major themes emerging from this long and complex research? Let me try to capture a few of them which struck the research group as particularly significant.

We made progress in isolating and measuring certain qualities in the therapeutic relationship which are associated with evidences of therapeutic involvement on the part of the patient, and with constructive social and personality changes. Two which we were successful in measuring, and which appear to have great significance for therapy, are the sensitively empathic understanding of the therapist, and the extent to which he is perceived as a real and genuine person by his schizophrenic patient.

It appears from our complex data that these relationship qualities are not entirely supplied by the therapist, nor are they simply elicited by qualities in the patient. They are, it would seem, a product of the interaction between the two. Obviously a great deal more needs to be learned before we can fully understand the nature of this interactional event. But a start has been made. Currently we would have to say that the best therapeutic relationship develops between a therapist who is understanding and real, and a client or patient who is able to be somewhat expressive, who is not too remote from his own experiencing.

It is a sobering finding that our therapists—competent and conscientious as they were—had over-optimistic and in some cases seriously invalid perceptions of the relationships in which they were involved. The patient, for all his psychosis, or the bright young college student with no knowledge of therapy, turned out to have more useful (and probably more accurate) perceptions of the relationship.

A significant theme of our findings is that much the same qualities of relationship are facilitative for the schizophrenic individual as for the neurotic. What differences there are do not appear major. This would seem to justify an intensive focus on the interpersonal relationship as perhaps *the* most important element in bringing about personality change in any group. It suggests that whether we are dealing with psychotics or normals, delinquents or neurotics, the most essential ingredients for change will be found in the attitudinal qualities of the person-to-person relationship.

Another encouraging fact emerging from our study is that it appears possible to identify and assess the qualities of client in-therapy behavior which indicate that change is in process. Our tools here are crude, and need refinement. Yet crude as they are, these indices of process level, and to a lesser degree of process movement, show a significant relationship to social and behavioral outcomes. The process construct receives much confirmatory backing from our study.

An important chain of events in the process of change emerges from our work. When a relationship possesses the dually determined qualities we have described, then indices of change are evident or become evident in the client, and an improved inner integration, a reduction in pathological behavior, and an improvement in social adjustment follow. The evidence for this chain is not entirely clear-cut. There are gaps and uncertainties in this evidence. Yet the above statement appears justified by the facts.

All of this points to the conclusion that an early assessment of the relationship qualities and the process level of any given relationship is a good prognosticator of the probability that constructive personality change will occur. This has far-reaching implications.

One of the unspoken themes of the research, largely evident through omission, is that it was quite unnecessary to develop different research procedures or different theories because of the fact that our clients in this investigation were schizophrenic. We found them far more similar to, than different from, other clients with whom we have worked. They appeared to respond constructively, as do others, to subtle and freeing elements in an interpersonal relationship, when they were able to perceive these elements. Though this fact shows up in no specific way in our evidence, it pervades all our data. It may be one of our more important findings.

PART II

The Theory Behind the Research

6. The Therapeutic Conditions Antecedent to Change: A Theoretical View

The conceptualizations on which this chapter is based were hammered out in staff interactions at the University of Chicago and the University of Wisconsin, and it would be impossible to name all of the individuals who helped in sharpening these interactions. The chapter was written, drawing on this experience, by Carl R. Rogers and Charles B. Truax.

In Part I an overall view of the concepts, the design, and the findings of the investigation has been given in condensed and general form. In Parts II, III, and IV, we will present, in a much more thorough and detailed way, the theories which constitute the underpinning of the research, and the data analyses of findings expressed in much more complete and complex form.

The first theoretical problem has to do with our views as to the elements which underlie change. What do we as therapists do that actually leads to constructive change in our clients or patients? This is a question of paramount importance to all who are engaged in helping relationships, for certainly only a small percentage of the events occurring in the therapeutic relationship make any real contribution to the work of psychotherapy. What, then, are the essential ingredients in effective psychotherapy among all the attempts we make to help the patient resolve his conflicts and anxieties? Which of these efforts actually contribute to the individual's positive personality growth?

Many therapists have felt that the answers to such questions are so subtle as to be impossible of investigation. How can one be scientific about relationships which are completely subjective? When a previously suicidal woman says, "I was kept from destruction by the look in one man's eyes," how can one investigate such a situation with the blunt tools of current research? It seems clear that the therapeutic relationship differs from one therapist to another. With a given therapist it differs from one client to another. Thus a therapist finds himself using sophisticated, polite, and even academic language with one client, and vulgar and coarse terminology with another. He is blunt with one individual, gentle with another. Even with the same client his relationship differs over time, from the first interviews with their tentative testing and uncertainty on both sides of the desk to the later relationship, deeper and more knowing on both sides.

In the light of this it is a very real question as to how this can possibly be a field for research. How can one isolate those therapist behaviors which have any relevance for personal growth, especially since it is almost certainly not his *behaviors* which are relevant to the process of therapy? In spite of all these considerations we have elected to study certain elements in the therapeutic relationship, recognizing that the findings of research can never be as complex or subtle as the total experience, and yet recognizing too that investigation may point to certain generalities or commonalities which are important in furthering both our knowledge and our practice.

The Search for Common Elements

There appears to be general agreement as to at least some of the elements which are important in a helping relationship. Psychoanalytic writers (Ferenczi, 1930; Alexander, 1948; Schafer, 1959; Halpern and Lesser, 1960), eclectic therapists (Strunk, 1957; Raush and Bordin, 1959; Strupp, 1960; Hobbs, 1962; Fox and Goldin, 1963), and client-centered therapists (Dymond, 1949; Rogers, 1951, 1957; Jourard, 1959; Truax, 1961) have all emphasized the importance of the therapist's ability to understand sensitively and accurately the inner experiences of the client or patient. They have also stressed such qualities as the maturity of the therapist and his integration or genuineness within the relationship. Finally, they have stressed his warmth and his acceptance of the individual with whom he is working. Thus these three characteristics of the therapist as he enters the process of psychotherapy have been stressed in a wide variety of therapeutic approaches, even though they have been differently defined by different writers. Cutting across parochial viewpoints, they can be considered as elements common to a wide variety of therapies.

Some years ago, Rogers (1957) attempted an organized theoretical statement in which it was hypothesized that three characteristics of the therapist in the relationship, when adequately communicated to the client, constituted the necessary and sufficient conditions for constructive personality change. These three conditions were that the therapist be a genuine or self-congruent person within the therapeutic hour; that he experience an unconditional positive regard for his client; and that he experience and communicate a sensitively empathic understanding of the client's phenomenological world.

Though it would be difficult if not impossible to establish either the necessity or the sufficiency of these three therapist's "conditions" (Ellis [1959] has pointed out that any specific condition is unlikely to be either necessary or sufficient), this theoretical statement has had considerable heuristic value. It has been the springboard for a number of significant studies. By setting forth a rigorous and reasonably well-defined set of hypotheses, it has made possible a testing of the effectiveness of these three conditions.

Some Initial Assumptions

It was made clear in the reference mentioned above that there are certain initial assumptions which must be fulfilled if the hypotheses are to hold. The first assumption is that the therapist and his client have a psychological contact. This means simply that they have the minimum essentials of a relationship, namely, that each makes a perceived or subceived difference in the experiential field of the other. This difference may be quite minimal and in fact not immediately apparent to an observer. Thus it might be difficult to know whether a catatonic patient perceives the therapist's presence as making a difference to him. But it is almost certain that at some physiological level he does sense or subceive this difference.

The second assumption is that the client has some degree of incongruence between his awareness and his experiencing. What this means is that the percepts, concepts, and constructs regarding self, environment, and others which are present in the person's awareness are not entirely matched by the experiencing going on in him at the physiological level. This is indeed a minimal assumption, since such incongruence is to some degree characteristic of all of us as imperfect human beings. It does not necessarily mean that the individual is severely disturbed. Put in the more technical terms of Rogers' theory (1959), it indicates that he is "vulnerable" to anxiety, meaning that there is an incongruence but that the individual is defensively unaware of it. Or it may mean that he is "anxious," a state in which the incongruence between awareness and experiencing is approaching symbolization. When such a discrepancy enters awareness, a change in the construct system is forced.

When thus defined in technical terms, this assumption may sound elaborate or unusual. Actually it necessarily exists in every person who comes voluntarily for psychotherapy, since some dim awareness of such a discrepancy is the very problem which brings him to us. Even with most individuals who do not come for psychotherapy, such a condition is met. Our clinical experiences with "well-adjusted" industrial executives indicate that even their minimal degree of anxiety, tension, or incongruence between self and experience is quite enough to meet this assumption.

A final assumption which is basic to the theory is that the patient will perceive at least to a minimal degree the therapist-offered conditions of genuineness, warmth, and empathy. In ordinary relationships with normal or mildly disturbed individuals it can be taken for granted that such a perception exists if the conditions are indeed offered. Most individuals have a sufficiently realistic perception of their environment to have a minimal awareness of these conditions when they are present. In dealing with deeply disturbed and psychotic individuals this assumption cannot be taken for granted, and a phenomenologically based measure of the patient's perception is necessary to establish whether there is some degree of realistic appreciation of these therapeutic conditions.

The description of the therapeutic conditions which follows and the predictions related to them will take for granted that the assumptions described above are, in any particular relationship, already met.

Therapist Congruence

The order in which the three therapeutic conditions are described has some significance because they are logically intertwined. Perhaps this can be made clear. It is important that the therapist achieve a high level of accurate empathy. However, to be deeply sensitive to the moment-to-moment "being" of another person requires of us as therapists that we first accept and to some degree prize this other person. Consequently a satisfactory level of empathy can scarcely exist without there being also a considerable degree of unconditional positive regard. But neither of these conditions can possibly be meaningful in the relationship unless they are real. Consequently unless the therapist is, both in these respects and in others, integrated and genuine within the therapeutic encounter, the other conditions could scarcely exist to a satisfactory degree. Therefore it would seem that this element of genuineness, or congruence, is the most basic of the three conditions. The following paragraphs attempt to describe the meaning of this concept.

We readily sense this quality of congruence in everyday life. Each of us could name persons who always seem to be operating from behind a front, who are playing a role, who tend to say things that they do not feel. They are exhibiting incongruence. We tend not to reveal ourselves too deeply to such people. On the other hand, each of us knows individuals whom we somehow trust because we sense that they are being what they *are* in an open and transparent way and that we are dealing with the person himself, not with a polite or professional façade. This is the quality of congruence.

In relation to therapy it means that the therapist is what he *is,* during his encounter with his client. He is without front or façade, openly being the feelings and attitudes which at the moment are flowing in him. It involves the element of self-awareness, meaning that the feelings the therapist is experiencing are available to him, available to his awareness, and also that he is able to live these feelings, to be them in the relationship, and able to communicate them if appropriate. It means that he comes into a direct personal encounter with his client, meeting him on a person-to-person basis. It means that he is *being* himself, not denying himself.

Since this concept is liable to misunderstanding, it may be well to state some of the things that it does not imply. It does not mean that the therapist burdens his client with the overt expression of all of his feelings. It does not mean that he blurts out impulsively anything which comes to mind. It does not mean that the therapist discloses his total self to his client. It does mean, however, that he does not *deny* to himself the feelings that he is experiencing, and that he is willing *transparently to be* any persistent feelings which exist in the relationship and to let these be known to his client if appropriate. It means avoiding the temptation to present a façade or hide behind a mask of professionalism or to adopt a confessional-professional relationship.

It is not a simple thing to achieve such reality. Being real involves the difficult task of being acquainted with the flow of experiencing going on within oneself, a flow marked especially by complexity and continuous change. So if I sense that I am feeling bored by my contacts with this client and this feeling persists, I think I owe it to him and to our relationship to share this feeling with him. The same would hold if my feeling is one of being afraid of this client, or if my attention is so focused on my own problems that I can scarcely listen to him. But as I attempt to share these feelings I also want to be constantly in touch with what is going on in me. If I am, I will recognize that it is *my* feeling of being bored which I am expressing, and not some supposed fact about him as a boring person. If I voice it as my *own* reaction, it has the potentiality of leading to a deep relationship. But this feeling exists in the context of a complex and changing flow, and this needs to be communicated too. I would like to share with him my distress at feeling bored and the discomfort I feel in expressing this aspect of me. As I share these attitudes I find that my feeling of boredom arises from my sense of remoteness from him and that I would like to be more in touch with him, and even as I try to express these feelings they change. I am certainly not bored as I try to communicate myself to him in this way, and I am far from bored as I wait with eagerness and perhaps a bit of apprehension for his response. I also feel a new sensitivity to him now that I have shared this feeling which has been a barrier between us. I am very much more able to hear the surprise or perhaps the hurt in his voice as he now finds *him*self speaking more genuinely because I have dared to be real with him. I have let myself be a person—real, imperfect—in my relationship with him.

It should be clear from this lengthy description that congruence is helpful even when negative feelings toward the client are involved. Of course it would be most helpful if such feelings did not exist in the therapist, but if they do it is harmful to the patient to hide them. Any therapist has negative attitudes from time to time, but it is preferable for him to express them, thus to be real, than to put up a false posture of interest, concern, and liking which the client is likely to perceive, or subceive, as ungenuine.

It is not an easy thing for the client, or for any human being, to trust his most deeply shrouded feelings to another person. It is even more difficult for a disturbed person to share his deepest and most troubling feelings with a therapist. The genuineness, or congruence, of the therapist is one of the elements in the relationship which makes this risk of sharing easier and less fraught with dangers.

In view of the subtlety of this concept, it is not surprising that behavioral cues which permit us to measure the degree of congruence are also subtle. At a very low level of congruence the therapist may be clearly defensive in the interaction, as evidenced by the contradiction between the content of his message and his voice qualities or the non-verbal cues which he presents. Or the therapist may respond appropriately but in so professional a manner that he gives the impression that his responses are formulated to sound good rather than being what he really feels and means. Thus incongruence may involve a contrived or rehearsed quality or a professional front.

At the upper ranges of therapist genuineness, his openness to all types of feelings and experiences, both pleasant and hurtful, without trace of defensiveness or retreat into professionalism, is usually most evident from the quality of his voice and the manner of his expression. It is no doubt fortunate in trying to rate such a subtle quality that all of us have had a lifetime of experience in judging genuineness or facade in others. Hence we are able to detect extremely subtle cues in this respect.

Unconditional Positive Regard

A second condition which is hypothesized as essential for therapeutic movement and change is the experiencing by the therapist of an unconditional positive regard for the client. This means that the therapist communicates to his client a deep and genuine caring for him as a person with human potentialities, a caring uncontaminated by evaluations of his thoughts, feelings, or behaviors. The therapist experiences a warm acceptance of the client's experience as being a part of the client as a person, and places no conditions on his acceptance and warmth. He prizes the client in a total rather than a conditional way. He does not accept certain feelings in the client and disapprove others. He feels an *unconditional* positive regard or warmth for this person. This is an outgoing, positive feeling without reservations and without evaluations. It means *not* making judgments. It involves as much feeling of acceptance for the client's expression of painful, hostile, defensive, or abnormal feelings as for his expression of good, positive, mature feelings. For us as therapists it may even be that it is easier to accept painful and negative feelings than the positive and self-confident feelings which sometimes come through. These latter we almost automatically regard as defensive. But unconditional positive regard involves a willingness to share equally the patient's confidence and joy, or his depression and failure. It is a non-possessive caring for the client as a separate person. The client is thus freely allowed to have his *own* feelings and his *own* experiencing. One client describes the therapist as "fostering my possession of my own experience and that I am actually having it; thinking what I think, feeling what I feel, wanting what I want, fearing what I fear; no 'ifs,' 'buts,' or 'not reallys.' " This is the type of acceptance which is expected to lead to a relationship which facilitates the engagement of the patient in the process of therapy and leads to constructive personality change.

The question is often raised: But what about the therapist's attitude toward his client's asocial or antisocial behavior? Is he to accept this without evaluation? Sometimes this question is answered by saying that the effective therapist prizes the person, but not necessarily his behavior. Yet it is doubtful if this is an adequate or true answer. To be sure, the therapist may feel that a particular behavior is socially unacceptable or socially bad, something he could not approve of in himself, and a way of behaving which is inimical to the welfare of the social group. But the effective therapist may feel acceptant of this behavior in his client, not as desirable behavior, but as a *natural consequence* of the circumstances, experiences, and feelings of this client. Thus the therapist's acceptance may be based upon this kind of feeling: "If I had had the same background, the same circumstances, the same experiences, it would be inevitable in me, as it is in this client, that I would act in this fashion." In this respect he is like the good parent whose child, in a moment of fear and panic, has defecated in his clothing. The reaction of the loving parent includes both a caring for the child, and acceptance of the behavior as an entirely natural event under the circumstances. This does not mean that the parent approves such behavior in general.

Thus when the therapist prizes his client, and is searching for the meaning or value of his client's thoughts or behaviors within the client, he does not tend to feel a response of approval or disapproval. He feels an acceptance of what *is*.

Unconditional positive regard, when communicated by the therapist, functions to provide the non-threatening context in which it is possible for the client to explore and experience the most deeply shrouded elements of his inner self. The therapist is not paternalistic, or sentimental, or superficially social and agreeable. But his deep caring is a necessary ingredient in providing a "safe" context in which the client can come to explore himself and share deeply with another human being.

Accurate Empathic Understanding

The ability of the therapist accurately and sensitively to understand experiences and feelings *and their meaning to the client* during the moment-to-moment encounter of psychotherapy constitutes what can perhaps be described as the "work" of the therapist after he has first provided the contextual base for the relationship by his self-congruence or genuineness and his unconditional positive regard.

Accurate empathic understanding means that the therapist is completely at home in the universe of the patient. It is a moment-to-moment sensitivity that is in the "here and now," the immediate present. It is a sensing of the client's inner world of private personal meanings "as if" it were the therapist's own, but without ever losing the "as if" quality. Accurate sensitivity to the client's "being" is of primary value in the moment-to-moment encounter of therapy; it is of limited use to the individual if the therapist only arrives at this insightful and empathic understanding of the patient's experience as he drives home at night. Such a delayed empathy or insight may be of value if the therapist has a later chance to respond to the same theme, but its value would lie in formulating his empathic response to the patient's *immediate* living of the relationship.

The ability and sensitivity required to communicate these inner meanings back to the client in a way that allows these experiences to be "his" is the other major part of accurate empathic understanding. To sense the patient's confusion, his fear, his anger or his range as if it were a feeling you might have (but which you are not currently having) is the essence of the perceptive aspect of accurate empathy. To communicate this perception in a language attuned to the patient that allows him more clearly to sense and formulate his confusion, his fear, his rage or anger is the essence of the communicative aspect of accurate empathy.

At a high level of accurate empathy the message "I am with you" is unmistakably clear so that the therapist's remarks fit with the client's mood and content. The therapist at a high level will indicate not only a sensitive understanding of the apparent feelings but will *by his communication* clarify and expand the patient's awareness of these feelings or experiences. The communication is not only by the use of words that the patient might well have used, but also by the sensitive play of voice qualities which reflect the seriousness, the intentness, and the depth of feeling.

An accurate empathic grasp of the patient's conflicts and problems is perhaps most sharply contrasted with the more usual diagnostic formulation of the patient's experiences. This diagnostic understanding which is so different but so common involves the "I understand what is wrong with you" or "I understand the dynamics which make you act that way" approach. These evaluative understandings are external and sometimes even impersonal. While they may at times be very useful in developing external understanding, they are in sharp contrast to an accurate and sensitive grasp of events or experiences and their *personal meaning to the client*. The external and evaluative understanding tends to focus the client's being on externals or upon intellectualizations which remove him from an ongoing contact with the deeper elements of his self. The empathic understanding when it is accurately and sensitively communicated seems crucially important in making it possible for a person to get close to himself, to experience his most inward feelings, to maintain contact with his inner self-experiences, thus allowing for the recognition and resolution of incongruences. It is this self-exploration and consequent recognition and resolution of incongruities that we believe allows the client to change and to develop his potentialities.

Though the accuracy of understanding is central, the communication of intent to understand can in itself be of value. Even the confused, inarticulate, or bizarre individual, if he perceives that the therapist is *trying* to understand his meanings, will be helped because he will be encouraged to communicate more of his self. The very effort to understand communicates to the patient the value placed on him as an individual, thus conveying an element of unconditional positive regard. It gets across the fact that the therapist perceives his feelings and meanings as being *worth* understanding. It is in this sense that the intent to be empathic is of value. If the intent should continue without actualization, however, there is the possibility that it could become harmful. That is, if as a therapist I am consistently unable to understand the inarticulate or bizarre individual, he may become even more hopeless about the possibility of ever communicating himself.

There are many ways in which the therapist can communicate a low level of accurate empathic understanding. The therapist may be off on a tangent of his own, or may have misinterpreted what the patient is feeling, or may be so preoccupied and interested in his own intellectual interpretations of the client's behavior that he is scarcely aware of the client's "being." He may have his focus of attention on the intellectual content of what the client says rather than what the client "is" during the moment, and so ignores, misunderstands, or does not attempt to sense the client's current feelings and experiences.

The common element in a low level of empathy involves the therapist's doing something other than "listening" or "understanding"; he may be evaluating the client, giving advice, offering intellectual interpretations, or reflecting upon his own feelings or experiences. Indeed, a therapist may be accurately describing psychodynamics to the patient, but in a language not that of the client, or at a time when these dynamics are far removed from the current feelings of the client, so that there is a flavor of teacher-pupil interaction.

At a relatively low level of empathic sensitivity the therapist responds with clarity only to the patient's most obvious feelings. At an intermediate level, the therapist usually responds accurately to the client's more obvious feelings and occasionally recognizes some that are less apparent, but in the process of tentative probing, he may anticipate feelings which are not current or may misinterpret the present feelings. At a higher level the therapist is aware of many feelings and experiences which are not so evident but his lack of complete understanding is shown by the slightly inaccurate nature of his deeper responses. At this level he is simply "pointing" to some of the more hidden feelings. He is aware of their existence and so points to them but he is not yet able to grasp their meaning. At a very high level of empathic understanding the therapist's responses move, with sensitivity and accuracy, into feelings and experiences that are only hinted at by the client. At this level, underlying feelings or experiences are not only pointed to but they are specifically identified so that the content that comes to light may be new but it is not alien. At this high level the therapist is sensitive to his own tentative errors and quickly alters or changes his responses in midstream, indicating a clear but fluid responsiveness to what is being sought after in the patient's own explorations. The therapist's words reflect a togetherness with the patient and a tentative trial-and-error exploration while his voice tone reflects the seriousness and depth of his empathic grasp.

It is this sensitive and accurate grasp and communication of the patient's inner world that facilitates the patient's self-exploration and consequent personality growth.

The Theoretical Predictions

The three constructs defined in the preceding pages—empathic understanding, unconditional positive regard, and therapist congruence or genuineness—are central to the research. It is part of the theoretical background of the study that if these three conditions exist, then a process of therapy will occur in which the client deeply explores himself and comes to know and experience the full range of his being. As a consequence of the patient's engagement in this process of psychotherapy, personality growth and constructive personality change are theoretically predicted to occur.

Since these conditions—as offered by the therapist—vary in degree, and since the variables of process movement and therapeutic outcome also exist in varying degrees, the theoretical predictions are cast in the following form:

1. The greater the degree to which the therapist is congruent in the relationship, the greater will be the evidences of process movement in the client, and the greater will be the degree of constructive personality change in the client over therapy.
2. The greater the degree to which the therapist evidences unconditional positive regard for the client in the therapeutic relationship, the greater will be the evidences of the client's engagement in the process of therapy and his consequent personality change.
3. Finally, the greater the degree of accurately empathic understanding exhibited by the therapist toward the client, the greater will be the evidences of the client's engagement in the process of therapy and his consequent personality change.

These theoretic predictions are made with the understanding that three assumptions may be made about the therapeutic relationships in which these elements are studied. These are that the client and therapist are in psychological contact—that each makes a perceived or subceived difference in the experiential field of the other; that the patient is, at least to a minimal degree, incongruent and hence anxious or vulnerable to anxiety; and that the therapist's behavior communicates these attitudinal conditions so that they are to some degree perceived or subceived by the client.

Although the conditions are listed in the order of their theoretical importance, no specific predictions are made as to whether the conditions might be separately effective, or whether they are effective only when they exist together. The theory favors the view that each must be minimally present for effective therapy.

References

ALEXANDER, F. *Fundamentals of Psychoanalysis*. New York: W. W. Norton, 1948.

DYMOND, ROSALIND. A scale for the measurement of empathic ability. *J. consult. Psychol. 13:*127–233, 1949.

ELLIS, A. Requisite conditions for basic personality change. *J. consult. Psychol. 23:*538–540, 1959.

FERENCZI, S. The principle of relaxation and neocatharsis. *Int. J. Psycho-Anal. 11:*428–443, 1930.

FOX, R. E., and GOLDIN, P. C. The empathic process in psychotherapy: A survey of theory and research. Unpublished manuscript, 1963.

HALPERN, H., and LESSER, LEONA. Empathy in infants, adults, and psychotherapists. *Psychoanal. Rev. 47:*32–42, 1960.

HOBBS, N. Sources of gain in psychotherapy. *Amer. Psychologist 17:*741–747, 1962.

JOURARD, S. I–thou relationship versus manipulation in counseling and psychotherapy. *J. indiv. Psychol. 15:*174–179, 1959.

RAUSH, H. L., and BORDIN, E. S. Warmth in personality development and in psychotherapy. *J. study Interpers. Processes 20:* No. 4, 1957.

ROGERS, C. R. *Client-Centered Therapy*. Boston: Houghton Mifflin, 1951.

ROGERS, C. R. The necessary and sufficient conditions of therapeutic personality change. *J. consult. Psychol. 21:*95–103, 1957.

ROGERS, C. R. A theory of therapy, personality, and interpersonal relationships as developed in the client-centered framework. In S. Koch (ed.), *Psychology: A Study of a Science*. Vol. III, *Formulations of the Person in the Social Context*. New York: McGraw Hill, 1959, pp. 184–256.

SCHAFER, R. Generative empathy in the treatment situation. *Psychoanal. Quart. 28:*342–373, 1959.

STRUNK, O., JR. Empathy: A review of theory and research. *Psychological Newsletter 9:*47–57, 1957.

STRUPP, H. H. Nature of psychotherapist's contribution to the treatment process. *Arch. gen. Psychiat. 3:*219–231, 1960.

TRUAX, C. B. Therapeutic conditions. *Discussion papers,* University of Wisconsin Psychiatric Institute, 1961, No. 13.

7. The Process Conception and Its Measurement

The elucidation of a new view of the therapeutic process was largely the work of Eugene T. Gendlin and Carl R. Rogers. The implementation and testing of this theory through operational scales was carried out by many additional workers, especially the following: Emily Earley, Joe Hart, Marcel Heisel, Marjorie H. Klein, Philippa L. Mathieu, Richard Rablen, Paula Rohrbaugh, T. M. Tomlinson, Charles B. Truax, Alan Walker, and Ferdinand van der Veen. The chapter was written by Eugene T. Gendlin and T. M. Tomlinson.

Theoretical Background

Process as Compared with Outcomes

To date, theory and research on therapeutic effects have largely been concerned with how an individual is at a certain time, thus dealing with diagnostic categories, task performance, psychometric evaluation, personality characteristics, conflicts, complexes, and other similar elements. As a result, personality theory and measurement have become relatively sophisticated in defining an individual's characteristics and in formulating the needed changes ("perception is unrealistic," "personal relationships are avoided," "self-defeating patterns are repeated," etc.). Outcomes of psychotherapy are measured by applying these measures *before* and *after* therapy. They provide a statement about the sum of the overall changes—changes on psychometric tests, change in various kinds of personality manifestations and problems—which have occurred as an apparent product of psychotherapy. Far less attention has been given to delineating theoretically, and to measuring operationally, just what processes are the agents of change. "Working through" (Freud, 1959, 1936), "emotional learning" (Alexander and French, 1964), "abreacting" (Fenichel, 1945), are a few of the words with which some therapeutic orientations have referred to the process of change or movement, but little has been done to spell out their meanings.

The research program reported in this book was chiefly concerned with the *process* of psychotherapy and its conditions. Our main hypotheses were that the process of therapy would maximally occur under certain conditions of therapist behavior, that the process would occur more in therapy than in control clients, and that this process would be of the same kind in schizophrenics as in neurotics and normals. Our endeavor was to measure variables of *ongoing* psychotherapy. We felt that research into a phenomenon (psychotherapy) best succeeds when the phenomenon itself can be measured; one cannot indefinitely remain limited to measuring only before-and-after, leaving the phenomenon as such in a "black box." Without measures of the phenomenon itself one cannot know whether the phenomenon is really occurring between the before-and-after measures. For example, when one sets out to measure changes in a therapy group (as compared to a no-therapy control group), how can one know how many of the therapy group have really been in therapy? All those who entered a room with a therapist twice a week? Being in therapy requires more than mere physical presence, but what? One needs a definition of therapy. Thus the main purpose of the research was to advance to the point where we would be able to define and measure *ongoing psychotherapy,* and the conditions which determine when it does, or does not, occur.

The Trend Toward a Concern with Process

The various schools of therapy differ in what content they hold basic, for example: sex, power drives, interpersonal relations, self-concepts. Individuals also differ in what contents they discuss in their therapeutic struggles. Yet change occurs as well in clients of one therapeutic school as of another. Obviously, content is not the determining factor.

It was natural that a concern with process should develop in the client-centered orientation. Rogers had held that for purposes of therapy not only was diagnosis unnecessary (1957) but the therapist might be more effective without it. The therapist was urged to avoid generalized interpretations that might lead to a prematurely fixed impression, and to meet his client in an immediate, personal encounter, verbalizing the client's present, concretely-felt personal meanings. In this mode of responding, the client's sense of feeling had a central role. "Feelings" are not only emotive or affective states. They may also be felt personal meanings which the client has not yet fully conceptualized. As the therapist responds to these, refers to them, and helps put them into words, these felt personal meanings change. New aspects of them are differentiated, that is, become discriminable in terms of the felt change. As these are conceptualized in turn, still further aspects arise, and a self-propelled change process is put into motion.

The therapist responds to concrete felt meanings here and now, and he verbalizes felt meanings the client implies but does not say. Such implicit meanings are felt now by the client and recognized by the therapist. Hence they differ from deductions. A therapist could deduce from what is now being felt many other characteristics the client is *not* now feeling or talking about. Such deductions are useful for diagnostic categories but have little role in client-centered therapy.

Rogers' method of practice put the emphasis on the question, What is the ongoing feeling process now and how may it be therapeutically facilitated?

Secondly, Rogers' theory of human nature tends, from another direction, to stress the process aspects of psychotherapy. Adjustment and maturity are not artifacts of the shaping and censoring of society. Development of the self, of values, of socialization, the enjoyment and consideration of others—all are viewed as natural processes of a human organism. Neurotic and psychotic difficulties are viewed by Rogers as flaws in the wholeness of the organism, as resulting from "incongruences," estrangements between the experiencing individual and the cognitive maps—the self concepts—by which he operates. According to Rogers, if the individual is surrounded by a climate of certain conditions —acceptance, understanding, and genuine personal response—he will *naturally,* as a part of his own species nature, *move toward* more openness to his organismic experience, toward healing the inner estrangement, toward a more mature adjustment. These basic concepts of personality and human nature imply a natural *process* of positive change and growth. What occurs in therapy is thus, for Rogers, not an imposition on the individual of some possible shapes. Rather it is a natural chain of events akin to the biological growth processes, which is always essentially the same for a given species. In these ways the client-centered mode of responding and the view of human nature foreshadow the "process" concept.

A third source of the concept is the role Rogers assigns to "experience" in his theory. Rogers took over from other theories the view that personality is fashioned by the attitudes and values of others, but he terms this aspect of personality "neurotic." His position is that optimal functioning occurs only when the individual's own bodily experience is the basis for his personality organization, his value judgments, his perceptions and reactions. Therapy is viewed as the client's increasing use of his ongoing experience in developing new and optimal ways of expressing, perceiving, and organizing himself. Maladjustment is viewed as the incongruity between the individual's actual experiences, and his introjected judgments and perceptions held in place by reward and punishment. Therapeutic reorganization requires using direct experience and bringing concepts and values into line with it.

From the formal theory statement written in 1953 (Rogers, 1959*b*) here is the brief summary of twelve directions of therapeutic movement:

1. The client is increasingly free in expressing his feelings, through verbal and/or motor channels.
2. His expressed feelings increasingly have reference to the self, rather than nonself.
3. He increasingly differentiates and discriminates the objects of his feelings and perceptions, including his environment, other persons, his self, his experiences, and the interrelationships of these . . . his experiences are more accurately symbolized.
4. His expressed feelings increasingly have reference to the incongruity between certain of his experiences and his concept of self.
5. He comes to experience in awareness the threat of such incongruence. This experience of threat is possible only because of the continued unconditional positive regard of the therapist, which is extended to incongruence as much as to congruence, to anxiety as much as to absence of anxiety.
6. He experiences fully, in awareness, feelings which have in the past been denied to awareness, or distorted in awareness.
7. His concept of self becomes reorganized to assimilate and include these experiences which have previously been distorted in or denied to awareness.
8. As this reorganization of the self-structure continues, his concept of self becomes increasingly congruent with his experience; the self now including experiences which previously would have been too threatening to be in awareness.
   a. A corollary tendency is toward fewer perceptual distortions in awareness, or denials to awareness, since there are fewer experiences which can be threatening. In other words, defensiveness is decreased.
9. He becomes increasingly able to experience, without a feeling of threat, the therapist's unconditional positive regard.
10. He increasingly feels an unconditional positive self-regard.
11. He increasingly experiences himself as the locus of evaluation.
12. He reacts to experiences less in terms of his conditions of worth [or introjected values] and more in terms of an organismic valuing process. (Rogers, 1959*b*, p. 216)

This statement represents the starting point from which our thinking about process in therapy has gone forward.

Steps Toward a Process Theory

Rogers saw as one of the chief problems of this formulation the impossibility of observing or checking "congruence" between awareness and experience. If one could only measure the contents of experiences one could then check the client's increasing congruence between his experiences and his conceptualizations. But one side of this equation was, by definition, unobservable: the contents of experience.

Gendlin and Zimring (1955) took the next step. They began with the observation that during psychotherapy feelings and personal meanings—until then supposedly "in" experience but not "in" incongruent awareness—not only emerge but change as the client attends to them, expresses them, and is responded to. They viewed personality not as made up of contents ("experiences") but as an ongoing process of experiencing, an ongoing feeling process. They introduced the term "direct referent" to describe the feeling which the client is concretely and immediately experiencing (Gendlin and Zimring, 1955; Rogers, 1958. See also, Rogers, 1960; Gendlin, 1962, 1964). The client (and the therapist) employ words to point to the client's experiencing. The client guides his words in accordance with the "felt meaning" which is implicit in his experiencing. The verbal content may be about the past, but the meaning is contained in the client's present experiencing as he now feels it and as it guides his symbolizing in words.

As a person engages in this process of directly grappling with his experiential meanings, these *change*. Man is not made up of pre-set "contents," ideas, or emotions such as anger, shame, fear of "X," etc. Rather, there is an experiencing process and as responses and words carry this process forward, change takes place. Fear of "X" turns out to be a feeling that "when 'Y' happens I am hurt." More exactly, it then becomes not so much hurt at "Y" as "helplessness in the face of 'Z.' " All the while there is ongoing experiencing.

The Experiencing Process

To make this conception of process clearer, and to bring home just where and how it occurs, an example from a common experience other than psychotherapy will be helpful, although the similarity to psychotherapy will be evident.

Suppose you have been listening to a discussion and you now are about to say something relevant and important. As you wait for the chance to speak, let us say your attention is distracted for a moment and you lose hold of what you were about to say. You never did have the words you were about to say. You had a felt sense of being about to say something, and now you strive to get hold of that felt sense again. What do you do to regain such a sense of what you were about to say? Where do you look for it?

Now suppose you do get hold of it again. You say, "Oh!—just a moment—I've got it!—" Again at that moment, although you "know" what you are about to say, you don't know it in words.

Thus one can have, lose, and regain a felt sense which, all along, has not been in the form of words. This is a "felt meaning," the direct referent.

Such a felt meaning or direct referent may seem to be located in one's stomach (like "butterflies in your stomach"), or wherever a given individual feels fear, hunger, or joyful excitement. Whatever its body location, it is best defined in terms of the kinds of activities or the sequence of events in which we use it: how we refer to it, look for it, phrase it. Let us, therefore, note what we do when we have lost the sense of what we were about to say.

How does one get back the sense of what one was about to say? One may become quiet, receptive, hoping that what one was about to say will come back. Or, one can actively grope for it. Or one can purposely think of something else or do something else, to get rid of the strain of trying. Or, one can ask oneself questions like, "Was it something about . . . ?" Or, one can very systematically try to trace logical connections ("It would have had to be about . . . it must therefore be something about . . ."), or the sequence of events ("It was right after Mr. A said . . . but it was before Mr. B said . . .").

In all these examples whatever we deliberately do is done in the hope that suddenly there will be an "unfolding" (Gendlin, 1964), and the whole thing will flood back. We depend upon it to come back. So long as it doesn't, we haven't remembered what we were going to say, no matter how likely our suggestions, or how good our tracing. We cannot deduce what we were going to say. In these examples about remembering it is quite clear that the direct referent is capable of independent movement. Only this gives success to our efforts.

When we do get back the sense of what we were going to say, there is a physically felt release which tells us that we've got "it." This release is a change in our bodily felt condition.

We guide our search for what we were going to say by the degree of intensification which we directly feel. We concentrate on the felt sense we do have. Sometimes we sense it getting stronger for a moment. We then feel close to it. At other moments it may recede, seem to be lost again. If something we verbalize has the effect of intensifying the felt sense, we cling to it strongly. Even if it is a rather unlikely phrase from a logical point of view, we prize the phrase if it brings us closer. The felt sense we have responds something like the children's game: "warm; warmer! warmer!! colder; colder; oh, ice cold; warmer!" etc.

As we "focus" (Gendlin, 1964) our attention on what we were going to say and grope in this fashion, the directly felt sense plays a central role. We guide our verbalizations by it. The direction of search is determined by the intensification of feeling, the "referent movement" (Gendlin, 1964) we feel.

The interplay between what we say or think and the direct referent cannot be determined by any imposed logic or value system. What we suggest to ourselves may be the "best" or "most interesting," or the most sensible, yet it may produce no referent movement. We thereby know we are not getting hold of what we were going to say. On the other hand, some phrase may produce referent movement in spite of making little logical sense. Thus the interplay between verbalization and direct referent contains its own inherent direction, its own sense and value direction.

When we finally get hold of what we were going to say, when there is "unfolding," we may be quite disappointed. It may not be at all interesting or good. Perhaps it is hardly worth saying after all. Perhaps what we were about to say now seems plainly false. Nevertheless, if we have felt a physical release and flooding back, we cannot doubt that we have reached what we were going to say.

In the above situation we all clearly know the distinction between those moments when we speak with mere logic, and those moments when we have also a directly felt response or referent movement. Everyone knows how unsatisfying it is when we try to recall what we have forgotten and get no referent movement. We have only probable conceptions. We then usually say, "I think it *must* have been . . . , but I can't be sure." The "must" indicates a conceptual, logical sureness very different from, and basically unconvincing compared to, that sureness of the physically felt release of remembering, unfolding, flooding back. Similarly, in psychotherapy when the client says, "It *must be* that I have to keep myself from succeeding in order to prove . . ." the words "must be" indicate that there is not a directly felt referent movement and unfolding.

The variable we tried to measure in the research was the degree to which the individual employs directly felt experiencing in his verbalizations. *This is process.*

A felt sense, when verbalized, is always many things. For example, when I get hold of what I was going to say I may find that I need one or two paragraphs to express it.

Similarly (to change the example to one more pertinent to psychotherapy), suppose a client is trying to explore what it is that bothers him about "X" (where "X" is a situation or a person). He may go through several sequences of focusing on a direct referent, feeling referent movement, unfolding, and release; focusing on a new and different direct referent, and so on. In this process he finds he feels as he does because certain facets of the situation have certain meanings to him because they involve certain circumstances which, in turn, affect certain other needs of his in such a way that he now has difficulties which discourage him because he knows he ought now to do something else, but if he tries he knows that what will happen is . . . , and so on and so on. Always a complex texture is verbalized as the direct referent unfolds.

The way in which the direct referent interacts with verbalization and guides it is much more refined than any diagnostic or evaluative conceptions the individual may have. It is also quite independent of such concepts and values. No matter how undesirable or infantile, silly or shameful or otherwise unvaluable it may seem to him that such and such should bother him about "X," nevertheless that is the direction which referent movement indicates (Rogers has termed this the "organismic valuing process") and only as he focuses on it, as it unfolds and releases, can the process of psychotherapy proceed.

Not realizing the essential role of the direct referent in determining the direction of movement in therapy, many writers treat therapy as a purely theoretical problem. They assume the therapist or the client must decide on the goals of therapy, on the direction of the whole course, and on the choices at every step. It is not so. One's best evaluating and deciding may produce no referent movement. The answer may be, ". . . colder, colder, ice cold!" The process of therapy depends on attending at every point to the direct referent and following the direction of the referent movement.

In our example of trying to get back the sense of what we were going to say, we spoke of focusing on the direct referent and of its referent movement as it may intensify or even finally release and unfold. We focus directly on such a felt sense—and yet we have lost that felt sense which constituted what we were going to say! It seems as if we have to invent more and more "things" to read into the human person: now there will have to be two direct referents—the one we lost hold of and search for, and the one we do have and employ.

This little problem illustrates a basic aspect of process theory: we should not make a "thing" out of a felt sense, an experience, a direct referent. Experiencing is a process, not a box full of thing-like entities.

In such a process what we concretely feel is not one "thing," nor many separate "things." There is not one "feeling of this" and another "feeling of that," or one "experience of this" and another "experience of that." There is an ongoing physically felt life process. Thousands of potentially separable (but not separate) facets "function implicitly"

(Gendlin, 1964) in any one moment of this sentient process and are implicit in one "this feeling." To verbalize always involves carrying forward the experiencing process. Verbalization does not just represent experience. It does not just take a picture of experience. It is not just *about* experience. Verbalization responds to experiencing and carries it forward. Thereby the concretely felt experiencing is changed; we have felt referent movement. After referent movement, some aspect of experiencing may now be present which was absent before, as experiencing is now more fully ongoing than before. Verbalization is "feedback" (if you like this way of putting it).

Not only words but also events, other peoples' responses and actions, and many other kinds of things can produce referent movement. Such referent movement is experiencing going on further or more broadly than before. This referent movement is not just any arbitrary change. Rather, it is a "carrying forward" of experiencing in some respect in which it was previously blocked or narrowed or restricted. In various theories this phenomenon has been called a release of inhibition, something breaking through from the unconscious, the release of an anxiety bond, etc. Elsewhere a more experiential theory of it has been formulated (Gendlin, 1964). What is important is to note that "carrying forward" is an experiential change process. It may occur when we say exactly what is implicit in a feeling, or when we focus directly on the feeling, or when another person responds to it. It does not always occur. In fact, usually it does not. There are all sorts of responses and reactions which have no referent movement and carrying forward. In such cases we may have done, said, thought, explained, and heard much —yet in regard to the specific question we are just where we were before. Referent movement and carrying forward are rare, and always welcome! However unwelcome the words and content may be, there is directly felt relief and easing in the moment of referent movement and carrying forward. Even if what we were going to say turns out to be very disappointing, the feeling, "That *is* what it was!" is in itself a good feeling.

Carrying forward often occurs in interaction between the client and the therapist, whereas it did not occur in the individual's lone thinking or feeling. Often he has thought and struggled in regard to something for months without any referent movement whatever, yet there may be a felt "give" when he hears the therapist's response (even though that response may not be particularly brilliant or novel in content). Sometimes referent movement occurs at the instant the client is about to speak, or even before he does.

It isn't always in terms of the content of therapy that referent movement is noticeable. The client may feel freer in general, more open, more firm, more deeply alive in a relationship than alone (or, he may feel less so, more constricted).

Just as the individual's own attention, direct reference, groping and verbalizing, isn't just *about* experience (but rather, carries experiencing forward) so also interpersonal responses are not merely the content of the words. T's response carries C's experiencing forward, affects it, changes it, enables it to be more fully ongoing.

This interactive response was formulated by Rogers in terms of the therapist's consistent attitudes or "conditions," which we attempted to measure in this research.

We hypothesized that as successful therapy progresses, the role of experiencing in all the regards described would generally increase; the individual would more often "freshly phrase" his feelings (that is to say, put words to a direct referent, rather than use words only conceptually, or only about situations). His notions about himself, his chain of thought, his reactions to things, would more often be based on the role played by his directly felt experiencing. Note that all we have described here concerns roles which directly felt experiencing can play together with words, thoughts, statements, and interactive behaviors. Thus we can say that the individual is "remote from" his experiencing if he usually speaks, thinks, judges, and reacts without his directly felt experiencing having played such a role. This is comparable to someone trying to figure out what it was he was about to say *without* reference to his directly felt sense of it (without letting it come, or groping for it, or tracing it, or phrasing it and without depending upon *it* to "unfold," "release," or show referent movement).

In contrast, the more the individual's experiencing plays these central roles in his thinking, speaking, and reacting, the higher he moves on the "process continuum."

In developing this approach (Gendlin, 1962, 1964), "contents" (*what* one experiences) came to be considered "process-aspects," symbolizations of aspects of the directly felt process. Where the process of experiencing is narrowed or stopped, symbolizations of it will also be limited. The theory of the unconscious is thereby reformulated. We observe that individuals when responded to in certain ways engage in a process in which aspects of feeling and experience "become aware." They will say, "Only now do I realize this and this, *which I have long felt, but not known.*" For example, a man may long have felt some discomfort in a certain situation. Only now does he become aware that it was anger he felt. The older theory concludes that the anger was "repressed" or "denied to awareness." The present theory emphasizes that certain feelings were, all along, in awareness, but the experiencing moved no further and hence "anger" was not an aspect of it that could be conceptualized. Only as he is responded to, and as his experiencing is carried forward in a fuller manner, does he "become angry," and only then can he conceptualize anger as an aspect of his present experiencing. Earlier, anger did not exist as a package or content hidden "under" awareness. Rather, at the earlier time, he *did* experience and *was aware* of a feeling of discomfort. The process of experiencing was narrowed or stopped and did not go to its completion. The process is carried forward during therapeutic responding, and there is an ongoing change. One does not merely dig out what was there, unchanged.

The Testable Nature of This Theory of Process

In the process theory the emphasis is placed not upon what the client says but upon how he engages his inward concretely felt data as he speaks. The question is, then, can one observe whether, and measure to what extent, his words refer to concretely felt experiencing. The clue that this can be done lies in the fact that in clinical practice we are able to distinguish between the individual who is really engaged in therapy and the individual who is merely intellectualizing. Obviously if we can make this distinction in therapeutic practice it must be by means of observable aspects of in-therapy behavior.

For example, verbal behavior can be examined for its sequential connections. Do the sentences each relate to the proceeding in that they are all about the same situation, follow the time sequence which the events followed, or are logical implications one from the other? If so, experiencing probably plays a minor role in the verbalizing. Or are the connections between the sentences "felt connections"? Does it seem that the individual is having to refer inwardly to something directly felt which intervenes between one sentence and the next? If so, it is likely that an experiential referent is being employed. Consider the following sentences:

T: So an important bad thing happened when I didn't notice you, that time, when I walked out of the building.

C: That's right.

T: I guess it felt like I didn't want to see you.

C: No! No, no, no. Very much not that. Any part of it which felt like that is a completely different kind of thing.

T: I see. Go ahead. Go ahead with the thing it really is.

C: [*pause*] If I could explain how, really it's exactly the same kind of thing we have been talking about. And I don't know where it fits. But it does.

T: About not feeling real? Do you mean that if I don't see you then you're not real — that type of thing?

C: M-hm — yeah — it's that, but it's not clear "in that last mirror" and that's the only analogy I can think of and it's not enough.

T: It doesn't really say what it is at all, but you've got it named that way. That you've got a whole series of mirrors facing each other, and when it gets way, way, way inside somewhere in the last one where it really counts, there is where it isn't clear.

C: Yeah. [*long pause*] And all that analogy does, is it keeps me from losing it.

T: When I walk by and don't see you, in some way-inside sense, something is lost.

C: And this is where I don't understand it, because seeing you lets me be someway inside me, and then when it turns out you didn't see me, then it is like I wasn't that way.

These sentences do not follow one another in a purely logical way, nor can they be deduced from one another. The sequence makes sense only if we assume that the individual was referring to a concrete felt meaning and thereby was guided through this sequence of verbalizations.

Other observable indices are illustrated here. Note the metaphoric way of speaking. Such speech makes sense only if considered to refer to directly felt meanings. If we take it literally and logically, no real meaning can be assigned to it. Also, note how the direct referent guided the individual's choice of words; the formulation is not yet correct, it only "keeps me from losing it."

Thus there are observable aspects of process which can be indicated on rating scales. Taken together the scales would then measure the degree to which directly felt experiencing plays such central roles for the client as those illustrated above.

The Beginning of a Process Scale

On the basis of the theory regarding experiencing (Gendlin, 1955, 1957) Rogers undertook to identify the specific observables of the therapeutic process. He started by immersing himself in naturalistic observation. "I used myself as a tool . . . I have spent many hours listening to recorded interviews—trying to listen as naively as possible. I have endeavored to soak up all the clues I could capture as to the process, as to what elements are significant in change" (Rogers, 1958, p. 142). The result was a "Process Scale" (Rogers and Rablen, 1958) consisting of seven parallel variables. These were: (1) "feelings and personal meanings," (2) "manner of experiencing," (3) "degree of incongruence," (4) "communication of self," (5) "the manner in which experience is construed, (6) "the relationship to problems," (7) "the manner of relating to others." For each of these seven variables, or strands, the Process Scale describes seven stages. At the low end of the scale, the seven variables are seven distinct aspects of behavior. Here they are approximately as described by Rogers in several of his writings and in the Rogers and Rablen Scale (Rogers and Rablen, 1958).

1. "Feelings may at times be *exhibited* in ways which seem quite obvious to the observer, but they are unrecognized as such by the individual," or are "described as unknown past objects, external to self."
2. "The individual is very remote from his experiencing and unable to draw upon it or symbolize its implicit meanings."
3. "There is no awareness whatever of . . . discrepancy," or "when the client voices contradictory statements about himself . . . [there is] little or no awareness that these represent contradictions."
4. ". . . we find the individual . . . avoiding any expression which seems in any way revealing of self." "There may be expression about self as an object and about self-related experiences as objects."
5. "Personal constructs are extremely rigid, unrecognized as constructs, and thought of as external facts. The individual is unaware that he has construed experience as having a particular meaning."
6. "No problems are recognized," or "problems . . . are perceived as external to self."
7. "Close relationships are perceived as dangerous. The individual avoids close involvements with others."

These aspects blend as the meaning of all the terms becomes experiential in nature. This blending is evident in Rogers' description of the high end of the scale, the sixth and seventh stages:

1. ". . . feelings are experienced and expressed freely in the immediate moment with a deeper sense of ownership and acceptance."
2. ". . . experiencing is an accepted inner referent to which he can turn for accurate meanings . . . using it comfortably as a major referent for his behavior."
3. ". . . aspect(s) of incongruence [are] vividly experienced . . . The individual is vividly aware of the inaccuracy with which he has symbolized his experiencing" . . . and "is able to symbolize and conceptualize the meanings which are implicit in the immediate moment."

4. "The self exists in the experiencing of feeling. At any given moment, the self *is* the experiencing."
5. "In the moments of movement which occur . . . there is a dissolving of significant personal constructs in a vivid experiencing of a feeling which runs counter to the constructs. There is the realization that many personal constructs which have seemed to be solid guides are only ways of construing a moment of experiencing."
6. "The individual is living some aspect of his problems in his experiencing." The problem is not "an object in itself."
7. "The individual risks being himself in process in his relationship to the therapist. [He risks] being the flow that is himself and trusting another person to accept him as he is in this flow."

To give a clearer picture of the way in which the scale is constructed, the several stages on the strand relating to feelings will be briefly described (Rogers and Rablen, 1958). The Feelings and Personal Meanings (FPM) strand refers to "the relationship of the individual to the feelings and personal meanings which exist within himself." In stage 1 of this continuum, "the individual is largely unaware of his feeling life. Even in a receptive climate feelings are not described. Feelings may at times be exhibited in ways which seem quite obvious to the observer, but they are unrecognized as such by the individual."

In stage 2, "feelings are sometimes described as unowned, past objects external to self. There is a strong tendency to shrug off rather than to explore feelings."

At stage 3, "there is much description of feelings and personal meanings which are not now present. In describing these distant feelings they are not pictured as acceptable but as bad or abnormal."

Stage 4 is recognized by the fact that "feelings and personal meanings are freely described as present objects owned by the self. There is considerable acceptance of these known described feelings. Feelings of an intense sort are still described as not now present. Occasionally feelings are expressed in the present but this occurs as if against the individual's wishes. There is often a dim recognition that feelings previously denied to awareness may break through into the present but this seems to be a frightening possibility."

Stage 5 has further characteristics. "In this stage we find many feelings freely expressed in the moment of their occurrence, and thus experienced in the immediate present. These feelings are owned or accepted. Feelings which have been previously denied now tend to bubble through into awareness, though there is fear and distrust of this occurrence. There is a beginning tendency to realize that experiencing a feeling provides a direct referent to which the individual can turn for further meanings."

In stage 6, "feelings which have been previously denied to awareness are now experienced with immediacy and acceptance. This immediately experienced feeling is something which *is,* not something to be denied, feared, or struggled against."

Stage 7 is rarely reached, certainly not by patients in this research. At this level, "new feelings are experienced with richness and immediacy and this experiencing is used as a clear and definite referent from which further meanings may be drawn. Feelings are rarely denied to awareness and then only temporarily. The individual is able both to live in his own feelings and personal meanings and to express them as an owned and accepted aspect of himself."

An Account of Research Using the Process Scale

When the initial version of the scale was completed, some pilot studies were carried out to determine whether it could be used reliably, and whether it had validity. An informal study by Heisel involved the use of five recorded interview segments taken from different interviews in a case in which it was judged clinically that movement had occurred. (In this study, and in all those which followed, the data consisted of samples or segments of interviews, never the entire interview.) The judges—students in a seminar who had been discussing the process concept—were asked to indicate, using the paired comparisons technique, which of each pair of samples represented the higher position on the Process Scale. The fact that there was a significant degree of concordance among these essentially untrained judges encouraged further work with the scale.

Using the improved scale, Walker, Rablen, and Rogers (1959) undertook to rate 24 samples taken from two early and two late interviews of six cases. These cases were externally rated for outcome (this means that the measures of outcome used had no direct relationship to psychotherapy) and afforded an opportunity to make the first statement regarding the scale's validity. The segments were given to two judges in random order. Neither judge knew the time of occurrence of the interview, the case the sample came from, or the rated outcome of the particular case. Ratings were made in terms of stages and the correlation of these ratings between the two judges yielded an r of .83. The six cases were then ranked according to their externally rated outcome and compared statistically with ranks derived from the process ratings. The correlation between these two sets of ranks was .89 (rho), significant at an .02 level. These studies suggested that the strands of the Process

Scale described behavior which could be reliably rated, and which appeared to be associated with other criteria of improvement.

The next study, by Tomlinson (1959), was designed to expand on the preliminary results provided by Rablen and Walker. The material for rating came from the University of Chicago Counseling Center (Halkides, 1958) and consisted of segments of varying length chosen from each of 40 interviews representing twenty cases. In all, 360 segments were rated, 9 from each interview, 18 from each case. Of the twenty cases, ten were judged to be more successful and ten were judged less successful (using external criteria). Each case was represented by an early and a later interview, and each interview from a more successful case was matched with the interview of the same number from a less successful case.

There were three judges. One judge rated all the 360 segments and the remaining two judges rated portions of the segments selected at random. Reliability coefficients ranged from .47 to .63. The results showed no clear difference between process scores of early and later interviews, regardless of rated outcome. It seemed that matching the later interviews for number between the two groups distorted the evidence of significant change in individual cases (change being defined as the difference between process ratings of early and late interviews from a given case). As an example, one more successful case with 108 interviews was matched with a less successful case containing only 15 interviews. The interview-matching forced interview 15 to be used as a "later" interview in both cases, thus removing whatever effect therapy may have had in the remaining 93 interviews of the successful case.

The results did show significant differences between process scores of the two groups, the higher ratings being associated with the more successful cases. However, it was determined that this significance was due entirely to the different starting points of the more successful and less successful cases, and not at all to an increase in process ratings over time. This seemed to suggest that the successful client enters therapy at a higher level of process than his less successful counterpart.

Puzzled by the contrast between the low interrater agreement found by Tomlinson, and the high agreement found between judges in earlier studies, Hart (1961) undertook an investigation which focused on the reliability properties of the Process Scale. By systematically varying certain conditions of rating and the rating materials he sought to identify the optimal circumstances for reliable ratings. His results indicated that the Process Scale, when used by experienced raters under optimal conditions, is a highly reliable measuring instrument (interrater reliability: $r = .72$ to $.95$). Inter- and intrajudge reliability stemming from the use of both tape and typescript units was superior to the reliability of ratings made using either tape units or typescript units alone. Also non–time-limited ratings yielded higher inter- and intrajudge agreement than ratings which were time-limited. Thus when raters spent as much time as they wished on each segment, the results were better.

At this point a second validation study was undertaken (Tomlinson and Hart, 1962), incorporating suggestions stemming from the findings of the above studies. For example, following Hart's recommendation, the raters in this investigation were experienced and made non–time-limited ratings of simultaneously presented tape and typescript units. The interview samples, following a suggestion of Tomlinson's, were selected to represent end points of therapy rather than being matched according to number. Using the second interview and the next to the last interview in each case made it possible to compare cases in terms of "real" process change (late process ratings minus early) regardless of case length.

The study was based on ten cases, considered representative of the University of Chicago Counseling Center clients. From the second interview and the next to the last interview of each case, nine two-minute samples of therapy were selected. The sampling units were arbitrarily chosen at every three-minute interval within the interview, e.g., three-minute interval, two-minute unit; three-minute interval, two-minute unit; three-minute interval, two-minute unit; and so on. The 180 units obtained were coded to disguise their origin from the raters, and randomly assigned to eighteen ten-unit groups. For every two-minute unit a tape recording and a typescript of the tape recording were given to the judges for ratings.

Two raters were used, both of whom had participated in previous studies on the Process Scale. Both raters had previous experience in psychotherapy and were considered sensitive to in-therapy events. These two experienced raters rated all 180 units, assigning one rating to each two-minute sample. The rating period extended over eighteen days, since each rater rated ten of the 180 units per day. The raters made the ratings at separate times and were not allowed to discuss their ratings with one another, or with others.

As mentioned previously, the raters used both tape recordings and typescripts to make their ratings of the two-minute units. Typescripts were necessary because of the poor fidelity of some of the tape units. Tape recordings were used in addition to the typescripts to provide such cues as tonal quality, rate of speech, emphasis, and the like.

Of the ten cases selected, five were considered more successful and five were considered less successful on the basis of a multicriteria success score. The criteria included therapist ratings of outcome, patient ratings of outcome, and an adjustment score based on a self-concept Q-sort. The more successful and less successful cases were randomly assigned to rating groups and all cues in the tape segments concerning the number of the interview or the satisfaction of the client with the therapy were eliminated.

The judges were instructed to rate each unit as a separate entity. The judges reported no influence in their ratings due to hearing previous segments from the same case, although it was impossible to assess this objectively within the design employed.

The results of this and previous studies can be summarized as follows:

1. Interjudge agreement was always significantly better than chance, as estimated by parametric and nonparametric statistics. Interjudge reliability appeared to have a minimum correlation of about .60. Under some conditions this could be improved.
2. The Process Scale distinguished between more successful and less successful cases at a high level of statistical significance ($p < .01$).
3. The process ratings indicated that more successful cases began as well as ended at a significantly higher level of process than less successful cases ($p < .01$).
4. There is evidence that there was significantly greater change (movement) in process level during the period of therapy in more successful than in less successful cases ($p < .05$). The absolute difference, however, was only modestly significant.
5. There was a tendency for the process level of the second half of each interview to be rated higher than that of the first half. This tendency towards intra-interview change was definitely significant (sign test) in the more successful cases ($p < .01$).

The third result above merits a brief discussion before continuing further. From these two validation studies one of the clearer findings has been that the more successful case almost invariably starts therapy at a higher stage of process than the less successful case. In the study just reported, using the Mann-Whitney U-test to test the significance of the difference between early more successful and early less successful cases, we found that the differences were significant in the expected direction at about the .02 level. These results are similar to previous studies. Again the more successful clients seemed to enter therapy at a higher stage of process than the less successful ones. This suggests that there may be some characteristics which each client must possess in some minimal degree to profit from psychotherapy, and that clients below this minimum will not progress in psychotherapy. This conjecture is similar to and supports findings by Kirtner and Cartwright (1958*b*). High levels of the Process Scale characterize the *successful* client's behavior throughout therapy; the unsuccessful client does not mount the scale— apparently because he is too low in "process behavior." Thus, initial process levels may be a good predictor of success or failure. The scale appears to define change-producing behavior.

In a further analysis of thirty-eight clinic cases of neurotics (Gendlin, Klein, Tomlinson, 1962), it was found that:

1. There was no relationship between the client's *initial process level* and the degree of his *positive* process movement over therapy.
2. There was a significant correlation between *initial process level* and degree of process movement *regardless of direction* over therapy. Clients starting at a higher process level showed more variability, more change both positive and negative, than clients starting at a lower level.
3. More successful cases showed significantly more absolute process movement *regardless of direction* over therapy than less successful cases.
4. When the cases were divided into those which showed positive process movement, insignificant change, or negative process movement, more successful cases were significantly more likely to be found in the first group.

The conclusion was warranted that not only are more successful and less successful cases significantly different in process level, but that a significant though quite modest process movement occurs in the more successful as compared to the less successful group.

The Improvement of Instruments for Assessing Process

When we began to measure process in the present research on schizophrenics, we still thought that the Process Scale could be used only by raters who had some experience with psychotherapy and were highly empathic, sensitive persons. However, we found that the ratings of such individuals agreed with each other only to a moderate extent. The early Process Scale appeared to be too global, and some of the strand descriptions were imprecise. In the words of one rater: "Many [strand] descriptions seem based on the client's previous position at the previous stage." This is partly true in that the descriptions were defining one stage as only "more" of a particular variable than the last stage. Thus: stage 1: no "X" at all; stage 2: very little "X"; stage 3: still not much "X"; stage 4: beginning of "X"; stage 5: "X" now quite often striking, etc.

We realized that there were two important revisions to be made. One was to anchor each stage of the Process Scale in a more specific description. The other was to measure each of the several variables in the scale separately, so that an individual higher in one strand than in another strand could be reliably rated.

In improving the scaling process, we found that the raters were often the vanguard. When raters disagreed on a rating the solution usually lay in better specification of just what they observed and used as reasons for their ratings. What on the scale bears *one* name is used by the raters for *several* different sorts of events which they notice and agree to place on a certain point of the scale. The scale would then be revised and these more specific behavior descriptions would be incorporated into the official scale. In this way developed the sequence of scale revisions referred to throughout this book.

This method of scale revision has some important implications; often what seems a fuzzy or subjective variable is really only too general. An intuitive person may claim that he simply "picks up" such and such an "impression" as though by magic, yet careful discussion will reveal the observable cues. For example, such and such a tape recorded segment may strike a rater as very clearly indicating that an ongoing experiential process is playing a major role. Why? In answer he may point to the metaphoric form of words, to the sharp intake of breath, to the pauses and the search for words, to the transition from one statement through a silence to another statement which relates to the first, but not in a logical way, etc. As long as the scaled variable is only general, a rater noticing these observable marks will rate the variable high. A rater who does not notice these things (perhaps he has noticed different things) may rate it low. Thus scales become more objective the more specific they become. The specific aspects of a seemingly subjective variable are objective.

We were not always as systematic as the above description implies. Some of our scale revisions moved forward to increasing specificity and objectivity. Other revisions moved back again toward more global ratings. The pressure to obtain findings conflicted with the desire to develop an adequate instrument. Rater reliability (statistically calculated agreement between raters) did not invariably improve by greater specificity in scale definitions. Raters who train together may informally obtain very high reliability with only a globally defined scale. It is obvious, of course, that in such a case, reliability is due not to the scale but to the informal rater consensus arrived at in training. One can replicate a study using the same scale, but one cannot replicate such informal consensual training. Thus, the immediate advantage of global scales plus training is balanced by the disadvantage of nonreplicability. The whole development might be summarized by saying that genuinely behavioral measures of therapeutic process used with full application of quantification methods are possible, though not yet fully achieved.

The same kind of irregular development occurred in our movement from one scale in which seven variables dovetailed toward a number of scales each for a single process variable. A small study by van der Veen (1960) indicated that reliability and validity improved when raters employed each strand separately. He divided Rogers' original Process Scale into seven separate sections and (using the same descriptions throughout) compared separate ratings on each variable with global ratings using all descriptions simultaneously.

On the other hand, later, Tomlinson (1962), using the more specific, newer, simple strand scales of Experiencing, Personal Constructs, Problem Expression, and Manner of Relating (see Appendices C.1, C.2, C.3, C.4), found the correlations between the scales to be as high or higher than reliabilities between raters on the same scale. In terms of research economy this finding dictated that we eliminate three of four scales which seemed to measure the same thing. But, for the long-term aim of defining useful variables a question remains: Could the finding have been a genuine correlation of variables? These apparently quite different scales produced correlated findings! Was Rogers right in his original idea that these variables of process are distinct, but occur together? Or were we encountering a rater set, an inability to discriminate what really determined the ratings quite apart from what a given scale contained?

Another consideration of importance is the fact that some of the individuals who developed and revised these scales (not the raters, of course) were, at the same time, the therapists of the schizophrenic patients later to be rated. Thus they could not help employing their increasing experience with their patients in the development of scale definitions. In this, as in so many other ways, the novelty of the research put a limit on the definitive conclusions which could be reached from this project. It was all the more necessary to develop replicable instruments, since only replications of these studies on a new population of patients would produce conclusive findings.

We cannot say at this time whether the several aspects of the process variable are indices of one process or not. As will be seen later, the findings indicate that the manner of relating is somewhat independent of the other variables, while manner of experiencing, relationship to problem expression, manner of forming personal constructs, all seem to measure the same thing. This suggests the interpretation that the similar scales all scale the same question: Are the client's *verbalizations* grounded in an ongoing experiential process? The Relationship Scale differs in that it concerns the manner in which the client's experiential process grounds his relating of himself to the therapist. While this is also measured from tape-recorded verbalizations, cues for the Relationship Scale are different, while a cue for the Experiencing Scale is likely also to function as a cue for the other scales. However, in the long run, only reliable and replicably defined scales can answer the question. The development has gone far enough to assure us that such scales are possible.

References

ALEXANDER, F., FRENCH, T. M., *et al. Psychoanalytic Therapy.* New York: Ronald Press, 1946.

FENICHEL, O. *The Psychoanalytic Theory of the Neuroses.* New York: W. W. Norton, 1945.

FREUD, S. Recollection, repetition, and working through. (1914) *Collected Papers,* Vol. II. New York: Basic Books, 1959, pp. 375–376.

FREUD, S. *The Problem of Anxiety.* (1926) New York: W. W. Norton, 1936.

GENDLIN, E. T. A process concept of relationship. *Counseling Center Discussion Papers,* III, 2. Mimeographed. Chicago: University of Chicago Library, 1957.

GENDLIN, E. T. Experiencing: A variable in the process of therapeutic change. *Amer. J. Psychother. 15:*233–245, 1961. Also included in *Counseling: Selected Readings.* Columbus, Ohio: Charles E. Merrill & Co., 1962.

GENDLIN, E. T. *Experiencing and the Creation of Meaning.* New York: The Free Press of Glencoe, 1962.

GENDLIN, E. T. A theory of personality change. In P. Worchel and D. Byrne (eds.), *Personality Change.* New York: John Wiley & Sons, 1964, pp. 100–148.

GENDLIN, E. T., JENNEY, R. H., and SHLIEN, J. M. Counselor ratings of process and outcome in client-centered therapy. *J. clin. Psychol. 16:* 210–213, 1960.

GENDLIN, E. T., KLEIN, MARJORIE, and TOMLINSON, T. M. *Process Scale Movement in Neurotic Cases,* Mimeographed research report, University of Wisconsin Psychiatric Institute, October, 1962.

GENDLIN, E. T., and ZIMRING, F. The qualities or dimensions of experiencing and their change. *Counseling Center Discussion Papers,* I, 3. Mimeographed. Chicago: University of Chicago Library, 1955.

HALKIDES, G. An investigation of therapeutic success as a function of four variables. Unpublished Ph.D. dissertation, University of Chicago, 1958.

HART, J. T. Some inter-rater and intra-rater reliability properties of the Process Scale. Unpublished M.A. thesis, University of Wisconsin, 1961.

KIRTNER, W. L., and CARTWRIGHT, D. S. Success and failure in client-centered therapy as a function of client personality variables. *J. consult. Psychol. 22*:259–264, 1958*a*.

KIRTNER, W. L., and CARTWRIGHT, D. S. Success and failure in client-centered therapy as a function of initial in-therapy behavior. *J. consult. Psychol. 22*:329–333, 1958*b*.

ROGERS, C. R. The necessary and sufficient conditions of therapeutic personality change. *J. consult. Psychol. 21*:95–103, 1957.

ROGERS, C. R. A process conception of psychotherapy. *Amer. Psychologist 13*:142–149, 1958.

ROGERS, C. R. A tentative scale for the measurement of process in psychotherapy. In E. A. Rubinstein and M. B. Parloff (eds.), *Research in Psychotherapy*, Vol. I. Washington, D.C.: American Psychological Association, 1959*a*, pp. 96–107.

ROGERS, C. R. A theory of therapy, personality, and interpersonal relationships as developed in the client-centered framework. In S. Koch (ed.), *Psychology: A Study of a Science*. Vol. III, *Formulations of the Person in the Social Context*. New York: McGraw-Hill, 1959*b*, pp. 184–256.

ROGERS, C. R. Significant trends in the client-centered orientation. In D. Brower and L. E. Abt (eds.), *Progress in Clinical Psychology*, Vol. IV. New York: Grune & Stratton, 1960, pp. 85–99.

ROGERS, C. R., and RABLEN, R. A. *A Scale of Process in Psychotherapy*. Mimeographed manual, University of Wisconsin, 1958.

STANDAL, S. W., and VAN DER VEEN, F. Length of therapy in relation to counselor estimates of personal integration and other case variables. *J. consult. Psychol. 21*:1–9, 1957.

TOMLINSON, T. M. A validation study of a scale for the measurement of the process of personality change in psychotherapy. Unpublished M.A. thesis, University of Wisconsin, 1959.

TOMLINSON, T. M. Three approaches to the study of psychotherapy: Process, outcome and change. Unpublished Ph.D. dissertation, University of Wisconsin, 1962.

TOMLINSON, T. M., and HART, J. T., JR. A validation of the Process Scale. *J. consult. Psychol. 26*:74–78, 1962.

VAN DER VEEN, F. A strand analysis of the psychotherapy Process Scale. Unpublished research report, University of Wisconsin Psychiatric Institute, 1960.

WALKER, A., RABLEN, R. A., and ROGERS, C. R. Development of a scale to measure process change in psychotherapy. *J. clin. Psychol. 16*:79–85, 1960.

PART III

The Findings:

Data Analysis and Results

8. Measurement of Conditions and Process Variables

The final ratings of all the interview segments, and the analysis and interpretation of this voluminous data, were the sole responsibility of Donald J. Kiesler, Philippa L. Mathieu, and Marjorie H. Klein. Chapters 8 through 12 are all the product of the work of this team. They wrote these chapters, with Douglas Schoeninger assisting on Chapter 11.

The major hypotheses of this study required measurement of the various therapeutic conditions and patient process variables as they occurred in the therapeutic interaction. These variables have been conceptually described in Chapters 6 and 7. The purpose of the present chapter is to detail our methods for the measurement of process and conditions variables and to present data descriptive of their course and interrelationship in the therapeutic encounter.

Therapist conditions variables were measured from three viewpoints: that of clinically naive judges, applying rating scales to tape-recorded samples of therapy hours; that of the patients whose perception of the level of conditions offered by their therapists was assessed at regular intervals by a questionnaire; and that of the therapists whose perception of the relationship was assessed via the same questionnaire. Each viewpoint yielded an assessment of three different therapist conditions—accurate empathy, unconditional positive regard, and congruence—as well as an estimate of the overall quality of these conditions. The judges' ratings applied to discrete moments in the taped record of the course of therapy. The patients' and therapists' evaluations represented more global perceptions of the overall therapeutic climate. Patient process (experiencing) was assessed only by judges. Their data were the tape-recorded samples of the therapeutic interaction.

This chapter is divided into three sections. The first presents the various methodological problems involved in sampling from tape recordings of the entire course of therapy, and outlines our sampling and rating procedures. The second section contains information regarding the reliability of ratings of conditions and process variables and assesses their stability, trend, and interrelationship over the course of therapy. In the final section we examine the interrelationship of the several conditions variables including the relationships among rated conditions, and among patient and therapist perceptions.

Sampling and Rating Procedure

Two general problem areas confronted us in our attempts to develop and apply subjective rating scales to tape recordings of the therapeutic interaction. It was necessary to develop sound methods for sampling from the miles of tape that composed the basic data (in this study, 1,204 hours of recorded therapeutic interaction with 28 patients), and it was essential to construct rating scales that could be used reliably and would be applicable to many discrete therapy samples. Both sampling and rating procedures had to be practical, replicable, and at the same time compatible with the demands and assumptions of the hypotheses to be tested.

Segment Selection

Consider the problem of sampling or segmenting from the single recorded therapy hour. Logically there are two alternatives—one can take the total therapy hour as the sample, or extract shorter samples from it. While the total sample may be desirable for some research purposes, we decided that it would be inordinately difficult for judges to make reliable and valid ratings of the research variables we were concerned with from so large a slice of the therapeutic interaction. Not only would it require considerable training and experience for the judge to weigh and evaluate variable portions of the interaction in order to arrive at a global rating of conditions or process, but also it would be difficult for the judge to retain his impressions in the face of momentary variations within the therapy hour. Both factors were likely to jeopardize the reliability of the ratings. In addition it was possible that an intensive exposure to the entire therapy hour would introduce bias, insofar as judges might respond to irrelevant content and subjective factors when more material was present. Although the danger of bias is not completely eliminated in brief segments, it may be somewhat reduced. For these reasons we elected to take brief samples of the single therapy hour.

We were then faced with the alternatives of random or systematic sampling, both as a basis for selecting individual hours from the total course of therapy, and for choosing segments from each individual therapy hour. We decided on random sampling, not only because it was more practical than systematic sampling, but also because it was particularly compatible with our general theoretical orientation and assumptions. The conditions and process variables in this study, as theoretically conceived, are content free. They represent attitudinal and experiential components of the therapy relationship that are assumed to be omnipresent in the therapy interaction, being independent of specific topics or problems. Theoretically it is not the occurrence of any specific event at any special moment in therapy that is effective, but rather the general or cumulative operation of the attitudinal relationship (conditions) factors that leads to the therapeutic process and, in turn, to constructive personality change. Thus the sampling approach yielding the most generally representative ratings should produce the most appropriate assessment of the basic variables for this study.

It was decided to take the brief sample of the interaction from the second half of each therapy hour. This procedure increased the likelihood of tapping higher levels of conditions and process, thereby maximizing the range of ratings available for the relatively small patient sample.

Segment Length

A segment for use with a rating scale must be of adequate length to yield reliable ratings and to reflect the ratio of patient response, therapist response, and silence in the total interview. We needed the briefest possible segment which would at the same time fulfill these conditions. Reliability of ratings for therapist conditions, in segments of from 30 seconds to five minutes, had been considered in an unpublished pilot study by Bocchini, Farwell, and Hart (1960). They found that three- to five-minute segments yielded more reliable ratings than shorter excerpts. In a study comparing patient process ratings in segments of two minutes, four minutes, eight minutes, and sixteen minutes, Kiesler, Mathieu, and Klein (1964) found no difference in range or reliability of ratings between the longer segments and the shorter—two and four minutes. Thus both studies revealed that segments of a few minutes in length were appropriate and sufficient for reliability of ratings. The study by Kiesler *et al* also showed that process ratings from the shorter segments yielded the same ranking of patients as ratings from the longer samples.

Apparently it is necessary to use long segments only when the absolute value of process ratings is a concern. Longer segments tend to receive significantly higher process ratings, undoubtedly as a function of additional information. Since this study was primarily concerned with exploring the ranking of patients and therapists on process and outcome dimensions, and did not contain predictions regarding the attainment of absolute levels of process or conditions, we felt free to select the briefest possible segments (two and four minutes) for ratings.

Segmenting Procedure

The majority of the segments taken from therapy and sampling interviews of the fourteen experimental and fourteen control patients were of four minutes' duration. Each four-minute segment was extracted at random from the latter half of the therapy or sampling interview tape according to a standardized procedure.[1] First, each tape was timed and the midpoint determined. Then the last half of the tape was entered at a randomly determined time point, and a segment consisting of the four subsequent minutes was transcribed onto a small reel. There was only one prerequisite—the segment taken had to contain a minimum of two patient statements and two therapist responses. If this criterion was not met by the first entry, the segmenter was instructed to use his best judgment to find a segment meeting this criterion, first in another portion of the latter half of the therapy hour or in the first half of the hour. If it proved impossible to find sufficient verbal material at any place in a given therapy hour, that interview was skipped altogether.

This minimum requirement for the patient-therapist interaction was considered essential for valid ratings. It resolved an issue that was of particular relevance for a sample of schizophrenics, since many therapy hours with schizophrenics contain long periods of patient silence. We were aware, however, that this procedure could introduce bias in favor of the less verbal patient. While the verbal patient would be sampled at random, the "high" points of therapy with the more silent patient would be more likely to be represented. In spite of this possible source of bias, we felt it essential to obtain segments containing sufficient verbal cues for valid and reliable ratings.

Rating Scales for Conditions

Empathic understanding, congruence or genuineness, and unconditional positive regard are the three therapist conditions that Rogers holds to be necessary and sufficient for meaningful patient growth in the therapeutic relationship. Together they constitute the climate established by the therapist, consisting of the cumulative impact of his general attitudes and manner of response on the patient in the interaction. These three conditions constructs were operationalized for the present study into three discrete rating scales: Accurate Empathy (Truax,

1. The sixty-eight two-minute segments (in contrast to 652 four-minute segments) were selected systematically rather than randomly, being taken from either the 20–22 minute or the 30–32 minute points of the therapy interviews.

1961), Congruence (Kiesler, 1963), and Unconditional Positive Regard (Truax, 1962) (see Appendix B, Rating Scales for Therapeutic Conditions, for a copy of each of these scales).

Each of these scales was designed for use with recorded segments of the therapy interaction. They are meant to apply to the therapist's communications and are often anchored in terms of *his* behavior and responses in the interaction. Although the therapist's verbal behavior is obviously a component of the interaction, the constructs tapped by the rating scales are intended to represent the *therapist's* attitudes and responses as a party to the interaction rather than to describe the patient-therapist interaction itself. Ideally, these attitudes and responses can best be judged from recordings containing only the verbalizations of the therapist. This editing out of patient speech would have been prohibitively expensive for our project. Instead, the judges were generally instructed to draw the cue for their inferences from the therapist's behavior, and to ignore the patient's responses as much as possible. It should be made clear, however, that this technique does not permit rigorous control over the confounding effect of the patient's verbalizations or the general interaction tone but represents, in effect, our attempt to explore complex theoretical variables in what was essentially a naturalistic setting.

Accurate empathy (AE).—The range of this 9-point scale extends from a low point where the therapist manifests a virtual lack of empathic understanding of the patient (stage 1) to a high point where he shows an unfalteringly accurate response to the patient's full range of expressed and implicit affect (stage 9). A high level of accurate empathy requires in effect that the therapist understand the patient's phenomenal world, integrate this material fully into his own frame of reference, and communicate this integration to the patient. This is not to say that the therapist must respond with the same intensity or range as the patient does, but rather that he incorporates the patient's feelings into his own awareness. At a high level of accurate empathy the message "I am with you" is unmistakably clear—the therapist's remarks fit compatibly with the patient's mood and content. At a low level of accurate empathy the therapist may be off on a tangent of his own, may have misinterpreted what the patient is feeling, or may be so preoccupied with his own intellectual interpretations that he is scarcely aware of the patient.

Congruence (CONG).—This 5-point scale of therapist congruence or genuineness ranges from a point where there is an obvious discrepancy between the therapist's feelings about the patient and his concurrent communication to the patient (stage 1) to a high point where the therapist communicates both his positive and negative feelings about the patient openly and freely, without traces of defensiveness or retreat into professionalism (stage 5).

For the purpose of this research, ratings of congruence were limited to instances where the patient questioned, explicitly or implicitly, the therapist's feelings or opinions about him. In a direct question, the patient might ask, "How do you really feel about me? Do you understand what I am saying? Do you think I will ever get out of this hospital?" An indirect question might include moments such as, "It would be nice to know someone actually cared about me. Sometimes I wonder if I will ever get out of this hospital." Or the patient might indirectly question the therapist by implying that the therapist's past behavior had been unsatisfactory to him: "I wish you would talk more. I wish I could find a way to make myself understood." The therapist's response was rated according to the degree to which his feelings about the patient were freely and openly expressed.

Unconditional positive regard (UPR).—For this third condition a 5-point scale was used, defining five levels of unconditional positive regard, beginning with an almost complete lack of regard or acceptance (stage 1) and progressing to a high level where the therapist unerringly communicates to the patient a deep and genuine caring for him as a person with human potentialities—a caring uncontaminated by evaluations of the patient's thoughts or behaviors (stage 5). Thus at a high level the therapist places no conditions on his acceptance and warmth, being involved in a nonpossessive caring for the patient as a separate person with permission to have his own feelings and experiences. In contrast, at a low level the therapist evaluates the patient, expresses dislike or disapproval, or expresses positive regard only in a selective manner. Thus positive feelings toward the patient may be rated low on this scale if this acceptance is given conditionally.

Rating Scales for Process

Experiencing (EXP).—The evaluation of patient process movement in this study was cast in terms of the experiencing dimension proposed by Gendlin (1962). It is movement on this dimension of self-awareness that characterizes an important aspect of the patient's development during therapy. The therapeutic goal is the emergence of the patient as a spontaneous person—his development as a fully functioning person.

While the experiencing dimension was conceptualized in terms of a continuous progression toward an optimal state of self-awareness, neither Gendlin nor Rogers expected progress to be steady in the actual therapy course. A patient's experiencing may vary considerably at any given moment of therapy—he may reach peaks wherein he experiences himself in a new way, he may drop back to more familiar plateaus of self-involvement, he may suddenly retreat to very low levels of experiencing. Rogers and Gendlin agreed that despite these fluctuations experiencing was always measurable in the therapeutic interaction, that the construct was always relevant for understanding the therapeutic process, and that the general course of successful therapy could be characterized by some amount of positive movement along this important dimension of the therapy process.

The concept of experiencing was first operationalized in the form of a 7-point rating scale by Gendlin and Tomlinson. It was revised by Mathieu and Klein (1963) for this study (see Appendix C.1 for a copy of this scale). At the lowest stage of experiencing the patient is not able to "own" his affective involvement in what he says, and may relate a straightforward narrative in which there is no personal reference or little or no expression of feeling. The middle stages of the scale are marked by the patient's progressive ownership of his feelings and involvement in events to the point where he can freely express his feelings and explore them in search of their personal meaning. The upper stages of the Experiencing Scale represent the patient's deepening awareness of his feelings, his successful understanding of them, and their integration into his experiential framework. Thus the higher stages are independent of any specific narrative structure. The focus is on the patient's ability to experience freely, to have insight into the significance of his experience and to move freely and appropriately among aspects of his experiential framework.

Rater Selection

The raters used in this study were undergraduates drawn from the student body of the University of Wisconsin. The selecting of clinically naive, as against clinically expert, raters was a consequence of the data we were seeking. The theory basic to this research was that the therapeutic conditions are valid and effective only if they are communicated to the patient. The clinically naive rater would be freer to adopt the set necessary for rating conditions from the recipient's viewpoint than would the expert clinician who would be especially attuned to the intent and motivation of the therapist. The use of naive assessors had been studied by Arnhoff (1954) and Cronbach (1960) and their findings suggested that naive assessors are often more reliable in their judgments than expert clinicians, and are more likely to confine their judgments to the dimension at issue, rather than basing them on extraneous or tangential clinical inferences. As Cronbach concluded: "There is no evidence that psychological training gives the assessor an advantage [in predictions concerning psychopathology]. . . . This conclusion is supported by the frequent finding that peer ratings have validities as good as those of ratings by observers" (1960, p. 589). Although these findings did not refer directly to the rating of scale dimensions at issue here, they provided an additional justification for the use of naive judges.

The majority of raters were drawn from liberal arts departments, especially the departments of English, Art, History, and Speech. According to several pilot studies, students with these interests could be quickly trained to grasp the conceptual dimension basic to the rating scale and to apply this dimension reliably to the tape-recorded therapy interaction. Psychology students were not used as raters on the assumption that their set for the rating task would be different from that of the non-psychology students.

Rater Training

Once the raters were selected there were no special criteria determining their assignment to a given scale dimension. Each rater was assigned for training in the use of one, and only one, scale. Raters were not allowed to become acquainted with other scale dimensions, or with the nature and composition of the patient population. Techniques for training raters varied for different scales, primarily because of our desire to incorporate improvements suggested from training experience with one scale into subsequent procedures. The general goal was, of course, to develop a training technique which would insure adequate interrater reliability with a minimum use of staff time. It was believed that the rating scales should be so clearly phrased as to be self-explanatory, that staff members should not be called upon to impose additional conceptual structure on raters. Such scales, we felt, would be able to stand on their own, could be easily used by other researchers. Our training techniques fell roughly into two general categories, differing primarily in the degree to which staff members consciously undertook to train the raters to their viewpoint. In retrospect, however, it was the more structured approach to rater training that proved to produce the most reliable and stable ratings.

Informally supervised practice.—The UPR and AE scale raters were trained in informally supervised practice sessions. The purpose of this procedure was to permit the raters to develop a mutual scale conception and task set with a minimum of staff intervention. All training was done by a single staff member in individual and group sessions. Each rater was first given a copy of the relevant scale to study and was assigned to rate practice materials. Blocks of practice ratings (ten per block) for all trainees were then intercorrelated. When the interrater (Pearsonian) correlations reached .60 the raters were assigned to project data. In instances where the reliability did not rise quickly to this correlation value the raters were assembled and told that their ratings were not in agreement. Disputed tapes were played and the raters were allowed to discuss and resolve their discrepancies without interference from the staff member. At no time did the staff member offer opinions regarding the rating of a specific segment. Thus the raters were permitted to develop a mutual set and manner of applying the scale to the therapy data. Periodically the staff members assessed their general conceptualization of the scale by requiring them to define scale stages, as well as to define issues not relevant to each scale stage. The major criterion for training, however, was the interrater reliability.

Group discussion and feedback.—The purpose of this training procedure—used for the EXP and CONG scales—was to insure that the rater's scale conception and task-set was similar to that of the research staff. All raters were given copies of the relevant scale, and in the first group session segments illustrating the various scale stages were presented. In addition, the definitions of each scale stage and the overall scale dimension were discussed by the staff members. Trainees then rated training segments in blocks of ten. A group meeting devoted to a discussion of all interrater and rater-staff discrepancies was held after each block of training segments was rated. In each case the disputed segment was listened to, and the staff discussed the basis for the rating, the correct rating, and the source of the discrepancy. The staff members' viewpoint set the standard in all cases so that the discussion was directed to clarification of this viewpoint. Reliabilities were assessed concurrently, as an additional index of training progress. After approximately six blocks of training materials had been rated and discussed in this fashion, raters were given a final block of segments. At the same time, the raters were requested to characterize the various scale stages from memory. The final meeting before assignment to the project material was devoted to a discussion of the rater's versions of the scale and a reconciliation of any remaining discrepancies with the staff conception. If the reliabilities proved adequate, raters were assigned to their major rating task, the rating of the project data?[2] When the

2. In some cases more raters were trained than were necessary for the major project ratings. In such instances we chose those who were the most highly reliable and who also agreed closely with the staff.

reliabilities were substandard, additional training materials and discussion sessions were held until a satisfactory level of interrater and rater-staff reliability was achieved.

The rationale and purpose of these two training procedures were divergent, though the goal in each case was the attainment of reliable ratings from clinically naive judges.

While all four rater groups (EXP, CONG, AE, and UPR) reached an adequate level of interrater reliability before turning to the project data, the greater long-term reliability of the EXP and CONG raters (see Table 8.1) suggests that the more structured feedback training technique may be the most desirable for this type of rating task.

Rating Procedure

Four groups of judges, trained by the methods outlined above, made ratings of four variables of the therapeutic interaction (EXP, CONG, AE, UPR) from tape-recorded segments of therapy and sampling interviews. The judges for a given scale worked independently; discussion of ratings and scale conceptions was prohibited after the completion of the training period. All judges were informed that they must hold the therapy materials in strict confidence, and were required to sign an agreement that they would refrain from any discussion of the taped materials.

Tape-recorded segments were presented to all judges in a standard random order. That is, experimental and control, therapy and sampling, early and late therapeutic interviews were completely randomized. Further the raters had no information concerning the nature of the case rated, the type of interview, the location of a given interview in the overall course of therapy, or the outcome of the case. Raters were given no background material on patients or therapists—the only information available was that contained in the taped segments drawn from the therapy and sampling interviews.

There was a standard procedure to follow for difficult ratings. When in doubt about a rating on the first listening, raters were instructed to replay the segment and make their best estimate of the scale stage achieved. In the case of partially inaudible segments raters were requested to replay the material and attempt a rating from all audible portions of the interaction.

Ratings of Conditions: Raw Data and Average Score

The raw data for subsequent analyses of conditions and process ratings consisted of the ratings made independently by judges for three therapist conditions scales (AE, UPR, and CONG) and one patient process scale (EXP). This section will describe the specific data available from therapy and sampling interviews and the kinds of summary scores that were derived from them.

Therapy interviews.—Material used for ratings of therapeutic conditions consisted of segments selected from interviews 2–15 for each of the fourteen experimental (therapy) patients. After the fifteenth interview, every fifth interview was sampled across the course of each therapy case. Thus in eight cases, lasting approximately thirty to thirty-five interviews, the first half of therapy was (except for the initial interview) completely sampled for the purposes of conditions ratings.

Three groups of judges (three in each group) made independent ratings for each of the three conditions scales on a total of 337 therapy segments. The score for *each segment* consisted of the average of the ratings by the three judges for that segment. Thus we had a score on each scale, for each of the 337 interviews sampled. In addition, for each scale, two average scores were computed for *each case*. The first was the mean of the ratings for interviews 2–15 ($\bar{X}_{15}$).[3] The second was the overall mean of all interviews (two through fifteen and every fifth interview thereafter) ($\bar{X}_{TOT}$). The average of interviews 2–15 ($\bar{X}_{15}$) was considered to provide a meaningful estimate of the level of the therapeutic conditions established in the initial portion of therapy, where the influence of the therapeutic conditions is considered, on theoretical grounds, to be of particular importance. The overall average $\bar{X}_{TOT}$ was considered as a global estimate of the general therapeutic conditions level for each therapy case, although it was disproportionately affected by the level of the early interviews.

In the light of the unreliability of the UPR ratings (see p. 149) it was considered essential to devise a further procedure to obtain reliable estimates of this therapeutic condition. We examined the ratings of each judge for each segment, and selected, for UPR, only those segments in which there was either complete interjudge agreement or in which a judge deviated only one stage from the ratings of the remaining two judges. A total of 136 segments met this criterion. Table 8.1 contains the Ebel (Guilford, 1954) intraclass reliability estimates for these segments, selected on the basis of their reliability (see UPR B, p. 149). From these scores an average UPR B score for each case was computed ($\bar{X}_{TOT}$). This is the UPR score used in all subsequent analyses in this

---

3. While only fourteen scored interviews are represented in this mean, we have chosen to retain the designation "15" because of the importance of recognizing that there actually were fifteen interviews during this period, although only fourteen were rated.

book (with the exception of Tables 8.4, 8.7, 8.10, 8.11, 8.12 which are based on the full set of UPR ratings—UPR A).

As well as considering each scale separately, we also recorded a global estimate of the level of all three therapist conditions together. This was done simply by averaging the three conditions means for each case (after the appropriate z transformations to equate the different scales). The combined $\bar{X}_{15}$ score was the average of the z scores for AE $\bar{X}_{15}$ and CONG $\bar{X}_{15}$ (as reliable UPR $\bar{X}_{15}$ ratings were not available). The combined $\bar{X}_{TOT}$ score consisted of the average of the z scores for AE $\bar{X}_{TOT}$, CONG $\bar{X}_{TOT}$, and UPR B $\bar{X}_{TOT}$ for each therapy case.

The basic rated conditions data for the analyses to follow consist, then, of individual scale scores for each therapy interview segment (with three judges averaged); the average for each scale across interviews 2–15 for each case ($\bar{X}_{15}$); the corresponding overall interview average for each case ($\bar{X}_{TOT}$); the combined conditions scores for interviews 2–15 (COMB$_{15}$); and the combined conditions scores for the total interviews (COMB$_{TOT}$).

Sampling interviews.—A psychiatrist who had no other relationship to the therapy project held brief interviews at regular intervals with each of the fourteen experimental and fourteen control patients. Conditions ratings were obtained for segments taken from every sampling interview. In order to obtain an estimate of the general level of conditions offered by the sampling interviewer an $\bar{X}_{TOT}$ for each patient was obtained for each scale. It consisted of the mean of the scores for each sampling interview segment (three judges averaged) across each case.

Ratings of Process: Raw Data and Average Score

Therapy interviews.—The tape-recorded material used for EXP ratings consisted of segments selected from each of interviews 2–52, every fifth interview after this point, and the last five interviews for each case. As the majority of the cases lasted fifty interviews or less, most cases were completely sampled for purposes of process ratings.

Four judges made two EXP ratings for each segment: a modal rating describing the overall level of EXP in a particular segment, and a peak rating describing the highest level of EXP attained at any point, however briefly, in the segment. These scores will be analyzed separately in the remaining research chapters. For both modal and peak ratings two mean EXP scores (with four judges averaged), one for interviews 2–15 ($\bar{X}_{15}$), and one for the total therapy interviews ($\bar{X}_{TOT}$), were computed for each case.

In addition, estimates of EXP trends and change in the course of therapy were obtained by various procedures as follows:

Early-late change.—The most stringent and literal estimate of EXP change over the course of therapy was based on the difference between the average of EXP ratings for the first five consecutive therapy interviews sampled (interviews 2, 3, 4, 5, 6) and the average of EXP ratings for the last five consecutive therapy interviews prior to termination. Change scores were computed by subtracting the early from the late means so that a positive value stands for an increase in EXP.

Interviews 2–30.—In order to obtain a fairly detailed picture of the trend of EXP in therapy, average scores were drawn from interviews 2–30 in each therapy case. Six averages were made for ratings of interviews 2–30 representing the averages for each block of five (four in the first block) consecutive interviews ($\bar{X}_{2-5}$, $\bar{X}_{6-10}$, $\bar{X}_{11-15}$, $\bar{X}_{16-20}$, $\bar{X}_{21-25}$, $\bar{X}_{26-30}$). As approximately half of the cases in the present study ran about thirty interviews and half for longer periods, this procedure did not give full coverage to all cases and did not sample equally for all phases of therapy in long and short term cases. It did, however, permit a fairly detailed examination of EXP trends in an initial portion of therapy.

Total therapy course.—In order to obtain an estimate of the global or gross trend of EXP in the total therapy course that would be comparable for long and short term cases, average scores for EXP over consecutive thirds of therapy were obtained. First, each case was divided into thirds according to the number of therapy interviews held. The average value for each third was then obtained by averaging all available EXP ratings for segments within the appropriate period. If, for example, a case ran for sixty interviews, $\bar{X}_{\frac{1}{3}}$ would be based on the ratings for consecutive interview segments 2–20; $\bar{X}_{\frac{2}{3}}$ on the average for interviews 21–30, 35, and 40; $\bar{X}_{\frac{3}{3}}$ on every fifth interview in the series 45 through 55 and the last five interviews 55–60. Thus the thirds average scores were based on all of the available segments for each case divided into early, middle, and late thirds according to the actual number of therapy interviews held. These scores provided a very global estimate of EXP trend in therapy when case length was adjusted so that long and short term cases were equated.

Sampling interviews.—Sampling interview segments ($N = 128$) were rated according to the same procedure used for therapy interviews. A modal and peak score were available for each sampling interview, consisting of the average of the ratings of the four EXP judges. For each of the fourteen therapy and fourteen control patients a mean of the total sampling interviews ($\bar{X}_{TOT}$) was calculated, representing the global level of EXP attained by a given patient in the sampling interview interaction.

Two additional procedures were employed to provide data descriptive of the trend of EXP over the sampling interview series, as follows:

First three sampling interviews.—EXP ratings of segments taken from the first three sampling interviews for each patient provided one fairly detailed picture of the trend of sampling interview process in roughly a nine- to twelve-month period for each case. This procedure did not equate long-term and short-term cases nor make adjustments for differences in the timing of the interview relative to the therapy course, the length of intervals between interviews, or the total number of interviews held.

Thirds of the sampling interview series.—In order to derive a general estimate of EXP trends over the total sampling interview series, each case was divided into thirds on the basis of the amount of time covered by the course of therapy. EXP ratings from any sampling interviews falling within each third were then averaged. This procedure, based on elapsed time rather than on the number of interviews held, was necessary in order to adjust meaningfully for irregularities in the timing of sampling interviews in some cases, and for missed sampling interview contacts. This procedure yielded a global picture of the trend of process in all interviews for each case, in contrast to the more detailed information available from the first three sampling interviews.

Summary of Conditions and Process Ratings

A major portion of the data for this study consisted of ratings made for three scales of therapist conditions (Congruence, Accurate Empathy, and Unconditional Positive Regard) and one scale of patient process (Experiencing). These ratings were made for brief tape-recorded segments (generally four minutes) taken at random from the latter portion of therapy hours. Interviews 2–15 for each case and every fifth interview thereafter were sampled for conditions ratings; interviews 2–52, every fifth interview, and the last five interviews were sampled for process ratings.

Each therapy segment was rated for each scale by a different group of judges (three for conditions ratings, four for process ratings) who worked independently and without any information regarding the nature of the interview, case diagnosis, or outcome. Rating scale scores for each interview segment always consisted of the average of the judges' ratings. These scores were used in turn as the basis for various summary scores, including the average for interviews 2–15, the average for all interviews (for all conditions scales separately as well as in combination), the average for thirds of the therapy and sampling interview course, the average for six interview blocks of interviews 2–30, and the scores for the first three sampling interviews (for EXP scale ratings).

Reliability, Stability, and Interrelationship of Conditions and Process Scale Ratings

Reliability of Conditions and Process Ratings

The reliabilities of judges' ratings for each of the four rating scales are presented in Table 8.1. Intraclass reliabilities were computed according to Ebel's (Guilford, 1954) formula, yielding an estimate of the reliability of the means of the judges' ratings (r_{kk}), and an estimate of the average intercorrelation of all judge combinations (r_{11}). If we consider

Table 8.1—Ebel intraclass reliabilities for the conditions scales (AE, UPR, CONG) and the patient process scale (EXP) for the therapy and sampling interviews

Scale	No. of judges	No. of seg- ments rated	r_{kk}	r_{11}
		THERAPY INTERVIEWS		
Experimentals				
AE	3	323	.63	.36
UPR A	3	335	.21	.08
UPR B	3	136	.99	.96
CONG	3	336	.77	.53
Modal EXP	4	592	.76	.45
Peak EXP	4	594	.79	.48
		SAMPLING INTERVIEWS		
Experimentals				
AE	3	67	.60	.33
UPR A	3	68	.35	.15
UPR B	3	36	.74	.49
CONG	3	65	.70	.43
Modal EXP	4	64	.74	.41
Peak EXP	4	66	.81	.51
Controls				
AE	3	59	.55	.29
UPR A	3	54	.40	.18
UPR B	3	15	.75	.50
CONG	3	52	.67	.41
Modal EXP	4	53	.84	.56
Peak EXP	4	55	.82	.54

the results presented in Table 8.1 it is apparent that good intraclass reliabilities were obtained for the EXP and CONG scales. The reliability of the AE ratings was somewhat less but still adequate. The UPR Scale ratings, however, were highly unreliable (See UPR A). Since the experiencing and congruence raters received directive training, it would seem that the more structured training techniques were more effective for these rating tasks.

In order to obtain an estimate of the stability of ratings for the various scales, judges were asked to rerate the first block of study segments (consisting of 79 to 100 segments) that they had rated. Six of the thirteen judges for the four scales were available for this task. Their rate-rerate correlations are presented in Table 8.2. The coefficients

Table 8.2—Rate-rerate Pearson correlations for six judges for the AE, UPR, CONG, and EXP scales

Scale	Judges	No. of segments rerated	r ($p \leq .01$)
AE	First	79	.75
AE	Second	79	.51
UPR B	Third	100	.41
CONG	Fourth	79	.65
EXP	Fifth	88	.52
EXP	Sixth	97	.67

ranged from .41 for the less reliable UPR ratings to .75 for AE ratings. Most fell within the .50–.69 range. These values were equivalent to the estimated interrater reliability coefficients (see r_u, Table 8.1) suggesting that the order of intrarater reliability obtained for this lengthy rating task was comparable to the level of reliability across judges.

Range and Variability of Conditions and Process Ratings

The scales tapping variables of patient and therapist behavior referred to the full range of events theoretically postulated for the therapy process. One would not expect to find all scale points represented in any study employing a small number of subjects from one diagnostic category. Thus it is of interest to present data showing the range and distribution of ratings for each of the four scales for the present sample of therapy and control patients. Figures 8.1 through 8.10 present the frequency distributions of scale stages used in ratings of the four scales in both the therapy interviews (Figures 8.1 through 8.5) and the sampling interviews (Figures 8.6 through 8.10).

The majority of EXP ratings (Figures 8.1, 8.2, 8.6, 8.7) fell at stages 1 and 2, yielding a highly skewed distribution. A decreasingly small proportion of segments received ratings of 3 or above. Thus this schizophrenic patient population, chosen randomly for participation in

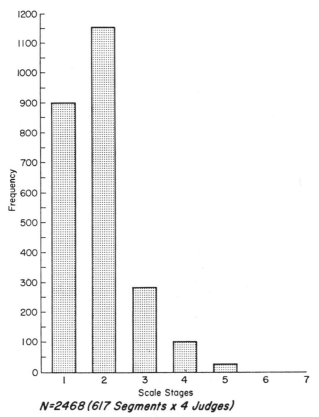

N=2468 (617 Segments x 4 Judges)

Figure 8.1—Frequency distribution of the modal EXP ratings at each scale stage, for four judges, for the total rated therapy interview segments.

therapy and control groups, showed a low level and range of experiencing in the therapy and sampling interviews. However, it is crucial to point out that movement, whatever its magnitude and location on this continuum, is theoretically meaningful. In terms of the rated scale stages in this study, movement from stages 1 to 3 indicated that the patient who entered therapy with an extreme level of denial of personal involvement had developed the capacity to express and own his feelings, but was not yet engaged in a steady process of self-exploration.

If we turn to the distribution of CONG ratings (Figures 8.3 and 8.8) we see that this variable of therapist behavior was distributed bimodally with the majority of ratings falling at stage 5. In effect the therapists and the sampling interviewer in this sample were judged either highly congruent or neutral, with no therapist being judged as phony or defensive.

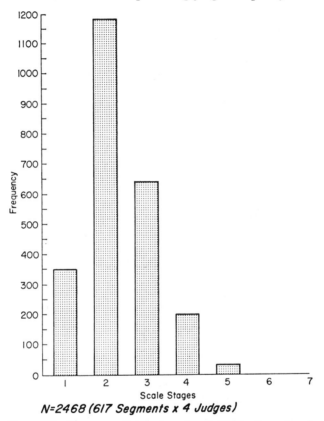

N=2468 (617 Segments x 4 Judges)

Figure 8.2—Frequency distribution of peak EXP ratings at each scale stage, for four judges, for the total rated therapy interview segments.

This striking bimodality is perhaps most parsimoniously viewed as a possible artifact of the rating instructions. Judges were generally instructed to make congruence ratings only in instances where the patient was questioning, directly or indirectly, the therapist's feelings about him. According to the specific scale construction, however, it is likely that many occasions where this issue did not arise may have been rated at stage 3, yielding, in effect, a differentiation between instances where the patient questioned the therapist and received a genuine response (stage 5) and occasions when he either questioned and received a neutral response or did not question the therapist's feelings at all (stage 3). To the extent that this is true, the present CONG Scale ratings may be useful as an index of one special class of patient-therapist interactions where congruence can be an important issue; but since it ignores other

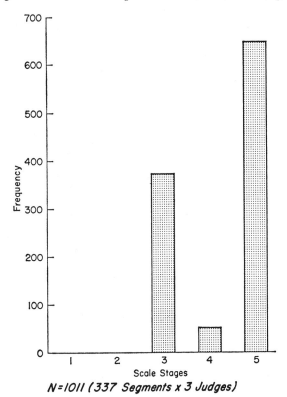

N=1011 (337 Segments x 3 Judges)

Figure 8.3—Frequency distribution of the CONG ratings at each scale stage, for three judges, for the total rated therapy interview segments.

classes of relevant interactions it likely represents only a rough estimate of the genuineness of the therapist's response.

For UPR ratings (Figures 8.4 and 8.9) the bulk of the therapy segments were rated at the upper range of the scale with a more normal distribution for sampling interviews. The stage most often rated in either case was stage 3, representing a generally positive but nonintense orientation of the therapist to the patient. Few ratings fell at the lower scale points. Thus the majority of segments were judged as indicative of a moderate to high level of the therapist's regard for the patient. The AE Scale ratings (Figures 8.5 and 8.10) were more normally distributed for both therapy and sampling interviews. They covered nearly the full range of the scale, with a midpoint at the natural midpoint of the scale, stage 5 for therapy interviews and stage 4 for sampling interviews. Thus the majority of therapy segments were judged to

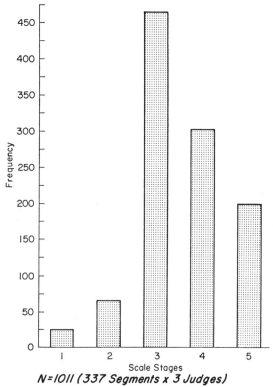

N=1011 (337 Segments x 3 Judges)

Figure 8.4—Frequency distribution of the UPR–B ratings at each scale stage, for three judges, for the total rated therapy interview segments.

represent the therapist's fairly accurate awareness of the patient's feelings with moderate probes and no misunderstanding. Sampling interview segments were judged slightly lower in this variable of therapist behavior.

Thus the behavior of the therapist throughout the therapy hours and of the interviewer in the sampling interviews was generally close to the theoretical averages of the Accurate Empathy and Unconditional Positive Regard scales. High and low points for these factors covered almost the full theoretical range, but were relatively infrequent moments in the cases sampled. The bimodality of the Congruence Scale reflected, most probably, the extreme difficulty of operationalizing this highly subjective construct. The narrow range of experiencing observed was

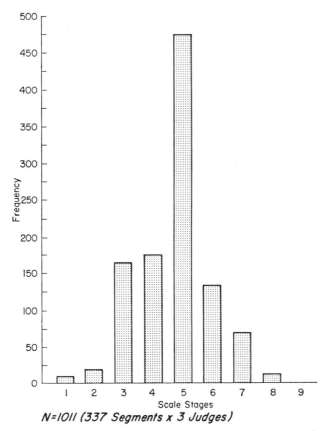

Figure 8.5—Frequency distribution of the AE ratings at each scale stage, for three judges, for the total rated therapy interview segments.

not unexpected, considering the low motivation of the hospitalized schizophrenic patient population.

Stability and Trend of Conditions

A basic question arising in regard to the nature of the therapist conditions was that of their stability over the course of therapy, as well as their general trend over the therapeutic course. Rogers conceived of the therapeutic conditions as stable attitudes of the therapist in the relationship. To the extent that the therapist's behavior is governed by his therapeutic goals and attitudes, the level of conditions rated in discrete interview segments should remain relatively constant over the course of therapy despite fluctuations in the behavioral and substantive aspects of the interaction.

One way to approach this issue was to question the relative stability of

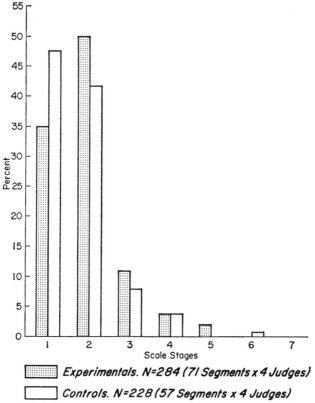

Figure 8.6—Relative frequency distribution of the modal EXP ratings at each scale stage, for four judges, for the total rated sampling interview segments.

conditions within our patient sample—to ask whether the therapy cases studied retained a constant ordering over successive therapy interviews. For this purpose conditions ratings of the fourteen patients for interviews 2–15 were intercorrelated. Each scale was considered separately, so that, for example, the CONG scores for each case for the second interview were correlated with the CONG scores for each successive interview, every interview being correlated with every other interview as well as with the average of interviews 2–15 ($\bar{X}_{15}$). Tables 8.3, 8.4 and 8.5 contain the intercorrelation (Pearson) matrices for each scale. Because of the low reliability of the UPR A ratings, only the results for AE and CONG are discussed.

Consider first the correlations for AE in successive interviews along the diagonal of Table 8.3. Apparently there was little relative consist-

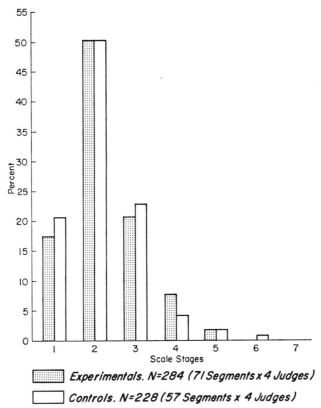

Figure 8.7—Relative frequency distribution of the peak EXP ratings at each scale stage, for four judges, for the total rated sampling interview segments.

ency in the level of accurate empathy offered by the therapist over the first few interviews. It was not until interviews seven and eight (then not consistently until the eleventh interview) that the level of AE in one hour could be predicted from that of the preceding hour. Initially, indeed, there was a negative trend for this condition. This suggested that the relative level of accurate empathy for the various cases reversed itself, before stabilizing gradually at about the seventh therapy inter-view. Comparing the relationship of each single hour with the average for interviews 2–15 ($\bar{X}_{15}$), however, we see that it was interviews four, five, and nine that were particularly atypical. Other interviews related positively to $\bar{X}_{15}$, to the point that the overall ordering of cases on the AE continuum could be predicted with a fair degree of accuracy from the majority of the initial interviews. The interrelationship among the

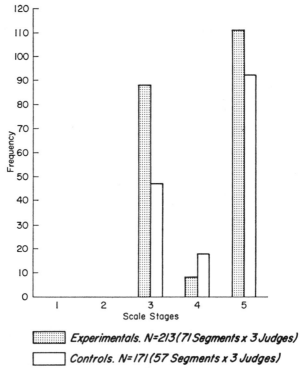

Experimentals. N=213 (71 Segments x 3 Judges)

Controls. N=171 (57 Segments x 3 Judges)

Figure 8.8—Relative frequency distribution of the CONG ratings at each scale stage, for the total rated sampling inter-view segments.

last five interviews was particularly high, suggesting that accurate em-pathy reached relative stability as the relationship progressed.

If we turn to Table 8.5 we see that CONG ratings were considerably less stable over interviews 2–15. With the possible exceptions of inter-views thirteen, fourteen, and fifteen the relationship between successive interviews was uniformly positive but low. Only six interviews, distrib-uted sporadically throughout the fifteen-interview period, significantly related to the overall level of CONG ($\bar{X}_{15}$). Apparently, therapist congruence was not stable from one interview to the next, although the moderately positive correlations suggested that the fluctuations in the relative ordering of cases were not drastic. It was only with the last three interviews (of the first fifteen) that the trend of this dimension of therapist behavior seemed to become at all stable. As to individual cases the stability of the conditions within each case resembled that

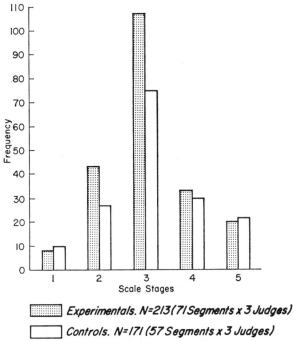

Experimentals. N=213 (71 Segments x 3 Judges)

Controls. N=171 (57 Segments x 3 Judges)

Figure 8.9—Relative frequency distribution of the UPR–A ratings at each scale stage, for the total rated sampling interview segments.

across cases. It was not until after the fifteenth interview that there was any recognizable consistency.

Interrelationship Among Rated Conditions

The theory basic to this research was that three therapist conditions are necessary and, in concert, sufficient for patient process movement and constructive personality change to occur. Yet the general level of interrelationship among these conditions was unspecified. While it was postulated that they are present in some measurable amount in all therapeutic relationships, there is no theoretical necessity that they covary in any systematic fashion in all therapy relationships. It is only in successful therapy, as indexed by the patient's process movement and personality change, that all three conditions are hypothesized to be uniformly high. In unsuccessful therapy the conditions can be either of variable level, or uniformly low. Nevertheless, it seems likely that these conditions, as conceptualized, will covary moderately in most therapy cases since they are mutually reinforcing to some degree. The therapist

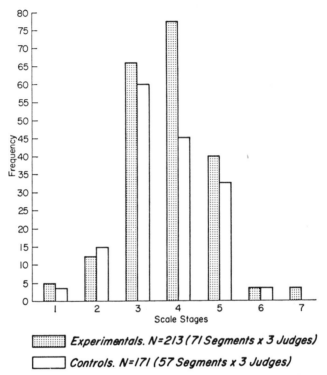

Experimentals. N=213 (71 Segments x 3 Judges)

Controls. N=171 (57 Segments x 3 Judges)

Figure 8.10—Relative frequency distribution for the AE ratings at each scale stage, for the total rated sampling interview segments of the study.

who is not congruent or genuine, for example, cannot logically achieve a high level of accurate empathy or positive regard, since his expression of these attitudes to the patient would probably not be convincing. Thus, in considering the interrelationships among therapist conditions we would predict moderately positive intercorrelations, rather than negative or zero values.

Two approaches were used to examine the extent of the interrelationship among the three rated conditions. First, average conditions scores for the three scales were intercorrelated, yielding an estimate of the

Table 8.3—Interview-by-interview rank-order intercorrelation matrix (14 × 14) for the means of three judges' ratings of therapy interviews 2–15 for the Accurate Empathy (AE) Scale

	3	4	5	6	7	8	9	10	11	12	13	14	15	$\bar{X}_{15}$
2	.42	.00	.60*	-.02	.42	.54*	.14	.31	.13	.03	.02	.30	.40	.48
3		-.23	.63†	.52*	.67†	.30	.11	.29	.29	.60*	.55*	.80†	.60*	.78†
4			-.15	.47	-.08	.12	-.13	.81†	.56*	.25	-.24	.27	-.07	.33
5				.22	.42	.18	-.02	.05	-.10	.03	-.05	.40	.66†	.42
6					.43	.02	.15	.58*	.60*	.46	.33	.66†	.16	.64†
7						.54*	.61*	.11	.52*	.26	.53*	.44	.32	.70†
8							.30	.35	.56*	.40	.28	.40	.52*	.63†
9								-.04	.44	-.10	.45	.18	-.13	.32
10									.71†	.51*	.12	.64†	.18	.65†
11										.56*	.66†	.59*	.29	.78†
12											.59*	.68†	.48	.69†
13												.51*	.36	.60*
14													.71†	.88†
15														.64†

* $p \leq .05$
† $p \leq .01$

Table 8.4—Interview-by-interview rank-order intercorrelation matrix (14 × 14) for the means of three judges' ratings of therapy interviews 2–15 for the Unconditional Positive Regard (UPR) Scale

	3	4	5	6	7	8	9	10	11	12	13	14	15	$\bar{X}_{16}$
2	-.20	.23	.23	.07	-.26	.11	.17	-.36	.07	.18	.33	-.18	.00	.17
3		-.09	.63†	.13	.49	.14	-.35	.61*	.22	.08	.30	-.31	.48	.42
4			.09	-.06	.56*	.55*	.76†	.11	.30	.54*	.47	.41	-.14	.67†
5				.52*	.26	.40	.07	.55*	.22	.56*	.51*	-.07	.60*	.73†
6					.12	.44	.42	.10	-.06	.34	.26	.17	.22	.48
7						.28	.15	.52*	.11	.21	.15	-.04	.15	.55*
8							.51*	.17	.20	.42	.41	.04	.40	.64†
9								-.20	.07	.37	.18	.64†	-.26	.56*
10									.46	.58*	.51*	.12	.44	.63†
11										.54*	.20	.35	-.37	.55*
12											.79†	.42	.19	.82†
13												.00	.51*	.68†
14													-.51*	.37
15														.24

* $p \leq .05$
† $p \leq .01$

Table 8.5—Interview-by-interview rank-order intercorrelation matrix (14 × 14) for the means of three judges' ratings of therapy interviews 2–15 for the Congruence (CONG) Scale

	3	4	5	6	7	8	9	10	11	12	13	14	15	$\bar{X}_{15}$
2	.20	.06	−.14	−.45	−.38	.24	.38	−.29	−.08	−.50*	−.28	.16	−.23	−.04
3		.36	.21	.21	.06	−.02	.12	.14	.14	−.40	−.27	.23	.23	.38
4			.34	−.11	.39	.37	−.14	.48	−.31	−.52*	−.22	.30	.26	.46
5				.25	.28	.41	−.20	−.08	−.02	−.30	.34	.24	.02	.40
6					.04	−.31	−.34	.23	.01	.48	.25	.12	.10	.24
7						.41	.25	.66†	.32	.39	.13	.35	.72†	.74†
8							.32	−.20	.08	.00	−.07	.18	.08	.37
9								.28	.33	.15	.18	.32	.57*	.55*
10									.01	.20	.26	.23	.76†	.60*
11										.34	−.01	.12	.31	.37
12											.05	−.01	.28	.18
13												.43	.45	.41
14													.74†	.65†
15														.84†

* $p \leq .05$
† $p \leq .01$

relative ordering among the various cases for each of the three conditions dimensions. Second, the average relationship among the conditions in discrete interviews was examined by correlating scores for each scale for each of interviews 2–15 separately and then computing the average correlation value. Thus the first procedure touches upon the relationship among the three conditions at a global level; the second considers the question of the typical momentary association among these therapist variables in the course of the therapy interaction.

Consider the intercorrelations among the average conditions scores. Since a reliable $\bar{X}_{15}$ estimate for UPR was not available it was only possible to intercorrelate the mean of interviews 2–15 ($\bar{X}_{15}$) for AE and CONG. The rank-order correlation obtained between AE_{15} and $CONG_{15}$ was .38, which failed to reach significance. Therefore, there was no dependable relationship between these two variables of therapist behavior when interviews 2–15 were considered, although the direction of relationship was positive.

If we consider the relationship among $\bar{X}_{TOT}$ (AE $\bar{X}_{TOT}$, CONG $\bar{X}_{TOT}$, UPR B $\bar{X}_{TOT}$) scores for each scale (Table 8.6), we see that the

Table 8.6—Spearman rank-order intercorrelations among the three conditions scales (AE, UPR, CONG) for the means of the total therapy interviews, for the fourteen experimental patients

	UPR B$_{TOT}$	CONG$_{TOT}$
AE$_{TOT}$	.50*	.28
UPR B$_{TOT}$		.51*

* $p \leq .05$

relationship between AE and CONG was lower still. While the positive direction of the relationship suggested a general similarity in the global level of conditions, this association was of such low magnitude that the ordering of therapists on the two dimensions was different. UPR B was significantly correlated with both AE and CONG. That is, the relative ordering of cases on the UPR dimension was similar to that obtained for AE and CONG respectively. How could this relationship be interpreted in the absence of a significant association between AE and CONG? The UPR B scores used in this analysis consisted of the most reliable ratings available for this variable. Therefore, the most parsimonious interpretation of the association between the UPR B ratings and the overall level of AE and CONG would be that the UPR judges' estimates of the regard dimension, when in agreement, were heavily loaded with the other therapist variables (empathic responsiveness to the patient and genuineness of involvement). Despite the fact that the UPR judges were unaware of the other scales and scale conceptions, their ratings may have been based on a generalized reaction to the therapist, including some combination of his genuineness or personal expressiveness and sensitivity to the patient. On the other hand it was equally possible, because the UPR ratings were made independently, that this relationship reflected a valid and meaningful pattern. Perhaps accurate empathy and congruence, as defined, could not coexist consistently in the same brief (four-minute) therapy sample. A therapist who was reflecting the patient's feelings at a given moment might not have sufficient opportunity at the same time to express his own feelings extensively. He might, however, be able to convey acceptance of, and regard for, the patient whether his focus was upon understanding the patient or reacting in a more personal context.

It was also important to examine the association of the three conditions variables at discrete moments in the therapy relationship. For this purpose, conditions scale ratings for segments taken from each of therapy interviews 2–15 were correlated. The coefficients were also averaged, yielding an estimate of the general relationship among conditions in discrete therapy interviews. The values for each interview as well as the average coefficients are presented in Table 8.7.

Table 8.7—Segment-by-segment Pearson inter-correlations among the three conditions scales (AE, UPR, CONG) for the respective means of each segment from therapy interviews 2–15 ($N = 196$: 14 patients $\times$ 14 segments)

	UPR	CONG
AE	−.08	.21
UPR		−.04

It was clear that there was no consistent pattern of association among the three conditions factors when specific and discrete interview ratings were considered. The average coefficients were modest, and gave only the most minimum support to the associations between UPR and AE and CONG reported for more global conditions estimates. The correlations obtained for discrete interviews suggested even more strongly that there was no consistent pattern of relationship among these conditions variables in the present sample of interviews. While some coefficients were significant, the direction of association was positive in some cases and negative in others. Values of moderate size occurred but were equalled in number by zero correlations. Further, there was no striking pattern for any of the variables paired and no meaningful trend that emerged consistently over time. Thus it was clear that while conditions ratings were sometimes positively related in therapy interviews, there was more often no relationship whatsoever, and, even instances of a strong negative relationship in our sample of therapy hours.[4]

Overall Assessment of Rating Scales

The purpose of this section has been the separate assessment of the process and conditions scale ratings. Experiencing ratings were found to meet the criterion of reliability and to cover a meaningful, but low, range of the scale for this schizophrenic sample. AE ratings also met our standards for reliability and were found to be normally distributed for this therapist sample over a fairly wide range of the scale. CONG and UPR ratings, however, raised serious interpretive problems. Many UPR ratings for discrete therapy segments were unreliable and had to be disqualified as adequate indices of this therapist condition. Although some segments rated reliably for UPR were combined to provide a global UPR B score, an uneven representation of therapy interviews for each case resulted, and the resultant scores needed to be interpreted cautiously. Finally, the interpretation of the more reliable CONG ratings was complicated by the fact that these ratings were inextricably confounded with the occurrence of certain types of patient questioning throughout therapy.

4. Whitehorn and Betz (Betz, 1962), using the Strong Vocational Interest Battery, have been able to identify differences in personal interest patterns and attitudes between their A (more successful) and B (less successful) therapists. SVIB scores were available for all the therapists of this study. The predictive screen used by Whitehorn and Betz (high score, Lawyer, CPA; low score, Printer, MPST) was applied to our therapists' scores. This screen yields a 5-point scale (0–4), with a score of four meeting the "successful therapist" criterion perfectly, and zero indicating the "unsuccessful therapist" criterion. Only one of the therapists of this study received a score below three. As a result, our therapists consisted of those who met the Strong pattern perfectly and those who missed the criterion on only one of the four Strong scales. The high and low conditions dichotomies were compared with the Strong patterns by Fisher exact probability test. Neither of the obtained probabilities (for AE_{15} and the congruence subscale of the initial patient Relationship Inventory) approached the .05 level. Moreover, the nonsignificant relationship to conditions tended to be inverse—i.e., the Whitehorn and Betz "successful" therapists tended to have a lower level of both rated and perceived conditions.

The validity of our more detailed explorations of the trend and interrelationship of the conditions factors was seriously curtailed by the questionable validity of the CONG and UPR ratings. Only for accurate empathy could we meaningfully pursue the conditions trend over therapy. An analysis of interviews 2–15 showed that this condition varied considerably in the early portion of therapy, stabilized at about the seventh or eighth interview, and remained relatively constant through the fifteenth hour.

Further, it was quite difficult to interpret the meaning of the significant association found between average AE and UPR scores for the total therapy course. Since there was no corresponding relationship for discrete therapy segments (indeed considerable evidence for a lack of association among conditions factors in discrete therapy hours) it was impossible to decide whether the more global relationship obtained reflected an unknown bias present in the selected UPR B ratings or a valid general association between accurate empathy and unconditional positive regard.

In summary, it was impossible to have confidence in the UPR and CONG ratings, and so it was premature for us to attempt to draw conclusions regarding the interrelationship of rated conditions at this time. On the other hand, the accurate empathy and experiencing ratings both appeared to be reliable indices of conditions and process respectively. The ratings were reliable, and the scores were distributed over a meaningful range of the scales yielding fairly stable differentiation of cases in the present sample.

The Interrelationship of Rated and Perceived Conditions

According to Rogers' theory, the conditions of accurate empathy, congruence, and unconditional positive regard are effective in producing process movement *only* if they are perceived by the patient. While a therapist may offer a given level of conditions in the relationship, this effort is effective only to the extent that it is communicated to the patient. In a relationship that is not successful it is possible that the therapist has been unable to create the necessary climate, or that the *patient* has not responded to his attempt. To test this theory, it was essential in this study that the level of therapeutic conditions as perceived by the patient be assessed, and equally important that the therapists' self-evaluations be tapped.

In order to assess the level of therapist conditions as perceived by patients and therapists, the Barrett-Lennard Relationship Inventory (Barrett-Lennard, 1962) was administered to all patients and therapists at intervals throughout the course of therapy. This questionnaire yields five scores, corresponding approximately to the conceptual dimensions tapped by the rating scales. Thus the regard (R) and unconditionality (U) subscales of the Relationship Inventory (RI) correspond roughly to the UPR Scale conception; congruence (C) to CONG; and empathic understanding (E) to AE. The total (T) RI conditions score, the sum of all four subscales, is roughly analogous to the combined conditions score (COMB) derived from judges' ratings.

Both patient and therapist were asked to complete the Relationship Inventory at various time points. The patient was asked to assess the attitudes he felt the therapist was expressing; the therapist, the attitudes he felt he was communicating to the patient. While the focus for the rating task was primarily upon the momentary state of the relationship, the reply may very well represent a composite of the preceding total interaction, with somewhat greater weight given to recent events in the relationship.

In the analyses which follow, the data from the Relationship Inventory have been restricted to two time points, due to the variability of case length and the difficulty in administering the instrument to all patients at regular intervals. The first assessment of the therapeutic relationship was made at a point shortly after the initiation of the therapy relationship. The second, the terminal Relationship Inventory, corresponded as closely as possible to the final interview for each case. It was possible to obtain an N of 8 and 13 respectively for the initial and terminal patient Relationship Inventories; an N of 11 and 14 for initial and terminal therapist assessments.

With this data on patient and therapist viewpoints, we were able to explore a number of issues, considered in the following sections: (1) We could assess the stability of patient and therapist perceptions of the therapeutic relationships by correlating initial and terminal RI subscale scores. (2) By examining the interrelationship among RI subscales at different time points we could assess the relationship among therapeutic conditions as perceived by each of the therapy participants, as well as consider any changes in this perception over time. (3) We could assess the degree of correspondence between patient and therapist perceptions by intercorrelating patient and therapist RI subscale scores at comparable time points. (4) We could assess the degree of correspondence between rated and perceived conditions by examining the relationship between judges' ratings of therapy segments and Relationship Inventory perceptions as expressed by patients and therapists. Thus we could weigh the patient and therapist perceptions, if divergent, against the viewpoint of an "outside" observer, the judge. The data also provided anchorage for the judges' ratings by showing the extent to which their ratings reflected the patients' or the therapists' viewpoints.

Stability of Perceived Conditions

To investigate this stability of patient and therapist assessments, initial and terminal RI scores were intercorrelated for patients and for therapists. The results of these rank-order correlations are presented in Table 8.8. The values are highly significant for they show that both

Table 8.8—Intercorrelations of initial with terminal Relationship Inventory subscales (Regard with Regard, Empathy with Empathy, etc.)

Subscale	Patient RI scores	Therapist RI scores
Regard	.91	.85
Empathy	.81	.88
Congruence	.91	.76
Unconditionality	.80	.78
Total score	.93	.94

patient and therapist perceptions of the therapeutic relationship were highly stable over the course of therapy. Thus the therapist's evaluation of his attitudinal efforts, and the patient's assessment of him, did not change from early to late in the relationship. This may indicate either that the same general attitudes were communicated by the therapist across discrete moments in the therapy interaction, or it may suggest that patient and therapist Relationship Inventory responses were global assessments reflecting the long-term cumulative impact of the interaction in addition to the state of the relationship at the time the questionnaire was administered.

Interrelationship among Perceived Conditions

The patient Relationship Inventory data permitted us to examine the associations among therapist conditions from the patients' frame of reference. Table 8.9 presents the rank-order correlations among the RI subscales for 8 initial and 13 terminal patient Relationship Inventories. Table 8.10 shows the corresponding means for the RI subscales. If we consider the matrix for the *initial* patient RI's we see that the four subscales were positively but moderately interrelated. Three of the six rho's were significant at or beyond the .05 level. One of these sig-

Table 8.9—Spearman rank-order intercorrelations among the patient Relationship Inventory subscales, for the initial and terminal Relationship Inventory protocols

	Empathy	Congruence	Uncondi-tionality	Total score
INITIAL RI SCORES				
Regard	.43	.83*	.68	.95†
Empathy		.48	.39	.64
Congruence			.77*	.88†
Unconditionality				.73*
TERMINAL RI SCORES				
Regard	−.13	.27	.40	.66*
Empathy		.26	.22	.58*
Congruence			.38	.70*
Unconditionality				.68*

* $p \leq .05$
† $p \leq .01$

Table 8.10—Mean values of the patient and therapist Relationship Inventory subscales, for the initial and terminal Relationship Inventories

	Patient RI scores		Therapist RI scores	
Subscale	Initial ($N = 8$)	Terminal ($N = 13$)	Initial ($N = 11$)	Terminal ($N = 14$)
Regard	22.25	27.38	37.73	38.78
Empathy	19.25	23.85	28.18	28.86
Congruence	22.88	20.92	35.09	36.14
Unconditionality	16.25	15.85	23.91	21.57
Total score	81.75	88.00	124.91	125.36

nificant relationships was between the two subscales tapping aspects of the therapist's positive feelings toward the patient, regard (R) and unconditionality (U). This finding was consistent with the conceptual emphasis placed on the joint operation of these factors. Neither regard variable was significantly related to the therapist's communicated level of empathic understanding (E). That is, early in therapy the patient's perception of the therapist's positive feelings was relatively independent of his perception of the therapist's level of understanding. Congruence (C) on the other hand appears to have been more closely associated with the therapist's ability to communicate acceptant feelings, since both regard factors correlated significantly with the perceived genuineness of the therapist.

Among the mean RI subscale scores (Table 8.10) for the initial patient RI, congruence (C) scored relatively high. This, in conjunction with the close association of congruence and perceived regard, might be interpreted to indicate that the patient early in therapy perceived as most meaningful to him the genuineness of the therapist's acceptance of him as a person. The perceived level of empathy (E) on the other hand was relatively low, and was not associated with the acceptance-regard-congruence cluster.

Finally, it was apparent from the uniformly significant correlation of the subscales with the total (T) RI score that each separate subscale was significantly related to the overall level of conditions as perceived by the patient early in therapy.

For the terminal Relationship Inventory there was no significant relationship among the various RI subscales although again all subscales related significantly to the total scale score. While regard, unconditionality, and congruence still tended to cluster, the relationships were of lower magnitude. An inspection of the subscale means for the terminal patient RI (Table 8.10) shows that the level of empathy had increased relative to the congruence dimension, so that regard and empathy replaced congruence and regard in relative prominence. One way to view this shift in emphasis was to interpret the greater prominence of empathy as indicative of the patient's growing concern with the definition and exploration of his problems as the relationship approached termination. It may be meaningful to view the lower interrelationship among terminal Relationship Inventory subscales as indicative of the patient's increasingly differentiated perception of the therapist. It was only after the relationship had been in existence for some time that the patient seemed to develop a differentiated sensitivity to those related but distinguishable aspects of the therapeutic relationship.

It is interesting to compare these findings for our sample of hospitalized schizophrenics with Barrett-Lennard's results for a psychoneurotic group seen in a counseling center setting (Barrett-Lennard, 1962). Since Barrett-Lennard administered the first RI after the fifth therapy interview, his data can be most meaningfully compared with the results for the initial Relationship Inventory in our study.

Unconditionality was judged by Barrett-Lennard's neurotics to be relatively independent of the other three perceived therapist conditions, particularly the therapist's level of regard, and while it was significantly correlated with empathy, congruence, and the total RI score, the magnitude of the relationship was somewhat less than that found for other subscales. In our schizophrenic population, on the other hand, unconditionality was highly associated with regard, congruence, and the total RI score. This discrepancy for two diagnostic groups may indicate that this variable plays a more pervasive role in the schizophrenic patient's perception of the therapy relationship.

In addition, Barrett-Lennard reports that empathic understanding and congruence were highly intercorrelated in his neurotic sample. From this he concludes that "although theoretically and operationally separate and distinct, the two scales are, in this instance, empirically indistinguishable" (Barrett-Lennard, 1962, p. 13). This pattern, however, was absent in the present schizophrenic sample, where the association between empathy and congruence was lower and insignificant.

In short, perceptions of components of the therapeutic relationship seem to cluster differently in neurotic and schizophrenic samples. Neurotics associate the therapist's genuineness with his communicated level of empathic understanding while schizophrenics tend to view genuineness and regard factors as related. This difference may well reflect the relatively greater focus on self-exploration rather than on relationship formation occurring in the initial perceptions of neurotic patients, in contrast to the schizophrenics' placement of more emphasis on the therapist's potential for a genuine understanding of them.

Further, in an early study, made in connection with this research, of responses to the Relationship Inventory, van der Veen (1962) compared our patients with the Barrett-Lennard psychoneurotic group. The comparison, made at the twenty-fifth interview for the neurotic group and at approximately the twentieth interview for our group, revealed striking differences. Our more disturbed patients perceived significantly less congruence, positive regard, and unconditionality than did the clinic clients. There was, however, no significant difference in the degree of empathic understanding perceived. (Is this because this judgment is less based upon inference?) There was no significant difference between the two groups of therapists in their perception of their own attitudes. Since the therapists working in our project were somewhat more experienced, and might be considered more competent to provide the therapeutic conditions, it seems reasonable to conclude that the more disturbed patient was simply less able to perceive the subtle therapeutic attitudes of the therapist, though he was able to assess the empathic behavior of his therapist.

Relationship of Rated and Perceived Conditions

The relationship between judges' ratings of therapist conditions variables and patient Relationship Inventory assessments of the same variables was meaningful in determining both the degree of commonality between the rating scales and the RI and the degree of similarity in the viewpoints of patients and judges. Two sources of data were relevant to this question. First, we investigated the association between patient perceptions and the level of rated conditions for those interviews contiguous to the patient RI assessment, tapping the extent of the patient-judge agreement at a given moment in the course of therapy. Secondly, we examined the relationship between the average level of rated conditions and patients' RI perceptions, inasmuch as the patient RI perception was apt to be also heavily influenced by his total therapy experience.

Momentary agreement between rated and perceived conditions.—In order to examine the relationship between patients' perceptions of the therapeutic relationship and judges' ratings at comparable time points, the average of the judges' ratings of the three interviews most immediately contiguous to the time of administration of the Relationship Inventory was obtained for each scale and correlated with the patient RI subscale and total scores.

Rank-order correlations for both initial and terminal RI data points are presented in Table 8.11. First consider the correlations between

Table 8.11—Spearman rank-order intercorrelations of patients' perceived conditions with rated conditions, both moment-by-moment, and average values over the rated therapy interviews

| | INITIAL RI SCORES ($N = 8$) | | | | | | | |
| | Moment-by-moment | | | | $\bar{X}_{15}$ | | | |
Subscale	AE	UPR	CONG	COMB	AE	UPR	CONG	COMB
Regard	.76*	.54	.00	.76*	.83†	—	.14	.60
Empathy	.88†	.17	.26	.81*	.71*	—	−.07	.31
Congruence	.67*	.38	.33	.69*	.81*	—	.31	.71*
Unconditionality	.46	.33	.36	.42	.52	—	.14	.40
Total score	.88†	.57	.21	.88†	.93†	—	.24	.69*

| | TERMINAL RI SCORES ($N = 13$) | | | | | | | |
| | Moment-by-moment | | | | $\bar{X}_{TOT}$ | | | |
Subscale	AE	UPR	CONG	COMB	AE	UPR B	CONG	COMB
Regard	.34	.62*	−.06	.50*	.58*	.60*	.26	.55*
Empathy	.56*	.38	−.32	.46	.38	.21	−.11	.24
Congruence	.74†	.49*	−.21	.57*	.81†	.50	.27	.63*
Unconditionality	.36	.59*	−.17	.42	.39	.25	.09	.26
Total score	.59*	.62*	−.23	.57*	.68†	.53*	.20	.56*

* $p \leq .05$
† $p \leq .01$

rated AE and the patients' perceptions of the therapists' behavior as
shown on the Relationship Inventory. Initially the rated level of AE
was highly correlated with all but the unconditionality (U) subscale and
was most highly associated with its RI counterpart (E) and the total
conditions level (T). Later in therapy, it was the therapist's communicated level of congruence (C) that was most strongly associated with
rated AE. The relationship between rated AE and the RI, E, and T
subscales continued at this point to be positive and significant, but was
of lower magnitude than that obtained initially. On the other hand the
initially high correlation between rated AE and the patient's perception
of the therapist's regard (R) dropped out altogether. Thus, initially,
judges' ratings of the therapists' AE agreed rather closely with the
patients' perceptions of their empathy, regard, and genuineness. Later
in therapy the patients' RI perceptions of the therapists' regard was no
longer related to the judges' AE ratings, although their perceptions of
empathy and congruence continued to be. Most importantly, these
findings suggested that at any point in therapy judges' ratings of therapist AE agreed significantly with the patients' assessment of therapist
empathy and congruence, as well as with the overall level of conditions
offered in the therapeutic relationship.

Reliable UPR ratings were available only for segments close to the
terminal RI data points (see Table 8.12). At this time, near the
termination of therapy, there was evidence (Table 8.11) for a high
association between rated UPR and most of the RI subscales and with

Table 8.12—Ebel intraclass reliabilities for the means of judges'
ratings (3 segments for each patient) for the moment-by-moment
data intercorrelated with therapist and patient Relationship Inventory scores

Scale	Initial RI scores		Terminal RI scores	
	r_{kk}	r_{ll}	r_{kk}	r_{ll}
JUDGES' RATINGS CONCURRENT WITH PATIENT RI SCORES				
AE	.57	.31	.75	.50
UPR	.00	.00	.49	.24
CONG	.84	.63	.83	.62
JUDGES' RATINGS CONCURRENT WITH THERAPIST RI SCORES				
AE	.60	.34	.76	.51
UPR	.00	.00	.44	.20
CONG	.86	.67	.82	.61

the total, with a slight tendency for UPR to correlate most highly with the relevant R and U dimensions. This association of the UPR ratings with most of the RI subscales could be most parsimoniously interpreted in terms of a halo effect on the part of either the UPR judges or the patients. In either case the UPR ratings agreed rather grossly with the patients' momentary assessment of the therapeutic climate, rather than in a more differentiated fashion with the patients' perception of the therapists' positive and acceptant feelings.

Judges' ratings of therapist CONG were not at all associated with patients' perceptions. Indeed the relationship between rated CONG and all RI subscales tended to be inverse as therapy approached termination. This lack of association between rated CONG and any of the RI subscales may have indicated the divergence of the judges' CONG ratings from the patients' viewpoint. This discrepancy was difficult to ' interpret unequivocally, however, since the restricted focus of the Congruence Scale and the resultant bimodality of ratings may have minimized the probability of observing a strong association between judge and patient viewpoints. The patients' broader perspective for congruence (measured in the RI), undoubtedly based on a wider range of situations, may have been the primary factor accounting for the apparent independence of judge and RI assessments of congruence.

Finally, we see from Table 8.11 that the combined rated conditions (COMB) estimates correlated both initially and terminally with the R and C factors of the Relationship Inventory, as well as with the RI total (T) score. However, it is only for the initial data point that we see a significant association between rated COMB conditions and patients' perceptions of E.

In general these findings suggested that, with the notable exception of the Congruence Scale, both the raters and the patients were similarly evaluating events occurring within therapy. While the patients and judges did not perceive the relationships in the same differentiated manner, they were in general agreement regarding the gross level of therapist conditions being offered at a discrete moment in the therapeutic encounter.

Global interrelationship of rated and perceived conditions.—In order to assess the relationship between the patients' and judges' assessments of conditions in a large block of the therapy interaction, patient RI scores were correlated with the averages of judges' ratings for each of the conditions scales (initial RI with $\bar{X}_{15}$, terminal RI with $\bar{X}_{TOT}$). These results, also presented in Table 8.11, followed a similar pattern to those obtained for the momentary relationships. Again rated AE correlated highly but indiscriminately with patient RI evaluations of the relationship, while rated CONG remained independent. UPR B ratings were associated with R and with the overall conditions score (T).

Most strikingly, these findings suggested that of the various RI subscales, congruence and regard, as perceived by patients, were especially consistent predictors of both rated accurate empathy and the combined conditions ratings. Of the two factors, moreover, congruence was the more powerful predictor. This may be interpreted as demonstrating the particular importance of the congruence dimension (and to a somewhat lower degree, regard) in therapy with hospitalized schizophrenics. Also the correspondence of judges' AE and COMB conditions ratings with the patient's perception of the therapist as genuine and positively regarding strongly suggested that the ratings in this study validly reflected the gross level of therapist conditions as perceived by the patient and more specifically reflected the patient's view of the therapist as a genuine and warm individual in the therapy relationship.

Agreement Between Patients, Therapists, and Judges in Evaluating Conditions

We have just seen that there was general overall agreement between patients' and judges' viewpoints concerning the level of therapist conditions in the relationship. In order to obtain a more complete perspective of therapist conditions, it was important to investigate further the association between therapist and patient perceptions of the therapeutic relationship and between therapist and judge evaluations. Both patients and therapists completed the Relationship Inventory at the same points. In each case the therapist was asked to describe the attitudes he was communicating to the patient; the patient, the attitudes the therapist appeared to have in the relationship. The rank-order correlations between subscales of patient and therapist Relationship Inventories at initial and terminal points in therapy are presented in Table 8.13. The majority of the rho's were insignificant and tended toward the negative direction. Three of the negative correlations were significant. The most striking pattern of negative relationship between therapist and patient RI's occurred in the contrast between the patients' relative perceptions of therapist empathy and the therapists' relative self-ratings of congruence and regard. Therapists who rated themselves as relatively high on these factors of genuineness and regard (and these were the factors on which therapists gave themselves the highest ratings —see Table 8.10) were seen by patients as relatively low in empathy and in conditions generally. Further, there was disagreement between

Table 8.13—Spearman rank-order intercorrelations of the patient and therapist Relationship Inventory subscales, for the initial and terminal Relationship Inventory scores

	Regard	Empathy	Congruence	Uncondi-tionality	Total score
INITIAL RI SCORES					
Regard	−.07	−.28	−.60	−.26	−.27
Empathy	−.79*	−.53	−.74*	−.55	−.60
Congruence	.00	−.30	−.40	−.19	−.23
Unconditionality	.11	.10	−.28	.14	.11
Total score	−.29	−.41	−.69*	−.40	−.42
TERMINAL RI SCORES					
Regard	−.16	.34	.08	−.03	.05
Empathy	−.34	.02	−.42	−.24	−.30
Congruence	−.27	−.04	.12	−.02	−.12
Unconditionality	−.34	.15	−.15	.06	−.06
Total score	−.43	.08	−.17	−.17	−.23

*$p \leq .05$

patients and therapists regarding other aspects of the relationship, both initially and terminally, though it was not quite so striking at the terminal point.

If we inspect the RI mean scores for therapist evaluations presented in Table 8.10 we see that the therapist perceived himself as offering a relatively higher level of conditions than that perceived by, or communicated to, the patient. Thus therapists were not only divergent in their evaluations of the therapeutic climate and the focus placed on various components of it, but tended to ascribe a more favorable level of conditions to the interaction. While it would clearly be premature to draw conclusions regarding the relative validity of the various viewpoints, the gross divergence between therapists and patients and judges in this sample has clear implications for this research. Different results certainly would emerge for any analyses employing Relationship Inventory scores as a function of whether the therapist or patient viewpoint was considered.

These findings, while somewhat more extreme, were generally consistent with results reported by Barrett-Lennard for a psychoneurotic population. He found that therapists viewed the relationship more positively than patients and that patients' and therapists' RI scores intercorrelated insignificantly. The general trend, however, was positive. From this, Barrett-Lennard concluded ". . . that there is little linear correspondence between the way the clients view their therapists, and the therapists' view of themselves" (Barrett-Lennard, 1962, *p.* 13). Our findings with a schizophrenic population were more extreme insofar as there tended to be an *inverse* relationship between therapist and patient perceptions of the therapist's attitudes. This direction of discrepancy was most probably a function of the differences in the diagnostic groups, schizophrenics being more divergent in assessing others' attitudes than a less severely disturbed neurotic sample.

In a separate study on our schizophrenic patient sample, Spotts (1962) examined the interrelationship of patient and therapist evaluations of the relationship when the sample was divided according to therapy outcome. In general his findings indicated that in successful therapy there is a significant positive correlation between patient and therapist evaluations of the relationship, specifically the dimension of positive regard, while in less successful cases therapist and patient assessments are more divergent, correlating negatively with one another. His study suggested that it was possible for therapists and schizophrenic patients to agree in their relative perception of the relationship, and that a relatively high order of agreement was associated with a favorable outcome. The divergent perceptions were limited to less successful therapeutic relationships. There was no evidence, however, bearing on the causal nature of the relationship between therapeutic outcome and the congruence of patient-therapist viewpoints. We can only conclude that these perceptions are generally important variables in therapy.

The question immediately arising in light of this divergence of patient and therapist assessment was, whose view was the more accurate? The perceptions and evaluations of therapists have been given great weight in past therapy research, but the discrepancy emerging between patient and therapist perceptions in this study cast some doubt on the wisdom of this practice. One way of evaluating the relative accuracy or validity of patient and therapist perceptions was to compare their evaluations with those made by independent observers. In this study it was possible to compare therapist and patient evaluations of the relationship with ratings made by judges from tape-recorded segments of the therapeutic interaction. The results of this comparison of patient-judge perceptions have been discussed in detail on pages 172–176. In general we found that patients and judges were in agreement regarding the overall and global level of conditions. It was apparent that the patients' general evaluation could be predicted with considerable accuracy from judges' AE ratings, from reliable UPR ratings, and from a combined conditions

Table 8.14—Spearman rank-order intercorrelations of therapists' perceived conditions with rated conditions, both moment-by-moment, and average values over the rated therapy interviews

	INITIAL RI SCORES $(N = 11)$							
	Moment-by-moment				$\bar{X}_{15}$			
Subscale	AE	UPR	CONG	COMB	AE	UPR	CONG	COMB
Regard	−.57*	.08	.20	−.14	−.52		−.21	−.34
Empathy	−.67*	.12	.03	−.33	−.66*		−.39	−.60*
Congruence	−.73*	.12	.25	−.26	−.66*		−.21	−.41
Unconditionality	−.50	−.09	−.20	−.36	−.52		−.48	−.54*
Total score	−.59*	.12	.00	−.25	−.57*		−.39	−.52

	TERMINAL RI SCORES $(N = 14)$							
	Moment-by-moment				$\bar{X}_{TOT}$			
Subscale	AE	UPR	CONG	COMB	AE	UPR B	CONG	COMB
Regard	−.34	.13	.21	−.02	−.42	−.02	−.10	−.18
Empathy	−.08	.34	.19	−.25	−.12	.15	−.11	.00
Congruence	−.16	.14	.03	−.01	−.02	.23	.09	.19
Unconditionality	−.29	.13	.25	−.05	−.18	.06	.13	−.04
Total score	−.24	.14	.21	−.08	−.19	.04	−.16	−.07

*$p \leq .05$

estimate, but that judges' evaluations of the therapist's congruence were generally unrelated to the patients' perception of the relationship.

Let us see then the extent of agreement between *therapists'* and judges' perceptions of the relationship. Table 8.14 presents the rank-order correlations between initial and terminal therapist Relationship Inventories and judges' ratings of conditions.

We see that therapist RI evaluations and judges' perceptions of the relationship initially were negatively associated. Regardless of whether we were dealing with ratings from interviews close to the RI administration point or with the average of ratings over interviews 2–15, an inverse relationship emerged for AE, combined conditions ratings, and therapists' assessments. The association between rated CONG and therapists' evaluations was not consistently negative, but it was at no time strongly positive. Relationships between terminal therapist RI's and judges' votings were of the same order as those observed initially, though the negative trend was not significant. In general the results in Table 8.14 were consistent whether the rated average of conditions or the ratings of interviews at the time of the RI administration were considered. The only discrepancy was the emergence of a very low positive trend in the association between therapist RI subscales and rated congruence in the terminal momentary RI matrix. In general, however, there was little correspondence between the judges' perception of the therapist's conditions and any aspect of the therapist's assessment of his communicated attitudes.

A possible explanation of this divergence came from the fact that judges rating tape-recorded segments of the therapy interaction employed three rating scales constructed specifically for the rating of tape-recorded material. While the subscales of the Relationship Inventory were derived from the same theoretical orientation as the conditions scales it is possible that differences in the way in which the conditions variables were operationalized in the rating scales might account in part for the discrepancy between judges' and therapists' assessments of the therapeutic relationship. A study conducted by van der Veen (1962, rev. 1965) shows that this is not the case. Here raters listened to the whole interview closest in time to the administration of the Relationship Inventory, and made their ratings on the same instrument (the RI) used by patients and therapists. In general van der Veen's findings agreed with those reported above. Judges and therapists did not agree in their perception of the therapeutic relationship even when the same rating instrument was used by both. Judges' ratings agreed more positively with patients' perceptions, but the correlations were not of the magnitude obtained when the judges' estimate was based on a larger number of tape-recorded materials. In any event we reached the general conclusion that the naive judge and the patient agreed in their assessment of the therapeutic relationship, and that the therapist's view was divergent.[5]

Overall, these findings indicate that there was, at best, no reliable relationship between the therapists' evaluations of therapy and the relative ordering of cases yielded by judges' evaluations of the same relationship. Similarly we found no commonality in therapist and patient perceptions unless the variable of outcome was controlled. There was, on the other hand, a positive association between patients' perceptions

5. It should be made clear that it is in the relative *ordering* of the relationships that this sharp discrepancy occurs. Van der Veen (1962, rev. 1965), in his study, has shown that the *mean* scores of the therapists were much closer to the mean scores of the judges than were the mean scores of the patients. Thus the negative correlations cited in this section were clearly due to individual personality differences in the therapists as to the degree to which they saw themselves offering the therapeutic conditions.

of the gross conditions level offered by the therapist and an independent and objective rating of these same conditions made on rating scales from tape-recorded data. Thus the evaluations by patients and by judges produced the same relative ordering of cases on dimensions of therapist conditions, an ordering which was generally divergent from that emerging from the therapist's evaluation of his performance.

This finding had several implications for the study and for therapy research generally. Most generally, it suggested that very different results could emerge from research employing therapist evaluations of the relationship than from studies based on the ratings made by patients or judges. Secondly, the high level of agreement between clinically naive judges and patients in their assessments of therapist conditions suggested that the conditions scale ratings for the present study were made from a frame of reference close to that of the patient. This rating perspective was compatible with Rogers' emphasis on the importance of the patient's perception of therapist conditions as a prerequisite to personality change. Thus the rating scales used to provide the bulk of the basic data for the major analyses of this research represented an important and theoretically valid perspective of the therapeutic interaction. Finally, the low agreement between therapists and both judges and patients might indicate that the therapists were evaluating the relationship divergently, employing different criteria, or using a different frame of reference to evaluate the relationship. Because of these differences it is difficult to draw meaningful conclusions from studies employing the therapist frame of reference without also exploring the patient's point of view.

Overview

The detailed exploration of the interrelationships among judges', patients', and therapists' perceptions of the same therapeutic interactions reported in this section has yielded results with important implications both for assessing the commonality among these perspectives, and for evaluating the power and validity of the scales and instruments employed.

First we have seen that, unlike conditions scale ratings, patient and therapist Relationship Inventory perceptions remained highly stable over therapy. This suggests, most parsimoniously, that the conditions assessments on the Relationship Inventory were made by patients and therapists at a more global level than that possible for judges working with discrete interview segments.

In considering the relationship among patient perceived conditions factors we found a strong intercorrelation among Relationship Inventory subscales early in therapy indicating perhaps that the patient's evaluation of his therapist was somewhat generalized at this time. Congruence, regard, and unconditionality were most strongly associated. They were not, however, significantly related to perceived empathy. This clustering, when viewed in conjunction with the high scores ascribed to the congruence and regard dimensions by these patients, suggests that the schizophrenic may place particular stress initially on the therapist's potential as a trustworthy relationship object. As therapy progresses, however, this general emphasis diminishes somewhat as the patient's perception of conditions becomes more highly differentiated.

When conditions scale ratings and patient Relationship Inventory evaluations were compared we found gross confirmation for the validity of the AE and UPR scales as conditions measures. AE and UPR ratings were related, not only to their appropriate Relationship Inventory counterparts, but also to perceived congruence and to the global (total) conditions level. This suggests that while the rating scales were functioning in a somewhat more general or global fashion than was intended, they were sufficiently powerful to differentiate the relative conditions level in the present cases from a perspective that was generally similar to that of the patient. Further, it is noteworthy that AE Scale ratings and patient-perceived congruence assessments were strongly related to one another. This, when viewed in conjunction with the evidence suggesting that the patients in this sample found therapist congruence particularly meaningful, gave further confirmation to the general validity of the AE Scale. That is, while AE Scale ratings might not be limited to the empathy construct, they appeared to have considerable commonality with the patient's global evaluation of the relationship and a particularly strong association with congruence, the predominant therapist factor in the relationship from the patient's viewpoint. While there was some evidence that the less reliable UPR ratings functioned in the same global fashion, the absence of complete coverage of the therapy course for these ratings weakened the data based on this scale. The general unreliability of the UPR ratings made even the more reliable UPR B ratings drawn from them difficult to interpret validly. The complete divergence between CONG Scale ratings and patient assessments of the quality of the therapy interaction highlighted the fact that ratings for the present CONG Scale could not be meaningfully anchored and were, therefore, extremely difficult to interpret.

It seemed clear at this point that the reliable AE ratings would perhaps provide the most adequate and meaningful assessments of the general level of conditions in the relationship. Yet it seemed equally clear that any relationships between accurate empathy and other variables could not be unequivocally interpreted in terms of the specific operation of accurate empathy, but had to be seen more globally in terms of the general quality of the therapists' attitudes and involvement in the relationship.

Finally, the close, though general, association between ratings of accurate empathy and patient perceived conditions became still more meaningful in light of the clear divergence of therapist views of the relationship from the views of both judges and patients. This negative correlation with both patient and judge perceptions, in conjunction with the clear tendency of therapists to make considerably more favorable evaluations of the interaction than their patients, suggested that the therapists, in this sample at least, were divergently optimistic in their assessments of the patient-therapist relationship. While it was difficult to pinpoint exactly the source of this discrepancy, it seemed clear that different results would be obtained as a function of the particular viewpoint of therapy considered.

Conclusion

In this chapter we have attempted to spell out in detail our methods for assessing conditions and process variables, to explain the various summary scores derived from process and conditions ratings of discrete therapy segments, and to explore the interrelationship of conditions ratings and the commonality of different measurement perspectives. This procedure has enabled us to understand more clearly the nature of the conditions and process ratings as well as the particular way in which these factors operate over the course of therapy.

Several conclusions are suggested by the findings of this chapter. The Experiencing Scale ratings were reliable and fairly well distributed over the appropriate lower range of the scale. Congruence Scale ratings, although reliable, were bimodally distributed and therefore were difficult to interpret. They seemed to depend crucially upon the occurrence of certain kinds of patient questions; and since they did not correlate with Relationship Inventory conditions, they did not offer us a straightforward assessment of the therapist's genuineness. Unconditional Positive Regard Scale ratings had been found to be unreliable, so that even when a subsampling of reliable (UPR B) ratings proved to correlate meaningfully with patient Relationship Inventory perceptions, the scores were difficult to interpret. Accurate Empathy Scale ratings were the most reliably rated and meaningfully distributed of the three conditions scales, and related positively to patient RI perceptions of the therapy relationship.

Two related factors suggested that a more general interpretation of the Accurate Empathy Scale was appropriate. First, the patient Relationship Inventory perceptions themselves were quite global—they changed little over therapy and each specific subscale score was highly correlated with the total RI conditions score. Second, the accurate empathy ratings were particularly highly associated with the RI total conditions estimate, and in particular with the patient perceived congruence estimate—rather than with its specific Relationship Inventory subscale counterpart (empathy). While the interpretation of accurate empathy ratings will be considered in greater detail in Chapter 12, here the pattern of relationships can be most conservatively viewed as suggesting that the Accurate Empathy Scale for this study tapped a more global conditions quality of the therapist which was clearly related to his communicated therapeutic commitment as well as the genuineness of this involvement.

While it was not possible meaningfully to examine the trend of either congruence or unconditional positive regard ratings in the therapy course, or draw any conclusions regarding the interrelationships among rated conditions, we were able to draw the following tentative conclusions regarding the Accurate Empathy Scale. It seemed apparent, for this sample, that this condition achieved stability by approximately the eighth therapy interview, and remained fairly constant at least until the fifteenth interview. It was equally clear that the accurate empathy ratings represented only the patient's perspective (since therapist assessments were very discrepant) and stood for a more global quality of the therapist (apparently his communicated genuineness and involvement in the relationship, rather than his specific empathic understanding).

References

ARNHOFF, F. N. Some factors influencing the unreliability of clinical judgments. *J. clin. Psychol. 10:*272–275, 1954.

BOCHINNI, R., FARWELL, ROBERTA, and HART, J. T., JR. The reliability of different segment lengths. Unpublished paper, 1960.

BARRETT-LENNARD, G. T. Dimensions of therapist response as causal factors in therapeutic change. *Psychol. Monogr. 76,* No. 43 (Whole No. 562), 1962.

BETZ, B. J. Experiences in research in psychotherapy with schizophrenic patients. In H. H. Strupp and L. Luborsky (eds.), *Research in Psychotherapy,* Vol. II. Washington, D.C.: American Psychological Association, 1962, pp. 41–60.

CRONBACH, L. J. *Essentials of Psychological Testing.* 2d edition. New York: Harper & Brothers, 1960, chapter XIX.

GENDLIN, E. T. *Experiencing and the Creation of Meaning.* New York: The Free Press of Glencoe, 1962.

GENDLIN, E. T., and TOMLINSON, T. M. Psychotherapy process rating scale: Experiencing (EXP) Scale. Revised by Philippa L. Mathieu and Marjorie H. Klein. Unpublished manuscript, 1963.

GUILFORD, J. P. *Psychometric Methods.* 2d edition. New York: McGraw-Hill, 1954.

KIESLER, D. J. Psychotherapy conditions rating scale: Congruence. Unpublished manuscript, 1963.

KIESLER, D. J., MATHIEU, PHILIPPA L., and KLEIN, MARJORIE H. Sampling from the recorded therapy interview: A comparative study of different segment lengths. *J. consult. Psychol.* 28:349–357, 1964.

SPOTTS, JULES E. The perception of positive regard by relatively successful and relatively unsuccessful clients. Unpublished research report, University of Wisconsin Psychiatric Institute, 1962.

TRUAX, C. B. A scale for the measurement of accurate empathy. Unpublished manuscript, 1961.

TRUAX, C. B. A tentative scale for the measurement of unconditional positive regard. Unpublished manuscript, 1962.

VAN DER VEEN, F. Conditions offered by the therapist as perceived by clients, therapists, and judges. Unpublished manuscript, University of Wisconsin Psychiatric Institute, 1962, revised 1965.

VAN DER VEEN, F. Perceived therapist conditions and degree of disturbance. Unpublished research report, University of Wisconsin Psychiatric Institute, 1962.

9. Therapist Conditions and Patient Process

Donald J. Kiesler, Marjorie H. Klein, Philippa L. Mathieu

The theoretical framework basic to the hypotheses of this research has been presented in Chapters 1, 6, and 7. This chapter is devoted to the findings which bear upon the first of these hypotheses: *The greater the degree to which the conditions of therapy exist in the relationship, the greater will be the evidences of therapeutic process or movement in the client.*

This hypothesis is deceptively straightforward, seeming to require measurement of two factors only: therapist conditions (theoretically defined in terms of three separate dimensions) and patient process movement. Chapter 8 suggested, however, that therapist conditions are perceived rather differently by patients and judges in contrast to therapists. In addition, there are various ways of combining and defining the conditions in a composite index; and both conditions and process can be tapped at many discrete time points in the course of therapy, and can, as well, be averaged over varying periods. Each separate viewpoint of therapist conditions, each method of combining conditions, and each sampling of data points represents but one of many possible operational definitions of the theoretical factors. Therefore, before presenting our results, it is necessary to discuss the issues inherent in the selection of alternative tests of Hypothesis I and to weight various approaches on an a priori basis. The first section of this chapter is devoted to this. The next sections present those analyses that serve as the most central tests of the hypothesis, as well as more exploratory analyses.

Theoretical Issues and Operational Definitions

Views of Conditions

As stated in Chapter 8, therapist conditions were measured from three different viewpoints: that of judges who applied rating scales to tape-recorded segments of the therapy hour; that of the patients who evaluated the ongoing therapy relationship on the Relationship Inventory (Barrett-Lennard, 1959, 1962); and that of the therapists who used this same questionnaire to describe the therapy interaction. Patients and judges were found to agree quite closely regarding the overall level of conditions present, while the therapists' viewpoints were found to be quite discrepant. Moreover, patients and therapists were making a global assessment of the therapy encounter, while judges were evaluating discrete four-minute segments of many hours in the course of therapy. Any summative score of judges' conditions ratings, then, represented an average of discrete ratings over the therapy interaction, while patient and therapist Relationship Inventory assessments represented their global evaluations of the total encounter.

Whose view of conditions was most central to Hypothesis I? Which type of assessment (global or summative) most appropriately represented the situational therapeutic climate? Regarding the first question, Rogers had emphasized clearly that therapist conditions must be communicated in order to be effective, and that the patient must perceive them, "at least to a minimal degree." Therefore it would seem that the most central test of this hypothesis rested with the patient's perceptions, with the view of objective judges next in importance. The therapist's view of his own behavior seemed theoretically least central. Regarding the choice between global or summative conditions estimates, Rogers suggested that the therapist's general attitudes, rather than any discrete behaviors, were the effective agents in patient process movement and personality change. Thus, it was important that we take an appropriately representative conditions estimate from a large portion of the therapy course.

Accordingly, the patient Relationship Inventory estimate of therapist conditions provided the most theoretically compatible test of Hypothesis I, since it represented the patient's perception of the overall therapeutic climate. The judges' ratings stood next in importance insofar as they too represented a type of recipient viewpoint. This was so since their instructions had been to focus on the patient's frame of reference. The findings reported in Chapter 8 suggested that the judges' frame of reference was indeed close to that of the patient. However, since judges' ratings were based on discrete, brief therapy segments, it was in keeping with the theoretical stress placed on the therapist's general attitudes to use averages of ratings of many segments for judges' conditions estimates.

In the following analyses, therefore, we have placed greatest weight on the patient Relationship Inventory measures of conditions, considering judges' average ratings ($\bar{X}_{15}$ and $\bar{X}_{TOT}$) next in theoretical importance. Therapist Relationship Inventory perceptions, we felt, provided the least central test of the predicted relationship between therapist conditions and patient process movement. The considerable attention paid to ratings for other analyses was a function of the fact that the most comprehensive coverage of the therapy course was provided by this data.

Separate vs. Combined Conditions

The second theoretical ambiguity revolved around the question: Did Hypothesis I require that each of the conditions dimensions relate separately to patient process movement, or was it more important to consider all three conditions factors in concert? In Chapter 1 Rogers explicitly stated that both approaches were necessary for the test of Hypothesis I: "The hypothesis states that a higher degree of these conditions—singly or in combination—will be antecedent to a higher degree of those client behaviors characteristic of movement in therapy." In the subsequent analyses, therefore, we have tested the relationship of conditions, considered singly as well as in combination, with patient process change. The separate conditions approach would seem to provide a more stringent test of the hypothesis, whereas the use of a combined index was perhaps more in keeping with the theoretical formulation of these variables.

Combining Therapist Conditions

Rogers postulated that the three conditions factors may operate jointly to influence patient process movement, but did not specify any hierarchy of procedures for weighting and/or combining these conditions into a single overall conditions estimate. Therefore, it was necessary to consider the implications of alternative procedures for combining conditions and to establish an a priori hierarchy among them. In Chapter 8 we described the most parsimonious method of combining conditions, a simple averaging of the three conditions variables. This approach, treating each condition with equal weight, provided the most literal test of the joint importance of the three therapist attitudes in relation to process movement. Other approaches, however, were also compatible with the underlying theory.[1] Of the three conditions, congruence seemed to play an especially central role since, as pointed out in Chapter 6, accurate empathy and unconditional positive regard cannot be meaningful in a relationship unless they are real. Thus, therapist congruence or genuineness seemed to function as a precondition, being

---

1. For an exploratory study the model of choice here would be multiple regression, yielding separate beta weight coefficients for the three conditions. This approach was not feasible for the present sample, since the small number of therapy patients would have made the obtained beta coefficients extremely unreliable and impossible to interpret.

prerequisite for the effective communication of accurate empathy and unconditional positive regard. Therapists high both in congruence and the remaining two conditions would then be expected to effect the highest levels of patient process movement. Those relationships that were either low in all conditions, or high in congruence and low in the remaining two conditions, would not show comparable process movement.

Secondly, the theoretical statement held conditions to be "necessary and sufficient" for patient process change. One implication of this position was that an inordinately low level of any one of the three conditions would cancel out or minimize the power of the others. One way to test this proposition was to consider the lowest (basal) level obtained by a therapist for any given condition as being especially critical in relation to process movement. Analyses based on the basal conditions score might then yield more conceptually meaningful tests of Hypothesis I than analyses based on either the average or altitude (highest level obtained) estimates of conditions.

Finally, the range or variability of conditions for a particular therapist over the therapeutic interaction might be an important factor interacting with the level of conditions obtained in the relationship. The therapist who manifested a *consistently* high level of conditions over the entire interaction would be more effective than a therapist with a similarly high average conditions level who showed greater variability in his attitudes.

Thus, more than one method might be necessary to provide a complete or definitive test of Hypothesis I. The most precise test of this hypothesis, using combined conditions scores, depended on a simple average of the three factors, equally weighted. The more complex combinations—treating congruence as a precondition, considering the basal conditions level, or using a complex estimate of the level and variability of conditions over the therapy encounter—were theoretically relevant, but did not constitute the most central tests of the hypothesis. Each focused on but one aspect of the complex theoretical formulation for conditions, and highlighted certain special relationships among them.

Defining Process Movement

Hypothesis I suggested that various facets of patient process behavior in therapy as well as changes in patient personality might be meaningfully related to the level of therapist conditions. The focus of the present chapter is on one process construct, that of experiencing. This construct, theoretically and operationally described in Chapters 7 and 8, relates to a patient's manner of self-experiencing and mode of handling and examining his feelings in the therapy hour.

While the primary focus of Hypothesis I was on process movement, there was also an implicitly predicted relationship between conditions and the general process level throughout the therapy course. Thus, while the major test of this hypothesis required consideration of patient experiencing change scores, other analyses based on overall or momentary estimates of process level would play a role, even though a secondary one.

Hypothesis V was related to Hypothesis I, and predicted a relationship between therapist conditions and change in patient personality. This conception, implying that the conditions-outcome association is mediated for the patient by factors of the therapy process itself, could be tested by examining the relationship between conditions and change scores for objective personality test behavior. Analyses relevant to this issue are considered in Chapter 11.

Conditions and Process Movement

Three sets of patient in-therapy EXP data were used as the basis for the central analyses of this section. These different operational forms were necessary inasmuch as the theoretical formulation did not specify the exact time points where significant process movement occurs in therapy. The traditional approach had been to use very early and very late interviews for this assessment of change, with the prediction that late therapy hours would evince significantly higher levels of process than early therapy hours.

We used this early-late approach for the EXP data since it was traditional and represented the most straightforward test of Hypothesis I. However, to make up for the fact that this kind of analysis ignored much of the raw data of the therapy interaction, we also looked at more detailed process data between these extreme interview points. That is, since no therapy case had a duration of less than thirty interviews, we examined EXP ratings for every interview of this large portion of the therapy interaction. Since several therapy cases had much longer durations, we also examined EXP ratings covering the total therapy course for each case.

Conditions with Early-Late EXP Change

Early and late EXP scores were obtained by averaging the EXP ratings for the first and last five interviews sampled in each case. Modal and peak EXP scores were treated separately. The Ebel intraclass

Table 9.1—Ebel intraclass reliabilities of the modal and peak EXP ratings for therapy interviews 2–6, and last five therapy interviews, for the fourteen experimental patients

EXP ratings	No. of judges	No. of segments rated	r_{ll}	r_{kk}
INTERVIEWS 2–6				
Modal	4	68	.33	.66
Peak	4	68	.46	.77
LAST FIVE INTERVIEWS				
Modal	4	69	.44	.76
Peak	4	69	.52	.82

reliabilities of ratings for the segments used to obtain these scores are presented in Table 9.1. It was apparent that the reliabilities of this subsample of ratings were comparable to the overall reliability of the modal and peak ratings reported in Table 8.1.

Several factors were relevant to our evaluation of the power of these early and late EXP scores to reflect change. The correlation of the early and late scores, for both modes and peaks, was quite high (.73 and .79 respectively), and the magnitude of EXP change for the fourteen therapy patients as a group was quite small (changes for modal ratings ranged from −.45 to +.55 with a mean of +.11; for peak ratings from −.45 to +.85 with a mean of +.11). These small changes in patient experiencing between the initial and the terminal five sampled therapy interviews indeed were no greater than what one might expect solely as a function of random fluctuations in the judges' ratings, a suggestion supported by an estimate of the reliability of the EXP change scores obtained by means of Mosier's formula (Guilford, 1954). The zero reliability values obtained (.02 and .00 for modes and peaks respectively) indicated very strongly that this extremely parsimonious method of assessing EXP change could not provide data of sufficient reliability to test Hypothesis I fairly or adequately. Therefore, the table of correlations between the conditions measures and early-late EXP change has not been presented or discussed.

It is interesting to speculate as to why the early and late therapy interviews did not reflect process movement. At the very end of therapy one can not reasonably expect the patient to reach his highest level of self-experiencing since he is more likely to be focusing on the termination phenomenon itself. Similarly, there is no reason to expect that the patient will always manifest a very low level of experiencing in initial interviews when he may be devoting considerable time to a detailed account of his problems and past experiences. Indeed it seems most likely that this variable of patient process fluctuates considerably over therapy as the patient focuses on a given problem area, resolves it, and takes up new issues. The EXP level may drop in periods of high threat and defensiveness, and rise sharply when a specific issue approaches resolution. As the relationship approaches termination a high level of experiencing may be unlikely, and in some respects impossible, as the focus shifts to a consideration of the patient's environmental situation, to consolidation of new defensive modes, or to a general recapitulation of the issues covered in therapy. To test this speculation, data was required that would give more comprehensive coverage of the trend of patient experiencing and that would reflect meaningful change for this dimension.

Conditions with EXP Trend in the Total Therapy Course

Our next step was the measuring of patient process or experiencing over the total course of therapy. With this more comprehensive data we were able not only to test that aspect of Hypothesis I predicting a relationship between conditions and process movement, but also to consider the suggested relationship between conditions and overall process level, as well as to explore the alternative possibility of a relationship between conditions and nonlinear process change. While Hypothesis I implied that the level of conditions was related to a positive linear trend in process, the relationship might prove to be more complex so that the trend of process change might not be consistently linear over the course of therapy.

In order to consider these relationships a series of Alexander-Grant trend analyses of variance (Grant, 1956; Edwards, 1962) were applied to EXP data representing the average level of EXP attained by each patient in each third of the total course of therapy. In these analyses, scores for the various conditions measures were used as independent variables—that is, they provided the basis on which we divided the fourteen experimental patients into high and low conditions groups.

Conditions had been defined and measured in many different ways in this study (see Chapter 8). Taking each rated conditions scale, each patient and therapist RI subscale, and only the most straightforward methods of combining those measures, we had a total of seventeen different (though not independent) conditions scores as a basis for dichotomizing patients into high and low conditions groups. In making the following analyses, we used each of these seventeen scores as a basis for dichotomization. In each case the high group consisted of patients whose conditions level was above the group median, the low group of those below the group median. The EXP modal and peak scores were treated separately. This series of analyses, in which the conditions criterion changed but the EXP scores remained the same, yielded information concerning the power of various conditions factors to predict differential trends or process levels over the course of therapy.

The Alexander-Grant trend analyses of variance for the seventeen dichotomies for patient EXP over the thirds of the total therapy interaction are summarized in Table 9.2.

First consider the Groups × Trials *interactions* from the analyses of variance for each of the conditions dichotomies, and the differential trend components for high and low conditions groups. Hypothesis I

Table 9.2—Significant *F*-ratios for the 2 × 3 Alexander-Grant trend analyses of variance over the thirds of the total therapy interviews, for seventeen conditions dichotomies (high vs. low), for the peak and modal EXP ratings (only *p* values ≤ .10 or smaller are listed)

Conditions dichotomies	Groups effect	Trials effect	G × T inter- action	Trials trend components		G × T trend components	
				Lin	Quad	Lin[a]	Quad
PEAK EXP RATINGS							
Judges ratings							
AE$_{15}$	.01	.10		.10			
AE$_{TOT}$	.05	.10		.10			
UPR B$_{TOT}$		.10		.10			.10
CONG$_{15}$		.10		.10			
CONG$_{TOT}$		.05		.10			.05
COMB$_{15}$		.10		.10			
COMB$_{TOT}$		.05	.10	.10	.10		.05
Patient RI							
Regard		.10		.10			
Empathy		.05	.10		.10		.05
Congruence	.05	.10		.10			
Unconditionality	.10						
Total score	.05	.10		.10			
Therapist RI							
Regard		.10					
Empathy		.10					
Congruence		.05					.05
Unconditionality		.10					
Total score		.05					.05

[a] No significant results.

Table 9.2, continued

	MODAL EXP RATINGS		
Judges ratings			
AE$_{15}$	.05		
AE$_{TOT}$	.10		
UPR B$_{TOT}$			
CONG$_{15}$			
CONG$_{TOT}$			
COMB$_{15}$			
COMB$_{TOT}$			
Patient RI			
Regard			
Empathy		.01	.10
Congruence	.05		
Unconditionality	.10		
Total score	.05		
Therapist RI			
Regard			
Empathy			
Congruence			
Unconditionality			
Total score			

predicted a significant Groups × Trials interaction, with significantly greater linear slope for the high group. It is apparent from Table 9.2 that none of the Groups × Trials interactions reached an acceptable level of significance. Thus, whether modal or peak EXP ratings were considered, and regardless of the specific way in which conditions were defined, there was no differential movement or change in EXP as a function of the level of therapist conditions. While several interactions approached significance, none reached significance. Although five of the conditions dichotomies in Table 9.2 showed significant quadratic (U-shaped) components for the Groups × Trials interaction, the differential trends were inconsistent. In some cases the high conditions group showed a significantly greater quadratic slope; in others it was the low conditions group. Since the differential trends were inconsistent, it seems unlikely they represented meaningful differences for this set of data. In short, the level of therapist conditions did not predict any change or fluctuation in patient process when this factor was estimated from thirds of the total therapy course.

In the previous subsection we observed that the hypothesis regarding process movement could not be tested on EXP data drawn from early and late five-interview blocks because no reliable movement occurred for the patient group as a whole. This question is similarly essential here. It is difficult to evaluate the importance of the failure of the

Groups × Trials interaction to reach significance without further assessment of the sensitivity of the process data to reliable process changes. Consideration of the Trials effect and corresponding trend components sheds light on this question. Table 9.2 shows that none of the Trials effects for modal EXP were significant, and that neither the linear nor quadratic components of the modal EXP scores approached significance. Thus, in the case of modes there was no discernible EXP change occurring with any consistency across the patient group when EXP was averaged over thirds of the therapy course for each patient.

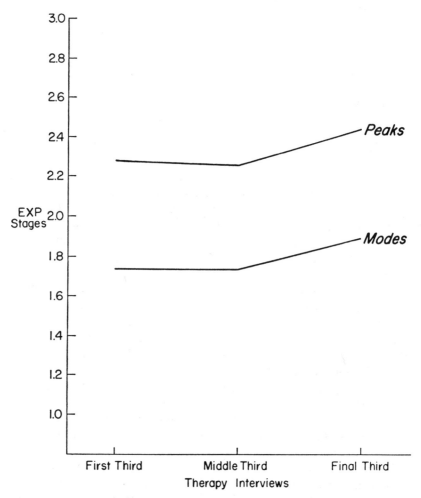

Figure 9.1—Trend of EXP modal and peak ratings for the fourteen therapy patients over the three thirds of the total rated therapy interviews.

Peak ratings of EXP did reflect changes in patient process as a function of time in therapy. Though the exact probability level varied depending on the conditions dichotomy used, it is generally apparent that the Trials effect for peak EXP ratings of successive thirds of therapy was significant. If we inspect Figure 9.1 presenting the curve for EXP peaks over the first, middle, and final thirds of therapy we see that while the level of EXP remained practically constant during the first and second thirds, it rose during the final third of therapy. The slope of this curve tended to be linear—the linear Trials component was significant at the .10 level. This, in conjunction with the significant Trials effect, suggested that the peak level of EXP did in fact change over the course of therapy, and that the direction of this change tended to be a positive linear function of time.

If we turn to a consideration of the Groups effect for the various conditions dichotomies in Table 9.2 we see that there was a significant relationship between the overall *level* of patient process in the course of therapy and certain of the conditions offered by the therapist in the relationship. Patients whose therapists were judged by raters to show a high level of accurate empathy demonstrated a generally higher level of experiencing over the entire course of therapy. This relationship held whether the conditions estimate was drawn from the initial interviews (AE_{15}) or from the total therapy course (AE_{TOT}). In addition, two aspects of the patient Relationship Inventory perceptions were related to overall process level. Those patients who saw their therapists as having a high level of congruence (C) or a high level of overall conditions (T), showed higher levels of experiencing in therapy. These differential EXP level effects are shown in Figures 9.2 to 9.4. These relationships were difficult to interpret in the absence of an association between conditions and process movement. Their interpretation will be considered more fully in the subsequent section when more detailed tests for the degree of relationship between conditions and experiencing levels are presented.

Conditions with EXP Trend for the First Thirty Interviews

The preceding analyses of the trend of patient experiencing over the three thirds of the therapy course did not substantiate Hypothesis I, although the peak EXP scores showed significant process change (significantly linear in slope) for the therapy group as a whole. Now we turn to a still more detailed test of Hypothesis I based on EXP ratings from each of the second to the thirtieth interviews.

Six EXP means were calculated for each patient across interviews 2–30: means of interviews 2–5 ($\bar{X}_1$), 6–10 ($\bar{X}_2$), 11–15 ($\bar{X}_3$), 16–20 ($\bar{X}_4$), 21–25 ($\bar{X}_5$), and 26–30 ($\bar{X}_6$). These values for each patient

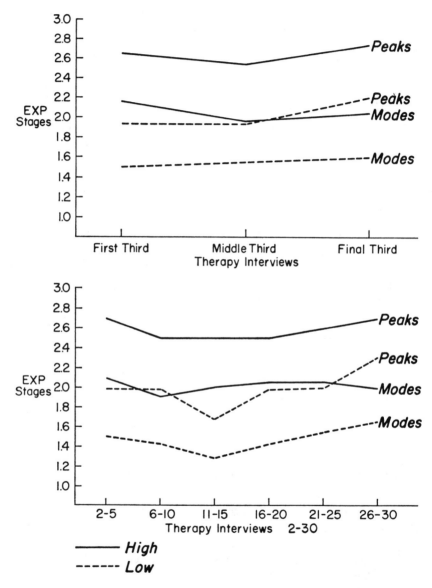

Figure 9.2—Trend of EXP modal and peak ratings for the high and low AE_{15} groups over the three thirds of the total rated therapy interviews, and over therapy interviews 2–30, divided into six interview blocks.

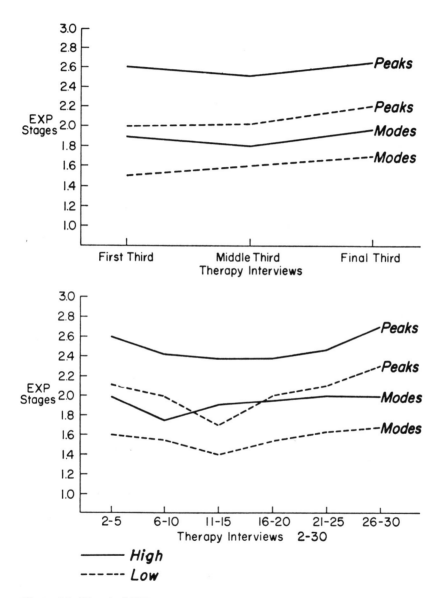

Figure 9.3—Trend of EXP modal and peak ratings for the high and low AE_{TOT} groups over the three thirds of the total rated therapy interviews, and over therapy interviews 2–30, divided into six interview blocks.

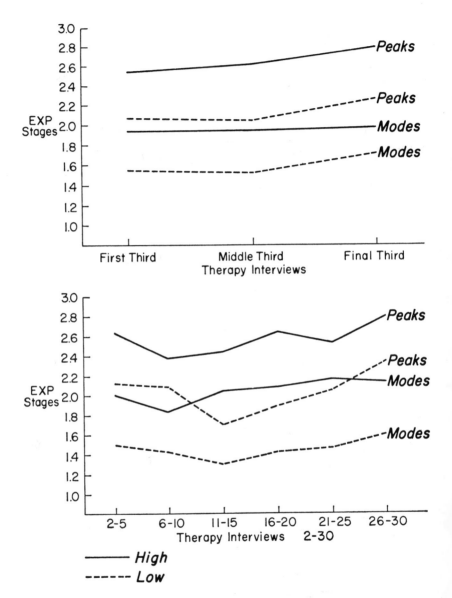

Figure 9.4—Trend of EXP modal and peak ratings for the high and low Pt-RI-C groups (and Pt-RI-T—dichotomies are identical), over the three thirds of the total rated therapy interviews, and over therapy interviews 2–30, divided into six interview blocks.

were then used in a series of Alexander-Grant trend analyses of variance employing the same conditions dichotomies as the preceding section. The results of these 2×6 trend analyses of variance, for the modal and peak EXP ratings, are summarized in Table 9.3.

Again, none of the Groups $\times$ Trials interactions or corresponding trend components was significant for either modal or peak ratings. Therefore, there was no support for the major aspect of Hypothesis I calling for a relationship between the level of therapeutic conditions and linear process movement.

However, when we consider the patient group as a whole, we find that process change did occur. The Trials effect in Table 9.3 was consistently significant for peaks ($p \leqq .01$) and tended toward significance for modes ($p \leqq .10$). This time, it was the quadratic (U-shaped)

Table 9.3—Significant F-ratios for the 2×6 Alexander-Grant trend analyses of variance over therapy interviews 2–30, for seventeen conditions dichotomies (high vs. low), for the peak and modal EXP ratings (only p values $\leq .10$ or smaller are listed)

Conditions dichotomies	Groups effect	Trials effect	G × T inter- action[a]	Trials trend components		G × T trend components	
				Lin	Quad	Lin[a]	Quad[a]
PEAK EXP RATINGS							
Judges ratings							
AE_{15}	.005	.01			.01		
AE_{TOT}	.05	.01			.05		
UPR B_{TOT}		.01			.05		
$CONG_{15}$		.01			.05		
$CONG_{TOT}$		.05			.05		
$COMB_{15}$		.01			.05		
$COMB_{TOT}$		.01			.05		
		.01		.10	.05		
Patient RI							
Regard		.01		.10	.05		
Empathy		.05			.05		
Congruence	.05	.005		.10	.05		
Unconditionality	.10	.05			.05		
Total score	.05	.005		.10	.05		
Therapist RI							
Regard		.01			.05		
Empathy		.05			.05		
Congruence		.01			.05		
Unconditionality		.05			.05		
Total score		.01			.05		

[a] No significant results.

Table 9.3 continued on page 202

Table 9.3, *continued*

	MODAL EXP RATINGS	
Judges ratings		
AE$_{15}$	.005	.10
AE$_{TOT}$	.10	.10
UPR B$_{TOT}$		.10
CONG$_{15}$		.10
CONG$_{TOT}$		.10
COMB$_{15}$		.10
COMB$_{TOT}$		.10
Patient RI		
Regard		
Empathy		
Congruence	.05	
Unconditionality	.05	
Total score	.05	
Therapist RI		
Regard		.10
Empathy		.10
Congruence		.10
Unconditionality		.10
Total score		.10

component, not the linear, that was significant. Figure 9.5 illustrates this marked difference in the peak EXP curve for the total patient sample in interviews 2–30, as compared with that for the total therapy course (see Figure 9.1). Here it is clear that while there was no overall initial-to-thirtieth-interview EXP increase, there was a discernible drop in EXP to the fifteenth interview, with a significant recovery by the thirtieth interview.

Thus, while the general trend of peak EXP for thirds of the total therapy course was linear over time, that is, the terminal experiencing level was greater than that found initially or at the midpoint, the trend of experiencing over 2–30 was not. Here, in the initial portion of therapy, we found a U-shaped curve of process, in which the level of experiencing dropped at the fifteenth interview point only to rise gradually again by the thirtieth interview. Taken together, these curves suggested that the general trend of patient experiencing over the course of therapy was complex. Apparently the patient's initial process level was not his lowest. Experiencing tended to drop off rather sharply during the initial portion of therapy before gradually rising to a terminal level that was slightly above that shown initially.

This type of fluctuation seems clinically meaningful. The most straightforward interpretation may be that the patient does not show his lowest level of experiencing initially since he is engaged in self-description, thereby exercising some selective control over the major focus and content of his communication. It is only when therapy is underway that the experiencing level drops, perhaps as the result of his defensive reaction to implicit or explicit pressures for the exploration of painful problem areas, or to the growing intimacy of the patient-therapist relationship. The slow increase in experiencing that follows this defensive phase may then represent the patient's slow and painful progress in the process of self-exploration as the relationship becomes more stable.

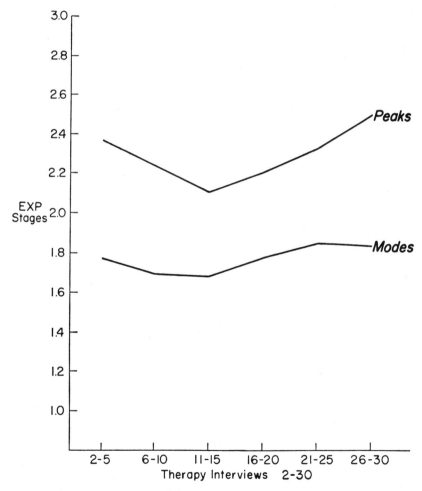

Figure 9.5—Trend of EXP modal and peak ratings for the fourteen therapy patients over therapy interviews 2–30, divided into six interview blocks.

Finally, the Groups effects reported in Table 9.3 show once again that certain of the therapeutic conditions were related to the overall level of process. As with analyses for the total therapy course, it was rated accurate empathy (AE_{15} and AE_{TOT}) and the patient's RI perceptions of therapist congruence (C) and total conditions levels (T) that predicted the level of process over the thirty-interview span. Figures 9.2 to 9.4 present these differential Groups effects. In addition, the perceived level of therapist unconditionality (U) was also related to the level of process attained in the first thirty interviews. Thus the more empathic the therapist was judged to be by judges, and the more congruent, unconditional, and generally therapeutic he was perceived to be by his patient, the higher was the overall level of EXP manifested in therapy interviews 2–30.

Alternative Methods of Defining Therapist Conditions

In light of the results reported in the preceding section it became increasingly important to insure that the aspect of Hypothesis I dealing with process change was fairly and exhaustively tested—by combining therapist conditions in more complex but still theoretically meaningful ways.

In the introduction to this chapter, three theoretically-derived methods of combining and defining therapist conditions were presented. Each method was directed toward one aspect of the basic theoretical model. Each could be useful for testing Hypothesis I in terms of certain special relationships among aspects of the therapist's behavior. In one procedure congruence was to be treated as a prerequisite or precondition, on the assumption that other therapist factors (accurate empathy and unconditional positive regard) are effective only when the therapist is genuine and open in the relationship. A second method would consider only the level of the lowest of the three therapist conditions factors, on the assumption that it is this basal factor that is crucial. A final procedure for combining conditions would consider both the level and variability of each therapist condition, on the assumption that the overall consistency as well as the quality of the therapist's behavior is essential in relation to process movement.

Using *congruence as a precondition,* cases were first dichotomized into high and low congruence groups, and then further subdivided on the basis of the combined level of accurate empathy and unconditional positive regard. For rated conditions three groups were thereby obtained: High CONG and high AE + UPR, high CONG and low AE + UPR, and a final group of low CONG and either high or low AE + UPR. For the Relationship Inventory perceptions, cases were grouped as follows: high C and high R E U; high C and low R E U; and a final group of low C and either high or low R E U. In order to group patients according to the *basal conditions level,* the standard (z) scores for each separate conditions scale were examined for each case, and the lowest value used as the basal score. Cases were then divided into high and low groups on this basis. Thus the high group might contain some cases with the basal value from the AE Scale, others with the basal value

Table 9.4—Significant *F*-ratios for the Alexander-Grant trend analyses of variance over the thirds of the total therapy interviews, for the basal dichotomies (high vs. low), the congruence precondition trichotomies (HH, HL, L), and the level and variability quad-richotomies (HH, HL, LH, LL) (only *p* values $\leq$ .10 or smaller are listed)

Alternative combinations of conditions	Groups effect	Trials effect	G × T inter-action[a]	Trials trend components		G × T trend components	
				Lin	Quad[a]	Lin[a]	Quad
PEAK EXP RATINGS							
Congruence as precondition							
RI		.10		.10			
Rated		.10		.10			.10
Basal conditions level							
RI	.10	.10		.10			
Rated		.10		.10			
Level and variability							
AE	.05	.10		.10			
CONG		.10		.10			
MODAL EXP RATINGS							
Congruence as precondition							
RI							
Rated							
Basal conditions level							
RI	.10						
Rated							
Level and variability							
AE	.10						
CONG							

[a] No significant results.

Table 9.5—Significant *F*-ratios for the Alexander-Grant trend analyses of variance over therapy interviews 2-30, for the basal conditions dichotomies (high vs. low), the congruence precondition trichotomies (HH, HL, L), and the level and variability quadrichotomies (HH, HL, LH, LL) (only *p* values ≤ .10 or smaller are listed)

Alternative combinations of conditions	Groups effect	Trials effect	G × T interaction	Trials trend components Lin[a]	Quad	G × T trend components Lin[a]	Quad[a]
			PEAK EXP RATINGS				
Congruence as precondition							
RI		.01			.05		
Rated	.05				.05		
Basal conditions level							
RI	.10	.01			.05		
Rated		.01			.05		
Level and variability							
AE	.05	.01			.05		
CONG		.05			.05		
		.05					
			MODAL EXP RATINGS				
Congruence as precondition							
RI	.10						
Rated					.10		
Basal conditions level							
RI	.05						
Rated			.05		.10		
Level and variability							
AE	.05						
CONG					.10		

[a] No significant results.

from the CONG Scale, etc. Finally, the *mean and variability* for each case were used to group the patients according to the level and consistency of two rated conditions scales, AE and CONG (UPR ratings were not sufficiently reliable to treat in this fashion). Cases were first divided at the median of the distribution for each scale and further subdivided according to the case variance.

The results of the Alexander-Grant trend analyses of variance of EXP scores for patients grouped according to each of the three methods are presented in Tables 9.4 and 9.5. Separate analyses were done for EXP estimates taken from successive thirds of therapy (for both modes and peaks), and for EXP scores for six-interview blocks from interviews 2–30 (for both modes and peaks). From the summary tables it is clear that Hypothesis I was again not supported. Only one Groups × Trials interaction, that for the basal level of rated conditions, reached an acceptable level of significance, but yielded no clear-cut trend effects. Similarly one Groups × Trials trend component, the quadratic for rated conditions with congruence as a precondition, reached significance; but here the direction of the differential EXP trends was not consistent with the hypothesis.

Significant Groups effects were obtained for rated conditions with congruence as a precondition (peak EXP in the second to thirtieth interviews), for accurate empathy, taking both the level and variability into account, and for the basal conditions score derived from the Relationship Inventory. Generally, however, these findings reflected the same effects emerging in previous analyses of this section when conditions were considered separately. The various Trials effects that were significant reflected the same general EXP trends discussed in the preceding section.

Overview

Three different sets of EXP scores were considered for tests of Hypothesis I. When EXP in the first and last five therapy interviews sampled was examined, change scores proved to be so unreliable that no meaningful test of the hypothesis was possible. Two other EXP measures drawn from successive sixths of therapy interviews 2–30 and from thirds of the total therapy course provided more reliable estimates of process movement, but there was no relationship between this movement and the level of therapeutic conditions. No matter how the conditions factor was defined—whether rated conditions, or conditions as perceived by either patient or therapist, were used as criteria for the formation of high and low conditions dichotomies, or whether theoretically derived methods of combining conditions were employed—there was no significant association between the level of conditions and the amount or trend of patient process movement. Clearly, the major proposition of Hypothesis I, calling for a relationship between conditions level and process movement, did not receive support in this sample of hospitalized schizophrenics.

Reliable process movement was discernible, however, for the schizophrenic group as a whole, although it was limited to peak EXP ratings. The trend of this movement was complex, with peak EXP taking a quadratic or U-shaped form in the initial interviews (2–30), and only becoming more regular over the total therapy course where a general linear function became apparent. Clearly then, the failure of any of the many conditions factors considered to predict differential EXP change was, in the case of the peaks at least, not attributable to the absence of reliable EXP changes in the patient sample as a whole.

In contrast, it was consistently apparent that the level of process (EXP) over therapy was related to several conditions factors. Higher levels of patient experiencing at all points in therapy were associated with high therapist accurate empathy (rated) and with high levels of congruence and overall conditions (as perceived by the patient). Further, the level of unconditionality (as perceived by the patient) was found to relate significantly with the level of EXP, but this relationship was limited to the first thirty therapy interviews. Because these relationships between conditions and process level occurred in the absence of more extended support for Hypothesis I, they cannot be interpreted in this context without more detailed exploration.

Conditions and Patient Process Level

Analyses in the preceding section consistently showed significant Groups effects for some of the conditions measures, indicating a positive relationship between these conditions and the level of patient experiencing manifested throughout the therapy course. It was necessary to examine further the nature of these obtained relationships.

Two approaches were relevant to this purpose. We could investigate the general relationship of conditions and process as they occurred in the overall therapy course or as they occurred at discrete moments in the therapist-patient interaction. These approaches, while answering slightly different questions, were complementary. The overall analyses assessed the relationship of the total therapeutic climate to the average level of patient experiencing manifested over the entire course of therapy. The momentary analyses tapped the immediate relationship between the therapist's behavior in a single four-minute segment of the therapy hour and the patient's concurrent level of experiencing. Thus the more gross procedure, based on overall means, or global perceptions, smoothed out within-case fluctuations of conditions and process, whereas the momentary procedure tapped the relationship between conditions and process at discrete moments.

It would also be meaningful, in understanding the conditions-process relationship, to examine the association between therapist conditions and patient process sampled outside of therapy. Analyses of the relationship of *in-therapy* conditions with patient process in the sampling interviews (which were conducted by one independent examiner) would show whether the conditions-process relationship was limited to the actual therapy interaction, or whether it could be transferred or generalized to an independent setting.

Overall Conditions Level with Overall Process Level

Two time periods were covered in these analyses. Data from interviews 2–15 ($\bar{X}_{15}$) and the initial RI, corresponding roughly to the initial half of therapy, permitted us to focus on the important formative stage of therapy; and data from the entire period of therapy ($\bar{X}_{TOT}$) plus the terminal RI provided a more general picture of the global conditions-process relationship. Table 9.6 presents the Spearman rank-order correlation coefficients for each set of conditions and process scores.

Rated conditions.—The results were quite consistent whether conditions scores from the initial portion ($\bar{X}_{15}$) or from the entire course of therapy ($\bar{X}_{TOT}$) were examined, or whether EXP scores were drawn from therapy or sampling interviews. First, EXP was significantly and positively related to the level of accurate empathy (AE_{15}) attained by the therapist in the *initial portion of therapy*. This relationship held for both EXP modal and peak ratings, and for EXP in the therapy and sampling interviews. The more accurate empathy the therapist manifested in the initial half of therapy, the more likely his patient was to exhibit a high level of experiencing both in the therapy interviews, and in an extra-therapy interview interaction. When therapist congruence ($CONG_{15}$) was correlated with EXP, no significant relationships were found. Since reliable ratings of therapist unconditional positive regard (UPR) were not available for the initial therapy period, its relationship with EXP could not be tested for interviews 2–15. As a consequence the combined conditions score ($COMB_{15}$) for this period was restricted to an average of AE and CONG. This estimate was only moderately related to EXP level. A significant positive relationship with EXP emerged only when the peak EXP behavior in the sampling interviews was tapped. Although this association was obviously influenced by the high AE-EXP relationship, it may be a particularly meaningful one. The purpose of the sampling interview was to provide a setting in which the patient's capacity for experiencing could be assessed independently of a specific therapist-patient relationship. Further, it was the task of the sampling interviewer to provide, in this standard setting, an atmosphere in which the patient could freely discuss any material he desired, in any way that was comfortable for him. Thus, it was encour-

Table 9.6—Spearman rank-order intercorrelations of perceived (RI) and overall rated conditions with overall patient process (EXP) level in the therapy and sampling interviews

Conditions measures	Therapy interviews				Sampling interviews	
	EXP ratings		EXP_{TOT} ratings		EXP_{TOT} ratings	
	Modes	Peaks	Modes	Peaks	Modes	Peaks
Rated conditions ($\bar{X}_{1b}$)						
AE_{1b}	.61*	.76†			.53*	.53*
$CONG_{1b}$	−.07	−.08			.12	.18
$COMB_{1b}$	.34	.35			.16	.52*
						.33
Initial Patient RI						
Regard	.90†	.81†			.38	.33
Empathy	.29	.48			.07	.05
Congruence	.83†	.69*			.62	.52
Unconditionality	.39	.23			.12	−.02
Total score	.79†	.76†			.33	.26
Initial therapist RI						
Regard	−.26	−.28			.00	−.34
Empathy	−.65*	−.64*			−.47	−.70*
Congruence	−.56*	−.50			−.13	−.37
Unconditionality	−.35	−.36			.00	−.26
Total score	−.49	−.47			−.18	−.49
Rated conditions ($\bar{X}_{TOT}$)						
AE_{TOT}			.54*	.73†	.44	.41
UPR B_{TOT}			.08	.20	.42	.48*
$CONG_{TOT}$			−.38	−.13	−.06	−.01
$COMB_{TOT}$			.18	.42	.44	.43
Terminal patient RI						
Regard			.20	.26	.10	.11
Empathy			.19	.38	.06	.09
Congruence			.51*	.71†	.46	.46
Unconditionality			.16	.14	−.08	.06
Total score			.30	.45	.20	.24
Terminal therapist RI						
Regard			−.26	−.26	−.22	−.38
Empathy			−.23	−.22	−.37	−.53*
Congruence			−.04	.01	.06	−.07
Unconditionality			−.13	−.24	−.18	−.34
Total score			−.18	−.22	−.21	−.38

* $p \leq .05$
† $p \leq .01$

aging that the overall level of conditions in therapy was at least associated with the peak EXP level attained when the patient was in a setting designed to tap his maximum spontaneous level of process. On the other hand, the more conservative view of these findings for rated conditions suggests simply that it was the association between the condition of accurate empathy and the level of experiencing that was predominant.

The same general pattern emerged when the association between the rated conditions level for the *total therapy course* and the level of EXP for the total therapy and sampling interviews was examined. Although the degree of this relationship was somewhat lower, therapist accurate empathy (AE_{TOT}) was again significantly and positively related to patient experiencing in therapy. The corresponding coefficients for sampling interview EXP only narrowly missed significance. Rated congruence ($CONG_{TOT}$) was again unrelated to the level of EXP and tended to be associated negatively. Unconditional positive regard (UPR B_{TOT}), representing the average of the reliable UPR ratings from various points in the therapy course for each case, was unrelated to EXP in the therapy interviews, but was associated with sampling interview EXP. While the association of UPR with modal EXP in the sampling interviews was moderate but insignificant, UPR was significantly related to peak EXP in the sampling interviews. Thus, the more warm and acceptant the therapist is judged to be towards his patient, the greater is the likelihood that a high level of experiencing will be manifested by that patient in interaction with a different and standard interviewer. Again it may be meaningful that conditions and peak process proved to be related in a setting where the patient's spontaneous experiencing capacity was tapped. Finally, the combined conditions ($COMB_{TOT}$) estimate for the total therapy course was only moderately related to therapy and sampling interview EXP. In no case were the coefficients significant, but therapy EXP peaks, and in the sampling interviews both modes and peaks, tended to be positively related to the general level of conditions in the total therapy relationship.

In summary, then, the results for the rated conditions showed a consistent positive association between the level of therapist accurate empathy and the level of patient experiencing. This relationship was quite constant for both therapy and sampling interviews, whether the conditions estimate was derived from interviews 2–15 or from the average of the total therapy course. That is, the more the therapist was judged to demonstrate an empathic and accurate understanding of the patient's problems and general frame of reference, the more deeply the patient tended to experience and explore himself. Other rated conditions were not consistently associated with the level of patient process. Therapist unconditional positive regard was associated with the patient's peak EXP level in the sampling interviews, but was unrelated to his in-therapy behavior. Therapist's rated congruence was wholly unrelated to EXP. The moderate relationship of EXP with the combined estimate is most conservatively seen as primarily reflecting the association between AE and EXP. In short, it seems that the therapist's level of accurate empathy was the best predictor of patient experiencing level when ratings of therapist behavior were considered.

Patient RI conditions.—When we turn to the correlations for therapist conditions as perceived by the patient we find that different conditions variables related to the patient's experiencing level. For the *initial* patient Relationship Inventory, regard (R) and congruence (C), as well as the overall conditions score (T), were significantly and positively associated with the level of EXP attained during therapy interviews 2–15 ($\bar{X}_{15}$).[2] Corresponding correlations with EXP in the sampling interviews were consistent, but only approached significance. The other RI subscales, empathy (E) and unconditionality (U), were only moderately and insignificantly associated with patient EXP in therapy, and were not at all related to the patient's sampling interview behavior.

Results for the *terminal* patient Relationship Inventory preceptions were similar, but the magnitude of the relationship was lower. Only the level of therapist congruence (C) or genuineness as perceived by the patient continued to be significantly associated with in-therapy EXP when the total course was considered ($\bar{X}_{TOT}$). Again, rated congruence tended to be associated with the level of patient experiencing in the sampling interviews, but the correlation values fell short of significance.

Thus, the results for conditions as perceived by the patient indicated that the more the therapist was seen as congruent, the deeper was the patient's level of experiencing. This relationship was not so strong for sampling interviews EXP. Other perceived therapist factors (i.e., regard and the overall conditions level) were related only to the level of EXP manifested in the initial portion of therapy. The degree of these relationships dropped for the terminal perceptions and the total EXP scores. As a result, despite the fact that patient perceptions of therapist attitudes remained highly stable over the course of therapy (see Table

2. This finding has recently been corroborated by a study of van der Veen (in press), in which he finds that patient-perceived therapist congruence relates significantly to the rated level on two other process scales—problem expression and degree of relating. Again a therapist attitude is found to be significantly related to patient in-therapy behavior indicative of the process of change.

8.8), the general association of the perceived level of conditions with experiencing dropped off somewhat over the course of therapy, so that only congruence remained associated with this variable of patient process.

Therapist RI conditions.—The correlations of various measures of patient EXP with conditions as perceived by therapists were strikingly dissimilar from those reported above. As Table 9.6 shows, therapists' evaluations of the level of conditions offered the patient were *negatively* related to patient process. This inverse relationship with EXP was fairly consistent in therapy interviews 2–15, in the total therapy course, and in the sampling interviews. It was particularly striking for EXP peaks, and quite consistent for all RI subscales, significantly so in the case of empathy. That is, the more the therapist viewed himself as showing empathic understanding (E) of the patient (and initially as manifesting a high level of genuineness [C]), the lower was the level of experiencing shown by the patient in the therapy and sampling interviews. The magnitude of this negative correlation between EXP and empathy decline somewhat at the terminal RI data point.

These findings are not startling if we recall that therapist perceptions of conditions were inversely related to patient and objective judges' perceptions (see Chapter 8). Indeed it now becomes clear that the patient-judge view of the therapy climate predicted patient experiencing, whereas the therapist's discrepant perception of the relationship was generally unrelated or inversely related to patient experiencing.

In summary, the following picture emerged for the relationship of the overall level of rated and perceived conditions with the overall level of patient experiencing in therapy and sampling interviews. For rated conditions, it was primarily therapist accurate empathy (AE) that was significantly and positively related to patient EXP. This association was especially strong in the initial portion of therapy, held over the total course of therapy, and extended to the patient's behavior in an independent interview setting. Neither unconditional positive regard (UPR) nor congruence (CONG) related to EXP level, although the latter condition tended to show an inverse relationship with EXP. For conditions as perceived by patients, only congruence (C) was consistently and positively related to EXP level. This relationship was more striking in the therapy than in the sampling interviews. While the perceived level of regard (R) and the overall therapist attitudes (T) were related to EXP initially, this relationship tended to decline over therapy. Finally, therapist self-rated conditions were inversely related to patient process, particularly in the case of the therapist's assessment of the level of empathic understanding (E) he offered his patient.

Momentary Relationship of Conditions with Process

The preceding analyses have dealt with the association between therapist conditions and patient process when these variables were averaged over the therapy interaction. It is also interesting to assess the degree of relationship between these variables at discrete moments in the therapy interaction.

Rated conditions.—In order to obtain an estimate of the relationship of rated conditions and EXP as they covaried in each therapy hour, the following procedure was used. AE, UPR A, and CONG were each correlated with the level of EXP in each of interviews 2–15, and the coefficients across the interview series were averaged for each scale. For example, fourteen Pearson coefficients were obtained (the first therapy interview was not recorded) for the correlation of AE and EXP modes, one for each of interviews 2–15. These coefficients were then transformed into z scores and averaged, and the mean z value was transformed back to a single r value, representing the average of the conditions-process correlations of each of interviews 2–15. Table 9.7 contains these average r values for each of the three conditions scales, representing an estimate of the momentary relationship of conditions with process.

Table 9.7—Momentary relationship between rated conditions and process (EXP) for therapy interviews 2–15

Rated conditions	EXP ratings	
	Modes	Peaks
AE	.38†	.45†
UPR A	−.08	.02
CONG	−.06	−.12

†$p \leq .01$

The rated level of therapist accurate empathy (AE) was significantly ($p \leq .01$) and positively correlated with level of patient experiencing in the therapy interaction. On the other hand, congruence and unconditional positive regard were unrelated to level of experiencing. Thus, the picture was the same whether rated estimates of conditions and process were based on single interviews or averaged over the entire course of therapy—only accurate empathy was consistently and positively associated with the level of patient experiencing.

Patient RI conditions.—As a way of assessing the momentary relationship of EXP with conditions as perceived by the patient it was necessary to examine EXP scores representing each patient's EXP level at the corresponding Relationship Inventory time points. EXP ratings, averaged from the seven interviews occurring at the time of the initial and terminal RI's, were correlated with their respective RI subscale and total scores (see Table 9.8). The reliability of these particular EXP ratings (see Table 9.9) was comparable to that for the total body of EXP ratings from which they were drawn (see Table 8.1).

Again, the results were similar to those employing averages of the perceived conditions and process variables. Initially the regard (R) and congruence (C) subscales, as well as the overall conditions estimate (T), for the patient RI's were positively and significantly related to the level of patient EXP occurring at the same period in the therapy interaction. Once more the relationship of patient-perceived conditions and process dropped somewhat at the terminal data point, where R, C, and T were only moderately and insignificantly related to EXP. Instead, it was the perceived level of the therapist's empathy (E) that was related to the peak level of EXP obtained in the terminal portion of therapy.

Therapist RI conditions.—Correlations of the therapist RI perceptions, initially and terminally, with the concomitant EXP ratings for the same time periods are recorded in the lower portion of Table 9.8. Again, as for the correlations for overall conditions and process, we see that the

Table 9.8—Momentary Spearman rank-order intercorrelations of initial and terminal Relationship Inventory conditions with EXP level (mean of seven contiguous interview segments) at each RI data point

Relationship Inventory	Initial EXP		Terminal EXP	
	Modes	Peaks	Modes	Peaks
Patient	($N = 8$)		($N = 13$)	
Regard	.67*	.69*	−.26	−.10
Empathy	.43	.43	.42	.58*
Congruence	.73*	.64*	.34	.47
Unconditionality	.17	.12	.15	.22
Total score	.64*	.64*	.15	.33
Therapist	($N = 11$)		($N = 14$)	
Regard	−.33	−.29	.01	−.02
Empathy	−.67*	−.60*	.07	.04
Congruence	−.63*	−.55*	−.07	−.05
Unconditionality	−.34	−.38	−.03	−.04
Total score	−.55*	−.50	.01	−.02

$p \leq .05$

Table 9.9—Ebel intraclass reliabilities for the means of the four judges' momentary EXP ratings (seven concurrent segments for each RI data point for each patient) for the initial and terminal patient and therapist RI data points

RI data points	No. of judges	No. of segments rated	r_{ll}	r_{kk}
PATIENT RI				
Initial (N = 8)				
Modes	4	51	.44	.76
Peaks	4	52	.46	.77
Terminal (N = 11)				
Modes	4	68	.54	.83
Peaks	4	69	.46	.77
THERAPIST RI				
Initial (N = 11)				
Modes	4	70	.53	.82
Peaks	4	71	.54	.82
Terminal (N = 14)				
Modes	4	80	.54	.82
Peaks	4	81	.50	.80

therapist's self-evaluations were negatively associated with the obtained level of patient process. Indeed, initially the levels of empathy (E), congruence (C), as well as the level of the combined conditions (T) which the therapist attributed to the relationship were significantly and inversely related to EXP. At the terminal time point, however, these relationships were no longer significantly negative, but shifted to zero.

Overview

In summary, the pattern of association between different measures of conditions and the level of patient process was roughly similar, whether these relationships were assessed over the whole of therapy, or at more discrete time points. The level of accurate empathy attributed to therapists by *judges* was significantly associated with the level of patient experiencing. The levels of congruence, regard, and combined conditions perceived by *patients* were similarly associated with patient experiencing in the initial phase of therapy. Only perceived congruence continued to relate to experiencing as the relationship neared termination. *Therapists'* assessments of their own performances in therapy were inversely related to the level of patient experiencing initially, but were unrelated to EXP as the relationship neared termination.

These findings were especially meaningful in relation to the pattern of intercorrelations, reported in Chapter 8, between judges', patients', and therapists' viewpoints of the therapy relationship. We saw there that the more the therapist viewed himself as offering a high level of conditions in the relationship, the more his patient, and objective judges, agreed in their view of him as manifesting relatively low levels of conditions. In this chapter, where we have been considering the association of conditions with process variables, we have found that the therapist's self-perceptions were negatively related to the level of experiencing manifested by the patient in therapy and sampling interviews. In contrast, both patient and judge evaluations of the therapy climate were positively associated with patient EXP. Although judges and patients seemed to stress different conditions factors (judges, AE; patients, C) in relation to patient process, these differential perceptions were in general accord. That is, the more positively the therapist was viewed by patient and judge in the relationship, the more likely his patient was to show a high level of experiencing and self-exploration throughout the course of therapy. Thus, of the discrepant viewpoints of the therapy relationship, it was the patient-judge assessments that predicted the level of patient process attained both over the course of therapy and in an independent interview setting.

The Causality Issue

In the foregoing discussion we have sidestepped the issue of the implied causal relationship between therapist conditions and patient process. Such a causal association between therapist attitudes and patient behavior was suggested in Hypothesis I. The design of this study and the procedures of analysis, however, did not permit a systematic test of this proposition. Therapist conditions were not controlled or applied systematically. Therapists were not required to maintain or attain a given set over the course of therapy. Patients and therapists were paired randomly without consideration of initial conditions and process levels. Hence analyses of the conditions-process relationship were essentially correlational, and therefore were not amenable to interpretations regarding the direction of any obtained relationship. Even when the level of conditions was made an independent variable, to be used as a basis for conditions dichotomies in the analyses of variance in this chapter, this constituted an *ex post facto* use of conditions and did not reflect a systematic manipulation of these factors. Hence, it is essential to stress that the major analyses of this study can only be interpreted in terms of the sheer level of relationship between conditions and process. No unequivocal conclusions regarding the causal direction of the relationship can be tested.

Conclusions

The significant findings emerging from the analyses reported in this chapter were that certain therapist conditions factors, particularly rated accurate empathy and patient-perceived congruence and total conditions, were associated with the *level* of process shown uniformly by patients over the total course of therapy and sampling interviews. Despite the fact that reliable process *movement* was found in the sample as a whole for peak EXP ratings, the predicted relationship between therapist conditions and this process movement did not emerge.

Thus, it is clear that we failed to find support for the major proposition of Hypothesis I—that there would be a relationship between conditions and process movement. In the context of this failure, it was difficult to interpret the positive association between conditions and process levels as supporting that aspect of the hypothesis which specifies such a general relationship. Certain issues had to be resolved before these latter findings could be viewed as theoretically supportive. First, it was important to consider the possibility that other characteristics of high EXP patients might account for the high conditions obtained from their therapists, or that other therapist variables were more basic than conditions. It was essential to explore the possibility that the availability of the full interaction (both patient and therapist verbalizations) to the independent groups of conditions and process judges might have contributed to the conditions-process relationships observed. Finally, it was important to demonstrate the therapeutic importance or validity of the conditions-process relationship by exploring its ties to variables of therapy outcome. Since these issues will be considered in Chapter 11, extensive interpretation of the conditions-process level relationships reported in this chapter will be deferred until all the material is available for our consideration.

We also had no sound basis, at this time, for weighing the *implications* of our failure to find any relationship between conditions and process movement. Interpretive possibilities ranged from issues having to do with the validity of the conditions scales, to the very real obstacle raised by the modest level of process improvement observed generally in this small sample of extremely withdrawn patients. These issues made it difficult to consider the nonsupportive findings reported in this chapter as contradictory to the hypothesis, although at the same time they underscored the need for greater specificity in the theoretical statement. These interpretive difficulties will be deferred until Chapter 12 when all the data of this study will be available.

References

BARRETT-LENNARD, G. T. Dimensions of perceived therapist response related to therapeutic change. Unpublished Ph.D. dissertation, University of Chicago, 1959.

BARRETT-LENNARD, G. T. Dimensions of therapist response as causal factors in therapeutic change. *Psychol. Monogr. 76,* No. 43 (Whole No. 562), 1962.

EDWARDS, ALLEN L. *Experimental Design in Psychological Research.* New York: Holt, Rinehart & Winston, 1962, chapter XIV.

GRANT, D. A. Analysis-of-variance tests in the analysis and comparison of curves. *Psychol. Bull. 53:*141–154, 1956.

GUILFORD, J. P. *Psychometric Methods.* 2d edition. New York: McGraw-Hill, 1954, p. 395.

VAN DER VEEN, F. Basic elements in the process of psychotherapy: a research study. *J. consult. clin. Psychol.* In press.

10. Process Movement in Therapy and Sampling Interviews

Donald J. Kiesler, Philippa L. Mathieu, Marjorie H. Klein

One purpose of this chapter is to present evidence bearing on the relationship between process movement and therapeutic outcome (Hypothesis V), and the applicability of this relationship to different diagnostic groups (Hypothesis II). The more general focus, however, will be on our exploration of trends of process in the therapy course and on an assessment of the general validity and utility of the process conception and related measurement techniques in describing a range of events in the therapy interaction.

Let us consider first the problems involved in defining and measuring process movement and the general predictions for process factors that can be derived from the basic theoretical formulation. The overall process construct and the substrands of process basic to the therapeutic interaction have been described in Chapters 1 and 7. Conceptualized in terms of the patient's in-therapy behavior and attitudes, and covering various aspects of patient functioning in the therapy interaction (e.g., relationship with others, manner of self-experiencing, mode of problem expression), each strand of the general dimension is considered to constitute a continuum of personality change and growth. Indeed, the process of therapy itself can be defined and described in terms of the patient's progress or movement along these various dimensions. Theoretically, in successful therapy the patient moves to progressively higher process levels over time, so that he becomes increasingly able to engage in therapeutically productive self-experiencing, self-exploration, etc. In less favorable therapy the patient may show only minimal process movement, or manifest no discernible departure from a low process level throughout the therapy course, or may even backslide in process over time. In line with this formulation, therefore, one might predict a positive linear trend in process over the course of therapy generally, and certainly a marked positive linear trend for more productive cases. One might also extrapolate to the individual therapy interview, predicting a slightly higher process level for the end of the traditional fifty-minute hour.

It is important, however, to consider several possible qualifications to this general prediction of positive linear process movement in therapy.

First, there may be points within the course of therapy where process movement becomes irregular, or where backsliding, sudden spurts, or periods of relatively uneven progress may appear. While these irregularities may often be highly idiosyncratic, they may also occur with sufficient consistency to recommend qualification of the theoretically linear process function. Second, it is possible that linear process movement may be characteristic of therapy that is markedly successful, not only by theoretical standards (which in this instance are circular) but also by independent, external criteria. That is, the validity and utility of Rogers' process conception is dependent in part upon its meaningful linkage to other more traditional and general conceptions of therapeutic behavior and outcome.

An implicit, and perhaps the most far-reaching, assumption underlying Hypothesis II is that therapy can be conceived as a dynamic process, with a lawful progression that is independent of the particular diagnosis or problem area presented by the patient. The process conception is assumed to be relevant for therapy with all patient types, despite the presence of minor group or individual variations in process that may occur at specific points in therapy. Thus, valid or successful therapy will be characterized by movement along the same dimensions or strands of process, regardless of whether the patient is schizophrenic,[1] psychoneurotic, or normal.

This latter formulation can be explored in various ways. In this study we elected, not to compare the predictive power or appropriateness of the Rogerian process conception with other conceptualizations of therapy, but to delineate the lawful operation of this theoretical process variable in a variety of therapy cases. Simply stated, it was our intent to show that whatever type of theoretically meaningful process movement is generally characteristic of therapy (or successful therapy), will be true regardless of the specific diagnostic designation of the patient. Some process movement, in short, should be discernible for therapy with any diagnostic group—or at least for successful therapy, regardless of specific patient type.

There is, however, no theoretical requirement that this movement take place within the same range of the process dimension for all groups, or that all patient groups show an equal amount or rate of improvement. That is, all patients need not initiate therapy at the same process

1. Since it is highly probable that our schizophrenic sample did *not* represent the endpoints of the acute-chronic continuum but was, rather, a quite homogeneous sample from the mid-range of this continuum (see Chapters 2, 3, and 12), the acute-chronic differentiation of schizophrenics stated in the hypothesis has been disregarded.

level, nor must they terminate similarly, change a specific amount, or even reach or surpass any fixed point on the general continuum. Indeed, it is quite consistent with the nature of the process conception itself, insofar as it constitutes a continuum of mental health, that different diagnostic groups may at least *initiate* therapy at different process levels. Normal, well-adjusted patients, if sufficiently motivated, should be capable of higher initial process levels than psychoneurotics. Schizophrenics may show the lowest level of process initially by virtue of their more profound personality disturbance. Likewise, different rates of change, amounts of change, and terminal points for the various diagnostic groups may similarly reflect differences in the needs and capacities of the patients for change in therapy. Any such variations are theoretically admissible provided that overall positive movement also occurs for all cases or successful cases.

As the scope of this hypothesis goes beyond the schizophrenic sample employed in other sections of this report, this chapter will summarize several independent studies for comparisons of process in different diagnostic groups. Likewise, since the scope of the process conception goes beyond the experiencing construct that serves as the primary process measure for the research presented in other chapters, we will also include results for other process measures. Our primary interest and focus, however, as well as the bulk of elaborative material, will be centered around Experiencing Scale ratings, since this scale is the most widely used and most theoretically general of the various specific process scales in current use.

General Process Trends

Process Within the Therapy Hour

While there is no theoretical requirement for major process movement within the single therapy hour, it is consistent with the process conception to expect some slight process change over the course of any given therapy interview. While intra-interview variations in process need not cover a wide range of the process continuum, minor variations or fluctuations, indicative of shifts in the quality of the patient's involvement and participation in therapeutic process, are quite likely.

Three independent studies, employing slightly different process rating scales and segmenting procedures, have considered this issue of process movement within the therapy hour. Tomlinson and Hart (1962) compared ratings of segments drawn from the first and final thirds of individual therapy hours, taken equally from early and late interviews of ten psychoneurotic counseling center cases. The ratings, made by two judges, were global ratings although they were based on the original Process Scale in which the various factors or strands of process were defined (see Rogers and Rablen, 1958). The interrater reliability of these global ratings was adequate—Pearson r of .65, estimated Ebel intraclass reliability of .79. Contrary to their general expectations, Tomlinson and Hart reported no statistically significant overall change in global process when first and last thirds of the interview hour were compared. Nonsignificant trends, however, suggested that intra-interview process movement was related somewhat to both time (early vs. late interviews) and outcome (successful vs. unsuccessful cases). Using a series of sign tests, holding time and judges as well as outcome and judges constant, the authors reported a greater likelihood of process movement in later interviews ($p \leqq .01$ vs. $p \leqq .08$ for late and early interviews respectively) and in successful cases ($p \leqq .01$ vs. $p \leqq .02$ for successful and unsuccessful cases respectively). That is, for a psychoneurotic sample slight positive intra-hour process change was more likely to occur within later interviews and/or within hours with successful-outcome clients.

A more comprehensive study by Tomlinson (1962) failed to replicate these trends. For this study Tomlinson employed four separate process scales representing four strands of Rogers' global process conception (problem expression, personal constructs, relationship, and experiencing). Four judges made independent ratings on each scale in turn. Segments were drawn from initial and final thirds of both early and late therapy interviews with fourteen schizophrenic and fourteen psychoneurotic cases, each group divided equally with respect to outcome. The interrater reliability of the ratings for all four scales was adequate—average Pearson r of .65, estimated Ebel intraclass reliability of .88. Analyses of the ratings showed no discernible process movement within the therapy hour for any of the four scales examined. Also, intra-interview process change was not associated strongly with either time, diagnosis, or outcome.

In a third and more complex study of intra-interview variations, process trends within the therapy hour were examined in greater detail (Kiesler, Klein, and Mathieu, 1965). Five successive, eight-minute segments were drawn from a therapy hour of eight normal, eight psychoneurotic, and eight schizophrenic cases. Half of the therapy hours sampled for each diagnostic group were taken from the early part of therapy, and half near therapy termination. Four judges made independent ratings of patient EXP, using a revised yet highly similar version of the scale used by Tomlinson. Interrater reliabilities were adequate, and comparable to those obtained by Tomlinson—Ebel intraclass reliability $r_{kk} = .85$ and $.87$, $r_u = .59$ and $.62$, for modal and peak ratings respectively.

Again, analyses of variance showed no consistency in process movement within the therapy hour for all patients—the main effect for Trials

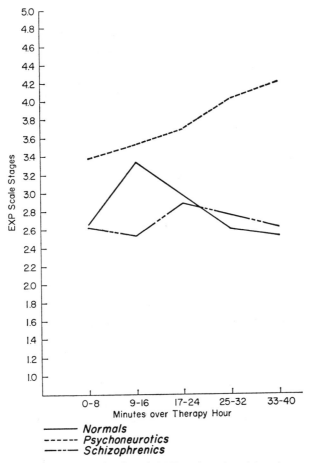

Figure 10.1—Trends of peak EXP ratings for eight-minute segments over the recorded psychotherapy hour for three diagnostic groups ($N = 8$ in each group).

(fifths) was not significant. Further, process change within the therapy hour was unrelated to the location of the hour in the therapy course, that is, early or late. It was only when patients were divided as to diagnostic group that significant differential process trends emerged. The Groups × Trials (fifths) interaction, indicating differential process trends for normals, psychoneurotics, and schizophrenics, was significant for both modal and peak EXP ratings ($p \leqq .01$).

Figure 10.1 presents the EXP curves for the three patient groups, over successive fifths of the therapy hour (data was plotted for peak ratings only, but the modal curves were identical). Here it was apparent that normals, psychoneurotics, and schizophrenics manifested divergent trends over the course of the individual therapy interview. Only the psychoneurotic group exhibited a type of positive linear process movement consistent with theoretical expectations. Schizophrenic and normal patients not only showed little positive process change, but manifested idiosyncratic fluctuations in EXP. That is, normals showed some initial process movement during the hour, but this increase was followed by a gradual decline in EXP so that normal cases terminated the therapy interview at a process level equal to or even below that shown initially. Schizophrenics, on the other hand, showed an immediate decline in EXP, followed by a recovery and stabilizing at the initial process level.

It was interesting to speculate regarding these differential trends. The psychoneurotic process curve (positive linear movement), indicating that this type of patient engaged in an increasingly deeper level of self-experiencing and involvement as the therapy hour progressed, was clearly consistent with theoretical expectation. The normal curve, with its initial peaking and subsequent decline, seemed to indicate a progressive retreat from involvement. The normal interviewee, despite his capacity for positive process change as demonstrated by his initial increase, apparently backslides as the interview progresses, perhaps either from lack of motivation or from his desire to keep his habitual defenses intact. On the other hand, the curve for the schizophrenic group did not suggest a comparable capacity for positive process change over a particular therapy hour. The initial backsliding and recovery of this group may reflect the more immediate defensiveness and retreat of the psychotic patient in the therapy relationship, and illustrate the slow and arduous pace of psychotherapy with such severely withdrawn cases.

In summary, these studies of intra-interview variations in patient process suggest that there is no *general* trend common to all therapy hours even when factors such as early vs. late in therapy, and therapy-outcome are considered.

Process Trends in the Therapy Course

Several studies are relevant to the question of whether some orderly trend of process movement is characteristic of the course of all therapy cases, and to the more general empirical problem of describing meaningful process trends in various patient groups. Findings emerging from these studies comparing process scale ratings in therapy hours spanning the entire therapy course are conflicting, and suggest that positive linear process movement is not a universal phenomenon in therapy. Rather, process seems to be a more complex function of time, diagnosis, and outcome.

Tomlinson and Hart (1962), in their study described above, reported general process improvement for a sample of psychoneurotic cases. Interviews occurring late in therapy were rated significantly higher on Rogers' global Process Scale than interviews occurring early in the course of therapy. Similarly, in our study of fourteen schizophrenic patients, linear process improvement was apparent for Experiencing Scale ratings of segments taken from the entire course of therapy. As we have seen in Chapter 9, when many interviews drawn from successive thirds of the total therapy interaction were in turn averaged, the peak EXP level of these schizophrenic patients was a significant linear function of time (see pp. 193–204 and Figures 9.1 to 9.4). More specifically, the patient's EXP level at the terminal third of therapy was significantly higher than that shown initially or at the therapy midpoint. This movement did not cover a wide range of the experiencing continuum, however, and was not equally apparent for modal EXP ratings.

A third study failed to replicate these general process trends when neurotic and schizophrenic patients were considered together. Tomlinson (1962) reported no general Trials (early-late) effects for analyses of variance of ratings for any of the four process scales considered in his study. More complex interactions did reach significance suggesting that positive process movement may be limited to cases of successful outcome and that process change may be more complex in cases with different levels of disturbance.

Other data from our research with schizophrenics illustrated the complexity of process change and suggested very strongly that studies examining only early and late interviews could not adequately depict the phenomenon. When the second through thirtieth therapy hours for the fourteen schizophrenic cases were divided into six successive blocks of interviews and each block averaged, the curve of experiencing that emerged was clearly nonlinear (see Chapter 9, pp. 204–208, and Figure 9.5). The trend of EXP over interviews 2–30 took a quadratic (U-shaped) rather than a linear form. Instead of increasing gradually and consistently to a higher process level, our schizophrenic sample dropped or backslid during interviews 2–15, and only later began to regain the initial level. The EXP level at the thirtieth interview was not significantly higher than that shown initially, but it did represent an improvement over the process status of the period around the fifteenth patient-therapist interaction. Moreover, these schizophrenics continued to show process movement beyond this point as the curves for the total course (thirds) indicate. Thus while process movement is not absent in a schizophrenic sample, its course is more complex than a simple examination of initial and terminal data points might suggest.

Overview

In summary, these studies of process trends within the therapy hour and across the therapy course indicate that the various process scales are sensitive to meaningful variations in patient behavior. When the single interview was considered, theoretically consistent linear process trends emerged for psychoneurotic patients. More complex curves for normals and schizophrenics could be meaningfully interpreted, suggesting that the process conception was indeed appropriate for characterizing a wide range of events within the therapy hour with all patients. When the total course of therapy was examined, positive process movement was apparent for both neurotic and schizophrenic cases, but only when process was assessed fairly grossly at initial and terminal interviews. However, these trends were not evident in one study in which both neurotics and schizophrenics were considered and only two interviews sampled, and they were shown to be more complex still in a detailed examination of experiencing scores for interviews 2–30 with schizophrenics.

In general, then, these studies suggest that while theoretically consistent process movement may occur in many therapy cases, other nonlinear variations in process (e.g., backsliding, sudden spurts, and plateaus) may be equally apparent and meaningful in reflecting the course of events in the complex therapy interaction. This in turn suggests the importance of obtaining fairly detailed process data if one is to draw meaningful conclusions regarding the similarity and differences in process trends for different diagnostic and outcome groups.

The Relationship of Process in Therapy to Outcome

While process movement seems to be an identifiable feature of the therapy course, the timing and rate of this movement varies, and may in some cases be a complex function of diagnosis and case outcome. Further exploration of the relationship between case outcome and process, therefore, is of considerable theoretical importance. If the process conception is to serve its theoretical function as a pivotal variable of therapeutic progress, its correspondence with at least some of the important criteria of therapeutic progress must be affirmed.

Regardless of fluctuations and idiosyncracies in the pace and timing of process movement, the general conception would require this type of improvement to be more clearly manifest in successful therapy cases than in less successful cases. Similarly, the basic theoretical stress placed on the process dimension as a continuum of mental health would require an association between terminal process level and other independent indices of personality adjustment. Both of these predictions are, in fact, very close to the general intent of Hypothesis V: *The greater the evidences of process movement in the client in therapy, the greater will be the evidences of constructive outcome.* Despite the reversal of approach taken in this section, any relationships obtained between outcome and process movement can be considered as support for this fifth hypothesis. Thus, any relationships shown between outcome and either process movement or terminal process level will serve the dual purpose of supporting the theoretical status and power of the process conception and of affirming the construct validity of various process scales.

Outcome Evidence from Related Studies

The three process studies described in the previous section also considered the association between various outcome criteria and the process trends over the therapy course. Despite differences in the specific outcome criteria, patient samples, specific process scales, and the location of segments in the therapy course, there was agreement in the findings of these studies. By and large they suggested that more successful therapy cases show both a higher level of process throughout therapy and more positive process movement from early to late in therapy than do less successful cases.

Both Walker, Rablen, and Rogers (1960) and Tomlinson and Hart (1962) focused exclusively on process movement in psychoneurotic cases drawn from a counseling center population. For both studies the success-failure outcome criterion consisted primarily of therapist judgments. For both studies, ratings of early and late therapy segments were made on Rogers' global Process Scale (Rogers and Rablen, 1958, Rogers, 1959). The primary difference between the two studies was in the composition of the outcome groups—Walker, Rablen, and Rogers selected cases representing extremes of success and failure, while Tomlinson and Hart selected cases representing a more moderate range of outcome.

The findings from both studies were that those cases judged to be successful by their respective therapists showed a consistently higher process *level* throughout the therapy course. When early and late therapy ratings were averaged, Walker, Rablen, and Rogers found no overlap between the Process Scale ratings of the success and failure cases. Tomlinson and Hart, while not reporting so clear-cut a process level difference for their outcome groups, also found a significant difference ($p \leqq .01$) for the success and failure groups in overall Process Scale level, amounting to roughly one scale stage.

In both studies the evidence for differential process *movement* in the more and less successful groups was not as clear-cut. Walker, Rablen, and Rogers did find a considerable association between positive Process Scale movement and outcome (a rank-order correlation of .89 between process movement scores and outcome rank) for their extreme groups. The trends found for the more restricted outcome groups examined by Tomlinson and Hart were somewhat weaker. While more Process Scale movement was reported for their more successful cases, this trend (as evidenced by the Success × Trials interaction) only reached the .10 level of significance, and the obtained change did not cover as wide a range of the Process Scale as that tapped by Walker, Rablen, and Rogers.

In general, then, the uniformity of trends reported in these three studies when different process scales and outcome criteria were considered represented consistent support for the theoretical expectation of greater process movement for successful therapy cases.

Outcome Evidence from the Present Study of Schizophrenics

When ratings from our study were examined more exhaustively for general process trends, it became clear that the process movement phenomenon is quite complex and can occur in different ways at different points of the therapy interaction. It seems important, therefore, to examine the relationship between process movement and case outcome, using the detailed data of this study.

The greater number of data points used in this study provided a considerably more comprehensive picture of the therapy course than had been obtained in previous studies. The Experiencing Scale ratings were obtained from a large number of therapy and sampling interviews by the procedures described in Chapter 8. Both modal and peak EXP ratings were made by four judges. These ratings were averaged across the four judges, and combined to form three blocks of data: (1) the average of successive five-interview blocks (first block, four interviews) over therapy interviews 2–30; (2) the average of all interviews within successive thirds of the total therapy course; (3) the ratings of the first three sampling interviews.

In order to examine the relationship between process (experiencing) and outcome, we divided the fourteen schizophrenic cases according to a number of different prognostic and outcome criteria. These various measures, described in detail in Chapter 11, represented a range of outcome indices and perspectives. The measures included change scores for MMPI subscales, clinical assessments of change made from examination of initial and terminal test batteries, hospital staff ratings of manifest symptomatic disturbance (Wittenborn Psychiatric Rating Scales), a Q-sort measure of the patient's self-concept, therapists' ratings of case success, and an objective index of hospitalization status. The prognostic indices were those relating to the patient's openness to change and his capacity to engage in the type of verbal interaction that is assumed to be basic to the therapy relationship.

While it was our general assumption that process movement would be related to favorable prognosis and outcome, it seemed somewhat unrealistic to expect that this host of different criteria and perspectives, which in many cases were themselves unrelated, would either consistently or to the same degree be associated with patient experiencing. Hence, we focused on trying to ascertain which outcome and prognostic indices did seem to relate to systematic trends in the patient's psychotherapy process behavior.

For the following analyses, each criterion of prognosis or case outcome was used in turn as the basis for dichotomizing the patients into more successful and less successful groups. The EXP scores for both the therapy and sampling interviews were then examined in a series of Alexander-Grant trend analyses of variance (Grant, 1956; Edwards, 1962), which would reflect differential EXP levels as well as differential EXP trends over the therapy and sampling interview series. The EXP data available for the no-therapy control patients in the sampling interviews also permitted us to consider the importance of the interaction between treatment type and outcome, and the resultant effect on process trends. While it was difficult to make specific predictions for these analyses, it was our general expectation that greater process movement, as well as a higher overall process level, would be apparent in the more successful patients (both therapy and control) generally, and for the more successful therapy patients in particular. Tables 10.1 to 10.3 summarize the results of these analyses. Only those main effects and interactions relevant to the relationship between process and outcome are presented.

Outcome and EXP level.—First, consider the main effect of case outcome (more successful vs. less successful) which bears directly on the problem of the relationship between therapy outcome and the overall

Table 10.1—Significant *F*-ratios and corresponding EXP means for the Groups effect—more successful (m.s.) vs. less successful (l.s.)—in the therapy and sampling interviews (only *p* values ≤ .10 or smaller are listed)

Outcome index	Therapy interviews 2–30		Total (thirds) therapy interviews		First three sampling interviews	
	Modes	Peaks	Modes	Peaks	Modes	Peaks
MMPI Hs						
p	≤.10					≤.10
m.s.	2.02					2.36
l.s.	1.66					1.97
MMPI Sc						
p	≤.05	≤.05	≤.10	≤.10	≤.10	≤.10
m.s.	2.05	2.61	2.04	2.67	1.98	2.41
l.s.	1.62	2.15	1.72	2.25	1.59	1.99
MMPI Pd						
p					≤.10	
m.s.					2.02	
l.s.					1.62	
Q-sort						
p					≤.10	
m.s.					1.99	
l.s.					1.55	
Truax-Liccione-Rosenberg assessment						
p	≤.10	≤.10		≤.05		
m.s.	1.98	2.54		2.62		
l.s.	1.63	2.18		2.20		
Wittenborn DS						
p	≤.05	≤.05	≤.05	≤.05	≤.10	≤.05
m.s.	1.63	2.12	1.65	2.13	1.63	2.09
l.s.	2.04	2.63	2.08	2.71	2.00	2.54
Therapist outcome						
p				≤.10		
m.s.				2.41		
l.s.				2.04		
Hosp. status (6 mos.)						
p					≤.05	≤.01
m.s.					2.03	2.53
l.s.					1.57	1.94
WAIS verbal IQ						
p	≤.10	≤.10		≤.10	≤.10	≤.10
m.s.	2.01	2.58		2.65	2.09	2.18
l.s.	1.64	2.11		2.17	1.64	1.64

Table 10.2—Significant F-ratios for the Success × Trials interactions and trend components for EXP ratings of the therapy interviews (only p values ≤ .10 or smaller are listed)

Outcome measures[a]	Therapy interviews 2-30						Total (thirds) therapy interviews					
	Modes			Peaks			Modes			Peaks		
	S × T[b]	Lin[b]	Quad	S × T[b]	Lin	Quad[b]	S × T[b]	Lin[b]	Quad	S × T	Lin[b]	Quad
MMPI												
K									.10			
Pa			.05							.10		.05
Sc					.01							
Wittenborn, MS										.05		.05
Therapist outcome												.05

[a] The following outcome measures yielded no significant trends: MMPI subscales F, Hs, D, Ma, Si; MMPI profile sort; Q-sort measures; the Truax-Liccione-Rosenberg assessment; Wittenborn subscales DS, SE, PC, PS, HS; therapist change scores; hospitalization status (6 mos.); WAIS verbal IQ; Phillips Premorbid Scale; Kirtner-Cartwright Scale.

[b] No significant results.

Table 10.3—Significant F-ratios for the Outcome × Trials (O × T) and Treatment × Outcome × Trials (T × O × T) interactions, for EXP ratings of the first three sampling interviews (only p values ≤ .10 or smaller are listed)

Outcome index[a]	Modes				Peaks			
	O × T Lin	O × T Quad	T × O × T Lin	T × O × T Quad	O × T Lin	O × T Quad	T × O × T Lin	T × O × T Quad
MMPI								
K	.10	.10						
Sc		.10						
Pd			.10			.05		
Wittenborn								
SE			.10	.10				
PC	.05	.05	.01		.01	.05	.05	
PS	.10						.05	
HS			.05	.05			.10	.10
Hosp. status (6 mos.)			.01				.01	.10
WAIS verbal IQ			.01	.01			.01	.10

[a] The following outcome measures yielded no significant trends: MMPI subscales F, Hs, D, Pa. Ma. Si; MMPI profile sort; Q-sort measures; the Truax Liccione-Rosenberg assessment; Wittenborn subscales MS, DS; therapist change and outcome scores; Phillips Premorbid Scale; Kirtner-Cartwright Scale.

level of EXP attained in therapy. Table 10.1 presents a summary of the means and corresponding significance levels associated with the outcome main effect for both the therapy and sampling interview EXP scores, when outcome is defined by a variety of different indices. Although it is apparent from Table 10.1 that many criteria were not associated with patient EXP level, it is also equally clear that several case outcome variables consistently showed a differential EXP level for the more and less successful groups.

The supportive findings from the psychometric indices were as follows. A strong relationship between outcome (more successful vs. less successful) and EXP was found for the MMPI schizophrenia (Sc) subscale, whether EXP was tapped in the therapy or sampling interviews, and whether initial stages only or the entire interview series was considered. That is, those patients showing the greatest reduction in schizophrenic pathology tended also to manifest the highest level of experiencing throughout the therapy interactions. Two other MMPI subscales also supported this relationship. Patients showing the greatest decrease in abnormal somatic concern (Hs) or in sociopathic attitudes (Pd) tended also to evince a slightly higher level of EXP in the therapy and sampling interviews—although the relationship was not as strong or consistent ($p \leqq .10$) as that for the Sc subscale. Similarly, clinicians' assessments of positive personality change, based on the total psychometric battery, showed a modest relationship to the patient's EXP level. Finally, there was a tendency for patients showing the most improvement in self-concept (self-expert Q-sort) to manifest a higher level of EXP in the first three sampling interviews ($p \leqq .10$).

Several nontest outcome criteria also related to experiencing level. There was a very modest association between the therapist's judgment of outcome and the patient's peak EXP level during the therapy course ($p \leqq .10$). The relationship between EXP and hospital release was stronger but was limited to the sampling interviews. This finding indicated that those patients, either therapy or control, who spent the most time out of the hospital manifested a consistently higher level of EXP in the sampling interviews.

One of the prognostic measures thought to be associated with the patient's general level of experiencing in both the therapy and sampling interviews was the patient's verbal intelligence score (WAIS). As Table 10.1 shows, this was indeed the case, for the verbal IQ measured at the initiation of therapy tended to be related positively to subsequent in-therapy EXP level. This suggests that the patient's verbal aptitude and/or his motivation to communicate verbally may be important correlates of in-therapy process behavior. This relationship of EXP to patient verbal intelligence will be explored further in Chapter 11, when the confounding role of this and other variables will be assessed.

Of the other outcome indices, the Wittenborn depressed state (DS) subscale showed a *negative* relationship with patient EXP, seeming to contradict the theoretical expectation. Those patients showing the least change in depressed symptomatology manifested the highest level of experiencing. However, examination of the initial DS scores for the outcome groups revealed that those showing least improvement on this Wittenborn index were significantly less pathological initially on this index, i.e., showed a low level of depression. Thus the negative relationship found between EXP level and change on these indices might have been primarily the result of a ceiling effect, which worked against positive change for the group initially less pathological. In fact the negative relationship obtained seemed to represent a positive association between initially low DS pathology and subsequently high EXP level in therapy. (Chapter 11 deals in more detail with this relationship of EXP level and initial psychometric measures.)

In summary, some outcome indices in Table 10.1 either were not related to overall EXP level in the therapy and sampling interviews or were associated only for certain sets of EXP data. It nevertheless seemed clear from the findings that several important, independent, and objective measures of outcome or personality change were associated with the general level of therapy and sampling interview EXP. It was significant that fairly consistent evidence had been found for an association between reduction in schizophrenic pathology, favorable hospitalization status, and clinical assessments of change and outcome, on the one hand, and the patient's experiencing considered essential to therapeutic progress, on the other. While the patient's initial verbal capacity may have played a limiting, prerequisite, or confounding role in these relationships, nevertheless the emerging association, for our schizophrenic population, between meaningful test change and the level of patient process gave encouraging support to the validity of our concern with the experiencing variable of patient behavior in the therapy relationship.

Outcome and EXP movement.—The process trends or process movement for the various outcome dichotomies provided a similarly encouraging picture. Evidence for many outcome indices supported our expectation of greater process movement in more successful cases, but variations in the pattern of process movement suggested that movement was taking place in the context of other process fluctuations which might also be important in therapeutic progress. Let us first consider the differential EXP trends for the various more and less successful experimental patients over the therapy interviews only. Then we will discuss the differential trends for both the experimental and control patients in the sampling interviews.

Table 10.2 presents the significance levels for the various Success × Trials interactions in the *therapy* interviews—the direct test of our expectations regarding differential EXP trends in the therapy interviews. The most consistent and theoretically supportive trends of in-therapy EXP emerged for success-failure dichotomies formed from two MMPI subscales (K and Pa) and from therapists' ratings of case success. Although the effect was somewhat weaker in the case of the MMPI K scale, a definite tendency existed for differential quadratic (U-shaped) trends to occur for the more successful and less successful therapy groups, as defined by these criteria. Those patients considered more successful by their therapists, and those evincing the greater reduction in MMPI defensiveness and paranoid pathology, showed a generally positive linear curve over the course of therapy. On the other hand, groups showing the less favorable outcome by these same criteria manifested a more complex process trend, which assumed a U-shaped pattern. That is, instead of rising immediately or steadily in process, the less successful patients showed negative process movement from the early to the middle period of therapy. Only in the final third did they begin to recover and gradually rise in EXP to a level greater than that shown initially. A typical picture of this differential pattern of experiencing for the more successful and less successful groups is shown in Figure 10.2, using therapists' rating as the outcome criterion. Only in the case of the MMPI Pa scale did the process movement for the less successful patients allow them to exceed the terminal EXP scale level of the more successful patients.

In general, then, while these findings did not allow us to conclude that there was more process movement for the more successful cases, or that the terminal level of the more successful and less successful therapy cases was consistently different, they clearly suggested that EXP movement was more monotonically consistent for the more successful therapy patients.

This general pattern of experiencing was also supported somewhat by findings for the MMPI Sc subscale. Of course, the most striking difference in these groups was the generally higher level of EXP for the more successful patients discussed above. However, the curves presented in Figure 10.3 indicate that portions of the trends for the more successful and less successful groups were quite similar. Both groups showed backsliding in the initial period of therapy, followed by process movement to a level above that shown initially. The significant linear component of the Success × Trials interaction for peak ratings of interviews 2–30 (supported by a near-significant trend for the thirds data) suggested that process movement for the less successful patient group was sharper than that for the more successful group, which followed a more gradual curve. Although this did not take the less successful patients to the level of the more successful group, it indicated considerable process

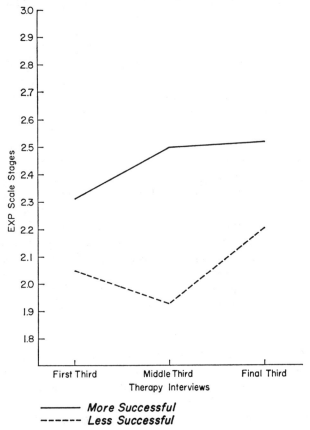

Figure 10.2—Differential trends of peak EXP ratings over the thirds of the therapy interviews, for more successful and less successful therapy groups as defined by therapists' ratings of case outcome.

movement on their part. Apparently what differentiated the high and low Sc change groups, then, was not the occurrence of process movement, but the level and abruptness at which it took place.

This finding was similar to those for the MMPI K and Pa subscales as well as for the therapists' ratings of case outcome. In general, backsliding and/or abrupt process movement in the initial two-thirds of therapy were characteristic of the less successful group. While both outcome groups showed process movement at some points, it was the initial consistency and overall stability of this movement that seems to have been the important differentiating factor.

Finally, differential EXP trends which were difficult to reconcile with the above findings appeared when the criterion of outcome was reduc-

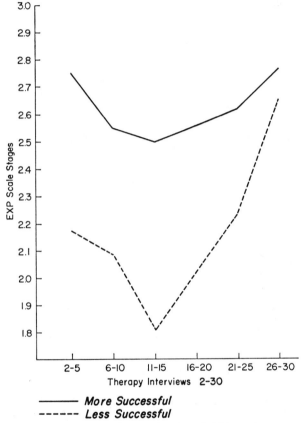

Figure 10.3—Differential trends of peak EXP ratings over therapy interviews 2–30, for more successful and less successful therapy groups as defined by MMPI Sc change scores.

tion of manic state (MS) symptomatology on the Wittenborn scales. For the MS subscale it was the more successful (greater reduction of manic symptoms) group that showed the U-shaped trend, in contrast to the more consistent monotonic EXP movement for the less successful group (see Figure 10.4). While there were no group differences in general EXP level, it was clear that the steadier EXP trend found for the more successful cases with other indices of outcome did not emerge when this type of behavioral rating (MS) was considered.

The trend of experiencing in the *sampling* interviews presented a somewhat more complex picture, not only because with these interviews

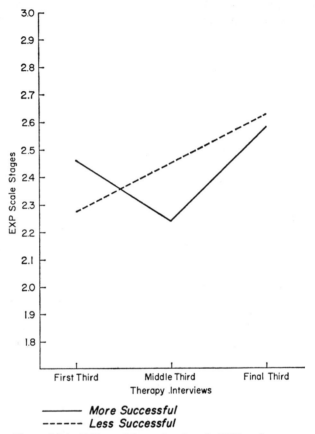

——— *More Successful*
------ *Less Successful*

Figure 10.4—Differential trends of peak EXP ratings over the thirds of the total rated therapy interviews, for more successful and less successful therapy groups as defined by Wittenborn MS change scores.

different patient groups were examined, but also because of the possibility that the sampling interview itself may have had different implications for the experimental and control patients. Since both the experimental and control patients participated in the sampling interviews, the pattern of EXP could be examined in four patient groups: the experimental-success cases, the experimental-failures, the control-successes, and the control-failures. Table 10.3 presents the significance levels of the *F*-

ratios for the Treatment × Outcome × Trials interaction effects of the sampling interview EXP data for the various outcome indices.

There was a clear tendency for favorable outcome to be associated with positive process movement, whether outcome was defined in terms of reduction in Wittenborn symptomatology (particularly paranoid condition [PC], paranoid schizophrenia [PS], and hebephrenic schizophrenia [HS]), by decreases in MMPI pathology (especially on the Pd and K subscales), by an objective criterion of hospital status (per cent time out of the hospital), or by a prognostic index of verbal aptitude (WAIS verbal IQ).

For some of these relationships it was the Success × Trials interaction that yielded significant differences in the EXP trends (MMPI K and Wittenborn PC and PS). For this first-order interaction the more successful group showed positive EXP movement that was either consistently linear, or that was marked by some initial backsliding with a subsequent recovery. Thus, this group's EXP level at the third sampling interview was clearly higher than that shown initially, and higher than that for the less successful cases (see Figure 10.5). The EXP curve for the latter group showed a contrasting pattern in which some initial process movement was followed by definite backsliding to a point well below both their initial EXP level and that of the more successful patients. Thus, despite the fluctuations apparent at the second sampling interview point, the general curves of EXP were different for the more successful and less successful groups (both experimentals and controls), and supported our expectation of an association between successful outcome and positive process movement.

Trends for the more complex second-order interaction (Treatment × Outcome × Trials) also yielded theoretically congruent findings for the one group predicted to show the most favorable process trends, that is, the experimental-successes. The other three groups showed contrasting patterns. Figure 10.6 presents typical curves over the first three sampling interviews for the outcome dichotomy yielding the most typical group differences (Wittenborn HS) among these four groups. Similar trends were found for hospitalization status, Wittenborn HS,[2] MMPI K and Pd subscales.

Of the four groups, the *experimental-success* patients showed the

---

2. Findings for the Wittenborn schizophrenia subscale tended to show reverse trends. For this subscale the major positive process movement occurred for the experimental-failure group, with the other three groups showing positive move· ment initially (from the first to the second sampling interview) with subsequent backsliding (from the second to the third). Examination of the initial group scores for this subscale yielded no evidence regarding the source of this inconsistent trend.

clearest (and generally the only) positive process movement, particularly from the second to the third sampling interviews. Moreover, the EXP level they attained at the third interview was clearly above their initial level as well as above the terminal levels of any of the other three groups.

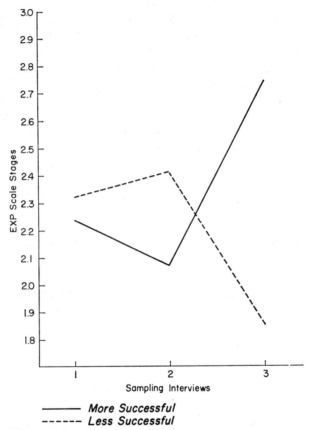

Figure 10.5—Differential trends of peak EXP ratings, over the first three sampling interviews, for more successful and less successful groups, therapy and control patients combined, as defined by Wittenborn PC change scores.

The curve for the *control-success* patients was frequently the converse of that for the experimental-successes. It was either somewhat negative in overall slope or showed an initial increase followed by a sharp decline in EXP. The control-success group showed the highest process level both initially and at the second sampling interview, before dropping to a relatively low level at the third interview. This initial depth in self-experiencing shown by the control-success cases indicated a capacity for self-exploration on the part of these patients who were not in therapy, but who nevertheless showed positive outcome change.

The trend of experiencing for the *experimental-failure* group in Figure 10.6 was quite similar to that for the control-success patients, with

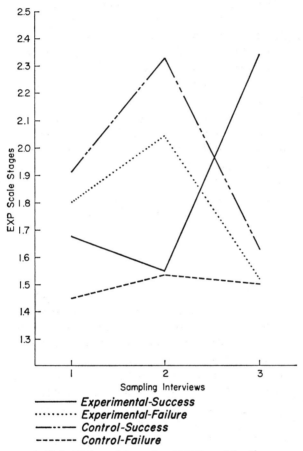

Figure 10.6—Differential trends of EXP modal ratings over the first three sampling interviews, for experimental-success, experimental-failure, control-success, and control-failure groups, as defined by Wittenborn HS change scores.

the exception that the general level of process was lower. Moreover, the experimental-failure curves never showed as sharp an increase in EXP as the control-success curves, suggesting a steady decline in EXP over the sampling interviews for the former cases. Also, while the experimental-failure group was at some times superior to the experimental-success and control-failure groups, by the third interview their terminal EXP level was consistently below that of the experimental-success group, and was either equal to or below that of the control-failures. This pattern seemed to suggest that while the therapy relationship could sustain for a time the level of experiencing evinced initially by the experimental-failure group, an eventual decline in EXP followed.

Lastly, the EXP curve for the *control-failure* group was consistently and strikingly below that of the other groups (although in some instances the second-interview backsliding of the experimental-success patients took them close to or below the control-failure patients). The predominant pattern was one of little or no process movement for this unsuccessful control group. In the instances where the control-failure group did show discernible EXP movement (such as that depicted in Figure 10.6), the level attained was barely equal to that of the experimental-failure and control-success groups, and then only at the third interview point. Generally, the trends for this group revealed their initial lack of, and failure to develop, a level of process comparable to that shown by patients who either had had the opportunity to engage in therapy, or demonstrated a capacity for constructive personality change or both.

Overview

It seems clear that while not all outcome indices and test subscales examined in this section were associated with experiencing, a considerable number did show theoretically meaningful relationships both to the general level and to the trend of this patient process variable. Although the scope of this data was not sufficient to support detailed interpretations of specific outcome-process relationships, the findings did seem consistent enough to warrant more general conclusions regarding the relationship between therapeutic outcome and patient process. These conclusions while taking into account the findings of the related studies presented at the beginning of this section, are based primarily on the more extensive data from this study of hospitalized schizophrenics.

First, in most instances there is a clear relationship between the *level* of patient process throughout therapy or sampling interviews and case outcome. More successful patients both start and end therapy with a higher level of experiencing than less successful patients. This general finding, consistent for both psychoneurotic and schizophrenic samples, suggests that there is a qualitative difference between the in-therapy behavior of more and less successful patients—that more successful cases not only end therapy with a deeper capacity for self-experiencing, but actually begin the relationship with superior self-orientation. This conclusion lends support to the general validity of the process construct stated in Hypothesis V. Moreover, the finding that a process level difference is present very early in the therapy interaction suggests that process variables (particularly experiencing) may have some value as prognostic factors insofar as they reflect the patient's readiness for constructive personality change, or for constructive therapy involvement.

Second, a relationship seems to exist between long-term process *movement* and favorable case outcome. However, the interpretation of this association is complicated by divergent fluctuations that occur for more successful cases as well as by the periodic presence of process improvement in their less successful counterparts. In this regard, data from therapy interviews 2–30 and from the first three sampling interviews of the present study yielded generally consistent findings. While process improvement did occur for the more successful patients in each setting, positive change was not exclusive to this group. Indeed, it seems that it was not the occurrence of movement, or of any given amount of movement, that distinguished more and less successful patient groups, but rather the pattern, abruptness, or general context of the movement. Both groups showed backsliding in the initial therapy interviews, but it was followed by process recovery. The fluctuations were sharper for the less successful group and occurred generally within a lower range of the EXP scale. Hence, the process movement of more successful patients seemed to be timed so that improvement was predominant toward the end of the initial therapy phase. In other words, whatever deterioration or nonimprovement did occur for these cases was superceded by positive change as therapy progressed. In the less successful group process movement was considerably less stable. In therapy it occurred with the same general timing as for more successful patients, but at a lower level and in the context of greater fluctuations. In sampling interviews it was restricted to very early interviews, and was later undercut by process deterioration.

By contrast, the smoothed curves for successive thirds of the therapy course approximated the theoretical formulation and the process function predicted for more successful patients. Cases meeting various criteria of favorable outcome consistently showed a positive linear trend of process change with improvement that was maintained in the terminal period of therapy. The curve for the less successful group was clearly divergent, showing backsliding or process deterioration until the midpoint of therapy. Although this backsliding was gradually superseded by process improvement, the change was rarely within the range of process characteristic of the more successful patients. Again, the major difference between the outcome groups seemed to lie in the timing rather than magnitude of process movement, in the abruptness and pervasiveness of backsliding, and in the general level of process manifested throughout the therapy course. That the cases of favorable outcome showed a linear curve for thirds of the total course seems to have been due, not to the absence of nonlinear fluctuations in this group, but to the fact that these fluctuations were less extreme, and were more rapidly superseded by process recovery.

These findings for our schizophrenic subjects were generally consistent with those reported in the related studies of psychoneurotic and schizophrenic patients. However, they also illustrated the greater complexity of process trends when more detailed information was available from extensive data points in the therapy course. The findings, which so consistently showed an association between positive process movement and more successful cases, and which emerged from analyses of early and late data points only, were roughly congruent with those for our more complex analyses; but they represented an oversimplification of process trends which could lead to unrealistic conclusions regarding more and less successful therapy cases.

A recent study by van der Veen (in press), based on the same population of schizophrenics under study here but using somewhat different methods, tended to agree with the major findings from this analysis. He found only slight relationship between process movement, measured on three scales, and a combined score of client outcome. On the other hand, the client process *level* was found to be associated with personality change.

The findings of this section, therefore, as well as those of related studies, seem to support the validity of the Process Scale, as well as the general prediction (Hypothesis V) of a relationship between outcome and process movement. The findings that process trends are more complicated for different outcome groups than might be predicted, or that some backsliding occurs for more successful patients early in therapy, need not be seen as a contradiction to the general expectation of process improvement from early to late in therapy. The process construct is not intended to bear a one-to-one relationship with theoretically extraneous criteria of therapeutic progress, nor is the course of therapy conceived of exclusively as a steady linear progression. In other words, there is room in the process conception for considerable variation in process throughout the therapy course. Indeed, it seems a tribute to the Experiencing Scale that it can reflect meaningful variation in process over the therapy course yet still reflect overall process improvement that is commensurate with the theoretical stress placed on the continuity between in-therapy process behavior and independent conceptions of healthy personality functioning.

Trends of Process in Therapy as a Function of Diagnosis

At this point let us reconsider the evidence of this chapter as it bears directly on the second major hypothesis of this study, which holds that the same variables of process movement will characterize the in-therapy behavior of neurotics and schizophrenics. This rather straightforward formulation can be viewed and tested at several different levels of abstraction. Most generally it can be interpreted as suggesting that the same variables will be appropriate for characterizing therapy regardless of patient type, that is, without any need for detailed intergroup similarities in all aspects of process or at all stages of therapy. At the other extreme, this hypothesis can be very precisely construed so that only point-by-point similarity of process trends is sufficient for its support. A more moderate position might require that a general trend of positive process movement be found in all cases of successful therapy outcome regardless of diagnostic group, yet still allow room for meaningful intergroup variation in the general process level, the amount of range of process movement, its pace and timing, and the pattern of other fluctuations. In this vein, moreover, one might not specify any commonality whatsoever between process curves for less successful cases in the different nosological groups, and might even expect considerable heterogeneity in the process profiles of cases not meeting criteria for favorable outcome. This more moderate position seems to us the most reasonable compromise because it allows us to retain the general spirit of the hypothesis—the spirit that governs our interpretation of the studies discussed in this final section.

The central research addressed to Hypothesis II and to a direct comparison of process in different diagnostic groups was Tomlinson's study (1962) of four dimensions of process in two patient groups, counseling center psychoneurotics and hospitalized schizophrenics. Approaching the general theoretical formulation from the same frame of reference as that outline above, Tomlinson predicted that process movement would be equally a function of success for neurotics and schizophrenics, but that the absolute process level for neurotics would exceed that for the psychotic group.

These predictions received moderate support from some of his measures of patient process. In the absence of significant Groups × Trials interactions which would have indicated differential process movement for neurotics and psychotics, he found, instead, significant Outcome × Trials interactions for the Personal Constructs and Relationship scales, supporting his prediction that process movement was a function of success, and was independent of diagnostic category. These results were supported by more modest trends for the Experiencing and Problem Expression scales, indicating that more positive process movement from early to late in therapy occurred for the more successful cases in both diagnostic groups, in contrast to the flatter or negative curves for less successful cases in both groups.

Significant Groups effects for the Personal Constructs and Problem Expression scales (supported by similar trends for the Experiencing and Relationship scales) supported Tomlinson's prediction of a generally higher process level in psychoneurotic cases. That is, regardless of the fact that successful cases in both diagnostic groups shared greater process movement (relative to less successful cases), this movement was taking place within different ranges of the process continuum as a function of disturbance level. The less disturbed neurotics entered therapy at a higher level of process than the more disturbed schizophrenic cases, and, when successful, moved to an even higher stage. While successful schizophrenic cases also showed considerable process movement, this movement never took them to a level comparable to that achieved by neurotics in the course of therapy.

Conclusions

It seems clear that there was a general positive relationship between process movement from early to late in the therapy course and case outcome. Though not all success or change indices examined were equally related to process movement, it is apparent in all studies reported in this chapter that the process level at the end of therapy for successful cases was higher than that shown initially. The general trend in less successful cases was more variable. In some cases less successful therapy was marked by a negative process trend, in others by no change or by lower-level process improvement. In general, however, the positive relationship between success and process improvement is apparent both for neurotics and schizophrenics, with no striking group differences in the general nature of this global trend.

This straightforward conclusion, however, is based largely on studies employing only two therapy data points—initial and terminal. While it is generally substantiated by grossly estimated trends emerging from a much more detailed examination of the therapy course, there is nevertheless evidence to indicate that the course of patient process is at times highly complex. Variations in the pace, timing, and context of process movement, as well as other patterns of backsliding and deterioration found in the detailed consideration of process for the schizophrenic sample, clearly open the possibility that other fluctuations may occur with process movement, and that these variations may consistently differentiate outcome or diagnostic groups.

Process improvement is not unique to successful cases. There is evidence that positive process movement may also occur in less successful therapy, but that its timing will be different and, perhaps more importantly, that its general level will be lower. At the same time, fluctuations and periods of backsliding or deterioration can characterize more successful cases, appearing to occur relatively early in the course of therapy with schizophrenics. Though comparable, detailed information is not available for a neurotic sample, it would not be particularly surprising to find similar fluctuations, perhaps with different patterns, for successful neurotics. Most simply, the limited evidence regarding detailed trends within the therapy course for more and less successful cases points to the complexity of therapeutic process even in cases that are successful by independent and objective criteria. Such complexities may not be inimical to therapeutic progress; and indeed, certain patterns of process fluctuation, particularly if occurring in the context of therapeutically meaningful shifts in focal content, defensive structure, and changes in adaptation, may be important phases which facilitate the eventual progress. Certainly there is room in the process conception for variations in process curves for successful cases, provided that any negative trends for more successful cases are subsequently superseded by process improvement, reflecting the presence of an implemented growth capacity that is clearly operative at the terminal portion of the therapy course.

By the same token, there is room within the general conception regarding different diagnostic groups for idiosyncratic fluctuations. While the evidence for such fluctuations is incomplete, the patterns observed in the detailed examination of schizophrenics as well as the differential diagnostic group trends that emerged for within-interview analyses, hint that in therapy the course of patient process may be more complex for schizophrenics than for neurotics. Other complexities and other patterns may emerge for other case types. Each can be meaningfully reconciled with the general process conception if, at the same time, therapeutic progress is related to general process improvement, or if process improvement is predominant at times when constructive personality change is particularly evident.

At their most general level, the studies summarized in this chapter provide meaningful support for the general validity of the process conception as a reflection of general therapeutic progress. More general relationships between diagnosis, outcome, and process level also reinforce the status of this construct as a continuum of mental health, and suggest its possible role as a predictive index of readiness for therapy. Further, it seems apparent that the process scales, particularly the Experiencing Scale, are quite sensitive to within-therapy variations in patient involvement, and that further attempts at empirical description of patient process trends, carried out in conjunction with a more detailed theoretical elaboration of the process conception, would contribute importantly to our increased understanding of the therapeutic process.

References

EDWARDS, A. L. *Experimental Design in Psychological Research.* New York: Holt, Rinehart & Winston, 1962, chapter xiv.

GENDLIN, E. T. *Experiencing and the Creation of Meaning.* New York: The Free Press of Glencoe, 1962.

GRANT, D. A. Analysis-of-variance tests in the analysis and comparison of curves. *Psychol. Bull.* 53:141–154, 1956.

KIESLER, D. J., KLEIN, MARJORIE H., and MATHIEU, PHILIPPA L. Sampling from the recorded therapy interview: The problem of segment location. *J. consult. Psychol.* 29:337–344, 1965.

ROGERS, C. R. A tentative scale for the measurement of process in psychotherapy. In E. A. Rubinstein and M. B. Parloff (eds.), *Research in Psychotherapy,* Vol. I. Washington, D.C.: American Psychological Association, 1959, pp. 96–107.

ROGERS, C. R., and RABLEN, R. A. A scale of process in psychotherapy. Unpublished manual, University of Wisconsin, 1958.

TOMLINSON, T. M. Three approaches to the study of psychotherapy: Process, outcome, and change. Unpublished Ph.D. dissertation, University of Wisconsin, 1962.

TOMLINSON, T. M., and HART, J. T., JR. A validation study of the Process Scale. *J. consult. Psychol.* 26:74–78, 1962.

VAN DER VEEN, F. Basic elements in the process of psychotherapy: a research study. *J. consult. clin. Psychol.* In press.

WALKER, A., RABLEN, R. A., and ROGERS, C. R. Development of a scale to measure process change in psychotherapy. *J. clin. Psychol.* 16:79–85, 1960.

11. Constructive Personality Change
for Therapy and Control Patients

Donald J. Kiesler, Marjorie H. Klein, Philippa L. Mathieu, and Douglas Schoeninger

This chapter deals in part with the last of the three major hypotheses of the study: *The process of therapy will occur to a significantly greater degree in a group of individuals to whom therapy has been offered than in a control group, paired and matched to the therapy group, to whom therapy has not been offered.* This hypothesis was focused primarily on in-therapy patient process behavior, although it had clear implications for other concomitant personality change in therapy patients. It was our expectation that experimental patients exposed to a therapeutic relationship would show a higher level of process (experiencing) than control patients receiving no therapeutic relationship over and above the general hospital milieu and consequently having no opportunity to develop in self-exploration. This theoretical difference was predicted to be manifest even in the patient's brief sampling interview contacts with a standard interviewer, whose purpose was to create an atmosphere that would reveal each patient's current mode and quality of self-expression.

The most parsimonious test of Hypothesis III consisted simply of a comparison of sampling interview experiencing scores for experimental and control group patients. However, it followed from the initial hypothesis of this study that a more theoretically meaningful analysis must also take account of the level of the therapeutic conditions available to the experimental group, on the assumption that the quality of therapist conditions would have the same relationship to the patient's behavior outside therapy as it had to his in-therapy experiencing. This more complex, conditions-outcome approach to Hypothesis III (subsequently referred to as Hypothesis III–A) permitted a more differentiated assessment of the effectiveness of therapy by emphasizing the importance of variations in the quality of the therapeutic relationship. The wording of this Hypothesis III–A is as follows: *Those individuals receiving a higher degree of the conditions of therapy will exhibit a greater degree of the process of therapy than will those individuals receiving a lower degree of therapeutic conditions, or those individuals constituting the paired and matched control group.*

251

It was further implicit in Hypothesis III that the process behavior manifest in the therapy and sampling interviews would be equally related to other constructive personality change. This formed the basis for Hypothesis IV: *Evidences of positive outcome will be greater in a group of individuals to whom therapy has been offered than in a control group, paired and matched to the therapy group, to whom therapy has not been offered.* This hypothesis could be tested by comparing the objective performance of experimental and control patients on a number of extra-therapy indices of personality change and adjustment.

An even more powerful and theoretically meaningful probe of this issue was demanded by Hypothesis IV–A, which states that *the greater the degree to which the conditions of therapy exist in the relationship, the greater will be the evidences of constructive outcome.* This required differentiation of the experimental group on the basis of the conditions level offered in therapy.

The first and second sections of this chapter, then, will be devoted to comparing the sampling interview experiencing and outcome-adjustment behavior of the control patients with that of the experimental group, the latter treated as a whole as well as subdivided according to the level of conditions received in the therapy relationship. The final section will consider various issues important for the interpretation of any differences emerging from these comparisons. For despite our efforts at matching therapy and control groups on theoretically extraneous variables such as age, sex, and socio-economic background, not all potentially confounding factors were thereby controlled. The extent to which such potentially confounding variables were active must be statistically estimated prior to any interpretation of therapy-control group differences or conditions-process or conditions-outcome relationships.

Process Movement in the Sampling Interviews
Hypotheses III and III–A

In order to test the hypothesis that therapy patients will show a higher level of process and process movement than no-therapy control patients, sampling interview EXP scores of the experimental and control patients were compared in a series of 2×3 Alexander-Grant (Grant, 1956; Edwards, 1962) trend analyses of variance. Additional 3×3 analyses compared high and low conditions patients, dichotomized according to six global conditions estimates,[1] with the control cases. Two kinds of

---

1. Experimental patients were divided according to each of six conditions factors representative of the global level of each conditions variable from each of three viewpoints (patient, therapist, judges). These included the overall means for

sampling interview EXP data were employed in these analyses: (1) EXP scores for the first three sampling interviews (initial, three months, six months) for each patient; and (2) scores for each third of the sampling interview series for each patient. Modal and peak ratings were treated separately in each case (see Chapter 8 for a more detailed description of the sampling interview procedure and for information regarding EXP Scale reliability).

First Three Sampling Interviews

The trend analyses for sampling interview EXP scores of therapy and control group patients gave little support for Hypotheses III or III–A. There were no significant Groups effects or Groups × Trials interactions or component trends, indicative respectively of differences in process level or process movement for the experimental patients, considered either as a group or as divided by six conditions factors, when compared to the control patients. However, there were two Groups × Trials quadratic effects which approached significance, that for the experimental group as a whole in contrast to the control group, and that for the high and low conditions (Th-RI-T) groups in contrast to the control group.

Figure 11.1 shows the means for each group at the initial, three months, and six months interview points. It suggests that the trend of experiencing for the control group tended to be negatively quadratic (inverted U-shaped), in contrast to that for the therapy group considered as a whole, which was positively quadratic (U-shaped). When the experimental group was divided according to the level of conditions the therapist attributed to the relationship (Th-RI-T), the EXP curve for the low conditions group was notably different in direction from that for the high conditions and the control groups. While both high conditions and control groups showed a modest rise and drop in EXP over the course of the first three sampling interviews, the low conditions group showed the converse—a sharp drop followed by a sizeable increase in the level of experiencing. This trend, a clear reversal of theoretical expectations, apparently reflects the consistently discrepant findings of the previous chapters regarding the therapist's viewpoint, showing a negative relationship between therapists' perceptions, on the one hand, and conditions and process factors, on the other.

---

rated accurate empathy (AE_{TOT}), unconditional positive regard (UPR B_{TOT}), congruence ($CONG_{TOT}$), and the combined score for rated conditions ($COMB_{TOT}$), as well as the total conditions score (T) on the terminal patient and therapist Relationship Inventories. These specific measures were chosen as most parsimoniously representative of the different viewpoints of the conditions variable estimated from the total therapy interaction.

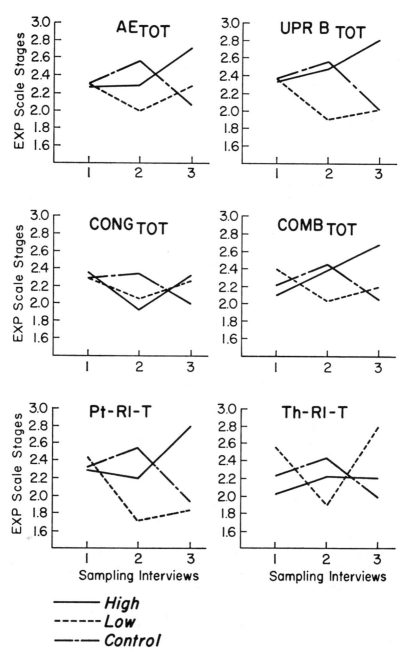

Figure 11.1—Differential patient EXP trends (peak ratings) over the first three sampling interviews for high conditions and low conditions therapy patients (as defined by six separate conditions measures) and for the control patients.

The trends for the other high-low conditions differentiations were considerably more consistent, and in line with theoretical expectations. None of the relevant trends reached significance but Figure 11.1 suggests that while all three groups had similar experiencing levels initially, their subsequent trends were divergent. The general trend for the high conditions group was positive. By contrast, the low conditions group showed a negative trend that was closer to that of the control group with its ultimate drop in experiencing level over the sampling interviews.

Total Sampling Interview Series

From the results of trend analyses of EXP scores for successive thirds of the total sampling interview series, it is apparent that the majority of the Groups effects and the Groups × Trials interactions and trend components necessary for support of Hypotheses III and III–A fell short of significance.

The division of the experimental group according to the level of rated accurate empathy (AE_{TOT}), however, yielded Groups × Trials quadratic trend components that were significant at the .05 level for modal EXP, and that approached significance for peak EXP. In both cases it is apparent from Figure 11.2 that the trend for the high accurate empathy group was particularly distinct, having a negative quadratic (inverted U-shaped) slope, in contrast to the more similarly flat curves of the control and low accurate empathy groups. While all three groups showed approximately the same level of experiencing initially, only the patients receiving the highest level of accurate empathy in therapy showed an increase in self-exploration at any point in the sampling interview series.

The Groups effect, when the conditions dichotomy was based on the level of rated unconditional positive regard (UPR B_{TOT}) in therapy, approached significance ($p \leqslant .10$). Figure 11.2 suggests that this effect was a reflection of the uniformly higher level of experiencing apparent for the high conditions patients in contrast to both low conditions and control group cases. Thus, the level of unconditional positive regard tended to be associated with a more consistently high level of experiencing at all points of the sampling interviews for these high conditions patients.

Overview

The preceding analyses of sampling interview experiencing ratings yielded few statistically significant results in support of Hypotheses III or III–A. Whether the total experimental group was compared with the control group, or whether the therapy group was further differentiated

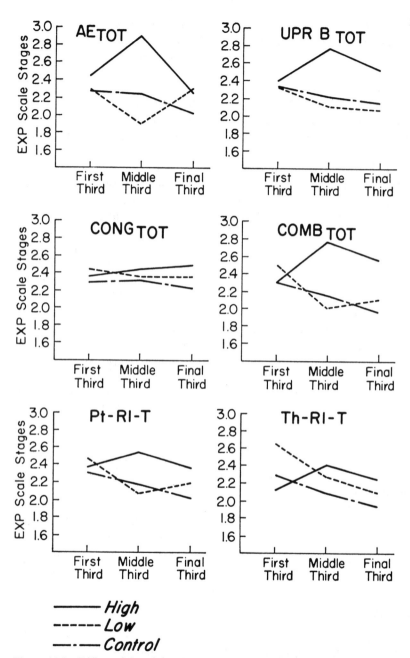

Figure 11.2—Differential patient EXP trends (peak ratings) over the thirds of the sampling interviews for high conditions and low conditions therapy patients (as defined by six separate conditions measures) and for the control patients.

according to the level of conditions in therapy, differential trends were not sufficiently reliable to warrant unequivocal support of the hypotheses. However, the trends for the various conditions and control groups, although statistically weak, were consistent with our expectations. Perhaps most important was the fact that the one measure of

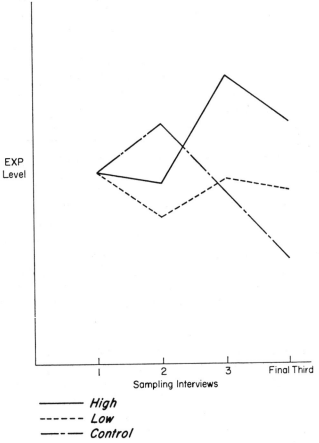

Figure 11.3—The trend of patient experiencing over the sampling interviews (combining the first three and thirds data), for the high conditions and low conditions therapy patients, and for the control patients.

therapist conditions (accurate empathy) that was powerfully and consistently related to in-therapy process behavior was also significantly associated with EXP in the extra-therapeutic setting.

Figure 11.3 presents our extrapolated curves of experiencing for the three patient groups over the total sampling interview series, based on the above estimates of the level of EXP over the first three sampling interviews as well as over the final third of the sampling interviews. First, it seems clear that it was meaningful to differentiate the experimental group according to the level of conditions received in the therapy relationship. Although the general shape of the curves for high conditions and low conditions therapy groups is similar, the level of experiencing of the two groups was different. While both groups initiated the sampling interview series at approximately the same level of process, it was the high conditions group that subsequently manifested a generally higher level of experiencing. The variations of the high conditions group were preponderantly within a range that was higher than their initial level; whereas the fluctuations for the low conditions group were consistently within a lower range of EXP than that shown initially. This difference suggests that the quality of therapy (high or low conditions) may have an impact on the depth and quality of self-exploration shown by the patient in a one-to-one relationship outside therapy.

Second, it is clear that the phenomenon of therapy, as compared with no therapy, may relate to differential trends in self-experiencing. While the level of EXP for the control group was generally below that of the high conditions therapy patients in the bulk of the sampling interviews, it was primarily the *course* of experiencing that differentiated control from experimental patients. Regardless of conditions level, therapy patients' experiencing showed a tendency to drop at the second sampling interview point, only to rise consistently thereafter. Conversely, the control group showed an increase in experiencing at the second sampling interview point that was followed by an uninterrupted decline over the remainder of the sampling interview series.

The initial decrease in sampling interview EXP for both therapy groups, in contrast to the initial increase of control groups, may be attributed to differences in these groups' perceptions of, and expectations for, the sampling interview. To therapy patients, in the context of their newly-begun therapy relationship, the sampling interview may have been perceived as either a research test or an unwanted interruption. In either case it is possible that they would not be likely to respond with their deepest capacity for self-exploration. Later, after the therapy relationship had crystallized, the sampling interview would not have seemed so threatening. At this stage it could more validly serve as a reflection of their actual capacity for self-exploration, and could tap the experiencing level as a function of therapist conditions. Control patients, on the other hand, would have been likely at first to see the sampling interview either as a potentially supportive relationship or as a means of help in leaving the hospital. Whichever was the case, it is understandable that the control patient might have attempted to express himself initially as fully as possible. Later in the interview series, as the control patient realized that the sampling interview could serve no satisfactory ameliorative or manipulative function, there would no longer have been reason for self-expression and his experiencing level would have dropped considerably.

Thus, while it is apparent that for this study the sampling interview did not serve as a statistically powerful test of experiencing differences in experimental and control patients, the trends that did emerge were theoretically meaningful. High quality therapy relationships (conditions) were apparently related to high levels of sampling interview experiencing, at a point in time when the therapy relationship was well established and when it was clear to the patient that the sampling interview represented no specific threat. Low conditions therapy apparently retarded or inhibited the development of a high level of experiencing just as in the therapy interviews. No-therapy control patients, in contrast, showed a type of gradual decline in experiencing over the sampling interview series that could be attributed to their lack of opportunity to develop or sustain the capacity for self-exploration in the absence of a therapeutic relationship. While there was some evidence to suggest that the sampling interview, as a measuring instrument, declined in effectiveness over time, it did tap, at some points, differences among high conditions, low conditions, and control groups that were consistent with theoretical expectations, but that were not of sufficient magnitude to permit unequivocal support of our hypotheses.

Constructive Personality Change for Therapy and Control Groups Hypotheses IV and IV–A

In this section our interest goes beyond variables of interview behavior to a consideration of evidence of differential constructive personality change for the therapy and control patients. In the following we will first describe the rationale for our selection of the various outcome measures. Next we will present the statistical tests of the hypotheses that therapy patients as a group (Hypothesis IV), and most particularly high conditions therapy patients (Hypothesis IV–A), would show a higher level of outcome-adjustment, or greater constructive personality change, at the termination of therapy than those in a matched, no-therapy control group.

Rationale for Selecting Measures of Personality Change

At the initiation of this study, various measures were selected in order to tap change in different aspects of the patient's personal and social adjustment. For example, the Butler-Haigh Q-sort was included to assess change in the patient's self-concept; the MMPI, to reflect change in psychopathology; the Wittenborn Psychiatric Rating Scales, for variations in observable symptomatology; and the Therapist Rating Scale (van der Veen, 1959), for the therapist's evaluations of in-therapy behavior and outcome. These measures not only tapped different aspects of the patient's adjustment behavior, but also assessed each patient from perspectives representative of the different participants in the care and treatment of the hospitalized schizophrenic. Other criteria of outcome were studied from factual sources, such as hospital records, which could serve as objective indices of the patient's hospital status.

Originally, the test and rating scale outcome battery included the MMPI, the Rorschach, the Thematic Apperception Test (TAT), the Wechsler Adult Intelligence Scale (WAIS) in its abbreviated form, the California F Scale, the Wittenborn Psychiatric Rating Scales, the Stroop Interference Test, the Butler-Haigh Q-sort, the Truax Anxiety Scale, and the Therapist Rating Scale. According to the original schedule, all self-report measures were to be administered at six-month intervals, with Wittenborn ratings to be made by ward personnel every three months. As the research progressed, however, many situations arose making it difficult to adhere rigorously to this schedule. Some patients left the hospital, others refused testing, and still others gave obviously invalid responses to specific tests. It was also difficult to test every patient at exactly the appropriate time point demanded by the testing schedule. As a result most cases had missing data.

For this reason it was necessary to use the test data in a more limited fashion than had been originally intended by (1) using only those test batteries yielding fairly complete coverage of the experimental and control group patients, and by (2) using only the pre-therapy (initial) and terminal test scores. This latter decision presented the additional difficulty that the schedule calling for retesting at fixed time intervals provided no guarantee that so-called terminal batteries would be administered at the actual time of termination of the therapy relationship. As Table 11.1 illustrates, there were sizeable discrepancies between the administration of some tests and the terminal interviews. The question of how large a time deviation to permit, between test termination and actual termination was solved by arbitrarily deciding to include as terminal tests only those measures administered within four months of the terminal interview. Applying these two criteria to the original test battery, only the MMPI, Q-sort, and Wittenborn instruments were available as final indices of personality and behavioral change for the therapy and control patients. Other outcome criteria, such as therapist ratings and hospitalization indices, were not affected by the difficulties of maintaining the test schedule described above.

The selection of appropriate control subgroups for test comparisons raised a second problem. Although it was our original intention to compare outcome-change scores for the entire experimental and matched control groups, subject attrition in the groups, as well as the problem of missing data, forced us to a more complicated selection of control patients for test data analyses. Specifically, it seemed clear that the time interval between initial and terminal test protocols was an important matching variable. Since very few of the matched control and therapy patients were retested at the same time intervals, any compari-

Table 11.1—Time difference in days, for the experimental patients, between termination of therapy and the test time point closest to termination: (−) test time point occurred before termination; (+) test time point occurred after termination

Experimental patient	MMPI	Q-sort	Wittenborn
PUF	−46	−42	−12
VAC	−324	−319	−259
RUD	+38	+40	−5
WIL	−4	−10	−59
NUF	−21	−23	+34
KEN[a]	—	—	−53
RAC	−64	−69	−289
GOS	−212	−206	—
SOC	−91	−102	−170
CUF	−224	−213	−222
LYN	+105	+219	−44
FIP	+19	+27	+8
FAS	+29	+14	+30
DEM[a]	—	—	—

[a] KEN and DEM refused all psychological testing.

son between experimental and control patients originally matched for "stratifying" variables would not take into account the possibly more important factor of the size of the time interval between initial and terminal tests. Accordingly, it was decided to match experimental and control patients in terms of the amount of time elapsed between initial and terminal tests for each test instrument.

Finally, it is important to note that since cases varied in length, the number of times each test was administered to each patient varied. In longer cases the terminal test battery may have represented the third or fourth administration of a given instrument whereas in shorter cases the

Table 11.2—A listing of the experimental and matched control patients with the number of tests between initial and terminal testing for each patient, for each outcome measure

Experimental patient	No. testings between	Matched control patient	No. testings between
		MMPI	
PUF	0	MIK	0
VAC	3	LIV	2
RUD	0	SAR	0
WIL	1	QIL	1
NUF	1	PEL	1
RAC	3	ORD	2
GOS	2	GUL	0
SOC	0	TAG	0
CUF	3	MAC	3
LYN	0	ZAG	0
FIP	0	HAV	0
FAS	0	FEL	0
		Q–SORT	
PUF	0	MIK	0
VAC	3	LIV	2
RUD	0	SAR	0
WIL	2	QIL	1
NUF	1	JAN	0
RAC	2	ORD	2
GOS	2	GUL	0
SOC	0	TAG	0
CUF	3	MAC	3
LYN	0	ZAG	0
FIP	0	HAV	0
FAS	0	FEL	0
		WITTENBORN	
PUF	1	GUL	1
VAC	5	CUL	3
RUD	0	SAR	0
WIL	4	QIL	1
NUF	3	MIK	4
KEN	4	LIV	4
RAC	4	ORD	3
SOC	0	DOZ	0
CUF	4	MAC	6
LYN	0	ZAG	0
FIP	0	HAV	0
FAS	1	FEL	1

terminal battery was more likely to have been the second administration. Table 11.2 shows the number of times each test was administered to each patient. While it is difficult to assess the exact influence of different numbers of retests on the various test scores, the reader should be aware of these variations.

Description of Outcome Indices Used in Analyses

Minnesota Multiphasic Personality Inventory.—The MMPI was used to provide two different assessments of change or outcome— MMPI subscale scores and MMPI profiles. Raw scores (corrected for K) for those subscales especially pertinent to the schizophrenic sample (F, K, Hs, D, Pa, Sc, Ma, Si, Pd, and Barron's ES Scale) were compared to assess change in the patient's specific psychopathology. Barron's Ego Strength Scale was included as an exploratory attempt to apply this index to our psychotic population. The ES scale was originally designed to predict the response of psychoneurotic patients to psychotherapy. Its use as an index of change is not yet well substantiated. However, to the extent that this scale could tap "constructive forces in the personality" (Barron, 1953), it might relate to differential change over therapy for our schizophrenic population.

MMPI profiles also provided the basis for more global clinical assessment of pathology and personality change. Four MMPI diagnosticians[2] were asked to make independent, blind evaluations of the MMPI profiles of both the experimental and control patients. Each diagnostician was given the initial and terminal profiles for the therapy and control patients, without information as to which were which, and without any identifying or other data, and each was asked to perform two judgmental tasks. The first was to judge each profile as falling into one of six diagnostic categories (undifferentiated schizophrenic, paranoid schizophrenic, manic state, sociopath, psychoneurotic, or normal) without information as to the pairing and timing of the profiles. Given this latter information, but not knowing which patients were experimentals and which controls, the diagnosticians were then asked to assess each case as improved (+), not changed (0), or deteriorated (−). As Table 11.3 shows, interjudge agreement for these tasks was quite acceptable—48.1 per cent unanimous, 65.4 per cent majority agreement for the diagnostic classification task; 46.2 per cent unanimous, 96.2 per cent majority agreement for the profile assessments of change.

2. The authors gratefully acknowledge the assistance of Robert R. Carkhuff, Samuel H. Friedman, and George S. Welsh in this evaluation and rating task. Donald J. Kiesler was the fourth diagnostician.

A composite index of change was derived from these assessments. In those instances of majority agreement regarding both initial and terminal diagnostic classification, a patient was considered to show improvement (+) if his terminal diagnosis was closer to "normal" along the following continuum: schizophrenic < sociopath = manic state < psychoneurotic < normal. A diagnostic change from schizophrenic to sociopath, for

Table 11.3—Frequency of different levels of interjudge agreement for judges' diagnostic classification of initial and terminal MMPI profiles (K = 4 judges), and for judges' ratings of initial-terminal adjustment change from the MMPI profiles (K = 3 judges)

Patient group	Two or less agree	Three agree	All four agree	Total
JUDGES' DIAGNOSTIC CLASSIFICATIONS				
Experimentals	8	4	14	26
Controls	10	5	11	26
Total	18	9[a]	25[b]	52
JUDGES' RATINGS OF ADJUSTMENT CHANGE				
Experimentals	1	9	3	13
Controls	0	4	9	13
Total	1	13[c]	12[d]	26

[a] Per cent three of four agreement = 34/52 = 65.4 per cent.
[b] Per cent unanimous agreement = 25/52 = 48.1 per cent.
[c] Per cent two of three agreement = 25/26 = 96.2 per cent.
[d] Per cent unanimous agreement = 12/26 = 46.2 per cent.

example, would be considered improved (+), in contrast to the change from manic state to sociopath which would be considered no change (0). In the cases where there was no majority agreement among the judges, their change ratings were used to determine the outcome category. By this procedure each patient was finally classified as either improved (+), no change (0), or deteriorated (−).

Thus there were two types of assessments available from the MMPI test data: discrete subscale scores providing an estimate of specific psychopathological change, and clinical assessments of profile change approximating the manner in which this test is frequently used as the basis for decisions in clinical practice.

Butler-Haigh Q-sort.—The Q-sort was employed primarily to serve as a measure of the patient's self-concept. Each patient was instructed to "sort these cards from those least like you to those most like you as you see yourself today." Eighty items were chosen from the 100-item Butler-Haigh sort used in a previous study of psychotherapy (Rogers and Dymond, 1954), and were sorted on a 9-point scale. Two scores were obtained. The first was a self-expert correlation, representing the correlation between the patient's self-sort and an ideal standard sort reflecting the conception of clinical psychologists as to the theoretically well-adjusted person. A high correlation indicates that the patient's self-sort was very similar to the experts' conception of the well-adjusted person. The second, an adjustment score, was obtained in the following manner. Items given a value of four on the expert-sort were scored zero, since they represented the median of the scale stages. Of the remaining items, those rated 0–3 on the expert-sort were scored one point each for the patient if he placed them between stages 0–3 on his self-sort. Likewise, those items rated 5–8 on the expert-sort were scored one point each for the patient if he rated them between 5–8 on his self-sort. The adjustment score, then, was the sum of all the items scored one point. This latter scoring procedure was identical to that used by Rosalind Dymond Cartwright in the 1954 Chicago study.

Clinical assessment of change from the total test battery.—These clinical assessments (hereafter referred to as the Truax-Liccione-Rosenberg[3] assessment) of change provided an index of patient personality change made from a global evaluation of test materials, similar in technique to the procedure adopted for the MMPI profile analyses. This approach was of particular value as a supplement to the more specific test scores, and approximated the manner in which various psychological tests are frequently used in the process of clinical decision-making. Two clinical psychologists were asked to make independent and blind assessments, from the test protocols, of the amount and direction of patient change. They used a 9-point scale, ranging from extreme improvement to extreme deterioration in psychological functioning. The initial and terminal test batteries were provided each judge. Although they were informed as to which batteries were from the same patient, and which of the two batteries was initial and which terminal, the judges were not informed as to the therapy or control status of the patients. They were free to base their evaluations on any test or combination of tests they found useful and meaningful. Despite the

3. The authors gratefully acknowledge the assistance of John V. Liccione and Marshall B. Rosenberg in this evaluation and rating task.

flexibility of instructions, the level of agreement for this task was acceptable (82 per cent for agreement within one scale point).

Wittenborn Psychiatric Rating Scales.—These scales consist of item
clusters that provide a descriptive assessment of the patient's symptomatology based primarily on observations of his ward behavior. For this
study these ratings were made periodically by hospital staff members
who were acquainted with the ward behavior of the patient. Subsequent
analyses are focused only on those scales most relevant to our patient
sample (manic state, depressed state, schizophrenic excitement, paranoid
condition, paranoid schizophrenia, and hebephrenic schizophrenia). In
each case initial and terminal ratings provided the contrast between the
patient's behavior at the beginning and at the end of therapy as it
appeared to ward staff members.

Therapist Rating Scale.—This data, available only for therapy patients, was collected only at termination. The function of the scale was
to assess the therapist's view of the outcome of therapy and the extent of
personality change in his patient. Therapists were asked to rate their
patients on ten items covering various aspects of outcome and change.
For the purposes of our analyses only two of these subscale ratings were
considered. The first was an 11-point scale of change for which the
therapist was specifically instructed to "rate the amount of change you
feel the client has made, either positive or negative." The second was a
9-point scale of outcome of therapy on a dimension ranging from
marked success to complete failure.[4]

Hospitalization status.—In addition to test scores and clinical judgments a more community-oriented criterion of outcome—the patient's
hospital status—was needed. While it is difficult to pinpoint the many
different factors contributing to a patient's leaving the hospital and
remaining out, such information provides, nevertheless, a highly meaningful and realistic criterion of success. For this study three indices
were culled from hospital records. These were the number of days
spent out of the hospital during the first six months after therapy
termination; the number of days spent out of the hospital during the first
full year after therapy termination; and the number of days spent out of
the hospital over the period extending from the initiation of therapy to
three years. Comparable scores for control patients were also calculated. For instance, if an experimental patient spent five months in
therapy, the interval used to estimate the hospitalization rate for his
matched control began five months after the control patient received his

4. For an analysis of the relationship of all aspects of the therapist rating
scale to both process and outcome measures, see van der Veen and Stoler, 1965.

initial test battery. This procedure was considered necessary in order to equate the time interval used as a base for the computation of the hospitalization rates for the experimental and control patients.

Analyses of Initial to Terminal Outcome Change

In order to test hypotheses IV and IV–A regarding differential personality change in therapy and control patients, several sets of repeated measures analyses of variance of initial and terminal psychometric scores were calculated: for therapy patients as a group in contrast to the controls (Hypothesis IV); and for therapy patients differentiated according to the level of therapist conditions, in contrast to the controls (Hypothesis IV–A). Two conditions measures, rated accurate empathy (AE_{15}) and the patient's perception of therapist congruence (Pt-RI-C), were used to differentiate the high and low conditions groups.[5]

MMPI subscale and Q-sort indices of improvement.—Table 11.4 summarizes the results of the 2 × 2 repeated measures analyses of variance of initial and terminal MMPI subscale and Q-sort adjustment scores for the therapy patients as a group in contrast to the controls. Tables 11.5 and 11.6, and Figures 11.4 and 11.5, summarize the 3 × 2 repeated measures analyses of the test scores for the AE_{15} and Pt-RI-C dichotomies. (Since the Pt-RI-C dichotomy yielded trends highly similar to those of the AE_{15}, only the latter trends will be presented in the figures.)

First, it is apparent that none of the Groups × Trials interactions

5. Only those conditions factors significantly associated with in-therapy patient experiencing (AE_{15} and Pt-RI-C) were used to form dichotomies for analyses of outcome-adjustment scores. The rationale for this focus was complex. A very basic assumption of this study was that any positive outcome manifested outside therapy was associated with antecedent process movement in the therapy setting; and that this process movement was a function of the level of conditions in the therapy relationship. Our concern with outcome factors, then, was both to test the general proposition that therapy has a beneficial effect over no-therapy, as well as to affirm the power and validity of the experiencing variable in relation to constructive personality change. Thus, when focusing on the association between conditions and outcome we were theoretically most interested in those therapist conditions factors that related positively to patient process in the therapy setting— that is, in demonstrating that conditions factors associated with in-therapy patient process behavior were also associated with extra-therapy adjustment indices. As this was our primary interest we elected to limit our focus to the question: Do patients receiving high levels of conditions known to relate to process in therapy also show particularly high levels of outcome-adjustment when compared to both low conditions and no-therapy control patients? This approach did not permit us on an a priori basis to examine the relationship between other factors and outcome.

indicative of differential change in the control and total therapy groups reached significance. There were, however, several significant Trials effects, suggesting that for both groups of patients reliable change did occur for the MMPI F, K, and Sc subscales. Specifically, these changes suggested a reduction in the patient's vicarious approach to the test task, a strengthening of reality-oriented defensiveness, and a reduction of bizarre cognitive behavior, occurring equally in both therapy and control groups. The other MMPI subscales and the Q-sort indices of improvement did not reliably reflect change for the groups, although the overall trends for both groups was toward a reduction in psychopathology.

Table 11.4—Significant F-ratios for 2 $\times$ 2 (experimentals vs. controls) repeated measures analyses of variance of the initial and terminal test scores for the MMPI and Q-sort outcome measures (only p values $\leq$ .10 are listed)

Outcome Measures[a]	Groups effect[b]	Trials effect	G $\times$ T interaction[b]
MMPI			
F		.05	
K		.05	
Sc		.05	

[a] MMPI Hs, D, Pa, Ma, Si, and ego strength subscales, and Q-sort-r, Q-sort adjustment measures not significant.
[b] No significant results.

When the therapy group was differentiated according to the level of accurate empathy (AE$_{15}$), a significant ($p \leq .05$) Groups $\times$ Trials interaction emerged for the MMPI Sc subscale. Only one other Groups $\times$ Trials interaction approached significance, that for the MMPI Hs subscale. As Figure 11.4 shows, this trend was most likely a reflection of an initial difference in the Hs scores of the three patient groups, rather than of differential change or terminal test differences. Patients attributing a low level of congruence to their therapists appeared to enter therapy with less concern for somatic ailments than the other groups. All groups, however, converged over time and their Hs scores were quite similar at the terminal test point.

Although the Sc subscale finding represents the only interaction effect significantly reflecting differential personality change for the high and low conditions groups it seems clearly important in light of the diagnosis of our patient sample. As Figure 11.4 shows, the greatest reduction of

Sc pathology occurred for the patient group receiving high levels of accurate empathy in the therapy relationship. Low AE patients showed a contrasting trend, suggesting a slight increase in Sc subscale score, or at most no positive change in this dimension. While the control patients

Table 11.5—Significant F-ratios for 3×2 (high-low-control patients, high-low patients dichotomized via AE_{15}) repeated measures analyses of variance of the initial and terminal test scores, for the MMPI and Q-sort outcome measures (only p values $\leq$ .10 are listed)

Outcome measures[a]	Groups effect[b]	Trials effect	G × T interaction
MMPI			
F		.05	
K		.05	
Sc		.01	.05

[a] MMPI Hs, D, Pa, Ma, Si, and ego strength subscales, and Q-sort–r, Q-sort adjustment measures not significant.
[b] No significant results.

Table 11.6—Significant F-ratios for 3×2 (high-low-control patients, high-low patients dichotomized via Pt-RI-C) repeated measures analyses of variance of the initial and terminal test scores, for the MMPI and Q-sort outcome measures (only p values $\leq$ .10 are listed)

Outcome Measures[a]	Groups effect	Trials effect	G × T interaction
MMPI			
F		.05	
K		.05	
Hs			.10
Sc		.05	
Ego strength	.05		

[a] MMPI D, Pa, Ma, Si, and Q-sort–r, Q-sort adjustment measures not significant.

showed a slight trend for improvement over time, this trend was moderate in comparison to the sharp decrease in pathology observed in the high conditions therapy group. Thus, while the three groups did not differ initially in their Sc subscale scores, they did change differentially over therapy, suggesting that a high level of accurate empathy in the

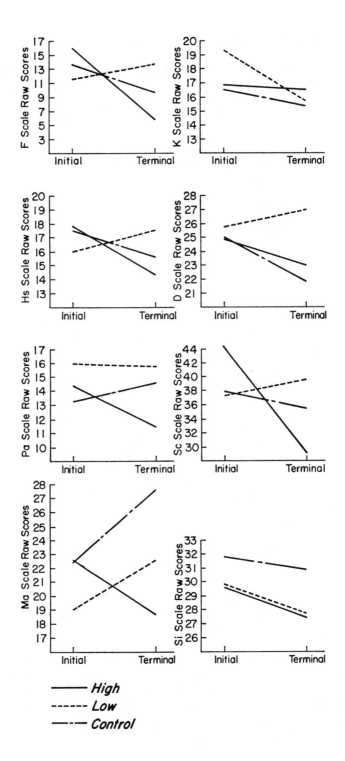

Figure 11.4—Differential trends of MMPI subscale change (initial to terminal) for the AE₁ₛ high and low conditions therapy patients, and for the control patients.

therapy interviews was associated with favorable outcome, and that this effect was particularly striking in contrast to the unfavorable outcome for the low AE group.

Additional support for the effectiveness of high therapist empathy can be drawn from an examination of the other nonsignificant trends in Figure 11.4, showing other MMPI subscale changes that were supportive of the significant Sc finding. The curves for the F, Hs, D, Pa, Ma, and ES subscales consistently show that the greatest improvement was for the high accurate empathy group, particularly in contrast to the negative change or lack of change for the low conditions group. Controls were intermediate, showing generally either moderate improvement or changes comparable to that of the high conditions patients. The K and Si subscales were the only exceptions. In the case of the K subscale, all three groups shared a uniform and statistically significant (see Table 11.5) decrease in defensiveness. Trends for the Si subscale suggest that a reduction in social isolation was somewhat characteristic of the patients undergoing therapy, but the trend was not of sufficient strength to differentiate them reliably from the controls.

The safest conclusion to be drawn from the MMPI data is that a low level of therapist accurate empathy was associated with a lack of improvement in therapy. While high conditions therapy was consistently associated with the greatest degree of positive MMPI change, test scores for the control group indicated moderate levels of improvement that frequently approached those of the high conditions group. The picture for the Q-sort was less clear-cut (see Figure 11.5). Slight initial differences among the three patient groups were apparent but not significant. Low AE patients seemed to initiate therapy with the most favorable self-concepts, particularly in contrast to the high conditions patients. The control group's adjustment and self-expert Q-sort scores fell between those of the high and low AE groups. These differences were not present at the terminal test point, so that the self-concepts of the three groups tended to converge over time.

Clinical assessment of test profiles.—Clinical assessment of patient change for our study took the form of two separate global assessments, as described in a previous section. One centered around MMPI profile change, and the other used the entire test battery (Truax-Liccione-Rosenberg assessment). Table 11.7 presents frequency tables for MMPI profile change designations, and the probability values associated with Fisher's Exact Test for therapy and control groups. In this case it was necessary to perform separate comparisons of the experimental and control and of the high and low conditions groups, since the small number of subjects in each cell prohibited the simultaneous comparison of all three subject groups.

It is apparent that there were no significant differences in improvement rates, either for the experimental-control or for the high-low

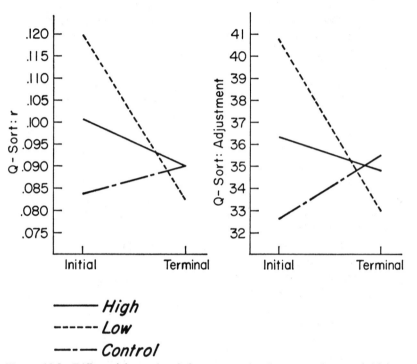

——— *High*

------ *Low*

—·— *Control*

Figure 11.5—Differential trends of Q–sort–r and adjustment change (initial to terminal) for the AE_{18} high and low conditions therapy patients, and for the control patients.

conditions therapy comparisons. None of the Fisher values reached the .05 level of significance. The trends, however, were consistent with both Hypotheses IV and IV–A. The majority of the therapy patients were classified as improved in contrast to control cases. Within the therapy group itself, five of the seven patients receiving high levels of accurate empathy showed MMPI profile improvement, while only two of five in the low accurate empathy group showed this type of favorable outcome.

Table 11.8 presents the analyses of variance of the Truax-Liccione-Rosenberg personality change scores assessed from the total test battery

Table 11.7—Fisher exact probability tests of the 3 × 2 (high-low-controls) classification of the experimental and control patients in terms of MMPI profile diagnostic assessment of positive change in adjustment for the AE_{15} and Pt-RI-C dichotomizations[a]: (+) positive change; (0) no change; (−) deterioration

Patient group	AE_{15}[b]		Pt-RI-C[c]	
	+	0 or −	+	0 or −
Experimentals				
High	5	2	4	2
Low	2	3	2	3
Controls	3	7	3	7

[a] The probability figures presented here all would have been slightly larger if the probabilities of the more extreme occurrences had been calculated and added. However, since none of the above figures was significant at the .05 level, the further superfluous task was omitted.

[b] Fisher probability
Experimentals vs. Controls $p = .147$
High vs. Low $p = .530$

[c] Fisher probability
Experimentals vs. Controls $p = .187$
High vs. Low $p = .325$

for each therapy and control patient. Again, it is clear that there were no significant differences for the experimental-control or for the high conditions, low conditions, and control comparisons. The mean outcome scores of the therapy and control groups were extremely close, and

Table 11.8—Means of simple analyses of variance for the high-low-control patients (the high-low conditions groups dichotomized via the AE_{15} and Pt-RI-C scores), for the Truax-Liccione-Rosenberg assessment[a]

Patient group	AE_{15}	Pt-RI-C
Experimentals	5.35	5.64
High	5.86	6.08
Low	4.75	5.10
Controls	5.46	5.46

[a] None of the p values was significant at the .05 level or less.

indicated virtually no improvement for either group—the scale midpoint of 5.0 indicates no change. Yet again, the means for the high conditions, low conditions, and control comparisons, while not statistically significant, were consistent with hypothesis IV–A. High conditions patients showed the greatest, control group members an intermediate, and low conditions patients the least amount of rated test improvement.

Therapist rating of change and outcome.—The therapist ratings of their patients' change and outcome, made at the termination of therapy, were available of course only for the experimental group. Table 11.9

Table 11.9—Means for high and low AE_{15} and Pt-RI-C patients (the high-low conditions groups dichotomized via the AE_{15} and Pt-RI-C scores), for therapists' ratings of patient change and outcome at the termination of therapy[a]

Therapist ratings	AE_{15}		PT-RI-C	
	High	Low	High	Low
Change	1.57	1.43	1.83	1.83
Outcome	5.17	5.14	5.17	5.17

[a] None of the *t*-test values was significant at the .05 level or less.

presents group means comparisons of the change and outcome ratings for high and low conditions groups. Whether accurate empathy or perceived congruence was used to determine the dichotomies, the high and low groups showed nearly identical mean values. In terms of the scale definitions, moreover, these means suggested that both groups were rated by their therapists as essentially unchanged. Thus, from the therapists' viewpoint at the end of therapy there was little discernible change in the patients, and certainly no differential change for the high and low conditions groups, suggesting that the therapists assessed therapeutic progress from the same discrepant perspective used in evaluating the quality of the relationship itself.

Wittenborn Psychiatric Rating Scales.—Analyses of variance findings for the Wittenborn subscale scores described in the previous section showed no significant differential change for either the therapy patients as a group, or for the high and low conditions patients, in contrast to the controls. None of the interaction effects necessary to support Hypotheses IV or IV–A reached or approached the .05 level of significance. Indeed, there was little change in the Wittenborn subscale scores for the patient sample as a whole. The strongest Trials (overall change) effect found was the trend at the .10 level for the hebephrenic schizophrenia subscale, suggesting a general reduction of hebephrenic symptoms in the total patient sample.

As Figure 11.6 shows, therapy patients as a group manifested a generally less severe level of paranoid symptomatology than did controls. Results of the more differentiated analyses showed that it was the high accurate empathy group in particular that manifested the least severe general syndrome (depressed state, hebephrenic schizophrenia, paranoid schizophrenia), with control and low conditions patients being rated as relatively more severe. Trends for the schizophrenic excitement scale were similar but not significant. While these group differences were apparent to some degree throughout therapy, they were especially marked at the initial rating period.

This data most clearly suggests that the variable of symptomatic severity may play a confounding role in the developing therapy relationship. This possibility will be considered in detail in the final section of this chapter. Meanwhile, it seems clear that differential symptomatic change, necessary to support Hypotheses IV and IV–A, did not occur when hospital staff ratings provided the index of change and outcome.

Hospitalization status.—Table 11.10 presents the means and F-ratios for analyses of variance comparing hospitalization status of the

Table 11.10—Means and F-ratios of simple analyses of variance for the experimental vs. control patients and for the high-low-control patients (the high-low conditions groups dichotomized via AE_{16} and PT-RI-C scores), for three measures of per cent time out of hospital

Patient group	Means			F-ratios		
	0–3 yrs.	6 mos.	12 mos.	0–3 yrs.	6 mos.	12 mos.
Experimentals	50.7	63.6	68.2	NS	NS	$p \le .10$
AE_{16} Dichotomy						
High	45.7	57.8	67.0	NS	NS	NS
Low	55.7	69.3	69.5			
Pt-RI-C Dichotomy						
High	55.2	79.5	89.7	NS	NS	$p \le .05$
Low	62.9	68.8	69.5			
Controls	46.9	40.0	39.8			

therapy group as a whole, and of the high and low conditons therapy patients, with those of the control group. First, it is apparent that while the F-ratios for the experimental-control comparisons did not reach significance, there was a strong tendency for the total therapy group to have a more favorable release than control group members. This was

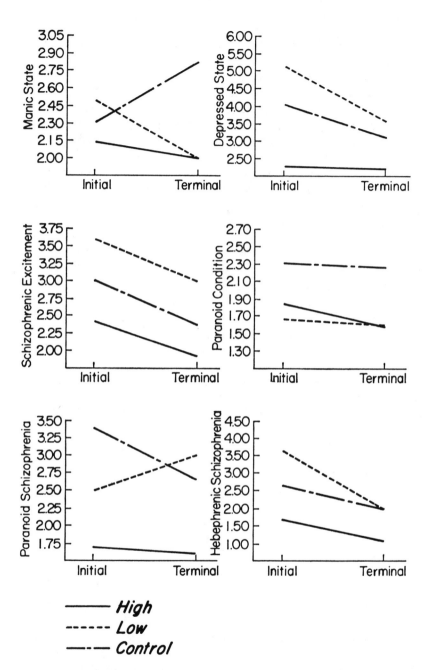

Figure 11.6—Differential trends of Wittenborn subscale change (initial to terminal) for the AE₁ₛ high and low conditions therapy patients, and for the control patients.

especially marked when the full year after therapy termination was used as the basis for the hospitalization status, suggesting the greater success of therapy patients in maintaining release from the hospital.

The role of the therapist conditions variables was considerably less clear-cut. If we consider the accurate empathy groups, we find that it was the low conditions group that showed the most favorable hospitalization status. When patient-perceived congruence was used to determine the conditions dichotomy, results were more consistent with theoretical expectations. At both the six- and twelve-months points the high congruence patients showed the greatest percentage of time out of the hospital, with low congruence patients being intermediate, and controls showing the least favorable outcome. This trend was statistically significant only at the one-year point. Duncan multiple range comparisons, however, indicated that this difference was clear only for the two extreme groups, that is, the high conditions and control groups. The intermediate low conditions group was not significantly different from either of these two groups in hospitalization status.

Two conclusions are suggested. First, it is apparent that therapy and control groups do not show differential release rates until considerable time has elapsed after therapy termination. Second, it seems clear that although more favorable hospitalization status occurred for the high conditions (congruence) patients, this emerges most clearly in contrast to the control group, rather than to the low conditions group.

Overview

When the preceding complement of personality change and outcome measures is considered, support for Hypothesis IV, which called for differential improvement in the therapy patients as a group in contrast to the controls, turns out to be quite limited. Only one criterion index revealed even a trend in support of the hypothesis—hospitalization rates one year after therapy termination showed that therapy patients as a group spent more time out of the hospital than did the controls, suggesting their greater long-term success in maintaining release or parole from the hospital. In all other respects the various outcome-change measures for the experimental and control groups were virtually identical.

When the experimental group was dichotomized according to the level of conditions received in the therapy relationship (thereby testing Hypothesis IV–A), we found a statistically significant positive relationship supportive of the hypothesis between the level of conditions and some measures of patient outcome. High conditions (accurate empathy) patients showed the greatest amount of positive change for the MMPI schizophrenia (Sc) subscale, controls, a moderate degree of positive change, and the low conditons therapy patients, a slightly negative trend. High conditions (patient-perceived congruence) patients also showed the most favorable hospitalization rates, although with this measure the positions of the control and low conditions groups were reversed, with the controls showing the least favorable outcome.

Generally, these two findings were supported by many consistent but statistically insignificant trends, not only for the additional MMPI subscales but also for global assessment of improvement made by diagnosticians utilizing the MMPI profile data alone, and other diagnosticians using the entire test battery. These trends showed that control group cases had a moderate level of improvement, in relation to the large improvement shown by the high conditions patients and the lack of improvement shown by the low conditions patients.

Therapist ratings of change and outcome, Q-sort self-ratings, and the Wittenborn hospital-staff ratings offered no support for either Hypothesis IV or IV–A. Therapist ratings were virtually identical for both high and low conditions groups. The Q-sort self-ratings and the Wittenborn hospital ratings reflected only initial or overall group differences and showed little overall change and no differential group change. Clear-cut trends emerged for three Wittenborn subscales, indicating that patients rated by the hospital staff as least severe in depression, paranoid schizophrenia, and hebephrenic schizophrenia also received higher levels of therapist accurate empathy. Yet, this same high conditions group tended to show the least favorable self-concepts both at the initiation and termination of therapy. The low conditions patients, on the other hand, tended to show the greatest level of symptomatic disturbance, and the most favorable self-concepts initially. The control patients fell consistently between these extremes. These findings suggest that variables such as the severity of symptoms and the nature of the self-concept may function as confounding factors in both the conditions-process and the conditions-outcome relationships.

Support for Hypothesis IV–A, therefore, was limited to two types of outcome measures: self-report test change and objective hospitalization rates. While not sufficiently reliable to lend unequivocal support to Hypothesis IV–A the results seem sufficiently consistent to warrant further study. It seems especially meaningful that the single MMPI subscale directly relevant to the shared diagnostic classification of all the patients in this study (the Sc scale) significantly reflected differential change for high conditions, low conditions, and control groups. The weaker trends apparent for other MMPI subscales may have reflected the relative lack of uniformity within our small patient sample for these more tangential areas of pathology.

While support for Hypothesis IV–A was modest it nonetheless quite consistently affirmed the greater efficacy of high conditions therapy, particularly in contrast to low conditions therapy. While test outcome differences for high conditions in contrast to control patients were not so sharp, the consistent trends suggest that high conditions therapy had a generally positive effect, and that this effect was more likely to have long-term implications for the patient's post-hospital adjustment than the more modest improvement for the control group.

The Assessment of Confounding Variables

The major purpose of this study was to demonstrate the relationship between therapist conditions factors and variables of patient process (Hypotheses I and III–A) and personality change (Hypothesis IV–A). We further attempted to explore the effect of therapy on process (Hypothesis III) and outcome (Hypothesis IV) by comparing in-therapy and control groups. We saw that the level of therapist conditions, particularly rated accurate empathy and patient-perceived congruence, was positively associated with patient experiencing level (but not with movement) in the therapy and sampling interviews. We found, further, that there were few differences in either process or outcome for therapy and control patients, unless the quality or level of therapist conditions was considered. When they were considered, improvement was consistently greatest for the high conditions therapy patients and least apparent for low conditions patients, with an intermediate level of improvement characterizing the no-therapy control group. These latter differences were theoretically consistent, providing meaningful, although limited, support for Hypotheses III–A and IV–A.

Yet, before even such limited conclusions could be drawn, certain interpretive issues had to be resolved. Findings reported in the previous section suggested that there may have been initial test differences between patients who subsequently received high and low conditions in the therapy relationship, and that therapy and control patients may have differed somewhat on these measures initially. If such differences existed, they may have had an important role in the differential process course or outcome characteristic of high conditions, low conditions, and control groups.

At this point, then, it was essential to control statistically for the possible confounding effect of such theoretically extraneous differentiating factors, before the conditions-process and conditions-outcome relationships could be interpreted as providing theoretical support.

Patient age, sex, degree of chronicity, and socio-educational status were considered of sufficient relevance to therapy prognosis that they were controlled in the design of the study. (See Chapter 2 for a detailed description of these stratifying variables.) Other patient variables were not controlled systematically but were perhaps equally important. A patient's level of verbal intelligence or initial openness to personal problems may crucially affect the quality of his participation in therapy. Likewise, factors such as the patient's location on the process-reactive premorbid continuum, or his degree of ego strength before therapy, may relate to his readiness for, or openness to, personality change in the course of therapy. Aspects of initial presenting pathology or self-attitudes may relate both to the quality of in-therapy behavior and to the nature of outcome. Lastly, the factor of case length, uncontrolled in the design of this study, may interact with the conditions-process or the conditions-outcome relationships. In this section any such variables differentiating patient groups have been controlled statistically in a reassessment of the significant conditions-process and conditions-outcome relationships obtained.

Measurement of the Extraneous Variables

The measurement procedures for many of the variables considered in this section have been described in detail in other chapters. The four stratifying variables of age, sex, chronicity, and socio-educational status were discussed in detail in Chapter 2. Psychometric measures including the MMPI subscales, Q-sort indices of adjustment, and Wittenborn Psychiatric Rating Scales estimates of ward behavior were described fully in the first section of this chapter. The procedures for measuring verbal intelligence and patient in-therapy verbalization rate, and for obtaining ratings of process-reaction, readiness for self-exploration, and initial mental health are presented below.

Wechsler Adult Intelligence Scale.—The measure of verbal intelligence for this study consisted of the composite score for the verbal subscales of the Wechsler Adult Intelligence Scale (abbreviated form), administered to each patient prior to his assignment to either the therapy or the control group.

Patient in-therapy verbalization rate.—The work of Saslow and Matarazzo (1959) has suggested that merely the average duration of the patient's talking in the therapy interview may represent an important determinant of the resulting relationship. Likewise, for this study we were concerned that our segmenting procedure (see Chapter 8) might have biased our sampling of patient-therapist interactions in favor of patients who talked less in the interview hour. For both these reasons it was deemed necessary to obtain a measure of patient talking rate in therapy. The measure decided upon was the per cent of patient silence in the second therapy interview for each of the fourteen therapy cases. This sample may or may not have been representative of the patient's behavior throughout therapy, but it did provide an estimate of his ability or willingness to verbalize early in the therapy interaction.

The Phillips Premorbid Scale.—The process-reactive continuum has proved of considerable value as a prognostic index for schizophrenic patients (Hunt and Appel, 1936; Blair, 1940; Kant, 1940; Wittman, 1941; Benjamin, 1946; Kantor, Wallner, and Winder, 1953; Brackbill and Fine, 1956). The Phillips Scale has been used rather extensively to define this continuum (Phillips, 1949, 1953; Garmezy and Rodnick, 1959; Zigler and Phillips, 1961a, 1961b). For this scale, various areas of the patient's premorbid history (sexual adjustment, interpersonal relations, and affective and cognitive functioning) are rated, yielding an index of the type of onset of disturbance. A patient is scored at the reactive end of the continuum if there is little or no evidence of long standing mental or emotional disturbance. The reactive schizophrenic, with a sudden onset, is considered to have a more favorable prognosis than the process schizophrenic, with the latter's contrasting history of long-term withdrawal and disturbance. The scoring on the Phillips Scale was performed by a staff member from an examination of available case records. The scorer had no knowledge of the treatment or outcome status of individual cases. For each patient two ratings were made: an optimistic rating based on a favorable interpretation of ambiguous case-history data, and a pessimistic rating for which ambiguities were resolved in the pathological direction. Since these scores correlated very highly (.91), only those for optimistic ratings are used in subsequent analyses.

Kirtner-Cartwright Scale.—This scale (Kirtner and Cartwright, 1958) is intended to provide an assessment of the degree of openness and the quality of problem exploration manifest in the patient's early therapy interview behavior. Attention is paid in particular to the manner and degree to which problems are defined by the patient as having personal anchorage and affective implications. The scale is very similar in conception to the Experiencing Scale, and can serve for this study as an independent assessment of the patient's initial capacity for self-exploration. The Kirtner-Cartwright Scale was applied to the second therapy interview for each experimental case by four judges trained specifically for this purpose. Interrater reliabilities were adequate—Pearson intercorrelation values ranged from .58 to .65. In the analyses that follow the average of the four judges' ratings of the second interview segments will be used.

Thematic Apperception Test mental health ratings.—The initial

TAT protocols of the experimental and control cases were rated by one judge, Rosalind Dymond Cartwright, on a 9-point scale of mental health developed and used by her in the Rogers and Dymond (1954) study. Factors such as creative and expressive quality, organization and structure, degree of disturbance, and affective tone in the content of TAT stories told were considered together for a global assessment of the patient's personality functioning. These mental health ratings were made blindly, so that the judge had no knowledge of the patient's treatment or outcome status.

Initial Differences in Experimental and Control Groups

The purpose of matching therapy and control groups for factors such as age, sex, chronicity, and socio-educational status was to insure that the two groups would be as similar as possible initially on any dimensions that might relate to their ultimate outcome, thereby making it probable that any differences in process or outcome were due to their differential treatments. As the preceding section has shown, however, our sample revealed no differences in process or outcome between experimental and control patients. Hospitalization rates constituted the sole exception. Consequently, we need consider the confounding effect of initial factors for only the experimental-control differences in hospitalization rates.

Table 11.11 presents the means and t-test values for initial comparisons of therapy and control groups on the various extraneous variables described above. While there were no significant differences between the groups on any of the measures, there was a trend for therapy patients to show a slightly higher level of initial ego strength, suggesting a more favorable prognosis. Generally, however, the lack of initial differences for therapy and control groups suggested that the selection procedure by which the groups were matched for stratifying variables did, in fact, yield comparable groups.

In order to assess the contribution of the initial ego strength trend to the different hospitalization rates for the experimental and control groups, a simple analysis of covariance was performed. With this procedure, the magnitude of the group difference was considerably diminished. The original F-ratio for the therapy-control difference dropped from 4.53 ($p \leq .10$) to 2.71 ($p \leq .25$), and the group means moved closer together (71.2 per cent and 40.7 per cent, in place of the original 73.5 per cent and 37.4 per cent for therapy and control groups respectively). Thus, it seemed probable that the discrepant ego strength scores for therapy and control groups accounted for their different hospitalization rates. While the therapy group continued to show a greater percentage of time out of the hospital, the difference was no longer statistically significant. Thus, when initial ego strength was controlled, the resultant findings became consistent with those for other outcome measures, indicating no differential improvement for the experimental and control groups.

Table 11.11—Means and *t*-test values of comparisons of the experimental and control patients on initial measures of patient extraneous variables

Extraneous variables	Means		*p*
	Experimentals	Controls	
MMPI			
F	14.8	15.9	NS
K	17.3	17.0	NS
Hs	16.8	18.1	NS
D	25.7	25.5	NS
Pa	15.2	14.3	NS
Sc	41.9	39.6	NS
Ma	21.5	23.5	NS
Si	30.8	30.7	NS
Ego strength	41.6	36.3	$\leq.10$
Q-sort-r	.10	.09	NS
Q-sort adjustment	38.2	32.6	NS
Wittenborn			
MS	2.3	2.4	NS
DS	3.8	3.8	NS
SE	2.9	3.0	NS
PC	1.8	2.4	NS
PS	2.2	3.6	NS
HS	2.8	2.6	NS
WAIS verbal IQ	104.5	103.0	NS
Phillips Premorbid Scale	37.9	40.1	NS
TAT mental health ratings	4.0	3.2	NS

Initial Differences in the High and Low Conditions Groups

Since there was no attempt in this study to control the level of therapist conditions offered a particular patient, it was essential to consider the extent of association between the level of conditions subsequently attained and any initial patient factors that might have influenced these therapist variables. This was particularly important for the clear interpretation of the relationship obtained in Chapter 9 between two measures of therapist conditions (rated accurate empathy and patient-perceived congruence) and the general level of patient experiencing. It was also pivotal in considering the interrelationship of these same conditions variables with three measures of patient outcome: hospitalization rates, MMPI Sc change, and MMPI profile change. In this section, then, we will first compare high and low conditions groups (AE$_{15}$ and Pt-RI-C dichotomies) on the initial patient measures, and will then attempt to control statistically for the effect of any significant differences regarding these extraneous factors on the conditions-process and conditions-outcome relationships.

Comparison of high and low conditions groups.—Table 11.12 presents the 2 × 2 frequency counts and corresponding Fisher exact probability values for the four stratifying variables (age, sex, socio-educational

Table 11.12—2 × 2 frequency counts for the high and low conditions patients (AE$_{15}$ and Pt-RI-C dichotomies) on the four stratifying dichotomies of the study—socio-educational status, sex, chronicity, and age (*p* refers to the probability values resulting from Fisher's Exact Test)

Stratifying dichotomy	AE$_{15}$		Pt-RI-C	
	High AE	Low AE	High C	Low C
Socio-educational status	(*p* = NS)		(*p* ≤ .10)	
High	5	3	5	2
Low	2	4	1	4
Sex	(*p* ≤ .10)		(*p* ≤ .05)	
Males	5	1	5	1
Females	2	6	1	5
Chronicity	(*p* = NS)		(*p* ≤ .10)	
Acutes	3	5	2	5
Chronics	4	2	4	1
Age	(*p* = NS)		(*p* = NS)	
Young	3	4	3	4
Old	4	3	3	2

status, and chronicity) compared for the two conditions dichotomies (AE$_{15}$ and Pt-RI-C). This table shows that the patient's sex was significantly related to both conditions factors, indicating that therapists of male patients manifested higher levels of accurate empathy, and were attributed higher levels of congruence, than were therapists of female patients. Likewise, socio-educational (SE) status and chronicity were moderately associated with the two conditions measures, although not to a significant degree. High therapist conditions tended to be more likely for high SE status patients, and, surprisingly, for chronic rather than acute cases.

Further inspection of the relationships in Table 11.12 suggests that the three variables of sex, SE status, and chronicity interacted cumulatively in relation to therapist conditions—so that it was the high SE status, chronic, male patients whose therapists provided the higher conditions levels; whereas therapists of low SE status, acute, female patients showed lower conditions levels. In order to examine this interaction more systematically, a composite index for these three stratifying variables was derived. Each of the three factors (male sex, high SE status, and chronicity) independently associated with high therapist conditions was arbitrarily weighted one point toward a composite stratifying score. For example, a male, high SE status, chronic patient received a score of three; the male, low SE status, chronic patient, a score of two; the female, low SE status, acute patient, a score of zero. The positive correlations obtained for this composite stratifying index and the level of conditions (.41 with AE_{15}; .71 with Pt-RI-C, $p \leq .01$) suggested rather strongly that these factors did interact cumulatively in relation to therapist conditions, and that they were associated particularly with the patient's perception of his therapist.

The finding that high SE status was related to constructive therapy was consistent with previous research (Imber *et al.*, 1956; Rubinstein and Lorr, 1956; Rosenthal and Frank, 1958; Hollingshead and Redlich, 1958; Brill and Storrow, 1960; Raskin, 1961; Srole *et al.*, 1961; Langer and Michael, 1963). Our results for the sex and chronicity variables however, were somewhat more unusual. Since all but one of the therapists of the study were male, it is possible that the similarity of background and outlook more probable for same-sex patient-therapist pairs could account for the obtained association between sex and conditions level. However, the relationship between chronicity and high conditions was more unexpected. Two aspects of the original selection procedure could account for this seemingly discrepant finding. First, chronicity was indexed solely by length of prior hospitalization (more than eight months) and not by any psychometric or behavioral criterion of psychological regression or deterioration. The deficiency of this indexing is suggested by the fact that we obtained a negative trend in the relationship between chronicity and the Phillips process-reactive measure, indicating that the chronic patients in our sample tended to receive higher *reactive* ratings than acute patients. Consequently, the chronic patients actually tended to have a more favorable prognostic rating. Second, all patients with a history of extensive EST or IST were ineligible for the study, so that many of the most severely disturbed and/or deteriorated chronics in the hospital population were automatically excluded. This selection procedure may have biased the chronic sample so that it included patients whose apparent deficit was as much a function of lack of stimulation from prolonged hospitalization as it was of any psychotic deterioration. Thus, it is possible that the chronic patient in our study not only had a more favorable prognosis than the acute patient, but also represented the most well-adapted and non-deteriorated segment of the long-term hospital population. In either case, it seemed probable that the relatively high conditions levels obtained for chronic patients were in part a function of this subgroup's greater capacity for change, or greater responsiveness to the stimulating impact of the therapy relationship.

Table 11.13 presents the means and t-test values for high and low conditions group comparisons on a number of other initial patient

Table 11.13—Means and t-test values for the high and low conditions patients (dichotomized via AE_{15} and Pt-RI-C) comparing differences on initial measures of extraneous variables

Extraneous variables	AE_{15} Means			Pt-RI-C Means		
	High	Low	p	High	Low	p
MMPI						
F	16.0	13.2	NS	14.7	15.0	NS
K	16.9	18.0	NS	19.0	15.7	NS
Hs	17.9	15.4	NS	18.7	15.0	NS
D	24.9	26.8	NS	24.2	27.2	NS
Pa	14.3	16.4	NS	13.2	17.2	NS
Sc	44.4	38.4	NS	42.5	41.3	NS
Ma	22.6	20.0	NS	20.8	22.2	NS
Si	29.6	32.4	NS	30.7	30.8	NS
Ego strength	41.1	42.2	NS	42.5	40.2	NS
Q-sort–r	.10	.12	NS	.11	.10	NS
Q-sort adjustment	36.3	40.8	NS	38.2	38.2	NS
Wittenborn						
MS	2.5	2.6	NS	1.2	3.4	$\leq$.10
DS	2.4	5.6	$\leq$.05	2.7	4.2	NS
SE	2.4	3.6	NS	1.5	4.2	$\leq$.10
PC	1.9	1.8	NS	1.5	2.2	NS
PS	1.7	2.8	$\leq$.01	1.7	2.6	NS
HS	1.7	4.2	$\leq$.05	1.5	4.0	$\leq$.05
WAIS verbal IQ	109.1	99.2	$\leq$.10	112.5	94.7	$\leq$.01
Phillips Premorbid Scale	34.6	41.3	NS	37.8	41.7	NS
Kirtner-Cartwright Scale	3.6	4.0	NS	3.9	3.6	NS
TAT mental health ratings	4.7	3.0	$\leq$.10	4.8	3.2	$\leq$.10
No. months in therapy	19.0	12.4	NS	20.3	10.8	NS
No. therapy interviews	85.3	63.4	NS	93.3	51.5	NS
Length of second interview	49.3	43.4	NS	50.5	43.0	NS
Per cent silence of second interview	15.4	39.7	$\leq$.01	16.5	43.2	$\leq$.01

variables. Several initial differences appeared consistently for both high and low accurate empathy (AE_{15}) and perceived congruence (Pt-RI-C). High conditions patients apparently entered therapy with a relatively higher level of verbal intelligence, were more talkative in the second interview, and received more favorable ratings for TAT stories and for ward behavior (Wittenborn hebephrenic schizophrenia subscale). Other initial differences were limited to only one of the conditions dichotomies. Those cases subsequently rated high in accurate empathy received less severe disturbance ratings for the Wittenborn depressed state and paranoid schizophenia subscales. On the other hand, patients perceiving a high level of congruence showed less disturbance initially on the manic state and schizophrenic excitement subscales of the Wittenborn, but these differences only approached significance ($p \leqslant .10$). Hence, while there were minor variations in the specific symptom areas stressed for the two conditions dichotomies, it was clear that patients receiving and perceiving high therapist conditions showed less severe symptomatic disturbance at the initiation of therapy.

The other differences for these groups were consistent for both conditions variables, and suggested that high conditions patients exhibited a relatively greater verbal facility and general expressiveness upon entering therapy. This generalization regarding the high-low conditions group differences in verbal IQ, per cent silence in the second interview, initial TAT mental health ratings, and the stratifying index seemed justifiable in light of the high intercorrelation among these factors (see Table 11.14). That is, the high intercorrelations among these different measures suggested that they all tapped some aspect of the patient's general verbal facility and/or productivity. The positive relationship of this cluster to the stratifying index suggested a close association between

Table 11.14—Pearson intercorrelation matrix for the extraneous variables showing initial differences for the high and low conditions patients

	IQ	Per cent silence	MS	DS	SE	PS	HS	TAT
					Wittenborn			
Stratifying index	.635	−.672	−.108	−.305	−.156	−.174	−.439	.496
WAIS verbal IQ		−.547	.077	−.179	.108	.206	−.238	.495
Per cent silence			−.191	.510	−.139	.105	.168	−.420
Wittenborn MS				.382	.968	.692	.654	−.053
Wittenborn DS					.470	.646	.635	−.593
Wittenborn SE						.829	.695	−.208
Wittenborn PS							.636	−.355
Wittenborn HS								−.438

this initial expressive productivity and the patient's general educational background (high SE status), his probable commonality of background with the male therapist (sex), and his chronicity (likely reflecting, for this sample, the patient who was particularly eager for a relationship, rather than one who was severely regressed or deteriorated). The negative association between the TAT mental health rating and various Wittenborn scales also suggested that this expressive productivity factor reflected in part the patient's relative freedom from gross symptomatic disturbance. Together, these initial patient differences formed a pattern which could be interpreted as indicating that the patient receiving high therapist conditions enters therapy with a greater verbal facility and expressive capacity (verbal IQ, per cent silence, TAT ratings) that is associated with his general background and openness to the therapeutic relationship (stratifying index) as well as to his level of symptomatic disturbance (Wittenborn subscales).

This interpretation was further supported by the strong associations found between this cluster of initial factors and a TAT measure of "emotional distancing" developed by Barrington (see Chapter 14). This highly objective procedure for rating TAT stories taps a continuum from extreme emotional distancing to affective immediacy regarding the patient's involvement in his story. Barrington's TAT score correlated substantially with the initial patient-factor cluster (with the exception of the patient's initial verbal IQ score, although even here the correlation was low positive). The pattern of association suggested that the patient who had a low level of initial Wittenborn disturbance but a relatively high TAT mental health rating, who was relatively verbal during the second therapy interview, and who rated high on the stratifying index, was unlikely to show emotional distancing in his TAT stories.

Control for initial differences in conditions-process relationships.— In order to assess the extent to which the initial patient differences reported above influenced the relationship obtained between therapist conditions and patient process, partial correlations between rated accurate empathy, perceived congruence, and experiencing were calculated. Each factor initially differentiating the high and low conditions patients was treated in turn as the control variable. This procedure yielded an estimate of the variance in the conditions-process relationship that could be accounted for by the operation of the control variable, and provided an assessment of the residual conditions-process covariance. In cases, for example, where the conditions-process relationship was confounded by initial patient differences, the correlation coefficient for AE-EXP or Pt-RI-C–EXP became smaller after the effect of the initial differentiating factor (control variable) was removed.

Table 11.15 presents partial correlation coefficients showing the degree of residual relationship between accurate empathy (AE_{15}) or patient-perceived congruence (Pt-RI-C), and experiencing (EXP_{TOT}) when factors such as verbal IQ, second-interview silence, etc. were controlled. Of the eight initial factors considered, four contributed considerably to the conditions-process relationship. When initial verbal IQ, per cent silence in the second interview, initial TAT mental health ratings, and the initial level of depressive symptomatology (Wittenborn Scales)

Table 11.15—Partial correlation values for the conditions-process relationships (AE_{15}-EXP_{TOT}; Pt-RI-C–EXP_{TOT}), holding constant extraneous variables showing initial differences for the high and low conditions patients

Extraneous variables	Zero-order correlations			Partial correlation values	
				AE_{15} - EXP_{TOT}	Pt-RI-C–EXP_{TOT}
	AE_{15}	Pt-RI-C	EXP_{TOT}	$(.545^*)^a$	$(.664^*)^a$
Wittenborn					
MS	−.112	−.199	−.178	.567*	.652*
DS	−.640	−.397	−.616	.250	.581*
SE	−.203	−.232	−.189	.528*	.649*
PS	−.296	−.173	−.234	.513*	.651*
HS	−.562	−.460	−.255	.502*	.637*
WAIS verbal IQ	.500	.635	.555	.371	.485*
TAT mental health ratings	.577	.632	.470	.380	.536*
Per cent silence second interview	−.572	−.584	−.625	.292	.472*
Stratifying index	.410	.710	.534	.502*	.476*

[a] These values represent the original zero-order correlation coefficients for the AE_{15}-EXP_{TOT} and Pt-RI-C–EXP_{TOT} relationships.

* $p \leq .05$

were partialled out, the relationship between AE_{15} and EXP_{TOT} was reduced so sharply that it was no longer significant. On the other hand, none of these factors influenced the obtained relationship of Pt-RI-C and EXP_{TOT}. These latter variables continued to be significantly related, even when the initial, theoretically extraneous, factors influencing the AE_{15}-EXP_{TOT} relationship were held constant.

The patient factors seriously confounding the conditions-process relationship, then, were those reflecting aspects of the patient's verbal productivity and expressiveness at the initiation of therapy. This confounding, however (at least insofar as the variables measured were concerned), was limited to the relationship between *rated* therapist accurate empathy and *rated* patient experiencing. It was not present when the patient's perception of conditions (congruence) was considered. Thus, the confounding was present only when ratings made from the same tape-recorded segments of the therapy interview were intercorrelated.

How was this confounding to be interpreted? There seemed to be several alternative explanations. One was that the patient's verbal fluency affected the therapist's behavior in the therapy interaction itself. That is, the empathic quality of the therapist's reflections or interpretations of the patient's experiential field might depend largely on the quality or amount of the patient's communication. A second possibility was that the quality or amount of the patient's verbalization influenced the judges' ratings of the therapist, not because therapist empathy actually was dependent on the expressive quality of the patient, but because the judges used, as an important cue for rating therapist empathy, the patient's clarity of expression and response to the therapist. A third possibility was that both accurate empathy and experiencing ratings reflected a third factor, perhaps some more general quality of the patient-therapist interaction. In each case, however, it seemed clear that the major source of the confounding of the conditions-process relationship stemmed from the fact that both variables were rated, albeit by different judges, from the same tape-recorded interaction containing verbalizations of both participants.

In any case, it seemed clear that the relationship between accurate empathy and experiencing was difficult to interpret. Neither rating could be considered an independent assessment of patient or therapist behavior, and the covariance found could not be viewed as a significant association between independent factors. This methodological situation and the theoretical implications of a more complex, interactive association between accurate empathy and experiencing will be considered more fully in the following chapter, where an interactive interpretation of these therapist and patient variables is presented.

Control for initial differences in conditions-outcome relationships.— In order to examine the contribution of initial patient differences to the conditions-outcome relationships, partial correlations were calculated for these associations, with each of the initial differentiating patient factors serving in turn as the control variable. The two conditions-outcome relationships that proved (in the previous section of this chapter) to be significant were considered. Table 11.16 presents the partial correlation coefficients showing the degree of residual relationship between accurate empathy (AE_{15}) and MMPI Sc change, and between patient-perceived congruence (Pt-RI-C) and the twelve-months index of hospitalization status, after each of the eight factors initially differentiating the high and low conditions groups was controlled.

It is apparent from this table that the unadjusted correlation values for these particular conditions-outcome relationships did not reach a level of significance comparable to that yielded by the analyses of

Table 11.16—Partial correlation values for the conditions-outcome relationships (AE$_{16}$-Sc change; Pt-RI-C–hospitalization status), holding constant extraneous variables showing initial differences for the high and low conditions patients

					Partial correlation values	
	Zero-order correlations				AE$_{16}$-Sc change	Pt-RI-C– Hosp (12 mos.)
Extraneous variables	AE$_{16}$	Sc-change	Pt-RI-C	Hosp (12 mos.)	(.369)^a	(.327)^a
Wittenborn						
MS	−.112	−.234	−.199	−.550*	.355	.265
DS	−.640*	−.228	−.397	−.272	.298	.248
SE	−.203	−.273	−.232	−.564*	.333	.244
HS	−.562*	−.586*	−.460*	−.518*	.060	.117
WAIS verbal IQ	.500*	.295	.635†	.370	.267	.128
TAT mental health ratings	.577*	.050	.632	.252	.417	.224
Per cent silence second interview	−.390	.059	−.588*	−.158	.426	.293
Stratifying index	.386	.318	.680†	.186	.281	.278

* $p \leq .05$
† $p \leq .01$
^{a} These values represent the original zero-order correlation coefficients for the AE$_{16}$-Sc change and Pt-RI-C–Hosp (12 mos.) relationships.

variance of the preceding section. This reduction of significance level was undoubtedly due to the reduction of degrees of freedom resulting from the necessary elimination of the control group of patients from this matrix. Regardless, it seems clear from Table 11.16 that the respective conditions-outcome relationships were generally reduced when the effect of the theoretically extraneous factors initially differentiating the conditions dichotomies was considered. The only clear exceptions occurred for patient second-interview silence and initial TAT mental health ratings apropos of the accurate empathy-Sc change relationship. Here, the first-order coefficients were increased, although they did not reach the .05 level of significance.

Most generally, these analyses suggested that the initial patient differ-

ences in verbal productivity, expressiveness, and gross level of symptomatic disturbance which had proved to differentiate high and low conditions groups, and to influence the conditions-process relationships, also
influenced the conditions-outcome associations reported in the second
section of this chapter. Hence, although a significant association between therapist conditions and constructive patient change had been
found which could possibly have supportive theoretical implications, the
clear importance of initial patient factors in these relationships suggests
the need for a careful evaluation of the entire network of relationships
among initial patient differences, conditions, patient process, and patient
constructive change variables emerging from this study, and for the
development of a more complex, interactive interpretation of the total
pattern.

Overview

In this section the relationships previously reported between therapist
conditions and patient process, as well as the associations between
conditions and outcome, have been examined in conjunction with other,
potentially confounding patient variables. Certain initial patient factors
proved to be significantly associated with the level of therapist conditions the patient experienced in the therapeutic relationship. More
specifically, it was found that a relatively higher level of conditions
(rated accurate empathy and patient-perceived congruence) was generally related to the following initial patient factors: high socio-educational status, male sex, chronicity, high verbal intelligence, high verbal
productivity in the second therapy interview, high mental health rating
on the initial TAT, and a generally low level of manifest psychotic
disturbance on the Wittenborn Psychiatric Rating Scales. The higher
conditions level found for male patients was viewed in terms of the
greater probable similarity of outlook in like-sex, patient-therapist
pairs. The higher conditions reported for chronic cases was considered
to reflect the fact that chronicity was defined, for this study, in terms of
hospitalization length only, so that the more chronic (but not more
deteriorated) patients may have been somewhat more eager for, and
receptive to, the therapeutic contact. The prominence of the remaining
verbal and disturbance factors was interpreted as indicating the initially
greater verbal productivity and expressive capacity of the high conditions patient group, coupled with their relative lack of the type of gross
symptomatic disturbance which would have made therapeutic communication difficult.

When the effect of these initial differentiating factors on the conditions-process and conditions-outcome relationships (obtained in the pre-

vious section) was examined, we found that these variables did indeed, in many cases, influence the association between in-therapy and outcome variables. Initial conditions group differences in verbal productivity, verbal expressiveness, and symptomatic disturbance proved to have a confounding effect on both the accurate empathy-experiencing and congruence-experiencing relationships, and also on the accurate empathy-MMPI Sc change and congruence-hospitalization status associations. In the light of this, it seems clear that a straightforward interpretation of the theoretically important conditions-process and conditions-outcome relationships is difficult, and that the more complex evaluation, in the next chapter, of the entire pattern of association between patient variables, therapist conditions, patient process, and personality change is in order.

References

BARRON, F. An ego-strength scale which predicts response to psychotherapy. *J. consult. Psychol. 17:*327–333, 1953.

BENJAMIN, J. D. A method for distinguishing and evaluating formal thinking disorders in schizophrenia. In J. S. Kasanin (ed.), *Language and Thought in Schizophrenia.* Berkeley: University of California Press, 1946, pp. 66–71.

BETZ, BARBARA J. Experiences in research in psychotherapy with schizophrenic patients. In H. H. Strupp and L. Luborsky (eds.), *Research in Psychotherapy,* Vol. II. Washington, D.C.: American Psychological Association, 1962, pp. 41–60.

BLAIR, D. Prognosis in schizophrenia. *J. ment. Science* [now issued as *British Journal of Psychiatry*] *86:*378–477, 1940.

BRACKBILL, G., and FINE, H. Schizophrenia and central nervous system pathology. *J. abnorm. soc. Psychol. 52:*310–313, 1956.

BRILL, N. Q., and STORROW, H. A. Social class and psychiatric treatment. *Arch. Gen. Psychiat. 3:*340–344, 1960.

EDWARDS, A. L. *Experimental Design in Psychological Research.* New York: Holt, Rinehart & Winston, 1962, chapter XIV.

FRANK J. D., GLIEDMAN, L. H., IMBER, S. D., NASH, E. I., JR. and STONE, A. R. Why patients leave psychotherapy. *Arch. neurol. Psychiat. 77:* 283–299, 1957.

GARMEZY, N., and RODNICK, E. H. Premorbid adjustment and performance in schizophrenia: Implications for interpreting heterogeneity in schizophrenia. *J. nerv. ment. Dis. 129:*450–465, 1959.

GRANT, D. A. Analysis-of-variance tests in the analysis and comparison of curves. *Psychol. Bull. 53:*141–154, 1956.

HOLLINGSHEAD, A. B., and REDLICH, F. C. *Social Class and Mental Illness: A Community Study.* New York: John Wiley & Sons, 1958.

HUNT, R. C., and APPEL, R. E. Prognosis in psychoses lying midway between schizophrenia and manic-depressive psychoses. *Amer. J. Psychiat.* *93:*313–339, 1936.

IMBER, S. D., FRANK, J. D., GLIEDMAN, L., NASH, E. I., and STONE, A. Suggestibility, social class, and the acceptance of psychotherapy. *J. clin. Psychol. 12:*341–344, 1956.

KANT, O. Differential diagnosis of schizophrenia in the light of concepts of personality stratification. *Amer. J. Psychiat. 97:*342–357, 1940.

KANTOR, R. E., WALLNER, J. M., and WINDER, C. L. Process and reactive schizophrenia. *J. consult. Psychol. 17:*157–162, 1953.

KIRTNER, W. L., and CARTWRIGHT, D. S. Success and failure in client-centered therapy as a function of client personality variables. *J. consult. Psychol. 22:*329–333, 1958.

LANGER, T. S., and MICHAEL, S. T. *Life Stress and Mental Health.* New York: The Free Press of Glencoe, 1963.

PHILLIPS, L. Personality factors and prognosis in schizophrenia. Unpublished Ph.D. dissertation, University of Chicago, 1949.

PHILLIPS, L. Case history data and prognosis in schizophrenia. *J. nerv. ment. Dis. 117:*515–525, 1953.

RASKIN, A. Factors therapists associate with motivation to enter therapy. *J. clin. Psychol. 17:*62–65, 1961.

ROGERS, C. R., and DYMOND, R. F. (eds.). *Psychotherapy and Personality Change.* Chicago: University of Chicago Press, 1954.

ROSENTHAL, D., and FRANK, J. D. The fate of the psychiatric clinical outpatients assigned to psychotherapy. *J. nerv. ment. Dis. 127:*330–343, 1958.

RUBINSTEIN, E., and LORR, M. A comparison of terminators and remainers in outpatient psychotherapy. *J. clin. Psychol. 12:*345–349, 1956.

SASLOW, G., and MATARAZZO, J. D. A technique for studying changes in interview behavior. In E. A. Rubinstein and M. B. Parloff (eds.), *Research in Psychotherapy,* Vol. I. Washington, D.C.: American Psychological Association, 1959, pp. 125–159.

SROLE, L., LANGNER, T. S., MICHAEL, S. T., OPLER, M. K., and RENNIE, T. A. C. *Mental Health in the Metropolis,* Vol. I. New York: McGraw Hill, 1961.

VAN DER VEEN, F. The therapist rating scale. Unpublished manuscript, University of Wisconsin Psychiatric Institute, 1959.

VAN DER VEEN, F., and STOLER, N. Therapist judgments, interview behavior, and case outcome. *Psychotherapy: Theory, Research and Practice 2:* 158–163, 1965.

WITTMAN, PHYLLIS. Scale for measuring prognosis in schizophrenic patients. *Elgin State Hospital Papers 4:*20–33, 1941.

ZIGLER, E., and PHILLIPS, L. Case history data and psychiatric diagnosis. *J. consult. Psychol. 25:*458, 1961a.

ZIGLER, E., and PHILLIPS, L. Social competence and outcome in psychiatric disorder. *J. abnorm. soc. Psychol. 63:*264–271, 1961b.

12. A Summary of the Issues and Conclusions

Donald J. Kiesler, Philippa L. Mathieu, Marjorie H. Klein

In this chapter we will attempt to develop and present an integrated interpretation of the findings of the preceding four chapters, as well as assess the empirical evidence for the major hypotheses of the study. For both tasks it is necessary to consider and weigh the theoretical, methodological, and statistical strengths and weaknesses of the research and of the data on which the analyses are based. Thus, in this chapter we will reconsider the theoretical status of the various major hypotheses, examine the various factors imposing limitations on the interpretation of our results, and, finally, present an overview of the empirical findings in which we will attempt to take the various issues and limitations into account.

Some Ancillary Findings

Before proceeding with this task, let us present briefly the positive findings which were not predicted from the original theoretical formulation of the study. Some of these results were highly provocative, suggesting leads regarding design modification for future studies of psychotherapy process.

A major finding of the study was that it is possible and indeed profitable to sample tape-recorded therapy interactions in a project of this size. Our study demonstrated that by appropriate sampling procedures one can incode the process data of entire therapy interactions of many cases in a meaningful (and relatively economical) way. In other words, it seems that studies of psychotherapeutic process need not be limited to relatively molecular portions of the therapy interaction (e.g. one or several interviews only). This conclusion seems to apply, at least, to studies concerned with Rogerian variables; studies originating within other theoretical frameworks will likely have their own unique sampling problems to solve.

Second, it seems possible to develop rating scale measures for the kind of dimensions Rogers postulates as necessary and sufficient for psychotherapeutic improvement. Our study showed that clinically naive judges can be trained to rate at least one dimension of process, patient experiencing, to a point of high interjudge reliability. Although much less success was attained with ratings of the therapist attitudes or conditions, there is, nevertheless, promise of success even with these variables.

Third, our data emphasizes the importance of comparing patient and therapist viewpoints of the ongoing therapy interaction. The study clearly found that objective judges and patients agreed as to the level of therapist conditions being offered to the patient throughout therapy. Yet both tended to disagree with the therapists' assessments of their own behavior, the therapists as a group manifesting a decidedly more optimistic perspective. However, when only successful cases were considered, the patient-therapist dyads showed a moderately positive relationship in viewpoints (instead of the overall discrepancy in perception found for the therapists as a group), while the failure cases showed a markedly negative association of patient and therapist viewpoints. In other words, when both patient and therapist were perceiving the relationship in the same manner, successful outcome tended to eventuate.

Further, both patients' and therapists' viewpoints of their interaction showed high stability from early to late in the therapy interviews. Evidently both participants in therapy form their impressions of the interaction early, and their impressions remain relatively fixed throughout therapy. The data for the therapist conditions ratings supported this conclusion, although here the stability of therapist conditions was less clear-cut. For the rated conditions measures, it seems that near the eighth therapy interview the ranking of the therapists in terms of accurate empathy and congruence tended to become fixed, and to remain relatively constant thereafter.

Finally, contrasting our Relationship Inventory findings with those of Barrett-Lennard (1962) on his group of psychoneurotic subjects, we found that therapist relationship factors were relatively more crucial for schizophrenic patients. While therapist congruence seemed to be equally crucial for both groups, the schizophrenics focused additionally on therapist positive regard, while the psychoneurotics tended to emphasize the therapist's empathic understanding. In other words, the actual relationship with their therapist seems more pivotal for schizophrenics, while psychoneurotics tend to focus more on the therapist's empathic understanding capabilities.

In summary, we succeeded in encoding an enormous body of tape-recorded process data on twenty-eight schizophrenic patients by the use of sampling procedures. This encoding process permitted the application of rating scales, developed to assess therapist and patient variables, to the ongoing therapy interaction. While we were relatively successful in assessing patient process (experiencing), we were less successful in assessing therapist conditions variables. By including the Relationship

Inventory measure of conditions (tapping the perceptions of both therapists and patients) we were able to demonstrate meaningful findings regarding the pattern of agreement among therapist, patient, and objective judges rating the recorded interview samples. Finally, by comparing our Relationship Inventory data with that obtained on a psychoneurotic population we showed that different therapist variables are important for schizophrenic and psychoneurotic patients respectively.

A Critical Re-evaluation

A Hindsight View of the Theoretical Formulation

In retrospect it now seems apparent that the high level of generality of the hypotheses that guided this research was both an asset and a liability. The advantage of greater theoretical inclusiveness was offset by a multiplication of methodological obstacles. The difficulties of operationalizing broad theoretical variables and of applying a complex theoretical formulation to an intricate naturalistic setting served as both a stimulus and challenge for this research program.

If we consider the hypotheses of this research we see that they were not of equal status in the theoretical framework. Hypothesis I was an apparently stringent yet wide-ranging proposition regarding the causal relationship between three theoretically central therapist conditions variables and patient process movement. It held a central position in the theoretical superstructure and served as the most direct and certainly the pivotal test of the parent theory. Hypotheses II through V served primarily to amplify and clarify the assumptions basic to the first hypothesis. Hypothesis II affirmed and defined the general importance and status of the process construct as applicable to therapy with many different patient types. Its logical extension, Hypothesis V, went further, calling for an essential commonality between the process of therapeutic involvement and extra-therapeutic manifestation of growth and change. Together these hypotheses endorsed the role of the process construct as a continuum of mental health applicable to a wide range of patients. In the empirical setting, they served the important ancillary function of providing anchorage and validation for the process construct. Hypotheses III and IV spelled out the assumption most basic to Hypothesis I, that the therapeutic relationship is the important vehicle for constructive personality change. The greater weight we placed on their modifications in terms of Hypothesis I (Hypotheses III–A and IV–A) further underscores the central theoretical stress placed on the quality of the therapeutic relationship as the central agent in constructive personality change.

This research program, in short, was built on the assumption that the therapeutic relationship is the important vehicle for personality change, and that within this relationship certain specifiable yet general attitudes, held and communicated by the therapist, are the necessary and sufficient conditions for therapeutic progress. In the light of the importance attached to the causal implication of Hypothesis I it is regrettable that many of the conceptual and procedural obstacles encountered in examining this proposition rendered impossible its definitive test. Hypotheses II and V, affirming the general validity of the process construct, and Hypotheses III–A and IV–A, endorsing the importance of therapist conditions for extra-therapy criteria of patient change and outcome, did receive consistent but qualified support. Yet, in the absence of any evidence clearly confirming Hypothesis I we were able to endorse only the intent of the theory and to highlight only the particular importance of therapist attitudinal variables. We were unable to provide detailed support for the theoretically crucial interrelationship between these conditions and patient process movement. Thus, we find ourselves in the uncomfortable position where the results cannot be taken to refute the primary hypothesis, and the consistent body of empirical relationships that do exist cannot be used with confidence as a basis for theoretical modifications. Those conclusions suggested by the data of this study must be interpreted with caution because of the conceptual and methodological limitations of the research.

General Limitations of the Study

As we look back over the study with the wisdom of hindsight, it now seems clear that several aspects of our research design and data made it difficult for this study to provide a powerful test of the parent theory. The practical decision to employ a correlational approach to an essentially causal issue is an example. That is, patients were randomly assigned to therapists, and the therapy relationship was permitted to develop naturally, without any attempt at systematic control of therapist variables. The design of this study did attempt to control experimentally for several patient variables by matching experimental and control groups on the factors of age, sex, socio-educational status, and chronicity. This degree of matching went far beyond most that had hitherto been attempted in psychotherapy research. But it is not possible to match along all potentially confounding dimensions, and as a result no attempt was made to match the patients on the process variable. Hence, since our study was an "experiment of nature," the evidence our data could provide regarding the causal statement of Hypothesis I was limited to the degree of relationship between therapist and patient factors, with no indication possible regarding the causal direction of that relationship. On the other hand, some of the real strengths of our design derived from the very fact that we selected patients randomly, rather than selecting only those with good prognosis or those who desired psychotherapy; and that our therapists were not allowed to select only patients who seemed personally congenial to them.

The limited size and range of our patient sample, and the fact that the patients did not volunteer for therapy (were assigned randomly) may have made extensive process movement and constructive personality change unlikely. Our patient sample was drawn from a somewhat restricted range of the population of a single state hospital. The absence from this hospital of both very acute and extremely chronic cases resulted in a sample that was quite homogenous in severity and length of disturbance and general prognosis. Patients of our sample fell within the middle range of the process-reactive and acute-chronic continua. The relatively long-standing disturbance of, and modest prognosis for, this sample gave us little basis for anticipating high responsiveness to therapy, deep involvement in the process of self-exploration, or extensive personality change. In addition, the random selection procedure resulted in the recruitment of patients who had not volunteered for therapy and hence who had relatively poor motivation for a deep, growth-producing involvement in the therapy relationship. It is unfortunate, yet not surprising, that the overall level of process movement in this sample was extremely modest, occurring with good reliability but only within a restricted range of the Experiencing Scale, and was not of sufficient magnitude to provide an appropriate range of data for testing the theoretical statement contained in Hypothesis I.

Although the sample was homogeneous regarding premorbid history and prognosis, much heterogeneity existed regarding the symptoms presented by these patients. Patients were considered for inclusion in the sample if they showed the hospital designation of schizophrenia and met only a minimum of additional matching criteria. They were not screened or matched for specific symtomatology or for any other potentially relevant factors such as ongoing treatment plans, initial motivation for therapy, and verbal expressivity. It is not surprising, especially in light of the small number of cases involved, that so potentially diverse a patient group showed little initial homogeneity of symptoms, nor would such a group be expected to respond to therapy by manifesting uniform patterns of personality change. This factor minimized the probability of observing consistency of change sufficient to support the predicted relationships of process with conditions and/or different criteria of change and outcome.

Further, it is possible that the relatively small number of therapists, homogeneous in level of experience and general orientation, may not have permitted a sufficiently wide range of conditions for an adequate test of theoretical expectations. The data clearly shows that the extremes both of very high and very low therapist conditions were absent in this small group of therapists sharing similar concerns, values, and commitments to their patients. This range restriction of the therapist sample could only work against the establishment of the predicted conditions-process association.

The relatively high quality of the care offered all patients of the hospital, as well as the availability of a favorable ward milieu to most patients, and even the offering of concurrent group psychotherapy for some, may have mitigated any clear-cut effect of low therapist conditions, and may have undercut or diluted the impact of the more intense patient-therapist relationships. That is, the high quality of the extratherapy milieu may have acted not only to minimize the differences between therapy and control groups but also to obscure differences within the therapy group. It is heartening in this respect that the relationship between conditions and outcome emerged as clearly as it did, and not surprising that the distinction between high and low conditions groups, or therapy and control groups, failed to appear dramatically in the present sample.

Finally, there were statistical aspects of our data that posed difficulties. The number of subjects composing our patient and therapist samples was quite small. Compounding this inadequacy was the fact that the number of independent and dependent variable measures used in the study was rather large. Combined, these factors constituted a research situation where the reliability of obtained regression coefficients was low, and the opportunity for chance results was quite large (Humphreys, 1958). This situation suggests rather strongly that some of our "significant" findings may have been chance effects alone, and also that the obtained regression coefficients would have shrunk if a new sample had been taken. Also, because of the large number of tests of statistical significance calculated for the same body of empirical data, the researcher did not know, after the first test of significance, exactly at what level of significance he was operating, regardless of the table values given. These statistical limitations further necessitated a cautious approach in interpreting the results.

An Attempt at Integration

In spite of the limitations we have been describing there has emerged from this research a consistent body of relationships among certain therapist attitudinal variables, patient process level, and some indices of positive therapeutic outcome. These were discussed in detail in Chapters 8, 9, 10, and 11. While these relationships cannot be interpreted unequivocally, their pattern does appear consistent with our global theoretical expectations and consonant with traditional clinical lore.

Most generally, the results of this study suggested that the two therapist conditions variables accurate empathy and patient-perceived congruence (themselves highly interrelated) were associated with the overall level of experiential involvement that the patient maintained both in therapy and sampling interviews; and that both conditions and experiencing factors were related to various indices of positive personality change and favorable therapeutic outcome. More specifically, these two conditions variables were associated, not only with the average level of patient experiencing in the total therapy interaction, but also with experiencing at discrete moments in the therapy course. These relationships extended, furthermore, to the sampling interviews, so that the level of experiencing shown in this extra-therapy contact by the therapy patient was related, not to the conditions level offered by the standard sampling interviewer, but rather to the conditions quality of the original therapeutic relationship. The specific pattern emerging was that the deeper the level of the therapist's empathic understanding and genuineness with his patient, the more his patient would exhibit a deeper level of self-experiencing and self-exploration at every point of both the therapy and sampling interviews. This was indeed an intriguing finding. While the correlations for patient-perceived congruence were not quite so pervasive as those for rated accurate empathy, they were sufficiently consistent to indicate that the association of both conditions variables with patient experiencing level was stable and general.

These same conditions factors, moreover, were associated consistently with therapeutic outcome. Although only two of these relationships (those for accurate empathy with MMPI Sc scale change, and for congruence with hospital release) reached statistical significance, a number of other outcome and change indices yielded supportive trends. Most generally, patients receiving high conditions levels showed positive personality change and outcome, while patients with lower conditions showed no change or, in some cases, negative change eventuating in an outcome worse than that observed for no-therapy control patients.

Finally, it is apparent that these conditions-outcome relationships were generally similar to those emerging when experiencing-outcome relationships were explored. Experiencing *level* was related, not only to MMPI Sc scale changes, but to a variety of other criteria of outcome and change. That is, patients more involved in the process of self-experiencing and self-exploration showed not only a marked decrease in schizophrenic behavior as measured by the MMPI, but also a greater likelihood of remaining out of the hospital and of showing improvement on various other criteria of constructive change. The more limited and complex association between outcome and experiencing *movement* was also supported by a number of different outcome criteria both for therapy and sampling interviews. Patients described as more successful by various outcome indices tended to move towards deeper levels of self-involvement and self-exploration over the course of therapy.

Thus, therapist attitudinal variables, patient experiencing, and therapeutic outcome were interrelated more or less equally. However, two issues stand in the way of any firm interpretation of these relationships. First the confounding, both conceptually and operationally, of therapist and patient variables tended to obscure the exact nature of the association among conditions, process, and outcome. Second, the presence of uncontrolled but systematic initial differences for patients receiving and perceiving high and low therapist conditions made it particularly difficult to pinpoint the exact status of therapist conditions factors in the therapeutic process. Both issues raised problems for the interpretation of specific conditions scores, and particularly complicated the view of our conditions-process-outcome network. Let us consider in some detail each of these issues.

Confounding of Therapist and Patient Variables

Interpretive problems were most clearly delineated for the evaluation of the conditions ratings (accurate empathy in particular), and for the conceptualization of the obtained relationship between these conditions ratings and patient experiencing.

Conditions are seen as reflecting the therapist's attitudes in the therapy interaction and are thought to be functionally independent of the patient's specific contribution and of the quality of the joint interchange. Nonetheless, these therapist variables are anchored in the dyadic interchange. Not only are they conceptualized exclusively in reference to a specific patient-therapist interaction (i.e., not as general, pervasive therapist characteristics), but they are thought to become effective only as their communication is perceived by the patient. In regard to this conceptual confounding of therapist, patient, and interactional variables, the parent theory did not systematically elaborate the role played by the patient or by the dyadic interchange as interactional variables in the causal relationship postulated between therapist attitudes and patient process movement.

Similarly, the authors of the rating scales for the operational measures of the conditions constructs at times incorporated into the scale-stage definitions cues from the patient's verbalizations, or from the interactive aspect of the relationship. As a result, although theoretically these conditions should be manifest in therapy independent of cues from the patient or from the overall interaction, the scale definitions did at times rely on these cues.

Further, a closer inspection of the conditions scale definitions in light of the low interjudge reliability obtained when the scales were applied suggests rather strongly that the current conditions scales are multidimensional. The Accurate Empathy Scale, in the form used in this study, generally defines the overall impact of the therapist's response to the patient's specific comments. However, this impact seemed to contain distinct aspects: the accuracy and refinement of the therapist's understanding of the patient's phenomenological frame of reference, his implicit as well as expressed desire to understand the patient from this perspective, and his skill in communicating an empathic grasp of the materials presented by the client. The Unconditional Positive Regard Scale appears similarly complex, including not only the therapist's affective responses (i.e., his expressed warmth and affection for the patient), but also the degree of conditionality shown in his reaction to specific components of the patient's personality and symptomatology. The Congruence Scale measures what is in some respects the most elusive and many faceted of the three conditions factors, consisting of the therapist's communicated genuineness as a person and dependent in turn both on his reaction to the patient and on the maturity and appropriateness of his sharing of himself in the therapeutic relationship. Thus, not only are each of the conditions variables defined so that they are in some degree dependent on either the patient's stimulus value or the quality of the interaction, but each has been conceptualized in multidimensional terms for the specific rating scales.

In view of the conceptual anchorage of therapist conditions in the concrete patient-therapist relationship as well as the multidimensionality and patient-cue anchorage of specific scale definitions, it was impossible to assess the relative contribution of patient and/or interactional factors to the conditions ratings themselves. These same factors made it difficult to decide whether the obtained correlation between accurate empathy and patient experiencing level reflected an association between two independent measures, or was a spurious correlation. The accurate empathy-experiencing relationship may have been determined by the common roots of both factors in a more general interactional variable, by the more specific dependence of therapist empathy on the experiential quality of the patient's verbalizations, or by the relation of both factors to the complex of initial patient characteristics that differentiated high and low accurate empathy groups. Moreover, the availability of the recorded patient-therapist interaction to both conditions and process raters not only clouded further our ability to differentiate the alternatives just offered, but also made it impossible for us to reject the likelihood that the accurate empathy-experiencing relationship was merely an artifact of the rating procedure. That is, the obtained accurate empathy ratings may have reflected such contaminating interactional variables as gross amount of patient verbalization in the segment, or the intensity or pace of the dyadic interchange, or may have stemmed simply from the unwitting reliance of accurate empathy raters on patient experiential cues.

As long as we are aware of these difficulties, our data does permit us to sharpen our understanding of exactly what was being measured by the Accurate Empathy Scale. If we consider the definitions for the scale stages most frequently used by the judges in this study (stages 3 to 6), we can see two alternative interpretations for these scores. According to the definitions the judge had two possible bases for his ratings. Either he could evaluate the accuracy of the therapist's understanding of the patient's specific communication, or he could assess the therapist's avowed desire or willingness to be understanding. This latter alternative, apparently included for instances of sparse patient communication or for occasions when the therapist was honestly and openly groping to achieve a better understanding of the patient's problems, clearly focused the judge's attention on the therapist's *motivation* for empathic understanding, as well as on his willingness to become involved with the patient in the relationship.

While we cannot conclude that one of these alternative sets was predominant in the judges' accurate empathy ratings, two pieces of evidence suggest that the motivational focus may have been the more dominant. At the same time the judges were to make the complex empathy ratings, they were also to judge, on a single, 7-point Likert scale, the degree of genuineness of the therapist's motivation to understand the patient. These motivational assessments (M) were very highly correlated with the accurate empathy ratings (rho = .92 and .79 for AE_{15} and AE_{TOT}), suggesting that the empathy ratings were indeed heavily loaded with the rater's evaluation of the therapist's motivation for understanding. Further, when we consider in detail the specific items making up the congruence subscale of the Relationship Inventory (also highly correlated with both accurate empathy ratings and the M scores) we see that many items on this scale are so worded that the patient's endorsement of them can be construed as an index of the therapist's motivation for and commitment to the relationship. Some items, for example, tap the patient's perception of the therapist's honesty in the relationship (e.g., "I feel that I can trust him to be honest with me." "I feel that he is being genuine with me."). Other items more directly reflect the patient's evaluation of the therapist's openness regarding his opinions of, and reactions to, the patient (e.g., "He does not try to mislead me about his own thoughts and feelings." "He does not avoid anything that he thinks or feels about me."). Other RI items might be construed as representing the patient's evaluation of the therapist's *desire* for a mutually open and understanding relationship (e.g., "At times he is not aware of the way he feels about me." "What he says gives a false impression of his total reaction to me.").

In general, the relationship of M scale ratings and RI congruence scores to accurate empathy suggests that the latter ratings were heavily loaded with the rater's evaluation of the depth and genuineness of the therapist's more general commitment to the therapeutic relationship, and the honesty and openness of his sharing of his perceptions and reactions in the relationship. In other words, rather than reflecting the accuracy and refinement of the therapist's responses, the Accurate Empathy Scale seems to have been tapping a more global therapist quality—the therapist's communicated commitment to the therapy interaction and involvement in the problems of a specific patient in the interaction. While this interpretation does not free us from the possibility that these evaluations may have been confounded or determined in part by patient responses and interactional variables, it does offer us a meaningful alternative to the interpretation that these ratings were determined by the rater's response to patient cues.

At first glance it would appear that none of the procedural contaminations found for the accurate empathy-experiencing relationship applied to our questionnaire measurement of patient-perceived congruence and its significant association with patient experiencing in the therapy and sampling interviews. The congruence measure derived from a questionnaire filled in by patients, while the experiencing scores were the result of ratings by objective judges. Their measurement ought thereby to have been independent, since different subjects were involved in the assessment of the two variables. Unfortunately, this was not entirely the case, although it was certainly more the case for the congruence than for the accurate empathy ratings. There still remains the possibility that whatever patient factor led the judges to rate him at a deeper level of experiencing in the therapy interviews was the same factor leading that patient to perceive his therapist in a relatively good light—i.e., as communicating a high level of genuineness. In other words, the congruence score may not have been therapist-anchored at all, but rather may have derived from the same patient variable responsible for the patient's receiving a high experiencing rating. Therefore, it seems plausible that the experiencing ratings and the patient's measured perceptions of the therapist were not independent, but in fact interdependent, both being measured manifestations of the same patient variable. This interpretive ambiguity for the congruence-experiencing association will be discussed further in the next section.

When we consider the specific interpretation of the Experiencing Scale ratings we find ourselves on firmer ground, by virtue of their more explicitly defined independence of both therapist and interactional factors. Likewise, as we saw in Chapter 10, there is considerable evidence affirming the general validity of the process construct and the experiencing ratings made for the sample under study. The level of experiencing manifested by the schizophrenic patients over the therapy and sampling interviews was related to a number of meaningful criteria of change and outcome. While the association between experiencing *movement* and outcome was more modest and complex, the trends suggest somewhat greater overall process movement in cases of favorable outcome.

When we examine the conceptualization basic to the experiencing construct and the definitions of the specific scale stages rated most frequently in this sample, we arrive at a more explicit interpretation of our process ratings. As generally stated, the experiencing construct refers to the depth and quality of the individual's involvement in the process of self-awareness and self-exploration. This process has both a behavioral component (i.e., the specific experiential level manifest in the patient's verbalizations) and a more implicit motivational aspect (the patient's degree of involvement in or commitment to the process of affective exploration). This dual nature of the experiencing construct was especially predominant in the range of the scale most frequently used in this study. Patients receiving relatively high experiencing scores were primarily at stages 3 and 4, indicating their acknowledgment of their affective involvement in their narrative. Implicit in this is the individual's commitment to, and motivation to view, his experiences in this affective light. On the other hand, at the lower stages (1 and 2) the patient is manifestly uncommitted and uninvolved in the process of self-exploration—that is, he clearly does not refer explicitly to his feelings, and in some cases fails to acknowledge or even denies the personal relevance of situations or events.

Thus the experiencing scores, as well as the accurate empathy ratings, may be interpreted in motivational terms as reflecting the patient's more general motivation for, or commitment to, self-exploration. The ratings may be considered an index, not only of the patient's capacity, but also of his set, for self-experiencing.

In summary, our research program went much further in the measurement of such subtle variables as attitudinal conditions in the therapist and process qualities in the client than any study of which we are aware. Yet we must conclude that the definitional and procedural contamination of patient and therapist cues in the conditions scales presents obstacles to interpreting the relationship between conditions and overall process level. It leaves us no basis for deciding whether the conditions-process association reflects the empirical covariance of independently measured constructs, or whether it stems from the built-in conceptual interdependence of these related but distinct facets of the dyadic interaction, or whether it is a more direct artifact of the rating procedure. At this point, the methodological obstacles do not allow us to choose among these alternatives. Nevertheless, while we must be and are aware of the limitations involved in our attempt at conditions and process measurement, we must state as well our opinion that for its time it represents a landmark.

Finally, there is some evidence to suggest that the conditions-process relationship is not entirely artifactual, did not result entirely from the rating procedure. First, there were instances in some discrete therapy hours, and generally throughout the sampling interviews, where accurate empathy and experiencing were independent of one another, or even negatively correlated. Second, the relationship between empathy and experiencing, observed for the individual therapy segments, held also over the total therapy course, and was equally apparent in the independent sampling interviews segments. Third, it seems feasible to conclude from the high relationship of accurate empathy ratings with patient perceptions of therapist overall conditions, and the particularly high association with perceived congruence, that the rater using the empathy scale was assessing a therapist quality that was also perceived or responded to by the patient. Hence, while certain non-therapist aspects of the interaction may have been important in empathy ratings in some instances and may have figured prominently in determining the patient's evaluations, these accurate empathy ratings do not appear to have been solely dependent on such factors at all moments of the therapy interaction, and do indeed seem to have differentiated among therapists from a viewpoint close to that of the patient.

Confounding from Initial Patient Variables

The second major interpretive issue inherent in the findings of the study came from the pattern of initial patient differences associated with conditions, process, and outcome. As Chapter 11 made clear, patients who subsequently received high conditions (accurate empathy and perceived congruence) from their therapist, who showed high experiencing throughout therapy as well as more favorable outcome at termination, differed from low conditions-process-outcome patients on several other measures. The high-conditions, high-process, and successful schizophrenic patients tended to be males, from higher socio-economic backgrounds, who in addition manifested initially greater verbal ability (high verbal IQ) and expressive productivity (less silence in the initial interview), less symptomatic disturbance (Wittenborn ratings), and more satisfactory TAT productions (mental health ratings). This network of initial differences suggests that more integrated therapy candidates are characterized by a more favorable prognosis, a relatively higher verbal ability, and greater expressive productivity. While it is difficult to decide whether this complex of factors reflects a stable trait system or a transitory motivational state, either interpretation is congruent with the implicit demands of the therapy situation and would explain more favorable therapeutic outcome.

More detailed analyses in Chapter 11 showed that these initial case differences accounted for a considerable portion of the variance in both conditions-process and conditions-outcome relationships. While these patient factors did not account for the entire variance in these relationships, their role was nevertheless prominent and pervasive. However, we have no empirical basis for assessing the precise nature of the relationship of initial patient factors with therapist attitudes, patient process, or case outcome. Consequently, the interactive view presented in the following section should be considered a tentative attempt to account for the total network of consistent relationships in our data. Since we clearly cannot at present generalize beyond our schizophrenic sample, this attempt must be viewed, not as a formal conceptualization, but as an exploratory reconciliation of the general theoretical constructs with the specific pattern of findings emerging from the present study.

An Interactive View

It seems apparent that initial patient factors and therapist attitudes can interact complexly, setting the tone of the therapeutic relationship. In those cases where the patient enters therapy with a fair degree of expressive capacity and/or motivation for self-exploration, the therapist's corresponding involvement may be enhanced. That is, the more initially expressive the patient, the richer will be the material in which the therapist can anchor his empathic efforts. The more motivated the patient for the therapeutic process, the easier it will be for the therapist to become correspondingly involved in, and committed to, the relationship. The more responsive the patient, the more likely it will be that the therapist can communicate the genuineness of his concern for, and interest in, the patient as a person. On the other hand, patients lacking these capacities for therapeutic participation will generally fail to evoke similar therapist involvement. That is, the unmotivated, defensive, and reluctant patient from a different (lower) socio-economic background may not provide the therapist sufficient opportunity to deepen the relationship, and may thus severely limit the therapist's ability to communicate and function effectively. While skillful and sensitive therapists may succeed in involving even the initially reluctant patient, and more remote or superficial therapists may dampen the motivated patient's initial enthusiasm, it seems apparent from this sample that the patient's presenting capacities and motives contribute heavily to the establishment of a climate in which the therapist can function effectively.

These same initial patient factors can also be viewed as relating to patient process behavior throughout therapy and to more general case outcome. In instances where a high level of therapist involvement reciprocates the patient's motivation and expressive capacity, a relatively high experiencing level is sustained, and such patients have more favorable outcomes. In contrast, when effective therapist involvement and commitment is lacking and the patient is also initially unmotivated or unresponsive, his low experiencing level remains essentially unchanged, and no further personality change, or even negative outcome, may result.

As we have stated previously, we lack sufficient empirical basis for definite conclusions regarding the specific way in which this network of initial patient differences, therapist attitudes, and patient process interact and relate to case outcome. Nevertheless, it seems apparent that these facets of the interaction are interdependent and mutually reinforcing. While the patient's capacities and motives provide the structure for the therapist's effective functioning, the therapist's attitudes in turn may constitute the primary factor in sustaining the patient's self-exploration over the therapy course at a level which allows meaningful personality change to occur. While the initial differences observed for high and low conditions groups do account for a portion of the variance in case outcome, the equally strong association of these initial patient factors with in-therapy variables highlights the complexity and mutually reinforcing nature of the entire network. In other words, as the therapy interaction progresses, general patient capacities, motives, and level of experiencing, are so inextricably bound together with therapist attitudes that it seems most appropriate to conceive of therapy outcome as a complex function of their dynamic interaction.

This interactive view, while departing from our original theoretical position, seems to make the most sensitive use of the data of the study and to accommodate most appropriately the relationships obtained. This view is also compatible with the global nature of the research variables and the general interpretation considered for our present rating scales. Other, more parsimonious, interpretations for the relationships are possible, but seem less consonant with the complexity of the therapy setting. The number of variables can be reduced, for example, if we assume that both therapist conditions and patient process ratings are tapping the same variable—perhaps an interactional variable such as the greater intensity or pace of therapist-patient communication, or the greater percentage or activity of patient verbalization, in more productive therapy relationships. The interactional view, however, seems to give importance to all variables in the present network, is consonant with the global nature of our present measures and ratings, is consistent with previous findings in therapy research, and is congruent with traditional clinical experience. It seems reasonable to conceive of the therapy relationship as built upon, but not completely limited by, initial patient characteristics; to postulate that therapist attitudes grow in importance as the relationship is established, and play a central role in sustaining the patient's self-examination; and to conclude that aspects of the patient's background and symptom picture, as well as various facets of the patient-therapist interaction, contribute jointly to case outcome.

It is evident that the results of this study have not been interpreted as supporting in detail our theoretical specifications of a causal relationship between therapist conditions and patient process movement. Because of the limited patient and therapist sample investigated and in light of the experimental and statistical obstacles preventing a sufficiently powerful test of the more stringent theoretical statements, this lack of support is not surprising. Despite these limitations the results emerging from this study seem meaningful, consistent with other research in this area, and generally encouraging. In their present state they represent further elucidation of the very realistic complexity of the therapeutic relationship, therapeutic goals, and the host of factors impinging on them in the empirical setting.

It must be noted, moreover, that our findings do seem to provide some support for the parent theory, affirming the importance of the therapeutic relationship for personality change and the particular contribution of general therapist attitudes to the interaction. Our results relating process level to outcome appear to support the general validity of the former construct and demonstrate its continuity with other criteria for personal growth. The association of therapist empathy and congruence with both process and outcome seems to confirm the theoretical emphasis placed on therapist attitudinal variables over and above specific technique.

Generally, the fact that we have been able to differentiate more and less productive relationships by tapping conditions and process variables, and have shown the association of these factors to more familiar criteria of prognosis and outcome is indeed encouraging, showing the importance of concern with variables of this type. Finally, although the lack of sophistication in the measurement of conditions, process, and outcome variables has made it impossible to test the precise status of these factors, we can conclude from this study that therapist attitudes and patient experiencing do represent important facets of the interaction, and should prove a fruitful and meaningful focus for future research.

Implications for Future Research

In the future, studies of issues emanating from client-centered theory will require more detailed definition and elaboration of both conditions and process factors, as well as their conceptual integration with other aspects of the therapy setting (including patient and therapist characteristics, interactional factors, and empirical phenomena). Such factors will then require more rigorous experimental control. Before this is possible, however, more extensive methodological research will be necessary in order to resolve the many issues presented by the complex process phenomenon.[1] When, as in this study, theoretically central variables prove to be imbedded in a more complex framework, exploratory studies will be necessary to evaluate which of the many theoretically extraneous factors in the setting require particular consideration and control. Only with such pilot information, and with validly anchored instruments for the assessment of therapy variables, can more definitive experimental studies be undertaken.

References

BARRETT-LENNARD, G. T. Dimensions of therapist response as causal factors in therapeutic change. *Psychol. Monogr. 76,* No. 43 (Whole No. 562), 1962.

HUMPHREYS, L. G. Methodological problems in research on objective tests of personality. Unpublished manuscript, 1958.

1. For a detailed discussion of the many and varied issues that confront one in a study of psychotherapy such as this one, see Donald J. Kiesler, Basic methodological issues implicit in psychotherapy process research. Paper presented at the Association for the Advancement of Psychotherapy's 3rd annual conference on "An Evaluation of the Results of the Psychotherapies," held May, 1964, at Los Angeles. *American Journal of Psychotherapy 20:*135–155, 1966.

PART IV

Special Studies

Editor's Note

A great many individual studies were made by various staff members during the life of the research program. Many of these are finding their way into journal publication. The three studies chosen for this section seemed most appropriate to include because of the special light they cast on different aspects of the central data analysis contained in Chapters 8 through 12.

13. The Therapeutic Process as Related to Outcome

Working independently and utilizing four scales of process movement, T. M. Tomlinson set out to analyze process as related to outcome. Many members of the research group aided in supplying the data, but special help was given by Paula Rohrbaugh and raters Emily Earley, Jerry Hubbard, and Wendy Spotts. The study was conducted and this chapter written by T. M. Tomlinson.

Beginning with a paper by Rogers (1958) the process conception of therapeutic personality change has been expanded and now includes a rather large array of research (e.g., Walker, Rablen, and Rogers, 1960; Truax, 1961; Tomlinson and Hart, 1962) and theoretical advances and modifications (e.g., Gendlin, 1964; Gendlin and Tomlinson, Chapter 7 in this book). A major change has also concerned the development of more sensitive scales for the measurement of the strands of behavior hypothesized to change in therapy. It is the purpose of this chapter to carry forward this work in two ways: by using and evaluating four different process scales, presumed to measure different facets of therapeutic change, and by determining the course of process movement in therapeutically more successful and less successful schizophrenic patients.

The Study

Background

Before embarking on the present study, it will be useful to summarize briefly the earlier research done with the original scale. In substance, these studies (Walker, Rablen, and Rogers, 1960; Tomlinson and Hart, 1962) provided evidence that reliable and significant distinctions could be made between more successful (hereafter abbreviated m.s.) and less successful (hereafter abbreviated l.s.) neurotic clients, and between early and late interviews within these two groups of cases. Generally, it may be said that m.s. clients received higher process ratings than l.s. clients. There was modest but significant evidence of change in process level during the course of therapy. The m.s. clients entered therapy at a significantly higher level of process than did the l.s. clients and maintained that advantage throughout the course of treatment. The change in process itself took the form of slight increases for the m.s. clients, and rather more distinct decreases for the l.s. clients.

The foregoing studies served to establish the Process Scale as a useful and valid instrument for the measurement of the therapeutic process. The outcome of these studies also indicated that the theory of process was viable and invited further explorations into the nature of the therapeutic interaction. Moving in this direction, Truax (1961), using a group of hospitalized schizophrenics, took a bold step by employing the scale and the process theory as a major aspect of an investigation into the process of group therapy. Defining the process measurements as an index of intrapersonal exploration, Truax (1961) found a significant positive association between the process ratings and measures of a variety of therapeutic conditions. Among these conditions were those hypothesized by Rogers (1957) to be necessary and sufficient for the production of positive personailty change, as well as others related to the accuracy of communicated empathy, group cohesiveness, ego involvement of group members, and leadership. Truax's results indicated that the process measures reflect client behavior that is significantly associated with positive therapy outcomes, i.e., interpersonal and intrapersonal exploration of feelings and the meanings of experience. The generally positive nature of these results was the more impressive because the ratings were made on group behavior rather than individual client-therapist interaction. In addition, the range of client behavior susceptible to process analysis was now extended to include a sample of hospitalized schizophrenics.

The study to be spelled out in the remaining pages was a logical next step in the exploration of the client-centered conception of the therapy process, building in part on an earlier study (Tomlinson, 1962). It examined the nature of process and process change in schizophrenics within the customary therapeutic dyad of client and therapist. On the basis of results of prior research, it was expected that data obtained from schizophrenic patients would be qualitatively similar to that obtained from neurotics. Therefore, the following predictions were made.

Predictions

1. Positive process change in therapy (increase in process scores between early and late points of therapy) will be greater for the clients rated m.s. than for those rated l.s;

2. Initial process levels will be higher for those clients rated m.s.

than for those rated l.s. The outcome of this hypothesis will also provide a test of the "readiness to change" concept suggested in Chapter 7. Clients who manifest relatively high levels of process may be signaling a greater preparedness or motivation to change themselves and their current life situation. If so, it might be expected that this greater readiness will be reflected in their initial approach to experience, problems, relationships, etc., i.e. differences in initial process level.

Since four scales of process were to be individually examined and since there was previous evidence of covariation among the strands of behavior represented by each scale, it was postulated that (1) measures taken with any one scale would be duplicated in essence by those from any of the remaining scales, and (2) a combined process score representing the average of the ratings with all four scales would yield the most powerful, that is, discriminating, measure. In this case, power was defined as the sensitivity to differences in process level between cases, and to changes within a case over time.

Process Scales

Following the research outlined in Chapter 7, the original Process Scale was altered with the result that four scales came into being, each describing a different strand of behavior. The four scales represented expanded versions of the original strands of experiencing, personal constructs, problem expression, and manner of relating.[1] Briefly, the scales may be described as follows:

The Experiencing Scale (EXP.).—This scale has been described in Chapter 7, and the description will not be repeated here. Suffice it to say that it was designed to assess the degree to which a client is aware of the process of experiencing within himself, and is able to use his sense of having experience as a guide or referent for behavior. Low process ratings are assigned to those clients judged to be remote from their experiencing, while high process ratings are given to those clients judged to be using their immediate awareness of their feeling state as a behavioral referent.

The Personal Constructs Scale (PC).[2]—Each individual has a construct system to which he refers his experience for the interpretation of its meaning. To varying degrees, he "sees" his experience in terms of his construct system and behaves in accord with the resulting interpreta-

---

1. These four scales will be found in Appendix C.
2. The phrase "personal constructs" was borrowed from George Kelly's theory of personal constructs (1955). The elaboration of the concept into this particular scale form is entirely the responsibility of the author's.

tion of its meaning. If the individual's constructs are rigidly held, then he will tend to interpret his experience in a highly predictable, stereotyped way. Such a person depends heavily on his construct system to provide meaning to his experience. When personal constructs are more loosely held, the individual tends to react more directly to his experience and depends less on reference to this construct system to supply meaning. Placed on a continuum of manner of interpretation of experience, the lower extreme would be occupied by the individual who always checks his experience against his constructs, and the upper extreme would be occupied by the individual who always checks his constructs against his experience. In the former case, meaning is not given by experience, but by the construct system, and this system is unalterable. In the latter, meaning is always given by experience, and if experience disagrees with, or is not consistent with, the personal constructs, the constructs themselves are altered to agree with the experience.

Rogers postulated (1959) that clients at the beginning of therapy usually express themselves in ways characteristic of the lower end of this continuum. Part of the process of therapy is the loosening, reinterpreting, and often reformulating of the old construct system. During effective therapy the client will move from the lower end toward the upper end of the continuum.

The Problem Expression Scale (PES).—The original conception of the influence of approach to problems on eventual outcome of therapy came from papers by Kirtner and Cartwright (1957), and by Rogers (1959). In essence, they stated that the successful client tends to deal, from the first, with feeling-in-relationship problems and is able to localize the sources of his difficulties. He is internally focused and has a strong drive to generate and examine impulses, thoughts, and ideas. The failing client, on the other hand, tends to discuss only external manifestations of internal difficulties or discusses feelings as external objective things to be intellectually named, labeled, or categorized.

Using this evidence as a guide, van der Veen and Tomlinson constructed the Problem Expression Scale which is somewhat different in format from the other three. Instead of detailed behavioral descriptions at each stage against which the client's behavior is to be matched for rating, this scale uses a format of mutually exclusive steps. That is, different points on the scale refer to distinctly different ways of verbalizing or talking about problems. At each step, except the first and last which have only one, there are two descriptions, one positive and one negative. The negative description at one point becomes the positive description for the next point, so that the successive points are mutually exclusive. The total scale uses six pairs of opposite descriptions ranging from "not talking about a problem" at the lower end, to "talking about an actual resolution of problems" at the upper end.

The Relationship Scale (REL).—This scale, devised by Gendlin, concerns itself with the nature of the therapeutic relationship. It is proposed that relationships in therapy vary in quality and that cues are available from client-therapist interaction that suggest the nature of the relationship. Such subtle variables as the meaningfulness or importance of the relationship, the type of communication that is appropriate, and the degree of personal caring have been scaled in quantifiable form, and aid in identification of the degree to which a relationship has been established.

The REL Scale, using the 7-stage format, describes behavior in somewhat the following order: stage 1 deals with behavior which suggests that the individual refuses a relationship and refuses or does not perceive the likelihood or desirability of a close personal relationship. From this point, the client moves successively through behavior which indicates partial or intermittent acceptance of the relationship, to the final stage denoting total acceptance through the explicit sharing by the client of intimate personal and self-focused communication.

In sum, these four process scales were constructed so as to tap four independent but covarying strands of client behavior which were believed to be associated with therapeutic change. The scales differed somewhat in format and complexity, but all were concerned with the manner of client expression rather than the content of what he said.

Outcome Measurement

To provide optimum conditions for a clear test of the process conception, it was decided that only cases with relatively clear outcomes would be used. To tap as broad a range of outcome statements as possible, a cross section of outcome measures seemed desirable. To this end the following measures were selected: the Truax Final Outcome (FOC),[3] which represented an outcome statement based on a clinical evaluation of a composite of objective and projective measures (Rorschach, TAT, MMPI, Q-sort, WAIS, Wittenborn Psychiatric Rating Scales, and the Truax Anxiety Scale), the therapist rating of outcome, outside clini-

3. The Truax FOC was an outcome index based on a composite of five measures: (*a*) a measure of test change made from clinicians' judgments of time-separated Rorschachs; (*b*) per cent time spent out of the hospital; (*c*) a general anxiety factor reflecting change in anxiety scores on the Anxiety Reaction Scale; (*d*) an index (Constructive Personality Change Index) which tends to reflect ego strength or self-confidence, and was derived from the MMPI; and (*e*) change in self-expert Q-sort correlations over time for each client.

cians' ratings of change in the Rorschach (Truax-Liccione-Rosenberg assessment), MMPI profile change, change in self Q-sort as compared with an expert's Q-sort for the "adjusted person," and two "time out of hospital" statements. With the exception of the Truax FOC, each of the foregoing measures is discussed in other parts of this book, and therefore will not be dealt with in detail here. Suffice it to point out that each measure taps a somewhat different dimension of test behavior, ranging from composite statements based on several tests (the Truax FOC), to therapist and patient self-ratings, to time actually spent out of the hospital. The criteria and the 14 patients who were judged by them, are presented in Table 13.1

The patient DEM presented a special problem. He would not co-operate with the testing procedures, and thus test data available from him were incomplete. Both the Truax FOC statement and the therapist's rating of outcome placed him unambiguously in the less successful category, and there he was assigned for purposes of this study. The paradox in the case of DEM is clear; he was one of the patients who managed to stay clear of the hospital for both follow-up checks and yet he was classified a therapeutic failure. This dilemma is not unique to this study, and no satisfactory resolution is offered by this research. However, the position taken was that the independent evidence provided by the therapist and the test performance represented the most reliable picture of the patients' *hospitalized* personality make-up and therefore was the data upon which the decision of outcome rested.

Aside from DEM, the decisions as to success were made by counting each of the indices. A case was selected for analysis only if it was given a clear majority of votes as more successful or less successful, i.e., a plurality of at least two to one. By this criterion, RAC (7–0), SOC (7–0), GOS (6–0), FIP (5–2), VAC (5–2), and PUF (4–2) were chosen as more successful, while LYN (2–5), RUD (2–5), FAS (1–6), WIL (1–6), DEM (2–2), and KEN (0–5) were chosen as less successful. CUF (3–4) and NUF (3–4) were omitted from the analysis because of the ambiguity of the outcome of their cases. Thus, twelve of the fourteen original project cases were admitted for analysis, equally divided between more success and less success on the basis (except for DEM) of a composite vote of a variety of outcome measures.

Sampling Procedure

The material to be rated for process was taken from early, intermediate, and late interviews from the twelve schizophrenic patients selected as experimental subjects. The original plan called for only an early and a late interview, namely the fifth interview from the beginning of therapy

Table 13.1—Outcome indices employed in the determination of more successful, indeterminate, and less successful cases

Patient	Truax final outcome		Therapist rating of outcome		Truax-Liccione-Rosenberg assessment[a]		MMPI profile change		Self-expert Q-sort		Time out of hospital 6 mos.		12 mos.		Total outcome votes		
	m.s.	l.s.	m.s.	l.s.	m.s.	l.s.	m.s.	l.s.	m.s.	l.s.	Yes	No	Yes	No	m.s.	l.s.	no data
More successful																	
RAC	X		X		X		X		X		X		X		7	0	0
SOC	X		X		X		X		X		X		X		7	0	0
GOS	X		X		X		X		—	—	X		X		6	0	1
FIP	X		X		X		X		X			X		X	5	2	0
VAC	X		X			X	X			X	X		X		5	2	0
PUF	X			—	X		X		X			X		X	4	2	1
Indeterminate																	
CUF		X	X			X		X		X	X		X		3	4	0
NUF		X	X			X		X		X	X		X		3	4	0
Less successful																	
LYN		X		X		X		X		X	X		X		2	5	0
RUD	X			X	X			X		X		X		X	2	5	0
FAS		X		X		X	X			X		X		X	1	6	0
WIL		X		X		X		X		X		X	X		1	6	0
DEM		X		X	—		—		—	—	X		X		2	2	3
KEN		X		X		X	—		—	—		X		X	0	5	2

[a] Made by Dr. John Liccione and Dr. Marshall Rosenberg on the basis of the before and after test data. They had no connection with the research, and knew nothing of the cases or their outcomes.

and the fifth from the end. However, due to considerations of time and economy the first twenty-four interviews (twelve early and twelve late) were extracted before five of the cases had actually terminated. Consequently, if we were to tap the true end-points of the five prolonged cases, we had to take another interview from the other seven cases so that all cases would be equally represented. We thus added twelve inter-

Table 13.2—Average process ratings and interview numbers for early, intermediate, and late interviews from more successful and less successful patients (Both the initially selected and the additional segments are included)

Patient	Early		Intermediate		Late	
	Process rating	Interview number	Process rating	Interview number	Process rating	Interview number
More successful						
RAC	3.39	5	3.97	91	3.44	137[a]
SOC	1.61	5	3.31	37[a]	3.34	41
GOS	1.85	5	2.57	68	4.00	104[a]
FIP	3.05	5	3.50	26[a]	2.79	31
VAC	2.18	5	1.94	109	3.12	157[a]
PUF	4.06	5	3.89	21	4.06	23[a]
Mean	2.70	5	3.17	59	3.46	82
Less successful						
LYN	3.39	5	3.31	18[a]	1.86	23
RUD	3.11	5	3.06	20[a]	3.12	24
FAS	2.97	5	2.72	244	1.69	324[a]
WIL	3.64	5	3.69	41	3.31	42[a]
DEM	1.92	5	2.90	23[a]	1.99	27
KEN	3.37	5	2.60	114	2.20	188[a]
Mean	3.07	5	3.05	77	2.37	105

[a] Additional interviews.

views to the original twenty-four. These additional interviews were selected by Rohrbaugh as part of an independent study.[4] They consisted of interviews from the true terminating points of the five prolonged cases, and interviews from a point between the true early and late interviews of the seven early-terminating patients. Thus, each case was represented by three time-separated interviews for sampling. The interview number associated with each data point for each patient is shown in Table 13.2.

Except for the extended cases (over fifty interviews), the intermediate interviews did not represent the exact mid-point of the therapy. For the shorter-term cases the intermediate and final data points tended to be

4. The author wishes to thank Miss Paula Rohrbaugh for making the segments available.

located within the last third of the total number of interviews held in the case. Thus the bias, if any, was in the direction of oversampling of the last half of therapy.

Two four-minute segments were extracted from the same arbitrary points within the first and last thirds of the tape recordings of the thirty-six interviews. The segments were transferred onto separate spools and typescripted. Each of the seventy-two segments was edited for cues which might betray the temporal position of the interview, the name of the patient or the therapist, or the length of the interview. Two different random orders were prepared since the judges would be required to rate all but the additional segments four times.

Lastly, all the segments, except the additional twenty-four samples, were mixed with fifty-six filler segments, identical to those from the schizophrenics, but taken from clients diagnosed neurotic. The judges believed that all the segments were equally important in the rating process, and they were not alerted to the differences in psychopathology.

Judges and Rating Procedure

Four judges were used to make the ratings of process. Two of the judges had had very limited experience as therapists, but two had been very active in previous studies involving the assessment of process. Two of the judges (one experienced in process measurement and one not) were laymen with no formal training in psychology. The other two were graduate students in clinical psychology (one advanced and one beginning). No training was given to the two inexperienced judges, the aim being to tap directly the necessity for rater training by comparing the reliabilities of the experienced and inexperienced judges. The only contact with the process concept for the two inexperienced judges was a familiarization procedure given to all judges prior to rating with each scale. This involved having each judge rate a practice set of twenty segments extracted from interviews other than those used for this study.

To make the ratings of process, the segments were given to the judges in alternate random sequences, and each judge started his ratings at a different point within the body of segments. In this way the judges were never rating the same segments in the same order. The judges were required to play the tape-recorded segment and simultaneously read the accompanying typescript of the interaction; then locate on the assigned process scale the position which best reflected the behavior he was judging; and finally assign a numerical rating (1–7) which corresponded to the selected stage of process. Each judge repeated this procedure four times, once for each of the behavioral scales being rated. At the fourth rating, the twenty-four additional segments were randomly inter-polated and the ratings made in the customary manner. Learning effects and contrast of new segments with old should have been minimized in view of the randomizing procedure and the sheer number of segments and ratings.

In sum, seventy-two four-minute segments of patient-therapist inter-action were extracted from the first and last thirds of early, intermediate, and late recorded therapy interviews from twelve schizophrenic pa-tients. Forty-eight of these segments were randomly mixed with filler segments from a neurotic population and presented in random order to judges for process rating. All of these segments were rated by four judges using each of four scales. At the fourth and final rating, twenty-four additional segments were randomly interpolated and rated by four judges, each using a single but different scale.

Results

Reliability

Tables 13.3 and 13.4 present the various interjudge and interscale correlations. Judgmental reliability (Table 13.3) was assessed using

Table 13.3—Intraclass reliability of all judges' ratings of process (Experiencing, Personal Constructs, Problem Expression, and Rela-lationship scales) for both multiple, and single plus multiple, rated segments

Process scales	Multiple rated segments ($N = 48$)	Multiple plus single rated segments ($N = 72$)
EXP	.89	.85
PC	.88	.86
PES	.88	.88
REL	.88	.87

Ebel's (1951) intraclass method and the agreement between judges was uniformly high. Since the Rohrbaugh segments were rated only once by each judge, in contrast to the other segments which were rated four times, it might appear that the reliability of the added data would be open to question. However, in view of the high interscale correlations pictured in Table 13.4 (ranging from .57 between EXP and REL to .85 between PC and EXP using Pearson's method), it appears that the ratings reflected the same dimension, or very highly correlated dimensions, of behavior. Thus the ratings of the added data were for practical purposes all made in terms of the same dimension of behavior. Coupled with that fact was the judges' own high reliability, both on the original forty-eight segments (.85–.92 depending on the scale) and on the twenty-four Rohrbaugh segments (.85–.87). The judges' high agreement on two-thirds of the process ratings suggests the likelihood that they would have agreed similarly on the remaining one-third (the added

Table 13.4—Interscale correlations

	EXP	PES	PC
REL	.57	.66	.68
EXP		.71	.85
PES			.83

segments). This is borne out by their agreement on the additional ratings despite the use of different scales. The average correlation for all segments of .87 further buttressed the claim of equivalence between the two sets of data.

Thus, the use of the added process ratings was justified on the following grounds: demonstrated agreement between judges on one set of data implied the likelihood of their agreement on a second, and this was supported by the results. The fact that only one judge rated the added data with each scale did not mitigate the usefulness of the ratings. These single ratings came after demonstrated agreement on two-thirds of the segments and suggest that if all had rated the added segments the results would have been materially unchanged. In sum, the judges were demonstrably reliable and the scales were highly correlated.

The Factor of Rating Experience

Apparently the experience of the judge in making ratings was of no consequence. The two inexperienced judges were approximately as reliable with each other ($r = .85$) as they were with the two experienced judges ($r = .79$). The simple training procedure as well as the absence of rating experience implies at least two alternative conclusions: that the behavior described in the scales was sufficiently clear and was closely enough related to the observed behavior that training was unnecessary to attain a high degree of reliability; or that the behavior was so gross as to be readily seen by even naive observers. However, it should be kept in mind that the strands (experiencing, personal constructs, etc.) were scaled separately expressly to gain simplicity of judgment.

The descriptions at each level are couched in ordinary language and attempt to characterize only behavior believed to be associated with given levels of process. Presumably any reasonably sophisticated individual should be able to identify behavior which mirrors the strand descriptions, and assign the correlated numerical rating. Apparently this was the case; that is, the judges were able, even in the absence of formal training, to identify the scale description which most closely matched the observed behavior. One of the advantages of the process concept may be that given a moderate level of psychological sophistication, little training is needed to achieve satisfactory reliability.

Analysis of Process Ratings

Five analyses were carried out: an overall analysis of variance based on the mean process ratings from all judges and scales, and an analysis of variance of the process ratings for each of the four process scales. In each of the latter analyses the statistical test was performed on the mean of the four judges' process ratings which stemmed from the same scale.

Figure 13.1 represents a plot of the mean process ratings from each of the four scales and four judges for each of the three data points. Figure 13.2 is a plot of the average for each of the four scales; each data point represents the average rating by four judges using one of the four scales. As can be seen the trends are similar across scales and are summarized by the overall plot in Figure 13.2.

Analysis of Combined Process Ratings

The summary of the analysis of variance (Table 13.5) indicates that there were no significant effects due to outcome alone. Apparently the

Table 13.5—Overall analysis of variance for combined process ratings

Source	df	MS	F	p
Between subjects				
Success (S)	1	.75	.88	NS
Ss/Success	10	.85	3.40	< .01
Within subjects				
Interviews (I)	2	.42	.21	NS
I × S	2	1.62	6.48	< .01
Residual	20	.25		

overall mean differences were sufficiently reduced by the initial differences between m.s. and l.s. patients (Figure 13.1) to wash out the marked differences in process level of the terminating interviews. Similarly, the crossover of the m.s. and l.s. process ratings over time reduced the mean differences between early and late interviews; thus the main effect "interview" was not significant.

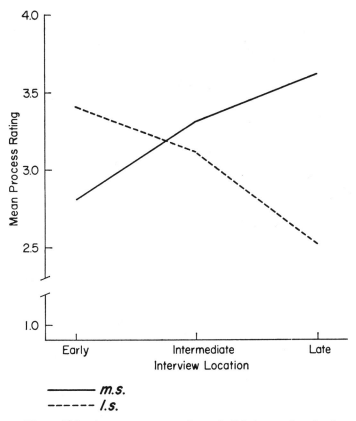

Figure 13.1—Average process ratings of all judges and scales for early, intermediate, and late interviews of more successful and less successful schizophrenic patients.

The interaction between interviews and outcome did reach significance ($F = 6.48$, $df = 2/20$, $p < .01$), and indicates that the process ratings changed significantly during the course of therapy as a function of the rated success of the case. From Figure 13.1 it is clear that the patients rated m.s., though starting at a somewhat lower level of process than those rated l.s., overtook and ultimately significantly exceeded the

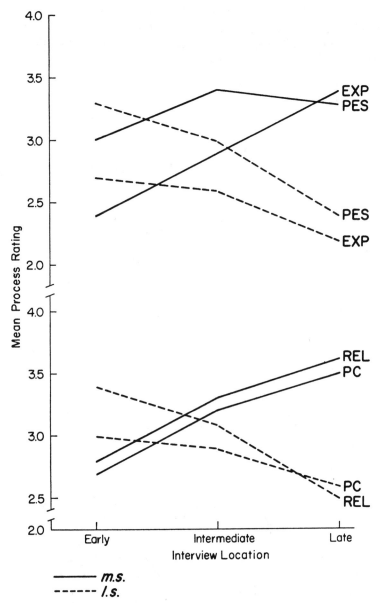

Figure 13.2—Mean process ratings from more successful and less successful patients for the Experiencing (EXP), Problem Expression (PES), Relationship (REL), and Personal Constructs (PC) scales.

process level of the l.s. cases. Figure 13.1 also suggests that the difference between m.s. and l.s. was not solely a product of the increase in process level of the m.s. patients. The l.s. patients showed a pronounced drop in their process level over time, although the difference between early and late mean ratings of the l.s. patients was not by itself significant.

Analysis of Individual Scale Ratings

With the exception of the PES scale, results similar to those obtained in the overall analysis were obtained with each of the process scales. The results for each scale are given below.

Table 13.6—Analysis of variance of process ratings made with the Experiencing Scale

Source	df	MS	F	p
Between subjects				
Success (S)	1	1.44	1.74	NS
Ss/Success	10	.83	2.59	< .05
Within subjects				
Interviews (I)	2	.22	1	NS
I × S	2	1.81	5.72	< .02
Residual	20	.32		

EXP Scale (Table 13.6).—There were no significant main effects, but the interaction between success and interviews was significant ($F = 5.72$, $df = 2/20$, $p < .02$), though slightly reduced in power relative to PC and REL.

Table 13.7—Analysis of variance of process ratings made with the Personal Constructs Scale

Source	df	MS	F	p
Between subjects				
Success (S)	1	1.29	1.24	NS
Ss/Success	10	1.04	4.73	< .01
Within subjects				
Interviews (I)	2	.11	1	NS
I × S	2	1.47	6.82	< .01
Residual	20	.22		

PC Scale (Table 13.7).—As with the overall analysis the main effects "success" and "interviews" were not significant. The interaction between success and interviews indicates that there was significant change ($F = 6.82$, $df = 2/20$, $p < .01$) in process level over time as a function of the outcome of the case, i.e., the process ratings increased over time for the m.s. patients and decreased during the same time span for the l.s. patients.

Table 13.8—Analysis of variance of process ratings made with the Problem Expression Scale

Source	df	MS	F	p
Between subjects				
Success (S)	1	.94	1	NS
Ss/Success	10	1.68	3.81	< .01
Within subjects				
Interviews (I)	2	.36	1	NS
I × S	2	1.21	2.76	NS
Residual	20	.44		

PES Scale (Table 13.8).—There were no significant differences between the main effects, nor was there a difference in the interaction of these effects. Thus the PES Scale did not distinguish, at an acceptable level of significance, differences in process level between m.s. and l.s. patients between time-separated interviews, or the interaction of these two variables.

Table 13.9—Analysis of variance of process ratings made with the Relationship Scale

Source	df	MS	F	p
Between subjects				
Success (S)	1	.62	1.12	NS
Ss/Success	10	.55	1.40	NS
Within subjects				
Interviews (I)	2	.08	1	NS
I × S	2	2.15	6.81	< .01
Residual	20	.32		

REL Scale (Table 13.9).—The results essentially duplicated those found with the PC Scale. There were no significant main effects, but the interaction between outcome and interview position was highly significant ($F = 6.81$, $df = 2/20$, $p < .01$). There was significant change in process level over time as a product of the outcome of the cases being rated.

In terms of the predictions stated at the beginning of this chapter these results may be summarized as follows:

1. The first prediction was that positive process change over therapy would be greater for m.s. than for l.s. patients. The significant interaction between success and interviews found in all the analyses except that for PES confirms this statement. Speaking only from the results of the overall analysis it seems clear that there was a significant difference in the amount of change as a function of the outcome of the case. The m.s. patients showed a marked upward trend in their process level from early to late interviews, whereas the l.s. patients showed a moderate downward trend. The combination of these two events eventuates in the observed differences between the two groups in terms of the amount of change in process level over time.

2. The second prediction, regarding the expectation of an initially higher process level for m.s. than for l.s. patients cannot be accepted. Not only did the prediction fail to receive statistical support, but the m.s. patients started at a lower level of process than the l.s. patients. It is worth noting that the initial difference between m.s. and l.s. groups was itself not significant. Nevertheless the "readiness to change" concept offered as an explanation for the data from neurotics needs qualification when schizophrenic patients are involved.

3. A third issue concerned the redundancy of the scales. It was postulated that the ratings made with any one scale would essentially duplicate the ratings made with any of the remaining three. The interscale correlations support such a conclusion. However, the PES Scale failed to pick up differences between the m.s. and l.s. patients in terms of amount of change in process level, and thus may be viewed as the least sensitive instrument. From the standpoint of power to discriminate the PC and the REL Scales seemed to be the most sensitive to the changes in patient behavior which were reflected in the process ratings. Of the scales which reliably discriminated change, the REL and EXP had the lowest interscale correlation, .57, and therefore they may represent the best combination of ability to discriminate plus scale independence.

4. The second postulate, that a combined process score representing the average of ratings with all four scales would yield the most discriminative measure, does not seem to be acceptable. Two of the scales, the PC and the REL, detected differences in change as a function of success with power equivalent to the overall measure. Further, since the overall measure failed to provide any other indications of superiority, e.g., discriminations between main effects, there is no apparent reason to prefer a mean of all the scales over either the PC or REL alone.

Discussion

It seems clear that the process measures are capable of distinguishing client behavior in terms of change and outcome. Apparently the process conception, as reflected in the various scales, does indeed tap dimensions of behavior which are susceptible to therapeutic influence and which varies as a combined product of outcome and time.

If a single dimension is sufficient to account for all the variance it may be broadly identified as the client's "approach to his experience." For example, if he seems reasonably fluid in the interpretation of his experience and able to relate reasonably well, he is rated higher than a client who is more rigid and less willing to enter into the relationship. Clearly, clients do range along such dimensions, and it is quite plausible that these behaviors would influence the client's capability for change. It is conceivable that "approach to experience" may be separated along a number of component dimensions all of which are related and may be expected to covary. The sum of these components is the client's "manner of experiencing" and thus the ratings from any of the scales can be viewed as tapping the client's expressive method of conceptualizing his experience. The results lend support to the notion that clients vary in their styles of approach to experience and an alteration of the expressive manner of this approach signals significant change in psychotherapy.

Perhaps the single most important finding of this study was the evidence of a systematic relationship between some variables of client expressive behavior and the outcome of psychotherapy. The dimensions that compose the process conception were shown to vary in a predictable and significant manner with independent criteria of therapeutic improvement. Obviously the results do not permit assumptions of a causal relationship between process change and outcome. Nevertheless, one can say conservatively that it was a successful attempt to identify and quantify some of the variables which change during the course of therapy and which at the same time are significantly related to the measured success of the case. The data are thus offered as evidence confirming Rogers' (1958) conceptualization of the process of personality change, and, more specifically, as evidence of significant therapeutic change in the patients who made up the experimental sample for this study.

As is generally the case when between-groups comparisons are made some of the characteristics of individuals required separate identification. For example, of the six m.s. cases shown in Table 13.2, two (GOS and SOC) rather dramatically increased in process level over time while a third (VAC) changed considerably. A fourth (PUF) did not change over time, but his mean process level was higher than any other at each temporal position. Thus four of the six patients rated m.s. either changed considerably or were consistently rated high in process level. One m.s. patient (FIP) declined in process level over the period of therapy, and the last (RAC) remained unchanged at an intermediate level of process.

Among the patients rated l.s., three (FAS, KEN, and LYN) showed marked decrease in process over time, while another (WIL) decreased slightly. The remaining two (DEM and RUD) remained at about the same level. The only noteworthy increase in process level by an l.s. patient was DEM's intermediate score relative to his early rating. His rather precipitous decline at the terminating interview in contrast to his intermediate score probably mirrors the indecision and confusion regarding his mental status at the termination of therapy.

Thus if one were to arrange the twelve patients on a continuum of improvement in therapy they would distribute themselves continuously over the range of the scale. As in most studies of this type, some patients improved, some deteriorated, and some remained unchanged. However, none of the l.s. schizophrenics improved and only one m.s. patient declined, whereas four m.s. patients improved and four l.s. patients declined. On the basis of these considerations the process conception seems to be a valid measure in terms of individual characteristics as well as of differences between groups.

A disturbing note in these results is the decline in process level of the l.s. patients. Whether the decline in process level over time was a product of the therapy itself, or whether it occurred and would have occurred independently of the intervention cannot be known from these data. It is perhaps sufficient to acknowledge that a decline did, in fact, take place. However, if therapy is cited as the agent of positive change in the m.s. patients, then presumably it must also be cited for the negative change in the l.s. patients. From this point of view the therapy must then bear the onus of contributing to the deterioration of some of the patients. If this is the case, then this study provides evidence of the harmful as well as the salutary effects of psychotherapy.

Therapy, it seems, should no longer be viewed as either helpful or safely benign. Continued or additional decline, at least from the standpoint of the process conception, i.e., the client's approach to his experience, does occur in some instances. Whether or not therapy is the agent of this decline, it is clear that it may not always be the treatment of choice. Thus the problem of client selection for therapy is now expanded to include identifying and selecting out those who may be expected to react adversely to a given type of therapy experience. It has been suggested (Schofield, 1961) that given therapies may be suitable for some clients, but ineffective (and in this case deleterious) for others. It seems plausible, for example, that an approach which does not hinge on intrapersonal exploration might be more suitable and change-producing for those clients who are not self-oriented and not introspective. By itself a suggestion of this sort is neither unique nor particularly insightful. However the implication it carries for future professional conduct is of considerable importance, suggesting as it does that therapists may have to abandon the rather ethnocentric stand they customarily take regarding their treatment approach.

The evidence to date is that all therapeutic approaches yield some evidence of success, but seldom is that record of success sufficient to discriminate the more from the less effective treatments, or even to buttress the claim that therapy is better than no therapy. One of the reasons for the ambiguity surrounding treatment efficacy may center on the fact that most of the outcome studies offered a single treatment to all the participating clients. The clients who failed in empirical tests of the efficacy of psychotherapy might have succeeded if a different approach had been used, and conversely those who succeeded might have failed.

Although we do not know enough yet to make valid decisions about the role of individual differences in suitability to given therapeutic approaches, it might be useful to begin to collect data along those lines. For example, the most obvious sorting procedure would place those clients with the intellectual equipment and attitudes necessary for self-exploration with one type of therapy, e.g., an "insight" (London, 1964) approach, and those without these attributes with an "action," i.e., behavior change approach. Though oversimplified, it seems possible that the major objection to such a position might not be in terms of the problems of client selection but might come, rather, from therapists of various persuasions resisting the implication that their therapy is not the only legitimate method. This resistance would be compounded by the tendency of some therapists to rule out certain therapy approaches on philosophical and/or moral grounds, e.g., behavior therapy is antihumanistic or insight therapy is asocial and breeds irresponsibility in its patients. Out of this controversy only one group of people, the clients, are truly disadvantaged, for it is they who ask for help. If, for petty reasons, representatives of the various therapeutic positions evade the necessary collaborative research then they, as spokesmen for the therapeutic enterprise, will also have evaded their primary responsibility as clinicians, namely, to provide their clients with the treatment best suited to the achievement of the clients' goals. Thus this chapter ends with a plea for communication and understanding, not between client and therapist, but between therapists of different theoretical and procedural persuasions. Intramural alienation serves no useful professional purpose and, in the final analysis, it is the client who suffers.

References

EBEL, R. L. Estimation of the reliability of ratings. *Psychometrika 16:* 407–424, 1951.

KELLY, G. A. *The Psychology of Personal Constructs.* New York: W. W. Norton, 1955.

KIRTNER, W. L., and CARTWRIGHT, D. S. Success and failure in client-centered therapy as a function of client personality variables. *J. consult. Psychol. 22:259–264,* 1957.

LONDON, P. *The Modes and Morals of Psychotherapy.* New York: Holt, Rinehart & Winston, 1964.

ROGERS, C. R. The necessary and sufficient conditions of therapeutic personality change. *J. consult. Psychol. 21: 95–103,* 1957.

ROGERS, C. R. A tentative scale for the measurement of process in psychotherapy. In E. A. Rubinstein and M. B. Parloff (eds.), *Research in Psychotherapy,* Vol. I. Washington, D.C.: American Psychological Association, 1959.

SCHOFIELD, W. *Psychotherapy: The Purchase of Friendship.* New York: Prentice-Hall, 1964.

TOMLINSON, T. M. Three approaches to the study of psychotherapy: Process, outcome, and change. Unpublished Ph.D. dissertation, University of Wisconsin, 1962.

TOMLINSON, T. M., and HART, J. T., JR. A validation of the Process Scale. *J. consult. Psychol. 26:74–78,* 1962.

TRUAX, C. B. The process of group psychotherapy: Relationships between hypothesized therapeutic conditions and intrapersonal exploration. *Psychol. Monogr. 75,* No. 7 (Whole No. 511), 1961.

WALKER, A., RABLEN, R. A., and ROGERS, C. R. Development of a scale to measure process change in psychotherapy. *J. clin. Psychol. 16:79–85,* 1960.

14. The Differential Effectiveness of Therapy as Measured by the Thematic Apperception Test

Though the data for the focused study reported in this chapter were collected by many members of the project staff, the study itself was entirely independent of the project. Dr. Byron L. Barrington, of Wausau, Wisconsin, interested in psychotherapy and psychotherapy research, requested permission to use the project data. This permission was gladly given. Dr. Barrington presents the results of the study in this chapter. His analysis has given valuable new perspective on the degree of personality change in our different groups. We are indebted to him.

Frequently projective test scores have yielded contradictory or inconclusive results when used to evaluate psychotherapy. This is especially true in studies comparing the therapist's rating of case success with other outcome measures (Henry and Shlien, 1958). It was the author's opinion that these results, at least in part, reflected a lack of agreement in the personality theory and expectations for change held by the therapists and those individuals analyzing the tests. In addition, most studies using the Thematic Apperception Test have measured change in terms of improvement on some global rating of adjustment. These ratings, though often fairly reliable, involve subjective interpretation and the combination of a number of different variables from the TAT.[1]

The purpose of this study was threefold: to select a set of fairly objective TAT variables that would theoretically be related to the type of attitude and behavior change occurring with successful psychotherapy; to use these measures to establish the degree to which change occurred in a group of hospitalized patients in psychotherapy; and to establish the relationship, if any, between change on the TAT and other measures available on these cases.

1. I wish to express my appreciation to Dr. Eugene Gendlin for arranging to have the TAT records and other data sent to me. I would also like to thank the other members of the project staff who took the time to collect, summarize, and send to me the data on which this study was based.—B. L. B.

To accomplish these aims, specific variables were selected from TAT records that would reflect particular attitudes or behaviors said to change with successful client-centered therapy. Though all the therapists did not necessarily use this theoretical framework, it was the approach most representative of the group.

The specific TAT variables used were individually scored and summarized and therefore, to the extent that they had the hypothesized psychological significance, it was possible to see in which areas of functioning change occurred. The independent use of the various measures minimized the tendency for differential changes in several areas to cancel each other out. However, the possible usefulness of an overall change score was recognized and one was computed by combining the results from the individual measures. In addition, several of the measures that were theoretically measuring psychologically similar behaviors were also combined. In this way, both change in specific areas and overall change could be examined.

Methodology

The Measures

The particular TAT variables selected, and their assumed psychological significance, are listed in Table 14.1.[2] It will be noted these measures involve a minimum of subjective judgment. In most instances scores were obtained by counting members of some easily defined category, e.g., number of stimulus elements used. Consequently, the reliability of the judgments is less of an issue than it would be if a generalized rating of adjustment had been used.

Some elaboration on Table 14.1 might give a clearer picture of the individual measures. The first measure, *number of stimuli used,* was obtained by counting the number of stimulus elements of the cards mentioned by the subject as he told his story. The stimuli counted were those listed by Henry (1956) as "usually" or "frequently" noted in stories for the particular cards used.

Emotional distancing was measured by counting the number of times the subjects minimized the personal relevance or immediacy of the story by qualifying it with such phrases as "this is a story about . . ." or "this is a picture of . . ." Also counted were stories where it was stated that the setting for the story was a distant time or a foreign country.

2. Several other measures were originally selected but had to be dropped because the records did not contain sufficient data in these areas.

Number of feelings expressed was tabulated by counting the number of times words were used that described emotional reactions. The words included in that category were those appearing on a list of emotional words compiled by the author for a previous study (Barrington, 1963). Variance in number of feelings expressed was based on the same data, but was obtained by computing the variances for the subgroups of cases for pre- and post-therapy.

Table 14.1—TAT variables and assumed psychological significance

TAT variables	Assumed psychological significance
Number of stimuli used	Openness to experience and ability to accept intellectually and use stimulus elements
Emotional distancing	Defensive avoidance of threat; inability to cope directly with experience
Number of feelings expressed	Sensitivity to, and use of, emotional reactions as significant influences in behavior
Variance in number of feelings expressed	Appropriateness of emotional expression—emotional reactions are neither overwhelming nor strongly denied
Length of record	Intellectual productivity
Self-critical and self-depreciating comments	Degree of negative self-evaluation
Number of introduced authority figures	Dependence, lack of autonomy, oversensitivity to authorities
Number of introduced non-authority figures	Interest in, or desire for, social contact
Emotional tone of introduced non-authority figures	General emotional attitudes toward relations with people other than authorities
Number of direct interpersonal relations	Confidence in ability to deal with people in a direct face-to-face relationship
Tone of interpersonal relations	Expectation of the degree of satisfaction or dissatisfaction in direct social contacts

The length of each story was measured by counting the number of lines of type that were used in the story. In two records where the subjects went into long discussions of personal events unrelated to the card or story being told, only that material related to the story was counted.

Self-critical and self-depreciating comments reflected the number of times the person used the comment "I don't know," or criticized his story or himself with comments such as "I don't have a very good imagination."

Number of introduced authority figures was the number of people introduced into the story who did not reflect a figure represented on the card, and who had an authority role in the story, e.g., a mother telling the little boy to practice the violin in Card No. 1. Introduced figures were tabulated separately for authorities and others. "Others" would be peers or people of equal status to the main character in the story, e.g., "one of his friends comes and asks him to come out and play ball, but he has to stay in and practice." Authorities included figures such as parents, bosses, doctors, judges, or other people who would be likely to have control or authority over the main character in the story.

Emotional tone of introduced non-authority figures was judged from the way the introduced figure behaved in the story. If he argued with, or tried to control the hero, or was associated with physical or emotional discomfort, he was rated as negative. If the person was helpful or associated with pleasurable experiences, he was rated as positive. If both elements were present he was rated as neutral. In the final tabulation, positive and neutral figures were combined.

Number of direct interpersonal relations was the number of times characters in stories directly interacted, that is, talked to each other, hit each other, etc. Statements where a relationship was stated, but no direct interaction occurred, were not counted, for instance, Card No. 2 described as a "farm family" but with no direct contact among the people in the story.

Tone of interpersonal relations referred to the type of direct interpersonal relationship which occurred. Positive relationships were those that were helpful or satisfying to the main character. Negatively toned relationships were those that were undesirable or unwanted by the main character.

Procedure

The measures were applied to sixty-six TAT protocols from thirty-three subjects. The records generally consisted of stories from eight cards.[3] Analysis of the records was blind, the author having no knowledge of the number of experimental and control cases, nor which records were pre- and which post-therapy.[4] There were three records where

3. In some cases not all eight cards were administered before and after therapy. Scores for these records were prorated where necessary. The cards used were Nos. 1, 2, 3BM, 4, 10, 7BM, 16, and 19.

4. "Post-therapy" testing of the control cases reflected time intervals equivalent to experimental cases. Unfortunately, administrative problems often prevented post-testing immediately after termination. The records used were those obtained closest to the time of termination, but in some cases the discrepancy between post-testing date and actual therapy termination was over one third the total therapy time. Seven of the eleven experimental "post-therapy" records were actually obtained prior to termination. It would be more accurate to say comparisons were

comments were made in the stories about having taken the test before. This of course implied they were post-test records though the subject might have taken a TAT prior to the research project. It might also be added that the author had very little knowledge about the type of subjects included in the sample. In fact, the scoring was completed before the author learned that ten of the subjects were non-hospitalized controls.

Following the scoring the records were decoded and grouped as hospital experimental (HE), hospital control (HC), and non-hospitalized (N). The first group (HE) contained twelve subjects, the second (HC) eleven subjects, and the third (N) ten subjects. Pre-therapy comparisons were made between the total hospital and normal groups and between the separate HE, HC, and N groups. This was an attempt to establish the usefulness of the measures in discriminating between non-hospitalized subjects and individuals the severity of whose problems, or whose methods of handling them, lead to hospitalization. Similar group comparisons were made after the conclusion of therapy.

Of more primary concern were the change scores computed for each individual by comparing pre- and post-scores on each measure. Hypotheses regarding changes for individuals in the three groups were tested. For most measures this was done by ranking the individuals before and after therapy and applying a Wilcoxon signed rank test. Comparison of the relative amount of change for the HE, HC, and N groups was generally made by applying a Mann-Whitney test to the change scores.

A total directional change score was computed for each individual by adding up the number of measures where change was toward better adjustment and subtracting the number of measures moving in the opposite direction. If a positive value was obtained the overall record was felt to show improvement. If a negative value was obtained, it was assumed the person had, on an overall basis, moved toward a poorer adjustment. A sign test was applied to the number of individuals in each of the three groups moving toward better adjustment.

A comparison of overall change for the HE and HC groups was also made by ranking the total hospital group for change on each measure. A mean rank for all measures was then obtained and a Mann-Whitney

---

made between pre- and late-therapy or post-therapy records. This complicates the analysis of the results, but especially in view of the high percentage of records taken prior to actual termination it was felt that any error introduced would tend to go against the hypothesis of change resulting from therapy, i.e., reduce the likelihood of obtaining significant positive results.

test used to compare the mean ranks of individuals in the HE and HC groups.

A mean rank for change scores was also used to establish the relative amount of change for individuals in the HE group. This measure of overall change was then correlated with two other measures available on these cases: therapists' ratings of success, an outcome variable, and initial Kirtner-Cartwright Scale ratings, considered a predictive measure. The therapists' ratings of success were also compared to three individual measures that were felt to be most likely to reflect attitudes and behaviors that would be openly manifested in the therapy relationship and also of importance to the therapist in his attempt to evaluate the success of the case.

Several comparisons were also made between three TAT measures most sensitive to change resulting from therapy and the conditions ratings.[5] Pre-therapy TAT scores were correlated with therapist's conditions to establish the influence of the patient's attitudes as he entered therapy, on the behavior of his therapist. Secondly, level on the conditions over therapy was compared with change from pre- to post-therapy on the three TAT measures to establish whether the observed change in these particular areas was related to the three conditions rated.

Although the measures are quite objective, the issue of rater reliability was considered and a rate-rerate reliability check was run on five of the measures most likely to involve some subjectivity. A sixth measure, emotional distancing, was also checked because of the number of significant results associated with it. The second scoring was made about one year after the initial ratings, using fifteen randomly selected records.

Results

The rate-rerate reliability scores are presented in Table 14.2. The values given are rank-order correlations (rho). Considering the length

Table 14.2—Rate-rerate reliability for six TAT measures

Measure	rho*
Emotional distancing	.90
Number of introduced authority figures	.88
Number of introduced non-authority figures	.89
Positive emotional tone of introduced non-authority figures	.96
Number of direct interpersonal relations	.90
Positive emotional tone of interpersonal relations	.78

$* p < .01$

5. Ratings of the degree of accurate empathy, congruence, and unconditional positive regard shown by the therapist.

of time between the two ratings, the generally high scores indicate ratings of these variables can be reliably made.[6]

The pre-therapy comparisons of the combined hospital group and the non-hospital controls are summarized in Table 14.3. The plus or minus sign indicates whether the results were in the predicted direction of poorer adjustment for the hospital group prior to therapy. It will be noted that eight of the eleven measures went in the predicted direction, but only one—number of stimuli used—showed a statistically significant difference between the two groups (one-tailed test probability less than .025).

It would appear that although most of the measures went in the predicted direction they are of limited value in discriminating between individuals who have been hospitalized and those who have not.

Table 14.3—Pre-therapy differences on TAT measures between hospital and non-hospital cases; (+) indicates the results were in the predicted direction of better adjustment for the non-hospital cases; (−) indicates the reverse

TAT measure	Direction of difference
Number of stimuli used	+*
Emotional distancing	+
Number of feelings expressed	−
Variance in number of feelings expressed	+
Length of record	+
Self-critical and self-depreciating comments	+
Number of introduced authority figures	−
Number of introduced non-authority figures	+
Emotional tone of introduced non-authority figures	+
Number of direct interpersonal relations	+
Tone of interpersonal relations	−

* One-tailed $p < .025$.

The second use of the measures was to establish the presence, or absence, of change from the first to the second testing. Comparing change scores for individuals in the three groups would give information regarding the relative importance of various influences. Change in the non-hospital group would reflect the effects of taking the test a second

6. The rho value of .90 associated with emotional distancing was somewhat lower than expected considering the objective nature of the measure. In comparing the records where first and second rating differences occurred, it was found that the word "scene" was counted in the second scoring but not in the first. This, combined with a few errors in the form of missed references to "picture," produced the variation.

time, and perhaps the effects of general life experiences over time. Change for the HC group would reflect the factors operating on the N group plus the additional effects of hospital life and the general treatment program of the institution. Change for the HE group would reflect all the factors operating on the HC group plus the added influence of individual psychotherapy.

Table 14.4—Direction of change on TAT measures for hospital experimental, hospital control, and non-hospital control groups; (+) indicates movement toward better adjustment; (−) indicates movement toward poorer adjustment

TAT measure	Hospital experimentals	Hospital controls	Non-hospital controls
Increase in number of stimuli used	+	+ (*p* < .05)	−
Decrease in emotional distancing	+ (*p* < .025)	−	+
Increase in mean number of feelings expressed	−	+	−
Decrease in variance in number of feelings expressed	+ (*p* < .05)	−	no change
Increase in length of record	−	+	− (*p* < .01)
Decrease in self-critical and self-depreciating comments	+	+	−
Decrease in number of introduced authority figures	+	−	+
Increase in number of introduced non-authority figures	+ (*p* < .01)	+	−
Increase in positive tone introduced non-authority figures	+	−	+
Increase in number of direct interpersonal relations	+	−	+
Increase in positive tone of interpersonal relations	+ (*p* < .025)	−	−

Table 14.4 shows the direction, and statistical significance, of change on each measure for the three groups. A plus indicates movement in the direction of better adjustment. A minus indicates the reverse. It will be noted that on nine of the eleven measures the HE group showed a positive change and on four of these the change was great enough to be statistically significant. These were: decreased emotional distancing, less extreme emotional expression, more non-authority figures introduced, and an increased positive tone in interpersonal relations.

The HC group showed positive change on five measures and poorer adjustment on six. One change, increased number of stimuli used, showed a statistically significant amount of improvement for the HC group.

The non-hospital group showed negative change on seven of the eleven measures, positive change on three, and no change on one. Only one of these changes was statistically significant and that was a decrease in the length of the record. Because the length of the record would have tended to influence a number of the other measures it is likely that the negative trend on several other measures may have been a by-product of the decrease in record length for the N group. In interpreting this result it would appear likely that the N group was less motivated in the later testing, perhaps because the novelty of taking the tests and being part of a research project had worn off.

This decrease in motivation with repeated testing did not appear to have had as much influence on the hospital groups, as they showed no significant change in productivity. There could be at least two possible explanations for this. The hospital groups may have become less psychologically constricted so they could respond more freely to the cards and elaborate on their stories, and/or they may have been more concerned about doing well on the tests in the hope that it would influence plans for their discharge. These two influences could have made up for any reduced motivation because of less interest in the test the second session.

Table 14.5 shows the results of adding, for each individual, the number of categories where improvement was noted and subtracting the

Table 14.5—Number of hospital experimental, hospital control, and non-hospital control groups showing overall change toward better adjustment on TAT measures

Group	Improved adjustment	No change	Poorer adjustment
Hospital experimental	10*	1	1
Hospital control	6	1	4
Non-hospital control	3	0	7

* One-tailed $p < .02$ (sign test).

number showing negative change.[7] If the resulting value was positive the person had shown general improvement, if negative he had moved toward poorer adjustment. It will be noted that ten of the twelve HE

7. Only ten measures were used for this, as change scores for individuals would not be available for variance on emotional words.

cases improved, while one remained the same (positive and negative change balanced out), and one decreased. A sign test on these values produced a one-tailed test probability of less than .02, indicating significant improvement for the HE group.

The HC group also showed more individuals improving than moving the other way (six positive, four negative, and one no change) but this trend was not great enough to be statistically significant. The N group showed a non-significant trend toward poorer adjustment. As mentioned above, this probably reflects in part their decreased productivity.

These results suggest that the HE group improved more than did the hospital patients who did not have psychotherapy.

Table 14.6 gives a comparison of the amount of positive change on the various measures for the HE and HC groups. The HE group showed more positive change on eight measures. For three of the eight —decreased emotional distancing, less extreme expression of emotions, and fewer introduced authorities—the difference was statistically significant. The HC group showed more positive change on three of the eleven measures, but for none of these three was the difference significant.

When the measures were originally set up it was felt there were several broad areas of behavior into which the individual measures could be grouped. These were: openness to experience; free and appropriate use of emotion; intellectual productivity; self-trust or self-reliance; and sociability—the capacity to enter into and effectively handle interpersonal relations.

Length of record was the only measure assumed to primarily reflect intellectual productivity and was therefore alone in that category. Use of emotion had two related measures but one of these, variance on emotional words, did not produce scores for individuals. It was therefore not possible to combine measures for these two areas. For the other three areas, the ranks on each measure were averaged for each individual and the HE and HC groups were compared by applying a Mann-Whitney test to the mean ranks for the individuals in the groups. As the second column in Table 14.6 indicates, the HE group showed more change than the HC group in all three areas where measures were combined, and in one of the three, improved interpersonal relations, there was a statistically significant difference.

A similar procedure was used to obtain a mean rank for each individual over all the measures. The HE and HC groups were then compared using these scores. The HE group was higher, but for this measure of overall change the improvement of the HE group was not significantly greater than that of the HC group. From these results it would appear that the HE group did change significantly in a number of areas, and showed a significant movement toward better adjustment on an overall basis. In addition, in several areas the HE group showed significantly

Table 14.6—Comparisons of amount of change on TAT measures in hospital experimental and hospital control groups

TAT measure	Direction	Directions with measures grouped
Increase in number of stimuli used	HC > HE	
Decrease in emotional distancing	HE > HC*	
Openness to experience		*HE > HC*
Increase in mean number of feelings expressed	HE > HC	
Decrease in variance in number of feelings expressed	HE > HC[a]	
Use of emotion		—
Increase in length of record	HC > HE	
Intellectuality		—
Decrease in self-criticism and self-depreciation	HC > HE	
Decrease in number of introduced authority figures	HE > HC*	
Self-reliance		*HE > HC*
Increase in number of introduced non-authority figures	HE > HC	
Increase in positive tone of introduced non-authority figures	HE > HC	
Increase in number of direct interpersonal relations	HE > HC	
Increase in positive tone of direct interpersonal relations	HE > HC	
Sociability		*HE > HC†*

* One-tailed $p < .025$
† One-tailed $p < .05$
[a] Scores for all categories but variance on number of feelings expressed were computed by ranking all individuals in the HE and HC groups on their change pre- to post-therapy and testing for group differences by applying a Mann-Whitney test to these scores. For variance in feelings expressed the designated value reflects the level of significance of the difference in variances for the HE and HC groups post-therapy. There was no significant difference on this measure pre-therapy.

more improvement than the HC group. In no area did the HC group show significantly more improvement than the HE group, and in no area did a significant proportion of the group move toward better adjustment on an overall basis as was noted for the HE group.

The lack of a significant difference between HE and HC change, when overall scores based on mean ranks were used, indicates that the TAT record reflects rather diverse attitudes and behaviors. Therefore, change on an overall adjustment score is likely to involve the combination of different areas of experience which in some cases tend to cancel each other out.

The third use of the measures was the correlation of them with other indices available on the cases. Although differential amounts of change on the various measures was quite apparent, an overall change score

Table 14.7—Correlations of overall TAT change with other measures

Other measures	Combined TAT change
Therapist rating of success	−.11
Initial Kirtner-Cartwright scale score	.18

based on mean ranks was compared to pre-therapy scores on the Kirtner-Cartwright Scale and to the therapist rating of success. The Kirtner-Cartwright Scale has been used as a predictor of success, while the therapist ratings are an outcome measure that has often been found to have low correlations with measures of change based on projective test materials. As the TAT variables used in this study were selected because of their assumed relevance to attitudes and behaviors modified by successful therapy, it was thought more agreement might be found.

Table 14.7 shows the correlations between overall change on the TAT, as measured by mean rank over all measures, and two non-TAT variables. It will be noted that the Kirtner-Cartwright Scale does not effectively predict change when the overall score is used.

The correlation between therapist rating of success and TAT change was much lower than expected; in fact, a slight negative relationship was found when overall change scores were used. This lack of agreement obviously indicates that the therapists were rating something other than the type of change reflected in the overall TAT score.

In an attempt to establish what areas of change were used by the therapists, three TAT variables were selected which were assumed to reflect behaviors or attitudes that would be overtly shown during the therapy hours. To the extent this was true, and to the extent the therapists considered these behaviors of significance, they could be expected to show a higher relationship to the therapists' ratings than an overall score reflecting many areas not readily observable in the therapy relationship.

Table 14.8 gives the correlations between the three selected TAT variables and success ratings. Two of the measures, increased productivity and amount of self-criticism and impotence, produced non-significant relationships. The third measure, change in the amount of emotional distancing, produced a much more significant correlation of .72 (one-tailed test probability less than .01). From this result it appears that an increase in the client's willingness to, or ability to, deal directly and immediately with his experience is a major factor in the therapist's rating of the success of the case.

Table 14.8—Correlations of three selected TAT measures with therapist rating of success

TAT measure	Therapist rating of success
Decrease in emotional distancing	+.72*
Increase in length of record	−.23
Decrease in self-criticism and self-depreciation	+.25

* One-tailed $p < .01$ (*t*-test approximation).

The value of emotional distancing in this area is interesting as this was one of the measures on which the HE group showed significant improvement, and significantly more improvement than the HC group. It would appear that this measure touches a type of behavior or attitudinal change that is quite significant to the therapeutic process.

Three of the measures which showed significant change for the experimental group from pre- to post-therapy were also compared to the ratings of the degree of congruence, empathic understanding, and unconditional positive regard shown by the therapist. Two types of comparisons were made: ratings of the therapist's behavior with client change, and pre-therapy client attitudes with subsequent therapist behavior.

The first set of relationships are given in Table 14.9. With a few exceptions, the correlations all went in a negative direction, that is, higher therapist conditions were associated with less client change on the three TAT measures. Only congruence scores for interviews 2–15 correlated with change in emotional tone of interpersonal relations showed a significant relationship in the predicted direction, and the essentially zero correlation obtained with the congruence score over all interviews casts doubt on the meaningfulness of this result. It would appear that the significant change in these TAT variables with therapy does not bear a simple relationship to the three rated therapist conditions.

Table 14.9—Changes in TAT measures over therapy correlated with three therapist conditions; $(\bar{X}_{15})$ mean rating based on interviews 2–15; $(\bar{X}_{TOT})$ mean rating over all interviews

| | Therapist conditions | | | | |
| | Congruence | | Accurate empathy | | Uncondi- tional posi- tive regard[a] |
TAT measure	$\bar{X}_{15}$	$\bar{X}_{TOT}$	$\bar{X}_{15}$	$\bar{X}_{TOT}$	$\bar{X}_{TOT}$
Emotional distancing	−.43	−.12	−.54	−.40	−.16
Number of introduced non-authority figures	−.19	−.43	−.25	−.27	−.43
Tone of interpersonal relations	.52*	.06	−.07	.14	−.22

[a] Mean ratings for UPR for interviews 2–15 were not available.

* One-tailed $p < .05$.

However, interpreting the results given in Table 14.9 is complicated by the correlations between client pre-therapy attitudes and the subsequent conditions established by their therapists. As shown in Table 14.10, high relationships are found with two of the three TAT measures indicating that initial client attitudes are clearly related to the ability of the therapist to be empathic and congruent in the relationship.

If we attribute causal relationships to the correlations in Table 14.10,

Table 14.10—Rank-order correlations between patient pre-therapy scores on TAT measures and therapist's behavior; $(\bar{X}_{15})$ mean rating based on interviews 2–15; $(\bar{X}_{TOT})$ mean rating over all interviews

| | Therapist conditions | | | | |
| | Congruence | | Accurate empathy | | Uncondi- tional posi- tive regard[a] |
TAT measure	$\bar{X}_{15}$	$\bar{X}_{TOT}$	$\bar{X}_{15}$	$\bar{X}_{TOT}$	$\bar{X}_{TOT}$
Emotional distancing	−.32	−.29	−.76*	−.58‡	−.40
Number of introduced non-authority figures	.69†	.57‡	.59†	.53‡	.64†
Tone of interpersonal relations	−.29	−.01	−.17	−.01	.24

[a] Mean ratings for UPR for interviews 2–15 were not available.

* Two-tailed $p < .01$ † Two-tailed $p < .025$.   ‡ Two-tailed $p < .05$.

it would appear, from the results with emotional tone of interpersonal relationships, that whether or not a patient expected interpersonal relationships to be satisfying had little bearing on the therapist's response to him in the areas rated. However, the correlations involving number of introduced non-authority figures and emotional distancing were much higher. These indicate that the more the patient desired, or was concerned about, interpersonal relationships, the more likely it was that his therapist would show congruence and empathy in the relationship. Similarly the *less* a patient defensively avoided involvement (lower emotional distancing scores) the more his therapist responded with accurate empathy.[8] As one would expect, the pre-therapy patient attitudes seem to have had less influence later on in the therapy relationship, though the correlations with ratings based on all interviews are still fairly high.

Discussion and Summary

The results indicate that the TAT measures used in this study are capable of detecting changes in various aspects of personality which are modified by psychotherapy. In addition, the sensitivity of the measures to change in specific areas appears useful in establishing the kinds of behaviors or attitudes that are reflected in the therapist's rating of case success, and in predicting therapist in-therapy behavior from client pre-therapy attitudes.[9]

A clinical interpretation of the significant changes that were obtained gives the following picture: (1) The hospital experimentals reduced their need to deny, or emotionally distance themselves from, their experience. The hospital controls showed a non-significant movement toward increased defensiveness. (2) The hospital experimentals showed

8. It is interesting that the only relationships in Table 14.10 that do not follow the pattern are in areas that did not show a negative relationship in Table 14.9.

9. An additional analysis (not given in the results because of the small number of cases and because it was not a part of the original predictions) suggests that certain kinds of defensive client attitudes prevent the client from accurately perceiving the attitudes that are expressed by his therapist. The HE patients were split into those highly defensive and those less defensive, using the pre-therapy emotional distancing scores. The less defensive patients showed a correlation (rho) of .70 between their perception of their therapist's empathy as measured by Barrett-Lennard's Relationship Inventory and "objective" ratings of accurate empathy based on tape recording of the therapy hours. The highly defensive patients, on the other hand, appeared to be less accurate in their perception of their therapists as indicated by a rho of .35. Though these values are not statistically significant they suggest it might be valuable to further investigate client attitudes that interfere with the recognition and acceptance of positive therapeutic conditions when they are offered.

significant improvement in the appropriateness of their emotional expression. The hospital control group showed a non-significant trend toward more extreme emotional expression and the differential change in the two groups was great enough to produce a statistically significant difference after therapy which was not present before therapy. (3) The hospital experimentals showed an increased capacity to handle interpersonal relations in a personally satisfying manner, and there was significantly more change in this area for the HE group than for the hospital controls. (4) A significant proportion of the HE group moved in the direction of better adjustment on an overall basis. A majority of the HC cases showed a similar overall improvement but the proportion was not great enough to be statistically significant.

In general it appears that the patients receiving therapy were less psychologically vulnerable at the conclusion of therapy, and in turn more capable of facing themselves and their environment. The hospital control cases tended to remain about the same or to move toward a more defensive adjustment. This interpretation is to some extent supported even by the one area in which the hospital control group showed significant improvement. This measure, number of stimuli used, would be influenced by a tendency to talk about details in the card, perhaps in an attempt to avoid dealing directly with the significant theme or meaning associated with the card. Several of the records of the control group have this defensive "card description" tone. It should be noted, though, that this interpretation is subjective and it may be that the increased number of stimuli used does reflect the initially hypothesized increased sensitivity to the environment.

In summary, it would appear that the relatively objective TAT variables used in this study were sensitive to patient attitudes of significance in the therapy relationship, and to resulting therapeutic change. However, an overall change score, computed by averaging change over all measures, produced non-significant results. This suggests that the patients were differentially changing in various areas, and these changes were lost in a simple combination of scores.

References

BARRINGTON, B. L. A list of words descriptive of affective reactions. *J. clin. Psychol. 14:*259–262, 1963.

HENRY, W. E. *The Analysis of Fantasy.* New York: John Wiley & Sons, 1956.

HENRY, W. E., and SHLIEN, J. Affective complexity and psychotherapy: Some comparisons of time-limited and unlimited treatment. *J. proj. Tech. pers. Assess. 22:* 153–162, 1958.

15. The Effects of the Therapist and the Patient on Each Other

This study was based on the ward-availability project described in Chapter 3. Many individuals aided in the study: William Rhinehart III in the preparation of interview samples; Edgar Anderson in statistical analysis; Shirley Epstein, Marilyn Geist, George Talbot, and T. M. Tomlinson as raters. Eugene T. Gendlin, Douglas Schoeninger, and David Grant advised on the design.

Ferdinand van der Veen designed and carried out the study and wrote this chapter. The study was presented in the Journal of Consulting Psychology, *1965, Vol. 29, pp. 19–26, and the permission to use it in a slightly altered form in this volume is gratefully acknowledged.*

In clinical experience with emotionally disturbed persons it has long been recognized that certain patients are more difficult to work with than others, and that certain patient-therapist combinations work better than others. These observations, while apparent in clinical practice, have been difficult to study and verify. One practical obstacle has been the fact that therapy is pervasively a one-to-one relationship, so that it has not been possible to analyze a patient's behavior with several different therapists, or the behavior of a number of therapists with the same group of patients.

Also, theory in psychotherapy has dealt with how the therapist influences the patient, but has given little systematic attention to how the patient influences the therapist. While this focus has helped to clarify the therapist's role, it has obscured the reality of the truly interdependent nature of the therapy relationship.

In this study we have considered three possible sources of determinants for the behavior of each of the participants in the therapy relationship: the participant himself, the person with whom he interacts, and the particular combination of the two. Each of these sources of determinants is considered important for an understanding of what occurs in therapy. If the participant's behavior were completely independent of the other person, he would be totally uninvolved and mechanical in the relationship. If his behavior were totally dependent on the other, he would not exist as an independent influence. If what he did depended only on idiosyncratic elements in the particular relationship, the relationship events would be entirely unique and generalizations unfounded. While these alternatives taken singly are unreal, together they represent significant and complementary vantage points for considering the determinants of therapy behavior.

Method

Design of the Study

A study of the effects of several patients and therapists on each other's behavior was possible as a result of an unusual project for undertaking psychotherapy with chronic hospitalized schizophrenic patients (see pp. 57–62). It was arranged for a number of therapists to spend a few hours a week on one ward, and patients could come to see them or not as they wished. This procedure permitted the patients tentatively to engage in therapeutic contacts, without committing them to a structured and formal therapy relationship with one individual. It thus avoided pressuring the patient, while it also provided for an efficient use of therapist time.[1] The procedure also permitted a patient to see several therapists concurrently. An office with a tape recorder was available on the ward for recording the interviews.

A report on the clinical aspects of the project has been published (Gendlin, 1961). The present study is a research analysis of the interview recordings.

Eight therapists participated in the project and saw at least twenty-five patients for a total of almost 600 recorded interviews, in addition to many on-the-ward contacts that were not recorded. The length of the interviews varied considerably, from a few minutes to over an hour. Also, a number of the patients formed regular, long-term therapy relationships, which accounted for a large proportion of the recorded interviews.

From the recorded interviews that were obtained, interviews were selected for three patients, each of whom had seen the same five therapists at least two times. Two interviews were used for each therapist-patient pair, as close as possible to the first and fourth meeting for

1. The widespread acceptance of ongoing therapy contacts supported the basic idea of the project—of twenty-five patients on the ward, at least eighteen patients were seen more than five times and ten were seen more than fifteen times by the eight therapists that participated. From a practical viewpoint, it was felt that fewer therapists spending more time on a ward, rather than a large number spending only a few hours each, would probably be as effective and certainly more feasible as part of a regular hospital program.

each pair (see Table 15.1). Three four-minute segments were taken randomly from consecutive sections of each interview: one segment from the first third of the interview, one from the second third, and one from the last third, giving a total of 90 segments. A criterion for selecting a segment was that both the patient and the therapist spoke at least twice during the segment. The average length for the thirty interviews was 23 minutes, with a range of from 4 to 44 minutes.[2]

Table 15.1—Design of the study showing interview numbers for the particular therapist-patient combinations

	Therapist				
Patient	A	B	C	D	E
1	1,4	1,4	1,3	1,4	1,4
2	1,4	1,3	1,4	1,4	1,4
3	1,2	2,4	1,2	1,2	1,3

Table 15.2 presents the number of weeks which elapsed from the earliest to the latest interviews sampled for each patient and each therapist, the number of therapist-patient relationships each formed on

Table 15.2—Total number of interviews, weeks from earliest to latest interview, and therapy relationships for each patient and therapist

	Patients			Therapists				
	1	2	3	A	B	C	D	E
Number of interviews	57[a]	37	17	18	30	15	47	57
Weeks from earliest to latest interview	7½	18½	24½	13	13	4	24	16
Number of therapists	7	8	6					
Number of patients				5	6	6	11	15

[a] Patient 1 very actively sought out contacts with the therapists and as a consequence averaged more than one interview per day over the period of interviews sampled.

the ward during this time, and the overall number of interviews engaged in during the period. All interviews occurred within a time span of six months. All initial interviews for the fifteen therapist-patient pairs occurred during a two-week period. There was no apparent pattern in which patient saw which therapist at what point in the period.

2. The four-minute interview yielded only one segment, which was reproduced and rated three times. This lessened the chance of finding an effect due to the section of the interview; however, as will be seen later, the section of interview effect was clearly non-significant for all but one of the scales.

The design constituted a 3 x 5 x 2 x 3 orthogonal factorial one, with the factors consisting of the patient, the therapist, the interview, and the section of the interview. Five therapists had seen each of the three patients for two separate interviews, and a segment from each third of these interviews was rated on the patient and therapist variables.

Patient and Therapist Variables

The rated variables were derived from client-centered psychotherapy theory and research. The two scales for the patients, Experiencing and Problem Expression, were elaborated and revised versions of two sub-scales of the Process Scale developed by Rogers and Rablen in 1958 (Walker, Rablen, and Rogers, 1960; Tomlinson and Hart, 1962). The Experiencing Scale, developed by Gendlin and Tomlinson in 1961, refers to the individual's exploration of his immediate experience. It has seven stages which range from no concern with personally relevant material at the low end, to the direct reference to a continuous flow of inner events at the high end. The Problem Expression Scale refers to the recognition of and concern with personal problems. It also has seven stages—from no recognition of problems or difficulties at the low end, to the ongoing resolution of problems in terms of changes in the experience of the individual at the high end.

The therapist scales, Congruence and Accurate Empathy, were de-rived from Rogers' statement of the necessary conditions for personality change (Rogers, 1957), and the scales developed by Halkides (1958) to test this theoretical statement. The 5-stage Congruence Scale was one developed by Hart in 1960. It concerns the degree to which the therapist's expressions represent an accurate, open, and appropriate expression of his experience of the client, of himself, or of their interac-tion. At stage 1 of this scale the therapist is presenting a façade with marked discord between the feelings and the content of his expression. At stage 5 the therapist is freely and deeply himself, with full integration of the feelings and the content in his statements. The 9-stage Truax Accurate Empathy Scale refers to the accuracy of the therapist's ex-pressed understanding of the present thoughts, feelings, and experience of the patient. At the low end of the scale the therapist is unaware of even the most conspicuous of the patient's feelings, while at the high end he responds accurately to the patient's full range of feelings.[3]

Two judges rated the patient scales and two others rated the therapist

3. All the scales mentioned will be found in the appendices, except the Congruence Scale. This was an earlier form devised by J. Hart, 1960, and differs slightly from the revised scale by Kiesler.

scales. Judges practiced on training segments until they understood the scales and were proficient in their use. The segments were edited, with identifying information deleted. Judges used typescripts in addition to the recorded four-minute segments. The order of the segments was randomized, with a different order for each scale for each judge. Due to practical limitations, the two patient scales were rated concurrently by each judge, in an alternating order over the ninety segments. While some contamination could not be avoided by this procedure, the scales were sufficiently dissimilar to avoid confusion. Also, a segment could be listened to as many times as necessary in order to arrive at a rating on a particular scale. Judges worked completely independently of one another.

General Hypothesis

The general hypothesis of the study was that the therapist and the patient influence each other's therapeutic behavior, and that the therapeutic behavior of one is positively related to the therapeutic behavior of the other. "Therapeutic behavior" refers to the behavior of the therapist, insofar as it promotes personality growth in the patient, and to the behavior of the patient insofar as it promotes his own personality growth. It is operationally defined in the present study by the rated variables which were derived from client-centered theory (Rogers, 1957, 1958).

The relevance of this hypothesis for the therapeutic process is twofold: It concerns directly the basic assumption of therapy that the therapist has an effect on the behavior of the client. We wanted to test this assumption by comparing the effects of different therapists, who presumably would offer different levels of therapeutic conditions, on the behavior of the same client. The hypothesis also directly concerns the experience of the clinician that the degree to which a therapist is able to be therapeutic depends on the particular patient. The following specific hypotheses and the analysis of the data are organized according to the model for the determinants of the behavior of the therapy participants which was described above.

Specific Hypotheses

Two hypotheses concerned patient variables. Hypothesis A–1 stated that *the levels of problem expression and immediacy of experiencing of the patient are a function of both the patient and the therapist.* A subsidiary hypothesis, A–1a, was that *the effect of the patient is greater than the effect of the therapist.* Hypothesis A–2 stated that *the patient's level of problem expression and experiencing are also a function of the particular patient-therapist combination.*

A second pair of hypotheses concerned therapist variables. The first of these, Hypothesis B–1, stated that *the levels of congruence and accurate empathy of the therapist are a function of both the patient and the therapist.* According to the subsidiary hypothesis, B–1a, *the effect of the therapist is greater than the effect of the patient.* Hypothesis B–2, was that *therapist levels are also a function of the particular therapist-patient combination.*

Finally, Hypothesis C concerned the relationship between therapist and patient variables. It stated that *the therapist and patient variables are positively related to each other: when one is higher the other also tends to be higher.*

Results and Discussion

The Patient Variables: Problem Expression and Experiencing

The correlation between the two judges over the 90 segments was .46 on the Problem Expression Scale and .58 on the Experiencing Scale. These correlations, both significant at the .001 level, indicate considerable agreement between the two judges as well as a considerable area of difference in the application of the scales. To achieve more stable values, the ratings of the two judges were averaged and the averages used in the following analyses.

The reliabilities of these averages, estimated by the Spearman-Brown formula as suggested by Guilford (1954, p. 397), were .63 for the problem expression ratings and .73 for the experiencing ratings. The agreement between the judges on the thirty interviews, rather than on the individual segments, was .60 for problem expression and .82 for experiencing.

The results of the analysis of variance for the Problem Expression Scale are presented in Table 15.3. The main effect of the patient was highly significant. Also, the main effect of the therapist was significant. None of the other effects reached an acceptable level of significance.[4]

4. For the purposes of the present study—an exploratory one with a small, non-representative group of patients and therapists—the design is considered to be completely orthogonal, with all main effects as fixed rather than random variables. In this sense, the therapists and patients can be considered as different treatments. The error term for the F-ratios is the residual or fourth-order interaction. This does not provide an exact F distribution, though it is likely that the significance estimates are conservative. As a precaution, the .025 rather than the .05 level is taken as the acceptable minimal level of significance for the present study (the .05 level is indicated in parentheses on Table 15.3).

Due to the design, generalizations beyond the particular sample are not war-

Table 15.3 also presents the results for the analysis of variance of the Experiencing Scale. The main effects of patient, therapist, and interview were highly significant. Also, the interactions of patient by therapist, patient by interview, and therapist by interview were significant. Mean values for the significant sources of variation are given in Tables 15.4 and 15.5.

Table 15.3—Analysis of variance of patient scales

Source	df	Problem Expression			Experiencing		
		MS	F	p^a	MS	F	p
Patient (P)	2	46.186	38.90	.001	34.786	72.87	.001
Therapist (T)	4	4.840	4.08	.025	4.118	8.62	.001
Interview (I)	1	2.500	2.11		5.625	11.78	.005
Section of interview (S)	2	1.336	1.12		1.769	3.71	(.05)
P × T	8	3.072	2.59	(.05)	1.814	3.80	.025
P × I	2	4.908	4.14	(.05)	2.558	5.36	.025
P × S	4	2.136	1.80		.611	1.28	
T × I	4	2.424	2.04		2.076	4.35	.025
T × S	8	2.263	1.91		1.443	3.02	(.05)
I × S	2	.025	—		.358	—	
P × T × I	8	2.176	1.83		.676	1.42	
P × T × S	16	1.548	1.30		.686	1.44	
T × I × S	8	1.563	1.32		.581	1.22	
P × I × S	4	1.008	—		.542	1.14	
Residual	16	1.187			.477		
Total	89						

a See Note 4, p. 358, regarding acceptable significance levels.

The analyses of variance indicate that levels of problem expression and experiencing of the patient were a function of the therapist as well as of the patient, and that the effect of the patient was greater than that of the therapist. Particularly for the level of experiencing, the therapist and patient effects were modified by the particular patient-therapist combination, and by differences between the patients and the therapists in their variation over the two interviews. These results provide support for Hypotheses A–1, A–1a, and A–2.

___

ranted. It should be noted that a particular analysis of variance is *either* for a patient *or* for a therapist variable; it is possible, therefore, to determine the effects of both patients and therapists on any one variable.

An inspection of the means in Tables 15.4 and 15.5 reveals that the patients differed fairly consistently from each other over all therapists and both interviews, as well as over the therapists and interviews taken singly. Patient 2 was most sensitive to individual therapists, showing a greater range of behavior than the other two.

Table 15.4—Mean values for main effects in the analyses of variance of patient scales

Scale	Patient			Therapist					Interview[a]	
	1	2	3	A	B	C	D	E	Initial	Subse-quent
Problem Expression (7-stage scale)	4.0	3.6	2.8	3.3	3.4	3.4	3.9	3.3	NS	NS
Experiencing (7-stage scale)	3.0	2.4	2.0	2.2	2.5	2.4	2.8	2.5	2.6	2.4

[a] Usually the first and the fourth (see Table 15.1).

The therapists showed more uniformity than the patients, with therapist D outstanding as the one with whom the highest levels of patient behavior were obtained. The effect of this therapist was noticeably dampened with one patient (3), however, as were the effects of the other therapists. In the variation over the two interviews, patient 1 increased in his level of therapeutic behavior while the other two decreased.

Table 15.5—Mean values for the patient-by-therapist and patient-by-interview interactions in the analyses of variance of the patient scales

Patient	Therapist					Interview	
	A	B	C	D	E	Initial	Subse-quent
PROBLEM EXPRESSION SCALE							
1	4.2	3.8	4.1	4.4	3.5	3.8	4.2
2	2.8	3.8	3.2	4.3	3.7	3.8	3.4
3	2.8	2.6	2.8	3.0	2.7	3.0	2.6
EXPERIENCING SCALE							
1	2.8	3.0	3.0	3.6	2.8	3.0	3.1
2	2.0	2.5	2.0	3.0	2.8	2.7	2.2
3	1.7	2.0	2.2	2.0	2.0	2.1	1.8

The Therapist Variables: Congruence and Accurate Empathy

The correlations between the two judges were .46 for the Congruence Scale and .55 for the Accurate Empathy Scale. As with the patient scales, these correlations were taken to indicate a significant area of agreement (beyond the .001 level), but also that there were differences between the judges in the interpretation of the scale. In the following analyses the ratings of the two judges were averaged. The reliability estimates for the averaged ratings were .63 for congruence and .71 for accurate empathy, using the Spearman-Brown formula. Intercorrelating over interviews rather than segments yielded correlations of .62 for congruence and .66 for accurate empathy.

The results for the analyses of variance of the therapist scales are presented in Table 15.6 The main effects of therapist and patient were significant for both scales. The variation due to the therapist was consistently greater than that due to the patient. The therapist-by-interview interaction was significant for congruence and of borderline significance for accurate empathy. The therapist-by-patient interactions

Table 15.6—Analysis of variance results for therapist scales

Source	df	Congruence			Accurate Empathy		
		MS	F	p	MS	F	p
Patient (P)	2	7.519	8.78	.005	38.811	10.59	.005
Therapist (T)	4	25.247	29.49	.001	106.083	28.95	.001
Interview (I)	1	1.878	2.19		17.778	4.85	(.05)
Section of inter-view (S)	2	.211	—		1.078	—	
P × T	8	1.495	1.75		2.825	—	
P × I	2	.169	—		3.744	1.03	
P × S	4	.769	—		6.361	1.74	
T × I	4	3.419	3.99	.025	11.472	3.13	(.05)
T × S	8	1.135	1.33		2.050	—	
I × S	2	.744	—		4.544	1.24	
P × T × I	8	1.159	1.35		5.814	1.59	
P × T × S	16	.933	1.09		4.292	1.17	
T × I × S	8	.953	1.11		3.239	—	
P × I × S	4	.436	—		3.261	—	
Residual	14[a]	.856			3.664		
Total	87						

[a] The degrees of freedom for the total and the residual are reduced by two. Two of the segments from the initial interview of therapist A with patient 2 did not contain therapist speech, and could therefore not be rated on the therapist scales.

were not significant, indicating that the particular therapist-patient combination was not found to affect the therapist's behavior on these variables. These findings support Hypotheses B–1 and B–1a, but not B–2. They also indicate that the therapists differed in the direction and degree of change in their therapeutic behavior over the early therapy interviews.

The means for significant sources of variation (see Tables 15.7 and 15.8) showed some consistency across scales and interviews, with thera-

Table 15.7—Mean values for main effects in the analyses of variance of the therapist scales

Scale	Therapist					Patient			Interview	
	A	B	C	D	E	1	2	3	Initial	Subsequent
Congruence (5-stage scale)	2.8	3.6	3.0	4.4	3.6	3.8	3.4	3.3	NS	NS
Accurate Empathy (9-stage scale)	3.9	5.2	4.6	7.1	5.7	5.8	5.3	4.7	5.1	5.5

pist A showing a uniformly lower level of therapeutic behavior and D being consistently the highest. The high therapist also elicited the highest levels of patient behavior (see Table 15.4). The effect of increasing familiarity with the patient, if the interview effect may be so interpreted, varied considerably. Three therapists increased while two

Table 15.8—Mean values for the therapist-by-interview interactions in the analyses of variance of the therapist scales

Therapist	Congruence		Accurate Empathy	
	Initial interview	Subsequent interview	Initial interview	Subsequent interview
A	2.6	3.1	3.4	4.3
B	3.7	3.6	5.4	5.0
C	2.9	3.2	3.9	5.2
D	4.6	4.1	7.3	6.8
E	3.4	3.8	5.2	6.2

decreased from the initial to the subsequent interview. Patient 1 received consistently higher therapist behavior than the other two patients. It is of interest that this patient also showed the highest level of patient behavior. It should be noted, however, that the covariation of patient and therapist levels was far from perfect, a point which is taken up in more detail below.

The Relationship Between Patient and Therapist Variables

The basic data for testing the hypothesized relationship between patient and therapist behavior (Hypothesis C–1) were the ratings on the 90 individual segments and the mean ratings for the thirty interviews. Table 15.9 presents the intercorrelations of the patient and therapist scales. Relationships between the patient and therapist scales were uniformly significant though moderate. This finding is consistent with the expectation that the behavior of one member of the therapy dyad would be an important, but not the primary, determinant of the behavior of the other member.

Table 15.9—Intercorrelations of patient levels and therapist levels for segments ($N = 90$) and interviews ($N = 30$)[a]

| | Therapist scales | | | |
| | Congruence | | Accurate Empathy | |
Patient scales	Segments	Interviews	Segments	Interviews
Problem Expression	.36	.46	.44	.54
Experiencing	.38	.45	.48	.54

[a] $p < .01$ for all correlations.

Additional Findings

Change by the patient from the initial to the subsequent interview was not found to be related to change by the therapist over the two interviews. Change by the patient on immediacy of experiencing was, however, positively related to the therapist's mean level of behavior over the two interviews, for both of the therapist scales (r's of .52 for congruence and .49 for accurate empathy, for the fifteen therapist-patient pairs).

Since the length of the interview was determined primarily by the participants themselves, probably more so by the therapist than the patient, interview length in minutes was correlated with the therapist and patient scales. This provided an estimate of the relationship between the interview's manifest therapeutic qualities and its duration. Patient scales were not significantly correlated, but therapist scales showed a moderate relationship (.35 for congruence and .46 for accurate empathy, $N = 30$).

The reverse was found regarding the motivation of the patient to seek out therapy. The patient scales, but not the therapist scales, correlated significantly and negatively with elapsed days from a fixed date to the date of the interview (−.32 for problem expression and −.47 for experiencing for the thirty interviews). In other words, patients were higher in their therapeutic behavior when they sought interviews sooner. Comparing Tables 15.2 and 15.4, it may also be seen that the patients' level of therapeutic behavior was directly related to the frequency of their interviews over the periods sampled. It appears that therapists remained with patients longer in the interview when they functioned more effectively, and that patients were more motivated to seek out therapy contacts when they could make more effective use of them. Elapsed time between the initial and subsequent interviews did not show a relationship with any of the variables.

Limitations of the Study

The basic limitation of the study was inherent in the design. Neither patients nor therapists were selected randomly, and they were not exposed to systematically varied conditions. The generality of the results is therefore limited. The study was, in essence, an intensive analysis of the therapeutic interaction between three patients and five therapists.

Several limitations were inherent in the rating procedure. Scales were used which showed only moderate reliability, and though there were many indications of validity in the findings of this and other studies, the method of using persons as instruments always leaves room for unknown subjective elements. Also, judges heard both therapist and patient on the tape segments when making the ratings, so the possibility exists that the rating of the patient was influenced by the level of therapist behavior, and the rating of the therapist by the level of patient behavior. A number of the results in the present study indicate the independence of patient and therapist ratings, such as the reverse trend from initial to subsequent interviews for patient levels as contrasted with therapist levels, and the different pattern of therapist-by-interview interactions for the Experiencing Scale in comparison with both therapist scales. There is also evidence from other studies, as well as the subjective impressions of the judges themselves, that patient and therapist levels of therapeutic behavior can be rated independently. Nonetheless, a possibility for bias was present in the rating procedure and needs to be recognized.

Conclusions

A model has been proposed for conceptualizing the determinants of the behavior of each of the therapy participants, in terms of three primary sources of determination: the participant himself, the person with whom he interacts, and the particular combination of the two. Accordingly, the hypotheses of the study were (1) that the patient's level of therapeutic behavior is a function of the therapist and the therapist-patient combination, as well as of the patient himself; (2) that the therapist's level of behavior is a function of the patient and the therapist-patient combination, as well as of the therapist himself; and (3) that the levels of therapeutic behavior of the therapist and the patient are positively related to each other.

The first two hypotheses were supported for all of the therapist and patient variables, with the exception of the effect of the therapist-patient combination on therapist behavior. The third hypothesis was also supported for each therapist and patient variable.

In addition it was found that change in patient level of experiencing from the initial to the subsequent interview was a function of the particular therapist as well as the patient, and also that it was a function of the therapist's level of therapeutic behavior. Change in therapist congruence over interviews was a function of the particular therapist.

The duration of the interview was found to be positively related to the level of therapist behavior, but not to the level of patient behavior. There was also a significant tendency for the patients to seek interviews sooner when their levels of therapeutic behavior were higher.

Within the limitations of design, rating procedure, and rater reliability discussed above, the findings suggest the following conclusions:

1. The patient, the therapist, and to some extent the particular patient-therapist combination were determinants of the therapeutic behavior of the patient.
2. The therapist and the patient were determinants of the therapeutic behavior of the therapist.
3. More therapeutic behavior by one participant was associated with more therapeutic behavior by the other, though there was no corresponding association between changes in the behavior of the two participants over the two interviews.
4. Both patient and therapist to some extent influenced the amount of change in the patient's behavior over interviews, while change in the therapist's behavior tended to be influenced only by the therapist. Change by the patient over the interviews was associated with the degree of therapeutic behavior of the therapist.
5. The duration of the interview was related to the therapeutic activity of the therapist, and the proximity of the interview was related to the therapeutic activity of the patient.

The results supported the general hypothesis that the therapist and the patient influence each other's therapeutic behavior as well as their own, and that the therapeutic behavior of one is positively related to the therapeutic behavior of the other.

References

GENDLIN, E. T. Initiating psychotherapy with "unmotivated" patients. *Psychiat. Quart. 35:*1–6, 1961.

GUILFORD, J. P. *Psychometric Methods.* New York: McGraw-Hill, 1954.

HALKIDES, G. An experimental study of four conditions necessary for therapeutic change. Unpublished Ph.D. dissertation, University of Chicago, 1958.

ROGERS, C. R. The necessary and sufficient conditions for therapeutic personality change. *J. consult. Psychol. 21:*95–103, 1957.

ROGERS, C. R. A process conception of psychotherapy. *Amer. Psychologist 13:*142–149, 1958.

TOMLINSON, T. M., and HART, J. T., JR. A validation study of the Process Scale, *J. consult. Psychol. 26:*74–78, 1962.

WALKER, A. M., RABLEN, R. A., and ROGERS, C. R. Development of a scale to measure process changes in psychotherapy. *J. clin. Psychol. 16:*79–85, 1960.

PART V

Therapists at Work:

The Clinical Picture

16. Therapeutic Procedures in Dealing with Schizophrenics

One of the frequent topics in staff discussions had to do with the new ways in which we found ourselves dealing with our often hopeless, often silent, schizophrenic clients. Drawing on experiences in which we all participated, Eugene T. Gendlin gives, in this chapter, detailed descriptions of ways in which he —and we—endeavored to reach these individuals, thus expanding and extending ourselves as therapists, and our point of view about therapy.

Even before its application with schizophrenic patients, client-centered therapy had been moving toward an "experiential method" which has now become central. The special characteristics of schizophrenic patients have greatly accelerated this trend.

Similar developments have been occurring in the other therapeutic orientations. In the last two decades the emphasis has shifted from the different verbal contents and techniques toward a common experiential focus (Gendlin, 1961a).

Psychotherapy has become less technique-oriented, less mechanical, less cognitive, less limited to the best adjusted and most verbal patients, and less divided along the old lines. Therapists of many orientations sense a common movement which transcends the divisions between "reflection of feeling" and "interpretation," between "analytic" ("exploratory") and "supportive," between emphasis on sex and emphasis on self-concepts, power strivings, will struggles, interpersonal feelings, or other favorite *contents*. Very gentle and receptive therapists and very active and interventive therapists agree that when they are successful a similar experiential process transcends differences of words and techniques.

The roles of patient, therapist, and relationship are coming to be viewed in terms of concrete experience. In the patient, psychotherapy no longer aims exclusively at one kind of content (oedipal conflicts, self-concepts, etc.). Although various orientations still favor one or another of these kinds of content ("vocabularies," I would call them), a basic experiential feeling process is widely held to be what really consti-

tutes psychotherapy. Without this feeling process there is mere intellectualization or rationalization.With this feeling process, patients change
concretely, whatever vocabulary is employed. The therapist can aim his
responses at the patient's concretely felt meanings: the pre-verbal, preconceptual experiencing. Of course, the therapist will conceive and
phrase whatever he senses, and will employ words and concepts that
make sense to him. However, the object of the words and concepts will
be the concrete, felt experience in the patient. The therapist's chief aim
will not be to devise objectively correct sentences to describe the patient,
but rather to get the patient to attend directly to the concretely felt
experience he has there in the immediate moment. In psychoanalytic
terms, this is called the "pre-conscious," what one *can* feel and verbalize
if attention is drawn to it. As the concretely felt "pre-conscious" is
carried forward and responded to, more and more facets *become* pre-
conscious, that is, they become directly felt and thereby capable of being
verbalized. If the patient will attend to, and work through, what he
directly and feelingly has there (to which the response points), then
therapy will move and succeed, whatever the vocabulary of the response. With this emphasis on this concretely felt "working through"
process, therapists have come to agree that how one points one's response matters more than the terms in which the response is phrased.
Therefore, we commonly say today that a different therapist with a
different conceptual vocabulary may do psychotherapy as well as those
who share our own vocabulary. What matters is whether he can engender the experiential concretely felt "working through" process in the
patient.

Within the therapist, too, conceptual, professional machinery and
technique have yielded to an emphasis on the therapist's real person in
the interaction. Mere techniques are seen as self-defeating. By their
very formality, inhumanness, mechanical or abstract character, they will
fail to point at, and carry forward, the patient's unformed personal
meanings. The therapist must use his actual personal responses and
actual felt impression of what is happening. The therapist uses his own
felt experiencing of the moment, much as he aims his responses at the
patient's felt experiencing of the moment.

Finally, the interaction between patient and therapist is seen as an
ongoing experiential process in which both persons change and are alive
in new ways. Only a concretely felt new interaction can bring about
newly emergent facets of feeling in the patient so that he is alive in new
ways and actually *changes,* rather than merely finding out how he *is* and
has been.

Client-Centered Developments

Client-centered therapy was first defined in terms of the discovery that a deep, self-propelled therapeutic process arises when the therapist "reflects feelings." In this type of therapist response, discovered by Rogers (1942), the therapist freshly phrases his sense of the client's implied affective message or felt personal meaning (Rogers, 1951). For a time this was hard to distinguish from mere repetition by the therapist of what the client *says*. Seeman (1956) moved further toward an experiential formulation by clarifying this question. The therapist does not repeat what the client says or clearly feels. Rather, he "reflects the *unformed* emotional experience" (my italics) of the client. The therapist aims at the client's directly felt, not yet formulated, experiential meanings (Gendlin and Zimring, 1955; Gendlin, 1961a, 1961b, 1962b).

On the therapist's side, the same experiential development meant that he would no longer hide his own person behind a screen. Rather than mechanically "reflecting," the therapist was becoming more "spontaneous" (Butler, 1958), tending to voice his "immediate" feelings and responses to the client. Finally, Rogers (1957) redefined psychotherapy entirely in terms of therapist "attitudes" ("necessary and sufficient" for psychotherapy, regardless of the technique and orientation). Among these attitudes, the most important was genuineness or "congruence" of the therapist, eschewing any false front, screen, artificial maneuvers or techniques as such. The therapist was to be "himself," as he really is and reacts within this relationship.

Thus during this period client-centered therapy, like other orientations, moved toward emphasis on experiential concreteness in client, therapist, and their interaction.

Characteristics of Schizophrenic Individuals in Regard to Psychotherapy

Work with the hospitalized schizophrenic patient greatly accelerated the experiential trend in client-centered therapy. This was partly because of the way we selected these individuals for therapy. We did not consider their desire or suitability for therapy, or the hospital staff's recommendations. Individuals selected on the basis of such considerations are those likely to succeed because of their desire for help, because of "suitable" (i.e., good) prognosis for therapy, or because they have been able to attract staff interest. Instead we chose clients by strict research criteria (age, sex, social class, length of hospitalization), and so obtained much more typical (and much less hopeful) individuals. Here are a few of the characteristics we frequently met in our patients:

Silence.—Over and over again we met hours of solid silence. This was not the kind of silence we value in psychotherapy when the individual deeply explores himself inwardly. Rather, it was a silence of emptiness, resistance, of not knowing what to do. Another type of "silence" was non-stop talk about trivial and external matters.

The sense for an exploration process missing.—Whether silent or talking, the patient would not share the therapist's "set" of searching for what is wrong, of exploring or helping with what is wrong. The patient had no such "exploration set." He might be totally silent, or speak incessantly, but if he spoke, it would be about the bad hospital food, the troubles of his ward, his desire to go home, or that nothing was wrong with him. The therapist's attempts to reflect or interpret troublesome feelings would be rejected by the patient, or would puzzle the patient. He would see no point in focusing on such feelings. The patient was not asking himself questions, was not embarked on an endeavor to explore himself or to understand or change himself. What seemed missing was not just a specific feeling. The patient did not see the *relevance* of a therapist's *sort* of concern, for exploration was missing.

No self-propelled process.—Perhaps because of the lack of explorative set, perhaps for other reasons, the usual self-propelled therapeutic experiential process did not take place. (With more usual clients, such a process usually moves of its own accord after an initial period of therapy. At first, the therapist must pull the process along, must always refer anew to the experiential, felt aspect of what the client says. But, soon, more and more personal felt meanings emerge of their own accord, and both client and therapist are pulled along by "it," the concrete felt meaning which next emerges.) With these hospitalized patients, a therapy-like process might occur on a rare day, yet the next time it would be as though that had never happened. No continuous, self-propelled process developed.

Rejecting the therapist.—With great regularity both silent and verbal patients would reject therapy and the therapist. Such rejection was not part of the give-and-take of interview encounter as we are used to it. Rather, it was a total refusal to meet with the therapist. The message, often said explicitly, was: "Go away and leave me alone. I do talk to some people but not to you. Don't you have other patients you can go to see? I am not coming anymore. Don't come to see me." And this might be the patient's consistent attitude over a number of months. Had it not been for research, we would not have continued with these patients and would not have learned how to continue without violating their personal rights.

The Challenge to the Therapist

These patient characteristics greatly accelerated the already developing experiential method. For example, a therapist accustomed to "reflecting" feelings is confronted by ten or twenty hours of absolute silence —what feelings shall he "reflect"? Or if the therapist usually "interprets," what will he do after he has variously "interpreted" the continuing silence? Whatever the therapist's techniques, he sees himself failing to reach the patient's feeling life. He does not know much about it specifically (it is probably deadened, or sore, highly chaotic, and unknowable even to the patient), yet he must somehow reach it, point at it, relate himself to it, ask about it, *respond to it even without specifically knowing what it is.* Thus, these patients force therapists to point themselves at the directly felt, concrete, pre-verbal experiencing in the patient.

Let us say the therapist decides that exploratory techniques are not indicated, and employs supportive therapy instead. The distinction may mean that the therapist ceases even to try to respond to implicit meanings. But then, silence. Nothing happens. Or let us say the patient speaks in a highly autistic way with personal meanings and events compressed into hardly interpretable masses. The supportive therapist just "lets him talk." Not only is this not supportive, it is positively harmful: the patient's rather desperate efforts to communicate continue to fail with a therapist who "lets him talk" or gives only broad suggestions. The therapist is forced to give up both abstract exploration and mere support. Instead, he must respond in such a way that the patient can bear it, can concretely feel and know what is meant, can attend better to his own immediately available feelings, and can experience himself as perceived by, and understandable to, another person. There is no way to do that by simply using or simply avoiding interpretive insight. There must be explorative response, but of a different kind. The therapist must try to sense the patient's presently available felt referents, and must show the patient that this is what the therapist values and responds to. With long-hospitalized schizophrenic individuals, experiential referents are often deadened, painful, chaotic, and frightening masses of feelings and meanings. These are pre-verbal and felt, but only capable of being carried forward gently in terms of (any) verbal vocabulary.

Thus, the characteristics of these patients lead therapists to transcend the old techniques. From whatever point the therapist starts, he moves toward responding to the patient's directly experienceable, felt referents, even when these have to be verbalized in very tentative and concrete words.

Similarly, these clients lead the therapist to employ his own concretely felt experiencing as a source of his response behavior. At first, the therapist may notice only that many difficult and unaccustomed feelings occur in him with these clients. But soon he comes to use these feelings to create interaction. In another place I described this development in these words:

The client is silent, or talks of trivia. Attempts to verbalize his implicit communications make him angry, fearful, or withdrawing; or, as we try to respond to a deeper level of feeling, we find that the client simply has not meant to look at himself more deeply—and misunderstands us. We have all sorts of impressions and images of what the client feels. Perhaps we only imagine these, or perhaps sub-verbally the patient does communicate. We wonder what to do with all this richness of events which occurs in our own moment-to-moment experiencing, as we sit quietly or converse superficially. We feel much empathy but can show little. As we go along on a casual level, or in silence, we wonder if we aren't allowing ourselves to be just as helpless as this fearful person. We are in conflict, not knowing whether to push harder or to attempt being even safer. We blame ourselves for too much helpless waiting, then, minutes later, for too much interruption, pressure, and demand. We wonder whether the client is doing anything significant with us, whether we are failing him. We become impatient and angry at giving so much inward receptivity while so little of it seems communicated. We value deeply what little or trivial communication he gives us, and we do not want to push that away. Yet we feel dishonest when we seemingly assent to silence or to this trivial level of communication (Gendlin, 1962a).

We then become able to *use* these many feelings, images, and impressions. They are our impressions of the patient and our incipient *moves toward the patient*. In suppressing them, we suppress our incipient interaction with the patient. Each minute we suppress five or ten such potential moves. Since the patient is unable to initiate a meaningful interaction, it is left to us to do so. Genuine starts for such interaction occur within us constantly. And so we learn to use our own experiencing as therapists. But our feelings and images do not always come to us already shaped and verbalized in usable form. Therefore, we must focus on our own directly felt meanings and go through "a few steps of self-attention" (Gendlin, 1961b) to fashion a usable response to the patient.

Finally, we also learn from these patients that new, concrete interaction can precede new feelings and new words. When the patient cannot yet verbalize, or hear much verbalization, therapeutic movement depends on positive relationship events. The many difficulties which arise in relating to a hospitalized patient offer the therapist opportunities to relate to his patient as to a valuable and sensible person. For no matter how objectively wrong and obnoxious a patient's behavior may be, it can be met and opposed in a person-to-person encounter, and (while the behavior itself is stopped) the therapist can search for, find, and respond to, a positive thrust and integrity implicit in the patient's behavior.

Thus, just the difficult characteristics of these patients most highlight the role of experiential concreteness in patient, therapist, and interaction.

Therapeutic Procedures

Different therapists' styles vary greatly. Each therapist finds different behavior to convey *himself* directly and spontaneously. My descriptions present the *scope* and the *kind* of therapeutic procedures we learned in working with these schizophrenic individuals.

I am going to describe in detail the processes that occurred in me as I worked with these patients, my attitudes, steps of thought, and private procedures. I believe that in this way you can best evaluate what I do, take from it anything useful, or be stimulated by it toward something different.

We must develop *a vocabulary—a science—about the therapist's personal procedures;* we cannot leave these private and unnamed. Without detailed vocabulary about what we do inwardly, we cannot talk to each other or train new therapists. We need a science of doing psychotherapy, and the first step is to develop a vocabulary that names some of the procedures we employ both within ourselves and externally. That is what this chapter attempts to do with a series of descriptions of situations, and methods of handling them, which grew out of my work with schizophrenic patients.

Three Categories of Patient In-therapy Behavior

Not everything I describe here would be appropriate for every patient. Much of it has the form: "If the patient at the moment does so and so, then I find it helpful to do so and so." Such formulae create categories, classifications of patient in-therapy behavior. These are different from the usual categories of psychopathology.

Few terms from psychopathology tell us what to do in psychotherapy. For example, if the patient is "schizophrenic—undifferentiated tendencies," what does that tell me about how to approach him? Little can be said about what to do which would be applicable to all who are given this label and not applicable to many patients with other labels. Compare this diagnostic label with the category: "If the patient is quite verbal, but speaks only about externals and daily events . . ." This category requires certain kinds of therapist procedures, and allows us to discuss what we do. Notice that this is not a category of psychopathology! Some schizophrenic individuals, some neurotics, and some normals will present a therapist with this problem. Nor is it a class of patients. The same individual who presents one type of in-therapy behavior now may present a different sort later. Why settle on any one patient-class for an individual? After all, we hope he will change! I group my various descriptions under three categories of in-therapy behavior, not of patients.

These categories are:

I. The patient is totally *silent and unresponsive,* giving me no feedback at all, either verbal or gestural or postural. He sits or stands silently, unchanging and unmoved throughout.

II. The patient is *silent, but responsive;* his face, gestures, and rare words respond in continual, subverbal interaction.

III. The patient is *verbal but externalized;* he never speaks about feelings or personal meanings, only about others, situations, events without their affective aspects.

Interview Behavior I: Silent and Unresponsive

Throughout this section picture the patient sitting somewhat bent over, looking down at the floor between his feet, never stirring, never looking up or giving any sound or body indication that he hears. Imagine him in this position when we begin, and throughout. (This may be in my office, in the hallway, or where he sits in the day room.) When I leave he is still sitting in the very same position. He has made no sound, and has not moved.

No feedback demand.—I used to depend on what the patient said to lead me to the next thing I would say or do. I needed the patient's response to let me know whether what I did was good or effective. I now think therapists should have *many* patients so that their sense of effectiveness does not depend on any one given patient at a given time. I can continue to work, speak, and act without the patient's showing me that he hears me, that he agrees, or denies, or commits himself in any way.

The "sensible person" assumption.—I always assume that I am speaking to a sensible person, there, inside the patient. This assumption has never failed of later confirmation, but in the face of *this* person's total unresponsiveness it is an assumption requiring imagination. I imagine I know I am talking to the person in there, somewhere—a fully human, almost certainly suffering, person—half lost and weird, perhaps —unable and unwilling to send up any sign—but there. I think of it as throwing something over a wall to someone. I cannot hear it land there, and I cannot tell if it is any good to him. I throw it over the wall without expecting to hear anything for some time.

My ways of being expressive as a therapist seem rather radical to me and have seemed so to some other therapists. I seem to be "out on a limb," not knowing if I imagine the patient, or if he is really there. But much later the patient will say: "Why were you so silent? Why did you take so long? Why didn't you say much more of that kind of thing? Seemed like you knew I couldn't talk, and still you often didn't do much."

From such statements I know that my assumption is not really very doubtful at all.

The therapist is self-grounded.—I make clear that I speak and act on my own responsibility, because I want to say it or do it. Since the patient gives no response or commitment of wanting to meet with me, I tell him that I will continue to meet with him because I have decided to. Since he does not respond to what I say, it will stand simply as what I want to say. Since he says nothing when I tell him what feelings I imagine he feels, I make it clear that these are my imaginings. ("I don't know how *you* feel about it. You haven't said. This is just what *I* think of it.")

Ownership of feelings is specified.—When I intend to refer to *his* feelings, I make that clear. When I speak about *my* feelings, I make that equally clear. I specify who is the owner of the feeling.

This distinction lets the patient know that I point at whatever *he actually* feels. Or when it is something *I* feel or want to say and do, I make that clear. It leaves him uncommitted. It does not require that his feelings be already clear to him, or bearable enough to look at. The patient is rarely disturbed by whatever I am, think, feel, or want to do, if I can keep it clear that this is me and leave him uncommitted.

The concrete silence.—I talk about silent sitting together as something concrete. In ordinary social intercourse we must fill time with words. In a living room with others, even 30 seconds without talk brings strong discomfort. We *must* say something.

We usually think we are doing nothing (at least, nothing useful) if we just sit in silence next to someone. Sitting down next to a silent patient, one feels one's own implicit demand: "Say something!" Especially if the therapist has spoken, the eventuating silence builds a tension. The patient knows he should say something, but he won't. The time is a bad time, much like the rest of hospital time, wherein the patient refuses and resists while staff loudly or silently demand and criticize. Therefore, there is relief for the patient (I believe) when I say, as I usually do, "It's all right to be quiet. I'll just sit with you a while."

Perhaps after some time, I may say, "Now I'll sit with you a little longer, then I'll go. I'll be back on Tuesday."

When I sit with someone, I know that *is something,* even if I have nothing valuable to say. I no longer need constant evidence that I am being effective and helpful. I can just sit and give my company. I have been in situations where my pain could not be understood, and I have taken comfort just being with someone willing to *be* with me, who required nothing, could not grasp my torn-up feelings, but was human company—like a place to go when you are down and out, a human presence, civilization after wilderness. It is a lot when I just sit with someone. But I believe it helps to *say* that I mean to sit in silence. It helps to make it something.

Manifesting presence periodically.—I speak every few minutes when I sit in such a silence. I let myself be heard from. I feel the patient needs to hear me often, to find himself in touch with me even while he cannot yet reach out for me, or establish interaction. I do not want to be forgotten, so that he returns to isolated aloneness even while I am with him. What I say usually demands no answer. If I do demand an answer (and get none), I indicate it is all right. ("I wish you'd tell me, but it's all right for you not to.") My statements, every few minutes, are often about myself, about what is going on in me, what I think, feel, imagine, wish, or do inside myself, as I sit there.

Usually in therapy with neurotics, the transcripts of the tape-recorded interview show what therapist and client say alternately: *T. C. T. C.,* etc. The sort of transcripts which come from the above, when it is tape-recorded, run: *T. T. T. T. T. T. T. T. T. T.* throughout a whole interview! The patient may say something once, or twice, or not at all. The therapist says something every few minutes.

Actual response processes.—My actual trains of thought and feeling are the source of my responses. I think many things of all kinds in these minutes of silence. A minute of silence is a very long time! I could never possibly say all I think and feel—even if thoughts and feelings came in little verbal units, ready to be spoken. Actually they come in felt masses, only little of it in words. I put *some of* what I feelingly think into words for myself, as I sit there. After a time, one or another of these thoughts seems fitting to tell the patient. Perhaps I still mull about it, ponder it, see other sides of it, find a simpler way of phrasing something. But I do not stick at this or that phrasing. I let it run on in my mind. When I decide to say it (whatever "it" is, "this" thought or feeling), I won't have all the words pre-arranged for it. It will come out of my mouth spontaneously.

I will now describe several sources for such responses.

What the therapist might *have expressed.*—Some of my responses come from a chain of thought that is well known to every therapist, though few use it as a source of responses. This is my thinking about what I just said or did, and why I should perhaps have done otherwise.

Especially with silent and unresponsive patients, if the therapist says something and gets no response he can think of ten reasons why it might have been a stupid, wrong, or threatening thing to say. These feelings used to burden us as therapists, but they have become a source of responses instead. In the following I will describe my intervening thoughts to show how such a sequence of thoughts leads me to something further which I can tell the patient.

Suppose I had said (as I just described), "I'll just sit with you a while. It's all right to keep quiet."

Now I might find myself thinking: Silence is very well for me but he needs help. What if my saying that silence is "all right" means to him that I don't care to help, don't even know something is wrong, that I don't realize the silence is really terrible, awful, horrible, and not a bit "all right." Maybe he wishes he *could* say something, but he can't. Now I have quite a lot I want to tell him. There's no hurry. It is only a few seconds later. I mull it a while. Somehow I am going to tell him that I know he is suffering and that I want to help, although I do not need speech from him right away. I know from his sitting there like that, head down, looking at his feet, that he is suffering, discouraged, hopeless, something like that. But I do not *know* about him, and I do not want him to think I know all about him, have read his record, or am connected with one of the people in his life. I will have to tell him also that I do not really know anything about him. Now I feel I know what I want to tell him, something like: I think he is suffering; I don't really know that; I'd like to help; I need nothing special right now. After a while of mulling, I might simply say, "Most people in here are really suffering pretty badly. I'd like to help you. Sometime maybe I can."

But he does not know I mean help via his talking to me. Perhaps he thinks I could "help" him "sometime"; I'm not doing it now because I don't feel like doing it yet. I'll have to tell him I want to hear from him what is wrong, what to help with. After a while, I might say, "Sometime I hope you'll tell me something about how you came to be in this hospital." Then I think, What if he thinks I want an explanation or a defense? After all, I want to hear about his feelings, not the events as such, objectively. I might say, after a while, "I bet you went through a really tough time. I don't know anything about you, that's just my guess."

Then I might think, Perhaps he'll take that as curiosity, my trying to find out about him, wanting to hear dirty stories or embarrassing facts. So I might say, after a while, "Whatever hurts inside you and makes you feel bad, that's what I would care to hear about, whatever has you so silent and sad."

Then I might think, But what if he isn't sad at all, just lost, or sullen, or what not? So I might say, after a while, "To me you seem sad, sitting there so silently with your head down. Of course, I don't know how you really feel."

Words like "sad" or "angry" or "rough time" turn an individual's thoughts to his own feelings, rather than to other people's views of him and condemnations of him. Many patients expect to talk in the frame of reference of what they should have done, or not done, have been condemned for, or are innocent of. "To me you seem sad" indicates my wish to talk and think about him, his feelings, not about outward events, condemnations, and excuses. Inside himself he might find for a moment what he *does* feel, not sad, but . . . , and this will help. For an instant, he might feel like stirring and answering me, to correct me: "Not sad, just flat, empty, hopeless," or perhaps, "I wish I did feel sad, it would be something." My patient here says nothing, does not stir, but I feel it helps to talk to him about his feelings and to indicate that I am thinking about his feelings, even if I have to call them by misnomers. I make it plain: "I realize I don't know what your feelings really are."

Perhaps he does not know himself. I might tell him that, too, after a while: "Often people's feelings are all mixed up, they don't know just what they feel, except maybe just bad. It might be that way with you, or anyway that's what I was just thinking." It lets him know I was thinking about him, about how he feels.

But now I think further: Maybe he knows exactly what he feels, just can't *say* anything. What if he is quite ready to say it, except that it's the sort of thing you *never* say to anyone? Perhaps he doesn't know that the kind of thing he *would* say is appropriate to say to me. I wish he would say it! I want him to know that. And I want him to know I am a therapist, a feeling-doctor. I want him to know what I am doing here and that the sort of thing he feels is the right kind of thing to say to me. How can he know that? I have to tell him.

I might say, after a while, "I'm the kind of doctor that understands about people's feelings. Of course, I don't know yours, but I know a lot about this kind of trouble. That's the kind of doctor I am. Sometime I hope you'll tell me what you feel that bothers you. I might help with it."

Then perhaps I think: What if he is ready to talk *now,* why do I keep saying *sometime?* So I might say, after a while: "Anything at all, whatever it is, that you would care to tell me, I'd care to hear it." And then, as the silence continues, I might think, What if he wants to and can't? Then I might say: "If it's too hard to talk now, that's O.K." And then I might think that I'm just encouraging his flabby, heavy, discouraged tendency to do nothing, and so I'll say, after a while, *"I* sure wish I'd hear more from you."

From these descriptions you can see the thought sequence which leads me to responses. It is that familiar sequence in which the therapist has his doubts about whether what he just said was fitting, and wonders if it was perhaps stupid, hurtful, wrong, or misunderstood. We all have these thoughts, and they include the reasons *why* we doubt the worth of what we have just said. These need not be left as uncomfortable feelings. With silent and unresponsive patient behavior, we can use such sequences as a source of responses.

The "imagined patient" sequence.—Another sequence of thoughts which gives rise to responses concerns the patient. Later in therapy (perhaps the patient is still silent and totally unresponsive), I am active in many more ways. Among other things, I say more about him. So far I have used examples only from the first few meetings with patients who are silent and unresponsive. Here are some examples of what I might say a week or two later: "My God, you're sitting in the same place I left you last Friday! It seems awful that you would just sit and sit like that!" or, "I don't know, of course, but it seems to me you look *so* sad. I wonder if you're just feeling like you're hopeless, like it's no use."

Saying such things gives rise, in me, to a whole sequence of thoughts about someone who feels hopeless and no use. Of course I don't know if he feels that way (and I'll tell him that, too), but *the kind of interaction* we have as I talk is helpful, even if the *content* of my words may not fit him. I might say, after a while: "Sometimes a person can feel so no-use and no-good, he just tries to give up on himself."

I might ponder that a while, and then say: "But, you know, it doesn't really work to give up on yourself. Maybe you try and try to give up, but it only hurts."

And then, after a while, "Maybe it's hard to even think of picking things up again. Sometimes a person feels that to try again is like telling people it's all right that they hurt you."

And then, as I ponder that, I might say, "If they did hurt you, that's *never* all right."

And that will lead me, after a while, to another thing, perhaps: "Sometimes the ones that hurt you are just the people you most wish loved you. That's the hardest to take, I think."

Some of these sequences will fit anyone, but just as often the sequence will not fit the patient. These are responses to a person I imagine, a sad person, silent, broken, given up, hurt by those he cared about, in a state hospital, not cared for enough, or not understood. As I respond to such a person, all the while phrasing clearly that I do not know how the patient really feels, he experiences me reacting to him, much as he would if he were verbal. He experiences (he need not understand) my intention, which is to focus on his feelings, his hurts as they were to him, since that is the frame of reference of the things I say. His feelings may stir, become a little more alive, and perhaps a shade less unbearable and disorganizing than they were when he last could stand to look at them, which he did alone.

Then perhaps I shift. It strikes me that being hurt by those you care for and therefore not wanting to try again is too specific, probably wrong. Perhaps he is just out cold, too confused to feel anything, hearing my words as mere distant music, or noise from someone too frightening to hear. I begin to respond to his possibly global confusion. I might say: "Maybe what happened to you and what you feel is all one big mess that just hurts. Maybe you don't know *what* all it is." And so I begin another sequence, perhaps without specifically thinking of it as another sequence. It occurs to me that this global confusion might be full of crazy stuff, too. I say: "When a person gets *too* hurt, sometimes a lot of strange stuff goes on in him. I don't know about you but I know about *that kind* of thing."

Even a few minutes help.—Unless we *arrange* fifty-minute hours with a patient, he does not expect that. In a hospital, I leave myself free. I come when I can. Only if I really know that I certainly will be there on Tuesdays, do I tell the patient that. Often I do not say how long I am coming to stay. I do not leave abruptly. When I want to leave, I usually say I will go, and then I stay a little longer.

But this may be after ten minutes. Especially if I am tense, or the patient has been very violently rejecting of me (sometimes patients are totally silent *except* to say quite verbally, "Go away, don't come anymore, can't you understand that?"), I might impose myself on him only briefly, both for his sake and for mine. I might say, "I know you said you don't want me to come anymore. I won't stay long." Then I might stay only a few minutes.

Other patients, more verbal, may stop me in the hallway. I speak with them intensely for a few minutes. They may know that I cannot stay long. They accept my moving on quite soon, but I listen intently and respond deeply in the time I do spend. In this way I can carry a somewhat larger number of relationships than I otherwise could.

It is a mistake to think we should not respond therapeutically to patients if we cannot commit ourselves to them totally for many whole hours. This view comes from concern not for patients, but for therapists and clinical agencies. It is true that if you help someone open up his feelings he may then be more trouble than if he had not been responded to. (But he may also be less trouble as a result.) We are protecting *ourselves,* not the patient, when we say: "If you can't commit hours and months, don't respond at all." For the patient, a few minutes can be of crucial help. The experience of making sense to someone and living less autistically even for a few minutes may provide something the patient can keep and work with for weeks. I mention this here because one of the ways in which a few minutes can help involves a principle that is important in working with the silent and unresponsive patient. The principle is:

The continuing interaction.—The patient can live in interaction with me even when I am not there. Let us say I have spent a few minutes— fifty, twenty, or five—with my silent and unresponsive patient. Now I leave. He is more alive and upset, perhaps more of a "self" inside than before. He hates me (for example) because I make him hope and he cannot stand the pain that comes the moment he hopes. So he fights it down. He is again totally still, empty inside. He goes to lunch, waits in line, silently, thinking to himself, "Maybe, next time he comes, I'll hit him." He visualizes all that, sees and feels it, decides not to hit me. "Maybe I'll tell him I'm going to hit him." He experiences all this, imagines it, decides he won't say anything to me, ever. He eats lunch. He thinks maybe he will tell me he isn't any of the things I say, he is just angry at what "they" did to him (perhaps to himself he calls them "the jury" or "the machine" or what not), decides not to tell me because it will sound crazy. Decides never to say anything. Finds himself talking to me, saying this and that to me, justifying himself, explaining, wishing, demanding, carrying on; catches himself, decides to say nothing to me, ever. He returns to the day room and sits in his corner, as usual, looking at the floor. That reminds him of my having sat next to him. He kicks the chair hard, away from him. His heart pounds, he is live angry. The attendants come over. He subsides. Thinks of nothing or tries to think of nothing. Visitors are announced on the loudspeaker for another patient. His tears seem to want to come. He chokes them down, finds himself mentally telling me how busy his own folks are, why they can't come to visit him. Imagines that he finds himself crying with me, gets furious, decides to tell me nothing, ever, thinks perhaps he will tell me that nobody has any use for him. It is only one hour since I left.

Naturally enough, when I come the next Tuesday he is totally silent again, as if nothing had intervened. But a lot has happened, some of it in the context of talking to me, feeling with and at me.

For this reason, the *kind* of interaction I have with a patient seems to me much more important than exactly what I talk about. Even if he says nothing, and even if everything I say is foolishness and fits him not at all, I believe that this kind of interaction and pointing at feelings gives him a context to live in, imagine in, and relate in during the many, many hours when I am not there, as well as when I am.

Making contact.—Apart from these examples of what I might *say,* there are also things I *do* to make contact with my patient. I might get down on the floor in front of him and look up into his face for a moment. I might explain it as: "Sometimes I get to wishing you'd look up at me." I would not do it for long, but if our eyes met once, I would be glad, and say so.

I might put my hand on his shoulder, or I might grasp his hand. I might do this in some context or in my effort to reach him somehow. (Perhaps I first said, "I sure want to hear *something* from you.")

Isolated people need physical touch, especially children—one can pick these up and hug them. I think children are not different for being my patients from any other children. We deprive them of what we would easily give normal children (and these need more) when we refuse to hug them because they are patients. Similarly, with an adult physical touch is often the only way to make contact. I make my touching a mode that won't be confusing, sexual-like, or frightening. It is a message, a contact, a firm holding of hand. Or I hold shoulders, keeping my arms extended and stiff. It is a way of saying, "You. I am looking for you." It is important, then and later, that the patient is not threatened by, or forced to speculate about, the possibility of a sexual pass or overture. These are frequent in hospitals, and even more prevalent in patients' minds. However, other forms of physical contact, like being pushed about by aides, are just as prevalent. A firm grasp of a shoulder confuses few patients. In many contexts it is the only clear, fast, and impactful way of saying, "I am here, and I know you are here."

Interview Behavior II: Silent but Responsive

In this section please picture a patient who says very little. He may offer barely understandable, highly compressed, summary statements like, "Must be somebody has a use for a person," or, "I'd like to take them and shake them." For the most part, he is silent. However, he is highly responsive. He looks at the therapist at times, can look quickly away or down, and back again. He may stand, sit, walk away quickly, come back. He may jump backward three paces if what I say disturbs him. He may get angry and seem to walk at me as if to walk through me. His face tells every moment that something new is happening, though the therapist may have only a vague sense of what it is.

The "silent but responsive" patient today may be the same individual who was silent and totally unresponsive at first. Or the patient may be "silent but responsive" from the start. When he is quite silent for long periods, much of what I said in Category I will apply. "Silent but responsive" is a category of in-therapy behavior, not a category of patient. I will again present procedures applicable at the beginning, and then mention procedures appropriate later in therapy.

Accepting rejection.—It is all right with me—though I surely do not like it—when the patient rejects me. Suppose as I sit down, intending to keep the patient a few minutes of silent company, he gets up and sits down elsewhere. As I join him, he angrily moves away again. I call that "responsive," compared to no reaction at all. Now it is not the case that I have nothing to work with except what I bring. The patient is doing and expressing a lot. He gives me a lot to work with if I can tolerate it.

If he continues to leave wherever I go, then I stay where I am, and let him stay there. This is an interaction. He is there but he knows I am here, waiting. He won't join me, but he knows I am here. Much is happening. The whole day room may be tense with it. Or this may occur in an office: he walks out into the hall. Now he is out there and knows I am here. Or I may go out and stand next to him. If he leaves again, I may walk within sight of him and then stop and stay there. The ongoing interaction is a tensed rubber-band between us.

My assumption is that I can be rejected. It is not a bad thing for him, if I can take it. How often has he repeatedly rejected someone who nevertheless continued to want to know him? Almost certainly never.

A few minutes of this can be very important. After a while I can go. Before I go I want *some* contact with him. I might say loudly, "I'll see you Friday," and go. Or if he stays within closer hearing distance long enough, I might say, "I know you don't want me to, but I think I can help and I'll be back."

If he will stay where we can talk, I might say, "Why be so scared?" Or, "I wish you'd stay put for a minute." Or (if I see it on his face), "I guess you're mad at me for not leaving you alone," to which his face might say, "Damn right!" and I might then join in a harder-sounding way of talking: "Yeah, but what good is it if I leave you alone, you'd just stay in here. You've been here—how long? Whatever it is, it's probably long enough. What good am I to you if I leave you alone? That doesn't help anybody." Or his face might say, "You're strange; I don't get you at all; what are you doing?" to which I would say, perhaps, hard and briefly: "I'm a doctor and I sometimes can help people in here. Quit running away from me—I'm not gonna do anything to you." Or I'll just say, "It's all right. I'll be back Friday." Only a few minutes do I impose myself this way, but before I go I want a moment to indicate I have not been overly hurt. Perhaps I just wave good-bye from a distance, and go.

Often the patient will refuse to come to a therapy office, yet will be quite willing to meet the therapist in the day room or hallway. He knows he is free to walk away. Therefore, when he continues to stand next to me, I know I am not imposing upon his freedom if I stay. We stand in the hall. He says nothing. I say the same type of things I already have outlined, but his face and posture respond. Then I respond to that. "I don't know for sure, but maybe you feel . . ." whatever I get from his gesture or motions. I end many such responses with, "But, of course, I don't really know what you feel, that's just what I imagine"; or, "That's just what *I* was thinking maybe you felt, then, when you jumped away from me."

Many instances of rejecting the therapist require such an interim period of uncommitted hall meetings, in which the patient is free to walk away, but does not.

I must now mention a series of procedures that involve my actions, before I can deal more fully with this largely subverbal therapeutic interaction.

Being active.—If little therapy is happening, the broadest scope of action is desirable. I find it helps me to shift, move, get up, sit down, go for a Coke, tell about how my day has been (briefly), smoke, offer cigarettes (as I would do with anyone who is with me when I take out a cigarette), offer to buy a Coke (as I would with anyone when I buy a Coke), and generally widen what I might do to include whatever occurs to me.

Offering health-approaching activity.—Any patient activities closer to what healthy people do is probably a good thing. If the patient just sits, then looking up is probably a good thing. If he is always in the hospital, then going out on the grounds and to the canteen is probably toward health. If he will come to the nearby store with me (off the grounds) that is probably toward health. One can see the patient getting his land legs back. "Gee," he thinks, "I still know how to go to a store! I can still get around." Perhaps, at first, he is frightened, goes up to the counter, stands, lets others go ahead, backs off again, no cigarettes bought. Perhaps we walk into the store together and immediately he wants to leave ("It's too crowded."). But whatever move he can make toward ordinary health is probably a good thing.

Long before he is willing, I invite him to come outside on the grounds with me, to the canteen. He does not even answer, perhaps, but then I say that I think he might later want to, and *I'd* like that. *I* thought he might, some time. This process moves from the candy or Coke machine, downstairs to the canteen, to the store outside the hospital, to going downtown to a drug store, bar, or store.

Helping the patient reconnect.—Long before he is really ready, the patient needs to be invited and helped to reconnect himself to the outside world. We professionals have cut up the field so that one profession, "psychotherapy," is supposed to move the patient from the sick stage (occurring in the office) to the nearly-well stage. At that point another profession (social work) is supposed to help the patient with the world he returns to. Still another profession (vocational rehabilitation) works with his possible job, and so on. These other professions often refuse to help until the patient is "well enough," but the patient is not cut up into such slices. He is all one piece and often falls into the gaps between our professions. I have (rather painfully) learned that if I want my patient to move toward getting well, I have to be willing to do these things *before* he is "well enough." I will say, "Later on we will help you find a job in the city; you might want that then." I say this at a time when the patient cannot even talk. I also say, "I know you can't do that now, but you might be able to, later." Getting reconnected to the world (and perhaps in a situation different from that in which he became sick) is an essential part of the process of getting well. It must not be left "until the patient is ready," or he won't become so.

One of our very good therapists saw his patient for more than two years once or twice weekly. She was often silent and very quiet. Finally he became impatient and urged her to think about getting out of the hospital, perhaps with the aid of vocational rehabilitation set up by the therapist. Her response was: "I've been wondering if you'd ever want to *help* me." It seems she had much appreciated this nice man's coming to see her, and had silently hoped that sometime he might wish to help her. To her that meant help with her whole situation, not just some truncated separate part (her feelings or "illness").

"Schizophrenia" is being disconnected from the world, rather than in interaction with it. One cannot get well from it first, and then become reconnected and interact in the world.

I must invite the patient long before he is ready. After a time, we go to the Coke machine, the canteen, the store, the city, a job. (Of course, I have time for this only with some. I try to arrange for someone else who will do this with other patients.)

Opportunities for interaction.—When activities no longer serve as therapeutic vehicles, they can be stopped. Such stopping gives opportunities for therapeutic work. Patients get used to Cokes and walks, and therein lie two pitfalls: (*a*) that I shall have trouble bringing to an end for the patient a particularly desirable pattern—a convenient way of getting Cokes, cigarettes, time out of the hospital—when it ceases to be producing therapeutic movement. Making this break used to be difficult for me, but now I use my feelings of this difficulty just as I use my other feelings. For example: "I don't want to buy you Cokes anymore—it makes me think now that I'm just keeping things the same, when really you could go out and work and buy your own Cokes. So it doesn't seem right anymore. But I worry that I'm letting you down now, when I say this. After all, I was the one who first invited you to accept Cokes. In those days you didn't want to take anything from anyone. I kind of forced it on you and I know that." (*b*) that the patient will not begin therapy at all but will take me for a Gray Lady whose purpose is to make his life slightly better with Cokes and Canteen. To these patients I say often: "You know, what I am here for is to help you with what keeps you in the hospital," or, "And now it's time you tell me something of how you feel, if you can and want to." "Whatever hurts you and has you stuck, so you aren't getting out of here, that's what I'm supposed to help you with. I know you might not think you can get out of here, or maybe you don't want to, or you aren't sure what you want, but I guess you know, *I* want you out of here. I am looking forward to meeting you in town, in my office. I really can't stand for you to be in here."

Aside from constituting the movement toward health, candy and Coke machines and stores provide vehicles for ongoing interaction. You will see that many of my examples in the next section concern my interaction with a patient in front of the candy machine, or in the drug store, or in going from the day room to the machine downstairs. For these reasons, I have mentioned these things here.

Occupational therapy was once intended to be this type of vehicle— supplying events so that therapists could respond to patients. In most hospitals it has degenerated into making belts and wallets, usually in silence. (The patient usually does not need a wallet, let alone three!) It has been largely forgotten that such activities were intended to be situational occasions to help interaction occur so that therapeutic responding might thereby be possible.

But one *need* not do all this. Even with the patient I see occasionally for a few minutes in the hall, *there is a situation:* where we should stand, how he feels about others listening, my hurrying away so soon. His and my feelings in any *situation* are a vehicle for therapeutic responding, especially if the patient is only subverbally responsive.

Doubling back.—Some of my feelings about him in the situation are a good source of responses, if I tell them in a personal, detailed way. The patient we are speaking about may be silent or not, but he is responsive. Every moment something is happening with him, and he shows some of it. Perhaps I cannot be sure just what he feels, but I see he feels *something*. (Note: we are almost always wrong in guessing just what someone feels, but never in seeing visibly that he feels *some* reaction. One can talk to, refer to, and accept that reaction, whatever it is, without ever knowing *what* it is!)

One whole set of feelings I have for others in situations comes to me at first simply as discomfort. As I look to see why I am uncomfortable I find content relevant to the person I am with, to what we just did or said. Often it is quite personal. I was stupid, rude, hurrying, embarrassed, avoidant, on the spot; I wish I didn't have to go since he wants me to stay. I wish I hadn't hurried him out of the store in front of all those people; I feel bad that I don't know what to say; I am embarrassed that the nurses see us looking silent and stupid; I wish I had a chair to sit down on.

As we get outside the store—after I have had to insist that we leave: "Now I'm sad that I embarrassed you in there. I am always worrying about being late and I get rattled. But I wish I hadn't rushed you in front of all those people—that bad feeling is just what I wish you didn't have to put up with."

Or, as we arrive downstairs at the candy machine, where we are alone: "I am never as comfortable upstairs where everybody listens to us," or, "I didn't feel like saying this to you upstairs, I just didn't feel at ease with all the aides watching us."

Or, "Just then, when you made that face, I didn't say anything about it because I didn't know what to say, but now I wonder, Are you mad at me?"

Or, "I don't mind us standing here, but I am getting tired standing. I wish we could go to the lounge, downstairs, where I could sit down." And so, a week later, he leads us to the lounge. It is clear to both of us that this is not what *he* wants, we are doing that for *me* because I get tired standing. "I am very glad you want to do that for me. Thanks!"

Or, "I guess you're mad at me because I'm leaving. I don't feel good about it either. It just never feels right to me to go away and leave you in here. I have to go, or else I'll be late for everything I have to do all day today, and I'll feel lousy about that." Silence. "In a way, I'm glad you don't want me to go. I wouldn't like it at all if you didn't care one way or the other."

These examples have in common that I express feelings of mine which are at first troublesome or difficult, the sort I would at first tend to ignore in myself. It requires a kind of *doubling back*. When I first notice it, I have *already* ignored, avoided, or belied my feelings—only now do I notice what it was or is. I must double back to express it. At first, this seems a sheer impossibility! How can I express this all-tied-up, troublesome, puzzling feeling? Never! But a moment later I see that it is only another perfectly human way to feel, and in fact includes much concern for the patient, and empathic sensitivity to him. It is him I feel unhappy about—or what I just did to him.

A very warm and open kind of interaction is created in telling my feelings this way. I am not greatly superior, wiser, or better than the other people in the patient's life. I have as many weaknesses, needs, and stupidities. But the other people in his life rarely extend him this type of response.

The inward side of a feeling.—What I term the "inward side" of a feeling is the safest aspect to express. We tend to express the *outer* edges of our feelings. That leaves *us* protected and makes the other person unsafe. We say, "This and this (which *you* did) hurt me." We do not say, "This and this weakness of mine *made me be* hurt when you did this and this."

To find this inward edge of me in my feelings, I need only ask myself, "Why?" When I find myself bored, angry, tense, hurt, at a loss, or worried, I ask myself, "Why?" Then, instead of "You bore me," or, "This makes me mad," I find the "why" *in me* which makes it so. That is always more personal and positive, and much safer to express. Instead of "You bore me," I find, "I want to hear more personally from you," or, "You tell me what happened, but I want to hear also what it all meant to you." Instead of saying, "When you move so slowly and go back three times, it makes me mad," I say, "I get to thinking that all our time will be gone and I'll have to go without having done a thing for you, and that will bother me all day."

It is surprising how positive are the feelings in us which first come up as anger, impatience, boredom, or criticism. However, it is natural, since our needs with the patient are nearly all positive ones for him. I need to be effective in helping him. I need to be successful in helping him arrive at his truth and a way to live. I need to feel therapeutic. When my feelings are for the moment constricted, tense, bad, sad, or critical, it is because in terms of some of these very positive needs I have with him, we have gone off the track. No wonder, then, that when I ask "why" concerning my bad feelings, the emergent answer is positive feelings. I am bored because I want to hear more personal, feeling-relevant things from him. I am angry because our time is being wasted —the time on which I count to be an effective therapist. I am critical of him because I wish something better for him.

But often there is also a peculiarity of mine involved, and this must be expressed. Do such expressions make the patient feel that the therapist is weak, in need of help, or unreliable? I make sure the patient knows I can perfectly well stand what I feel. I will not say much about my unresolved personal problems or situations. I might say: "Today I feel rattled about something that happened to me. It isn't too bad, but it means I might have trouble with the people I work with downtown." Again, here, my way of saying it conveys that I know what it is and I can stand it.

Openness to what comes next.—A response is not in itself right or wrong. One must be sensitive to the *next* moment, the patient's reaction to the response. If I can respond sensitively and well to his reaction at the *next* moment, even if I just said something foolish, hurtful, or wrong, a meaningful and positive interaction will emerge.

I used to ponder whether I was about to say a right or wrong thing. Then, if it was wrong (as I could tell from the patient's reaction), I would not know what to do. Now, I spend moments letting my feelings clarify themselves, but once they feel clear, I no longer wonder so much whether it is right or wrong to express them. Rather, I have open curiosity, sensitivity, and a readiness to meet whatever reaction I will get. This may tell me what I said was "wrong," but all will be well if *now* I respond sensitively to what I have stirred. I now say whatever I now sense which *makes* what I said before "wrong." (It is not my admission that I was wrong which matters here. I rarely make a point of having been wrong. That matters only to me. I am the only one who cares how often I am right or wrong. But whatever it is in him which I now sense and which *makes* what I said wrong—I now see it in his further reaction—*that* is what I have to respond to at the next moment.)

Almost anything is an opportunity for further interaction.—Under these circumstances a very intense and eventful interaction occurs. Perhaps on the side of the patient it is nonverbal, but visible and active.

On the therapist's side, it involves both the concrete moves and facial expressions he cannot help, and the verbalizing of his thought processes. Many therapists have remarked about the schizophrenic patient's "exquisite sensitivity." There is a great deal of subverbal patient response. The therapist must respond further to make *further* interaction proceed with warmth and openness.

Therefore, when I have taken a patient out to some stores and then want to discontinue it, I may actually welcome the difficulty. It is an occasion for a close interaction. I will have to tell him that I feel bad about letting him down on a promise, perhaps say that I well remember it was I who first invited him. Perhaps he feels let down, betrayed, angry, disappointed, or what? Whatever it is, we won't hide from each other. I will also tell him I feel it is not a new breakthrough thing anymore. I want to see him well soon, and able to go places alone. I don't feel useful anymore, doing this, and I don't feel good if I think I am not useful. (Or whatever I do feel, in some form I can tell him.)

In these last sections, I have emphasized bad, troublesome, or difficult therapist feelings, because they offer rich sources of personal, positive responding. Of course, I also have many "good" feelings. And for these, too, I need a few moments to find a form in which to say them. It is most noteworthy, however, that just in those instances in which we feel stuck, or sense that we have just fallen down, or are strongly puzzled over what to do next, we have incipient therapeutic responses, if we allow what we sense to become clarified in ourselves. After all, the patient is someone who has difficulties in relating. The patient can move beyond these only if the therapist moves beyond them as he feels them in terms of himself.

If the patient cannot bear any response while he talks.—Sometimes a patient who says a few things after a long silence is sorely oversensitive and cannot bear anything I say in response. If he winces in pain at whatever I say, I am content to be silent. I just nod when I understand, or I ask for a repetition. I keep my responses and make them *later,* when he is no longer trying to say something to me. At that time, I make them *mine,* rather than loading them on him. I need not imply, "What *you* said meant . . . ," or "means to me . . ." Rather, I probably say, "I've been thinking—maybe you feel . . ." (as I would put it if it were all my own). Some patients can stand anything *I* think, but cannot bear the same statements as implications of what *they* have said. It is as if what they said is all that can be stood and *no more.*

Compressed, hard-to-understand patient speech can be responded to bit by bit.—When an isolated, autistic person at last tries to speak with someone, twenty significant allusions may trip over each other in one sentence. I will say: "Just a minute. I want to understand. I understood when you said so-and-so, and I know, I think, that this made you feel such-and-such. Is that right? (Yes.) And then you said '. . .', and I didn't know what you meant by that. I got you up to there. Tell me again from there. Did I hear it right?" The patient may have said ten or twenty things before I stopped him, and I grasped only the first little thing. But the patient is soon glad to repeat, and expand, as he senses that the therapist really wants to grasp each thing, and from then on I really do grasp each thing one by one.

I never let such a patient mumble on. The therapist's bit-by-bit solid grasp and response is like a pier in the patient's sea of autism and self-loss. As each bit is tied to another person who grasps it, the vast, lost, swampy weirdness goes out of things. It is not a matter of this or that content as much as the autistic, isolated manner of feeling and living. If I let him talk, I can then make only a general response which does not affect the patient's lonely autism. The therapist's bit-by-bit grasping and response is needed.

Interview Behavior III: Verbal but Externalized

The third type of interview behavior characteristic of many hospitalized individuals is free and reality-oriented verbalization, none of it "therapeutically relevant" in the usual sense. It is all about external events, about what others did or do, what happened during the week, etc. This third category of interview behavior is common not only in hospitals, but also in ordinary out-patient psychotherapy. Nearly every therapist has worked for a long period with an individual who spoke almost never about his feelings and affective meanings, almost always about situations and events. Coming to psychotherapy meetings can mean very much to these people. It can be like a life-raft for them. One knows something of importance is happening. But it is not psychotherapy, as the repetitions over the years eventually show. Without rejecting or destroying the desperately needed support which such a relationship does give, how can we bring into it the missing therapeutic process?

This "verbal but externalized" group included a number of our hospitalized patients, as well as most of our *normal* subjects! Thus one should not assume too quickly that externalized talking indicates abject fear, or "schizophrenic flattened affect," or unusually great repression. Perhaps externalized talking also indicates that the individual does not feel it to be appropriate to express his feelings. Whether the individual is labeled normal, neurotic, or schizophrenic, verbal but externalized interview behavior presents the same problem and demands some of the same kinds of response from the therapist.

The internal frame of reference redefined.—I respond in such a way that what I say about the individual's feelings *can be checked by him if he will directly refer to what he feels.* Quite often, unfortunately, he won't try to check what I say, won't try to pay inward attention to his felt meaning. But my responses are intended and phrased so that he *could* directly find and feel what I say. My response achieves its purpose if he refers directly to his felt meaning. My responses need not be correct; it is just as helpful if it results in: "No, it's really more like . . ."

Rogers (1951) called this type of therapist response "taking the client's internal frame of reference." As I define it, such a response says something which *could be* directly found and felt by the client. It is not an explanation, generalization, external observation, or behavior definition. What is it, then? It is a statement such that, if the individual will attend inwardly directly to his whole "feel" of what he is saying or doing just then, he will find there the feeling or meaning at which my response points. Or if I am not quite right, he will find there whatever *is* there.

This type of response moves from the sharply defined units of speech (in what he *says*) to the as yet undefined (but directly felt) mass of personal meanings and feelings he has as he speaks.

For example, the client is angry (says or shows it), or, more exactly, he *might be* angry (so often my first impression is wrong). But in addition to a well-defined unit (like "anger") there is always a whole mesh of feelings and meanings. He is angry *at* me *for* doing such and such *because* it seemed to prove I didn't care for him in a certain important way, and this upsets him *because* he had invested himself and now feels let down, which makes him feel desperate and makes him vow not to get "conned" again as he has so often before, when he . . . etc., etc., etc. This chain is just an example of the texture always implicit in felt meanings. Therapeutic movement in depth consists of such further steps into a felt meaning. I want to respond to the felt meaning, so that he will attend to it and move such steps. I can do that by pointing my words at "this whole way you feel" without knowing much about it. (Any bit I do sense helps me phrase a more specific pointer.) I *point* there and invite the client to look there. I would like to know what he really *does* find as he looks there. I am gladly corrected if he finds something different, or if other words seem to him to fit better.

For example, I say, "I guess you're scared." He checks against his feeling of it and says, "No, I'm not scared at all, I'm determined." I

accept that. The word "determined" better names what he has there.
Whatever he names it, I want to hear more from it. He continues: "—
determined not to let them get me, not this time, by God!" Now I am
hearing more from it. Again I respond, "They've always got you
before, but you've made up your mind, you won't give in now." "Right,
and another thing is —" (I prize this "and another thing is"; another
thing usually will come up when we move into felt meaning.) "And
another thing is — the way they get me is — I start to say, No, I won't
go along with it — but then I get mad and, I don't get mad like I should,
but instead I go to pieces, I get all nutty, I carry on, and then they've got
me."

Notice that if I am a stickler I can insist that of course this patient *is*
scared. I was right in the first place. But we would not get into felt
specifics if I stick at general words. It does not make much useful sense
to say he *is* or he *is not* scared. What he has there is always a texture of
much more specific felt facets. He is (if you insist) scared *of* that,
which he is "determined" to avoid. I am content with any words, and
any corrections of what I say, so long as we can keep *pointing* at his
present mesh of felt meaning, and taking concrete steps in it.

An imagined felt referent.—Even when I know perfectly well that
the client is not working on anything, I ask myself, What *might* he be
working on if he *had* said this given thing as part of a therapeutic
exploration? That leads me to sense or imagine an aspect of it which he
might feel and which can set a therapeutic process into motion.

Creating an "it".—Even when the patient does not indicate that he
has any felt meaning tissue there at all, I create it. I imagine it: a felt
sense of "all that" he has there, feels, and *could* pay attention to if only
he would! I have no sharp idea what it might be like, but I can
respond deeply, even with my vague sense of it. For instance, he says,
"She'll take me for every cent I've got" (meaning his wife, who is getting a divorce). I know he is not "working on" anything therapeutically
now. Yet, if he were, he might — what? — look at his whole texture of
felt meanings concerning his marriage, his being imposed upon, his
helpless feelings, his passivity, his important anger, his sense that some
of his perceptions are after all realistic and trustworthy. He is not
intending to look at, or work on, any of these themes, but I can invite
him to, just by responding, "And what's awful is, here you are, helpless
to do a thing about it." Perhaps his next remark enables me again to
point at a felt referent. I nearly always point at felt referents. If one in
a hundred opens out, that is an adequate percentage for movement.

*I refer my interpretations back to that speech or act of his which gave
it to me.*—Whatever general (diagnostic or other) conclusion or im-

pression I have of him, I received it *from him*—from his behavior and speech. I can give it to him best if I remind myself how he gave me this impression. Then I can respond to that more specific feeling, statement, or behavior, rather than giving him only the general conclusion. For example, I can say, "When you said . . . it got me to thinking . . ." Another example: "The way you stand there so sadly — it looks sad to me, I don't really know — it makes me wonder whether maybe you think they won't visit you, even though you say they will—"

Anything is "an opener".—I can choose to look at anything said as only an opener to a more personal communication. If the patient sees me smoking and says, "Smoking is bad for you," I take it as an opener to relate, to talk about me, touch me, discuss both his and my self-destructive behaviors, weaknesses, etc. Similarly, if the patient says, "Can you get me a weekend pass?" (I know I can't), this can become an opener to a conversation about me, him, wishing to get out of the hospital, home, the people he would see if he went home, whether they really want to see him or not, etc., etc. Of course, nine times out of ten my attempts at such a conversation fail, but the tenth time I succeed in developing it.

Retroactive responding.—If I wish I had responded some way a few minutes ago, or last week, I do so now. (I used to think I had to wait until the client brought it up again.) I might say: "You know, a while back, when you said such and such, well, now I think about that, and I think . . ." Or, "Last week, when I drove home, I thought that maybe you . . ."

Untwisting.—I will not remain what I call "twisted." If the patient has somehow gotten me to seem in a way I do not feel, then I no longer feel "straight." I feel "twisted." Perhaps I am responding socially, smiling, while actually I know we are avoiding something. Or perhaps I have promised something I do not wish. I feel "twisted" out of my own shape, and I will not stay that way. It may take me a few minutes to work my way out, but I won't silently let it pass. Soon I will say: "I think now that I don't want to do this thing, which I promised a while ago. I don't feel good about disappointing you, and maybe, if you're mad, you're right—but I won't do it." Or, "Well, a while ago that business about so and so seemed real fine, and we both said it was great, but now I wonder, maybe are you making it sound better than it is?" Such instances are opportunities for more direct relating between us.

No unmentionables.—Anything that seems unmentionable is really an opportunity for more direct relating. If the client implies (or I sense) some very painful, threatening thing, I respond to it. I believe the client *already* has and lives such a thing, if it is there (if, as he checks inside himself, he finds it there), and I cannot protect him from that. I have the choice only whether to leave him alone with it, or keep him interactive company with it. I won't wait until the client brings it up himself. He is probably doing just that, right now, as best he is able.

Often the patient refers to something which is unmentionable because it "dare not be," can not be tolerated—for example, "that they don't care for me," or "that I am crazy," or "that the therapist doesn't care for me," or "that I am ugly," etc. It helps if I speak these out loud. The patient is still here. He has not been shattered. I phrase it with a "maybe" so we can back out if need be. I say, almost lightly, "Maybe you're awful scared you really *are* crazy." Or, "Maybe I don't care for you at all," or, "Maybe you're too ugly for anybody to like." The result is usually relief. I respect the patient, not the trap he is caught in.

Two-sided compound.—The reasons against expressing something must also be included. Whatever in my feelings holds me back from expressing something, that too I can express, and in fact, I *can* express the two-sided compound, whereas I did not feel I could express just the one feeling.

For example, to say just, "I think maybe you're very scared that you really are crazy," might scare him all the more because he might feel that *I* think he is. Actually, he often makes very good sense about many things and if I express that, too, "Actually, you make very good sense about a lot of things," the first sentence becomes a safe one. This therapist expression becomes possible for me as I decide to voice also that which at first stopped me from expressing my feeling. Another example: "I don't like it when you do that, and I don't want you to do it anymore. *But I think you do it to . . . and I like that.*"

Positive recognition.—That last example illustrates a special case, the case where I need to set a limit or call a halt to some behavior. I can do this more easily (and, I think, more therapeutically) when I find and voice the patient's positive thrust in so acting. For example, I might not let a patient touch me or grab me. I will stop the patient, but in the same words and gesture I will try to respond positively to the positive desire for closeness or physical relations. I will make personal touch with my hand as I hold the patient away from me, contact the patient's eyes, and declare that I think the physical reaching out is positive and I welcome it, even though I cannot allow it. (I know at such times that I may be partly creating this positive aspect. Perhaps this reaching is more hostile, right now, than warm. But there is warmth and health in anyone's sexual or physical need, and I can recognize that as such.) The total effect of such stopping is therapeutic and positive, a moment of contact, because I have expressed not only the limit but I have also met the positive thrust.

We often find it difficult to set limits because we fear to hurt. I do not say, "I'm afraid to hurt your feelings," but rather I say what these feelings are in him (which one might fear to hurt). I can recognize these in him, and usually they are positive.

Therapist-supplied affective meaning.—The patient talks, perhaps gets much value from having a friendly caring listener, but nothing of therapeutic relevance is said. There is only talk about hospital food, the events of the week, the behavior of others, a little anger or sadness, no exploration.

I become the one who expresses the feelings and felt meanings. I say, "What a spot to be in!" or, "Gee, and they don't even *care* what *you* think about it," or, "I guess that leaves you feeling helpless, does it?" or, "Boy, that would make *me* mad," or, "It must be sad that he doesn't care more for you than *that*," or, "I don't know, of course, but I wonder, do you wish you *could* get mad, but maybe you don't dare?" or, "I guess you could cry about that, if you let yourself cry."

Sometimes I must retell the events in such a way that the probable felt meaning emerges. For example: "So your mother and your husband decide even which laundry you should send your stuff to. I guess they decide everything. Not much of a home of your own? Must be a helpless feeling?" (Patient says nothing.) "Maybe kind of *insulting* to you?"

Sometimes I say such things on my own responsibility: "I wish they'd care for you more than they seem to."

At first the patient's only reaction may be a brief blank look, after which he resumes his narrative, grateful that I let him (that I do not stop us and insist on the feelings to which I pointed). I am always willing to let him ignore what I say and go on; that helps him to stand my expressing such feelings.

Therapist truthfulness.—I try not to do anything phoney, artificial, untrue, distracting, or unreal, ever. Of course I do many phoney things before I even notice them, but that gives me a chance to double back and express the truth. We must help patients live with, in, and through what *does* confront them, the world they *already do* live in. The patient can successfully live only with what *is* there. There is no way to live with what is not, with falsehoods, with artificial roles played by psychologists. One cannot learn to live with the untrue, no matter how good its untruth might be. Really, the untrue is not there in a fullness that can be lived *with*. On the other hand, saying what is true helps because it is *already* there and one can learn to live with it better and differently.

For the therapist to be committed to the truth has another advantage: truth has its own check within the patient's (or the therapist's) felt mesh of experiencing. To seek truth we need not be bright, or guess rightly, or choose wisely.

The client-centered response.—Whenever there is anything to respond *to,* when the patient says, does, conveys, or acts out anything, then the best response is still the client-centered response. In such a response I attempt as plainly and purely as possible to voice my impression of what the patient means and feels at this moment. Nothing else is as helpful and powerful as that sort of response. It lets the patient know that he has been understood; it focuses his attention on his felt referents so that he can check what is said and carry it further; it shows him that I consider his felt meanings the ultimate deciding basis for what is true and what is not; it generates the therapeutic process of experiential movement; it tends to lead him to pay attention directly to his felt meanings without distorting them by what he or I may think; it lifts erstwhile private, hardly bearable aspects into the non-autistic interpersonal world; it lets the patient experience not only what he already knows he feels, but also what he almost but not quite feels (so that he feels it clearly, after it is spoken of); it keeps my own person and feelings clearly separate from his person and feelings so that there is room for both to be clear and undistorted; and it is the only way I know in which feelings that are too chaotic, weird, and sore to bear can come to be lived and borne. Such an interaction process provides solidity, clear intention, simplicity, respect and openness. Any feelings that are concretely lived in that manner become not only known, but also take on that manner. Therefore, their implicit sense and positive life thrust can emerge and the individual can come alive in a way that lessens the desperation and alters the very quality of these feelings.

Thus the various procedures I have described in this chapter are primarily used when the patient does *not* interact with me, is *not* (over a long period) saying, expressing, or acting out anything meaningful. When, through any of these channels, he *is* communicating meaningfully, then my response is the one long associated with client-centered therapy—the effort accurately to sense the client's felt meaning at that moment, and to communicate to him my understanding of that meaning as clearly as possible.

References

BUTLER, J. M. Client-centered counseling and psychotherapy. In C. Brower and L. E. Abt (eds.), *Progress in Clinical Psychology.* Vol. III, *Changing Conceptions in Psychotherapy.* New York: Grune & Stratton, 1958.

GENDLIN, E. T. Experiencing: A variable in the process of therapeutic change. *Amer. J. Psychother. 15:*233–245, 1961*a*.

GENDLIN, E. T. Initiating psychotherapy with "unmotivated" patients. *Psychiat. Quart. 35:*134–139, 1961*b*.

GENDLIN, E. T. Client-centered developments and work with schizophrenics. *J. counsel. Psychol. 9:*205, 1962*a*.

GENDLIN, E. T. *Experiencing and the Creation of Meaning.* New York: The Free Press of Glencoe, 1962*b*.

GENDLIN, E. T., and ZIMRING, F. M. The qualities or dimensions of experiencing and their change. *Counseling Center Discussion Papers,* I, 3. Mimeographed. Chicago: University of Chicago Library, 1955.

ROGERS, C. R. *Counseling and Psychotherapy.* Boston: Houghton Mifflin, 1942.

ROGERS, C. R. *Client-Centered Therapy: Its Current Practice, Implications, and Theory.* Boston: Houghton Mifflin, 1951.

ROGERS, C. R. The necessary and sufficient conditions of therapeutic personality change. *J. consult. Psychol. 21:*95–103, 1957.

SEEMAN, J. Client-centered therapy. In D. Brower and L. E. Abt (eds.), *Progress in Clinical Psychology,* Vol. II. New York: Grune & Stratton, 1956, pp. 98–113.

17. A Silent Young Man

Carl R. Rogers

It would surely be desirable, if it were possible, to give the reader some experience of the process of therapy as it was lived by each therapist in his interaction with his schizophrenic clients. Yet long descriptions of therapy in a variety of cases tend to be unconsciously distorted; the transcription of a whole case would be much too long for presentation (and misleading in its omission of voice qualities); and consequently some other solution must be found.

What I propose to do in this chapter is to present, in transcribed form, two significant and I believe crucial interviews in the therapy with James Brown (pseudonym, of course) together with my comments as therapist on this experience. This seems to be a doubly valuable approach since the two interviews presented here are available in tape recorded form to any professional worker through the Tape Library of the American Academy of Psychotherapists.[1] Also, in a subsequent chapter of this book there are presented fifteen segments of the tape-recorded interviews with Mr. Brown, taken at spaced intervals throughout the therapy. These segments are commented on by six experienced therapists who have listened to these recorded samples. Thus the person who is seriously interested in the interaction in this case can read and study these two interviews and my presentation of the meanings I see in them; can listen to the two interviews in order to judge the quality of the interaction for himself; can read and study an unbiased sampling of the whole therapy experience for this man; and can compare his own judgments and impressions with those of six other therapists who, like himself, have no personal investment in the research.

Let me give a few of the facts which will introduce James Brown. He was twenty-eight years old when I first began to see him as a part of the research. A coin toss had selected him as the member of a matched pair to receive therapy. He had been hospitalized three times, the first time for a period of three months when he was twenty-five. He had been hospitalized for a total of nineteen months when I first began to see him,

1. I am very grateful to Mr. Brown for his permission to make professional use of this material. The current address of the Tape Library of the American Academy of Psychotherapists is 6420 City Line Avenue, Philadelphia, Pennsylvania. In their listing this is "The Case of Mr. VAC."

and for two and one-half years at the time of these interviews. He is a person of some intellectual capacity, having completed high school and taken a little college work. The hospital diagnosis was "schizophrenic reaction, simple type."

Some readers will be disappointed that I am not presenting any of the facts from his case history. A superficial reason for this is that it might be identifying of this individual. A deeper reason is that I myself, as his therapist, have never seen his case history and do not know its contents. I should like to state briefly my reasons for this.

If I were trying to select the most promising candidates for psychotherapy from a large group, then an examination of the case histories by me—or by someone else—might be helpful in making such a selection. But in this instance Brown had been selected by the impersonal criteria of our research as a person to whom a relationship was to be offered. I preferred to endeavor to relate to him as he was in the relationship, as he was as a person at this moment, not as a configuration of past historical events. It is my conviction that therapy (if it takes place at all) takes place in the immediate moment-by-moment interaction in the relationship. This is the way in which I encountered Mr. Brown, and I am asking the reader to encounter him in the same way.

At the time of these two interviews, I had been seeing Mr. Brown on a twice a week basis (with the exception of some vacation periods) for a period of eleven months. Unlike many of the clients in this research the relationship had, almost from the first, seemed to have some meaning to him. He had ground privileges, so he was able to come to his appointments, and he was almost always on time, and rather rarely forgot them. The relationship between us was good. I liked him and I feel sure that he liked me. Rather early in our interviews he muttered to his ward physician that he had finally found someone who understood him. He was never articulate, and the silences were often prolonged, although when he was expressing bitterness and anger he could talk a bit more freely. He had, previous to these two interviews, worked through a number of his problems, the most important being his facing of the fact that he was entirely rejected by his stepmother, relatives, and, worst of all, by his father. During a few interviews preceding these two he had been even more silent than usual, and I had no clue to the meaning of this silence. As will be evident from the transcript his silences in these two interviews were monumental. I believe that a word count would show that he uttered little more than 50 words in the first of these interviews! (In the tape recording mentioned above, each of the silences has been reduced to 15 seconds, no matter what its actual length.)

In the two interviews presented here I was endeavoring to understand all that I possibly could of his feelings. I had little hesitancy in doing a good deal of empathic guessing, for I had learned that though he might not respond in any discernible way when I was right in my inferences, he would usually let me know by a negative shake of his head if I was wrong. Mostly, however, I was simply trying to be my feelings in relationship to him, and in these particular interviews my feelings I think were largely those of interest, gentleness, compassion, desire to understand, desire to share something of myself, eagerness to stand with him in his despairing experiences.

To me any further introduction would be superfluous. I hope and believe that the interaction of the two hours speaks for itself of many convictions, operationally expressed, about psychotherapy.

The Interviews

Tuesday

T: I see there are some cigarettes here in the drawer. Hm? Yeah, it is hot out.
[*Silence of 25 seconds*]

T: Do you look kind of angry this morning, or is that my imagination? [*Client shakes his head slightly.*] Not angry, huh?
[*Silence of 1 minute, 26 seconds*]

T: Feel like letting me in on whatever is going on?
[*Silence of 12 minutes, 52 seconds*]

T: [*softly*] I kind of feel like saying that "If it would be of any help at all I'd like to come in." On the other hand if it's something you'd rather — if you just feel more like being within yourself, feeling whatever you're feeling within yourself, why that's O.K. too — I guess another thing I'm saying, really, in saying that is, "I do care. I'm not just sitting here like a stick."
[*Silence of 1 minute, 11 seconds*]

T: And I guess your silence is saying to me that either you don't want to or can't come out right now and that's O.K. So I won't pester you but I just want you to know, I'm here.
[*Silence of 17 minutes, 41 seconds*]

T: I see I'm going to have to stop in a few minutes.[2]
[*Silence of 20 seconds*]

T: It's hard for me to know how you've been feeling, but it looks as though part of the time maybe you'd rather I didn't know how you were feeling. Anyway it looks as though part of the time it just feels very good to let

2. Long experience had shown me that it was very difficult for Jim to leave. Hence I had gradually adopted the practice of letting him know, ten or twelve minutes before the conclusion of the hour, that "our time is nearly up." This enabled us to work through the leaving process without my feeling hurried.

down and — relax the tension. But as I say I don't really know — how you feel. It's just the way it looks to me. Have things been pretty bad lately?

[*Silence of 45 seconds*]

T: Maybe this morning you just wish I'd shut up — and maybe I should, but I just keep feeling I'd like to — I don't know, be in touch with you in some way.

[*Silence of 2 minutes, 21 seconds*] [*Jim yawns.*]

T: Sounds discouraged or tired.

[*Silence of 41 seconds*]

C: No. Just lousy.

T: Everything's lousy, huh? You feel lousy?

[*Silence of 39 seconds*]

T: Want to come in Friday at 12 at the usual time?

C: [*Yawns and mutters something unintelligible.*]

[*Silence of 48 seconds*]

T: Just kind of feel sunk way down deep in these lousy, lousy feelings, hm? — Is that something like it?

C: No.

T: No?

[*Silence of 20 seconds*]

C: No. I just ain't no good to nobody, never was, and never will be.

T: Feeling that now, hm? That you're just no good to yourself, no good to anybody. Never will be any good to anybody. Just that you're completely worthless, huh? — Those really are lousy feelings. Just feel that you're no good at *all*, hm?

C: Yeah. [*muttering in low, discouraged voice*] That's what this guy I went to town with just the other day told me.

T: This guy that you went to town with really told you that you were no good? Is that what you're saying? Did I get that right?

C: M-hm.

T: I guess the meaning of that if I get it right is that here's somebody that — meant something to you and what does he think of you? Why, he's told you that he thinks you're no good at all. And that just really knocks the props out from under you. [*Jim weeps quietly.*] It just brings the tears. [*Silence of 20 seconds*]

C: [*rather defiantly*] I don't care though.

T: You tell yourself you don't care at all, but somehow I guess some part of you cares because some part of you weeps over it.

[*Silence of 19 seconds*]

T: I guess some part of you just feels, "Here I am hit with another blow, as if I hadn't had enough blows like this during my life when I feel that people don't like me. Here's someone I've begun to feel attached to and now *he* doesn't like me. And I'll say I don't care. I won't let it make any difference to me — But just the same the tears run down my cheeks."

C: [*muttering*] I guess I always knew it.

T: Hm?

C: I guess I always knew it.

T: If I'm getting that right, it is that what makes it hurt worst of all is that when he tells you you're no good, well shucks, that's what you've always felt about yourself. Is that — the meaning of what you're saying? [*Jim nods slightly, indicating agreement.*] — M-hm. So you feel as though he's just confirming what — you've already known. He's confirming what you've already felt in some way.

[*Silence of 23 seconds*]

T: So that between his saying so and your perhaps feeling it underneath, you just feel about as no good as anybody could feel.

[*Silence of 2 minutes, 1 second*]

T: [*thoughtfully*] As I sort of let it soak in and try to feel what you must be feeling — It comes up sorta this way in me and I don't know — but as though here was someone you'd made a contact with, someone you'd really done things for and done things with. Somebody that had some meaning to you. Now, wow! He slaps you in the face by telling you you're just no good. And this really cuts *so* deep, you can hardly stand it.

[*Silence of 30 seconds*]

T: I've got to call it quits for today, Jim.

[*Silence of 1 minutes, 18 seconds*]

T: It really hurts, doesn't it? [*This is in response to his quiet tears.*]

[*Silence of 26 seconds*]

T: I guess if the feelings came out you'd just weep and weep and weep.

[*Silence of 1 minute, 3 seconds*]

T: Help yourself to some Kleenex if you'd like — Can you go now?

[*Silence of 23 seconds*]

T: I guess you really hate to, but I've got to see somebody else.

[*Silence of 20 seconds*]

T: It's really bad, isn't it?

[*Silence of 22 seconds*]

T: Let me ask you one question and say one thing. Do you still have that piece of paper with my phone numbers on it and instructions, and so on? [*Jim nods.*] O.K. And if things get bad, so that you feel real down, you have them call me. 'Cause that's what I'm here for, to try to be of some help when you need it. If you need it, you have them call me.[3]

C: I think I'm beyond help.

---

3. Two words of explanation are needed here. He seemed so depressed that I was concerned that he might be feeling suicidal. I wanted to be available to him if he felt desperate. Since no patient was allowed to phone without permission, I had given him a note which would permit a staff member or Jim himself to phone me at any time he wished to contact me, and with both my office and home phone numbers.

T: Huh? Feel as though you're beyond help. I know. You feel just completely hopeless about yourself. I can understand that. I don't feel hopeless, but I can realize that you do.[4] Just feel as though nobody can help *you* and you're really beyond help.

[*Silence of 2 minutes, 1 second*]

T: I guess you just feel so, so down that — it's awful.

[*Silence of 2 minutes*]

T: I guess there's one other thing too. I, I'm going to be busy here this afternoon 'til four o'clock and maybe a little after. But if you should want to see me again this afternoon, you can drop around about four o'clock. O.K.? — Otherwise, I'll see you Friday noon. Unless I get a call from you. If you — If you're kind of concerned for fear anybody would see that you've been weeping a little, you can go out and sit for a while where you waited for me. Do just as you wish on that. Or go down and sit in the waiting room there and read magazines — I guess you'll really have to go.

C: Don't want to go back to work.

T: You don't want to go back to work, hm?

This is the end of the interview. Later in the day the therapist saw Mr. Brown on the hospital grounds. He seemed much more cheerful and said that he thought he could get a ride into town that afternoon.

The next time the therapist saw Mr. Brown was three days later, on Friday. This interview follows.

Friday

T: I brought a few magazines you can take with you if you want.[5]

[*Silence of 47 seconds*]

T: I didn't hear from you since last time. Were you able to go to town that day?

C: Yeah. I went in with a kid driving the truck.

T: M-hm. [*Voices from next office are heard in background.*]

[*Silence of 2 minutes*]

T: Excuse me just a minute. [*Goes to stop noise.*]

[*Silence of 2 minutes, 20 seconds*]

T: I don't know why, but I realize that somehow it makes me feel good that today you don't have your hand up to your face so that I can somehow kind of see you more. I was wondering why I felt as though you were a little more here than you are sometimes and then I realized well, it's

4. This is an example of the greater willingness I have developed to express my own feelings of the moment, at the same time accepting the client's right to possess *his* feelings, no matter how different from mine.

5. I had, on several occasions, given magazines and small amounts of money to Mr. Brown and loaned him books. There was no special rationale behind this. The hospital environment was impoverished for a man of Brown's sort, and·I felt like giving him things which would relieve the monotony.

because — I don't feel as though you're hiding behind your hand, or something.

[*Silence of 50 seconds*]

T: And I think I sense, though I could be mistaken, I think I do sense that today just like some other days when you come in here, it's just as though you let yourself sink down into feelings that run very deep in you. Sometimes they're very bad feelings like the last time and sometimes probably they're not so bad, though they're sort of — I think I understand that somehow when you come in here it's as though you do let yourself down into those feelings. And now —

C: I'm gonna take off.

T: Huh?

C: I'm gonna take off.[6]

T: You're going to take off? Really run away from here? Is that what you mean? Must be some — what's the — what's the background of that? Can you tell me? Or I guess what I mean more accurately is I know you don't like the place but it must be that something special came up or something?

C: I just want to run away and die.

T: M-hm, m-hm, m-hm. It isn't even that you want to get away from here *to* something. You just want to leave here and go away and die in a corner, hm?

[*Silence of 30 seconds*]

T: I guess as I let that soak in I really do sense how, how deep that feeling sounds, that you — I guess the image that comes to my mind is sort of a, a wounded animal that wants to crawl away and die. It sounds as though that's kind of the way you feel that you just want to get away from here and, and vanish. Perish. Not exist.

[*Silence of 1 minute*]

C: [*almost inaudibly*] All day yesterday and all morning I wished I were dead. I even prayed last night that I could die.

T: I think I caught all of that, that — for a couple of days now you've just *wished* you could be dead and you've even prayed for that — I guess that — One way this strikes me is that to live is such an awful thing to you, you just wish you could die, and not live.

[*Silence of 1 minute, 12 seconds*]

T: So that you've been just wishing and wishing that you were not living. You wish that life would pass away from you.

[*Silence of 30 seconds*]

C: I wish it more'n anything else I've ever wished around here.

T: M-hm, m-hm, m-hm. I guess you've wished for lots of things but boy! It seems as though this wish to not live is deeper and stronger than anything you ever wished before.

---

6. Clearly my empathic guessing in the two previous responses was completely erroneous. This was not troublesome to me, nor, I believe, to him. There is no doubt, however, that my surprise shows.

[Silence of 1 minute, 36 seconds]

T: Can't help but wonder whether it's still true that some things this friend said to you — are those still part of the thing that makes you feel so awful?

C: In general, yes.

T: M-hm.

[Silence of 47 seconds]

T: The way I'm understanding that is that in a general way the fact that he felt you were no good has just set off a whole flood of feeling in you that makes you really wish, *wish* you weren't alive. Is that — somewhere near it?

C: I ain't no good to nobody, or I ain't no good for nothin', so what's the use of living?

T: M-hm. You feel, "I'm not any good to another living person, so — why should I go on living?"

[Silence of 21 seconds]

T: And I guess a part of that is that — here I'm kind of guessing and you can set me straight, I guess a part of that is that you felt, "I tried to *be* good for something as far as he was concerned. I really tried. And now — if I'm no good to him, if he feels I'm no good, then that proves I'm just no good to anybody." Is that, uh — anywhere near it?

C: Oh, well, other people have told me that too.

T: Yeah. M-hm. I see. So you feel if, if you go by what others — what several others have said, then, then you are *no good*. No good to anybody.

[Silence of 3 minutes, 40 seconds]

T: I don't know whether this will help or not, but I would just like to say that — I think I can understand pretty well — what it's like to feel that you're just *no damn good* to anybody, because there was a time when — I felt that way about *myself*. And I know it can be *really rough*.[7]

[Silence of 13 minutes]

T: I see we've only got a few more minutes left.

[Silence of 2 minutes, 51 seconds]

T: Shall we make it next Tuesday at eleven, the usual time?

[Silence of 1 minute, 35 seconds]

T: If you gave me any answer, I really didn't get it. Do you want to see me next Tuesday at eleven?

C: Don't know.

T: "I just don't know."

[Silence of 34 seconds]

T: Right at this point you just don't know — whether you want to say "yes" to that or not, hm? — I guess you feel so down and so — awful that you just don't know whether you can — can see that far ahead. Hm?

[Silence of 1 minute, 5 seconds]

7. This is a most unusual kind of response for me to make. I simply felt that I wanted to share my experience with him—to let him know he was not alone.

T: I'm going to give you an appointment at that time because *I'd* sure like to see *you* then. [*Writing out appointment slip.*]
[*Silence of 50 seconds*]

T: And another thing I would say is that — if things continue to stay so rough for you, don't hesitate to have them call me. And if you should decide to take off, I would very much appreciate it if you would have them call me and — so I could see you first. I wouldn't try to dissuade you. I'd just want to see you.

C: I might go today. Where, I don't know, but I don't care.

T: Just feel that your mind is made up and that you're going to leave. You're not going *to* anywhere. You're just — just going to leave, hm?
[*Silence of 53 seconds*]

C: [*muttering in discouraged tone*] That's why I want to go, 'cause I don't care what happens.

T: Huh?

C: That's why I want to go, 'cause I don't care what happens.

T: M-hm, m-hm. That's why you want to go, because you really don't care about yourself. You just don't care *what* happens. And I guess I'd just like to say — *I* care about you. And *I* care what happens.[8]
[*Silence of 30 seconds*] [*Jim bursts into tears and unintelligible sobs.*]

T: [*tenderly*] Somehow that just — makes all the feelings pour out.
[*Silence of 35 seconds*]

T: And you just weep and weep and weep. And feel so badly. [*Jim continues to sob, then blows nose and breathes in great gasps.*]

T: I do get some sense of how awful you feel inside — You just sob and sob. [*He puts his head on desk, bursting out in great gulping, gasping sobs.*]

T: I guess all the pent-up feelings you've been feeling the last few days just — just come rolling out.
[*Silence of 32 seconds, while sobbing continues*]

T: There's some Kleenex there, if you'd like it — Hmm. [*sympathetically*] You just feel kind of torn to pieces inside.
[*Silence of 1 minute, 56 seconds*]

C: I wish I could die. [*sobbing*]

T: You just wish you could die, don't you? M-hm. You just feel so awful, you wish you could perish.
[*Therapist laid his hand gently on Jim's arm during this period. Jim showed no definite response. However, the storm subsides somewhat. Very heavy breathing.*] [*Silence of 1 minute, 10 seconds*]

T: You just feel so awful and so torn apart inside that, that it just makes you wish you could pass out.
[*Silence of 3 minutes, 29 seconds*]

---

8. This was the spontaneous feeling which welled up in me, and which I expressed. It was certainly not planned, and I had no idea it would bring such an explosive response.

T: I guess life is so tough, isn't it? You just feel you could weep and sob your heart away and wish you could die.[9]

[*Heavy breathing continues.*] [*Silence of 6 minutes, 14 seconds*]

T: I don't want to rush you, and I'll stay as long as you really need me, but I do have another appointment, that I'm already late for.

C: Yeah.

[*Silence of 17 minutes*]

T: Certainly been through something, haven't you?

[*Silence of 1 minute, 18 seconds*]

T: May I see you Tuesday?

C: [Inaudible response.]

T: Hm?

C: Don't know. [*almost unintelligible*]

T: "I just don't know." M-hm. You know all the things I said before, I mean very much. I want to see you Tuesday and I want to see you before then if you want to see me. So, if you need me, don't hesitate to call me.

[*Silence of 1 minute*]

T: It's really rough, isn't it?

[*Silence of 24 seconds*]

C: Yes.

T: Sure is. [*Jim slowly gets up to go.*]

[*Silence of 29 seconds*]

T: Want to take that too? [*Jim takes appointment slip.*]

[*Silence of 20 seconds*]

T: There's a washroom right down the hall where you can wash your face.

[*Jim opens door; noise and voices are heard from corridor.*]

[*Silence of 18 seconds*] [*Jim turns back into the room.*]

C: You don't have a cigarette, do you? [*Therapist finds one.*]

T: There's just one. I looked in the package but — I don't know. I haven't any idea how old it is, but it looks sort of old.

C: I'll see you. [*hardly audible*]

T: O.K. I'll be looking for you Tuesday, Jim.

Commentary

What has happened here? I am sure there will be many interpretations of this material. I would like to make it plain that what follows is my own perception of it, a perception which is perhaps biased by the fact that I was a deeply involved participant.

Here is a young man who has been a troublesome person in the institution. He has been quick to feel mistreated, quick to take offense, often involved in fights with the staff. He has, by his own account, no

---

9. As I have listened to the recording of this interview, I wish I had responded to the relief he must have been experiencing in letting his despair pour out, as well as to the despair itself.

tender feelings, only bitter ones against others. In these two interviews he has experienced the depth of his own feelings of worthlessness, of having no excuse for living. He has been unsupported by his frequently felt feelings of anger, and has experienced only his deep, deep despair. In this situation something happens. What is it, and why does it occur?

In my estimation, I was functioning well as a therapist in this interaction. I felt a warm and spontaneous caring for him as a person, which found expression in several ways—but most deeply at the moment when he was despairing. I was continuously desirous of understanding his feelings, even though he gave very few clues. I believe that my erroneous guesses were unimportant as compared to my willingness to go with him in his feelings of worthlessness and despair when he was able to voice these. I think we were relating as two real and genuine persons. In the moments of real encounter the differences in education, in status, in degree of psychological disturbance, had no importance—we were two persons in a relationship.

In this relationship there was a moment of real, and I believe irreversible, change. Jim Brown, who sees himself as stubborn, bitter, mistreated, worthless, useless, hopeless, unloved, unlovable, *experiences* my caring. In that moment his defensive shell cracks wide open, and can never again be quite the same. When someone *cares* for him, and when he feels and experiences this caring, he becomes a softer person whose years of stored up hurt come pouring out in anguished sobs. He is not the shell of hardness and bitterness, the stranger to tenderness. He is a person hurt beyond words, and aching for the love and caring which alone can make him human. This is evident in his sobs. It is evident too in his returning to the office, partly for a cigarette, partly to say spontaneously that he will return.

In my judgment what we have here is a "moment of change" in therapy. Many events are necessary to lead up to such a moment. Many later events will flow from it. But in this moment something is experienced openly which has never been experienced before. Once it had been experienced openly, and the emotions surrounding it flow to their natural expression, the person can never be quite the same. He can never completely deny these feelings when they recur again. He can never quite maintain the concept of self which he had before that moment. Here is an instance of the heart and essence of therapeutic change.

An Objective Look at the Process

If we look at the few client expressions in these interviews in terms of the hypotheses of this research, we can see that being deeply in therapy does not necessarily involve a ready flow of words. Let us take some of the feeling themes Brown expresses and look at them in terms of the process continuum we have conceptualized.

My feelings are lousy.

I ain't no good to nobody.

I think I'm beyond help.

I don't want to go back to work.

I just want to run away and die.

I ain't no good, so what's the use of living?

I don't care what happens.

I wish I could die.

Compare these themes with brief descriptions of the process continuum at stages 3, 4, 5, and 6 of the seven stages of the original Process Scale.

Stage 3. "There is much description of feelings and personal meanings which are not now present." "The experiencing of situations is largely described in terms of the past." "Personal constructs are rigid but may at times be thought of as constructs."

Clearly Mr. Brown's manner of expression does not fit this stage in any respect except that his concept of himself as no good is held in rigid fashion.

Stage 4. "Feelings and personal meanings are freely described as present objects owned by the self. . . . Occasionally feelings are expressed in the present but this occurs as if against the individual's wishes." "There is an unwilling fearful recognition that one is experiencing things—a vague realization that a disturbing type of inner referent does exist." "The individual is willing to risk relating himself occasionally to others on a feeling basis."

It is evident that this matches more closely Mr. Brown's experience in these hours.

Stage 5. "In this stage we find many feelings freely expressed in the moment of their occurrence and thus experienced in the immediate present." "This tends to be a frightening and disturbing thing because it involves being in process." "There is a desire to be these feelings, to be 'the real me.' "

This stage seems to catch even more of the quality of the experiencing in these interviews.

Stage 6. "Feelings which have previously been denied to awareness are now experienced with immediacy and acceptance . . . not something to be denied, feared, or struggled against." "In the moments of movement which occur at this stage there is a dissolving of significant personal constructs in a vivid experiencing of a feeling which runs counter to the constructs."

While some aspects of Jim's experiencing in these interviews come close to this description, it is clear that he is not acceptant of the feelings which well up in him. It appears that ratings of the stage he has reached in these interviews would probably cluster modally around stage 5, with some elements rated 4 or 6.

Perhaps this will give the reader some feeling for both the strengths and inadequacies of our conceptualizing of the process continuum and our attempts to capture it in an objective rating scale. It is relevant to what has occurred in these interviews, yet Brown's unique expression of his feelings is certainly not fully contained in the descriptions supplied by the original Process Scale, or the further separate scales developed from it.

This examination of the process aspect of these interviews may help to explain something which has mystified colleagues who have listened to the interviews. They often marvel at the patience I displayed in sitting through a silence of, say, seventeen minutes. The major reason I was able to do so was that when Jim said something it was usually worth listening to, showed real involvement in a therapeutic process. After all, most therapists can listen to talk, even when the talk is saying very little and indicates that very little that is therapeutic is going on. I can listen to silence, when I think that the silence is likely to end with significant feelings. I should add, however, that when I ceased to be patient, or ceased to be acceptant of the silence, I felt free to express my own feelings as they were occurring in me at the moment. There are various examples of this in these interviews. I do recognize, however, that it is easier for me to be patient than it is for a number of my colleagues. I have my style, and they have theirs.

Later Events

If one expects some quick and miraculous change from such a moment of change as we saw in the Friday interview, he will be disappointed. I was, myself, somewhat surprised that in the next interview it was as though these two had never happened—Jim was inarticulate, silent, uncommunicative, and made no reference to his sobbing or to any other portion of the interviews. But over the next months the change showed. Little by little he became willing to risk himself in a positive approach to life. Yet even in this respect he would often revert to self-defeating behaviors. Several times he managed to make all the necessary arrangements for leaving the hospital to attend school. Always at the last moment he would become involved in violent altercations (completely the fault of the other person, naturally!) which caused the hospital staff to confine him and which thus destroyed all the carefully laid arrangements. Finally, however, he was able to admit that he himself was terrified of going out—afraid he couldn't make good. When I told him that this was something to decide within himself—that I would see him if he chose to stay in the hospital, and that I would continue to see him if he chose to leave—he tentatively and fearfully moved out toward the world. First he attended school, living at the hospital. Then he worked through many realistic problems regarding a suitable room, finally found a place for himself in the community, and fully moved out.

As he could permit others to care for him, he was able to care for others. He accepted friendly gestures from members of the research staff, and it meant much to him to be treated as a person by them. He moved out to make friends of his own. He found a part-time job on his own. He began to live his own life, apart from any hospital or therapy influence.

The best evidence of the change is in a letter to me, a little more than two years after these interviews. At the time I was away for an academic year. I was seeing him very infrequently at the time I left, but I made arrangements for him to see another therapist (whom he knew slightly) if at any time he wished to do so. A few months after I left, I received the following letter from him:

Hi Doc,

I suppose you thought I had died, but I'm still here.

I've often thought of you and have been wanting to write but I'll use the old excuse that I've been busy.

Things are moving along pretty fast. I'm back in school, but things have changed slightly there. Mr. B. decided to quit teaching, so everything I had planned with him fell through.

(There follow three paragraphs about the courses he is taking and his pleasure at having been given—through the rehabilitation officer—an expensive tool of his trade. He also speaks of his part-time job which is continuing. Unfortunately, this material is too identifying to quote. He continues on a more personal note):

. . . I had a wonderful summer. Probably the best in years. I sure hate to see it come to an end.

I've met lots of people and made lots of friends. I hardly saw any of the kids from school all summer, and I didn't go out to hospital all summer.

Now, when I look back, it was like going down a different road. A very enjoyable one at that.

Also I haven't seen G. S. [substitute therapist in therapist's absence] at all this summer so far. As far as I could see it was good not seeing anybody, nor having to think about hospitals, doctors, and being out there. It was more or less like being free as a bird.

In fact, Doc, I was suppose to have gone up to the university and write those tests again. Some Mrs. N. has been calling and it irritates me because *I* think I did good and all that going up there will do is spoil the effect more or less. I don't mind seeing you, Doc. That's not the point. I still want to see you when you get back, but it is a good feeling not having to have to see anybody.

I can't really explain it, so I won't try.

I sure wish I was out there at this time. It's been down in the low 40's every night here lately and it's starting to rain a lot.

By the way, I finally went home. That was last Wednesday. I got there at noon and I could hardly wait to get back. Back to Madison, back to my room, back to my friends and civilization.

Well, Doc, I guess I've talked enough about myself and I guess about half way back, I'd have let you do all of it. Right?

All in all things couldn't be too much better for me, compared to what they have been. It sure feels good to be able to say, "To hell with it," when things bother me.

I'll write later when I have "time," Doc. Maybe I'll be mean and won't write until you do, because I did wonder how come I never heard from you before I did.

> Bye for now, Doc.
> Sincerely,
> JIM.

It is amusing that in his new-found independence he is refusing to take the final tests for the research project—amusing, but thought-provoking too. Perhaps when people accept themselves as persons, they refuse to be the objects of an investigation such as this one. It is a challenging, and in some deep sense a positive, thought.[10]

10. Perhaps this will cast a revealing light on one bit of dry statistics. If one looks at Table 11.1 one finds that the last battery of tests for this client (listed as VAC) was given more than 300 days before actual termination of therapy. This would appear to be an unforgivable lapse and discrepancy. It means that VAC was ruled out of the statistical consideration of outcomes, measured from pre- to post-therapy. This is unfortunate from the point of view of the findings, since the changes in him were unquestionably positive. But from a human point of view, his refusal to take the final test battery may well point to one of the best measures of his growth as a separate and self-directed person. In any event, many of the numbers in many of the tables have behind them stories as unique as this one.

Concluding Comment

In the case of Jim Brown, the progress he made appeared to grow primarily out of the qualities of the relationship. It appeared to have very little to do with fresh insights, or new and conscious self-perceptions. He *became* a new person in many ways, but he talked about it very little. Perhaps it is more accurate to say that he lived himself, used himself, in many new ways. In some fundamental characteristics he is still very much the same person. As of this writing he is completely on his own, functioning well, with friends of both sexes, entirely out of touch with the personnel of the hospital or the research group.

PART VI

An Evaluation by Outside Experts

18. The Client-Centered Process as Viewed by Other Therapists

The unusual idea of a sampling approach upon which this chapter was built was the contribution of Charles B. Truax. The therapists whose recorded interviews served as the foundation stones for the effort were Carl R. Rogers, Jack Teplinsky, and Charles B. Truax. The individuals responsible for selecting the tape segments were Edward Williams, Tanis Wallace, David LeRoy, Emily Earley, and Marjorie H. Klein. Tanis Wallace and Edward Williams were responsible for the transcriptions.

The outside therapists who voluntarily devoted their time and interest to listening to the cases and writing extensive comments, made the chapter possible. They are: Paul Bergman, Ph.D., Laboratory of Psychology, National Institute of Mental Health (now deceased); O. Spurgeon English, M.D., Department of Psychiatry, Temple University Medical Center; William C. Lewis, M.D., Department of Psychiatry, University of Wisconsin; Rollo May, Ph.D., Wm. Alanson White Institute, New York; Julius Seeman, Ph.D., Department of Psychology, George Peabody College for Teachers; and Carl A. Whitaker, M.D., Atlanta Psychiatric Clinic (now of the University of Wisconsin).

Charles B. Truax and Robert Carkhuff[1] organized this complex material and wrote this chapter.

A very real problem in psychotherapy and in psychotherapy research is that each case and each research project tends to be meaningful only to others sharing the same theoretical orientation. A question which deeply concerned us was, How can we break out of this provincialism? How can we obtain meaningful reactions and evaluations from individuals of other orientations? The methodology of research can more readily be understood and judged by others, but since the essential data is clinical, how can competent clinicians meaningfully react to the research without knowledge of the therapy itself?

1. As part of his work on a National Institute of Mental Health Post-Doctoral Research Fellowship.

It was obviously impossible to have others listen to hundreds of hours of partially inaudible, often silent, recorded interviews. It was at this point that a simple but new idea presented itself. The research, as has been evident, is built largely on brief recorded segments of interviews. Could a sampling of segments in the interviews provide a basis for clinical reaction and evaluation? If it could, it would allow for a reaction from therapists of other orientations. If it could not, then this would cast doubt on the meaning of the research itself, since most of the raw data was composed of these brief, arbitrarily selected segments of recorded interviews. In a sense, then, asking outsiders to come in to view and comment on the process of therapy in our research by asking them to react to brief recorded samples also involved an implicit invitation to evaluate the clinical adequacy of the raw data of the research. This clearly involved a risk, but a risk that seemed necessary.

The three selected cases were ones in which the therapists regarded themselves as more or less client-centered; the clients were ones showing improvement.

The therapy samples were selected by a modified random procedure. Two four-minute samples were randomly selected at each one-fifteenth of the case length. Effort was made to select from each pair the one sample having the highest audibility and the content most typical of the case. Thus fifteen recorded four-minute segments gave a one-hour "sampling summary" of each case. Because audibility was often far from perfect, typed transcripts of these segments were also prepared. This procedure yielded a systematic and representative sample of each of the three cases. Still, the one-hour "sampling summary" itself was an extremely small proportion of the total interaction, ranging from approximately three percent down to two-thirds of one per cent.

It should be clear that this modified random procedure tends to reflect the "average" moment in therapy, not the "most significant" or "deepest" moments, just as does the research itself. Thus we were taking the risk of allowing critical leaders in the field of psychotherapy to see fifteen glimpses of the ordinary interaction of our interviews, without any attempt to acquaint them with the better or more meaningful depths or peaks of that interaction. The whole venture was a very new one, and not undertaken without trepidation.

We were very fortunate indeed in obtaining the cooperation of six leading and creative therapists who differed rather widely in orientation. It was as much a new venture for them as it was for us. Drs. Paul Bergman, O. Spurgeon English, William C. Lewis, Rollo May, Julius Seeman, and Carl A. Whitaker were willing to pioneer. Their task was to focus upon three critical aspects of the therapeutic process: (1) What movement, if any, occurs? (2) What is the therapist doing that is helpful? (3) What is the therapist doing that is not helpful? No further structure was imposed.

The three cases selected for study involved young male schizophrenics but varied in length from 30 to 166 sessions. The therapists were of varying degrees of experience: at one extreme was a man who had had more than thirty years of experience as a psychotherapist while at the other extreme was a relative beginner, with only slightly more than two years of experience. They were alike only in that they were all relatively client-centered in approach.

The clinical consultants valiantly surmounted many of the obstacles inherent in the present exploration. Some flavor of the obstacles can be gained from reading typescripts of the same one-hour "sampling summaries" that they received. The printed scripts presented below cannot portray the therapeutic experience as vividly as the tapes, which included tonal and voice qualities, so the reader may have even more difficulty than the reviewers in sensing the flavor of the therapeutic transactions. If the reader has not had previous experience with transcripts of recorded conversation, the excerpts may strike him as extremely incoherent. This may be due to the natural incoherences and incomplete statements which are a part of all ordinary conversation. It may at times be due to a fault in the transcription, since complete accuracy is impossible, and sometimes a mistake in hearing one word can cloud the meaning of a whole statement. Finally, of course, some of the incoherence may be due to the nature of the patient. If the material is read with word-for-word literalness, it may be confusing. If it is read for its flow and its implicit patterns, it may prove more meaningful. Some readers may prefer simply to dip into the recorded material and to proceed at once to the commentaries which follow.

The Case of Brown[2]

James Brown, a young male schizophrenic who had been hospitalized for more than one and one-half years at the beginning of psychotherapy, was seen for a total of 166 interviews.

The following are the typescripts of the therapeutic samples:

Excerpt 1

C: Well, still I can't, couldn't start one thing and leave it and start something else and do it, it would bother me and be on my mind every, every — while I was doing something else.

T: But you just can't divide yourself — it's all or nothing at all for you.

C: [pause] I start doing something I know I ain't going to finish, but then I don't know when to stop. [laughs]

2. In our research code, this is the case of VAC. This is also the individual described in Chapter 17.

T: Mm — mm — you don't even want to get underway if you're not going to carry straight through to the, finish —

C: Unless, it's something I don't care about, what I got to do, then I don't care whether I start it or don't finish it but if it's something I like to do or something I don't mind doing why then —

T: Some — something that has any of *you* in it — I mean if you really choose to do it or something you're interested in, then if you get going on it like, I guess you've got to push it through. You just say if somebody else is making —

C: [*long pause*] It seems like I've got to be on the move all the time —

T: Mm.

C: I can't sit still for — maybe I oughta sometimes [*T:* Mm — Well that's —] and it's even hard for me sitting here, I mean just, just sitting here.

T: Well, I guess, as I say, don't think you always have to just sit, you — some of them walk around here.

C: It makes more sense.

T: But anyway, it's, it's hard for you, ah, to just stay put.

C: Yeah, as far as that goes, I was always on the go, I couldn't be in the same place twice — unless I was at work, about the only place it didn't happen, when I wasn't at work I was never in the same place twice, oh, after ten, fifteen minutes I'd have to get out of there and find someplace else to go to or something else to do.

T: The kind of a guy that's always on the go — huh?

C: I gotta, it's like some drive in me.

T: Mmm — mmm — You can't stay put, you've got to keep moving, moving, moving, moving —

C: Like cards, I can play cards for about five minutes and then I got to get up, do something else but after I do it I can always come back and play cards again.

T: Mmm — mmm.

C: I don't know, if it's just nothing that's interesting to me or what.

T: You really don't quite understand why you can't, ah, stick at one thing long or why you have to, well as you say you eventually come back to it, but you have to move around, you've got to be on the go [*pause*] and even right here it's darn hard to just sit. Well, as I say again, I've already said, you can always get up and walk around whenever you want to. I don't smoke, but if you've got cigarettes, why feel free to light up one.

C: I won't, [*laughs*], I won't, unless I can swipe a Chestie, I don't smoke enough, I don't smoke that much, if I, that's another thing I was going to cut out entirely, if I had the will power, haven't got enough will power.

T: You can't quite make it . . . .

Excerpt 2

T: You're trying to say, if I get the flavor of what you're feeling, sounds as though the feeling may be — "What's the use of anything, what's the use of doing anything, what's the point of talking, what's the point, ah, of anything at all, doesn't seem as though there is any point or purpose in anything" — is that your feeling?

C: Nothing makes sense anymore.

T: "There isn't any meaning in things — there's just no sense to anything."

C: It's just like a dream world.

T: You feel there's no sense to a dream world and there's no sense to this world— [*long pause*]

C: Well, even the life before I come in here, doesn't seem real any more, after being here.

T: "Even my real life, before I got here no longer seems to have any reality, it's just kind of a dream too, it doesn't make sense —" [*very long silence*]

Excerpt 3

C: [*sighs*] — Yeah.

T: You just got to get the hell out of here.

C: [*sighs, voice is partly crying*] — I was talking to the aide last night, he said nobody seemed to want me on the outside, and he said they didn't want me here so they was goin' to send me to the County[3] and I ain't goin'.

T: Mmm — Boy, that was a real blow. As if it weren't bad enough to feel that nobody wants you on the outside, then to feel they don't want you here, just going to kind of get rid of you, that just really cuts — [*long pause*] You just feel, well, "They *aren't* going to send me to the County —" [*long pause*]

C: [*sighs deeply, blows nose*] — I'd kill myself first— [*pause*]

T: You just feel "I would really do away with myself before I'd let that happen —" [*long pause*]

C: [*muttering*] Might as well, nobody wants anything to do with me so —

T: Would you repeat that again?

C: Nobody wants anything to do with me anyway so I might as well —

T: Mmm — You feel there isn't anyone that gives a *damn* about you— [*pause*] You just feel nobody wants to have anything to do with you— [*long pause*] Guess that must make you feel "Boy, am I ever *alone.*"

Excerpt 4

T: I see we just have a few more minutes left — [*clears throat*] — would you feel like sharing with me anything of what's been going on —

C: Oh, I just feel, ah — dead.

T: Hmm.

C: I just feel dead [*pause*] beat —

T: Discouraged and beaten, not feeling good physically and— [*clears throat*]

---

3. In this hospital, patients who were not responding to treatment, and who were regarded as having become essentially custodial cases, were transferred to one of the County Hospitals. Brown feels (with some evidence) that this decision has been made in regard to him.

[*long pause*] I feel as though perhaps you find something that you kind of like about being just able to come here and be as silent as you feel or as much within yourself as you feel— [*long pause*] And I do often wish I was better at guessing than I am. Do you prefer to have me keep still, or whether sometimes you like to be — jogged a little with the notion that maybe there might be something you'd care to share? [*long pause*] I guess you don't feel like commenting on that either. [*long silence*]

Excerpt 5

C: Yeah, the last thing is I've got ole Dr. C—— again and as far as I'm concerned I don't ever want nothin' to do with her —

T: You just feel you don't get on with her and you don't want to have anything to do with her —

C: Yeah, the other day I wanted to see her. I felt so damn lousy, I felt like goin' out and killing myself [*T:* Hmm] and I wanted to see her, and she said "I haven't got time for you" — that ole shit.

T: Mmm — I guess you're saying —

C: How scared I was —

T: You were saying, "Here I am at the very bottom ebb, just really frightened, fearing I might do away with myself and then what does she do — she says she hasn't got time enough to see me."

C: Well [*very low*], well, the Monday before Christmas I was so sick I thought I'd die, and I came over here to see her and she said, "It's all in your head — go on back," so I went back and I could hardly move so then I had my temperature taken and that was one hundred and three, wasn't a damn thing I could do about that except put up with it and —

T: I guess you feel she doesn't really care *either*— [*long pause*]

C: Yeah —

T: "Nobody really gives a damn about me —" [*long pause*] I guess it must sort of seem as though "What really is the use? — nobody cares about me at all —" [*long pause*]

C: Well, I really don't care no more myself, whether I'm dead or what the hell happens —

T: Mmm . . . .

Excerpt 6

T: I'm not quite sure what the "so" is. She has her way of thinking and you have hers.

C: No, she has her way of thinking and I have my own way of thinking.

T: Yes, that's right [*laughing*] — I guess I — got that mixed up, that's what I meant — ah, she has her way of thinking and feeling and you have your way so-o-o-o —

C: So, any way I tell her she still is goin' to have her own way.

T: The thing I can's quite decide is whether you're saying, "So, it's hopeless —"

C: So what good does it do to see her?

T: I see, you feel that there's no such thing as — communication I guess between people who hold different views. You feel "If she feels one way and I feel and think another way then there's no use talking to her, there's no use, they—" [pause]

C: Every time I go see her, I tell her what I think, how I feel, she tells me what she thinks and "You can leave now 'cause I ain't got my mind made up —"

T: So you feel, yeah, you communicate what you feel, but then what she feels is "it" so now you can go— [long pause]

C: One day I just about called the doctor for her too — I, I had that lump here and the first time I went to see her, ah, I told her about it and she laughs and I said "I don't think it's funny" and she says, "Well you know I always laugh a lot —" then and there I thought there was hope for me.

T: Mmm — mmm — mmm — I guess there's a feeling of real bitterness there that something that you felt real serious about, she just laughed at and it did make you feel — "Hell, she needs a doctor worse than I do —" [pause] Feeling, "I must be pretty good if she's that bad —" [long pause] I see I've got to stop pretty quick . . . .

Excerpt 7

C: Every time I turn around today they'll be slapping me in the face. [sighs]

T: You feel that, no matter what you do, everytime you move any direction, somebody will *slap you.*

C: No, no, not everybody.

T: Not everybody.

C: It's that idea of goin' to that *damn* County.

T: I see, I see, I see — mmm — it's just no matter what you try to do or try to think about or what not — Wow! Then this prospect of going to the County — will just rise up and slap you in the mug.

C: I know it as sure as I'm sitting here. [Voice sounds weepy.]

T: You just won't be able to get that out of your mind. It just hits you from right to left.

C: I tried to this morning and tried to yesterday afternoon.

T: You just try to do things to keep it out of your mind but in spite of anything you can do it just comes hitting back at you.

C: It just tears me down.

T: Mmm — mmm — mmm — You just feel that it — destroys you and your confidence in yourself and everything. It just tears you, and makes you — smaller — [pause]

C: It does. Makes me think what is there to look forward to besides that.

T: Every time it comes back to you, you feel, "Well, that's going to be my future, what else is there to look forward to —" [pause]

C: It's just the way I feel.

T: Mmm — You just feel as though "Really there's nothing ahead of me but the County Hospital —" [pause] I guess that's a real —

C: What else *can* I think?

T: Mmm — "How could I possibly think anything different than that? — What other alternative could there possibly be?"

C: Outside of running away.

T: Then, it's either the County Hospital or running away from here, those are the only two alternatives that seem to you possible.

Excerpt 8

C: Do you have any money I can borrow, Doc? [*blows his nose*]

T: I think so.

C: I was —

T: Mmm?

C: This guy here, I know [*blows his nose again*] [*T:* Mmm] been a good friend to me [*both speaking*] [*T:* Got a what —] not sure whether I can call him that or not —

T: I still couldn't hear you, your best friend?

C: I got here —

T: Yes.

C: I'm goin' to see if we can go to town Sunday.

T: See if you can go to town Sunday, with the best friend you've got here.

C: Well, he can go but —

T: He can go — mmm —

C: Go to the show or somethin'.

T: Mmm — is a dollar enough, hmmm?

C: I don't know what the show is — I want to take him — 'cause he ain't got any money either.

T: You want to take him. I see.

C: See if he'd go.

T: Well, how about two, will that do it?

C: Should — I'll see if Earl will take me, take us in— [*pause*]

T: So what you'd like to do is take him in and treat him to the show, if you possibly can, huh —

C: I can get in but I don't know about getting back.

T: Huh?

C: I can get in but I don't know about getting back.

T: Mmm — well, let's see, I've got three ones — you take them, if you don't need them you can give part of it back to me, but if you do need 'em you've got 'em. [*pause*]

C: We're goin' all day — [*very low*]

T: Huh?

C: We're goin' all day — Sunday.

T: You're going all day Sunday, is that what you said? You'd just like to really get away from here a little bit with a friend, huh?

C: Yeah, he's in the same boat I am.

T: Mmm — what boat is that?

C: Nobody'll come up to see him.

T: Mmm — mmm — no outside friends, or relatives or any of the family or anything that call on him any more than on you, so you might as well —

C: I know how he feels —

T: So you know how he feels — mmm — you sure do, don't you — so you might as well be friends to each other at least, hmm [*pause*] if he doesn't have a family that will come to see him you can be his family and if you don't have a family that comes to see you he —

C: No, but —

T: Hmm?

C: No, not that —

T: Not that — it's just that you know how he feels and how damn lonesome it is and you'd like to do something for him — is that more like it? [*pause*]

C: Yeah, maybe if it makes him feel better I'll feel better.

T: Mmm — mmm.

Excerpt 9

C: So, everybody that does know I can go in, why has gone —

T: What did you say?

C: Everybody that does know that she gave me permission to go to town has gone.

T: Mmmm.

C: The aide on the ward, Charlie, he's gone for a month's vacation.

T: Mmm — mmm.

C: Ralph is gone.

T: Mmm — you just feel that all the people whom you might have turned to for some corroboration are all out of the picture — [*long pause*] I guess I'd just like you to know that if you want me to speak to her on that, I would — [*long pause*]

C: She asked me, she says, "Do you think you're ready to go home?" I says, "I don't know," or ready to leave — She asked me about my folks, I says, "I don't see any of 'em and I don't want to see 'em." [*pause*]

T: But you tried to be honest with her that as to whether you were ready to leave, you really didn't know yourself.

C: I told her sometimes I felt like it, felt like it so much, but after a while — then I didn't feel I could again.

T: Mmm — mmm — it's as though it sort of builds up in you as a real hope and desire and so on and then when you don't leave why it kinda dies down again — is that it — mmm? [*pause*] What's the biblical verse, "Hope deferred maketh the heart sick," or something— [*pause*]

C: It ain't that I don't wanta go — [*very low*]

T: What?

C: It ain't that I don't wanta go — it's just the way I feel at times. I don't know.

T: M-hmm.

C: I'd sure as hell hate to come back here though.

T: M-hm — m-hm — if you leave you want it to mean that you really leave and ah, don't come back and I guess it's when that, when you think of whether you're ready to leave in that sense then it's, then you're not quite sure, huh— [*pause*] I guess it is, you want to get away from here all right, that's something you're clear enough about, but it's whether you're really ready to leave in the sense — of never coming back, that's — that you're not quite so certain of— [*pause*]

Excerpt 10

C: No matter how many chances I get I won't go. [*bitterly*]

T: M-hm — m-hm — m-hm — m-hm — "I am absolutely determined that I won't talk with her on my own initiative, and I won't go to town — no matter how many chances I get."

C: I could have gone in Saturday all day.

T: Mmm — you feel like —

C: She won't let me go, so — I just won't go at all.

T: "She won't let me go in my way, so I won't go in *any* way" — and I, I get a feeling behind that, "I'll show her somehow, I'll show her that —"

C: I'll show her that I just don't give a damn.

T: That's it, uh-huh, I wasn't quite sure how to finish that myself. "I'll show her that I don't care about anything — I don't give a damn about myself, about going to town, about her, about getting out, I don't give a *damn* about anything— [*long pause*] Sort of well, I'll punish her by becoming a person who doesn't want anything [*pause*] and that'll show her —" [*pause*]

C: It won't be hurting *me* any 'cause I *don't* care— [*long pause*]

T: I guess I hear different things in that, I, I hear you saying — I hear the words where you're saying, "It won't hurt *me* at all, *I* don't care, it doesn't, I don't give a hoot" — and I can also hear the bitterness and the hurt in that— [*long pause*]

C: I don't —

T: I guess you are saying, "I care that I was hurt."

C: I don't give a damn enough to even — know if it hurts or not —

T: M-hm — m-hm — m-hm — I guess you're saying everything, every other feeling is just covered over by the feeling, "I don't care about anything, I don't care, I am indifferent, I, it doesn't make any difference what happens — nothing makes any difference to me." . . .

Excerpt 11

C: ———— [the doctor] told me that too —

T: Huh.

C: ———— [the doctor] told me too —

T: You feel you'll hold out because of your pride, or will you go [*pause*] well, maybe I shouldn't ask, but let me, let me see if I've got the situation straight. Dan would like you to come, and I imagine you'd like to see him, wouldn't you? —

C: I suppose so.

T: And —————— [the doctor] was willing for you to go, but I suppose that all boils down to the question of whether you'd ride in the green car [hospital car] or not, is that it?

C: No, she says I could go by myself.

T: Oh, really? Well that's a change, isn't it? — I see, I see, so that isn't the issue, it's more the question of "Will I step outside of this place or not," huh? Or maybe that isn't the issue, I should probably keep my big mouth shut and let — you tell me, what, what is the, what are the angles of it?

C: I haven't thought much about it.

T: Huh— [*long pause*] I guess one reason I kind of jumped on that was that — just a minute before that I was thinking, I wonder if you really have considered the alternatives. If you have and made up your mind, O.K. I was thinking about more general alternatives. I was thinking, I realize how deeply you're committed to the notion, that you won't do anything but be indifferent, until someone opens doors for you, that by God you're not going to make any more efforts and get hurt — you're not going to try to do things and then have them slapped down so you will *sit* until something happens, at least that's the way I've gotten your feeling and, I can understand that certainly. All I was wondering was whether you really have considered the alternative possibility — oh, another part of that is, another part of the first one is, "And if they say I've got to go to school, O.K., then I'll go to school to get out of here even though I think it's a silly idea and don't want to do that." Ah, now the alternative to all of that would be a tough one, I realize, but it would be to decide *"I'm going to go to town and scout around and see if I could find anything in the way of a job. I'm going to go to town and visit Dan. I'm going to go to town and make the kind of contacts I would want if I did get a job"*— libraries or churches or whatever has any meaning to you—"I'm going to tell . . . ."

Excerpt 12

T: Want a cigarette? [*pause*] I feel as though I haven't been much help today — [*long pause*]

C: No, [*mumbling*] I feel like I want everything — at the same time I don't want nothin' — [*laughs*]

T: Mmm — So you feel, on a [mumble] like that, I'm not sure I get the whole thing — you say either you want everything at the same time or you don't want anything —

C: No, I want everything at the same time, or everything — at the same time I don't want it at all.

T: I see, I see, uh-huh, uh-huh, well that is true, isn't it? You want everything — you want to be out, and you want to have a job, and you want to have a girl, and you want to have all kinds of things and at the same time you feel, "I'm indifferent to everything — I don't really want anything— [*pause*] If I want anything I get hurt [*pause*] so I don't want anything —" [*long pause*] I guess that fits lots of things, I guess that's part of the reason why you're saying, "So I don't want Sally to come tomorrow, but if she comes I'll be glad to see her, but I'm indifferent," but I think another part of you probably says, "I hope very much she'll come, and I want to see her —" [*long pause*] Is it something like that? [*pause*]

C: No, it's all hodge — that or anything else in general [inaudible].

T: Mmm — you're just not thinking about anything much, huh?

Excerpt 13

T: Mmm — mmm — mmm — "When I make up my mind to go to school, I want to get admitted to school, I don't want to have this and that and the other all unfinished in regard to it." huh — mmm, mmm — I guess it's the — the unfinished part of it that's particularly hard to take — if you could plow through and do whatever you've got to do to get into school, O.K., but to have to have this hanging in mid-air and that hanging in mid-air — that really bothers you— [*long pause*] I guess the feeling is, "I'm a person who likes to plow through to the finish and I don't tolerate it well if I'm interrupted or if I can't wind the thing up, or if I can't — I hate to leave it with loose ends sticking out all over —" [*long pause*]

C: Yeah, I can remember ah, when I was outside I was painting this house for these people and you know what, I'd have painted all night long if I'd had my way.

T: M-hm, m-hm, m-hm, m-hm, m-hm; you just remember that as one sample of this. Ah, O.K., once you started painting their house you would have liked to just paint right through the night if necessary 'til you were finished— [*long pause*] I guess you hate the feeling of anything hung up in mid-air or unfinished— [*pause*]

C: Yeah, there's lots of times I start somethin' in the day and think I'll get done by night and never get it done, and it makes me so disappointed.

T: Mmm — mmm, mmm, mmm — that's really hard to take not to — not to plow right through from start to finish without a stop — if something makes that impossible then that's really disappointing to you.

Excerpt 14

T: Huh?

C: You set me up once.

T: I remember, so I would like to advance you a loan to take care of that — you can pay me back when you get your money if you want, ah — but you, ah — I just want to make sure that, ah, if you want to have, ah, if you want to be able to work on your stuff here, you'll be able to go in and pick up your books this afternoon, that'll give you something to do over the weekend — I do want you to be able to come in on Tuesday [*pause*] and I think I realize how you feel about the thing in general, I'm not trying to say anything about that and if you feel that you want to stay away from school until they get this squared away, O.K., and I really do understand how you feel about that. It's just on these two smaller things that I want to make sure that, ah, just the lack of bus fare that will stand in your way of either getting your books or coming to see me— [*pause*]

C: I'll need a bus going in and out.

T: There isn't any bus going in now?

C: Not today, starts tomorrow — the last one left at eight forty.

T: Mmm — and when does the school close up?

C: Runs all 'til ah, nine o'clock I guess 'til —

T: Until night —

C: Night school —

T: Well, I think I will be here about ah, quarter of three or three o'clock, and going in at that time, I'll be over here then — ah, there'll also be some other people from our group going in at about that time too, so if you wanted to you could go in then — is it open on Saturday?

C: No.

T: Well, I'm not trying to persuade you on that, I just felt more that the lack of a little bit of money would stand in your way of doing either one of those things.

C: Well, I knew I'd get back in.

T: Huh —

C: I knew I was going back in.

T: Yeah, it bothered you at first.

C: Yes, it sorta irked me off.

T: Mmm, felt kind of pissed off that they hadn't got this thing properly arranged.

C: Well, at least they coulda told me to start with, but no it's later, later, later, later, it's always later. Why didn't they say so in the first place — [*blows nose*] — so at least I'd know.

T: And what do they think now, that it won't come all next week?

C: 'Til next week, so next week it'll probably be next week — so I don't know [*pause*] so I guess when it gets here it gets here.

T: I would say, that if you're willing to take a loan which you would repay when you get it, I'd be glad to make you a loan— [*pause*]

C: I'll wait and see— [*pause*]

T: You want to wait until Tuesday to see if it —

C: Oh, I wanted to see ———— [the rehab worker] Monday, but —

T: Uh-huh.

Excerpt 15

T: Yeah, people really do create a lot ah, problems for you, but one thing that has a lot of meaning to me is that right now you're — you're facing the fact as well as you can that things that go on inside of *you* are damn upsetting to you sometimes, so much so that there are times when you would welcome being back in the hospital and I guess I feel two ways about that. I feel badly that ah, things have been that rough for you and I feel somehow sort of good about the fact that you're trying to figure some of this out and to really face whatever the elements are in you that ah, and in your situation that ah, get you upset or off the beam — and I'd say too that ah, one reason I keep pushing you today, I'm sure, is that, God damn it, one of the things I'm pretty good at is helping people to get at what is really troubling them! If we can, if we can at all get to the bottom of what it is that sets you off and makes you nervous and what the experiences are that, that ah, give you this feeling of nothing really getting to you [*pause*] why we may be able to lick that too— [*long pause*]

C: Yeah, it's hard fighting two different worlds.

T: It is hard to find two different worlds, isn't it?

C: No, fight 'em.

T: Mmm?

C: Fight 'em.

T: Fight them, fight two different worlds, I see — mmm — yeah, you're, am I getting it right? — naturally there's a lot on the outside world to fight and make your way in, and so on, and then to fight the inside world too is that what you mean?

C: No, not really.

T: Well, tell me a little more what you do mean when you say it's hard to fight two worlds.

C: You live in two different worlds.

T: Yeah, uh-huh, uh-huh, uh-huh — well if —

C: I live in one world with you, and in another.

T: Yeah, yeah, yeah, hmmm, and you know the thing that ah, I'm trying to tell you and I suppose I've been trying to tell you for a couple of years or more is that ah — I'd like to come into that inside world, that world of feeling and so on and you do let me in every once in a while and I don't think you keep me out ah, on purpose, I don't mean that but ah — the world of feeling or that inner world becomes a lot more possible to live in if you can let somebody else in too.

Commentaries

The evaluators focused on what they felt were more general and critical dimensions rather than the subtle nuances of their own particular theoretical stances. Although the purpose was not to set forth each of the particular theorist's views of therapy, their views were reflected by distinct differences in language and by differences in focus as well as differences in conclusions. Thus, while Bergman, the first theorist considered, sees no movement in the case of Brown, all other theorists perceive progress of varying degrees.

Bergman

Although Bergman, a psychoanalytically trained psychologist who sympathizes with the philosophy but not the technique of client-centered therapy, surmises from the content of the excerpts that the hospital staff considered Brown improved, he is not convinced that "the patient's attitude or mood changed to any degree at all." Bergman concludes that Brown "never achieved a trusting therapeutic relation-ship."

Concerning the activities of the therapist, Bergman suggests:

For the therapist . . . it must have been a miserable strain to see this unmotivated and recalcitrant patient for 166 hours. I think that occasionally signs of the strain are showing. In the main the therapist evidently holds to a line of reflecting feelings, but not infrequently he tends to slant his responses toward persuasion, the insinuation, or even the open presentation of an alternative point of view. It is not that I blame the therapist for not being consistently client-centered, I cannot imagine any human being not getting impatient and angry with Brown's stubbornness and unreasonableness. But I sense a certain deflection from the emotional to the intellectual sphere, when the therapist seemingly feels hopeless about the efficacy of reflection and turns to reasoning and argument. I wished he had bluntly expressed his irritation. It might have given him a more secure, less rigid stance, and might have improved his contact with the patient.

Bergman's tone is essentially negative. For Bergman, a very sick patient, rigid and recalcitrant in disposition, is treated by a therapist who is inhibited and inconsistent in approach. The interaction between therapist and patient is never really helpful for the patient. The thera-pist is frustrated and never trusts himself to be free in the relationship; the patient, consequently, never comes to trust the therapeutic relation-ship.

Let us attempt a rather formal summary of Bergman's reactions and clinical analysis, employing his language where possible. Some of the many messages of this rigid and recalcitrant patient are received by the therapist. The therapist strains to reflect these messages and some of these reflections are received by the patient, but with minimal positive impact upon the patient. Failing with some reflections, the therapist defers to the intellectual sphere of reasoning and argument and never really reaches the patient with words which "seem to have acquired too negative a meaning on the patient's part to be a suitable bridge for the relationship." The patient, in Bergman's judgment, shows no discerni-ble improvement.

Bergman's impressions provide a useful contrast with those of the other theorists, who discern positive movement, however minimal. While Bergman feels that the therapist, finding his reflections of limited effectiveness, deflects to persuasion and argument, English sees the therapist's initial attempt as being to "mastermind" the patient and this having failed, the therapist reverts to reflection of feeling and actually *succeeds* in helping the patient. Thus, the two major phases described by Bergman and English seem to be similar but in reverse order and lead to differences in judgments of success.

English

Although English, an eclectic yet dynamically oriented psychiatrist, compliments the therapist's initial understandings of the patient's feelings of loneliness and worthlessness and his "safely permissive" remarks and "friendly, relaxing" attitudes, English becomes immediately disgruntled with the therapist's "awkward guesses" aimed at constructing the world of the patient. "He is trying to mastermind the patient too much. He is assuming he knows the patient's mental construction and feeds him the words . . . In all this, he seems to be trying to carry the patient's thinking, rather than using a questioning technique that would help expose the patient to himself and the therapist."

English acknowledges that the therapist goes on to become helpful on occasion in enabling the patient by reflection to see and feel his experiences. This is not without *some* reservations:

. . . the therapist seems to be agreeing too much with the patient's mood in words of, "Yes, you are lonely, aren't you. No one cares about you and you don't give a damn about anything either." It is admittedly an important part of psychotherapy to help the patient to see and feel his sadness and despair. But, in this case it seems as if the therapist works too hard at this theme and ignores possibilities of other insights . . . In summary, the therapist seems to close off the possibility of exploring why the patient's negative concepts make him so sad and depressed. He never opens up the opportunity for an historical exploration as to the reasons for depressed moods and hopelessness.

English also points to the therapist's "warm, personal interest [which] tends to force the patient to make good his positive intentions." He concludes on a somewhat positive note:

Therapist begins with a speech a little over-long for patients generally, but he does point up the patient's ambivalence about going out in the world and functioning constructively or staying in the hospital. There is a discussion of two different worlds, neither of which either patient or therapist have clarified but which each assumes he understands. I did not get much of a picture of the patient's inner world or outer world from the tape or script. But this is one of the therapist's ways of constructing psychotherapy (every psychotherapist has them) and so we go along with this mode of expression even though it is not clear. But, patient and therapist seem in better rapport. Patient is planning to undertake activity and he indicates that he feels understood and supported by the therapist. Movement is positive in the last excerpt and the therapist has achieved a helpful position.

Lewis

Lewis, a psychoanalyst, has many questions to ask about the sampling method: the sampling method affords a glimpse into the atmosphere of the treatment relationship, but gives one hardly any idea of whether treatment has really begun, is half finished, or is successfully completed.

By way of introduction, Lewis offers these remarks:

The first impression I had on listening to the tapes was that something had indeed happened in the period of treatment which was discernible immediately, allowing for some ups and downs in the patient's mood, in his relation to the therapist, etc. One gets a general impression of more spontaneity, better contact, more communicativeness with each of the tapes as the treatment progresses. At some point in each one of the cases, material of some more than superficial emotional significance is touched upon. The patients appear to relax into some kind of therapeutic relationship. They seem less defensive, less tied to concrete reality, more inclined to talk about their feelings, their relationships with significant persons in their lives, etc. The problem in assessing this first impression is the degree of change shown. Is this the sort of "warming up" that one observes in an initial prolonged interview with a very sick patient, who is able to come off his defensive hostility, suspiciousness, guardedness, etc.; or does it signal an important change in the level of functioning of these individuals such as one sees after a long, intensive, therapeutic experience of the sort with which I am most familiar? Is it 3 per cent or 97 per cent?

Concerning all of the therapists in general, Lewis hastens to add:

The style of the therapist varies markedly also—to a degree quite surprising to me, since I had assumed that the simplicity of the client-centered method would tend to level out individual differences more than it does. There are marked similarities; it is certainly a familiar observation to anyone who has been around a large center of training that the junior members of the group tend to imitate the teachers and to copy automatically the smallest mannerisms of those they admire and respect and with whom they wish to be identified. . . . I suppose this is neither good nor bad if the patient does not interpret these engrafted mannerisms as engrafted mannerisms but rather as a genuine part of the therapist's equipment. However, some aspects of the . . . therapists' styles seem to me artificial and stereotyped and hence not representative of their "natural" selves.

Lewis concludes his introduction by suggesting:

[The client-centered method] . . . at one magnificent cut of the Gordian knot, abolishes most of the intricacies and stubborn sticky immobilities that one runs into in the treatment of schizophrenics or borderline schizophrenics. I am quite sure that anyone would welcome such a simplification if it worked. The question being asked the commentators is, *"Does it work* to limit one's scope so radically?" I don't know, and the reason that I don't know is because the material relevant to the question is simply not to be heard. The net impression given by these tapes is disappointing.

Turning to the case of Brown in particular, Lewis sees the patient as "a tortured man whose anguished sobs come through, whose utter despair is easy to sense and whose cycles of very tentative hopefulness alternate with the blackest gloom." Lewis goes on to suggest that those messages of the patient which the therapist receives appear to be reflected only minimally and with little impact upon the patient. At this point, the therapist actively reaches out: "[The therapist] . . . is more apt to express his own personal reactions to the patient rather than to reflect exclusively the patient's reactions. He does a great deal of active reaching and musing in an attempt to satisfy, I suppose, this patient's desperate need for some kind of closeness and dependency."

That the patient "is poignantly aware of the therapist's attempts to reach him, is apparent." However, it is clear that Lewis is dissatisfied with the overall adjustment of the patient and would concede only minimal, if any, improvement: "Though it is evident from what he says about his external life, that there has been improvement . . . , these cycles [of hopefulness and gloom] tend to go on right up to the very end without much evidence that I detect in the tape that the patient is feeling more free of suffering."

May

Whereas, the other evaluators emphasize differences between the three therapists, May, an existential analyst and theorist, views the process of client-centered treatment as being quite similar in the cases of Brown, Jones, and Smith. His introductory comments are generalized to all three cases:

Some indications of postive movement, in my judgement, are the following: Patient and therapist communicate more openly in later sessions; patient seems to talk more about his problems (and less about why he is in the hospital); the anxiety of the patient has not lessened—indeed, it may be increased—in the segments toward the end, but focuses more on the real problems.

For example, in the case of Brown, the patient comes to focus on getting a job or going to school.

Concerning *helpful* therapist activity, May again generalizes:

All three therapists show a genuine interest in the patients, a desire to listen and to hear (which are not the same thing) the patients' communications, and a clear desire to help. There is no doubt that the therapist cared about the patient and his welfare as a "self," which I am convinced all three patients sensed and appreciated. . . . The curative element rests, in the last analysis, on the genuine interest and concern shown in the relationship which give the patient his human world, communicated to the patient in terms that do not force him into the therapist's own world in terms of standards of health, social adjustment, etc. It could well be that for each of these patients it was the first time any human being was ever devoted to his welfare over a period of time. Using these tapes as a basis for judgment, it is indicated that the client-centered approach does give the therapist the dedication to the patient, and the skill and sensitivity necessary to hear the patient without forcing him into a preconceived mold.

With Brown in particular, May sees the therapist's loaning Brown money without insisting that it be accepted as a very minor but clear symbol of the therapist's genuine interest and concern for the patient's welfare. In addition, May notes the frank humility of the therapist who says to Brown, "I don't feel I've been of much help today," and, "Often I wish I was better at guessing," and asks the patient whether he prefers the therapist to jog him or keep still. May continues:

In answering the third question, "What is the therapist doing which is *not* helpful?" I come to the more concrete and controversial side of my reactions. I shall deal here with the predominant technique used throughout the sessions by all three therapists, namely that of reflecting back the communication to the patient . . . It is safe to say that the major part of the responses are of this sort. I am aware that the aim of such responses is to reflect the feelings of the patient. But I found myself when first listening in each tape to this reflecting of communication, feeling mildly irritated and offended, and later on not so mildly. I was aware within myself of the vague impression that the therapist was mimicking the patient (though I knew that was not at all what the therapist intended) or implying that the patient hadn't said it well (though in almost every instance, for the obvious reason that the patient is on the inside of the experience, the patient says it better).

But my major criticism of this technique is on a different basis. Despite its purpose, I felt that reflecting the feelings of the patient was precisely what the technique does not do. By and large the therapist reflects the words of the patient, not his feelings; words *about* feelings rather than the experiences themselves. We see this in the examples . . . when the therapist in effect repeats the patient's sentence, only substituting a synonym like "an animal" for the patient's word "dogs," and like the phrase "do away with myself" for the patient's "kill myself." (Note that the patient's words are more graphic, alive, penetrating.) Also the therapist very often reflects the projected *action* of the patient rather than feeling: "killing myself" rather than the deep despair, discouragement, or rage and resentment such as this act could convey.

May also emphasizes that "when the therapists do respond on the level of feelings, the range of affects picked up and dealt with is definitely limited." Seldom are the negative emotions of anger, aggression, hostility, and basic conflicts, especially those involving childhood relationships, reflected. Thus, when Brown tells of trying to see the woman physician at the hospital when he felt sick, but "that ole shit" wouldn't see him, the therapist reflects it as a feeling that "nobody cares":

The patient then goes on to talk of killing himself; the therapist reflects, "Guess that must make you feel, 'Boy am I ever alone?'" and responds when the patient says he can't talk to that doctor, there "is no such thing as . . . communication between people who hold different values." This seems to me an intellectualized reaction to the patient's real and pervasive rage and resentment toward "that ole shit" and probably other doctors, therapists and the world to boot.

Further, May is distressed with the therapist's over-identification with patient, something which seems to "take away the patient's opportunity to experience himself as a subject in his own right, to take a stand against the therapist, to experience being in an interpersonal world (I sometimes got the feeling there were not two people in the room)." To summarize, much of the potential dynamic of the relationship with the therapist is absent: "I think the lack of this dynamic of interpersonal relationships is a consequence of a misuse of the 'reflecting' technique, so that we get only an amorphous kind of identity rather than two subjects interacting in a world in which both participate, and in which love and hate, trust and doubt, conflicts and dependency, come out and can be understood and assimilated." May sees the effective and truly therapeutic moments in all three cases as those when the therapist did not merely reflect the patient but himself *added* something which came "out of his own subjective state, his own identity as one person in the relationship."

For May, the last paragraph from the excerpts of the case of Brown is particularly touching. When the patient is lonely and baffled by the "two worlds" now outside the hospital, the therapist responds, "I'd like to come into that inside world with you."

May's conclusion is positive—with some reservations:

My overall judgment, as stated at the outset, is that this is definitely good therapy, that the patients . . . are clearly moving in a positive direction, and that progress is traceable to specific things in the therapist, particularly in his *attitude* . . . This attitude toward therapy . . . is in my judgment more critical for the patient's progress than any technique as such. The harmful effects of the air of going along on the surface in some of the sessions, being two-dimensional, are avoided to a considerable extent by the fact that there is nothing whatever superficial about the therapist's concern for the patient; the patients were taken with complete seriousness, and they knew it. This is what has the profoundly powerful effect upon the other person. My belief, nevertheless, is obviously that the therapy would go along better, effect change on a deeper and more lasting level, if the underlying feelings, including the negative aggressive ones, were brought out and experienced directly in the relationship between patient and therapist.

For May, the case of Brown (as well as the cases of Jones and Smith) can be summarized by saying that those, "graphically alive and penetrating" messages of the patient which are received by the therapists are handled primarily in two ways: on the one hand, the therapist's tendency to reflect the patient's words and projected actions rather than the feelings behind the messages achieves minimal or even possibly negative effect in the patient; on the other hand, even when the therapist does reflect feelings he does so within an extremely limited range of affects and therefore, the impact upon the patient is extremely limited. What in the final analysis helps to achieve in the patient a greater capacity for relatedness and a shift from the symptoms of apathy and resignation to overt anxiety with a focus on problems is the communication by the therapist of his interest, concern, and dedication to helping the patient. The therapist actually gives of himself at times, rising above the over-identification implicit, for May, in the technique of reflecting as it is employed in these cases. This is positive movement for May.

Seeman

Seeman, a client-centered psychotherapist, presents a highly positive summary:

The case of Brown seemed to be one in which there was a long plateau and then a quick upward thrust late in therapy. The quality of the process in the patient took a quick initial turn from symptom to self. It then seemed to level off until Excerpt 8, where there was some evidence that Brown could feel concern for someone else.

The more emphatic change seemed to come at about Excerpt 12. In that excerpt I sensed more immediacy and outward drive; the focus changed from withdrawal to a more determined energy output. However, until the end there was a kind of ambivalence in Brown, a pushing out but also a feeling that the world was a hard place in which to cope.

The process in the therapist seemed to change at roughly the same time as that in the patient. [The therapist] seemed aware and sensitive . . . Starting about two-thirds of the way through therapy, there was a progressive deepening of personal involvement, which was expressed both in more sensitive moment-to-moment understanding and in acts of caring. The final excerpts indicated most clearly the attitude, "I'm with you and I want to do things to help."

Summarizing, the therapist is aware and sensitive throughout therapy and thus receives most of the patient's messages. The therapist expresses sensitive moment-to-moment understanding in his reflections of the patient's feelings. These reflections have a major impact upon the patient in helping him to explore himself. In addition, the therapist exhibits an attitude of personal involvement and acts of caring which communicate to the patient the feeling that the therapist is with him and wants very much to help. Thus, the patient is able to move from withdrawal and his other early symptomatic concerns to the self-concern and interpersonal exploration which culminates in a more determined energy output in conjunction with a deep concern for the therapist. While the patient continues to be ambivalent about facing the hard, cold world, it is clear that Seeman is impressed with the efficacy of the treatment process.

Whitaker

Whitaker, a promulgator of a dynamic relationship-centered analytic therapy, first introduces the reader to his view of the necessary conditions of an adequate therapeutic experience as he perceives them in relation to Brown:

In listening to the tapes, the therapeutic conditions which I think of as necessary for adequate experience on the part of the patient seemed to be well fulfilled. There is an isolation of the therapeutic experience, there is an absence of teaching, an absence of technical jargon. Furthermore, there seems to be a fair degree of functional clarity in the process that is taking place and a firm, maybe too firm, administrative structure. The character of the transference seems to begin in a competitive sibling pattern as is usual and it seems possible in most situations for the development of dependence and regression to a pre-verbal experience which we think is necessary.

Concerning the activities of the therapist in general, Whitaker suggests:

There seems to be some real question about the degree of involvement on the part of the therapist unless one were to consider his careful discipline of himself as a kind of involvement. I also questioned the degree of professional reality behind the functioning of the therapist. Is he trying to carry out a pattern rather than function as a person in a professional framework? The process and the movement within the therapy sometimes seemed like a bilateral unreality which I think of as helpful, but at other times I felt self-doubt on the part of the therapist and a confusion for which he compensated by using a technical response. Many times the reciprocal equilibrium within the relationship was upset by one or the other person and re-established at a new and higher level. We think this is necessary for psychotherapy, but many times the process appeared to have no breakthrough. It looked like a formal interchange with none of the "eureka" quality sometimes called insight.

Whitaker continues:

On the positive side, one gets a very strange sense of the patient developing an enjoyment of his own separateness (aloneness) and a gradual change away from being lonely. At times I wondered, Was this actually taking place or was the therapist by his example teaching the patient to adjust to life by becoming uninvolved. I became convinced that part of what was going on therapeutically consisted of the patient being forced to put himself into his words, and to face the fact that the therapist was trying to not put himself into words, and I wondered how much of the therapeutic process consisted in the contrast between these two.

In the case of Brown in particular, Whitaker was "impressed by the psychodrama quality of what goes on—the therapist functioning as an alter ego to the patient, his repeated use of stereotyped phrases indicating reassurance, encouragement to go on and quite deliberately stimulating the patient to a 'why' type investigation":

The reflection done by the therapist in this setting is similar to the psychoanalytic pattern. It's as though the therapist were trying by the quality of his verbal retort to get the patient to go behind the patient in the same way the analyst does by positioning his chair. There is an apparent lack of feeling in the reflecting quality of the therapist's reverbalization. Is the therapist protecting himself from over-involvement by not even using separate words from those of the patient? Is he bent upon a complete denial of himself in the interest of the patient?

Whitaker proceeds to elaborate upon what might be labeled a process of "confirmation without commitment" on the part of the therapist: a kind of consensual validation wherein the patient's evaluation of himself is expressed for him by the therapist in "first person, singular" language.

After acknowledging that during the last third of therapy the therapist finally seems "to break his vow and use his third ear," even developing real personal affect and actually expressing his own opinions, Whitaker searches for an adequate capsulation of the process:

. . . I got the impression that the therapist talking in the first person produces a kind of identification between the two of them that brings about what seems almost a *bilateral oral incorporation*. The closeness is obvious by the rapt attention of the therapist in his effort to reflect the patient's verbal formulation on the level of the therapist's own inner experience of the communication. Obviously, the therapist must be responding to much more than words. His involvement reflects this. The person of the therapist is not easily sensed by the listener but many times when the therapist talks back in the first person, it is obvious that the therapist's inner experience is very co-ordinate with the patient's inner experience. In this framework, their joint affect originates in the patient. The therapist suffers, but tolerates the pain. This willingness to experience the pain which the patient has not been able to tolerate tends to make the patient experience his affect and not try to avoid it to the same degree that he has on previous occasions.

The therapy becomes, for Whitaker, an unusual kind of ego-strength-ening process:

If the patient struggles to differentiate the "I" and "not I" then the therapist, in this bilateral incorporation, because he is symbolically involved with the patient and simultaneously able to control the in and out of his own ego boundaries, offers the patient an experience in breaking and repairing ego boundaries in the framework of verbal language. To say it in my words, the patient discovers he can be crazy inside and social outside and enjoy that too.

In summary, Whitaker acknowledges that progress has taken place, but not without again expressing the ambivalence which he has already made explicit throughout his critique:

As in all therapy, I must insist that even in client-centered therapy, the dynamics of the relationship are determined by the therapist even though the patient is the only one who appears above water. The process seems to repeatedly involve the therapist taking what the patient says and spreading it, that is, making a generalization, an abstraction and deducing from it, or adding to it, or personalizing it, or even questioning it, in a tone of voice which interprets the two. The patient thereby becomes tense and anxious and at one point talks of killing himself and does so in the sense of withdrawing and after that comes to fear the real behavior as he had previously feared the impulse. This I cannot explain on any other basis than a real therapeutic change. It makes me say again that the therapist does understand the disease and he conveys this to the patient, even though it's difficult for me to understand the conveyance.

Summarizing, then, a strong therapist, disciplined in self-denial, is attuned to many of the communications of a patient who feels lost and alone. However, the therapist handles the communications in different ways. On the one hand, "the therapist in his effort to reflect the patient's verbal formulation on the level of the therapist's own inner experience of the communication" displays an intense closeness in his rapt attention. Because the therapist suffers for the patient's pain yet is willing to experience this suffering, the patient is better able to experience previously intolerable affect. While Whitaker is not sure he really understands the conveyance, the therapist's ability to impart his understanding of the patient's disturbance is an effective therapeutic ingredient.

Even in the context of those joint affects originating in the patient, the therapist maintains and communicates an ability to break out of his own ego boundaries. The patient, consequently, is able to verbally experience a breaking and repairing of his own ego boundaries.

On the other hand, due perhaps to the therapist's persistent self-denial, many of the therapist's attempted reflections lack feeling and communicate a kind of detachment from life and its many conflicts. This therapist detachment, whether the motive be conscious or unconscious on his part, is to be distinguished from the therapist's "rapt attention" involved in achieving the "bilateral inner experience" of the patient. It is in this sense that the therapist becomes an alter ego. The detachment would seem to mean a lack of involvement as a real *second* person in the relationship. In a strange twist of what would be viewed by many as an undesirable therapist characteristic, the patient appears to benefit and become less intensely and pathologically involved with many of life's exigencies.

To recapitulate, the therapist's (*a*) communication of his coordinate inner experiences and understanding of the patient's psychopathology, and (*b*) exploitation of the apparent permeability of his own ego boundaries, and (*c*) maintenance of some detachment and self-denial, seem to converge efficaciously in a process in which the patient adjusts to his aloneness and gradually changes away from being lonely. A strengthened ego in greater contact with—but less intensely agonized by—his inner and his social self is beginning to emerge in the patient.

A Critique of the Case of Brown

The case of Brown is a useful point of departure in the study of the client-centered process with schizophrenics. In spite of the many handicaps involved, this representative client-centered case has served to generate formulations from a variety of different orientations describing the therapeutic process in client-centered therapy. While the difficulties inherent in the random selection of brief excerpts of psychotherapy may at times confound and even compound the differences, it may be that the differences would be even more profound than they are here portrayed if the theorists had the time and energy to observe the complete case.

Most interesting, perhaps, are the wide deviations in the evaluations of the primary question: (1) What movement, if any, occurs? At the one extreme, Bergman and Lewis, both of whom are analytically oriented, discern little or no progress in therapy for a very sick and despairing patient. At the other extreme, Seeman, a client-centered theorist, sees great and consistent movement in therapy, culminating in the patient's determined energy output.

In the middle ranges, English recognizes moderate patient gain from the process of feeling increasingly understood, supported, and in becoming action orientated. Concerning movement, May says: "Yes, but . . ." He sees positive movement in a formerly desperate but apathetic patient's greater capacity for relatedness and problem solving but hastens to add that more effective therapy and deeper and more lasting patient personality change might have occurred if the underlying feelings had been brought out and experienced directly. Whitaker acknowledges the patient's gradual changing away from aloneness which implies some growing ego strength. However, he professes a lack of real understanding of how the therapist makes the process happen.

In summary, then, two theorists see little or no progress while the four others perceive varying degrees of positive movement. In considering what makes for these differential evaluations, we might turn to the critical questions aimed at explicating the client-centered therapeutic process with schizophrenics: (2) What is the therapist doing that is helpful?, and (3) What is the therapist doing that is not helpful? An exploration of these facilitative and retarding conditions of therapeutic growth leads us to look at what has been posited by these various theorists as going on both within the therapist (as well as the patient) and between therapist and patient.

With the exception of Seeman all theorists take note of certain limitations and inflexibilities in the therapist, at least initially. However, May, Whitaker, and possibly English acknowledge some degree of therapist growth, primarily in terms of the therapist's somehow freeing himself within therapy. Again, Bergman and Lewis stand together, holding that the therapist's inflexibility dominates therapy.

It is clear that all theorists feel that when the therapist is rigid and inhibited his approach is not helpful. However, it is equally clear that rigidity does not have the same meaning for all clinical commentators. This was noted strikingly in the contrasting evaluations of therapist rigidity by Bergman and by English and, as should become increasingly clear to the reader, in the consideration of the critical interactions between therapist and patient. At only one point is this seeming deficit possibly seen as a potential asset: Whitaker's suggestion is that the therapist's persistent self-denial is communicated as a kind of detached attitude toward life and its mischances, and that "the therapist by his example [was] teaching the patient to adjust to life by becoming uninvolved."

On the positive side, the communication of the progressive freeing and deepening of *personal* involvement is seen by May, Seeman, Whitaker, and possibly English as a significant source of the patient's constructive personality change.

Again, in attempting to evaluate the meaning of the interaction between therapist and patient, there is disparity in the interpretations of effective and ineffective modes of accomplishing therapeutic personality change. Thus, while all theorists refer to the therapist's ability to reflect elements of the patient's self (and therefore, implicitly, communication of empathic understanding) they do not agree on either the context or the effectiveness of the role of reflection in the case of Brown.

Seeman, Whitaker, and English perceive the role of reflection, alone and in combination with other ingredients, as having had major impact upon the patient's self-understanding and adjustment. For varying reasons, Bergman, Lewis, and May emphasize the essential ineffectiveness of reflection as employed in the case of Brown. At one end, the reflection by the therapist of his coordinate inner experiences and his understanding of the patient's conflicts represents for Whitaker one of the conditions converging to affect the patient's adjustment to, and changing away from, his feelings of being alone in the world. Whitaker does, however, note that some of the therapist's attempted reflections lack feeling and actually connote a lack of involvement.

At another end, May feels that reflection fails because, on the one hand, only the words and the projected actions of the patient are reflected. Indeed, May even suggests that the therapist, however unintentionally, seemed to be "mimicking the patient" or "implying that the patient hadn't said it well (though in almost every instance, for the obvious reason that the patient is on the inside of the experience, the patient says it better)." Even when feelings are appropriately reflected, May sees the feelings as being within an extremely limited range of affects and the reflections, then, being of limited effect.

There are at least some constant threads running through many of the formulations. Reflection is frequently seen as occurring within a limited range of affects: the therapist thus selectively responds to only certain feelings and selectively fails to respond to other feelings. May and English, especially, stress the closing off of the possibility of exploring more negative emotions in the patient.

There is substantial concern with the notion that the therapist in his reflections is following some kind of model of what therapy should be. In many cases, this concern is related to the feeling that the therapist is rigid in approach. Whitaker bluntly asks: "Is the therapist trying to carry out a pattern rather than to function as a person in a professional framework?" Lewis concerns himself with what he terms "engrafted mannerisms" which he feels are not a genuine part of the therapist's equipment.

Of significance as an effective ingredient of therapeutic personality change is the role of the therapist's communication of certain attitudes. In the formulations of English, May, and Seeman a form of "therapeutic dedication" is a critical ingredient of effective psychotherapy. For May, the interest, concern, and dedication, in conjunction with the therapist's actions in "giving of himself" is the most significant process variable. For English and Seeman the therapist's warmth and involvement as expressed in acts of caring converge with reflection as the effective therapeutic ingredients. English actually suggests that the therapist's "warm and personal interest tends to force the patient to make good his positive intentions."

While Lewis acknowledges the therapist's attempts to reach out to the patient, he sees these attempts as personal reactions and musings, which, while they seem to offer some potential, never really produce anything more than the patient's beginning awareness of attempts to reach him.

Again, only Whitaker gives express treatment to the therapist's lack of involvement as a real second person in the relationship. While this stands in apparent contradistinction to the therapist warmth and intimacy underscored by English, May, and Seeman, Whitaker, himself, distinguishes this detachment from the therapist's "rapt attention" in accomplishing joint inner experiences with the patient.

The case of Brown does give rise to heuristic discussion from a variety of different viewpoints. Four of the theorists recognize some degree of movement while two do not. For those who discern no progress, this lack of movement seems tied to the essential ineffectiveness of the therapist's attempts toward reflection of feelings. For those who see therapeutic movement, and constructive personality change in the patient, two elements alone and in combination emerge most frequently as basic ingredients of their formulations of therapeutic personality change: (1) the therapist's effective reflection of feelings and communication of understanding, and (2) an attitudinal quality involving especially the therapist's warm and personal dedication.

In summary, then, the elements which emerge, alone and in their different combinations, often vary in their context, sometimes in their order, and usually in their emphasis. At the same time, it is clear that there *are* some common threads running through the formulations of outside clinicians and theorists.

The Case of Jones[4]

The case of Joseph Jones covered 47 interviews with a young male schizophrenic who had been hospitalized for less than eight months when psychotherapy was initiated. Following are the excerpts:

Excerpt 1

T: . . . as a result of it, this complaint or charge whatever it was but only for observation, from there on in the hospital.

C: Right, yes.

T: They gave you some tests then.

C: However, I understood that they weren't using that alone. It was combined and they were taking everything that was involved in my case before they decided.

T: Uh-huh. Yeah.

C: But if those tests, if they regard those tests as favorable I don't see how they could have kept me here.

T: Mmm.

C: At least I don't think, I don't think they would have.

T: Yeah — from your end at least the biggest kind of objective evidence that they have would be the testing.

C: Well, what they had before was the testimony of certain people and course the fact of the matter is that I wasn't allowed to testify in my own behalf at all but whatever they said, it didn't, wasn't proving anything. The note that I wrote was, did, did not contain any words that would incriminate me in any way, anda, so, kinda tests as you say constitute a tangible thing that you got in front of you that says this guy is, is either well or sick as his case may be.

T: Mmm.

C: Anda, but I understood that they were correlating the circumstances of the case with that test. That's why, that's the way I understood it.

T: M-hmm — mmm. So what they said anyway is that they took the testing along with everything else they could learn about you.

C: Yes, and they sorta drew a parallel between what the tests indicated and what their other evidence indicated.

T: Mmm — mmm.

C: They saw similarities or [*T:* Mmm — mmm] some, something similar, a, similar indication in both.

T: So that after the initial observation period was over then the hospital stepped in and said, well on the basis of this evidence that we consider as evidence anyway, we're going to keep you.

C: Yeah.

T: And here you are. Let's get back for a minute to something you said

4. In our research code, this is the case of SOC.

earlier on ah, ah first of all, I'm a psychiatrist ordinarily, not a psychologist.

C: You aren't a psychologist. I, I assumed, I, I thought it was, I figured this is, this as a psycho —

T: Yeah.

C: A psychology department here.

T: Yeah. I'm the only psychiatrist working in this outfit, ah —

C: However, perhaps you can still give me some idea.

T: Yeah, and I didn't mean to dodge that, I, ah, I don't know how much value is placed on psychological testing here.

C: Perhaps different values in different places by different people.

T: That's, that's been my experience.

C: Yeah, I think that would be understandable — However, I say that either, either ah, I, I'm, I, I say that they read the other ones wrong, what they, they read the indications wrong or else, anda like I said you can, I simply say that those tests don't prove anything.

T: M-hmm — I didn't catch a couple of things in there. One of them says, "God damn it, they did it wrong, I know me, they don't, and here they have all this crap over here and they say I'm sick when I know damn well I'm not." But I guess that right along with those answers are, are a kind of deep puzzlement saying, "Well really, what the hell is going on around here? Just what is going on with me? Do they, do they have something? I don't think so but — I don't know."

Excerpt 2

C: Yes, it's the attitude you take of me immediately more like you might think, might take for a person who's sick. Well, the attitude, I should say that the attitude of yours should be of me is, is the attitude you might very well take of a mental patient from there on. That's the way I see it.

T: So that you —

C: I, I don't see how you can assume that a normal person or at least a person, well, mature or normal or —

T: I see.

C: I mean I don't see how you can attribute that to a guy that you were sitting with just like yourself.

T: "I mean normal." See if this gets it, ah, are you saying to me, "Now you wouldn't act this way with someone who wasn't, who you didn't consider a mental patient or would you?"

C: Say a friend of yours.

T: Yeah. So you're saying to me, "You wouldn't talk like this to a friend or a relative, would you?"

C: I don't think you would. I don't think you would attribute that answer to a friend or relative.

T: Uh-huh. And, and tied on to that for you is ah, "The only possible people who would talk like you're talking is someone with, who thought himself to be an authority and other people to be patients or have ah, inappropriate ideas or feelings that should be discounted." That's right — say ah, I talk to my friends and relatives the same way I talk to you. I, I don't think I see them quite as you think I see them. The person you're seeing here now is the same guy that goes out and talks to other people too in the University. This is me.

C: Well —

T: I, I'm, correct me if I'm wrong. Isn't what you were saying, just kind of saying, "You're being false with me, Buster."

C: Well, whether or not you treat anybody else differently I don't know, but I still say that you're checking in me what isn't there.

T: Mmm — the important thing for you is that it seems that I look on you as though you have your own character traits that aren't there and as you say, "I'm not belligerent, I'm not hostile, I'm not isolated, I'm not a mental patient and you think I am all these things."

C: [*coughs*] Yep. 'Bout it. Course I can understand one thing for sure. I can understand uh, why you would, would, would not just, just assume that I was normal. Since I am in this place it's only natural for you to assume just the opposite. Ah I, I can understand that.

T: Mmm.

C: Fact it'd be to me, I suppose it'd really be strange if you really, if you were to assume I was normal.

T: Mmm.

C: 'Cause that would, that would, that would be what you, what you would ordinarily . . . .

Excerpt 3

T: I see.

C: I don't know whether, I don't know whether Shaw was thinking of something along the line of, of ah just purely intellectualism.

T: [Inaudible.]

C: I doubt whether he was thinking of that. I think he was thinking of artistic [*T:* Mmm — mmm] inspirations. You know how, how, how women would make a poet just go off in the skies.

T: Mmm — mmm.

C: You know, get real, real romantic and write all kinds of flowery things and so forth.

T: Can send him.

C: Yeah, I ah, course that, that's true of composers. They, they get real inspired and get terrifically uh, worked up by some woman and that just causes them to be so, so inspired that they write something real, real outstanding.

T: Mmm.

C: Anda, well I mean, you know just like I said the only difference that I can see between Shaw was referring as using a woman for his own ends rather than for her ends.

T: Mmm — mmm.

C: You see, his, his mental ends rather than her physical ends.

T: Mmm.

C: Ah, if you put it that way.

T: Mmm.

C: In other words, in other words the only difference I can see between his, what he was talking about and what I, what I'm saying is that, is that mine was more purely intellectual and I don't think he was thinking that kind of thing.

T: Mmm — mmm.

C: But it is the same insofar as it's just a purely, ah inspirational thing rather and it has no real physical reality of any kind, really.

T: M-hmm.

C: It's purely, purely a mental thing.

T: See if I get that. Ah, part of the uniqueness of this relationship or feeling that you had was not so much that you wanted her for her sake and her physical sake as well as her spiritual sake but because you wanted her for your sake or you needed her for your sake as a stimulant or inspiration of some kind.

C: It just, it just happened that way. I, I don't say that I consciously ah, wanted, you know wanted to [*T:* I see] use her in that way.

T: Mmm.

C: It happened that way. In, in the very, in the very beginning you see it was purely a romantic thing.

T: M-hmm.

C: But then as time went along more and more it became, it became less and less romantic and more and more just pure thinking.

T: M-hmm. Mmm.

C: As time went on I, I would say almost in great proportion to the time that, to the amount of time that passed.

T: M-hmm. M-hmm.

C: Amounted to the intellectual end of it.

T: But really there was a real kind of wanting her —

C: Yes.

T: For her sake, ah wanting to —

C: Just her.

T: Your need for her, then at times increased as you saw her over a period. That decided then that ah, stimulation to your own intellect grew.

C: That's right.

T: And, and you needed her for that rather than anything else.

C: Yes that it what is was — in other words, instead of, ah — gosh, well in a way it was, it was you know a revelation sort of.

T: Mmm.

C: Ah, only it wasn't the kind, it wasn't a revelation by, by I, means of ah, religious prophet or something like that you'd say, revelation from God. Well, to me it was revelation by means of her. Not from her because you know it isn't that way.

T: M-hmm. M-hmm.

C: She didn't tell me anything, or reveal any knowledge to me.

Excerpt 4

T: . . . get out of here. It seems that is simple.

C: Yeah, but I think ah, whatever they call it, I guess — reminds me of that little sign over there in the board room ah, cooperation and planning which you and I did together did something for me; well this is not quite the same but it's ah, a plan which the doctors and patients get together to do what the doctors want.

T: Mmm.

C: And — [*laughs*]

T: M-hmm. "As a patient I don't really have too many rights."

C: Nope.

T: "Not much freedom at all."

C: How do you feel about that? Do you think patients ah, should have any rights or do you think that the, that the status they have is what, without, without, will always prevail? Perhaps you would ra — not want to express an opinion, but I just wondered because I've been kind of talking, talking about this.

T: Yeah, I think you sensed probably that I don't hold to that feeling too much, to me the patient —

C: I don't think you hold the same feeling as I feel, as I have.

T: No. Well what, that is, I mean from my end, I've never worked in a state hospital. I don't —

C: Oh yes, that's right, yeah.

T: I've always been in a much smaller unit where ah, the patients were looked on differently than ah, from what you describe.

C: Yeah — [*clears throat*] S'pose you can't really answer that.

T: Well that's kind of a loaded question too.

C: It's what?

T: It's a loaded question —

C: Yes, I suppose it is, 'cause what, whatever you answer why, well if you answer not the way I want why —

T: M-hmm. I think I can come a little closer to it; I certainly don't want to feel, feel I'm dodging that. I would feel that's the reason, feel that way myself ah, well as you know, I feel that you as ah, well, in terms of thinking of you as my patient in a way ah, have a good many rights.

C: I have a good many rights?

T: M-hmmm. At least in terms of our relationship.

C: Yeah well, probably not the right just to walk out.

T: Yeah. [*Patient laughs.*] You have the right to walk out but I have the right to follow you.

C: [*laughs*] Well, see there you are, we have every right, but I might not want it.

T: Mmm — "And even here I don't have the kind of freedom that I want for myself and hope to have eventually."

C: Well, I don't think I do — Perhaps you have no idea that the thought of, I mean I've already answered that question I asked, you have to think about it. Er, you have to study the thing yourself somewhat.

T: Does it seem I haven't answered it yet, Joe?

C: I don't think you've answered it.

T: O.K.

C: I don't think you've said it in your own, given me a direct answer, yes or no, ah —

T: But I'm not sure that I got the question.

C: I just asked you whether, whether, whether ah, you thought that the status that I described as the patient as having and has very little or almost no rights, is, is, is the status that you think is proper for a patient to have or whether you think a patient should have more rights?

Excerpt 5

C: Maybe I'll feel better tonight — It's hard to get out of the habit once you've gotten into it — Maybe it's my own fault because after all couple months ago I was getting to sleep a lot earlier, then I started in gradually not getting to bed as early. I, I got started going to bed later and later and later and started sleeping in the morning and made up for it and that's what, what happened.

T: M-hmm. M-hmm — sort of crept up on you.

C: It's my own — indifferent attitude I guess —

T: Mmm.

C: And on top of that I haven't been eating breakfast. Last three or four days.

T: M-hmm.

C: Don't even get up in time for breakfast. [*coughs*] Can't figure out why. Seems as though I'm not, I'm not taking ah, feeding me, not taking the trouble to wake me up anymore.

T: M-hmm. M-hmm.

C: Mean I get, get, find myself getting in late and wonder how it got so late anda seems to me that they, if they, they really got me up I wouldn't, I wouldn't, I wouldn't be in bed that late. They don't seem to care what time I get up.

T: Almost, in effect you're saying, "Here I am kind of falling into, what I see as a bad habit by myself and I can't control it, or haven't been controlling it and nobody else is really interested enough to try to help me."

C: I don't know if, if the situation is changed over there.

T: M-hmm.

C: Used to be they, they ah, really they, really meant it ah, now they don't seem to do it.

T: Does it seem, Joe, that they've almost given up on you? [Inaudible.]

C: Huh?

T: Does it come through as feeling, "Well, they've given up on me?"

C: I don't know, I really don't know. Maybe they figure I'll miss breakfast couple times and I'll learn my lesson and I'll get up earlier. Furthermore, I know that I can't get up early — I don't know why.

T: Gotten to be a very mysterious thing.

C: Seems awfully mysterious ah — Well how much time do we have left?

T: Think most of the hour.

C: Hmmm?

T: Quite a bit.

C: Half hour?

T: M-hmm.

C: Too bad I ain't got a problem now.

Excerpt 6

T: M-hmm. Now on the other side of, I guess you're saying, is concerned, "Just because I'm average or only a little above average doesn't mean I can't do what I want to do. I might very well be a good anthropologist like other good anthropologists."

C: Just, just takes a certain amount of work and study, ah, well ninety per cent, you know the old expression about ninety per cent perspiration and ten per cent [*T:* M-hmm — mmm] expression. [*laughs*]

T: M-hmm. M-hmm.

C: Well, I think that's true of most any field ah, for, for most people.

T: Mmm.

C: Most people who ah, make a go of any field if you work hard at it, they aren't necessarily brilliant or outstanding or ah, I think my, probably why I agree with that sentence is my, is my broad-mindedness.

T: Mmm.

C: Or what I think is my broad-mindedness ah, my, my tendency to ah, not to stick along one rail so to speak, one narrow path that ah —

T: M-hmm.

C: To kind of branch out in different things.

T: M-hmm. M-hmm.

C: Kind of take a look at everything. In other words, I'm really not disappointed at the college, I, I try to have a look at number of fields, including psychology.

T: M-hmm. Not, not single-minded about the whole thing.

C: And that's my, I probably, I say that's probably my ah, my greatest asset; is my tendency not to ah, limit myself too much to one particular thing.

T: M-hmm.

C: I think that's ah, that's a bad thing for a person to do. Eh, sort of ah, get himself into a ah, niche, anda —

T: Mmm.

C: Anda, oh you know, dig a hole for himself or something.

T: Overspecialize.

C: Overspecialize.

T: Overspecialize right into the ground like —

C: That's what I mean.

T: M-hmm. M-hmm.

C: Ah, course I, you know you can't help but recognize that in a world like we, in a world like we have today why, can't, you just can't get out of that. You have to specialize.

T: Mmm.

C: The only question is what degree of specialization am I ah —

T: Mmm.

C: Whether it's real, real ah, ah technical or ah, expert ah, type work that, or whether it's gonna be ah, reasonably broad-angled. Mean I happen to know that there's ah, there are a number of men in college who have not limited themselves to one particular thing entirely at least.

T: M-hmm.

C: Uh, they may, even though they may more or less stick to one thing but they have interests in other fields as well as the one that they're uh, more or less specializing in. Ah, I don't if you've ever, probably heard of him, you may have read some of his works, ah, Carlton Cooley. You probably heard of him haven't you?

T: No, I'm afraid I haven't.

C: He's, he's very well known to the general public because he wrote a book ah, which was intended not so much for professionals so much as for, for the general public and that was really quite a general work, see.

T: Mmm.

C: Ah, cover, covered the whole more or less, the whole field of ah, of ah human culture and ah, human progress.

T: M-hmm. M-hmm.

C: Anda well of course, that story may be questioned whether I'd ever be as, as successful as, probably as he was.

T: Mmm.

C: Ah, that's something only the future can tell.

T: M-hmm. He's kind of the ah —

C: He's more or less exceptional —

T: The ideal —

C: He's more or less exceptional. Ah, when I was going to school I got the, I got the impression the professors I had were more or less men who specialized in a particular field.

T: M-hmm.

C: Ah, archeology, the professor I had for archeology, I felt was pretty much of an . . . .

Excerpt 7

[*They are playing cards.*]

C: Hmm, you got more diamonds than I have. No wonder, all you need is two bowers for cryin' out loud. I can't win that way. [*Both laugh.*] But the [inaudible] yeah —

T: Had both bowers.

C: I just chose the wrong suit that's all.

T: Yeah, I had both red, actually I had three jacks.

C: God!

T: I had both red and the jack of spades so when you refused the club I knew I was in.

C: Well I don't know, I could have tried clubs but I didn't think that I'd make it —

T: Even in clubs I'd have that —

C: Fact is I didn't have enough trump, sh–shouldn't do that without a bower really.

T: You're right.

C: I don't know what's the matter with me. I'm overbidding here, like right and left or something, ah I mean — oh, my deal?

T: M-hmm.

C: 'Cause I'm, I'm usually conservative about bidding.

T: M-hmm.

C: Ah, reasonably conservative; oops, I forgot. Well, well, well.

T: Humpff.

C: Geez, whata ya say? [*laughs*]

T: I'll pass that one.

C: Well, I don't know. [*Therapist laughs.*] I feel like, don't know whether to even try anymore. [*laughs*] — Well, I guess I will though. I don't care 'cause I may as well get set again. I've lost the game anyway — let's see, ah —

T: Come on, lead.

C: Yeah. [*Sound of cards being played.*] Well, I only made a point, I barely, just barely did make it.

T: Well, I just lost one.

C: See I, I was — I was so far off in my — [*Therapist laughs.*] [*Sounds of cards being shuffled.*] You maybe —

T: Yup. [*More shuffling, coughing.*] This time we go in for luck.

C: God! Pass.

T: Pass.

C: [*laughs*] Yeah —

T: Game of bridge, in the game of bridge somebody could pass, I don't know a good hand, I say pass.

C: I'll pass again.

T: Let's see, I'll call diamonds.

C: My lead though.

T: M-hmm.

C: [*clears throat*] Oops, you got that.

T: Yeah. [*Patient laughs.*] M-hmm.

C: Here we go again, eh what?

T: Mmm.

C: Jesus!

T: Eh —

C: Made it.

T: Right.

C: It was that last trump, that's what did it.

T: Just barely [inaudible].

C: Mean you got seven?

T: Yeah.

C: What'd you have before?

T: I had six.

C: In other words . . . .

Excerpt 8

C: I'm not going to go to the opposite extreme and say that you should make ah, snappy decisions without thinking about it.

T: No.

C: No, I'm not going to say that — but I am going to say that if you, if you, you ah, at least a reasonable time to think about it anda, a reasonable amount of, you know when, providing that you do give it enough consideration to it, why you shouldn't just, you know, that's like worrying. You go around in circles and, you don't get anywhere. Worrying, go around in circles, it's ah, that you get faced with a decision and you just keep muddling around about it and then don't even come to a decision why, the same thing really.

T: M-hmm.

C: It's just as bad.

T: M-hmm.

C: And ah, so in other words you think about it, you see what, whatever the possibilities are you, you should be able to make a choice.

T: M-hmm. Mmm. As long as you consider all the aspects, then the choice should be obvious then —

C: Fairly —

T: And easy.

C: Fairly obvious. I don't mean easy as, that ah, even though you may, may be undecided say between two, two or three alternatives, why ah there's always, seems like to me, in other words to put it more simply, it seems to me that there is a right decision whether you know it or not.

T: M-hmm.

C: There is a right decision whether you know it or not.

T: Mmm.

C: The whole thing is to find out what it is. It's hiding there somewhere.

T: M-hmm. M-hmm. "Somewhere among all the alternatives there is the one right one and my job is to find it."

C: Well that of course is I suppose — at least there is one, at least one will be right.

T: M-hmm.

C: There may be more than one but at least there's one.

T: M-hmm. M-hmm.

C: That's what counts.

T: There's always hope and there's always the possibility of finding the right one. At least one possibility — certainly takes up time.

C: Yup. Well I think probably seems rather ah, obvious to you, I mean ah, probably don't even mean what you would call ah, mere ah, ah well, self-evident stuff. I mean I think it would be self-evident that ah, for instance, I think it would be very self-evident when you say ah, in order, in order to know what you're gonna do with yourself you gotta know yourself.

T: Mmm.

C: See, this is, this seems rather obvious to me, I think it must be obvious to you — that's, that's really the whole thing.

T: M-hmm.

C: Ah —

T: "It kind of boils down to knowing what I want."

C: Knowing ah, what you are.

T: Mmm.

C: Knowing what you are, wh–what type are you? Where do you fit in?

T: M-hmm.

C: Whether you have ah, whether you have ah, in other words say you were filling out a ballot sheet —

T: M-hmm.

C: I've done the best I can. I'm satisfied.

T:.M-hmm.

Excerpt 9

C: After I, well for me it's just sort of a thing of the past. Now I don't worry about it so much. I mean ah, it doesn't, doesn't bother me because I'm not thinking of the past, in terms of the past that way.

T: M-hmm.

C: I'm, I'm not, not so concerned about it.

T: Shadows in the background are not as troubling to you as they once were.

C: At least I, I've ah, well I feel that I ah, I don't know what it means, I don't know if I know how to explain it — why it doesn't bother me anymore, it just ah, I guess I can say I, I've taken more of a philosophical attitude toward it.

T: Mmm.

C: I mean I, I don't ah, I just don't, I feel it won't do any good about it. I don't worry about it.

T: M-hmm.

C: Take care of something that's, that's past.

T: Guess there's even some troubling sensations, "I'm not really sure why I still don't worry about it because there's still shadows there."

C: They're there but they're not there what they were.

T: M-hmm.

C: Thank God!

T: M-hmm. Something haunting about the way they were.

C: It was terrible, the whole period, that whole period in my life ah, after he died and many years, period of ah, seemed like, what seemed like terrible times, terrible. Ah, a feeling of oh, I don't know just purely, truly too deep, really too ah, too horrible to describe too well. Just, just, it was just a feeling of what you'd call merciless. Like, like being in a big terrible, thick fog, not really knowing what, what you were going to do or —

T: Something comes to my mind: the sun was blotted out and darkness covered the face of the earth.

C: Yes, I, I, I, that describes it well. I didn't see anything but sadness.

T: Yeah. How long was there the feeling of groping and not knowing anything?

C: Not really knowing anything ah, not understanding either, not feeling secure, before —

T: Anyway was indescribable — indescribable.

C: I would even, I'm, I'm not going to even attempt to describe it very well. It's impossible to describe — so as I see it then the real trouble after that was the fact I didn't have a father.

T: M-hmm.

C: That about sums up everything from here, from then, there until now.

T: Mmm.

C: The fact that I had only a mother and no father — in, in order to ah [*loud noise makes recording inaudible*] my life.

T: M-hmm, I see, so in circumstance you're saying "That made my mother so important in my life and then kind of distorted it."

C: Distorted it . . . .

Excerpt 10

T: Well, I seem to be hearing you saying, "I'd like to pin you down."

C: That's it. Right, that's what I've been trying to do for a long time but I haven't been able to succeed very well. Apparently you just don't feel any need to say anything very definite, express any definite opinion about anything so I'd even given up hope. Huh, can't do anything about it.

T: "He's not giving anything so I may as well not expect anything much, I suppose."

C: Yeah, that's one, another thing that I would kind of expect, a rather foolish question if you don't mind my saying so —

T: Mmm — you know this is putting words in your mouth again, trying to see if that's your feeling. "I really am alone, for a while I hoped at least that he would share something with me, but I guess he is just, doesn't like to. I'm alone now as I was then actually."

C: Well, I don't know, I'm kinda puzzled about the whole thing. As to why, why I expect certain things that obviously ah, you don't, you don't think I should expect. I don't really know why I expect it.

T: Mmm.

C: Eh, eh, I guess it should be pretty obvious without having to spell out things just how, how you want things to be or how you think things should be. I suppose there's no point in asking about it.

T: It ah —

C: Well, I don't mean to create some problems. Mean as long as I feel all right now I, I look forward to things all right, being all right why I'm not so concerned. I might be more concerned if I felt I had more problems and troubles and worries and stuff but I, don't really feel I do so I'm not really as concerned about as I would be if that was the case.

T: M-hmm. M-hmm. Part of that anyway at least sounds like, "I don't really need too much of you now because I do feel pretty strong in myself, so God help me if I ever really needed you though because it doesn't look as if I'd get much more of you than I get right now. This whole problem, the whole relationship is, is kind of puzzling, perplexing, disappointing some-times [*C:* I have been —] discouraging."

C: I have been puzzled, I don't know why, but I have. I don't know — [*long pause*] Well I — like I said before I mean I just don't understand ah, psychiatric stuff, like what's psychotherapy supposed to be and all that. I, I, I don't understand why you figure there's a, what you think you're trying to accomplish with me and all that. I, I, if you don't want to explain, eh, eh clarify anything about it, well I guess there's nothing much I can say.

Excerpt 11

C: Ah, [inaudible] too many people — I mean, you know what I mean by fearsome, well they tend to be ah, something, there's something hard about them [*T:* uh-huh] something ah, well are you there or not — some-times but ah — you may, you, you know, you know that partly, nothing in me is hard or arrogant or what you'd call downright vicious. Vicious in a, in an unfriendly ah, ah well you, they act as though they hated me. [*laughs*] No, I wouldn't be afraid of them. I wouldn't, I wouldn't, I wouldn't make the mistake of returning that fear, wouldn't hate them just because they hated me.

T: M-hmm.

C: That'd be smart. See I, I figure ah, I'd just take my own attitude, they can have their attitude but I just take my own attitude.

T: M-hmm. "They can feel any way they want to, I don't have to be influenced by that."

C: Try, I try and be ah, well, impartial I guess. I try to ah, not get too personally involved.

T: M-hmm.

C: Not that enough, allowed my personal prejudices to be there, I mean everybody has them and I'm no exception but I try not to allow my prejudices, ah partialities or whatever you want to say or my, in other words my personal, my personal ah, ah beliefs or attitudes to get in the way of how I feel about people.

T: Uh-huh.

C: In other words, they, they can act any way they want to, ah they can act crazy or they, they can act foolishly or — but providing, providing they don't ah — providing that they don't ah — actually do any harm why, I mean I don't see anything to worry about.

T: Uh-huh.

C: But I mean, I don't feel that ah, they should probably you know, this whole problem a lot of it is family wrangling. I'm kind of wandering here but ah, this whole problem of what to do, would be me and me and Sammy — we had one for it, "Do you run, do you stand still, what do you do? How do you, how, how do you react to it?"

T: Mmm.

C: Ah, say if you have ability, are you firing away or do you wait until they come at you before you fire, or, or do you play it safe and run? Eh, same way with people.

T: Mmm.

C: They aren't all as bad as they seem to be, I think.

T: M-hmm.

C: They may seem to be bad, they aren't really as bad as they seem to be.

T: They may look like a feathered animal but looks are deceiving.

C: I think so.

T: No doubt you're saying that, something like, "I really try to be neutral, ah, as much as I can and not allow my irrational person . . . ."

Excerpt 12

C: Mean after all, you know ah — I'm no, I, I'm not a super-brain. I can't ah, I can't hardly think everything for myself, I can't really ah, I mean there are certain things that are bound to be far beyond me, and ah, I, I did get out of it one thing, I, I ah wondered, it's the same old thing. I wondered why, why it affected me more than other people.

T: M-hmm.

C: Ah, you see this thing, this problem that I had recently that's, that's the important thing that I realized. Same problem I had recently was the problem I had way back then, way back about ten years ago.

T: M-hmm. M-hmm.

C: Ah, do you have any idea what problem I might be referring to?

T: The only thing that occurred to me was relating to girls.

C: Yeah, you hit it right on the head. Course I forgot what adolescence, you right away think, ah, ah, adolescence is the time when you start getting in with girls.

T: M-hmm.

C: You, you were, you, you were getting the idea of what I was trying to get at.

T: M-hmm. M-hmm.

C: Ah, I don't think it surprises me, that you, that you would have thought of that, not really surprising but —

T: Not really surprising but I guess you were pleased ah, ah to see I was following you pretty closely.

C: Yeah.

T: Saying, "God, it's really very clear to me too that I really have the same thing, the kind of problem that brought me into the hospital this time, as long back as ten years ago almost exactly."

C: It's the same problem ah, I would say ah, I don't know, I, I can't help but feel if, if you have a say, if you have a problem one time, say, say you have a problem five years ago — ah, that, that's when it's going to be severe ah, at a point in the future, I mean ah, there, there'll be a certain carry-over from that, that same problem basically there'll be some carry-over from one problem eh, a more [inaudible] instance of it to the more recent.

T: M-hmm.

C: In other words, if you haven't really solved the problem then the darn thing is going to live to haunt you.

T: M-hmm. M-hmm. Mmm.

C: Anda, that's, that's one of the things that I, that I realized.

T: It's obvious that if you don't take, if you, if you're unable to master or mature through one phase of development, well then that's going to stick with you and crop up again and again until you do go through it.

C: In other words, until you really have, if, if it's a problem, the problem has to be solved.

T: M-hmm.

C: If you can't solve the darn problem, you're done. You can't, you, you, you just can't be, ah something that'll nag you all the time.

T: You'll be kind of a cripple.

C: Yeah, you, you'll, you'll be handicapped — may, maybe to put it more simply to say that you aren't mature. You just aren't mature. In order to ah, gain in maturity you have to win the problem you have to face, you have to [inaudible] you haven't really tried. If you don't you aren't mature. Any, any problem like that you have to find the right answer to.

T: Seems to be so much a part of growth, it seems to be such a basic problem, you're saying that "I'll never really eh, a person couldn't ever really call himself grown or matured until he has somehow solved it."

C: In other words, his, his attitude was right. Ah, has to have, have a certain, a person has to have a, a, ah, ah, a definite way of looking at it, ah a definite way of dealing with it. Ah, yeah, I'm, I'm right, thinking very much in sociological terms.

T: M-hmm.

C: Mean, it's, it's something that I think you could probably get this out of sociology, huh?

Excerpt 13

C: . . . quite account for the fact that, that I, that I think of myself as, as ah, establishing a more or less, ah — personal [inaudible] thing. I wonder ah — I don't know, I haven't always, I haven't always thought of it that way. Basically, I've felt my problem was just in, ah putting my thoughts more or less into why, what other people in the society at large, ah I'm problem solving eh, probably don't mean anything to me 'cause I need a new approach er, or ah, you don't really think of me that way do you? I mean I don't, I don't hardly think of myself that way, I don't, why you would think of me that way.

T: Mmm.

C: It may, it may sound that way at times ah, I, ah honest to God, I, I ah, I can't see that there's anything very different, except maybe some difference but — by and large I can't see that there is much difference.

T: M-hmm. "With some uneasiness I guess you found my ah —"

C: Mean, I, I imagined you're really having much of a compassion to my being or my trying to be in any way unique or something.

T: Mmm.

C: I don't imagine you're able to do such a thing.

T: I see. I feel that's very strongly the picture I got from what you were saying.

C: Maybe but — well let's put it this way. I think of myself as different, though I, mainly in a sense that I, feel there are too many, ah guys who cause irritation in here. That's really the main difference. [Inaudible] so gosh darn mean around here, I, I, just not what I would call well-educated people.

T: M-hmm.

C: I mean ah, they act like after all self-education that's true but, but by and large the, the level to me doesn't seem to be a very high level. You see, that's the thing I'm trying to get at. Ah, there's so many guys in here who just, who just, particularly guys like for instance, alcoholics. Uh, these guys ah — apparently they strike me as being very uneducated anda almost incapable of getting along by themselves. There seems to be not too much that can be done for them and they, and they just seem to come in here and go out but they come right back in again and they can't really make it go when they get outside. In other words, eh, I, I, I, I, I, I'd say the reason, that the way I think that the reason is that they are that way, is, that is that they aren't very trained or educated so that they can get along. Eh, it's obvious to me that the, the level of education in patients in here just isn't very high. A lot haven't even finished grade school.

T: M-hmm.

C: And I would say, and the majority haven't finished high school. This, this is not of course, there aren't many ah grownups, say like ah, ah 30 or 40 year olds, something like that, that I mean, like I said, I should let it go quietly but the thing that strikes me the most is that, that after once you do have a pretty good education and do have good training for a job and . . . .

Excerpt 14

C: Why was it? We seemed to drift off. We didn't, we didn't retain what you would call really ah, real comradely sort of thing.

T: "Why did I lose him?"

C: Why did I? How can you answer — Why, I mean if I lost, if I lost close connection with him, why, how could I have close connection with hardly anybody else? If you can't be friends with your own brother how you gonna be friends with other people — who aren't even your blood brothers? Isn't that a tough question — Now, I don't know, all I can say now is no. The answer is very simple or should be very simple. The truth is that I was so sick that I was incapable of being friendly. [*T:* M-hmm.] To anybody.

T: "Same symptoms of, same old kind of feeling that I, that I was just so arranged or disarranged —"

C: Disarranged.

T: "That I couldn't see anybody, any other person."

C: I seemed to be ah, well I guess that's the, that's the part that's ah, I mean I don't, whether you'd say, you know, generally I would say I remember facing it that way but, well anyway about my illness, my kind of illness, part, part of my kind of illness. You tend to ah, be, you know you ah, people tend to be wrapped up in yourself, not have too much regard for other people.

T: M-hmm. M-hmm. "This may not be universal but the symptoms are true for me."

C: That I know, I know, I know that much about ah, ah, that, that's kind of, that's kind of general — amongst the patients that they, either that they have, they have a hard time adjusting to other people, that's putting it more generally, adjusting to, adjusting to ah, not just people, just everything around.

T: M-hmm.

C: Everything around. People or — [*T:* Mmmm.] People or society or, they just don't get along with people and they don't get, they don't get along as far as ah, well working with other people I mean, you know. I mean I just, well I was, I was going along there without hardly any friends and, anda I had, as I had already said before that I had, I had, I won't go to, to ah mix with people anda join any kind of groups ah, anda of course no desire whatever to ah, most of all as I said the furthest thing from my mind was the idea that I would help other people by actually being a leader of some kind.

T: M-hmm.

C: You know, I mean in other words . . . .

Excerpt 15

C: . . . have to ah, oh expected to go in unless you got a straight shot. You have to have ah, my father often taught me to do that, to judge where the ball — [*T:* M-hmm. M-hmm.] Or the angle shot.

T: M-hmm — m-hmm — m-hmm.

C: See ah, thing is tough.

T: M-hmm.

C: Ah to me ah, it seems to me about 50, 50 per cent of the mistakes that you make when you're shooting are due to inability or ah, I don't know it, it's inability or chills or something. Ah, well anyway, not being able to hit the ball. Really on the spot you should hit it.

T: Mmm.

C: Mean you know, most of the time, I'd say 90 per cent of the time, you know, you know doggone well you can't hit the ball dead center. You don't have that good a shot.

T: M-hmm.

C: And the question is where besides dead center.

T: Mmm.

C: That's where, that's where the tricky stuff comes.

T: M-hmm.

C: You see what I mean.

T: Yeah, the biggest part of the game really for you is just in mastering the simple angle shot which in itself has enough difficulty.

C: To me it does because I find that I miss it about 50 per cent or more and more all the time.

T: M-hmm.

C: If you can't make those shots how you gonna be a good player?

T: M-hmm —

C: Ah you, to learn where to, where to hit the ball.

T: I guess you're also saying, "Let other people worry about stance and position and — My worry is that, fundamental dropping the ball in the pocket."

C: Then of course I'm only a beginner.

T: M-hmm.

C: I, you know naturally I, I wouldn't even know about these other things if the fellow hadn't told me.

T: M-hmm.

C: See I, I, in other words I said, I don't know whether it's true or not, but said something like it's almost better if I hadn't told those things because he said he'd confuse me.

T: M-hmm.

C: Try to learn all that at once, tend to confuse me.

T: M-hmm. Trying to get it all in at the same time, that's too much.

C: I thought it was. I still think it is — seems like, seems like that's true of a lot of things. It's trying, trying to learn too much at once, too, too much at once.

T: M-hmm.

C: Concentrate on more than one thing at a time eh, that's tough.

T: Mmm.

C: To think of more than one thing at a time ah, whew, it's bewildering.

T: M-hmm.

C: Yeh. That's what I felt —

T: Mean you try to take in too many things well then, everything gets confused, very puzzling to you.

C: There's so doggone many things you know and how, the difficulty is trying to say, almost is impossible unless you have some kinda, I don't know, some basis, some basis on which to choose among the things.

T: There is a note in what you said that I [inaudible] how much there is to know and how long it takes to learn them one by one.

C: The thing is if you can't learn them one by one, if you have ah, if you have more than one thing on your hands, if you try and master it, ah, it can be awful pressure I found.

T: M-hmm.

C: I found in trying to figure out my problems ah, trying to figure out how to live right there ah, there's there's to me most confusing things.

T: M-hmm.

C: The most bothersome thing, trying to ah, trying to fit things in where they belong.

T: M-hmmm. Trying to make a picture of the parts of something.

C: I don't know, I guess everybody has that trouble. [cough]

T: The grind is discouraging, frightening, kind —

C: Can be yes, but . . . .

Commentaries

Bergman

In considering therapeutic movement in the case of Jones, Bergman offers:

This man apparently had a psychotic disturbance when he entered the hospital, but already at Excerpt 1 he seems to have recovered. He talks coherently and neither his thought processes nor his affects seem to be severely disturbed at any time during the interviews. Nor do I see any particular movement either to or away from depths of feeling in the excerpts. That does not mean that I consider the interviews to have been useless. I rather believe that they have done some good.

Bergman hastens to add, however, that he finds it impossible to judge how much was accomplished in the interviews. That the sessions might have done some good is tied to "lukewarm" characteristics of the therapist: "After all, the therapist was well intentioned, non-judgmental, sympathetic and interested . . ."

Concerning therapist characteristics which were *not* helpful, Bergman has a great deal more to add:

The therapist seems to me to have adhered more faithfully to the letter than to the spirit of client-centered therapy. I find him somewhat less than open to his own as well as to the patient's experience. Frequently he gets entangled in the content of the patient's communication and misses important strains of feeling. At times he is defensive or concerned with the impression he makes on some audience—a supervisor, the researchers, himself? When the patient accuses him of evasiveness, it is hard to see from the excerpts whether the accusation is not justified. At any rate, I do not like the idea of meeting head-on questions of the patient regarding the therapist's attitudes with nothing but reflections of feeling. This therapist displeases me also with his tendency to use at times the language of psychological theory. My negative prejudice already aroused, I feel even suspicious when he inappropriately pauses or emphasizes in the midst of a sentence.

Bergman concludes with a specific example:

At one point we learn that the patient lost his father when he was young, and this was one of the traumata of his life. (At this point, incidentally, the therapist responds with deeper empathy than usual.) I imagine that to have a fatherlike person in the therapist and to be able to experience in relation to him some important feelings—negative as well as positive—may have been meaningful and beneficial to the patient even if the therapist did invite neither very deep trust nor the deepest possible exploration of feelings.

Thus, for Bergman, a defensive therapist, even if well intentioned, is not open to many of the communications of an already-recovering patient or to the feelings which the patient's messages arouse in himself. The therapist gets entangled in the content of those patient experiences which are received and achieves only minimally, or misses completely, the important threads of feeling. Thus, the therapist's activities have little therapeutic effect upon the patient except that it is helpful for the patient to experience positive and negative feelings about the person of the therapist. Some minimal "good" was accomplished.

English

For English, the movement oscillates continually between two extremes. During the very early stages of therapy the therapist appears to structure the patient's thoughts for the patient and even "then attacks the patient for his (the therapist's) own words and forces the patient to be apologetic for what he has been feeling."

However, English acknowledges, the therapist goes on to help the patient "define his feelings," or "clarify his thinking." In doing so, the therapist clearly "helps the patient find his own form of expression with less interference." A long swing toward understanding is thus achieved. There appears to be "movement toward better client-therapist rapport" and closeness.

Suddenly, during the middle sessions, the pendulum swings in the other direction. In a discussion of alternate decisions, the therapist assumes responsibility for finding the right one rather than leaving it to the patient and offering to serve only as an aid to the process. Finally, during the latter part of therapy, the patient's frustrations with the therapist emerge: "The patient is challenging therapist for not being willing to be 'pinned down' as to any opinion about things. Patient goes on to say that he apparently expects things the therapist doesn't think he should expect. As dialogue proceeds, therapist goes on trying to express patient's feelings of frustration for him rather than clarifying what the patient was *frustrated about* concerning therapist."

English expresses his own growing feeling of frustration: "It seems therapist is acting so as to prevent any self-discovery on the part of the patient rather than aiding such a process. When the patient tries to express himself in relation to the therapist, he is pushed away so that he is forced to continue contact with therapist by means of the emptiest sort of vague generalities or remain silent."

The remainder of therapy is characterized, for English, by the lack of clarification of the patient's vague allusions. There is little patient movement toward self-understanding. Often the therapist merely agrees and does not attempt to ascertain any personal examples of the patient's general complaints.

English has great difficulty discerning the therapist's framework of operation in therapy:

It seems as if the patient's original familial unstructured existence is allowed and therefore encouraged to continue in this kind of therapeutic relationship and the reviewer sees little relationship occurring, since relationship has to occur around something meaningful to the patient in his past, present or future. This phenomenon occurs in very few excerpts. When it does occur the reviewer fails to catch any continuity with subsequent excerpts.

English concludes: "This is the most unstructured dialogue the reviewer has ever encountered in observing therapy. This in itself would not necessarily be a criticism, if an effective relationship was occurring. But, the reviewer did not get the sense that an effective working relationship that would enhance problem solving or maturation is occurring as the case excerpts proceed . . ."

In summary, then, a confused and frustrated patient sends out many vague messages, some of which are received. In dealing with these communications, a restrictive therapist vacillates between attempting to help the patient find his own mode of expression, which only begins to have an effect on the patient, and leading the patient's thoughts, thus actually preventing his self-discovery. It is implicit that the course of helping the patient clarify his understanding would have had more impact if it were not for the dominating sway of the therapist's structuring. In terms of outcome, English is almost in complete agreement with

Bergman: The relationship is an ineffectual one which allows for little movement except for a more clear expression of hostility by the patient.

Lewis

For Lewis, the patient Jones, "starts out intellectualizing a great deal, sounds suspicious and hostile, but gradually warms up and gets together with his therapist." Lewis, as did Bergman, notes that Jones initially talks and acts "pretty 'sanely.' " "There is a quite striking and general absence of any reference to the kinds of things many acute schizophrenics think about and are concerned about, with perhaps the exception of loneliness and depression and helplessness—this triad of apathetic despair being couched in perfectly understandable terms and not disguised in some type of symbolic reference, etc."

However, in contrast to both Bergman and English, Lewis' reactions are generally favorable to the process of the Jones case. He finds the "atmosphere of calm, secure acceptance" to conform to a general standard of good supportive psychotherapy. Concerning the therapist's helpful activity, Lewis suggests: "The therapist limits himself to 'pump priming' much more, and I had the impression that he stayed with the patient on any content, on any level and with the patient's language, in a positive way. He appears to need less to reflect everything that the patient says . . . He seems to back off more and let the patient talk."

Lewis is clearly pleased with a "psychotherapy conducted in the style of dynamic psychiatry (which of course has a strong psychoanalytic coloration)." However, Lewis has reservations concerning the therapist's tendency to ignore the latent transference feelings and thus not make resistance interpretations:

None of this the therapist picks up as related to the patient's feelings toward him in this style of treatment, and the question is whether perhaps he might have given the patient a chance to resolve them a little more if he had done so. I do not mention this to raise objections to the strategy, but rather to point to a kind of dynamic movement within treatment which is evident . . . [and] which is the focus of scrutiny in other forms of psychotherapy, and which is so hard to get at by the present method.

Lewis concludes on a positive note: "Toward the end of the treatment I had the feeling that the patient was accepting the therapist and showing confidence in him and in himself to a greater degree than that shown in the early segments."

To summarize these views briefly, a suspicious and intellectualized but nevertheless recovered patient sends out many messages. The therapist receives many of these messages and operates quietly to encourage the patient to find his own mode of expression and self-discovery, an effective therapeutic agent for the patient. The therapist reflects only infrequently and these reflections have little or no impact upon the patient. Thus, in an atmosphere of calm acceptance, the patient through self-discovery comes to "settle down" and finally exhibits some improvement.

May

May's formulation of the process in the case of Jones is essentially the same as that for Brown. May clearly emphasizes movement in therapy as a process of change from concern with overt symptomatology toward anxiety mobilization with a problem-solving focus. For Jones, this means trying "to learn of life, the fundamentals of hitting the ball in the center!"

Again, May emphasizes the therapist's "reflection" of the patient's words and proposed actions rather than his feelings. The absence of much of the potential dynamic of the therapeutic relationship is due to this "misuse of the 'reflecting' technique" in the limited "range of affects picked up and dealt with . . ." May further suggests:

. . . nowhere is *anger* reflected by the therapist. Other negative emotions like aggression, hostility, and genuine conflict (as distinguished from mere misunderstanding) are almost entirely absent in what the therapist reflects. It seemed clear to me that the patient was angry . . . [W]hen . . . Jones is trying to pin the therapist down on whether he believes in rights for mental patients, isn't the patient trying to express a current of anger? The fact that this isn't brought out seems to me partially to account for the patient's consequent resignation and "I-can't-expect-anything" attitude. If this anger were brought out, assumedly, then the patient might have gone on to bring out what is behind his obsessional concern for "rights". . . But what I missed was a living-out of what the patient was experiencing in the world right there.

May again points to the effective and truly therapeutic moments as those when the therapist did not merely reflect the patient but added something which came "out of his own (the therapist's) subjective state, his own identity as one person in the relationship." Some dynamic interpersonal relationship is seen in the case of Jones, especially at the point when the therapist says to Jones, "I guess you were pleased to see I was following you pretty closely," or when the therapist asks, "Do I seem still to be dodging, Joe?" and Joe responds frankly with, "Yes." At other times the opportunity for such a relationship is missed:

. . . [W]hen patient Jones continues his obsessional grill of the therapist about whether he believes in patient's "rights," it would have been refreshing, and I think definitely good for therapy, if after a little while the therapist had reacted, "Christ, Joe, here we have a chance to talk about your problems, and you're going to keep me on the hot seat all afternoon?"

In summary, then, when a therapist of good intent and dedication is finally able to communicate his interest and concern and to rise above his hesitancy to be a second and real party in the relationship, the resigned yet desperate Jones is able to mobilize his anxieties and focus on his problems.

Seeman

Seeman found the case of Jones quite stimulating. He notes, as did Bergman and Lewis, the absence of severe pathology in the patient's speech and manner throughout therapy: "With regard to the patient, it seemed evident from the beginning that he was a person of relatively high intellectual ability. He also seemed to have a more complex and integrated personality organization."

The therapeutic process appeared to go through three phases for Seeman: ". . . especially in the early phases, [it] was an intellectual one, and I found myself waiting for a "direct experiencing" phase. The patient seemed to come nearer to this process in the latter phases of therapy . . . , though even here the movement was hesitant and tentative."

Toward the end of therapy, "the patient's sensitivity, perceptiveness, and ability to differentiate between self and non-self" became particularly evident.

Seeman appears puzzled about the therapist:

On the one hand, he seemed sensitive and direct, capable of close under-standing. On the other hand, I also sensed a distance, a barrier beyond which the patient could not penetrate. The therapist seemed to put a strict limit on his personal involvement. The patient made many bids for a closer give-and-take relationship, but seemed not to succeed in this quest. I found Excerpt 10 especially unsatisfying in this respect. The patient needed a transparent relationship at that point and did not get it.

To sum up, then, for Seeman the therapeutic process has been set in motion, although, to be sure, constructive patient personality change has not yet occurred. A sensitive but somewhat vacillating and defensive therapist presents a distinct barrier to some of the communications of a complex yet integrated patient. On the other hand, the therapist exhibits a real capacity for close understanding of many of the patient's communications. At times the therapist communicates sensitively and directly with significant effect upon the patient. At other times, the therapist clearly places a strict limit upon his personal involvement and transparency and thus many of his communications lose their effectiveness. The therapist's communication of his understanding facilitates the patient's movement from an intellectual experiencing of therapy toward a hesitant and tentative direct experiencing with greater sensitivity and perceptivity and an increased ability to distinguish between his self and non-self.

Whitaker

Whitaker acknowledges some movement in the case of Jones, although he emphasizes that the "therapeutic process seems quite conspicuously different from either of the other fragments." In therapy the patient discovers a capacity to get rid of the heavy "affect-load" of his life's conflicts. At termination, Jones is working at formulating a philosophy of living as well as an understanding of the dynamic pattern of his own pathology.

Whitaker relates the distinctiveness of the Jones case to the therapist's behavior:

One is struck by the "as if" quality of his language, yet as early as segment 2 there is strong evidence of the effective use of his role to reverse the patient's ambivalence. Is this reversal a defensive pattern or an actual new percept of the patient and his situation? I was having fantasies about the significance of the "uh-huh technique" and was equally divided between defining it as, "Oh yes, I see," or "Really, I didn't hear you," or in question form it meant, "Are you sure?" "Is that true?" "Could you really believe that?" At other times, I decided that the therapist was the patient's advocate in verbalizing to bind anxiety by supplying words for the patient to escape his feelings.

Whitaker suggests that "somehow out of this, there emerges bilateral meditation":

It's as though these two persons had developed the capacity to be alone together. Out of this, the patient feels free to disagree with his therapist without doubt and without anxiety. Thereupon the therapist adds one of his own associations.

It's as though the patient discovers himself when the therapist is not afraid. Out of this emerges the capacity on the part of the patient to get rid of the affect-load in his life choices. Problems are still problems but they don't feel like problems. That is, the choices are now real ones—they are less symbolic and are less loaded.

Finally, near the end of therapy the patient is "defining the big objectives in his life" and facing his own basic incapacities. During the last session "the patient finally gets down to saying that trying to learn too much at one time is bewildering." Whitaker is fascinated by this message from Jones: "This may well be one of the secrets of this kind of psychotherapy. The growth effort is primarily with the patient while the therapist spends his effort in maintaining restraint and control."

Whitaker labels the therapy in the case of Jones as "training in verbal communication," with the therapist operating to replay Jones's verbal and creative offerings. In this sense, Whitaker is in strong agreement with Lewis' concern for verbal retraining. However, Whitaker notes that the therapist is very real and humble during the later parts of therapy. At these points, "the therapist and the patient differentiate their roles and see each other as persons." While therapy is not "existential" for Whitaker during its early phases, directionality emerges "for a latter part of therapeutic movement where the therapist can more correctly be a real person and can recognize the patient's efforts as being personal and growth-oriented."

For Whitaker, then, a fearful patient's creative communications are received by the therapist and played back by the therapist. In effect the therapist "trains" Jones in verbal communication. In addition, in the course of this training, the therapist becomes Jones's "advocate in verbalizing to bind anxiety by supplying words for the patient to escape his feelings." A kind of "bilateral meditation" develops. Out of this, the patient risks himself, somehow feeling "free to disagree with his therapist without doubt and without anxiety." Thereupon the therapist takes courage and adds his own associations and thus becomes a second and real party in the relationship: from this the patient gets the courage to face himself because the therapist is no longer afraid. Thus, in an interactional process in which each party gets courage from the progressive freeing and self-risking of the other, the patient discovers himself and comes to be able to unburden himself of much of the "affect-load" in his life choices. Finally he works at formulating both a philosophy of living and the dynamic pattern of his own pathology.

A Critique of the Case of Jones

The case of Jones also elicited a variety of formulations. Concerning the major question of movement, there are significant differences in evaluations. Several of the commentators readily note the absence of any severe psychopathology on the part of the patient. Thus, initially it would appear that the patient has already recovered to some extent from his psychotic disturbance and that the prospects for therapeutic growth would be quite good.

However, not all of them discern growth. Bergman and English agree that the relationship is essentially an ineffectual one, except for the possible helpfulness of the patient's being better able to experience and express his negative feelings, especially toward the therapist. Lewis, on the other hand, sees a sane, but hostile and suspicious, patient moving with renewed confidence toward a gradual "settling down" and "warming up." May, again, sees a movement from resignation and despair toward a capacity for relating and problem-solving. For Seeman, a complex and integrated patient moves beyond experiencing therapy *intellectually* to a tentative but direct affective experiencing which involves greater perceptivity and increased self-awareness. Whitaker describes an initially fearful patient, who, after unburdening his life decisions of their affect-load, works at understanding himself.

Thus, two commentators sense essentially no movement while the others describe a therapeutic process moving in varying degrees toward greater self-understanding, direct experiencing, and problem-solving.

When the therapist's facilitative and retarding characteristics are considered, two qualities seem, at least initially, to emerge from the formulations. On the one hand, the therapist is described as well-intentioned, sensitive, and dedicated. On the other hand, he is a defensive and controlling person who seems not really free to be himself. For May and Whitaker, the hesitancy to be himself is to some degree finally overcome and indeed becomes for them an effective therapeutic ingredient.

In the formulations of the case of Jones, there is less concern with the technique of reflection per se. May has noted, for all three cases, the limited effectiveness of reflecting within a narrow range of affects. Both May and Bergman observe that the therapist often gets entangled in the content of Jones's messages and thus minimally receives, or misses completely, important feelings. Only for Seeman does the technique of reflection and the process of empathic understanding (which reflection attempts to communicate) have meaning as a significant element in enabling the patient to attain direct experiencing and greater perceptivity and awareness.

For Whitaker, reflection assumes an important role in initiating an interactional process which leads ultimately to patient self-discovery. A "bilateral meditation" evolves as a consequence of the therapist's "replaying" the patient's messages. Out of this joint inner experience of being "alone together" the patient emerges "free to disagree with his therapist without doubt and without anxiety."

Rather than reflection, which seems for many of these theorists to connote some kind of structural framework being imposed upon the patient's offering, English and Lewis note the therapist's quiet encouraging of the patient to find his own mode of expression and self-discovery. However, for English this encouragement is contradicted by the therapist's attempts at structuring the patient's thoughts. Unfortunately, this structuring dominates, with the result that the patient is prevented from self-discovery.

Again, much of the therapist's activity is seen as occurring within a range which is narrow and which is controlled by the therapist. Almost all the commentators are disturbed with the therapist for ignoring many feelings, especially latent transference feelings. Bergman offers the positive side of this consideration, that is, that the patient is better able to vent many of his feelings upon the therapist. However, English has difficulty in understanding the therapist's rationale for this. Little meaningful relationship is what English sees to be the consequence.

Whitaker accounts for the therapist's limitations in his suggestion that "the client-centered therapist is limited by using his two ears and his head":

Early in therapy the therapist as the mother surrogate must subdue his response to the patient except that he is alert and listening. I do not understand why this therapist does not offer the vision of his third eye or the hearing of his third ear in the latter part of therapy where the patient is struggling for growthful impulses from whatever source he is able to get them. Even though one starts out patient-centered it is feasible to assume that therapy can move to the place where it is relationship-centered and finally to an existential interrelating between two personal equals with differential responsibilities.

In summary, then, on the positive side is the evidence of a well-intentioned, sometimes sensitive, dedicated therapist. On the negative side must be counted his initial defensiveness and attempts to control, and his failure, on many occasions, to perceive not only his patient's experiences, but even his own.

Whitaker's formulations are perhaps unique here. The interactional process, seemingly initiated by therapist reflection, evolves to a point where both therapist and patient are able to be somewhat open in their experiencing and expression of feelings and where both therapist and patient have respect for their own as well as for each other's feelings.

The Case of Smith[5]

The case of Philip Smith involved 30 interviews with a young male schizophrenic who had been hospitalized for less than eight months. Following are the excerpts:

5. In our research code, this is the case of FIP.

Excerpt 1

T: You know it's almost as if, you're feeling "Well, gee, there's nothing at home to want to be here for — might just as well be in G——[6] as here," is that it?

C: Well, I've got something back in B—— before that — I just don't [*pause*] I don't know how to say it but — I do it — it don't bother me a bit.

T: I know, so you thought well, somewhere inside of you, "Well, everything is pretty hopeless or I'm hopeless or —"

C: I know I [*T:* "I can't win so —"] and I can't keep a job.

T: "I can't keep a job, what the heck can I do?"

C: I got this job and I worked a week and quit, I've never worked more than two weeks in a factory.

T: Mmm.

C: I farmed, the longest was nine months.

T: "I can't hold a job, I can't even support myself then — I might just as well be in G——, I guess, I can't make it myself" — is that it?

C: Yeah, I think that's pretty close to it, but I never figured, as a matter of fact I didn't even start to figure anything.

T: Mmm — You didn't really think this through at all — it just happened that way and you feel that way.

C: Yeah— [*long pause*] Do you know why the Doctor wrote to the court?

T: Why, he wrote?

C: Yeah.

T: The court requested —

C: I know but they will, just asked to send me back or something —

T: Mmm.

C: In it — They had a letter there, said they wanted me back here.

T: Oh, you mean — why would he write that kind of letter?

C: Yeah.

T: Suppose, pretty clearly he thought this would be even more helpful than G——.

C: Does he think I'm sick?

T: What do you have? I presume whatever he thinks, he thinks that the experience here would be helpful to you — I suppose I hope it will be too. What do you have, a fever?

C: What?

T: Do you have a fever?

C: Fever, why?

T: You asked if you were sick.

C: I meant in the head— [*pause*]

T: Now you feel, I don't know, sort of as though you had some kind of feeling about this. "What do these people do, write him letters saying I'm nuts or they mean what?"

6. A correctional institution.

C: My lawyer talked to me about it and he said, he said that I was emotionally upset — but I don't know what that means —

T: Mmmm.

C: That's about the same thing as being insane ain't it? [*pause*]

Excerpt 2

C: What good do you think this is gonna, what would anybody get out of this?

T: Yeah, quite true at that.

C: It's a kinda therapy?

T: Mmm — "Hey, what is there in it for me?"

C: What good could anybody get out of it.

T: Mmm — What you're saying right now, "I don't really feel I am getting anything."

C: No, I [*pause*] I guess I haven't been in here long enough —

T: Mmm — Your feeling in a way is that ah, the few times we have talked, "I don't really feel I've gotten much out of it."

C: Hmm — I ain't got nothin'.

T: Mmm — "And what is the use then to go on this way, or I don't believe I get anything — it's just pretty useless, pretty hopeless."

C: [*pause*] It seems to be hopeless.

T: It doesn't seem to do anything really — help with you at all.

C: I don't think this hospital ever done me any good yet — [*laughs*] — I think I got worse since I've been here.

T: You felt really worse, "I guess especially since I read last night about this other fellow."

C: Oh, I've always thought that.

T: Hmm.

C: Since a couple of weeks ago — I haven't been any better [*pause*] I, I just don't care for anything now.

T: "Not much interest in anything, so what happens, guess it happens."

C: I don't care if I live today or die tomorrow.

T: Nothing seems to have any meaning or purpose— [*pause*]

C: Seems funny, the whole world seems all funny.

T: Sort of distant or —

C: It don't even seem like it's real.

T: Mmm — is it sort of like seeing a movie or what?

C: No, it ain't like seeing a movie — you know it's real but you don't feel it.

T: Mmm — "And I know this is all there is, I know this is really real, but it don't seem that way."

C: It seems so crazy — [*laughs*]

T: "Logically, it doesn't make sense, but it sure seems that way."

C: It don't make no sense to me [*pause*] I don't feel like — like one person's gotta, like he could say — you get in and spend the rest of your life in prison. I don't see how you can judge another person like that.

T: More than one person made this decision.

Excerpt 3

T: Well, I guess I felt at times as though you were thinking about that.

C: Only, I was mostly counting —

T: Hmm.

C: I sit and count quite a bit.

T: Count what?

C: Oh, specks, little, like stuff like that — little spots.

T: Little specks of dust.

C: Yeah —

T: I guess in that time you must have counted up a bushel of them.

C: [*laughs*] — Yeah, I do quite a bit of counting.

T: As though this were some way to keep busy or something like that.

C: I guess that's why I do it for — keep my mind off of other things.

T: Mmm — So in a way, I guess in a sense saying, start thinking about things that were pretty darned unpleasant so I guess you started, "Counting and keep my mind off it" [*pause*] something like that?

C: I know upstairs, then I do quite a bit of counting, I counted all the tile — [laughs] — Boy, there's a lot of it.

T: I guess in a way it does sound sort of silly sitting around counting.

C: Yeah, they think I'm a crackpot or somethin' — [*pause*] That don't bother me when they think I'm crazy —

T: Mmm —

C: Why, if I am, I ain't alone. [*laughing*]

T: I suppose it wouldn't bother you.

C: Well, it sorta does.

T: "Well, I can say it doesn't bother me or somethin' like that — but it really does."

C: Yeah, well I guess nobody wants to be crazy.

T: Supposing part of — "What does it mean, does it mean I'm bad or evil or something like that?"

C: Well, I have a different version for crazy — people that can't control theirself.

T: Mmm — This is what's crazy, no control over what we do."

C: They know what to do, but they can't stop it.

T: I suppose in a way you're sort of saying, "I'm crazy —"

C: Mmm.

T: "This is what I do then, say I do something and I can't do anything about it and what does crazy mean well, that's what it means" — is that it?

C: Yeah— [*pause*]

T: I suppose I sense it means a lot of other things to you too.

C: [*pause*] Well there's quite a bit of difference in, kinda mean different kinda people that are crazy.

T: Mmm — "We're crazy in different ways," huh.

C: Yeah, take a sadist, he's a lot different — I mean different than others —

T: Goes around hurting people that are nice. [*C:* Or hurting himself.] Uh-huh — hurting himself.

C: I know I got shook up one day when a nurse called . . . .

Excerpt 4

C: If it wasn't for the court putting me here, I wouldn't be here.

T: "So being here is really a blow to my pride."

C: No, I didn't mean that, when I was up to G——, I joked about this place, quite a bit —

T: Mmm — mmm —

C: Told the guys I'd like to come here, but I don't think I really meant it.

T: "I wasn't really serious."

C: This guy that used to work here as an aide he told me about it — I guess he sensed that, he always says I was bumming here, told me I was bumming, but he didn't know more, no more about mugs than I do.

T: "I suppose what really does get to me, it's not ah, this is ah, for being here, means people won't respect me or trust me or ah, even think of me as a person" — is that it partly?

C: Yeah, that's right — I know the doctors don't [*names two doctors*] —

T: "They all look down their nose at me," huh.

C: I don't care for 'em anyway, they don't really like me.

T: I suppose even though, you say, "Well I didn't like them, yet it still does get to me that they think this of me."

C: [*pause*] I guess the only ones that ever did trust me was my mother and a guard at G——.

T: Mmm — "The only people I really felt and trusted —"

C: Maybe it was because I liked them and I thought, I know Dan trusts me, with just about anything he's got. The only thing I don't like about this place is that they, everywhere I go they have to have an aide tagging me.

T: Mmm.

C: I hate that.

T: "Being watched all the time as though I were some stupid child or something," huh.

C: Afraid I'm goin' to run away.

T: Mmm — mmm.

C: So I know if they keep that up then I will.

T: "It eats on me that they don't trust me and sort of watch me all the time like I'm going to run off or do something—" [*pause*]

C: Like when I get mad, the patients here they just keep away from me.

T: Mmm — As though something was wrong with you — or something.

C: Well I blew up one time, right here among the patients.

T: Mmm — and now they're sort of afraid to get close to you.

C: The only one that does is Jerry but he don't say much to me.

T: Mmm — "He's around me but we don't really talk much. We joke a little but —"

C: When he, he talks, he seems, he seems like he's watching everything he says.

T: He's afraid to say what he thinks, is that it?

C: Like, he's afraid I will blow up at him or something.

T: Oh . . . .

Excerpt 5

T: I suppose in a way it says, sort of says something very much like the one about R. T. [recreational therapy] or other things that, "I'm not going to be forced into it."

C: [*pause*] Well, that's the way I felt.

T: Mmm.

C: I didn't, I, I guess nobody likes to be forced into anything. Some will go along with and there's some that won't, and I'm just one of them that wouldn't.

T: Mmm — "Then if it's something I want to do then, let me do it, but don't try to make me do it."

C: Right. I'd do it if I was asked for it.

T: Mmm — mmm.

C: But I didn't ask for it.

T: Mmm.

C: I guess when a guy hasn't got them privileges, he want's 'em [*T:* Mmm] and when he's got 'em, he don't want 'em — [*laughs*]

T: Yeah.

C: That's the way I feel.

T: The grass always looks greener on the other side.

C: Yeah — and when you get on the other side, the other side looks better yet.

T: Mmm— [*long pause*]

C: Well, you know when we were talking about my own father —

T: Mmm.

C: My step-father — well, I thought I hated him then, don't seem to now.

T: "Well, at that time I felt very strongly like that dirty son of a bitch. I'd like to kill him and now, now No!" [*pause*]

C: I, I got to give the boy credit though —[*T:* Mmm.] He brought me up and all that.

T: I suppose in a sense even more than just giving him credit huh — yeah, "I find that I do like him too, and I'd like him to like me."

C: Yeah, I'd like him to but you can't make a horse drink — [*laughs*]

T: "I'd like very much if he would care for me and yet I, I don't think that, well he really does," is that it?

C: I don't know, I, oh think he sorta likes me in a way, but I don't think he could hate me all the way —

T: Mmm — the way he's acting, he must care somewhat.

C: You know he wouldn't even let me use any of his stuff.

T: Mmm.

C: He was sorta nice to me when I got out of G——.

T: Huh —

C: We didn't have any, no arguments or nothing this time.

T: You mean he went out of his way to be nice.

C: Yeah, maybe he thought I went through enough.

T: Mmm.

C: Before I got sent up to G—— he said, "I'll sure crown him."

T: "Before that he was always forever, forever riding me."

C: Always riding me ah, he did, he did it for his — he tried to do it for a good thing.

T: "Now, when I look back, I can see well, maybe he thought he was doing me a favor, sure didn't feel like it then, but maybe that's what he was trying to do."

C: I haven't wrote him a letter, not ever in my life I don't think —

T: Mmm.

C: But I think I'm goin' to do it one of these days.

T: "I never have gone out of my way to tell him how I feel or anything and . . . ."

Excerpt 6

C: Boy, she was soaked [*T:* Hmm—] [*pause*] we just laughed at her — [*laughs*] — We hated to see her lose it, but it seemed so funny you know.

T: You appreciated the fact that it was really something to her and yet it seemed so, so comical that —

C: I guess that's the biggest one she ever did hook onto, now she catches pretty good sized ones but they're all carp — [*laughs*]

T: [*laughing*] — Don't make good trout.

C: They ain't trout at all, they're just river bass, or whatever you call 'em.

T: Mmm — they ain't worth anything.

C: They ain't even worth skinning 'em on account of the scales — [*pause*] I enjoy fishing for carp more than I do any other fish —

T: Mmm —

C: You, you know you can get a carp — [*laughing*]

T: [*laughs*] — Very easy?

C: You just throw a piece of bread, you look and you got 'em.

T: "Well, that's one way I can really win —" [*pause*] [*laughs*]

C: It's just like when I go hunting, I don't like to hunt for squirrels —

T: They're hard —

C: They're too hard to see in the trees — I like to hunt for rabbits, 'cause I know I can get rabbits.

T: It's lots more fun hunting or fishing if I know I can catch something.

C: Well, before I, the first time I started hunting, I couldn't get nothin', but I still enjoyed it, 'cause I was learning about it —

T: Mmm.

C: And now I know quite a bit about it —

T: Mmm.

C: And they're easy to get now, if you know where, it just de — depends on the weather now, if you know where to hunt, it's the weather.

T: If you know how to hunt, well it's not so hard, it comes easy.

C: Like when it's real nice and warm out, even if it's cold to you but the sun is shining on you —

T: Mmm.

C: The old rabbits they ain't goin' to sit much, they ain't goin' to sit that much, that's why they appear in the open.

T: Sit in the sun?

C: Yeah, and people they trounce around in berry bushes and get all scratched up —

T: And you're out there.

C: They keep 'em on the run —

T: Kicking them around.

C: Once in a while I'll kick up one, it's all right if you just go out there and just walk slow and look under the little piles, they just leap a little bit around holes — [*Therapist laughs.*] — A little dark in there and you bend down and look and you can see 'em — a lot of times you just take the gun butt and bust 'em in the head.

T: Mmm.

C: I don't like to do it that way, I like to kick 'em out and let 'em run — that — they're clean suicide, doesn't matter — [*laughs*]

T: Too easy that way?

C: Yeah, you don't feel like you've really earned it.

T: Mmm.

C: Well, it takes just a little —

T: There's no, no real fun to it —

C: No, usually when you go out to kill a rabbit, they're sittin' and it's pretty hard to shoot 'em on the run, and that's the way I like it.

T: There's really more challenge to it.

C: Yeah, like this year when I got out — opening day got my limit on pheasant and rabbit — I suppose I mighta gotten my limit on squirrel, but I wasn't about to go in the woods —

T: Mmmm.

C: A lot of guys don't like to hunt with me because when I go hunting I hunt in all posted land.

Excerpt 7

C: And they had my name on last year's — Phil goes to Mendota for a mental checkup — [*laughs*] — oh, that sounds silly — [*still laughing*]

T: Yeah — "And the silly part of it is the realization well that's me, not just someone else, it's me."

C: They write so many lies in the paper though — they exaggerate and all that, they want to make a big thing out of nothing — sure I committed a crime [T: Mmm] but they don't have to build it up so big like I sound like I'm a regular dangerous criminal, I mean.

T: You sounded like an Al Capone or something— [*pause*]

C: Al Capone wasn't rough though, that was Dillinger — [*laughs*]

T: Yeah.

C: Al Capone had men, lots of 'em to do his dirty work, Capone wouldn't do nothin' —

T: Mmm.

C: Dillinger liked his own dirty work, you know.

T: "They built it up and as my father has built it up too huh, he sort of washed his hands of me or something and —"

C: Yeah.

T: "Doesn't want anything to do with me" — that must, that must really hurt.

C: Oh, not too much — [*laughs*]

T: Mmm.

C: If it does it makes me laugh every once in a while though, it sorta seems funny.

T: I guess it's not a funny laugh either.

C: Nope, [*laughing*] [*pause*] no that isn't it — [*laughs*] [*pause*]

T: Mmm.

C: I think a laugh does you good once in a while.

T: Mmm — "If it really bothers me then I laugh, don't let it bother me as though it were really funny and humorous."

C: Yeah, that's the way I am — [*laughs*] — I bet you think I'm a real gone nut.

T: No, guess I don't — I guess my feeling there was, that, that really must have hurt quite a bit, where you really had to laugh about it or be — oh, cry or something— [*pause*]

C: I don't think you've even — I don't think anybody's worth crying over, I'm gonna have to laugh it off and either, after you're done laughing you feel a lot better, before long you forget all about it [*pause*] some people are sensitive.

T: Mmm.

C: Oh, everybody's got a sensitive part in 'em.

T: I suppose it would strike me as a pretty odd thing would it, if you really weren't hurt by it? I guess by laughing you're saying, "I really am hurt but I don't want to feel it."

C: When I laugh I don't feel it.

T: [*pause*] "When I laugh I can almost feel good about it."

C: Al — almost — [*laughs*]

T: Almost.

Excerpt 8

T: "Maybe a big part of it sure is that they haven't written, maybe they don't care — and it does matter to me."

C: Oh, it'd help out I know.

T: Mmm — "I may try to say I don't care whether they write or not but I damn well do —"

C: I say it to other people but I don't say it like that to myself.

T: Mmm [*long pause*], "Because it really does hurt that I think they don't care" [*long pause*] I s'pose one of the things you were saying there was, "I may seem pretty hard on the outside to other people, but I do have feelings."

C: Yeah, I've got feelings. But most of 'em I don't let 'em off.

T: M-hm. Kinda hide them. [*C, faintly:* Yeah.] [*long pause*]

C: I guess the only reason I try to hide 'em, is, seein' that I'm small, I guess I got to be a tough guy or somethin'.

T: M-hm.

C: That the way I, think, I think people might think about me.

T: Mm. "Little afraid to show my feelings. They might think I was weak, 'n' take advantage of me or something. They might hurt me if they — knew I could be hurt."

C: I think they'd try anyway.

T: "If they really knew I had feelings, they, they really might try and hurt me." [*long pause*]

C: I guess I don't want 'em to know that I got 'em. [*T:* Mm.] 'Cause then they couldn't if they wanted to.

T: "So I'd be safe if I, if I seem like a, as though I was real hard on the outside. If they thought I was real hard, I'd be safe."

Excerpt 9

T: [*long pause*] I guess the way, only thing I sensed there was it seemed as if you got more uncomfortable, just before you pulled away or something like the closer you got to it the more uncomfortable you felt, was that it?

C: I don't think I was even getting close to it.

T: Mmm — let's us assume you'll get there.

C: [*pause*] I'm getting tired of sitting now.

T: [*long pause*] Mmm [*long pause*] that's the way you've been thinking, sort of running over in your mind things that have happened or feelings, or experiences or something like, sort of been looking at a blank.

C: It's more than a blank.

T: [*long pause*] You know, I just have this — [*laughs*] idea that, sort of going into a big empty room, and sort of looking around all over it, saying, well it must be here, it must be here. [*Patient laughs.*] So it, it seemed just sort of to fit this.

C: That might be it, I don't know [*pause*] maybe I'm looking for somethin' that ain't there.

T: Mmm.

C: And after I keep saying it's somethin' that ain't there, who'd blame me — [*laughs*]

T: [*laughs*] — That would go right with the chair wouldn't it — the sort of phrase I threw out was, "Whether I'm looking in the wrong room or whether it just isn't there."

C: [*pause*] I don't know what it is.

T: Mmm — It's not knowing where it is or exactly what it is.

C: Mmm.

T: Just a very strong feeling that there is something there.

C: I just got that feeling that there must be somethin' there.

T: Mmm — "If I'm this bothered well there damn well must be something big there to bother me."

C: Maybe I'm looking for something that's too big and it ain't that big.

T: Mmm — "Maybe I'm looking for something huge when it's really something that when you see it it's quite small."

C: [*very long pause*] I'm sorta gettin' tired now — [*laughs*]

T: Mmm.

Excerpt 10

C: It makes your record three, four times —

T: Mmm.

C: I don't see no sense in that, why can't one get it done with one trial.

T: "Why can't we get it over with?" [*long pause*] I suppose I sense some feelings about some other aspect of it too, maybe the other inmates there or guards or —

C: No, it's not the inmates or guards it's just that you get so damn lonely in them places.

T: Oh, being really cut off from people.

C: You're cut off from the whole world when you're in a cell— [*pause*]

T: Yeah, being terribly lonely and then you get sort of afraid too.

C: Well, I know they ain't goin' to take me back to no jail [*long pause*] I'm sick of this— [*pause*]

T: And when, when you're in a cell there being very much cut off from — one— [*long pause*] it gets pretty helpless there too.

C: You can't do much — unless you do it before they get you.

T: Oh — and once you're in there you're pretty much at their mercy, is that it?

C: I'm at nobody's mercy.

T: Mmm.

C: I let them do what they please.

T: [*pause*] I think I sense that that's the part that's really upsetting that — "The fact that you got me here I hate to have, to be in this position, I can't fight back."

C: Oh, I can change it, I'd just take a little walk, [*T: Mmm*] but that ain't goin' to get you nowhere [*T: Mmm*] 'cause I know there's no cell [*T: Mmm*] that's for sure.

T: You mean very strongly, "I'm not going to let them do this to me."

C: I did it too many times let 'em throw me in a — in a little ole cell.

T: Mmm.

C: [*long pause*] They don't even treat a person like a human in them damn jails.

T: Mmm.

C: Just like a bunch of dogs.

T: Once you get in there they just treat you like dirt, an animal —

C: Not just me, they treat everybody like that.

T: Mmm — You're feeling very strongly, "I'm not going to let them do this [*pause*] I just won't be treated this way."

Excerpt 11

T: I suppose I sense a sort of ah, ah more sad unhappiness about it this morning —

C: I don't think it's unhappiness.

T: "Some kind of feeling, I'm not sure what it is —" [*pause*]

C: It's just that the things I want to talk about I can't.

T: Mmm — There's a hopeless feeling about it.

C: Yeah.

T: You can't talk about them. "I want to and yet there is no use" [*pause*] is that it, ah?

C: I can't seem to do it— [*pause*]

T: Is there anything that I could do that would make it easier then?

C: M-hmm— [*pause*]

T: Do you think you could sit here and talk about it to the tape, if I left?

C: I dunno.

T: Would that make it easier? [*pause*] Would you like to try that? [*pause*]

C: It's the idea, it's just the idea of just saying it.

T: Mmm.

C: I don't know what would help.

T: I hope you're now saying that if you felt that would make it easier, you sure would be willing to do that — [*pause*]

C: It might and it might not, I dunno.

T: Mmm — Would you like to try it then?

C: I can try it, I guess.

T: When, when you get through if you'd like to talk to me some more, I'll be down the hall, if not you can just turn it off, there's a stop button on the recorder.

[*Therapist goes out.*] [*pause*]

Excerpt 12[7]

C: I think the biggest buck is that, I — feel sorry for myself [*pause*] I miss my parents too, so much [*pause*] I don't know if it's that they don't, that they don't love me any more, or they don't like me or I don't know what — that bothers me quite a bit I guess— [*pause*] When I was about sixteen, something just seemed to take hold of me, made me do things that I didn't want to do — I mean I still did it — it wasn't what I was doin' or

7. This is the material which the patient spoke into the tape recorder. It took about twenty minutes, but by eliminating all silences it has been condensed into a brief segment. This is also the only instance in which two excerpts are taken from one interview. In this respect, it is a more specially selected segment than any of the others in the three cases.

nothin' — [*pause*] I've always been curious of people, it just seems like nobody likes me [*pause*] they're always trying to make fun of me or somethin' — I just know that — after I get done talking here — [*fiddles with mike*] — that someone's gonna — listen to it and — that's why I have such a hard time — talking today I guess— [*pause*] [*clears throat*] I just wish I could talk to [*pause*] some other doctor to find out if somethin's wrong with me, with me when ———— ain't around — [*pause*] Well, I was talking about the time that I was sixteen that, I've always liked these, I've had quite a few relationships with queers [*pause*] I guess my biggest problem is from sex. Well, when I was six — sixteen [*pause*] [*sighs*] — I started to — molest young girls I didn't want to hurt 'em — I never hurt 'em neither — well I guess that's it — and I used to think quite a bit of it — I don't know why I did it but — [*speaks to Therapist*] Hello —

Excerpt 13

C: When I try to think, there's somethin' back there, but I can't bring it out —

T: Mmm.

C: But then I start counting — [*laughs*] — I start counting. [*speaks very low*]

T: Mmm — You're sort of saying, I don't want to, I don't want to even want to think about whatever it is, I'll just get away from it — start counting or something.

C: [*long pause*] And when I can't think of nothin' it bothers me.

T: Mmm — why can't I think of it, is that it?

C: Yeah— [*long pause*]

T: And yet it seems so easy to just start counting or —

C: Yeah.

T: Safely —

C: I mean there ain't nothin' wrong about counting, lot of people like to count — [*laughs*]

T: You sound like they're saying, "Oh, that's terrible." [*Patient laughs.*] I guess in a way, I do feel that way, not that it's terrible but, that's ah, well that's saying that you can't really be yourself and have to count instead. I don't know, does that make any sense to you?

C: I'd like to be myself instead of counting —

T: Mmm.

C: But it comes out just like an automatic — [*laughs*]

T: Mmm — "Just right away there I am counting."

C: Yeah, before I know it I'm at ah, five, six already.

T: Mmm.

C: What I never could figure out, it's puzzled me quite a bit, it seems like ah, like a lot of my dreams have come true and that.

T: Mmm — "I dream something and it happens."

C: Yeah [*pause*] like I dreamt this — one time I was sitting at a table with some person, there were two of 'em there I know and I — in my dream it — here I ended up arguing with 'em —

T: Mmm — [laughs] [pause]

C: But this time I avoided it. [laughs]

T: Mmm — this time it didn't come true.

C: Part of it did.

T: Mmmm.

C: What I — I had a dream before I even come here — I had a dream in G—— before I was even sent here — I was sitting in a long corridor.

T: Mmm.

C: And they were fixing the walls ah, taking plaster down and a bunch of us guys were sitting on the bunks joking around and all of a sudden it hit me I'd had that dream . . . .

Excerpt 14

C: I can't think that too much, the only thing that comes to my mind now is the things that I wanna do when I get out.

T: Right now, thinking of the future, huh.

C: Yeah.

T: It looks black to you, huh.

C: I wanna go out and go fishing — [laughs] — I think of pleasanter things I like.

T: Mmm — "Things that I'd really like to do."

C: Yeah.

T: "That's what I'm looking forward to—" [very long pause]

C: Do you know what day they gave me that ninety days, what was the date?

T: I really don't know what date it was.

C: But they do, about June I'll probably get out.

T: That's right.

C: I sure hope they don't give me another ninety days, after that — [laughs] [Therapist laughs.] Boy, them nineties, they give 'em pretty freely — [laughs]

T: [laughs] — Like, "Boy — this can go on forever."

C: It could if they wanted it to. What's the most they can keep it up at?

T: That, I don't know, ah, I don't recall ever doing this before.

C: Didn't anybody ever die in this hospital before.

T: Not that I've heard of.

C: You have now — [laughs]

T: Yeah.

C: [laughs] — Ninety days they said — that shocked me at first. [laughs]

T: Sort of like a sentence or something.

C: Yeah, without even, well I don't, it seems fair though — I didn't want to go back to jail and in a way I did though —

T: Mmm.

C: The only reason I wanted to go back though was so I could see my parents.

T: Mmm — "If I got back there at least I'd have a chance to see 'em."

C: Yeah — But they should have at least let the guy appear in court so they can give him the sentence, I mean not do it behind his back.

T: Mmm.

C: Maybe he's tired of looking at me — [*laughs*]

T: Well, I suppose if you really strongly objected to it you could write him a letter.

C: It won't do no good though — [*laughs*] I don't think I'd be — be out of here for a while if I did that now, unless I run away and that ain't goin' prove nothin'.

T: Mmm. I suppose —

C: You could gripe and moan all you want and they still wouldn't let you out — [*laughs*]

T: [*laughs*] — They got you.

C: Yeah — [*laughs*]

T: I don't know I suppose I have the feeling right now — that . . . .

Excerpt 15

C: The only thing I can figure out is mostly they — going from one foster home to another.

T: "I'm feeling pretty unwanted by now —"

C: Oh, I know different and all, but —

T: Mmm.

C: I really didn't know at that, at that time either.

T: Now you know one thing that, then this was pretty *real?*

C: Yeah — [*very long pause*]

T: Well, if — if other people who have had somewhat similar experiences usually feel pretty, well, pretty ah, I don't know whether afraid is a good word or ah, something like afraid of ah, of sexuality with people their own age —

C: I didn't —

T: Do you feel that way or . . . .

Commentaries

Bergman

Bergman sees Smith as initially a very sick patient. His progress is clear, yet Bergman is puzzled as to why therapy terminates where it does: "I think that Smith made a strong attachment to his therapist and I cannot see why the therapy should have ended soon after the last excerpt, unless some major external obstacles arose. Incidentally, I imagine that the later course of therapy would have been slow and difficult since Smith would find it hard to re-experience the aggressive, competitive, hostile, sadistic feelings which I surmise he gave up early in life."

In respect to the therapist's activity, Bergman offers: "I am very favorably impressed with the sturdy, firm, 'masculine' tone of the therapist. These qualities blend beautifully with the superb sensitivity of his comments, with his ability to hold the attention of the patient and the occasional free handling of the situation."

Bergman summarizes on an extremely favorable key: "It seems almost incredible to me that random excerpts from the therapy should contain as high a percentage of meaningful talk as these excerpts do. This is fascinating material." The messages of a very sick patient, then, are received by a sturdy, firm, but free therapist who communicates his understanding and facilitates a strong and meaningful relationship with extreme skill and sensitivity.

English

English observes much movement toward insight in a blocked and hostile patient. For English, a competent therapist helps to clarify Smith's thoughts and feelings by sensitive reflecting and leading, and skillful structuring of the patient's comments. The therapist tries to help the patient clarify his relation to reality, to be able to see "what others think of him." The therapist is helpful in enabling Smith to see that he has positive as well as negative feelings which he would like to express directly to significant others. Thus, initially, the therapist contributes considerably by constructing "the patient's feelings and presentation of self in words that sharpen mood and self-concept."

Just beyond the middle portion of therapy the therapist tries the helpful maneuver of "getting the patient to talk into a tape recorder while alone and state what would make his life easier in this institution":

At this, patient admits that he misses parents, that he feels no one likes him, that they even make fun of him. Expresses desire to see if another doctor thinks he is crazy. Goes on to admit that at age 16 he began to molest young girls. He doesn't know why he did it but earlier in his speaking into the tape recorder he said he was always curious about people.

When, during the next session, the patient blocks in thinking, he starts counting. The therapist initially facilitates Smith's exploration of this and then is sidetracked from his goal:

Therapist implies that counting is defense against thinking anything unpleasant. Patient pursues this quite a ways and then patient jumps over to dream and therapist goes along with him. Therapist gives up goal he was pursuing so well and accepts the patient's defensive maneuver of shifting the subject, since the patient obviously couldn't break into counting to defend himself against a discussion of the *meaning of counting.*

In general, while the therapist gets caught in some vagaries and defensive maneuvers, he is helpful in getting the patient's "true feelings out" about his past, his present, and his future, about others, his parents, and his therapist, but especially about himself. At termination English feels that Smith indirectly admitted his anxiety about sex activity with girls his own age "and that he isn't up to feeling it yet, but that the therapist will get him there."

English concludes by complimenting the therapist's ability to lead the patient to insight through the passive client-centered method. However, he hastens to add: "What the patient would *do* with the insight gained could not be determined from the tape."

Summarizing, a competent therapist receives most of the messages of a blocked and hostile patient. The therapist's sensitive reflections combine with his skillful structuring in effecting sharpened patient experience and expression. At times the therapist does get lost in the patient's vagaries and defensive maneuvers and is ineffective in reaching the patient.

Lewis

Lewis again notes his impression that whatever the therapist is responding to is often not apparent in the segments of the tapes that are sampled. Whereas Bergman notes the therapist's "superb sensitivity" and English emphasizes the therapist's skillful structuring, Lewis finds himself most critical of the therapy in the case of Smith, a "particularly trying" patient. Lewis clearly implies that he sees little or no movement and he attributes this, in part, to certain therapist behaviors:

It seemed to me that the therapist was continually running ahead of the patient, trying to put more complicated formulations in the patient's mouth than the patient was ready for, and he got a fair amount of resistance from the patient. I did not feel that he was always very close to the emotion of the patient but again it is hard to judge this because he may have been responding to all sorts of cues I do not have. Judging only from the verbalizations, the voice tone, the expression of feeling that I could pick up, etc. . . . , the therapist sounded in general as if he was determined to pull out of the patient depressive, lonely, apathetic, poignant feelings when the patient was rather flippant, shallow and teasing. Late in the tape the patient does finally admit that he has tender feelings underneath a "tough guy" exterior, but [the therapist] does not pick up the hostile resentment of the patient who is "sick of this" and stresses the patient's loneliness. He is not sensitive to the patient's wish to get out of the treatment situation although it does come up in the second segment to a certain degree. He appears to leave very little time between what the patient says and his responses for things to sink in. There is a kind of hurried quality in this tape and one gets the impression that whatever the therapist is responding to is not always apparent in the segments of tape that are sampled.

Lewis continues to elaborate on his impression "that this therapist has got the bit in his teeth to some degree and doesn't want to let it go":

One notes also the fumbling (which we all do) to try to get in touch with a complex utterance, such as is apparent in section 9, where there is a certain amount of floundering and shot-gun interpretations or reflections. . . . [B]ut it is significant that he did manage to say something critical about the therapist only when the therapist was not present. This is some indirect evidence that perhaps the therapist was blocking this expression without quite realizing it.

Lewis concludes by qualifying his more critical comments: "This is all perhaps excessively critical considering the fact that the patient is an extraordinarily difficult fellow to deal with, and most of us would find him quite trying."

In summary, then, Lewis believes that a determined but fumbling therapist actually blocks the expression of some of Smith's feelings. The therapist attempts to reflect those messages which he receives; however, his reflections are not close to the patient's emotions and thus have little positive effect upon Smith. The therapist then attempts a kind of "shotgun" approach in his interpretations and reflections with little impact. Thus, there is little movement and Smith remains difficult and resistant throughout therapy.

May

For Smith, as for Brown and Jones, May discerns some movement toward greater communication between therapist and patient. The resignation and despair of early sessions have been transmuted into overt anxiety and there is an intense focusing by the patient on his problems: "By and large I consider the shift in therapy from symptoms to 'open' possibilities which are faced with overt anxiety to be the most significant indication of positive movement in therapy." While May acknowledges the possibility of lasting positive movement for all three cases, he is "least confident about the lasting positive movement in the case of Smith who seems to have psychopathic characteristics."

Again, the therapist seems to have the "therapeutic intent" and respect for the patient which May considers to be basic "curative elements." However, May thinks that the therapist has many shortcomings. Like the other therapists he tends to reflect the words rather than the feelings of the patient. He almost mimics Smith:

Patient Smith remarks, "Maybe I'm looking for something that is too big and it ain't that big." Therapist responds, "Mmm . . . Maybe I'm looking for something huge when it's really something that when you see it, it's quite small!" Again, patient Smith says, ". . . They don't even treat a person like a human in them damn jails . . . Just like a bunch of dogs!" Therapist answers, "Once you get in there they just treat you like dirt, an animal."

As earlier, May notes the limited range of affects dealt with by the therapist and an absence of dealing with the relationship between patient and therapist. The use of the first person singular for reflecting the patient's statements has clear disadvantages:

I felt there was too much identification of therapist with patient, shown in the therapist's frequent use of "I" as though he were the patient. This is done almost all the way through in the case of Smith. I can see, of course, how this use of "I" for the patient can be a genuine and spontaneous experience of actual identity at certain moments. But when it is done constantly it seems to me to take away the patient's opportunity to experience himself as a subject in his own right, to take a stand against the therapist, to experience being in an interpersonal world.

The therapist seemed to hold Smith back from exploring the past. At times Smith wanted to talk about basic past relationships which meant much to him: "Whatever our theoretical position toward childhood relationships with parents, and even though we may not go along with the weight of genetic causality placed upon childhood experiences by classical Freudians, nevertheless it seems to me these relationships are power-laden centers of affect which are very important for the patient."

Concerning Smith's soliloquy into the tape, May has some very "special reactions":

Smith's tone of voice here seems authentic, searching, facing his problems as best he can without the bravado of other sessions. One might hypothecate that thus an interpersonal relation is not necessary to bring these things out; the patient only, ironically enough, has to talk into a machine! But I believe this would be an error. I believe that Smith could not have done this except that he *had been* talking with the therapist and knew it *would* be listened to by the therapist. In my own terms, I would interpret this experience as "Eigenwelt," the facing and dealing with one's self is possible by the bravado of defying someone else. But such "Eigenwelt" is in the context of, and inseparable, I assume, from the "Mitwelt" of the interpersonal world which the relation with the therapist has built up.

While May's overall judgment of all three cases is that this is "definitely good therapy," he has reservations in the case of Smith, who presents especially difficult problems. May traces whatever progress there was to specific things in the therapist, particularly in his attitude: ". . . the therapist's respect for the patient, desire to listen and to hear, commitment to the welfare of the patient and to the possibility of the patient's health, use of potentialities, etc. were very clear." The fact that there is nothing whatever superficial about the therapist's concern for the patient overcomes the potential harmful effects of "going along on the surface, being two-dimensional." May reiterates his belief that "deeper and more lasting" change might be effected "if underlying feelings, including negative aggressive ones, were brought out and experienced directly in the relationship between patient and therapist."

Seeman

Seeman qualifies the process movement which he discerns in the case of Smith: "My chief feeling about Smith was that a process of therapy had truly gotten underway but that Smith still had some way to go."

Seeman sees the therapist's consistency and perceptiveness in his relationship to the patient as having been helpful. However, "there were a few puzzling moments":

It seemed to me that in Excerpts 1 to 3 the patient was anxious to talk about being seen as "crazy" but that the therapist was slow to move into these feelings with Smith. For example, the therapist's question about the patient's having a fever seemed a denial of the patient's reference to the word "sick." Also, in Excerpt 3, the therapist's reference to "no control over what *we* do" moved a step away from personal confrontation. From here on, however, the therapist seemed very much "with" the patient.

In discussing the session where the patient met with the tape recorder, Seeman offers: "One other facet of the therapist's activity puzzled me, and that was in Excerpt 11 when the therapist seemed insistent on leaving the patient to himself. At the time I thought the therapist misread the patient's need. But when I heard Excerpt 12, I felt that the patient was making very active use of the time alone."

Seeman describes the case of Smith as a therapy which is in movement, but which was prematurely terminated: "One could argue with real cogency that the start Smith got in self-understanding could generalize and take him further on his own. This would be an uphill way, because it seemed that there were still some significant self-related attitudes that were being denied by Smith. On balance, my feeling is that there was a real self-search that had to have positive results, but that the search was still very much in process at the end."

In brief then, a consistent and perceptive therapist at times misreads the patient's messages. The therapist's consistency and perceptivity in understanding and communicating his understanding account for the patient's movement from concern over being seen as "crazy" to one engaged in the process of self-exploration.

Whitaker

In acknowledging that the patient gains his own growth impetus in therapy, Whitaker rather directly implies that this is done in spite of the therapist's activity rather than because of it. Yet the therapist's behavior, which has highly negative connotations for Whitaker, seems in some way to set the stage for the patient's "breaking" out of this relationship. Whitaker is angered and puzzled by the role of the therapist in relation to Smith.

Whitaker finds himself "immediately preoccupied with the carbon copy imitation of Carl Rogers." He goes on to say, "The voice tone has an eerie similarity although the therapist sometimes talks a little too fast. I found myself bored in the listening and with a similar kind of boredom to that which I get from listening to psychoanalytic tapes. I was concerned with the fact that the therapist's 'I' of identification with the patient seemed hollow."

The first person formulations of the therapist seem to infuriate Whitaker and he clearly sees the therapist as most effective when he drops that "role." He wonders: perhaps it is "an actual fantasy in the therapist himself." Indeed, it is a "joint fantasy state." Certainly, however, the therapist is "not a corrective mirror but a plain mirror." Whitaker becomes particularly distressed with the therapist's utilization of the "neutral response" and his complete denial of himself "in such a firm fatalistic manner that the patient seemed to be forced to deny himself."

This kind of unreal, exaggerated humility seemed difficult for me to tolerate. I also felt that in the therapist's denying his aggression, he forced the patient to also cover his own aggression. As a matter of fact, by segment 10, I had become preoccupied with the therapist's endless dampening of the patient's response and somehow the patient's threat of suicide seemed consonant with this. Yet in the final line of segment 10, it seemed as though there was a real person in the felt response of the therapist's tone of voice and in segment 11, this is confirmed when the therapist becomes personal and breaks out of his technical role. Here again, I found myself wondering if the long delay made the breakthrough more significant.

As therapy progresses, the patient is indeed able to stand in opposition to the therapist. Smith even comes to mock the therapist "as though somehow he had gotten strength in their relationship." In conjunction with the therapist's somewhat increased responsivity, one "gets the sense of strength produced by this separation between the therapist and the patient."

However, in general Whitaker questions the very limited and apparently aimless structuring of the relationship. The therapist becomes for Whitaker a kind of "teaching machine" which rapidly reinforces the patient's words and demands, in turn, immediate response to its formulations. Sometimes it seems even to be the punishing of the patient in "delicate and subtle ways."

In summary, Whitaker asks:

Why is this therapy so difficult to understand? Is the power of the therapy the endless denial by the therapist of his own person, even of his physical presence? It's as though he insists that he is only a voice, only an idea, as though no one is there. In contrast to this, the patient obviously can see that he is a person, he is a body. Is it possible that this peculiar kind of double-bind may be the basis for the establishment of a profound transference–counter-transference, an interlocking relationship? . . . Then he breaks it and in breaking gains his own growth impetus.

Thus, a self-denying therapist receives some of the messages of an ambivalent and hostile patient. The therapist's machine-like reflections are really only joint fantasy statements which have no corrective value. The therapist's endless self-denying role as the patient's alter ego, however, operates to somehow encourage the patient to break free of an unreal relationship. A somewhat stronger ego is in some unclear fashion the result.

A Critique of the Case of Smith

The case of Smith appears to have elicited some of the widest disparities in the formulations of the client-centered process with schizophrenics. The extremes in reactions are present for all critical questions.

At one extreme are Bergman and English. For them, positive movement is clearly discernible, and traceable to laudable therapist behavior. A blocked and hostile patient forms a strong and meaningful relationship in which insight, mood, and self-concept are sharpened.

While May and Seeman acknowledge movement, they are hesitant and tentative in their formulations about the lasting quality of the progress seen in therapy. May describes the possibility of positive patient movement from desperation toward a greater capacity for relatedness and problem solving for all cases. However, he is clearly least confident of the lasting nature of the positive movement in the case of Smith. Seeman perceives patient engagement in real and positive self-search for understanding—but he emphasizes that the engagement is "in process" and by no means concluded, if indeed successful process ever concludes.

For Whitaker, an ambivalent and hostile patient somehow gains growth impetus in spite of the activities and attitudes of the therapist. "Or could it be because of the activities and attitudes of the therapist?" Whitaker thoughtfully and ironically seems to ask.

At the other extreme in the evaluations of movement, Lewis sees Smith as a hostile and resistant patient who remains such throughout therapy because of the therapist's gross inadequacies.

Briefly, then, two theorists make out clear-cut and very positive movement in therapy, two other theorists see positive movement but fear it may not last, and a fifth reviewer sees positive movement but isn't sure whether this is in spite of or because of the therapist. The sixth reviewer sees no clear positive movement.

In the reviewers' reactions to the therapist, three central positive factors seem to emerge: (1) the therapist's presentation of high levels of skill and sensitivity throughout therapy; (2) the therapist's positive intent and dedication which is distinct from his skill or lack of it; (3) the therapist's rigid pattern of self-denial which is broken at times as he becomes somewhat more real as a separate self with the progression of therapy.

Again, explicit attention is accorded the technique of reflection. The picture which emerges is a bipolar one. Bergman, English, and Seeman assume a positive stance in their view that the therapist is consistent, perceptive, and sensitive in his understanding of the client and his communication of this understanding. Lewis, May, and Whitaker, in turn, take stands on the essential ineffectiveness of his attempts at reflection.

There is sharp disagreement in other dimensions. Thus while English perceives the therapist as skillfully leading and structuring the patient's comments "in words that sharpen mood and self concept," Lewis is distressed by the therapist's continual "running ahead of the patient," and "trying to put more complicated formulations in the patient's mouth than the patient was ready for . . ." To confound matters, Whitaker questions the overall lack of structure, not so much perhaps in the therapist's formulations as in his lack of substantive direction in therapy. It is implicit for Whitaker and explicit for Lewis that the therapist feels bound to carry out some sort of pattern which has been worked out prior to his first contact with the client. By contrast, Bergman and English are impressed with the occasional "free handling" of the therapy situation by the therapist which enables the patient to experience and express a more full range of feelings.

From such contradictions, what elements emerge as the effective therapeutic ingredients in the case of Smith? Clearly, the therapist's consistent and very sensitive communication of his understanding of the patient are the critical aspects of movement for Bergman and Seeman. For English, the therapist's communication of his perceptive understanding conjoins with skillful structuring to overcome the therapist's occasional meanderings in the patient's defensive maneuvers and to effect constructive personality change in the patient.

May sees the progress in therapy as traceable to the therapist's attitudes, that is, his respect for the patient and his "commitment to the welfare of the patient and to the possibility of the patient's health [and] use of potentialities."

Whitaker's formulations give the therapist's activities an ironical twist. His recognition of at least minimal growth in ego strength of the patient, combined with his negative evaluation of the therapist's "endless denial," pose a conflict for him. His tentative resolution, which is really a question, is worth requoting: "Is it possible that this peculiar kind of double-bind may be the basis for the establishment of a profound transference–counter-transference, an interlocking relationship which goes on undisturbed by the patient until the patient becomes bored with this unreal quality and this parent-child relationship? Then he breaks it and in breaking gains his own growth impetus."

An Overview

The attempt to bring outsiders who themselves are creative leaders in the field to focus their clinical and theoretic skills upon very brief recorded samples taken from three relatively "successful" client-centered cases was in a sense an attempt to break free of the context of client-centered theory and practice by drawing on external views of client-centered process. It also was an attempt to see if clinical meaning could be drawn from the brief samples which have formed the raw data of the research program. In short, could the real "stuff" of therapy be seen in randomly selected brief samples and could these be contained in the less than life-sized context of tapes and typescripts?

In these attempts the reviewers were asked to focus upon (1) what therapeutic movement, if any, occurred? (2) what therapist activities were helpful? (3) what therapist activities were not helpful?

The reviewers' responses to these questions have more than satisfied the initial hopes for this venture. New and fresh ways of looking at the client-centered process emerge from the outsiders' formulations of the dynamics and processes involved in these three cases. Client-centered therapy has had a chance to see itself as others see it and thus gain in perspective. More than this, new conceptualizations of therapeutic mechanisms have emerged and new perspectives on old mechanisms have been attempted.

Clearly, both clinical and research meaning can be found in the very brief, randomly selected excerpts of the tape recorded therapeutic process even though some of the reviewers regard it as an unsatisfactory basis for evaluation. The raw data for research, fragmentary as it is, can provide meaningful raw data for clinical formulations and insights.

The discovery that some meaningful understanding of the therapeutic relationship and process can grow out of listening to only an hour-long series of excerpts from a therapeutic encounter extending over a four year period is perhaps of itself of major importance. What new clinical insights and formulations might emerge from a similar viewing of psychoanalytic, existential, learning theory, or other therapeutic approaches? Would the same clinical formulations apply?

Therapeutic Movement or Progress in the Patient

Significant therapeutic movement, in varying degrees, was observed by the six reviewers in thirteen out of the eighteen clinical formulations (six reviewers for each of three cases for a total of eighteen evaluations). Thus the clinical evaluations tended to reaffirm the evaluations of relatively "successful" cases based upon outside criteria such as hospital discharge rates, gainful employment, and positive change on the diagnostic indices.

A careful look at the evaluations reveals that they have some pattern. On the one hand, Drs. Bergman and Lewis see significant positive therapeutic movement in only one out of the three cases. While Bergman concedes minimal movement in the case of Jones, Bergman and Lewis each discern significant movement in a different case. By contrast, Drs. May, Seeman, and Whitaker could each find clinical evidence for therapeutic movement in all three cases.

May, Seeman, and Whitaker are perhaps closest in their theoretical orientation to the client-centered position. Particularly are they closely allied in stressing the fundamental character of the relationship and the phenomenological or existential stance. One might ask: Could it be that their theoretical views are perhaps as important as the clinical materials from the excerpts of the cases themselves in determining evaluations of progress? This does seem a distinct possibility, particularly in view of the formulations of Bergman and Lewis who are in closer kinship with the psychoanalytic stance. Nevertheless, it seems as though all theorists employed evidence from different sources for deciding on the presence or absence or degree of therapeutic movement.

What, then, are the indices of therapeutic movement that the reviewers relied on in assessing progress in these three cases? Are the indices related to the research instruments measuring degree of self-exploration? Or experiencing? Does the tape-recorded material contain other potentially useful research indices?

A central common thread woven through the fabric of each theorist's formulation was the level of the patient's depth or extent of self-exploration. Thus, this seems to be a variable critical to the assay of therapeutic movement. Depth of intrapersonal exploration would, then, appear to be a goal in the therapeutic approaches represented by each of the clinical reviewers. A number of the formulations, though not all, made explicit the importance of openness to new and direct experiencing and thus defined this as both a goal to be aimed at in psychotherapy and an index of extent of therapeutic progress. Here, too, there is a common core of meaning in the research scales on the one hand and the clinical evaluation on the other.

Just as clearly, other indices of movement were underscored to greater or lesser degrees. Thus, changes in the general energy level of the patient, increased self-confidence, the development of insight and the focus on problem-solving are all stressed as evidence of movement or therapeutic personality change. With hindsight it seems strange that of these latter four indices the elements of increased energy level and self-confidence were not included in the research indices of therapeutic process.

In view of the general consensus on the indices of movement in therapy we must ask: How, then, are the differing evaluations of movement in the same case arrived at? Do different clinical reviewers place a differential weight on a given index of movement such as depth of intrapersonal exploration? Does a given concept, such as depth of self-exploration, have the same implicit meaning to a client-centered theorist as it does to proponents of other orientations? Can divergent questions of values find empirical answers and resolutions?

Perhaps another approach to explaining differing estimates of movement when the same indices appear to be used, lies in the difficulty of separating movement in the patient from evaluations of the therapist's activities. The research effort itself has had to deal with this very difficult question: Can evaluations of what the therapist is doing be distinguished clearly from evaluations of what the patient is doing? Whitaker's answer to this is a resounding "Yes!" He finds himself in the perplexing situation of seeing movement in the patient and yet feeling that the therapist is primarily a retarder rather than a facilitator. Thus Whitaker, in his formulations of the relationship between patient movement and therapist activities, sees the patient as adjusting to his loneliness in the manner in which the therapist appears to adjust to life's exigencies, or discovering himself, or growing in ego strength, by breaking free of the relationship, almost *in spite of* the therapist who is seen as the patient's "reflecting" alter ego.

The Therapist's Contribution

All reviewers respond to the therapist's activity of reflecting patient feeling as a central therapeutic approach in the client-centered process. For many of the commentators the evaluation of the therapist as helpful or unhelpful hinges upon whether he is effective or ineffective in reflecting the feelings of a particular patient. Reflection of feeling, which can range from inadequate reflection of content to an approach to "oneness" with the patient in depth reflections seems almost of necessity to involve a basic empathic understanding of the patient. Thus, although client-centered theorists have lately exhibited a growing concern with other dimensions such as therapist congruence or genuineness, the reviewers see empathic understanding as a central dimension in the client-centered therapeutic encounter with schizophrenic patients. There seems to be a clear correlation between the reviewers' assessments of progress and their assessments of the effectiveness or ineffectiveness of reflection (or communication of accurate empathic understanding). In only a few of the present formulations is positive therapeutic movement described in a relationship in which reflection (or empathy) seemed to have little therapeutic impact upon the patient. In most cases, patient progress goes hand in hand with effective reflection, that is to say, with communication of accurate empathy. It is significant, however, that in many of these evaluations empathy or reflection conjoins with other effective ingredients to constitute the significant sources of effect in patient personality change.

None of the reviewers describe any of the client-centered cases as ineffective where they see effective reflection by the therapists. This underscores the critical nature of reflection of feeling, depth of reflection, or empathy to the client-centered process.

The formulations of effective therapy in the context of ineffective reflection suggest other dimensions relevant to the helping process. Some of these dimensions would seem to be related to empathy.

The careful attention which English accords the therapist's skillful structuring in leading of the patient's thoughts and viewings is a case in point. The therapist in that case would indeed probably describe himself as engaging in depth reflection. In more client-centered terminology this structuring and leading is described as a reflection of the feelings implicit in the verbal and non-verbal communication of the patient: the attempts to reflect meaning conveyed by changes in voice, by small bodily movements, and by the other subtle cues offered by the face to face encounter, as well as the attempts to reflect the meaning of things avoided or simply left unsaid. Both go beyond what the patient is saying verbally, yet both emphasize a sensitive and empathic understanding by the therapist. Thus, a major clustering of clinical observations seems relevant to the research measures of accurate empathy.

A second clustering of the clinical evaluations of positive therapist activities seems relevant to the research measures of positive regard and unconditional positive regard. Rollo May in general, and English and Seeman particularly in the case of Brown, emphasize as critical dimensions of effective therapy the therapist's *interest, concern,* and *personal dedication.* Personal dedication, particularly when highlighted by acts of caring, appears central. Lewis, in turn, perceives the therapist's quiet encouragement in the communication of an attitude of attempting to help as the truly effective therapeutic element in the case of Jones (the case seen by him as most benefited). Lewis emphasizes the therapist's attempts to help Jones find his own mode of self-expression and self-discovery.

The element of personal involvement, while it clearly touches upon the hypothesized condition of unconditional positive regard or "nonpossessive warmth" also points to a slightly different dimension. It raises questions. Is the construct of unconditional positive regard adequate to include the meanings of the therapist's dedication and involvement? Is the therapist's dedication an emergent whole involving nonpossessive warmth, genuineness, and intensity and intimacy? Is the therapist's calm secure acceptance and quiet encouragement, described by Lewis, cut from the same fabric as the "rapt attention" of the intense and immediately-reflecting therapists described by Whitaker? Can these grow out of the therapist's self-congruence and maturity or are they something more?

The degree to which these elements exist in each of the three cases evaluated is controversial. The inherent ambiguity of the tape-recorded and transcribed material, taken from the therapeutic encounters themselves, leads to differing interpretations. Thus, while English, May, and Seeman emphasize the personal involvement of the therapist in the case of Brown, Lewis sees only the therapist's active "reaching out" with personal reactions in musings. Then, too, Whitaker notes that many of the therapist's verbalizations in the case of Brown lack feeling and communicate detachment rather than involvement. For Whitaker, in a strange twist of outcome, this detachment seems to combine with other elements to facilitate Brown's adjustment to his aloneness. In effect, it is implied that the patient is taught to become uninvolved with life's exigencies. While May emphasizes the therapist's involvement and dedication as a facilitative element in the cases of Brown, Jones, and Smith, Seeman reacts to the therapist's placing limits on his personal involvement in the case of Jones, and Whitaker stresses the therapist's self-denial in his relationship with Smith. Are these divergent perceptions really a function of the ambiguity of the tape recordings and typescripts or are they, at least in part, a function of the theoretic positions of the reviewers?

Thus, while there are threads of common agreement as to what constitutes a helpful relationship, there are divergent interpretations of the clinical material, the raw data. English and Lewis agree about the helpfulness of the therapist's encouragement of the patient to find his own modes of operating, but English, in the case of Jones, notes that the efficacy of this therapeutic mechanism is diminished by the dominating role of the therapist in overstructuring Jones's thoughts in a way which prevents self-discovery. English's description of the therapist as skillfully leading Smith and skillfully structuring in a way that promotes self-discovery contrasts sharply with Lewis' views of that therapist's continually "running ahead" of Smith and "trying to put more complicated formulations in the patient's mouth than the patient was ready for . . ." Thus some divergencies among the six reviewers in interpretation of the actual raw data occur even when there is an agreement on the important variables to be evaluated.

A third clustering of helpful therapist activities pointed to by many of the outside theorists is related to the research measures of self-congruence or genuineness of the therapists.

Several of the clinical reviewers point to the therapist's progressive freeing of himself to communicate with openness as an important happening. This openness and freeing of one's self involves an ability to step out of the narrow confines of the therapist's role and give personally of one's self. Although this clearly goes beyond the construct of congruence it just as clearly presupposes the existence of a high degree of congruence and genuineness. It is significant that the therapist in each of the three cases did not seem to enter the therapy encounter with complete freedom and openness. Is it that the therapist's freedom to be himself flourishes only after he has come to know the patient in some fashion, that is, after the relationship has been established?

The focus in the reviewers' formulations was, then, upon the change in the therapist toward a greater openness and a greater personal freedom in the therapeutic encounter. Is this a reflection of a precondition to a similar change in the patient toward openness and freedom to be one's self? Stated in the negative: Can the therapist expect openness and freedom to be one's self in the patient when the therapist himself is not open and free?

Perhaps the most surprising and striking aspect of the commentaries by the "outsiders" revolves around the construct of genuineness, self-congruence, or openness. The client-centered therapists, both individually and collectively, have advocated openness and freedom in the therapeutic relationship. They have emphasized as critically important the therapist's willingness for the patient to be himself in his own manner. The outside theorists, in their attempts to describe the process of client-centered therapy, often focus upon what they perceive as the therapist's rigid and controlling nature which closes him off to many of his own as well as to the patient's experiences. If only one reviewer were to focus on this it could be dismissed as a malperception, but clearly it is not. If it is in some sense a valid observation how does this apparent rigidity interact with the intent to be open and the verbal communication of a willingness for the patient to take the lead? Is the patient, as suggested, in a difficult "double-bind" situation when he encounters a therapist who verbally desires openness and freedom in the patient but cannot in actuality be free and open himself? Particularly striking was the observation by almost all the theorists that the client-centered process of therapy somehow avoids the expected and usual patient expressions of negative, hostile, or aggressive feelings. The clear implication is that the client-centered therapist for some reason seems less open to receiving negative, hostile, or aggressive feelings. Is it that the therapists have little respect for, or understanding of their own negative, hostile, or aggressive feelings, and are thus unable to receive those feelings from the patient? Do they simply "not believe in" the importance of the negative feelings?

Such a line of reasoning leads to a simple equation which might be inherent in the nature of the relationship between therapist self-congruence or genuineness, on the one hand, and an unconditional positive warmth or caring for the patient, on the other. Self-congruence or genuineness in the therapist means that the therapist is able to accept and respect both the positive *and* negative aspects of his own self and to value even the less desirable sides of his being, while unconditional positive regard means that the therapist is able to accept and even respect the positive *and* negative sides of the patient's feelings and experiences. Thus, the basic underlying acceptance and respect for all aspects of the self and all aspects of experiencing might tie together the two conditions of "unconditional positive regard" and "therapist congruence or genuineness." Are these two conditions simply two sides of the single coin of *respect* for human experiencing? If so, is this coin of "respect for experiencing" fundamental to accurate empathic understanding of others? Is freedom and openness of the therapist derivative of this respect for all human experiences?

Implicit in the discussion of the therapist's facilitating activities is the formulation of what is not facilitating. For the most part the outside reviewers see the therapist as most ineffective when he is being rigid in technique and in adherence to a preconceived role, rigid in placing limitations on personal involvement, rigid in avoiding the discussion of transference or of historical material, and rigid in avoiding aggressive and hostile feelings. A second and lesser point made by the clinical reviewers is the failure of the therapist to engage himself as a real second person in the relationship. This seems almost to preclude the dynamic interaction between therapist and patient which would allow for the development and perhaps resolution of transference feelings. At the same time, is it precisely this alter-ego role of the therapist, this self-denial in favor of the patient's being which constitutes the essence of client-centered therapy? The times when the therapist is flexible in his approach, however, seem to be a critical element.

In their comments, the clinical reviewers have sharpened our perspectives on the client-centered process of therapy. Some of them have gone far out on a limb to make suggestions toward radically new ways of looking at effective ingredients in client-centered therapy. It seems fitting to close this chapter by quoting again some of these comments:

. . . this willingness to experience the pain which the patient has not been able to tolerate tends to make the patient experience his affect and not try to avoid it to the same degree that he has on previous occasions.

. . . [The therapist] offers the patient an experience in breaking and repairing ego boundaries in the framework of verbal language . . . the patient discovers he can be crazy inside and social outside and enjoy that too.

The truly therapeutic moment is when the therapist added something which came out of his own subjective state, his own identity as one person in the relationship.

It's as though the patient discovers himself when the therapist is not afraid.

[Something therapeutic derives from] the sturdy, firm, 'masculine' tone of the therapist . . . and the occasional free handling of the situation.

. . . The curative element rests, in the last analysis, on the genuine interest and concern shown in the relationship which give the patient his human world, communicated to the patient in terms that do not force him into the therapist's own world in terms of standards of health, social adjustment, etc.

. . . one gets a very strange sense of the patient developing an enjoyment of his own separateness (aloneness) and [thus] a gradual change away from being lonely.

. . . What was going on therapeutically consisted in the patient being forced to put himself into his words, and to face the fact that the therapist was trying to not put himself into words and I wondered how much of the therapeutic process consisted of the contrast between these two.

This may well be one of the secrets of this kind of psychotherapy. The growth effort is primarily with the patient while the therapist spends his efforts at maintaining restraint and control. It's as though he [the therapist] insists that he is only a voice, only an idea, as though no one is there. In contrast to this, the patient obviously can see that he is a person, he is a body. Is it possible that this peculiar kind of double-bind may be the basis for the establishment of a profound transference–counter-transference, an interlocking relationship which goes on undisturbed by the patient until the patient becomes bored with this unreal quality and this parent-child relationship? Then he breaks it and in breaking gains his own growth impetus.

19. A Dialogue Between Therapists

Carl R. Rogers and Commentators

When we submitted interview samplings from three cases to six highly competent but extremely busy therapists, the most that we had hoped for was that we would obtain some reaction to this case material. To listen to fifteen four-minute segments from each case and to dictate a reaction to this material seemed to be all that we could reasonably expect. We found, however, that from a number of our therapists we received rich and thoughtful commentary on a variety of important issues in psychotherapy. These views deserve further presentation and also further comment. The preceding chapter has mentioned some of these issues but has focused primarily on the reactions of our "experts" to the case material. In this chapter I wish to let them expound some of their broader views, and also to enter into a dialogue with them. I would like to point up some of the differences between them, and also point up the differences between the views of the research group and those of some of our commentators. It is hoped that such a focus will better outline some of the important issues current in psychotherapy today as they are reflected in these cases and these therapists.

How and When Does Therapy Occur?

One issue which is vitally important and which crops up in a variety of ways both in the remarks of our commentators and in our own reaction to their remarks can be formulated in the following fashion: Does therapy occur, and can it be perceived, in the moment or does therapy occur only over a long sequence of time and can it be perceived only in this long period of time?

It is this issue, I believe, which is behind the differing reactions to the use of four-minute segments in giving an impressionistic view of the case. Some of our therapists—notably Bergman and Seeman—did not even comment on this aspect of it, simply accepting the fact that they could form some judgments from brief segments of the interaction. May had some initial scepticism but this was soon resolved. He says:

Before listening to these segmented tapes I had a good deal of doubt as to whether I could make anything out of them let alone give reactions which would be pertinent and valuable for the study but I had not listened for more than several minutes before I was surprised by my own involvement; I found it an engrossing and in some moments a fascinating experience. The material is of unusual interest and, I believe, fruitful for reaction and judgment.

Whitaker sees the matter as having both positive and negative aspects in it. He says:

To discuss someone else's method of doing therapy on the basis of four-minute samples from interviews spaced by dividing the process into fifteen segments seems to have created certain distortions but to have added certain advantages. The sampling is so restricted that one does not struggle with the problem of keeping the content in mind. One can identify with the therapist responding to the patient in such a short sample. The disadvantages, however, are fairly serious. One tends to interpolate and extrapolate both affect and content and to jump to conclusions thereby.

He feels that because of the need for closure the listener tends to fantasy the body movements, posture, and facial expression of both patient and therapist and the conclusions reached may be contaminated by such fantasy.

It is English and Lewis who seem to feel most strongly the deficiencies of the sampling process. English states that he feels "under some handicap in not having a history of the cases and knowing more of the psychopathology of the cases being treated." Obviously for him it is not really feasible to understand therapy without some kind of a longitudinal picture of the individual and of what is going on.

Lewis gives the strongest and clearest presentation of an orientation which makes the sampling procedure quite definitely inadequate. He says:

In the first place, many of the indices of movement which are familiar to those who work in the psychoanalytic framework cannot be found in these brief segments. They (the indices) depend on content as well as atmosphere. If one compares the utterances in a given hour to the twigs of a tree, which, as one proceeds to obtain a deeper and deeper understanding of the patient, can be discerned as the twigs of several main branches which join in a central trunk, I think it is fair to say that those who work in the analytic method tend to strike for the central trunk. The "twigs" will consist of a number of communications of the patient (explicitly verbalized), some non-verbal statements (in the form of various sighs and primitive sounds, gestures, facial expressions, vasomotor changes), and a host of behavioral manifestations in relation to the standard props of the therapeutic situation. Taking all of these into account, the analyst attempts to find some central core of meaning. He tries to understand what the patient is really driving at, behind his indirect, disguised, and displaced references to apparently unrelated things. This attempt is, of course, not always successful, but this is the endeavor. The actual responses of the analyst may often pertain to smaller branches than the main ones and particularly in the initial phase of treatment. It is likely to stay up amongst the twigs, just as the [client-centered] therapist does. However, as time passes and the recurrent cycles of behavior we class as the neurosis of the patient become clearer and clearer, a change in the depth of the comments of the analyst begins to occur. As the patient works through his initial resistances to treatment, his fears, suspicions, doubts, distrusts, discomforts, etc., and begins to talk of more deeply personal things, the analyst tends to encourage the production of looser and looser associations and to encourage the patient to bring in dreams. All of this makes for a longer-cycle scanning process than could be evident in four-minute excerpts.

This is an excellent statement which indicates that the concern about the brevity of the segments has to do at a deeper level with a whole orientation toward the concept of psychotherapy. Let me try to pose rather sharply (perhaps with excessive sharpness for the purpose of clarity) the differing views on this subject. In the view of Lewis and in that of many other therapists it is necessary, for therapy to take place, that a deep and profound *understanding* of the central core of the patient's difficulties must occur first and most significantly in the mind of the therapist. Then a similar understanding and insight can occur in the mind and experience of the patient if the interaction is skillfully handled by the analyst. Naturally, scattered four-minute segments from therapeutic interaction make it very difficult, if not impossible, to determine whether these conditions have been fulfilled.

There is, however, another point of view as to what constitutes therapy which is in general held by our group and by an increasing number of therapists in other orientations. This view holds that for therapeutic change to take place, an *experiencing* of the core distortions or discrepancies must occur in the *client*. Often the therapist understands what is going on, and understands these central incongruences, but it is not *his* understanding which is the essential element of therapeutic change. In the case of James Brown reported in a previous chapter, it is not at all the therapist's *understanding* of what was transpiring during his sobs which was important for therapy. It was the *experiencing* by the client of his despair and worthlessness, and at the same time his *experiencing* of being loved. Or quite probably this description in itself is grossly inadequate to convey the richness of his experiencing in that moment. Since he never really verbalized this experience it is not clear what the totality of its meanings was to him. It was, however, the experiencing which was crucial, not the insight, nor the words into which he might put those insights, nor the therapist's understanding of the whole event. Likewise in the case of Smith talking into the tape recorder alone, it was his open *experiencing* of some of his conflicted feelings which was important, not the question of whether the therapist understood those feelings or their relation to his personality structure.

Both of these orientations are entirely tenable, as is evident from the fact that many therapists hold to each conception of therapy. To those who feel that the therapist's understanding is primary, it is obvious that four-minute segments give little clue to the depth or completeness of this understanding, and hence little clue as to whether therapy is taking place. To those who see the primary element as the client's experiencing of discrepant elements within himself, four-minute segments can provide a variety of clues. Is the relationship providing a climate in which such frightening experiencing can take place? Does the client show evidence of coming closer to his own experiencing or is he still remaining remote from it? Is the conversation about past experiencing, or does it have to do with the here and now?

This section of the dialogue with our outside experts makes it clear that we need more consideration—both theoretical and empirical—as to what constitutes the essential elements of therapeutic change.

Spontaneity of the Therapist

Our several outside evaluators are frequently annoyed or repelled by what they see as a lack of spontaneity in our three therapists—a rigidity, a self-discipline, a withholding of self. Whitaker is perhaps most vocal on this. Some of his statements will indicate both his thinking and feeling about this point:

> If one assumes the process of therapy is in the person of the *therapist,* then the life theme of the therapist should be an essential characteristic and visible in any segment of verbal recording. I would formulate our theme as: the therapist says by his total functioning, "I am trying to grow, come and we'll both work at it together." I cannot see the personal theme of these therapists.

At another point he says:

> I expect to enjoy the patient. I expect to respond only if I feel emotionally spontaneous or if there is some necessity for structuring the relationship. The Rogerians here seem committed to respond at each point of the patient's verbalization. I watch and wait for the encounter. They seem to make an effort to start an encounter with each move of the patient. I feel that therapy is an opportunity and a responsibility for joining with the patient in an interaction around my convictions, possibly not in moral issues but in the issues of interpretation and evaluation of the current experience and possibly even of his historical experience. I feel free to challenge the patient if I feel personally related to what is going on. I do not feel this is true of the therapists here portrayed.

At another point he remarks:

The lack of spontaneity and the lack of flexibility in the therapist-as-a-person seemed an orientation very much like analysis. The therapist is standing behind the patient, unseen and almost non-existent. Does this denial of self actually imply an acknowledgment of the "other"? Is it possible that the patient is being taught to be more on guard because the therapist is so on guard? What is the effect on the therapist of not enjoying his relationship with his patient; of not being able to express himself personally?

In commenting on the therapist's offer of money to Brown he says:

For example the symbolic ghost-like person of the therapist in the middle of this procedure suddenly offers to loan the patient one, two, or three dollars for taxi fare. The contrast between this and his previous stereotyped formality is almost shocking and certainly must leave the patient with a peculiar expectation that it is possible for this person to be real and human and responsive, even though the therapist only chooses to do this on rare occasions and in a very subtle manner.

May, in commenting on some of the significant points in the case of Brown says: "Note incidentally that in each of these statements the therapist does not merely reflect the patient but states or adds something which definitely comes out of his own subjective state, his own identity as one person in the relationship." Speaking of his own view of therapy May says: "The therapist permits and helps the patient to create his own world by giving him as full and open an opportunity to do so as practically possible; but the therapist is fully present as the other being, still an identity in his own right, in this world."

I feel a little baffled by these comments, largely because I feel so deeply in sympathy with them. For more than a decade I have been trying to state that genuineness, or congruence, and the expression of such genuineness, is probably the most important part of the therapeutic relationship. I believe this is evident in the chapter in this book regarding the therapeutic conditions. So I feel that the therapists involved in these three cases would be very much in agreement with our commentators in feeling that the therapist as a real and spontaneous person should be present in the relationship. Why then do our views of these segments seem so discrepant?

In the first place it is probable that no therapist, including our commentators, is as spontaneous as he would like to be in any given therapeutic relationship. Thus it is almost certain that if each of our three therapists had been asked if they were completely spontaneous in the recorded segments which were presented they would have replied in the negative. Thus part of what our commentators are remarking upon is the failure of any therapist to live up to what he regards as the ideal goal of the therapeutic relationship. Consequently it is probable that many of their comments are justified in specific instances, and would be agreed to by the therapist being discussed. Another aspect of this question of spontaneity is that each person is spontaneous in his own way. It would be only natural to feel that another is not being spontaneous unless he is doing so in the same manner in which *I* would be spontaneous. In any event, this perception of rigidity in us as therapists, by several of our commentators, is something which we take very seriously, and which will cause us to examine our behavior with clients.

There seems, however, to be an additional dimension needing comment. The point which some of our commentators appear to overlook is that it is quite possible for a therapist to be spontaneously interested in the inner world of his client and to have this as the spontaneous and genuine focus of his attention. To limit my comments to the relationship in which I was involved, I am interested that to Whitaker my attempt to understand the feelings of Brown seemed so sharply at variance with my other feeling that I wanted to offer him money. For me, so far as I am aware, these were both very real. I genuinely wanted to understand his feelings, to live, as far as I was able, inside the world of his feelings. I also genuinely wanted to offer him money so that he would have more free choice in a given situation. It is important to me to be clear in the expression of my feelings. When my feeling is the desire to understand him, I want this to be clear. When my feeling is different from his, or springs entirely from myself, I want this also to be crystal clear so that the client can react meaningfully and in a self-defined way to my feelings. The fact that this is often achieved is partly exemplified by the willingness of our clients to differ with their therapists when they feel that the therapist is not understanding their own private world.

I am sure, however, that there is much that has not yet been said, thought, or experienced in regard to this matter of the therapist's genuineness. We have all of us come a very long way from the initial Freudian picture of the therapist as an impersonal screen. We have not yet formulated an adequate picture of the therapist as an experiencing person in the relationship nor have we carried through this concept adequately in practice.

The best expression of this groping comes from one of our commentators, Paul Bergman, who in a communication some time before his untimely death (separate from his comments on the cases) tries to express some of the changes going on in himself. He says:

Some time ago I began, at first cautiously and then more boldly, to experiment with expression of my own subjective reactions to my patients. [As a consequence] I have heard expressions of hope from people who suffered from the restricted, tightly circumscribed relationship, and I have also heard outcries of anxiety and upheaval which however were welcomed because the previous relative calm and freedom from anxiety were experienced as antiseptic sterility.

He says of the concept of genuineness:

This seems to be the condition that to my mind emerges as the one of central position and highest value. . . . I . . . experience it as a great relief to feel that I can meet my patients with some degree of trust in my feelings and it is my hope that in the future I will have more of such trust than I have at present and will have it possibly with more justification.

In these excerpts it seems to me that Bergman is describing the goal toward which most of us as therapists are striving. To the extent that we have not achieved it we would be as critical as are our commentators.

"Reflection of Feeling"

Our commentators have definite reactions to what they think of as "reflection of feeling." At the least they are perplexed; more often they are irritated or offended. Thus, English says, "I think a question here would be better than trying to tell the patient what he felt. This technique would arouse resentment in me, were I in the patient's place."

May gives meaningful examples of an actual, poor response, and his own version of a better and more empathic response. He says:

Patient Smith for example states that he gets no help from the therapy. The hospital "never done me any good yet" and concludes, "I don't care if I live today or die tomorrow." The therapist responds, "Nothing seems to have any meaning or purpose," which gets subsequently into an intellectualized discussion. . . . But I found myself asking, "Isn't it anger the patient is expressing, or discouragement, or sadness?" On the assumption of the first, his anger, I might have responded, "It makes you sore as hell to be shoved in here and nobody gives a damn."

I feel sure that the therapist would agree that this is a better response.

At another point May shows his fundamental sympathy with the intention of the therapist but feels the therapist has been lacking in skill:

I am aware of the dangers in the point of view I am supporting, that the therapist go beyond the actual words of the patient and respond to what the patient is trying to communicate but cannot. The chief danger is that the therapist will read into the patient's communications all kinds of theories of his own . . . which may have nothing at all to do with what the patient actually is experiencing. But the misuse of therapeutic insight and empathy should not make us throw out with the dirty bath water of dogma the baby of the potentially constructive function of the therapist. The central such constructive function of the therapist is to help the patient move beyond the limited words of his communication and his blocked-off experience with himself and others. . . . The patient is able progressively to experience the "feelings" which previously would have brought him destruction, such as anger, sex, disagreement with authorities, and which he has had to disavow and disown (repress). The therapist experiences with him the world he is building, "lives in it," and expresses this in what we call responding, interpreting, and so forth which will inevitably involve uncovering aspects or ways the patient is behaving and feeling of which he was previously unaware.

In most important respects there is not as much difference of opinion here as might be supposed. (Compare for example Gendlin's "Therapeutic Procedures" in Chapter 16.) I am (and this would be true of the other therapists working with me) as much opposed as our commentators to wooden "reflections," to therapists who merely restate the words or ideas of the client without understanding his deeper feelings. Like them, I am critical of points where the therapists failed to hear the feeling, whether it was anger, resentment, tenderness, conflict, or whatever. I have no apology to offer for the many instances of failure to live up to our own notion of what the therapist's response should be. I would only comment that none of us in practice is the equal of the therapist which we are in our thinking and imagination. I for example have heard tape recordings of interviews by four of our commentators and observed a fifth in a demonstration interview. In each case I was critical of the therapist for not living up to his own picture of the therapist's function, just as these commentators have been critical of us. It is simply a hard fact that when therapeutic interviews are available for careful listening we find that many, many errors are made, errors which the therapist regrets as much as his listener.

There is, however, one point in which I believe some of our commentators are seeing the situation erroneously. They persist in looking at the therapist's response from the outside, in terms of how it seems to them as outsiders. Viewed from this perspective what they are looking at is a "reflection of feeling," which seems to several of them to have little purpose. The experience is quite different when one is a client. From inside the client's experience the therapist's genuine effort to understand him, even though this is a groping and somewhat inaccurate effort, is reassuring, releasing, non-threatening. In my experience it is much less threatening and more effective than the questions which Dr. English would like to see used.

I can best illustrate this point by saying that if I were in conversation with one of our commentators at the moment when he was experiencing irritation at this kind of therapist response, and if I tried acceptantly to understand this attitude on his part, and said, "I guess to you these 'reflections of feeling' seem like a stupid, repetitive, and unhelpful aspect of the therapist's interaction," I am quite certain he would respond, "That's right!" and then would go on to expand his point of view, quite unaware that I had "reflected" his feeling. What I am saying is that I think several of our commentators tend to underestimate the value of a communicated, empathic understanding.

No doubt part of this is the fault of those of us in the client-centered orientation. If I had any part in terming this kind of response a "reflection of feeling" I certainly regret and apologize for this. It is definitely a misnomer. When it plays any real function, this kind of response is not a reflection of feeling, but an honest, groping attempt on the part of the therapist to understand fully, sensitively, and accurately the internal world of meaning, thought, experience, and feeling, of his client. When it has these qualities it is effective and definitely moves the therapeutic interaction forward.

The Process in the Client

In many ways our commentators and we the therapists in these cases see the process of therapy as it occurs in the client in ways that are very similar. Whenever there is more of an openness to experience, more loosening of constructs, more experiencing of denied feelings, more evidence of insight, we seem to be in agreement that this spells movement or progress.

In one important respect, however, our commentators are puzzled and ambivalent. They are perplexed by the immersion of the therapist in the experience of the client until, as they see it, there is almost an identity between the two. Whitaker expresses this most vividly. He says:

One colleague had the fantasy while listening to the tape that the patient was on the back of a bucking horse and the therapist was on the same horse with him. I had a fantasy that the therapist was like the guard on a basketball team, so close to the patient that it was hard for the patient to move or score what looked to me like baskets. However, there was "engagement" between these two people even though the use of words as real things was so specific that at times one had the feeling that the two of them were playing with words as though they were dominos.

At another point he says: "The therapist in effect has been a stand-in for the patient while the patient observes his own pathology."

These observers have at least discovered for themselves why this therapy has been called "client-centered." The original intent of this phrase was to communicate the fact that the process was centered in the client, and that the therapist immersed himself in this inner process. Though we have moved a long way from this as a complete description of therapy, and have placed much more stress on the relationship and the interaction in the relationship, and have come to stress the importance of the therapist's realness and genuineness in the expression of his own feelings, it is still true that the focus is upon what occurs in the client.

Although our commentators are perplexed, they do see certain advantages as well as possible disadvantages in this focus upon the client's experience almost to the exclusion of the therapist's experience. They recognize that it has a great deal to do with aiding the client in his own recognition of and acceptance of himself. Lewis says:

What seems to happen is that the patient's thoughts stay in *his* head; his feelings stay in *him* and are relatively uncontaminated by the therapist's responses and thoughts. In short, the phenomena of ego boundaries, boundaries of the self and so forth, might very well consolidate quicker in this type of treatment than in one in which more elaboration, interpretation, and so forth are brought into the treatment by the therapist. The very fact that the therapist does not tend to extract the personal meanings from the patient's reactions to people in the environment, but instead leaves those reactions exactly where the patient says they are, tends to keep the patient's boundaries intact. The tendency to read latent transference meanings into almost everything may be destructive to the schizophrenic who is trying somehow to establish who he is and what he thinks and feels.

Whitaker states, on a more ambivalent note: "The therapist works at the job. There is no sense of his ever being relaxed at any time. There is no lack of strength but he uses this strength to keep the patient endlessly responsible. He does this by way of silence, non-committal comments, as though to continue the silence, and by a process of subtle encouragement which endlessly says, 'You're at bat.' "

To me this last seems like a very perceptive comment. It is quite true that one of the real strengths of client-centered therapy is that it keeps responsibility clearly in the person of the client and that he comes quite quickly to recognize his own responsibility for his feelings, for the picture he holds of himself, for the choices he is to make as to his future, and for the stance which he takes toward the world. It is definitely the client who directs the show, not the therapist. The therapist is neither putting on a show of his own, nor is he giving reassurance, nor is he subtly reinforcing certain responses so as to shape the nature of future responses. He is not even saying that it is all right for the client to feel his feelings, whatever they may be. This would carry the implicit message that such permission should be given by the therapist or some important other in the future. It would not lead to the inner realization that "I can dare to express and to be my feelings, and this way of living seems to me valid, and a trustworthy way to be." It is in the hope that his client can achieve this realization that the client-centered therapist does endlessly communicate the message, "You're at bat." There is no doubt, however, that this aspect of the therapy is in some sense troubling to our commentators. Whitaker states:

It is as though the two were existing in some kind of common microcosm or isolation chamber or like twins in utero. These interviews are intensely personal for both of these individuals but only the patient's life is under discussion. This is so distinct that one sometimes feels there is only one self present and that self is the patient. It is as though the therapist makes himself artificially miniature. Sometimes this is so dramatic that I almost feel he disappears. This is in specific contrast to our type of therapy in which both persons are present in a rather specific sense and the therapeutic process involves the overt interaction of the two individuals and the use of the experience of each of them for the patient's growth.

I believe it might be correct to say that the direction in which client-centered therapists find themselves moving partakes of both of the elements which Whitaker mentions. There is no doubt that we are moving toward a freer expression of the therapist, his feelings and/or attitudes in the relationship. On the other hand we are trying to achieve this in a fashion which in no sense imposes on the client and which thus preserves the stress on the value of the client's *own* experience, his *own* locus of evaluation, and his *own* understanding of his life situation and the determination of his future.

Is Therapy a Verbal Retraining?

Two of our commentators see some aspects of the therapy as a type of verbal retraining. In this their thinking would be similar to that of psychologists interested in operant conditioning who frequently see therapy as simply the operant conditioning of the client or patient to use different words in regard to himself and his feelings. Whitaker says: "This therapy seems quite similar to what I would call training in verbal communication, by the therapist operating to replay the patient's verbal samples."

Lewis gives a much more extensive comment on this aspect. He says that the therapists—

stay very close to the *words* used by the patients and try very hard to find out what the patient means by these words. There is a gradual re-education of the vocabulary of these patients . . . What may be happening here with these patients is somewhat analogous to the learning of a language by a child (one thinks of Piaget's work). In the process of very carefully, as it were, "recalibrating" the meaning attached to certain verbal symbols again and again, a hidden movement may be taking place. The patients themselves are grateful for this and make several references to it . . . This ties in with the idea that the thought disorder of the schizophrenic is but a regression to early sensory motor levels of communication. Schizophrenics often use words as if they had a double meaning, one half of which is a motoric expression and the other a verbal symbol. What these therapists do, then, seems to be, among other things, a very careful, sensitive re-translation of the patient's utterances until the patient is quite sure that his words are getting across to the therapist and that a certain word has a very definite emotional connotation for the therapist. In the process of doing this the therapist avoids reference to anything more than what the patient is saying and stays away from any kind of abstract or symbolic references. This makes the whole process relatively simple and understandable to the patient.

One might equate this aspect of this treatment to getting acquainted with someone who speaks a different language from yours, or perhaps, to be more extravagant, to coming upon a dazed survivor from some type of cataclysmic explosion and helping him pick up his belongings and regain the meaning of the simplest things in his environment, in his home, and so forth—in other words, to begin to put the bricks together after a catastrophic disintegration. If these therapists have proved that this works, this is of importance because it affords the simplification of what the patients need, at least as a beginning of therapy.

I feel a considerable agreement with these commentators that a part of what is occurring is a re-training in the process of communication. For example, it has been a matter of surprise to all of us as therapists in this project that so tiny a fraction of the recorded interviews is filled with "crazy" talk. Some of our patients quite frequently on the ward displayed irrational language and language patterns. Yet this was rare in the interviews. I believe that one reason for this is that the therapist shows by his attitude and behavior that he fully believes that the patient is endeavoring to *communicate* to him. As this sinks in, as the patient comes to realize that here is a person who is listening to what he says, who expects that what he says will have meaning, the patient's statements become more meaningful. My only point of difference with these commentators would be that this kind of training is not only a re-training in verbal patterns, it is a training in the most fundamental aspect of any relationship, namely, the communication of meaning.

It might also be appropriate here to comment on the notion that therapy is simply the operant conditioning of the client or patient into new verbal patterns, since this is a view often expressed, though not by our commentators. I believe it might be said that client-centered therapy tends to reward the person for every expression of personal feeling, no matter what its content. Thus, gradually the client becomes more personally expressive, more expressive of feelings, and thus comes to define himself more in terms of all of his feelings and not simply a limited portion of them. He is rewarded at each step by the therapist's interest and understanding. This, as I see it, is one definition of the process of psychotherapy.

Some Conclusions

There are, I believe, some conclusions which may be drawn from this material. I will present first some conclusions on which I think the commentators and the therapists would be largely in agreement, shading into some views on which there would probably be less consensus.

A first and sobering conclusion is that as therapists we still have a long distance to go before we reach any kind of agreement as to what constitutes therapy. When commentators differ as sharply as they did in the preceding chapter and in this one, as to which events are therapeutic, which relationships promote therapy, and which cases show the most therapeutic movement, then it is clear that we are in an ill-defined field. It is obviously possible for one therapist to point to a particular aspect of a case and say, "This is clearly productive of therapeutic change," and for another therapist to point to the same aspect and say, "This is definitely non-therapeutic." A venture such as was embarked upon in the last two chapters leaves all of us more humble in our perception of the progress thus far made in understanding the process of constructive personal change.

One of the elements contributing to these sometimes divergent views is the conceptual difference as to the essence of therapeutic change. Is that essence the deep insight achieved by the therapist and communi-cated to the patient; is it the experiencing by the client of previously unrecognized feelings and meanings, in a relationship which makes such experiencing possible; or is it the interaction of two real persons, strug-gling to encounter each other in a relationship? Our commentators have helped to sharpen such basic questions.

One realization which grows out of this material is the distance we have moved from the orthodox Freudian view of the therapist. All— commentators and therapists—are, I believe, in agreement that it is when the therapist is spontaneous, real, genuine, drawing upon his experience of the moment, that he is most effective. It is when the therapist is reacting in a stereotyped, wooden, constrained way that he is most likely to be ineffective. The difficulty in *being* himself in the moment is amply demonstrated by what are perceived as frequent failures in this respect. Yet all would agree that this spontaneous realness is the goal.

One contribution made by the client-centered therapist—though not seen as such by all of our commentators—is that he has given a clear operational meaning to the communication of a sensitive empathic understanding. He has demonstrated the ability to move into, move about in, and to stay inside the phenomenal world of his client. This is a mode of interaction in which he is sometimes clumsy and sometimes wooden, but at his best he provides his client with the deepest kind of acceptance, in which he "understands all" and "accepts all."

Another contribution of the client-centered therapist—probably more completely recognized by our commentators—is that he has developed a mode of interaction which nourishes the self-hood of his client. By accepting the client's communications as significant, by keeping responsibility as much as possible with the client, by permitting the locus of evaluation to reside in the client, he encourages independence, and strengthens the client in a conception of himself as a worthy person, capable of coping with life.

PART VII

The Significance of the Program

20. The Social Significance of the Research

Eugene T. Gendlin

What did this research program contribute to the social problem that there are more than half a million people now in "mental hospitals"? How are the findings applicable to this problem, and what avenues of solution do they indicate?

Often in the past, research has measured only outcomes, but failed to define the "psychotherapy" which led to these outcomes. Thus one knew only that two people in a room did something quite undefined, called "psychotherapy" by one of them. The purpose of this research went beyond this. Its aim was to define the *"essential* conditions of psychotherapy"* (specifically those aspects of the therapist's behavior which make it therapy) and the "essential" indices of "process" in the patient (specifically those aspects of patient behavior which indicate that he is engaged in therapy). We then tested high therapist "conditions" and high "process" against the usual outcome measures, to see whether these really are essential factors of *effective* psychotherapy.

The peculiar characteristic of these essential factors is that they transcend different orientations of psychotherapy as well as different situational patterns such as individual therapy, group therapy, ward, family, occupational, and vocational therapy. The essential variables apply to all interpersonal situations of any sort, for example to normal work settings, family life, classroom situations, etc. These "conditions" have been investigated in a variety of situations, and there are a whole series of tentative research findings (Berlin, 1960; Thornton, 1960; Berzon, 1961; Emmerling, 1961; Hollenbeck, 1961; Rosen, 1961; Snelbecker, 1961; van der Veen, 1961, 1962*a,* 1962*b;* Barrett-Lennard, 1962; Appell, Gendlin and Klein, 1963; de Vault, *et al,* 1963; Clark and Culbert, 1964; Kagan and Huntgate, 1964).

We are beginning to show, as Rogers (1957, 1959) hypothesized, that genuineness, empathy, and unconditional regard are high in successful roommates, teachers, and mothers, as well as in group (Truax, 1961) and ward therapists (see Chapter 15). If you consider what these "conditions" are, you can see why they are applicable to all interpersonal situations: the "conditions" are fundamental attitudes of one person toward another. They define a quality possible in any personal interaction. Of course, specific behaviors differ for a teacher in a classroom, for a therapist, a work supervisor, or a ward aide. Yet, given the different behaviors appropriate in different situations, the same fundamental attitudes determine whether there is a therapeutic quality in the interaction.

The Significance of the "Conditions" for the Mental Hospital

If these are the necessary conditions of therapeutic relationships, and if they can occur in such a variety of situations, then the question is: In what kind of situational pattern can these conditions best be provided to a large hospitalized population?

Since our variables are essential aspects of all interaction, regardless of its setting, we are free to consider an unlimited variety of situational arrangements. That is the very nature of these variables.

It is true that the findings are tentative, not completely clear-cut, and in need of replication. (But, they are in a form in which they *can* be replicated. They have been defined and instrumented so that anyone anywhere can determine whether the "therapy" he studies does, or does not, involve these variables.) If these findings are replicated, and continue to be supported, then they imply the question: How can we, as a society, best house and treat our "mentally ill" population so that maximal levels of these variables are offered?

The Futility of Individual Therapy

It is clear from the nature of these variables, that one would not necessarily provide them through *client-centered* therapy, or through any *individually* structured therapy, since their basic nature does not imply anything one way or the other about specific therapist techniques or about individual, group, or other situational arrangements. Above all, it does not follow that we should retain the hospital system as is, and provide the "conditions" only by sending individual therapists into the present type of state hospital. That pattern would provide these conditions in only two of the patient's 168 hours per week in the hospital. Our findings show that even in that pattern the conditions can be effective—but our findings surely do not imply that it is the only, or best, way of arranging the situation.

If we thought only of the individual psychotherapy pattern added onto the current hospital pattern, the cost would surely discourage us. Individual psychotherapy as conducted in our program was long, often stretching into years. Could a professional psychotherapist (moreover, one who is able to create a relationship with high conditions) be provided for each patient now hospitalized?

Research is *laboratory* work. In a laboratory one often produces—at high cost and with years of effort—some product which, once found and defined, can then be mass-produced at little cost. If, in practical use, the cost of an item were what it first cost in the laboratory, most new products would remain prohibitively expensive and impractical.

To bring this home I want to tell about one of our therapists who, in one of our frequent moments of discouragement, divided the total amount of our research grant by the number of therapy patients in the research: $180,000 divided by 16 = $11,250 per patient. He said, "Why don't we just *give* each patient eleven thousand dollars? That would get them well for sure!" If our findings mean that an individual psychotherapist-researcher must be brought into the hospital individually for a half million patients, it would cost five billion dollars—too expensive to hope for.

Because of this well-known fact, we designed the research to define and measure what is *essential* for a psychotherapeutic process in these patients. Much of what any method of psychotherapy champions, another equally effective method specifically eschews. One suspects (Gendlin, 1964) that neither these nor those modes are really essential. If one could define what *is* essential one could then see how *that* can be provided for all those who need it.

An example: For many centuries it was known that roots of certain plants in India, when chewed, produced a quieting effect. But it was difficult to dig these plants up. It was too expensive and clumsy to provide such roots for mass use. Then came the discovery of the chemicals which were the essential calming agents, and means of producing them cheaply. Today we have tranquilizers and no longer need to dig up the plants.

The Generalized Use of the Conditions

If genuineness, empathy, and unconditional regard are the essential ingredients of psychotherapy, there is no doubt that we can produce and offer these conditions in many different situational arrangements more economically than in individual, office-based psychotherapy.

When we discuss the prohibitive cost of offering psychotherapy to hospitalized psychotics, we should remember that more or less well-functioning and well-paying patients in ordinary psychotherapy often require two years or more! Therefore, not only with psychotics, but also with neurotics, we are currently using a situational arrangement which makes therapy prohibitively costly for most people. Thus, the isolation of the essential effective ingredients, and the possibility of providing them in other, more economical situational arrangements, has great significance for psychotherapy generally, not only for hospitalized psychotics. We can begin to think of ways of offering these "conditions" to school children, to delinquents, and to many others, in each instance devising the situational patterns best fitted and most appropriate for these people and the schools or agencies concerned with them.

In many contexts we would wish that personal interaction were therapeutic, rather than the reverse. Once we know what essentials make interaction therapeutic, we can set about reorganizing many different social patterns so that they would include these therapeutic essentials. The day is nearer when the therapeutic ingredients can be given to society generally, rather than only to those few who hire an office psychotherapist for themselves.

In this chapter we will be concerned only with hospitalized psychotics. What might be appropriate situational arrangements to expose them to genuineness, empathy, and unconditional regard?

Therapeutic responding need not occur only in an office or in privacy, or for two hours weekly. In fact, our experience shows that this individualized pattern fits the hospital situation very poorly: (a) patients do not expect "an hour" of time. Ten minutes may be enough. Nor do patients always need or expect privacy; (b) the therapist may want to remain with the patient for two or even six hours and may thereby achieve in those rare times more than can be done in years of biweekly sessions rigidly lasting an hour and then rigidly stopped; (c) many patients are threatened by the rigid office situation and reject such psychotherapy; (d) initiation of psychotherapy is extremely difficult with discouraged, frightened, withdrawn, suspicious patients. Such patients need to see and hear therapeutic relating with other patients and to approach and withdraw from it repeatedly before they can bear to try out such a relationship themselves.

Not only in initiating psychotherapy but generally, when two people relate closely in the hearing and sight of others, these others are drawn in on an intimate level. They may be silent for a long time, or seem to ignore what occurs. However, the experience—and the possibility of similarly relating—remains with them. It does not seem an essential part of psychotherapy to shut ourselves away only with those patients with whom we relate. On a hospital ward, certainly, that is not necessary. The whole climate of the ward will be improved if we can bear to speak closely and intimately to a patient out in the open where others can hear us.

We tend to become locked into a given structural pattern of offering psychotherapy once such a pattern develops. We assume everything in the pattern is part of the therapy, part of the snakeroot that works. The great power of the "conditions" lies in what they do *not* include.

Among other things they do not include one given pattern to provide therapeutic interaction.

In our research program we attempted a different pattern of offering therapeutic relations, that is, the "ward-availability" plan (see Chapter 3). This pattern was specifically designed to meet the difficulty of initiating psychotherapy, but its considerable success points to a variety of possible patterns more natural to the hospital setting and population. It also made much more economical use of the time of therapeutically oriented people than the individual psychotherapy pattern. The ward-availability pattern may reduce the time needed for this population to no more than the length necessary for an average client population. In the old pattern, the really long time was taken by the resistance, hesitation, withdrawal, rejection, and silence—sometimes lasting many months— before a therapy process really began. Of course, this slow initiation is itself a kind of therapy, but it can be easily provided by the ward-available setting: a therapist can work with those who are willing— within sight and hearing of those who are not (who hesitantly and tentatively approach and repeatedly withdraw).

Another, broader pattern (we tried it informally with some success) is to provide one therapeutically oriented staff person to form relationships with patients. If patients are not told that therapeutic relating should take 50 minutes in an office it does not occur to them to need that, especially if the relating is plainly genuine and follows no rigid format. Thus one person can be available to relate more or less simultaneously with forty-eight to ninety-six patients, and can initiate and carry forward a great many relationships. Thus, the addition of one staff member whose job would be to relate to patients with genuineness, empathy, and regard would not really be so expensive. Consider that there is now on state payrolls one hospital staff person for every three patients, and relating to patients is the chief task of *none* of these.

Hospital psychiatrists are overworked in the administration and supervision of the many wards of which they have charge. In the main they must work through nurses. (They often complain of this, sometimes see one or two patients in therapy to keep up their skill and motivation.)

Psychologists are often occupied with testing. Sometimes they spend many hours in psychotherapy but always with this patient or that, or with a group for a set number of weeks, or in ward meetings. Rarely is a psychologist simply available even for a few minutes to a patient other than the few specially selected ones.

Social workers plan release, and then only when the patient is well enough. Occupational therapists provide an often very helpful atmosphere, but too frequently focus simply on activity. Nurses direct aides, give drugs, keep records. Aides do janitorial work and head up cleaning details. Even volunteers bring cookies, coffee, or cards, but rarely see their function as one of really relating to the patients with empathy (too often they are told to avoid painful topics, which are to be left for the doctor).

And so, even in a small, treatment-oriented, and excellently-staffed hospital (as was the one in which we worked), to relate to the patients is the primary task of not one of the wide gamut of professional specialties of the hospital. So much more true is this in the huge state hospitals (say 6,000 patients) in the big cities, and in badly understaffed hospitals out in the country.

It seems, from these considerations, that someone to relate with patients along the lines of the "conditions" can be provided for in many patterns (e.g., in some ward-available pattern) and is decidedly an economic possibility. It could often be fitted into current hospital budgets without seriously curtailing the other helping services now provided.

The Possibility of Training Laymen

Another major significance of these conditions is that they are attributes of the person, rather than of his knowledge. This does not mean that no training is required, but it is a very different kind of training. An M.D., Ph.D., or a university education is not a prerequisite for the capacity to offer high conditions.

This means that the basic population from which to draw people who can provide high conditions is the total population—everyone—not just a few expensively trained professional people. It means that the cost of providing someone to relate along these lines with every patient may be very much less than would be supposed.

At first it may seem a shocking notion that ordinary people can be trained to relate with high attitudinal conditions to patients. It seems to destroy the role of the professional. Actually, even with top-flight training, professionals are only sometimes successful and always deeply torn and worn by working with hospitalized psychotics. Could ordinary people do as well? The work of Margaret Rioch (1963) gives an answer by showing that some housewives, with a modest amount of intensive training, can be highly effective therapists.

An even more striking study is that carried out by Ernest Poser of McGill University (in press), in which it was demonstrated that college girls, without psychological training, related naturally to hospitalized schizophrenics, and these relationships proved to be very therapeutic. Actually their success with the patients was greater than that of professionally trained therapists working under identical conditions. Thus it is clear that individuals without expensive training can deal with psychotic individuals.

If we now consider the situation of the aides in state hospitals, we realize that these are untrained individuals, working under supervision, whose main responsibilities are menial. If ordinary people were trained to relate to patients with the "conditions" they too would work under supervision. If large numbers were trained, fully professional people would not be eliminated. They would have a more vital role than ever —to supervise these large numbers.

Plans of this kind are being tried in several places. In some hospitals, aides are being trained to relate more therapeutically. In other places, volunteers who visit patients one day a week are being trained (Veterans' Administration, 1965). Always, such training seems a daring venture till one stops to think that, as it stands, the people who now chiefly work with the patient have no training at all.

Such training need not be for a hospital staff job. It could be offered to anyone interested in *visiting* one or two patients regularly. Many people, for example, women whose children are grown (Gendlin, 1956; Rogers, 1956; Rioch, 1963), would welcome a really meaningful occupation and would accept training for it. There is always going to be a shortage of professional people but there is no shortage of people seeking meaningful activity.[1]

Possible Programs of Training

These developments could have come about long ago but for our ignorance as to how to train such people. Of course, no one research project can alone dispel this ignorance. At most, the findings point to the direction of definable therapeutic factors which make the training of ordinary people quite conceivable.

Possibilities of training are mentioned here, not to propose this or that plan (such plans depend on many factors), but to illustrate that if the "conditions" are indeed the essential therapeutic agents, then we know

1. Since our study had to do with one-to-one relationships, there has been little or no mention of groups. Yet the exciting work being done in basic encounter groups at various state hospitals (Camarillo State Hospital in California is an example) shows not only that a trained facilitator can provide high conditions in his relationship to the group members, but that increasingly the patients in such groups show more of these attitudes, and relate more therapeutically, *to each other*. This so greatly broadens the pool of people who may learn to be therapeutic for each other that it deserves separate explication by those who have been more closely involved in such work. It opens fascinating new doors for the utilization of the attitudinal conditions we have discussed.

what the essential training is and we do not require that all psychotherapists be highly trained professionals.

It is true that the research itself does not prove this, since all but one of our therapists were experienced Ph.D.'s and M.D.'s, or graduate students who, while inexperienced, were nevertheless professionally trained persons. To see the significance for a broad social application of the conditions, one must look at the conditions themselves with this question in mind: How much diagnostic and conceptual training does "empathy" require? We do not know for certain. It is likely that familiarity with the range of possible human patterns and feelings is helpful. However, in the main, as Rogers says (1957), diagnostic skill is not needed for therapeutic interaction. Margaret Rioch (1963) reports that college-educated women who had had no training in psychology or psychotherapy found it better *first* to listen and interact with patients, and *then* to learn psychopathological terms with which to name facets they observed. Thus the requirement for empathy seems to be not the technical vocabulary but the training to observe, to listen for, and to respond to, finer facets of feeling and reaction. (Most often, the unique, individual, and finely textured ways of feeling with which we must empathize have no technical names. There are only broader categories of which they are individualized instances.)

If training in empathy is conceivable without academic training, it is even more conceivable in genuineness and positive regard. There is much to learn about such responding (see Chapter 16 for only some of such learnings). But, none of these learnings require higher education. They require direct work with patients, supervision, and opportunities to discuss, differentiate, and resolve one's observations and reactions.

During the past few years we have trained a rather large number of totally inexperienced people. These included graduate students in psychology, psychiatric residents, undergraduates, and, most recently (in Illinois), volunteers. We began our training by taking the new people onto a ward in the hospital. They were asked to talk with those patients who approached them (some come up and initiate a conversation: "Are you a social worker?" "Are you a visitor?" "Do you know when I can go home?" etc.) They were told to be simply honest (when appropriate, to explain that they hoped to learn how to help people in hospitals, and that they would like to hear how the patient came to be here . . .). They were also told that it would be all right to sit next to a patient who remained silent, perhaps asking a few questions, then saying something like: "If you don't feel like talking now, that is really all right. You don't have to."

The purpose of beginning training in this way was to enable the trainee to speak naturally with patients. We have found repeatedly that the structured therapy situation is very tense for the beginning therapist. He wants very much to behave and respond "as a therapist," but not knowing what that is, his task is much as though he were desperately trying to be a "garoompf" (something extremely important but undefined). The result is tension, and suppression of his many natural responses which—just because they are simply natural—seem as if they couldn't be what was wanted. It may take years for the therapist to regain the natural ease which he gave up at the start. By beginning on the ward, without expectations, the trainee becomes comfortable in talking with patients. As a result, trainees can more quickly give themselves fully to listening and perceiving the patient.

Meanwhile the experienced therapist is also on the ward, talking with patients, sometimes joining this or that trainee for a few minutes in his conversation with a patient. In this way the experienced therapist can demonstrate how he works, again without the artificial pressure of having to do something well because it is a "demonstration." Genuineness, empathy, and unconditional regard apply directly also to training and supervisory relationships. After such a time on the ward, an excited and involved group of trainees discuss with the (hopefully) undefensive experienced therapist what they, and he, did and might have done. In this regard Rogers has led the way for many years—by discussing his difficulties and errors, by publishing a failure case, by participating in such meetings and thinking out loud about his own feelings and sometimes poor responses, all of which swiftly frees the tense beginner similarly to accept his inevitable personal difficulties and failures as these bear on responding to a troubled individual.

I have described this training because it illustrates the social significance of the conditions as essential variables of engendering the process of constructive personality change. The training described brings home the fact that academic training is not required (although experiential training *is* necessary, and perhaps selection also).

Another implication of these essential variables concerns the social problem as it bears on our present failure to provide help to patients from the lower socio-economic classes (Hollingshead and Redlich, 1958). The conditions are variables which, at least in principle, require none of the conceptual articulateness and verbal habits of the middle-class university professional. (A program to train selected lower-class individuals in the conditions is under discussion in Illinois at the time of this writing [Gendlin, 1965].) Perhaps it will soon be possible to give lower-class individuals the essential skills to help lower-class patients. This has been successfully tried in counseling of institutionalized delinquents and criminals in California.

Finally, and most broadly, we may view the mental patient population as one which has been abandoned and isolated by society. The "illness" seems to be, at least partly, the result of *no* empathy, *no* genuineness, *no* unconditional regard. It is most likely that professional people alone will not be able to "cure" this "illness" in so many people. Fortunately, there are already attempts, made by ordinary, socially conscious people, to bring these people back. As half-way houses, community clinics, day treatment centers, friendship houses, volunteer programs, etc. multiply, the "conditions," as essential variables of a therapeutic process and as practised by laymen, may become the scientifically defined way of bringing patients back to interhuman living.

A New Science of Psychotherapy

Research in psychotherapy has suffered from the fact that psychotherapy was not definable. This has meant that if an experimental therapy group was compared to a non-therapy control group, some of the supposed therapy subjects were not really receiving anything therapeutic at all. Similarly, some control subjects might have had a "high condition" relationship, but one not labeled "therapy." Averaging the changes in the experimental group as compared with the control group has often showed no significant differences. To bring this home, imagine trying to investigate the effects of a drug, with an experimental group taking the drug and a control group receiving a placebo. Imagine that some (perhaps half) of your experimental group are actually taking a preparation without the effective ingredient of the drug—and you don't know which ones these are—and that one or two of your controls are actually getting the drug on the side. Your experimental treatment group is not always getting the treatment and your controls are not truly controls.

Another difficulty in this research situation was that research in psychotherapy has, until now, not really been replicable. If in one research, psychotherapy was given and found successful (significantly more than in controls), the next research group had no way of repeating such successful therapy. They could only do whatever each of their therapists called psychotherapy, without knowing if it even resembled what was done in the earlier research, now being "repeated," or just how it differed. Perhaps in the repetition no positive outcomes or differences from the controls would be found.

The Significance of Defining the Conditions of Therapy

The conditions as measured by our instruments can be applied to any therapists. In this way any group can determine whether they are doing that which we investigated.

Since some of our findings are partial and unclear, and since in any case one study rarely provides definitive answers, it is important to notice not only the specific findings but also the *general* implications for the *sort* of variable which the conditions are. Even if future researches disprove our findings, the very *possibility* of such clear-cut disproof is a significant advance. This kind of variable and methodology allows therapist variables to be measured and can define "psychotherapy." Thus, if a different group of therapists views some aspect of what they do as "essential," then, by the same sort of methodology, the variable they choose can be instrumented and tested. It will be possible to replicate their "experimental treatment."

It is a major significance of this research that we have begun to define "psychotherapy" in researchable and replicable terms, so that we need no longer employ only the misleading definition of hours in a room.

Note that the conditions are variables of therapist behavior: they concern how the therapist does what he does. The direction is toward *a new science* about working with people—not a science which merely classifies types of people or pathological difficulties, but a science consisting of defined operations to employ with people who thereby change.

Every developed science has followed the path of first primitively classifying the phenomena as observed. (Physics began with the classes: the wet, the dry, the earthy, the fiery.) The development of science moves from classifying (and otherwise leaving unchanged) toward defined *procedures* to follow, and their predicted *consequences*. Developed science consists of operations. One predicts that, if the operation is performed upon the subject matter, certain changes will follow. Classifications are then readjusted and enormously improved in power.

Thus while our prediction—that the *same* operations would lead to the *same* change process in schizophrenics as in normals and neurotics —may seem strange, in fact the findings did indicate that the current psychopathological classifications are not very relevant to the therapeutic change process, or to the operations which bring it about. Perhaps new and better classifications may emerge (in a rudimentary way some more relevant classifications may be emerging). We should not be sad to see our current psychopathological classification becoming obsolete.

(It is still a good set of concepts to sensitize people to the variety of human ways of feeling.) The movement of science is—as it ought to be —toward variables of what we can *do* to the subject matter and what happens when we do it. A science of how to approach and relate to people is replacing a science that only classified people as they are.

We may hope to develop, in the next decades, a sophisticated and socially defined language about detailed therapeutic operations (attitudes, sets, and responses). As it is today, each therapist in each generation must begin at the beginning. While our present psychopathological science gives him sophisticated concepts about the patients, it gives him very few concepts about what he is to do to help the patients change. We have as yet very little such science, very few terms about a therapist's procedure which can mean the same to all and can be defined, observed, measured. The conditions variables are an early set of such terms.

It will also become possible to use the instruments which measure such therapist behavior variables as both training aids and training measures. We have already begun (Gendlin, 1962) to use the rating scales, backwards as it were, to define and illustrate for the trainee what the conditions variables are. We have a set of tape-recorded four-minute excerpts which illustrate the conditions at the various levels, and we use some of these to teach and some of them to test the progress of the trainee. The same rating scales can then be applied to their own tape-recorded interviews to establish how well such learning generalizes in their actual therapy behavior.

Finally, we ought to look at the findings in the context of the slowly increasing knowledge about how to cure schizophrenia. I say "cure" advisedly, because while we have no sure-fire "cure" as yet, this must be the objective.

Currently, government programs, community psychology, and social psychiatry are rapidly developing community approaches to the problem of mental health. The realization is now widespread, that "one-to-one" helping is insufficient, and that the structures of hospital and community must be worked with.

So strong is this new emphasis, that there is some danger we may lose the ingredient of the personal relationship. In many minds the personal relationship has become identified with office psychotherapy. It is therefore important that the therapeutic "conditions" measured here are applicable in other arrangements. Our own "ward-availability" pattern (see Chapter 3) is one such different arrangement. But in principle it should be possible *and economical* to build the therapeutic conditions into at least one relationship with at least one person, as part of the current community approaches.

It seems probable that patients will need at least one close relationship with at least one human being (however little actual time they may have with him). The findings imply that this is one essential ingredient which we should not lose, as we develop others.

There is a time lag today (though we may not yet have all the pieces of the puzzle) between what is discovered and what is used. Moreover, as the "conditions" show, work with psychotics—and people generally —depends very greatly on human qualities and attitudes. Thus, perhaps in one hospital everything conceivable is done to aid patients. The release percentage goes up and everyone is excited, publishes, and learns. But soon the staff changes and the hospital goes back to being an ordinary custodial institution. So much of our present way of working still depends on global devotion—on the "Hawthorne effect"— whereby any sustained major effort will bring improvement because *the attitudes* in such an effort are the effective change agents. The "conditions" define just these attitudes. It is a major step to define *them* (rather than the vast variety of different behaviors, methods, vehicles, and techniques which could implement them). Such definitions move beyond the present dependence on the happenstance of individual staffs, toward a socially defined set of procedures.

Society would change its present system if a better answer were reliably shown. We believe society will adopt better methods to the extent that their effectiveness is scientifically tested. The "conditions" are not at all new, but they have not been scientifically defined and tested before. Ever since the Quakers in 1794 established "moral" institutions for a more human treatment of the insane, it has been claimed by some that "insane" people need optimal human relationships. Why was this knowledge not taken up generally? Why would we expect it to be taken up now? The hope lies in measurable and tested effects of the conditions variables. As a society we accept scientific findings as a basis for social policy. When it was scientifically demonstrated and fully replicated that sunshine is not good for tubercular patients, the sunshine treatment was discontinued. When we found radiation to have bad cumulative effects, the X-ray machines were eliminated from shoe stores. There is a time lag, but not such a lag as that from 1794 to the 1960's. On the other hand, scientific verification in this area is extremely new, and we are not accustomed to it. It requires a certain discipline on our part as researchers. We need to build studies, one on top of the other, to use the same instruments with one step of improvement at a time, to replicate each other's experiments, to move toward genuinely rigorous tests of what we are already convinced of as people, and slowly to devise a scientific language of terms which define significant aspects of human interaction.

In this development the present findings are only one important, but very small, step.

The Implications of the Measurement of Process Behavior

Now let us turn to the social significance of the measurement of the client's process behavior. Our ability to measure this means that we no longer need to wait several years to know whether an individual's psychotherapy is now producing change. "Process" defines behavior indices of ongoing change. If these indices are present, change is now being produced. To be able to decide this from present interview materials has enormous advantages for research, and for training and administration. Instead of having to wait many years before a given case is defined as a "failure," something can be done about it in time.

The process measures now make it possible to study different methods and arrangements of psychotherapy in terms of the levels of process behavior they engender. Research studies need no longer take so many years of waiting for "outcomes" and "follow-ups." It is now possible to study just a few interviews, or specific kinds of therapist behavior within an interview. "What is the differential result of this or that procedure?", we have always wanted to ask. It is now possible to measure the effect of a given procedure on the immediately ensuing process level in that and the next interview. Such studies can be carried out in short periods of time.

The Broader Significance of the Use of Experiencing

A much wider social significance is implied in the findings. The individual changes if he gives his felt experiencing a basic role in his thinking, talking, interpreting, and reacting. We are becoming able to measure, that is, to make public and social, a method of thinking which involves the individual's experiencing. It has always been known that some individuals are creative, that is, that they do not remain only within given interpretations and constructs. Somehow they use something else with which to arrive at *new* interpretations and constructs. It has been a puzzle what they do, since it has seemed as if the given ways of construing experience is all we have. It does no good to say to someone, "Hold your constructs loosely," or "Don't get so tied to how you see it now," since, if I hold my constructs and interpretations ever so loosely and open-mindedly, that alone does not get me to something new or better. To say, "Hold the concepts loosely," only tells me what I should *not* do. It does not tell me what *to do*. The creative individual uses something else in addition to the constructs. He has something to work with when he lets go of a given way of seeing things. He uses not only the given interpretations and constructs, but also his concretely felt experiencing, his preconceptual impression, his whole sense of the situation he observes or thinks about. He attends to, responds to, and conceptualizes aspects of this felt experiencing. As long as we could not talk about something preconceptual, not yet structured and formulated, we could only say that creativity is holding constructs loosely, somehow easily getting to new ones. We could not say what else is involved.

The use of one's felt experiencing is a method of thinking. If we find that clients cannot succeed with personal problems without reference to, and movement of, experiencing, why would we wish to let thinking in the human sciences, social planning, historical thought, ethics, psychology, and other areas remain in the kind of helpless vacuum which, for clients, we term "intellectualization" or "rationalization"? Thus a revolution in the capacities of human thought is implied. We will still be able to move from concept to concept via logical and precise, event-determined connections, but we will also, when we wish, be able to move from concept to experiential felt meaning (thereby taking in a whole texture of relevant aspects not yet formulated), and thence to new and different concepts. In retrospect we can always give logical precision to such an experiential step, although in advance we cannot replace it by deduction and constructs only, since such a step moves beyond the given constructs and their implications.

But, this "method of thinking," this "skill," this using one's felt experiencing for thought and problem solving—is it not really a matter of personal growth? Is it not "defensiveness" which prevents so many people from using their experiencing? Would there not have to be major personality change and growth before people could use it.

At one time Rogers (1959*a*) and I thought that high process levels were a measure of optimal adjustment. Conversely, we thought that low process levels indicated defensiveness and poor adjustment. We predicted that as the successful client moved through therapy, his process level would increase more and more. He would begin therapy at a low level and terminate successfully at a much higher level of using his experiencing. The findings of this and other researches on both neurotics and schizophrenics have shown that the situation is not that simple. It is clear now that the use of one's experiencing may be the sort of behavior which *precedes* change, as well as being the sort of behavior which comes more strongly into evidence in the process of change. Quite poorly adjusted clients (both neurotics and schizophrenics) can be helped to engage in sufficient levels of process behavior to bring about change. We found consistently and significantly (with both neurotics and schizophrenics) that the level of this behavior is consistently higher for successful clients than for failures. There is a "working level" below which no change takes place. At the working level there is enough of this change-producing type of behavior to make therapy a success.

It seems, therefore, that the ability to so employ one's experiencing is not a function of adjustment. It is possible for extremely maladjusted people *near the beginning* of therapy! It is not the result of therapy—on the contrary, therapy takes place only through this change-producing behavior.

It seems that skill at the use of experiencing is not an index of health. Many people may be quite well adjusted (see our normals) without it. But it does seem that *if* such people do get into personal trouble they lack the skill to get out of it.

But then, if this type of behavior is so crucial in order to produce change, to resolve problems, to form new concepts and interpretations, and if one need not be well adjusted to use it, why then not teach it to everyone we can?

If process modes of problem solving and thinking can be taught (perhaps in high school or earlier), we would enable many people to resolve their own emotional problems, to carry their own experiencing forward, to overcome otherwise disabling situations without having to seek a professional therapist. Similarly (since use of one's own experiencing is vital in therapeutic responding to others), this skill would enable people to listen more helpfully to each other.

Can the skill be taught, and to whom? Instruments are now being developed on a pilot basis that instruct a step-by-step focusing on one's experiencing (both on personal problems and on intellectual problems), and a set of questions that can objectively establish whether these instructions were followed. (We had found, some time ago, that even a very short instruction to focus on one's felt meaning of a personal problem succeeded in producing significantly different GSR patterns (Gendlin and Berlin, 1961). Such instructions, questionnaires, and the instruments presented in this book bring us close to being able to define this "skill" objectively and socially, and to measure whether "teaching" it is possible. It also will enable us to answer the questions: At what developmental stage and school age is it best taught? Are there differences in how well subjects can learn it who are of different personality types, adjustment levels, socio-economic class, and genetic inheritance?

Such studies will probably lead to more and more universally applicable modes of teaching the focusing on one's experiencing (perhaps not only with middle-class verbal tools but also with images and actions).

Of course (as we said earlier about "conditions"), different types of situations may require different measurement instruments. The same basic process will have somewhat different observable indices. For example, if we wish to measure the extent to which small children in a classroom use their experiential process in their thinking about a subject, we may need somewhat different instructions and rating scales for the same basic variable. The basic question will still be: To what extent does the student refer to what he experientially senses? To what extent does he formulate freshly (as compared to using given concepts only)? To what extent is he basing his questions or comments on what we call "fresh thinking" (i.e., the use of as yet unformulated, sensed significance one *newly* formulates from out of one's directly sensed experience of what has been presented and discussed).

Thus we approach the time when this much more creative and powerful mode of thinking and dealing with oneself and others may become the property of everyone, taught in school by standard methods and its performance measurably tested.

The sort of society we have been evolving is more and more one in which highly specialized and complex role-slots are defined, and individuals must fit themselves into these. The individual is replaceable: someone else can be put into the same slot and perform exactly as the first one did. As society becomes more and more rationalized and complexly defined (irreversible in industrialization), we face more and more the problem of the individual person's relationship to these functionally defined roles.

To enable individuals to fill such roles, we give a highly sophisticated education to millions of them. Are we then to expect that they will shut down in themselves the (now richer than ever) experiential process so that they are only what the slot demands? It is not humanly possible. It would not be desirable. We want the individual person's creativity so that he is not only able to bear, but also able to change and improve the slot.

Similarly, we want a science which consists not only of given and rigid constructs (and just what follows logically from these) but also the experiential breadth of the individual thinker so that he can alter and improve concepts and create even better ones.

The measurement and definition of "process behavior," of giving one's felt experiencing process a basic role in one's thinking and interpreting, probably leads not only to a much improved research capable of improving psychotherapy, but also toward a more therapeutic society in which everyone might be enabled to employ the process and gain the power it adds to our more logical and conceptual modes of thinking and interpersonal responding.

References

APPELL, M., GENDLIN, E. T., and KLEIN, MARJORIE H. Teacher attitude variables and student explanation in three teaching methods. Unpublished research report, University of Wisconsin, 1963.

BARRETT-LENNARD, G. Dimensions of therapist response as causal factors in therapeutic change. *Psychol. Monogr. 76,* No. 43 (Whole No. 562), 1962, pp. 1–36.

BARRINGTON, B. Prediction from counselor behavior of client perception and of case outcome. *J. counsel. Psychol. 8:* 37–42, 1961.

BERLIN, J. I. Some autonomic correlates of therapeutic conditions in interpersonal relationships. Unpublished Ph.D. dissertation, University of Chicago, 1960.

BERZON, BETTY. Relationship Inventory pilot study. Research memorandum, Western Behavioral Sciences Institute, 1961.

CLARK, J. V., and CULBERT, S. A. *Mutually Therapeutic Perception and Self-Awareness in a T-Group.* Mimeographed paper, Graduate School of Business Administration, University of California, Los Angeles, 1964.

deVAULT, M. V., ANDERSEN, D. W., SAWIN, DOROTHY, CAUTLEY, PATRICIA, and BOEHLEBER, M. In D. W. Andersen (ed.), *The Wisconsin Teacher Project: Design and Instrumentation.* Mimeographed paper, University of Wisconsin, 1963.

EMMERLING, F. C. A study of the relationships between personality characteristics of classroom teachers and pupil perceptions of these teachers. Unpublished Ph.D. dissertation, Auburn University, 1961.

GENDLIN, E. T. Professional or Legal Certification of the Counseling Function. *Counseling Center Discussion Papers,* II, 8. Mimeographed. Chicago: University of Chicago Library, 1956.

GENDLIN, E. T. Some ideas toward measurement indices of therapist competence. *Int. Ment. Hlth. Res. Newsltr. 4:* Nos. 3 and 4, 1962.

GENDLIN, E. T. A theory of personality change. In P. Worchel and D. Byrne (eds.), *Personality Change.* New York: John Wiley & Sons, 1964, pp. 100–148.

GENDLIN, E. T. *Mental Health Field Worker Training Project* (preliminary draft). Chicago: Illinois Department of Mental Health, Department of Planning, 1965.

GENDLIN, E. T., and BERLIN, J. Galvanic skin response correlates of different modes of experiencing. *J. clin. Psychol. 17:*73–77, 1961.

HOLLENBECK, G. P. The use of the Relationship Inventory in the prediction of adjustment and achievement. Unpublished Ph.D. dissertation, University of Wisconsin, 1961.

HOLLINGSHEAD, A. B., and REDLICH, R. C. *Social Class and Mental*

Illness: A Community Study. New York: John Wiley & Sons, 1958.

KAGAN, M., and HUNGATE, J. I. (editors and project directors). *The Field Instructor-Student Relationship in Social Work.* A group research project of the Graduate School of Social Work, University of Texas. Bound, mimeographed report, April, 1964.

POSER, ERNEST. The effect of therapists' training on group therapeutic outcome. *J. consult. Psychol. 30:*283–289, 1966.

RIOCH, MARGARET J., ELKES, CHARMAIN, FLINT, ARDEN A., USDANSKY, BLANCHE S., NEWMAN, RUTH G., and SILBER, E. National Institute of Mental Health pilot study in training mental health counselors. *Amer. J. Orthopsychiat. 33:* 678–689, 1963.

ROGERS, C. R. Can we meet the need for counseling? A suggested plan. *Counseling Center Discussion Papers,* II, 6. Mimeographed. Chicago: University of Chicago Library, 1956.

ROGERS, C. R. The necessary and sufficient conditions of therapeutic personality change. *J. consult. Psychol. 21:* 95–103, 1957.

ROGERS, C. R. A tentative scale for the measurement of process in psychotherapy. In E. A. Rubinstein and M. B. Parloff (eds.), *Research in Psychotherapy,* Vol. I. Washington, D.C.: American Psychological Association, 1959*a*, pp. 96–107.

ROGERS, C. R. A theory of therapy, personality, and interpersonal relationships as developed in the client-centered framework. In S. Koch (ed.), *Psychology: A Study of a Science.* Vol. III, *Formulations of the Person in the Social Context.* New York: McGraw-Hill, 1959*b*, pp. 184–256.

ROSEN, H. H. Dimensions of the perceived parent relationship as related to juvenile delinquency. Unpublished M.A. thesis, Auburn University, 1961.

SNELBECKER, G. E. Factors influencing college students' person-perceptions of psychotherapists in a laboratory analog. Unpublished Ph.D. dissertation, Cornell University, 1961.

THORNTON, B. M. Dimensions of perceived relationship as related to marital adjustment. Unpublished M.A. thesis, Auburn University, 1960.

TRUAX, C. B. Process of group therapy: Relationships between hypothesized therapeutic conditions and intra-personal exploration. *Psychol. Monogr.* 75, No. 7 (Whole No. 511), 1961.

VAN DER VEEN, F. The perception by clients and by judges of the conditions offered by the therapist in the therapy relationship. University of Wisconsin *Psychiatric Institute Discussion Paper. 1:* No. 10(e), 1961.

VAN DER VEEN, F. Agreement among the perceptions by clients, therapists, and judges of the conditions offered by the therapist. Unpublished research report. University of Wisconsin Psychiatric Institute, 1962*a*.

VAN DER VEEN, F. Client process movement and perception of therapist conditions by clients, therapists and judges. Unpublished research report. University of Wisconsin Psychiatric Institute, 1962*b*.

Veterans Administration Voluntary Service, Report of the Annual Meeting, April 6–8, 1965. Washington, D.C.: Office of the Chief Medical Director, Veterans Administration. June, 1965, pp. 20–24.

21. The Relationship of the Research Program to Psychological Science

Carl R. Rogers

In view of the ideological differences which exist in psychology today (Wann, 1964) and more especially in the field of psychotherapy, which has been described as being in "chaos" (Colby, 1964), it seems appropriate, in this concluding chapter, to try to describe the place of this research in psychological science. How does it fit in? In many ways this study stands squarely in the middle of some of the disputes which divide the science of psychology. In other respects it has openly chosen certain directions with which not all would be in agreement.

In the first place we have dealt directly with human interaction, not with reductionist elements in the neurological, gestural, biological, or speech components of that interaction. We have endeavored to discover whether lawful order can be discerned in the verbally expressed meanings and emotionalized attitudes which are central to the relationship of two individuals. We have believed that the scientist can profitably enter the field of human behavior at any level of complexity—from a study of chemical reactions in the brain tissue, to a study of mass behavior in groups. The fruitfulness of a scientific endeavor does not depend upon the point of entry, but upon the manner in which the study is carried on. We have entered it at the level of the dyadic relationship between two persons, and have attempted to conduct the study at that psychological level rather than trying to treat it in terms of supposedly simpler neurological, biological, chemical, or behavioral units.

This is a naturalistically based research, resting upon the phenomena which naturally occur between the therapist and his client or patient. It grows out of the conviction that the most fruitful hypotheses develop out of a complete personal immersion in the range of phenomena being studied—in this case the therapeutic relationship with deeply disordered persons. This is not to say that we are in any way opposed to other approaches to investigation. Indeed it is hoped that out of such a naturalistically grounded research, hypotheses will emerge which can much more advantageously be tested in the laboratory.

In our overall view of what constitutes science, our perspective is very similar to that so persuasively advanced by Polanyi (1958) speaking from his rich experience in the physical sciences. We see the scientist's effort as consisting first of all of a dimly perceived but compelling pattern which the scientist, out of immersion in the phenomena of the field, believes to exist in reality. It is this informed, intuitive perception of intangible hidden connections between events which constitutes the basis for the scientist's hypotheses. In our case the whole course of the enterprise was set by the "hunch" (or "theory" if one wishes to be more presumptuous) that attitudinal qualities were the effective element in relationships that produce change.

In any science it is the scientist's disciplined personal commitment which helps to discover the fruitfulness or unfruitfulness of the initially perceived pattern. In this instance it is our judgment that the central hypotheses have proved fruitful, though by no means always correct.

There is another aspect of the program which is relevant to current disputes in the psychological field. Some of our constructs and measures have to do with strictly observable behavior (release from the hospital, for example); other fruitful constructs are clearly phenomenological in nature (the patient's perception of the therapist's genuineness, for example); still others are, like forgotten dreams or unconscious motives, difficult to categorize, because they are incapable of direct observation either by the person himself or the scientific observer (remoteness from one's own experiencing, for example). In short, our research program has been in no sense doctrinaire in the origin of its basic constructs. This, we feel, is as it should be in any true science. The constructs should be developed and cast in whatever form seems most appropriate to the dimly perceived pattern toward whose illumination we strive.

But when we come to the confirmatory aspect of science (which American psychologists so often think of as *all* of science), we have attempted to be as strictly rigorous as the slippery nature of our field of work will permit. We have endeavored to give operational definitions of each construct, such that the variable may be put to test. This means that for each of the subtle elements of the pattern we are trying to test we have been forced to look for external, observable cues, the measures of which are replicable. The measures are *not* the construct itself, any more than a streak on a photograph of a cloud chamber is an electron particle, but in each case the instrument is the best index of the construct itself we have thus far been able to devise. Thus we find ourselves "measuring" degree of empathy, rigidity of personal constructs, immediacy of experiencing, and other elusive concepts, in terms of the best external clues we can find. It may well be that one of the most significant outcomes of our research will be the use of the instruments we have devised, or the development of much improved instruments, for measuring constructs of this kind.

In the design of our research, and in our statistical analyses, we have again taken the best methods known to us to avoid deceiving ourselves in our findings. There are, we are sure, plenty of flaws in design and in method which will be spotted by sharp-eyed critics, but our commitment has been to the most rigorous methodology we have been able to achieve, letting the chips fall where they may.

In this combining of naturalistic observation with controlled research design, of elusive and unobservable constructs with operational methods of assessing these constructs, of clinical intuition with hard-headed empiricism, we believe that we are groping toward a new philosophy of the behavioral sciences—one which will be freed of the rigid confines of a strict behaviorism, but which will also be free of the irresponsibility of dogmatic speculation.

In still another dimension the research takes a stance with significant implications. In much of current American psychology man is regarded only as an object, a complicated machine in which cause and effect are inexorable, and behavior is therefore fully determined. We have repudiated this (to us) outdated Newtonian mechanistic conception of science. The approach we have taken is one which we believe is decidedly congenial with the view of science which has, over the past thirty years or more, been developing in the "hard" sciences (Kaplan, 1964; Matson, 1964). Our purpose is to discover objectively verifiable lawful relationships in human behavior, and thus in our practical efforts we are not far from the Newtonian model. But just as indeterminacy (the influence of the observation on what is being observed) has become a part of physics, so too, we believe, we cannot observe and study the deepest or most subtle aspects of human experience without altering the very phenomenon itself.

Just as physics has made some of the most exciting advances through strange new constructs regarding space—formulations of types of space never seen or seeable—so in psychology, we feel, there is no limit to the imaginatively conceived patterns of unobservable human dynamics which are possible, so long as the intent is to find ways of testing those imagined insights and patterns. This accounts for the very different, and very intangible, kinds of variables included in our study, sharply different from the point of view that every variable must be, in an *obvious* way, observable, countable, and measurable.

In another sense, too, our work is analogous to that of modern science in the more traditional fields. Just as complementarity has become an accepted aspect of those fields, so too there are aspects of human behavior, we believe, which can be fruitfully and precisely defined from two different vantage points—but in which the two views are irreconcilable. Thus the lawful behavior of the individuals in our study, in so far as we have been able to determine its lawfulness, stands in flat contradiction to the freedom of choice which is one of the most important elements when we attempt to understand these same events clinically. We are quite content to permit this paradox—of determinism as over against choice—to stand until it is resolved by some over-arching theory which can reconcile the contradiction.

Perhaps it will be evident from the foregoing that our conception of science permits free and creative thinking by the scientist about significant but subtly intangible phenomena. It also permits our clients to be more than puppets dancing only because jerked by external strings. It means, indeed, that our view of science emerges as having an unabashedly humanistic flavor.

This fact makes it less than surprising that implicit in our whole program is the view that "schizophrenics" are, first of all, persons. It is conceivable that they are suffering from a disease, and we would not wish to deny this possibility. It is conceivable that the interaction of their genetic constitution with their particular environment has created the condition labeled schizophrenia. But quite regardless of what evidence may emerge in the future in regard to either one of these possibilities, they are certainly disordered in their functioning as human beings, and it is with this human disorder that we have endeavored to deal.

Finally, it is clear from the whole thrust of the research that we regard the study of interpersonal relationships—the elements which may make for diminished functioning, for increased tension, for regression, as well as those which make for increased integration, increased fulfillment of potential, increased ability to cope with life—as one of the most crucial issues in the field of psychology. In this sense our research is only partially a study related to schizophrenic persons, only partially a study of psychotherapy. It is most importantly a study of relationships, and their potential for both harmful and constructive change. In this respect it may have implications far beyond the specific findings with a particular group.

We do not deceive ourselves into thinking that we have, through this research program, made enormous progress along the lines discussed above. We have moved in these directions. We have inched forward. We have, we hope, added strength to a more modern concept of psychological science. We have contributed to the ways of dealing with deeply disordered persons. We have, we believe, added significantly to knowledge regarding the complex field of interpersonal relationships. It is our hope and conviction that others, building upon what we have done, can carry these efforts further.

References

COLBY, K. M. Psychotherapeutic processes. In *Annual Review of Psychology, 15,* 1964, pp. 347–370.

KAPLAN, A. *The Conduct of Inquiry.* San Francisco: Chandler Publishing Co., 1964.

MATSON, F. W. *The Broken Image: Man, Science, and Society.* New York: George Braziller, 1964.

POLANYI, M. *Personal Knowledge.* Chicago: University of Chicago Press, 1958.

WANN, T. W., ed., *Behaviorism and Phenomenology: Contrasting Bases for Modern Psychology.* Chicago: University of Chicago Press, 1964.

APPENDIX A

The Form for Rating Degree of Disturbance

Editor's Note

It is believed that an important part of the value of our research program lies in the instruments and rating procedures which were developed for use in the program.

All of the major instruments are included in the appendices. A research worker who wishes to duplicate any of these instruments for his own work may do so without requesting specific permission, providing only that: proper credit is given to author, publication, and publisher; and that the material is not to be used for public dissemination or for profit.

Appendix A. The Form for Rating Degree of Disturbance

Irene A. Waskow and Vilma Ginzberg

The following aspects were taken into account in rating the degree of disturbance in matching the pairs of more chronic and more acute schizophrenic patients.

I. Behavior and Manner of Relating to Others
   A. Quality of affect (information obtainable both from the interview and the records)
      1. Inappropriateness
      2. Flatness
      3. Euphoria, depression
   B. Bizarre behavior (information obtainable primarily from the records, secondarily from interview)
   C. Ability to relate to others (interpersonal attitudes: warmth, openness, negativism, suspicion, guardedness, etc.)
      1. In the interview
      2. In general, as indicated by the records
   D. Behavior and Manner of Expression (information obtainable from the interview)
      1. Circumstantiality
      2. Coherence
      3. Ability to reach goal—ideas
      4. Rate and manner of speech, gesture
II. Thought and Reality Disturbances
   A. Awareness of surroundings and reality factors (information obtainable primarily from the records, secondarily from interview)
      1. Orientation (person, place, time)
      2. Unrealistic goals and expectations
      3. Denial of past occurrences
      4. Distorted perception or interpretation of interpersonal relationships
   B. Delusions and hallucinations (information obtainable from the records)
   C. Preoccupations (information obtainable primarily from the records, secondarily from interview)
III. Self-awareness, Self-structure, and Mechanisms (how patient operates and how he sees himself)

551

    A. Insight into illness (information obtainable from both interview and records)
      1. Reasons for hospitalization
      2. Awareness of need for help
    B. Ego-strength
      1. Amount of personality structure left intact
      2. Level of integration
    C. Strong defenses interfering with relating to self and others. (Information obtainable from the interview and from hospital records)

  IV. Estimate of Ability to Function in Community (information obtainable from hospital records)

On the basis of these considerations the rater made a disturbance rating for each candidate for the research design as follows:

  V   Very disturbed (roughly equivalent to a rating of 15 or below on the Luborsky Scale)
Vm   (roughly equivalent to a rating of 15 to 20 on the Luborsky Scale)
vM   (roughly equivalent to a rating of 20 to 25 on the Luborsky Scale)
 M   Moderate disturbance (roughly equivalent to a rating of 25 to 30 on the Luborsky Scale)

APPENDIX B

Rating Scales for Therapeutic Conditions

Appendix B.1. A Scale for the Rating of Accurate Empathy[1]

Charles B. Truax

The present scale is a refinement of a scale described elsewhere (The process of group psychotherapy: Relationships between hypothesized therapeutic conditions and intrapersonal exploration. *Psychological Monographs, 75,* 1961). It was designed to be used with tape-recorded interviews, but can also be used with motion picture recordings, video tape recordings, live observations, and, with only slight loss in reliability, with typescripts of psychotherapy interactions. This scale and its immediate predecessors have been used on psychotherapy interaction units involving as little as two therapist and one client statements and as much as four minutes of continuous therapist-client interaction. The present scale was designed to be used with therapist responses occurring in both individual and group psychotherapy, and to be used by both professional and lay persons.

The scale is an attempt to define nine degrees of accurate empathy, beginning with an almost complete lack of empathy and continuing to a level where the therapist unerringly responds to the client's full range of feeling and recognizes each emotional nuance and deeply hidden feeling.

General Definition

Accurate empathy involves more than just the ability of the therapist to sense the patient's "private world" as if it were his own. It also involves more than just the ability of the therapist to know what the patient means. Accurate empathy involves both the sensitivity to current feelings and the verbal facility to communicate this understanding in a language attuned to the client's current feelings.

It is not necessary—indeed it would seem undesirable—for the therapist to *share* the client's feelings in any sense that would require the therapist to feel the same emotions that the client feels. It is instead an appreciation of those feelings and a sensitive awareness of those feelings. It also, at deeper levels of empathy, involves an understanding of patterns of human feelings and experiencing so as to sense feelings

1. The author is indebted to Shirley Epstein and Edward Williams for suggestions and additions to the revised scale.

present in the client which are only partially revealed. From the therapist's experience and knowledge of patterns of human feelings and experiencings he can communicate what is clearly known to the client and can also voice meanings in the client's experience of which the client is scarcely aware.

At a *high* level of accurate empathy the message "I am *with* you" is unmistakably clear—the therapist's remarks fit in just right with the client's mood and content. The therapist's responses not only indicate a sensitive understanding of the obvious feelings, but serve to clarify and expand the client's awareness of his own feelings or experiences. This is communicated not alone by the language appropriate to the client, but also by the total voice qualities which unerringly reflect the seriousness and depth of feeling. The therapist's intent concentration upon the client is evident so that he is continuously aware of the client's shifting emotional content and can shift his own responses to correct for language or content errors in his own communications when he is not "with" the client.

At a *low* level of accurate empathy the therapist may be off on a tangent of his own or may have misinterpreted what the patient is feeling, and, at a very low level, may be so preoccupied and interested in his own intellectual interpretations that he is scarcely aware of the client's "being." The therapist at this low level of empathy may be even disinterested in the client, or may have his focus of attention on the intellectual content of what the client says rather than what the client "is" during the moment and so ignores, misunderstands, or does not attempt to sense the client's current feelings and experiences. At a low level of empathy the therapist is doing something other than "listening," "understanding," or "being sensitive"; he may be evaluating the client, giving advice, sermonizing, or simply reflecting upon his own feelings or experiences. Indeed, he may be accurately describing psychodynamics to the patient—but in a language not that of the client, or at a time when these dynamics are far removed from the current feelings of the client, so that it takes on the flavor of a teacher-pupil interaction.

Stages

Stage 1

Therapist seems completely unaware of even the most conspicuous of the client's feelings. His responses are not appropriate to the mood and content of the client's statements and there is no determinable quality of empathy, hence, no accuracy whatsoever. The therapist may be bored and disinterested or actively offering advice but he is not communicating an awareness of the client's current feelings.

Example 1

C: Sir, are you ready? [*earnestly*]

T: What about? [*mumbled*]

C: I want one thing to know — uh — is it or is it not normal for a woman to feel like that, like I felt — degraded — one thing right after the other from Sunday on — or is it a lesson? [*sadly, dramatically*] Is it immature to feel like this — is really maturity — what it says in the books, that one has to understand the other person — is a woman supposed to give constantly and — be actually humiliated? [*intensely, though softly*]

T: If she asks for it. [*casually*]

C: If she asks for it. [*registering surprise*] Did I ask for it? [*testily*]

T: Well, I don't know; I doubt — I don't think you did. [*mechanically*]

Example 2

C: I wonder if it's my educational background or if it's me.

T: M-hm.

C: You know what I mean.

T: Yeah.

C: [*pause*] I guess if I could just solve that I'd know just about where to hit, huh?

T: M-hm, m-hm. Now that you know, a way, if you knew for sure, that your, your lack, if that's what it is — I can't be sure of that yet [*C:* No] is really so, that it, it might even feel as though it's something that you just couldn't receive, that it, if, that would be it?

C: Well — I — I didn't, uh, I don't quite follow you — clearly.

T: Well [*pause*], I guess, I was, I was thinking that — that you perhaps thought that, that if you could be sure that, the, uh, that there were tools that, that you didn't have, that, perhaps that could mean that these — uh — tools that you had lacked — way back there in, um, high school [*C:* Yeah] and perhaps just couldn't perceive now and, ah —

C: Eh, yes, or I might put it this way, um— [*pause*] If I knew that it was, um, let's just take it this way — if I knew that it was my educational background, there would be a possibility of going back [*T:* Oh, so I missed that now, I mean now, and, uh] and really getting myself equipped.

T: I see, I was — uh — I thought you were saying in some ways that um, um, you thought that, if, if that was so, you were just kind of doomed.

C: No, I mean —

T: I see — [*interrupts*]

C: Uh, *not doomed*. Well, let's take it this way, um, as I said, if, uh, it's my educational background, then I could go *back* and, catch myself up [*T:* I see —] and come up —

T: Um.

Stage 2

Therapist shows a degree of accuracy which is almost negligible in his responses, and then only toward the client's most obvious feelings. Any emotions which are not so clearly defined, he tends to ignore altogether. He may be correctly sensitive to obvious feelings and yet misunderstand much of what the client is really trying to say. By his response he may block off or may misdirect the patient. Stage 2 is distinguishable from stage 3 in that the therapist ignores feelings rather than displaying an inability to understand feelings.

Example 1

C: You've got to explain so she can understand [*Therapist murmurs* M-hm, m-hm, *in bored tone*] — without — uh — giving her the impression that she can get away with it, too. [*excitedly*]

T: Well, you've got a job satisfying all the things that — seem important, for instance being consistent, and yet keeping her — somewhat disciplined and telling her it's good for her. [*conversationally*]

C: There's where the practical application of what we have just mentioned comes into being. [*laughs*]

T: M-hm, m-hm. [*sounding bored*]

C: And when it's a theoretical plan — [*T:* M-hm] — it's beautiful! [*shrilly*] [*T:* M-hm — m-hm] — but —

T: [*interrupting*] Something else about it that I feel *really* dubious about: [*banteringly*] What you can really do on the practical level? [*inquiringly*] —I sometimes say that's what — we're most encouraged about, too. [*mumbling*]

C: [*chiming in loudly*] Yes — uh — there are many — uh problems in our lives in the practical application of — trying to be consistent. [*informatively*]

Example 2

C: It seems that recently, uh, we, uh, set up our program for the next year, and, uh, outlined it, and concurred it by phone and all of this stuff, and I sent him a letter, a concurring letter, a letter to concur his phone call. I want him to send me a concurring letter to the letter that I concurred from to make more triply sure that I didn't — what's going on. So, I don't know what, uh, what's going on, what's going on in this guy's head. [*T:* M-hm.] 'Cause, uh, I assume at the outset then that this is a [*T:* M-hm] guy that reacts normally to acts, normally. Then, when a person *does* have something that is supposed to, or that he was going to be especially secretive about, [*T:* M-hm] that does have a definite meaning. Not a type that just promotes himself to — out of proportion like — let's say, uh, say a certain general. Perhaps, uh, this fellow likes servants.

T: Maybe you're saying that — I mean, what I see you doing now is, uh, escaping, considering — letting a — a justification — for — your feeling of anxiety in this situation —

C: [*interrupting*] Yeah, well, uh, I'm trying to figure out just how — well, just kind of what the outcome would be, what day do you think [*Therapist attempts to interject some comment, but Client does not yield*] I could go *on* with the delusions of trying to be a fortune teller, which I can't — [*T:* M-hm.] I can't stand that.

T: Then, I heard you say something else, uh, right at the beginning, I suppose this was, that uh, there it was a hot day, and you didn't think there was, you know, there was any calls coming downstairs.

C: Well, I — I would like to try to figure that out for myself, the feeling I — I sort of .get the feeling, you know, of — of getting to be triply sure, you know. Perhaps this is what I meant to convey here.

T: Well, uh — I don't know whether you really said this, but it's — you conveyed it to me, anyhow. And, I perceived the notion that, uh — you were feeling this way and, uh, sore and so on, and along comes this phone call and this situation [*C:* M-hm] to which, immediately, you respond with anxiety [*C:* Yeah] which, uh, you then felt was, uh, an indication of the insecurity of your level of confidence [*C:* Yeah] in yourself [*pause*] I'm very frank!

Stage 3

Therapist often responds accurately to client's more exposed feelings. He also displays concern for the deeper, more hidden feelings, which he seems to sense must be present, though he does not understand their nature. The therapist seems to assume the presence of deep feelings, although he does not sense their meaning to this particular patient.

Example 1

C: I'm here, an' uh — I guess that maybe I'll go through with it, and [*nervous laugh*] I'll have to — there's no use —

T: [*interrupting*] You mean you're here — you mean you're right here — I wasn't sure when you said that — [*C:* Well —] whether you meant you were — I guess you mean you were in — this is your situation. [*stumbling*]

C: [*interrupting*] I'm in — I'm in — I'm in the stage of suffering — well, yes, I'm here too because of that. [*Therapist murmurs* M-hm *after every other word or so.*] — An' — uh — [*sighs audibly*] — but, I can see where — uh —

T: [*filling in*] You feel it's — you feel it's a pretty tough situation to be in? [*inquiringly*]

C: Sometimes I do, sometimes I don't. [*casually*]

Example 2

C: Now that you're — know the difference between girls; I think they were about 9 to 8 years old, and, uh, they were just like dolls, you know, and [*laughs*] uh, I used to spend a lot of time with 'em. I used to go over there and would spend more time with these kids than what would with —

T: M-hm, hm.

C: But nobody ever told me why I was dragged in here. And I own my own place, I have my, my [inaudible] and my farm, I think I still own them. Because that, there was a little mortgage on it. And, uh [*pause*] my ex-wife but I don't see how in the world they could change that.

T: M-hm, hm.

C: But they sold my livestock and, uh, I, I worked with horses, and they sold them all, and, ah —

T: I think probably, should I cross this microphone? [*noise*]

C: And then I had a bunch of sheep.

T: M-hm, hm.

C: And they sold that stuff off, and the social worker, Mrs. ——— says to me, she says that uh, she says I was ill when I was brought in here.

T: M-hm, hm.

C: And that, which I know that I was not ill. Now, I'll tell you what she might've meant in what way I was ill. Now I'll tell ya, I batched it out there on the farm and I maybe just didn't get such too good food at the time. Now, whether she wanted to call that ill, or whether she wanted to call it mentally ill, that she didn't say.

T: M-hm, hm.

C: But she says I was ill, well, they could put that I was sick that I didn't have the right kind of food because I gained quite a bit of weight after I was brought in here.

T: M-hm, hm.

C: Yeah, but she didn't say which way she meant or how she meant that.

T: Uh-huh.

C: And she wouldn't give me any explanation and then I got mad at her [*T:* M-hm, hm] and of course I told her off. Then I asked her if she, they kept from me for a long time that my stock was sold and I thought quietly, anyhow, I says, I won't give my work . . . .

Stage 4

Therapist usually responds accurately to the client's more obvious feelings and occasionally recognizes some that are less apparent. In the process of this tentative probing, however, he may anticipate feelings which are not current to the client, as well as misinterpret some present feelings. Sensitivity and awareness of the therapist are present but he is not entirely "with" the patient in the *current* situation or experience. The desire and effort to understand are both present but accuracy is low. It is distinguishable from stage 2 in that the therapist does occasionally recognize feelings that are less apparent. Also the therapist may seem to have a theory about the patient and may even know how or why the patient feels a particular way, but the therapist is definitely not "with" the patient—they are not together. In short, the therapist may be diagnostically accurate, but not empathically accurate in his sensitivity to the current feeling state of the patient.

Example 1

C: If–if — they kicked me out, I–I don't know what I'd do — because — [*T:* M-hm.] I–I–I *am* really dependent on it. [*stammering*]

T: Even though you hate this part — you — say, "My God, I — I don't think I could — possibly exist without it either." [*C:* M-hm.] — And that's even the — that's the worst part of it. [*gently*]

C: [*following lengthy pause*] Seems that — [*catches breath*] — sometimes I — uh — the only thing I want out of the hospital — 's tuh have everyone agree with me [*T:* M-hm, hm] that's — I–I–I guess that if [*catches breath*] — everybody agreed with me — that everybody'd be in the same shape I was. [*seriously, but ending with nervous laughter*]

T: M-hm — well, this is sort of like — uh — feeling about the friend who — didn't want to do what I wanted to do; that — even here — if you agreed with me — this is what I want because if you don't agree with me, it means you don't like me or something. [*reflectively*]

C: Mmmmm — [*thoughtfully*] it means that I'm wrong! [*emphatically, quick breathless laugh*]

Example 2

C: . . . you know, I'll bet you tell that to all the girls. And when we would have oh, go out for department, frequently had parties and picnics and that sort of thing, and I knew his wife and, and, children and, uh there, there was no affair. It was, and, as a matter of fact, I, that was at the time that I had an affair with ———. [*T:* M-hm.] I didn't need a man because I had one. [*T:* M-hm.] How I, I don't think when I was living in ——— and working for the Welfare Department that even though I *hadn't* been having an affair with ———, I don't think that I would at that time have had an affair with ———. [*T:* M-hm.] I really don't.

T: One of the impressions I have [name] is that you, ah, your guilt feelings are *way* out of proportion — to what uh, they should be. In some ways you've got some real, ah, ah, victorian attitudes that you apply to yourself —

C: [*interrupting*] Well, I had an *affair* with a man and had an illegitimate baby and then go right ahead and have an affair with another married —

T: [*interrupting*] I'm not talking about that here. That's, that's serious. I mean, maybe you were indiscreet. Maybe uh, you were uh, you took chances that you shouldn't have taken, uh, what I'm saying is, uh, you have sexual feelings, you're going to have sexual feelings. It's a part of you because you're a person and, an —

C: [*interrupting*] But I didn't used to have them, Doctor!

T: [*going right on*] You want to, and you're going to want to find expression for them. And ah, and most people in your circumstance would find expression for them. And wouldn't have to feel so terribly guilty about it, as you do — they wouldn't have to go around hating themselves afterwards like you do. You've got built into yourself a good whip somewhere, [name], you whip yourself — [*pause*] I'm saying that compared to what most people in your circumstance, uh, what their feelings are like . . . .

Stage 5

Therapist accurately responds to all of the client's more readily discernible feelings. He shows awareness of many feelings and experiences which are not so evident, too, but in these he tends to be somewhat inaccurate in his understanding. The therapist may recognize more feelings that are not so evident. When he does not understand completely, this lack of complete understanding is communicated without an anticipatory or jarring note. His misunderstandings are not disruptive by their tentative nature. Sometimes in stage 5 the therapist simply communicates his awareness of the problem of understanding another person's inner world. Stage 5 is the midpoint of the continuum of accurate empathy.

Example 1

C: I gave her her opportunity — [*T:* M-hm] and she kicked it over. [*heatedly*]

T: M-hm — first time you ever gave her that chance, and — she didn't take it? [*inquiring gently*]

C: *No!* She came back and stayed less than two weeks [*T:* M-hm] — a little more than a week — and went right straight back to it. [*shrilly*] [*T:* M-hm.] — So that within itself is indicative that she didn't want it. [*excitedly*]

T: M-hm, m-hm — it feels like it's sort of thrown — right up in your face. [*gently*]

C: Yeah — and now I would really be — crawling — [*T:* M-hm] if I didn't demand some — kind of assurances — that that thing was over with. [*firmly*]

T: M-hm, m-hm — it would be — pretty stupid to — put yourself in that — same position where it could be sort of — done to you all over again. [*warmly*]

C: Well, it could be — yes! I would be *very* stupid! [*shrilly*] [*T:* M-hm] — because if it's not him — it might be someone else. [*emphatically*]

Example 2

C: Uh, it's really a store window there, uh, in Milwaukee.

T: Uh-huh. But this had been your idea, and you'd suggested it and then, lo and behold it comes out as —

C: Well, uh, you see, I have to investigate the contract I signed with the company, you know, these companies have to have a contract whereby they have rights to all patents and, and, copyrights uh, for uh, for so — so long a time after you leave the company, you know [*T:* Yeah] and uh, in other words, uh — [*talk together here*]

T: So you might have been all right in doing this but you're not really sure about that. You'd have to investigate that —

C: I'd have to investigate that and some other ideas I'd given them.

T: Uh-huh. And I know too, that, that this is another sign of how, another indication of how many things there were — that you need to track down. The drug was just one, this is just another, the movie camera, and [*C:* M-hm] and there are probably a number of others too.

C: Well, all those other ideas — [*Therapist talks simultaneously with Client here.*] Even before they [*silence*] When the, when the rocket, uh, was fired by a balloon the first time; I remember, uh, that, right after, uh, this time, that I had gotten into that trouble, I started a little office over in P—— and, and, uh, I submitted to the Department of uh, well, the National Inventors Council, *that* one particular idea. Well then, I just wrote in, an, asking uh, for a little recognition on it. [*T:* M-hm.] And of course, it was one of those ideas, like most of mine that any — anybody will think of and not many people will do anything about, you know [*T:* M-hm] and uh —

T: Not that hard an idea to think of but you were at least the one who did something about it and who tested it or something, but then didn't get recognition for it.

C: Well, they uh, they wrote me back and said they had nothing like that in their files. [*T:* M-hm.] Well, also uh, well, I had figured out a few, uh, affairs that, that, uh, amounted to sort of a gyroscope, uh, affair that I had submitted too, and, uh, they also didn't know anything about that. So, uh, I — I was pretty sick at that time, I, uh . . . .

Stage 6

Therapist recognizes most of the client's present feelings, including those which are not readily apparent. Sometimes, however, he tends to misjudge the intensity of these veiled feelings, with the result that his responses are not always accurately suited to the exact mood of the client. In content, however, his understanding or recognition includes those not readily apparent. The therapist deals with feelings that are current with the patient. He deals directly with what the patient is currently experiencing although he may misjudge the intensity of less apparent feelings. Often the therapist, while sensing the feelings, is unable to communicate meaning to these feelings. The therapist statements contain an almost static quality in contrast to stage 7 in the sense that the therapist handles those feelings that the patient offers but does not bring new elements to life. He is with the client but doesn't encourage exploration. His manner of communicating his understanding is such that he makes of it a finished thing.

Example 1

T: You're sort of — comparing — things you do do, things you have done — with what it would take to be a priest — is that sort of — the feeling? [*very gently*]

C: [*following long pause*] I don't know. [*meekly*] [*lengthy pause*]

T: Suppose we mean right now feeling real guilty? [*softly*]

C: [*sighs audibly*] Real small. [*very softly*] [*lengthy pause*] I can't see how I could feel any different — other than — feeling small or bad [*T:* M-hm] — guilty. [*softly*]

T: Things you've done just — so totally wrong to you — totally bad — you can't help sort of — hating yourself for it? [*assuming Client's tone*] — Is that the sort of quality? [*very gently, almost inaudibly*]

C: [*following pause*] And yet right now I feel as though I want to laugh — be gay — [*T:* M-hm.] I don't feel anything else. [*monotonously*]

T: [*speaking with Client*] Right at this moment? [*C:* M-hm.] — So — it's too much to really — feel — very miserable and show it? [*inquiringly*]

C: Yeah, yeah — [*urgently*] I — I — don't want to show it anyway. [*haltingly*]

Example 2

C: . . . gained a lot of weight, I'm way overweight, just the last couple of years, the more I, put on a lot of weight — I, well I *did* weigh around 160–165 now I weigh a little over 200; about 208 pounds or so. I really am overweight.

T: M-hm. You feel like [*C:* Yeah] you've got 40 pounds too much and you don't feel too good.

C: That's right. I washed medicine glasses for a little over three months the last summer so I, I feel like it right now, but some job, like *that*, that was — wasn't too hard, I could do it. [*T:* M-hm.] I done that four times a day and it'd take me about — oh, half an hour, three-quarters of an hour each time I done it, to wash, see to wash the medicine glasses first. All the different ones that take medicine, they give out medicine four times a day, I done that from, oh, the middle of May until the last part of August — the last day of August.

T: So you're saying, well, you're well enough to, to do some work.

C: Yeah, I went off — they wanted me to go on lawn detail last year but I didn't, I hardly feel that — I went out and shovelled snow last winter, just a day or two. If the work isn't too hard, I think I could do it all right. Now that really, that was really a nice good job for me, that washing glasses — I should've kept with that but uh, but oh I made the beds sometimes, about twelve or, something like that [*pause*] sometimes I mop the floor.

T: M-hm. Then you do feel well enough to, to do that sort of work [*C:* Yeah] around here and you're saying — [*pause*] You don't feel well enough or you don't really want to —

C: Well I don't really know, I wouldn't really be well enough to, I have to take medicine all the time and everything, to keep my nerves calmed, and uh —

Stage 7

Therapist responds accurately to most of the client's present feelings. He shows awareness of the precise intensity of most underlying emotions. However, his responses move only slightly beyond the area of the client's own awareness, so that feelings may be present which are not recognized by the client or therapist. The therapist moves on his own to more emotionally laden material. The therapist may communicate simply that the patient and he are moving toward more emotionally significant material. Stage 7 is distinguishable from stage 6 in that often the therapist response is a kind of pointing of the finger toward emotionally significant material with great precision in the direction of pointing.

Example 1

C: Th–the last — several years — it's been the other way around — I mean he'll say, "Well let's — go do this or that," and — and I — sometimes I actually wanted to, but I'd never go because — I feel like I'm getting my little bit of revenge or something. [*Voice fades at end.*]

T: By God, he owed it to you, and — if he didn't come through, you'll just punish him now — [*C:* Yeah] — now it's too late or — something. [*very softly*]

C: [*laughingly*] Yeah — that's — uh — that's just the way I — uh — *now it's too late* — It's your turn to take your medicine now. [*assuming Therapist's tone*]

T: M-hm — "I'm gonna treat you like — you've treated me." [*pause*] Uh —

C: M-hm — it's pretty — that's a — pretty childish way to think, but — I know uh — if I went home tomorrow, I'd do it tomorrow — if I had the chance. [*defiantly*] — If —

T: [*interrupting and overtalking Client*] One part of you could say, "Well — this is stupid and childish 'cause I — I *want* to be with him," — and yet another part says, "No, you gotta make him pay for it — you want *him* dangling there now." [*gently*]

Example 2

[*long silence*]

T: Are you interested in knowing any more about that or any more about your dreams or about anything else that has seemed important to you here in the hospital?

C: Oh, no, the last few months I haven't felt like having any recreation at all, I don't know why, it just doesn't appeal to me. And last night I almost had to force myself to go on a talent show.

T: Mm, m-hm. Just feel as though something like this, you just feel, oh, gosh, I'm not interested.

C: M-hm. I used to go to all the dances when I first came here, but now I don't care to now.

T: You sort of feel that even with things that at first you were quite interested in, now they seem less and less interesting.

C: M-hm.

T: I guess you're saying you don't quite know why that is but, uh, it seems that way.

C: M-hm.

Stage 8

Therapist accurately interprets all the client's present, acknowledged feelings. He also uncovers the most deeply-shrouded of the client's feeling areas, voicing meanings in the client's experience of which the client is scarcely aware. Since he must necessarily utilize a method of trial and error in the new uncharted areas, there are resulting minor flaws in the accuracy of his understanding, but inaccuracies are held tentatively. He moves into feelings and experiences that are only hinted at by the client and does so with sensitivity and accuracy. The therapist offers specific explanations or additions to the patient's understanding so that not only are underlying emotions pointed to, but they are specifically talked about. The content that comes to life may be new but it is not alien. While the therapist in stage 8 makes mistakes, mistakes do not have a jarring note, but are covered by the tentative character to the response. Also the therapist is sensitive to his mistakes and quickly alters or changes his response in midstream, indicating that he more clearly knows what is being talked about and what is being sought after in the patient's own explorations. The therapist reflects a togetherness with the patient in tentative trial and error exploration. His voice tone reflects the seriousness and depth of his empathic grasp.

Example 1

C: I'm getting *real* worried — b–because — I don't know just what I'm gonna have to face. [*insistently; raising voice to overtalk Therapist, who attempts to interject comment*] — I mean I can't even find — find what I'm gonna have to — uh — fight. [*last word barely audible*]

T: It must be something — pretty — God-awful terrible — and yet you don't even know what it is. [*gently*]

C: No — uh — I mean — someone could tell me that — I don't have enough confidence — uh — mmm — and I know I've — uh — I've always been afraid of — uh — *physical violence* — and — uh

T: [*interrupts*] That you've always been afraid of — being hurt — and I sort of sense, too, it's — being hurt by people — uh — that — physical violence like a — uh — *train* crashing in isn't frightening with you. [*gently*]

C: No — uh — [*reflectively*]

T: That a fight with people is upsetting? [*softly*]

C: Yeah! [*forcefully and registering surprise*] I — I think I'm — uh — afraid — uh — uh — I'm afraid of ever losing — uh — I think — not so much because of — uh the physical pain — but — the idea that — I lost and — uh — everybody knows it. [*haltingly*]

T: The idea that someone beat you — [*C:* M-hm] — That you were weak or something — [*very gently*]

Example 2

T: "The way she wanted me and I was always terribly afraid that she wouldn't put up with me, or would put me out, out." [*C:* Yeah.] I guess I can get something else there, too, "Now I was always afraid that she didn't really care."

C: I still think that though. [*T:* M-hm.] 'Cause I don't know for sure.

T: M-hm. "And don't really know for sure whether she cares or not."

C: [*pause*] She's got so many other, uh, littler kids to think about. [*T:* M-hm.] That's why —

T: "Maybe she likes them better or —"

C: No, it's not that, I think she likes us all. [*T:* Mm.] [*pause*] I think seein' that I'm the, I'm not the black sheep but, uh, the only one that served time [*T:* M-hm] and, that — 'n' got in the most trouble. [*T:* M-hm.] Seein' that I hurt her so much, that's why I think she's starting ta — she just don't care for me anymore.

T: You believe, "Maybe because I have hurt her so much, maybe she's fed up with me, maybe she's gotten to the point where she just doesn't care." [*long pause*]

Stage 9

Therapist unerringly responds to the client's full range of feelings in their exact intensity. Without hesitation, he recognizes each emotional nuance and communicates an understanding of every deepest feeling. He is completely attuned to the client's shifting emotional content; he senses each of the client's feelings and reflects them in his words and *voice*. He expands the client's hint into a full-blown but tentative elaboration of feeling or experience with unerring sensitive accuracy. Both a precision in understanding and a precision in the communication of this understanding are present. Both are expressed and experienced by the therapist without hesitancy.

Example 1

C: . . . uh — I've always been — so afraid — uh — show just how I — how I felt [*T:* M-hm] — and I — and I — I think —

T: [*interrupting*] Showing feelings is — weak or — something [*gently, fading until almost inaudible*]

C: Yeah — that's how it seems to me [*lengthy pause*] I know I — I've been in the TV room — and I — all of a sudden — had the feeling that — I was going to start crying — [*almost tearfully*] [*T:* M-hm] and — uh — I knew then I'd have to leave and go somewhere — [*T:* M-hm] — where nobody was; so in case I did start crying that nobody'd see me. [*bashfully*]

T: M-hm [*pause*] It'd just be — terrible to stand if you — if you ever did show this much feeling— [*sorrowfully*] [*long pause*]

C: The thing is — that — I'm — I'm afraid of — well, I'd be so embarrassed afterwards. [*ashamedly*]

T: M-hm — this would be — just — terrible — uh — a man wouldn't cry, a grownup wouldn't cry. [*C, almost tearfully:* Yeah.] — Or at least — [*leaves thought suspended*]

C: [*filling in for Therapist*] At least without an apparent reason [*T:* M-hm] [*long pause*] an', uh, an' — I don't have — an apparent reason. [*emphatically*]

T: It wouldn't only be weak, but — be crazy or something. [*very gently*]

C: [*chiming in*] Yeah! [*very positively*]

Example 2

T: . . . I s'pose, one of the things you were saying there was, "I may seem pretty hard on the outside to other people but I do have feelings."

C: Yeah, I've got feelings. But most of 'em I don't let 'em off.

T: M-hm. Kinda hide them. [*C, faintly:* Yeah.] [*long pause*]

C: I guess the only reason that I try to hide 'em, is, seein' that I'm small, I guess I got to be a tough guy or somethin'.

T: M-hm.

C: That's the way I, think, I think people might think about me.

T: Mm. "Little afraid to show my feelings. They might think I was weak, 'n' take advantage of me or something. They might hurt me if they — knew I could be hurt."

C: I think they'd try anyway.

T: "If they really knew I had feelings, they, they really might try and hurt me." [*long pause*]

C: I guess I don't want 'em to know that I got 'em.

T: Mm.

C: 'Cause then they couldn't if they wanted to.

T: "So I'd be safe if I, if I seem like a, as though I was real hard on the outside. If they thought I was real hard, I'd be safe."

Appendix B.2. A Tentative Scale for the Rating of Unconditional Positive Regard[1]

Charles B. Truax

The present scale is a refinement of a scale described elsewhere (The process of group psychotherapy: Relationships between hypothesized therapeutic conditions and intrapersonal exploration. *Psychological Monographs, 75,* 1961). It was designed to be used with tape-recorded interviews, but can also be used with motion picture recordings, video tape recordings, live observations, and, with only slight loss in reliability, with typescripts of psychotherapy interactions. This scale and its immediate predecessors have been used on psychotherapy interaction units involving as little as two therapist and one client statements and as much as four minutes of continuous therapist-client interaction. The present scale was designed to be used with therapist responses occurring in both individual and group psychotherapy, and to be used by both professional and lay persons.

The scale is an attempt to define five degrees of unconditional positive regard, beginning with an almost complete lack of unconditional positive regard and continuing to a level where the therapist unerringly communicates to the client a deep and genuine caring for him as a person with human potentialities, uncontaminated by evaluations of his thoughts and behaviors.

General Definition

Unconditional positive regard is the unitary dimension ranging from a high level where the therapist experiences a warm acceptance of the patient's experience as being part of that person and places no conditions on acceptance and warmth to a low level where the therapist evaluates a patient or his feelings, expresses dislike or disapproval, or when the therapist expresses positive regard in a selective evaluative way.

Thus, a warm positive feeling towards the client may be rated quite low in unconditional positive regard if this warmth is given conditionally. Unconditional positive regard for the client means an acceptance of the patient as a person with human potentialities. It involves a nonpossessive caring for the patient as a separate person and, thus, a

1. The author is indebted to Edward Williams for his contribution to the scale.

willingness to share equally the patient's joys and aspirations or his depressions and failures. It involves the valuing of the patient as a person without contamination from evaluating his behavior or his thoughts. Thus, it is possible that a therapist may evaluate the patient's behavior or his thoughts but still rate high in unconditional positive regard if it is quite clear that the valuing of the individual as a person is uncontaminated and unconditional. Unconditional positive regard at its highest level involves a nonpossessive caring for the patient—as a separate person with permission to have his own feelings and experiences; a prizing of the patient for himself regardless of his behavior.

It is not necessary—indeed it would seem undesirable—for the therapist to be a nonselective reinforcer in the sense that he gives sanction or approval to thoughts and behaviors that are disapproved by society. Unconditional positive regard is present when the therapist appreciates those feelings or behaviors and their meanings to the client or patient and voices a nonpossessive caring for him (not for his behaviors). The response of the therapist to the patient's thoughts or behaviors is a searching for their meaning or value within the patient and never a response of disapproval or of approval.

Stages

Stage 1

The therapist is actively offering advice or giving clear negative regard. He may be telling the patient what would be "best" for him, or may be in other ways actively either approving or disapproving of his behavior. The therapist acts in such a way as to make himself the locus of evaluation. The therapist sees himself as responsible *for* the patient.

Example 1

C: . . . and I don't, I don't know what sort of a job will be offered me, but — eh —

T: It might not be the best in the world.

C: I'm sure it won't. [T: And uh.] But —

T: But if you can make up your mind to stomach some of the unpleasantness of things [C: M-hm] you have to go through — you'll get *through* it. [C: Yeah, I know I will.] And, ah, you'll get out of here.

C: I certainly, uh, I just, I just *know* that I have to do it, so I'm going to do it but — it's awfully easy for me, Doctor, to — [*sighs*] well, more than pull in my shell, I–I just hibernate. I just, uh — well, just don't do a darn — thing.

T: It's your own fault. [*severely*]

C: Sure it is. I know it is. [*pause*] But it seems like whenever I — here —

here's the thing. Whenever I get to the stage where I'm making active plans for myself, then they say I'm high. An' —

T: In other words they criticize you that —

C: Yeah.

T: So tender little lady is gonna really crawl into her shell. [*C:* Well, I'll say "okay."] "If they're gonna throw, if they're gonna shoot arrows at me, I'll just crawl behind my shield and *I* won't come *out* of it." [*forcefully*]

C: That's right. [*sadly*]

T: And that's worse. [*quickly*]

C: [*pause*] But why don't they let me *be* a little bit high? Why — right now I'm taking —

T: [*interrupting*] Because some people [*C, talking with him:* 600 milligrams of Malorin, whatever that is, Malorin] because a lot of people here don't know you very well at all. And because people in general, at times, you have to allow they could be stupid. You, too. I mean you're stupid sometimes, so why can't other people —

C: So *much* of the time.

T: Why can't other people? I mean, you're an intelligent person and are stupid. Why, why can't you allow that other intelligent people can also be stupid? When it comes to you they don't *know* very much.

C: Mm [*muttered*].

Example 2

T: . . . another part here too, that is if they haven't got a lot of schooling, there may be a good argument, that, that they — are better judges, you know —

C: Yeah —

T: Now, I'm not saying that, that's necessarily true, I'm — just saying that's *reality.*

C: Yeah —

T: And you're in a *position* that you can't argue with them. [*pause*] Why is it that these people burn you up so much?

C: They *get by with* too many things —

T: Why should that bother you?

C: 'Cause I never got by with anything.

T: They're papa figures aren't they?

C: [noise] Yeah— [*pause*] I told the aides last night, I said, "You're making me — I *want to forget* the past and — you're making me think of my father again." [*pause*] They don't *understand.*

T: [*breaking in*] But you're bringing it into the present, I don't want to keep dragging up the past; the present seems to me — uh, the same thing you've been going through all your life [*C:* M-hm] — this fighting against this father.

C: [*pause with sigh*] So what will it take to straighten it out?

T: You're the only guy that can straighten it out.

C: But how?

T: You've got to understand —

C: [*breaking in*] I mean between me and the aides?

T: How could your dad straighten that out?

C: Tell 'm!

T: *Nah.* [*scornfully*]

C: He *would* do it.

T: It is up to you to change.

C: If them aides would listen to me, if the doctors knew what was going on. I was fighting my dad, I wasn't fighting the aides, because —

T: Yeah, but everybody realized you're fighting like this, they are not going to know it's your dad that you're fighting for. They are going to look at it and say, "My God, this kid is sick. Look at this, we — we tell him something and he gets *real* angry," or "The doctor won't allow fighting, who —"

C: [*breaking in*] — They are not going to do that on the outside. They do it in here.

T: Now look at this Doctor G——, now look —

C: At —— Hospital. I didn't get upset until I ran into G——.

T: I'm sure this is going to come up again. Now look at Dr. M——, whew, you — uh *tell* her that she's *not competent,* and you *rebel* against her, she's not thinking to herself, "Well, this kid, he's had problems with his dad, and he's carrying them over now," she's just gonna sit back and say, "My God, that's sick behavior!" And, uh, she's gonna prescribe the medicine [*pause*]

C: Did you tell Doctor P—— this?

T: *No,* I didn't tell Doctor P—— this!

C: No, but today, well, I'll bring it up.

T: Without even bringing it up, it's still up to you to handle this. People can't make allowance for your times, I mean, we can *understand it,* but it's up to you to understand it and *change your behavior,* so —

C: Why do they bring it up?

T: Why does who bring it up?

C: *The aides!*

T: What have they done, now?

C: They act too much like my daddy does.

T: Well, there's going to be a lot of people act like your dad — does — throughout life —

C: [*interrupting*] How do you think I can learn to live with that?

T: You've gotta learn how to, to respond to it, to handle it in a way it doesn't lead you to be *more* unhappy. Now you were very unhappy when they acted like your *dad* — but my guess is that you're a lot more unhappy *now* — because you responded the way you did.

C: I am —

T: So, uh — you've got to learn to live with it; you've got to learn some other way of handling [*pause*] people like this —

C: [*Yawns agreement.*]

Stage 2

The therapist responds mechanically to the client and thus indicates little positive regard and hence little unconditional positive regard. The therapist may ignore the patient or his feelings or display a lack of concern or interest for the patient. Therapist ignores client where an unconditional positive regard response would be expected—complete passivity that communicates almost unconditional lack of regard.

Example 1

C: [*speaking throughout in a woebegone voice*] You don't have to sit down and, and, and write like that but I thought he'd answer my letter. I thought, I didn't think he'd answer the letter, I thought he'd *come up* [*T:* M-hm] — and, and visit me; it's only 50, he hasn't been to visit me yet. It's only about uh, it's only about 50, 60 miles from here [*T:* M-hm] and I kind of expected him last Sunday but he didn't —

T: You were just sort of looking for him but he —

C: [*interrupting insistently*] Well, I wasn't, I wasn't, I was looking for him and I wasn't looking for him. I had a kind of half the way feeling that he wouldn't be up here. I know him pretty well and he's — walks around, you know, and thinks and thinks and thinks and — maybe it'll take him two or three weeks an' all of a sudden he — he'll walk in the house [*laughs*] — "Let's go see — so and so." [*nervous laughter*] He's a — he's a lot like I am — we're all the same, I guess. He probably — read the letter and — probably never said very much, walked out, forgot about it [*laughing nervously*] then all of a sudden it dawned on 'im [*nervous laughter*] and, ah, that's ah, that's about the size of it, as far as that goes. And uh, uh, so as I say, I [*pause*] I wouldn't be, I wasn't — too overly disappointed when he, when he didn't, ah, ah, ah, ah, *answer* it or come to see me. He probably will yet. [*laughs*] I'm an optimist, I always have been, he'll probably come and visit me some day. Maybe he'll come and let me go down there 'n' live. Maybe he won't, won't make much difference [*laughs*] one way or another.

T: Hmm. You can sort of — [*C:* Yeah] take things as they come. [*brightly*]

Example 2

C: [*sighs*] [*near hysteria throughout*] — Sometimes I get pressure in my head, and that's when I — *just* — lose control of myself — I can't —

T: You don't hardly know what you're doing at those times, is that it?

C: No, I don't!

T: It isn't your fault, is that the way it feels, what you're doing [*pause*] when you're like that?

C: [*with exasperation*] Yes, that's the way it is, it — it's been that way ever since I was a kid, I don't know why — I wanted to be normal like other kids, and I *tried hard but* — [*silence*] I went down to my sister's and it was a regular nut house down there, I couldn't work. I had good jobs working at the hotel — as a hostess — and I might just as well have been here, it was such a nut house. And my brother made us— [*silence*] But, I've been *threatened* with this place, ever since I was a kid. They come to take me once but my dad wouldn't let 'em. [*silence*] I mean it was such an upsetting home all of the time, and my brother said he'd go to the judge, and when I was 29, they'd take me. *I lived in fear all the time!* [*pause*] I *went to church* and I *tried to read the Bible,* and to — *pray* and — I took care of children. And a — and my dad would always say mean things to my mother and I tried to help and do what I could but— [*silence*] [*sighs*]

Stage 3

The therapist indicates a positive caring for the patient or client but it is a semi-possessive caring in the sense that he communicates to the client that what the client does, or does not do, matters to him. That is, he communicates such things as "it is not all right if you act immorally," "I want you to get along at work," or "It's important to me that you get along with the ward staff." The therapist sees himself responsible *for* the client.

Example 1

C: I still, you sorta hate to give up something that you know that you've — made something out of, and, and, uh, in fact, it amounts to, uh, at least, uh, what you would, uh earn working for somebody else, so —

T: [*enthusiastically*] O.K. What, well, eh, why don't — why don't we do it this way? That, uh, I'll kind of give you some homework to do. [*laughs*] And when you're going home these weekends, um, really talk to your wife and, ah, think yourself about *pretty specific possibilities* for you, considering what [*C:* Yeah] — some working on this in earnest. [*C:* Yeah.] And not just talk plans —

C: [*interrupting*] Well, I actually, I'd almost feel gettin' out right away but I, somethin' sort of holds me back, yet the season isn't — there [*T:* Uh-huh] and I don't know if it's good for me or not [*T:* Uh-huh] but I, ah —

T: O.K., but at least this next couple of months we can use in — *trying* at least to set something up or, or —

C: 'Cuz I feel that I, I don't know, I — feel I just want to do things again [*T:* M-hm] uh, 'cuz the longer you stay away from work, I was just reading about that psychologist James here the other day, an' it seems like if once you get into things and work, you feel better [*T:* Sure] and you don't, uh, it seems like, uh, the further you stay away from things, eh, you well, ah, you sorta think about it, put it that way.

T: M-hm. O.K. So, ah — in our thinking about it, though, that next few weeks, let's get closer to the doing of them. O.K.? [*warmly*]

C: Well, yes, that's — what —

T: Sound O.K. to you?

C: Yes. It sounds O.K. to me.

T: Good enough. [*amiably*]

Example 2

C: It's gettin' so I can't even — can't even sleep at night anymore — roll and toss all, toss all night long —

T: Pretty upset?

C: Oh, well, just lay there and think of everything — and some of the guys that come in after I did. There, there's some of them guys what of gone home, 'n' I'm still in here.

T: It's sort of up to you when you, as to when you go.

C: You can't do anything?

T: Well, I said, I sort of feel you have been — ah — you've been holding down that job — you still work in the kitchen, don't ya?

C: Yeah — [*mumbled*]

T: O.K., but you — you been holding that job, and you have your card, well, O.K. You fouled up somewhere, but you'll have your card again. And, well, you, in a sense showed the staff that you can handle these things, without getting into difficulties, *you* are on your way *home*.

C: That doggone kitchen detail, detail — seven cents a day — just ta scribble a bunch of junk. [*mumbled*]

T: Well, you're sure as hell not gonna get rich on it. — What about this trouble, talking about money — what about this trouble you were raising the last time? About borrowing some money from this gal, have you come to any decision on that?

C: Well [*pause*] I'd rather not say, I ain't gonna say nothin' as long as that tape recorder's on.

T: Want me to turn it off for a while? — It's a part of the project. That's why I sort of feel it's your responsibility to — to record these things.

Stage 4

The therapist clearly communicates a very deep interest and concern for the welfare of the patient. The therapist communicates a nonevaluative and unconditional positive regard to the client in almost all areas of his functioning. Thus, although there remains some conditionality in the more personally and private areas, the patient is given freedom to be himself and to be liked as himself. Thus, evaluations of thoughts and behaviors are for the most part absent. In deeply personal areas, however, the therapist may be conditional so that he communicates to the client that the client may act in any way he wishes except that it is important to the therapist that he be more mature or that he not regress in therapy or that the therapist himself is accepted and liked. In all other areas, however, unconditional positive regard is communicated. The therapist sees himself as responsible *to* the client.

Example 1

T: By — showing you that or trying to show you that — it isn't lack of things to talk about but it's, uh [*pause*] as far as I'm concerned your being unable to find something to talk about [*pause*] is the only, uh, a part of your inability to see me as a person — that you want to see — that uh —

C: You think it's wrong for me to see you as a doctor rather than a person?

T: Oh, no, no, I didn't mean that. Uh [*pause*] no, uh — no, what I meant was — that your inability, the fact there's nothing for you to talk about as far as you can judge. [*coughs*] All this means is you don't want to get close to me.

C: No, it doesn't mean that. No, you're mistaken about it. — It only means just what it says. [*curtly*]

T: Well, let me ask you, ah — would you object to getting close to me? Becoming, ah, friendly with me? Have *me* interested in *you?*

C: Why should I *object* to that?

T: I don't know. Would you?

C: No — [*pause*] But, how am *I* supposed to know, uh, what to say or what we should talk about that would accomplish that end?

T: Well, I don't know. Do you have trouble meeting friends, making friends on the, uh, outside?

C: What?

T: Do you have trouble making friends on the outside?

C: Trouble making friends? Is that what you're assuming about me?

T: I'm asking you, do you?

C: [*coughs*] No, I don't believe so. [*pause*] I have no trouble making friends.

T: O.K. Well, then, I expect you'd know what to say to someone, and how to talk to someone with whom you wanted to make friends, with whom you wanted to become close.

C: Well, of course the obvious thing is that we should — ask each other about — well, probably — *personal* matters.

T: O.K. — well, ask me about a personal matter. [*quietly*]

C: That and there again I question what good that does — There again, I'm, I'm apparently, you, you see me as — well, apparently you must think I'm [*pause*] somehow unable to see what, what to you m–must be more obvious. That, that *can* do some kind of good, but that I can't, but I just can't see it. I don't, I don't see how it can be used.

T: M-hm — Yeah, I know that. That's the kind of *damning* thing about this whole — attempt, as I see it. [*pause*] Becau — I — I just — uh, kinda get that feeling [*Client inhales and expels breath noisily*] for you it's a dead certainty that there's just no *point* in — getting friendly or trying to talk about anything 'cause there's nothing I can do for you. [*warmly*]

Example 2

T: One thing that occurs to me is I'm so glad you came. I was afraid you wouldn't come. [*pause*] I had everything prepared, but I was afraid you wouldn't come. [*pause*]

C: What — would you have thought of me then? — I guess maybe I shouldn't have, but I did anyway. [*rapidly*]

T: Is that — like saying, "Why or what?" But, partly you feel — maybe you shouldn't have come — or don't *know* if you shouldn't or "not should." There's something about — feeling bad that could make you — not want to come. I don't know if I got that right, but [*pause*] because if you feel *very* bad then — then, I don't know. Is there anything in that?

C: Well — I've told you before, I mean, you know, two things that, when I feel bad. I mean one that always — I feel that there's a possibility, I suppose, that, you know, that they might put me back in the hospital for getting that bad.

T: Oh, I'd completely forgotten about that, yeah — yet, and that's one thing. — But there is *another*?

C: Yeah, I already told you that, too.

T: Oh, yeah, you sure did — I'd forgotten about it — and the other you've already said, too?

C: I'm sure I *did* tell it. [*pause*]

T: It doesn't come. All I have when I try to think of it is just the general sense that if you feel — very bad, then it's hard or unpleasant to — but, I don't know — So I may have forgotten something — must have. [*pause*]

C: You talk — you always, hear what I'm saying now, are so good at evading me, you always end up making me talk anyway [T: You're right] and say what I'm saying.

T: You're right.

C: You always comment on the question or something, and it just doesn't tell me.

T: [*interrupting*] Right, I just instinctively came back — to you when I wondered — what I, well, felt like saying, because — that's what I felt like saying. You mean to — you mean to say that a few minutes ago we had decided that *I* would talk —

C: Well, you — you mentioned it, but [T: Right] that's as far as it got.

T: You're right — and I just — was thinking of what you're asking — I'm more interested in you right now than anything else.

Stage 5

At stage 5, the therapist communicates unconditional positive regard without restriction. There is a deep respect for the patient's worth as a person and his rights as a free individual. At this level the patient is free to be himself even if this means that he is regressing, being defensive, or even disliking or rejecting the therapist himself. At this stage the therapist cares deeply for the patient as a person but it does not matter to him in which way the patient may himself choose to behave. There is a caring for and a prizing of the patient for his human potentials. This genuine and deep caring is uncontaminated by evaluations of his behavior or his thoughts. There is a willingness to equally share the patient's joys and aspirations or his depressions and failures. The only channeling by the therapist may be the demand that the patient communicate personally relevant material.

Example 1

C: . . . ever recovering to the extent where I could become self-supporting and live alone. I thought that I was doomed to hospitalization for the rest of my life and seeing some of the people over in, in the main building, some of those old people who are, who need a lot of attention and all that sort of thing, is the only picture I could see of my own future. Just one of [*T:* M-hm] complete hopelessness, that there was any —

T: [*interrupting*] You didn't see any hope at all, did you?

C: Not, not in the least. I thought no one *really* cared and I didn't care myself, and I seriously — uh — thought of suicide; if there'd been any way that I could be sure that I could end it all *completely* and not become just a, a burden or an extra care, I would have committed suicide, I was that low. I didn't want to live. In fact, I hoped that I — I would go to sleep at night and not wake up, because I, I really felt there was nothing to live for — [*T, very softly:* Uh-huh.] Now, I, I truly believe that this drug they are giving me helps me a lot, I think, I think it is one drug that really does me *good*.

T: M-hm. But you say [name] that, that during that time you, you felt as though no one at all cared, as to what [*C:* That's right] what happened to you.

C: And, not only that, but I hated *myself* so that I didn't, I, I felt that I didn't *deserve* to have anyone care for me. I hated myself so that I, I, I not only felt that no one did, but I didn't see any reason why they *should*.

T: I guess that makes some sense to me now. I was wondering why it was that you were shutting other people off. You weren't *letting* anyone else care.

C: I didn't think I was *worth* caring for.

T: So you didn't ev — maybe you not only thought you were — hopeless, but you wouldn't allow people — [*Therapist's statement is drowned out by Client.*]

C: [*interrupting and very loud*] I closed the door on everyone. Yeah, I closed the door on everyone because I thought I just wasn't worth *bothering* with. I didn't think it was worthwhile for *you* to bother with me. "Just let me alone and — and let me rot that's all I'm worth." I mean, that was my thought. And I, I, uh, will frankly admit that when the doctors were making the rounds on the ward, I mean the *routine* rounds, I tried to be where they wouldn't see me. The doctor often goes there on the ward and asks how everyone is and when she'd get about to me, I'd move to a spot that she'd already covered —

T: You really avoided people.

C: So that, so that she wouldn't, uh, *talk* with me [*T:* M-hm] and when — the few times that I refused to see you, it was for the same reason. I didn't think I was worth bothering with, so why waste your time — let's just —

T: Let me ask you, ask you something about that. Do you think it would have been, uh, better if I had insisted that, uh, uh, you come and talk with me?

C: No, I don't believe so, Doctor. [*They speak simultaneously.*]

T: I wondered about that; I wasn't sure. [*softly*]

C: I don't — I, I, I . . . .

Example 2

T: "And I can sort of sense — *and when you want to,* when you feel like it, I'd be glad if you shared some of those —

C: What? [*abruptly*]

T: I said, when you want to, and when you feel like it, I'd be glad if you shared some of those feelings with me — [*Client, breaking in and speaking with Therapist:* Why, why — whoa, whoa, whoa —] I'd like to just sort of see 'm —

C: Why, you gettin' rich off this silent character or somep'n or what? [*raucous laughing sound*] Ten, fifteen, twenty dollars an hour? [*loudly*] Then he just sits here — an' that's it, huh? Oh, I know — [*mumbling*]

T: I'd say that's — that's a good point — what ya mean — [*softly*]

C: Oh, I don't know — [*pause*]

T: Well, that — uh, makes me say something stupid — uh [*laughs*] — I sometimes get paid fifteen, twenty dollars an hour, but that, I'm not getting paid —

C: [*interrupting loudly, overtalking Therapist*] Why, the state's paying ya that now, ain't they?

T: Not for you, no. I thought you might think that.

C: Who is, then? [*insistently*]

T: No, I get a salary from the University for doing research. [*calmly*]

C: Oh — *research!* [*incredulously*]

T: M-hm— [*pause*]

C: I think that's just a — roundabout way to put it — th–that's what, that's what I think.

T: Well, let's put it this way: I get it, but — I get exactly the same salary whether — I see you or not. [*gently*]

C: Oh, there, there probably is a — there probably is a — that type doctors there, but — uh, but I wouldn't call it *research!* [*scornfully*] — I, I, I, I, I, I, I don't know, I don' know, I don' care — I don' — I — [*ending in angry confusion*]

T: [*speaking with conviction*] Well, I'd like to *know you* — that, that's not research.

Appendix B.3. A Scale for the Rating of Congruence

Donald J. Kiesler

Dimension

Rate the degree to which the therapist communicates, honestly and without artificiality, his feelings toward the client at the moment of their occurrence in the interaction. The therapist's feelings or opinions about the client arise from the client's behavior at the moment—his verbalization about a particular topic, his voice quality or posture.

When the therapist is being *more* congruent he tells the client exactly how he feels about him at the time. When he is being *less* congruent he avoids communicating his exact feelings toward the client by the use of professional artificiality—by using clichés in a neutral or flat voice tone, without spontaneity; by the use of very abstract statements which fail to communicate; or simply by reflecting the client's own feelings. When the therapist is not being congruent *at all,* his communication to the client clearly contradicts his feelings toward him. In being incongruent, the therapist is presenting, knowingly or unknowingly, a façade to deceive the client about the therapist's feelings.

Stages

Stage 1

There is clear evidence of a discrepancy between the therapist's experiencing of the client and his current communication. The therapist contradicts the content of his verbalization with the voice qualities or nonverbal cues which are evident.

1. From the therapist's voice quality it seems evident he is irritated or disgusted with the client, or strongly attracted to the client, but he attempts to deny this by expressing the opposite or neutral feelings.
2. Nonverbally, it seems evident the therapist is uneasy, perplexed, or frustrated by the current interaction, but he attempts to deny it, or express the opposite feeling, i.e., that he is composed and in control.

Stage 2

The therapist communicates information to the client in response to the client's questioning, but his response has a phony, deceptive, or "half-truth" quality. The therapist does not speak openly and easily, but seems to be hedging, or covering up areas of ignorance, or avoiding revealing professional "secrets." There is a definite uneasiness and forced quality to his voice tone and pacing. He is not expressing accurately his uneasiness about not possessing the information the client wants, but is rather trying to express the picture of composure to the client, when this is not the case.

Stage 3

The therapist does not contradict his feelings about the client, but neither does he communicate his exact feelings toward the client. He is thus neither congruent nor incongruent, but *a*congruent.

1. The therapist may reflect or attempt to clarify what the client has said.
2. The therapist may respond in an artificial manner by the use of psychological or psychiatric clichés, or by habitual responses like "uh-huh," or "I guess what you mean is . . ."
3. The therapist may respond in a manner which is conceptually appropriate to the interaction, but with a flat or neutral voice quality, as though he were "miles away"—with no enthusiasm, intensity or spontaneity.
4. The therapist may ask the client for more information about the area being discussed.

Stage 4

The therapist communicates information to the client, either spontaneously or in response to the client's questioning, rather than withholding it for personal or professional reasons. The client may ask the therapist about mental illness generally, or some specific aspect of mental illness, about employment, about institutions or people known to both. The therapist communicates the information he has as well as he can. He speaks openly and easily, admits areas of ignorance, and is definitely not attempting to give the client information about which he is unsure. There is no attempt to fool the client.

Stage 5

The therapist communicates openly and freely his feelings, both positive and negative, about the client at a given moment—without traces of defensiveness, or retreat into professionalism.

1. Nonverbally, it seems evident the therapist is experiencing either positive or negative feelings toward the client, and he expresses these feelings. Instead of simply reflecting back the client's verbalizations, the therapist communicates that this is the way he has experienced the client at the moment.
2. Nonverbally, it seems evident the therapist is experiencing uneasiness, perplexity, or frustration in the current interaction and verbally expresses these feelings to the client.

Ways in Which Therapist Congruence May Appear

The momentary opportunities for the appearance of congruence can be: (1) the client's asking the therapist *directly* about his feelings or opinions of the client; (2) the client's implying *indirectly* that he would like to know what the therapist thinks or feels about him; (3) the client's implying directly or indirectly that the therapist's past behavior is unsatisfactory to the client; or (4) the therapist's spontaneous comments about his feelings toward the client.

Here are some examples of how a client might directly ask the therapist for his feelings about him:

How do you really feel about me?

Do you understand what I am saying?

Do you think I'll ever get out of the hospital?

How do you think I am progressing?

A client might indirectly ask for the therapist's feelings toward him in the following ways:

It would be nice to know someone actually cared about me.

Sometimes I wonder if I will ever get out of the hospital.

Sometimes I wonder if everyone thinks I am phony.

It would be nice to know that someone, anyone, really understood me.

The client might imply that the therapist's past behavior was unsatisfactory to him by saying:

I feel there should be some conversation on your part.

I wish I could find a way to make myself understood.

A therapist might spontaneously express his feelings toward the client by saying:

Today, I really feel good just talking to you.

I feel somewhat depressed that this is our last meeting.

The Rating Task

Only rarely will the therapist spontaneously elaborate on his exact feelings toward the client. It is your task to judge, in most cases, whether or not the therapist actually deceives the client about his feelings toward him when there is evidence that the client wants to know the therapist's feelings or wants to know some type of information. The following are situations for which you must make a judgment:

1. When the *client asks* directly or indirectly *for the therapist's feelings* toward him, the therapist's response should be judged a *1*, incongruent, if he seems to contradict his feelings. If the therapist reflects the client's asking back to him, or responds in a flat voice quality with a cliché, his response should be judged a *3*, neither congruent nor incongruent. If the therapist gives, openly and freely, his feelings to the client, the response should be judged a *5*, congruent.

2. If the *client asks for information* from the therapist, the therapist's response should be judged a *2*, inaccurate or partial information, if he seems to be deceiving the client. It should be judged a *3*, neither congruent or incongruent, if the therapist simply reflects the question back to the client by saying, for example, "I suppose you really would like to know . . ." The therapist's response should be judged a *4*, accurate information, if he seems to give the client, freely, as much of his knowledge of a subject as the client wanted.

3. When the *therapist reflects, spontaneously,* the client's previous verbalizations, simply goes along with him, attempting to understand, or uses professional clichés, or speaks in a neutral voice, the therapist's response should be judged a *3*, neither congruent nor incongruent.

4. The *therapist may on his own initiative express attitudes* about the client. If there is evidence he is deceiving the client, his response should be judged a *1*, incongruent, or a *5*, congruent, if he seems to be communicating honestly his exact feelings.

5. The *therapist may also spontaneously,* without questioning by the client, *communicate information* to him. If the communication of information seems free and open the response should be judged a *4*, accurate information, and, if not, it should be judged a *2*, inaccurate information, or incongruence on the therapist's part about not possessing the information, or about withholding information for personal or professional reasons.

APPENDIX C

Rating Scales for Therapeutic Process

The Process Scales: An Introduction

Carl R. Rogers

The four scales which follow are scales devised for measuring process level (degree of involvement in the process of change) and process movement (change in this level) during the course of therapy. It is believed that a word of introduction may be helpful.

The initial conception of a process scale by Rogers (1958) was brought into an operational form by Rogers and Rablen in "A Scale of Process in Psychotherapy"[1] (1958). This scale, and those which follow, have the purpose of providing an objectified instrument by which the level of therapeutic process in selected samples of interview material may be evaluated. The scales represent an abbreviated outline of the process continuum as it has been described in previous writings (Rogers, 1959, 1961). They encompass a broad range of interrelated behaviors which constitute the "stuff" of which psychotherapeutic interaction is made. In essence each scale represents a continuum of psychological activity which commences at one end with a rigid, static, undifferentiated, and impersonal type of psychological functioning and which evolves through distinctive stages to a level of functioning characterized by changingness, fluidity, and rich and immediate experiencing of personal feelings which are felt as deeply owned and accepted.

Behavior Samples Appropriate for the Scales

To the potential user of the process scales a word or two needs to be said about the experiential context from which the process conception and the process scales were derived and from which our rated examples have been obtained. A fundamental characteristic of our interview materials is that they represent samples of expressive behavior taken from situations in which there is an "acceptant atmosphere." From the standpoint of the therapist they have been settings in which the intent has been to provide an atmosphere of open, genuine, and unreserved acceptance of the client as a total person. From the client standpoint they have been settings in which the client has, in general, been able to experience the acceptance by the therapist of what has been expressed

1. This scale is obtainable at cost from the Western Behavioral Sciences Institute, 1121 Torrey Pines Road, La Jolla, California, 92037. Its distribution is limited to those interested in making research use of it.

up to the present moment (even though he may feel that what he will say next may not be acceptable to the therapist). It is our belief that those developments described in the process conception and in the process scales will be most readily observable in situations in which provision is made for this basic experiential context of acceptance. It appears likely that in atmospheres characterized by lesser acceptance or by threat, the expressive behavior of the individual will exhibit characteristics of a lower stage on the process scales than behavior drawn from an acceptant atmosphere. Hence if one is planning to use these process scales it should be kept in mind that they apply only to expressive behavior which has occurred in a situation in which the individual feels himself to be accepted.

It is hoped that these introductory remarks will help to place the four scales which follow in a suitable context.

References

ROGERS, C. R. A process conception of psychotherapy. *Amer. Psychologist. 13*:142–149, 1958.

ROGERS, C. R. A process conception of psychotherapy. Carl R. Rogers, *On Becoming a Person.* Boston: Houghton Mifflin, 1961, chapter VII (amplified version of above reference).

ROGERS, C. R. A tentative scale for the measurement of process in psychotherapy. In E. A. Rubinstein and M. B. Parloff (eds.), *Research in Psychotherapy,* Vol. I. Washington, D.C.: American Psychological Association, 1959, pp. 96–107.

ROGERS, C. R., and RABLEN, R. A. *A Scale of Process in Psychotherapy.* Mimeographed manual. University of Wisconsin, 1958.

Appendix C.1. A Scale for the Rating of Experiencing

Eugene T. Gendlin and T. M. Tomlinson
Revised by Philippa L. Mathieu and Marjorie H. Klein

Summary Rating Sheet

Process Rating Scale for Psychotherapeutic Interviews: *Experiencing Dimension*. The degree to which the client manifests inward reference in his verbalizations. The client is referring inwardly when he is referring to his own feelings and reactions—when he is searching for the meaning of the personal events, feelings, and ideas he is reporting.

Freedom to move among feelings and their significance from an experiential frame of reference.	7. The client does not need a narrative as a point of departure. He can travel freely among feelings and understands them quickly. The client has no difficulty in tying together what he is saying and presenting a clear picture of himself—what meaning his thoughts, actions and feelings have for him. He moves easily from one inward reference to another and is able to integrate them into his experiential frame of reference.	———
Able to arrive at a conclusion based on insight into the significance of his feelings.	6. Feelings become content. If there are situational associations they are understood in terms of the personal significance of the feelings associated with them.	———
Defines a problem in terms of feelings and attempts to explore this.	5. Exploration of (*a*) one situation or aspect of self-image involving many feelings and their potential relationship, or one feeling area (if well described) and its personal significance; (*b*) many situations examined in terms of the common feelings or significance involved.	———

Person communicates what it is like to *be* him.	4. Several ways it can be *4:* Either fluid expression of many feelings, or expression of one feeling and time spent elaborating on it in terms of the significance for self-image; or a specific expression of the fact that the feelings exist, but that help is required to express them.	————
Affective involvement *does* go beyond specific content but *passes by* deeper meanings.	3. Expressions of personal and "owned" feelings used as parenthetical comments to a narrative. Personal feelings are still (*a*) tied completely to situations in which they arise, or (*b*) unelaborated in terms of deeper personal meaning or significance.	————
Ownership of personal role in narrative.	2. Personal reference used to clarify that it is clearly *his* story.	————
No personal involvements.	1. No personal reference used. Narrative of events describing what amounts to a public picture. Denial or refusal of personal involvement.	————

Rater ————
Segment No. ————

Code √ = peak rating
x = modal rating

Stages

Stage 1

There is simply a narrative of events with no personal referent used. The client may be telling a story that he is connected with in some way but he does not use himself as a reference point—he says nothing about himself, or of his feelings, attitudes, or reactions. The story told is not "his" story.

If a personal referent is used, the content is such that the client reveals nothing private or tender about himself but merely describes the public aspects of his life. The manner of expression would tend to be matter of fact or to have a rehearsed quality.

Stage 2

The client establishes the association between the narrative told and himself by the use of personal referents, but he is involved in telling the story and does not go beyond it. Any comments he offers about the story do not contain personal reference but function only to "get the story across." Any emotions mentioned are described as part of the story, not the client, and are not elaborated beyond the level of pure description. There is no personal "ownership" of a reaction to the story.

The manner of expression at this stage may be less mechanical and more spontaneous than at stage 1. In some cases, however, the client may seem to be emotionally aroused or involved, but the level of this arousal will remain constant throughout and will not be referred to specifically.

Stage 3

The client is primarily involved in telling a story in which personal referents are used. He goes beyond the story at times to make parenthetical comments about his reactions and responses, but these associations are based on the external events only. Such comments can be an account of his feelings about the story, his feelings at the time of the events described, or comments about the personal significance of the events to him. These parenthetical comments must contain personal referents. The person's focus is upon telling his story "better" or elaborating upon it, but he does not use the story to show what he is like as a person.

Stage 4

The client is now clearly telling something about himself (his feelings, his image of himself), using himself as the referent for his comments. While these comments may be made in the context of a specific story, their function is not to modify the story but to *describe the self*. In some cases, the client may have great difficulty finding ways to describe himself and the expression of this difficulty alone is sufficient basis to rate *4*.

The client is now aware of his feelings and reactions and is able to express them. He is doing this in order to communicate what he is like; he is not engaged in a struggle to explore himself nor is he using his feelings as the basis for self-understanding.

Stage 5

The client is now using his feelings in a struggle to explore himself.

This may take one of several directions. The client may start with his feelings in a given area and work to understand these feelings, to differentiate them, or to understand how and in what situations they arise. The client may also start with some assumption he has about himself and work to understand how this assumption came about or clarify the implications that this assumption has for him.

The client at stage 5 is clearly engaged in a process of self-exploration in order to achieve self-understanding; this process may be extremely difficult for the client and may not be maintained throughout the segment. The expression of difficulty in achieving self-understanding is sufficient basis to rate 5 as long as the client is able to express and elaborate his feelings or to present clearly his self-image (as in stage 4).

Stage 6

The client is clearly examining the significance of his feelings or self-concept and is able to arrive at conclusions about them, or to use the results of this self-assessment as the point of departure for further self-exploration. His formulations about himself provide the links between any elaborations of events or expressions of feeling. In stage 6 the client is able to use the results of self-examination in specific areas to arrive at a deeper and more comprehensive self-understanding.

Stage 7

The client does not need a narrative as a point of departure. He can travel freely among feelings and understands them quickly. The client has no difficulty in tying together what he is saying and presenting a clear picture of himself—what meaning his thoughts, actions, and feelings have for him. He moves easily from one inward reference to another and is able to integrate them into his experiential frame of reference.

Appendix C.2. A Scale for the Rating of Personal Constructs

T. M. Tomlinson

Stages

Stage 1

The nature of the client's communication is such that no constructs (attitudes, beliefs, etc.) about either himself, others, or external situations, are reported. The client's verbalization is banal, trite, and irrelevant, e.g., he discusses the weather, baseball, etc., but nothing of a personally meaningful nature. The attitudes expressed are inconsequential in the determination of the nature of his construct system.

The client conveys the impression that he either can't, or does not want to, disclose his beliefs, attitudes, ideas, etc., to the therapist.

Indications

1. Much silence neither preceded nor followed by personally meaningful communication about attitudes, etc.
2. Inconsequential attitudes are expressed in which it is apparent that there is little self-involvement. The issues discussed have nothing to do with the present position of the client, e.g., weather, baseball, cars, the quality of hospital food, etc.
3. The entire tenor of the client's communication suggests he is simply trying to pass time and has no intention of expressing feelings about any but the most shallow and meaningless issues.

Stage 2

Personal constructs are extremely rigid, unrecognized as constructs, and thought of as external facts.

The individual seems unaware that the meaning imputed to his experience has come from himself and is not necessarily inherent in the situation. To him the meanings of external situations are facts, not experience subject to different interpretations.

Indications

1. Statements, particularly those expressing value judgments, are made in absolute, undifferentiated global terms.

2. The expressed constructs will for the most part be confined to external situations. Seldom will constructs about himself be verbalized. Sometimes the individual will make statements in which he tries in an objective remote fashion to characterize himself or his life; these statements seem to have the intent of placing the individual in a context which can be defined in terms of externals such as historical time, geographical place, and objectified (absolute) moral values.
3. The individual seems to place himself apart from external situations. He expresses attitudes about externals in a rigid way but fails to perceive his connection to these externals in that it is *his attitudes* that have defined the situation, not any characteristics inherent in the situation.
4. The interpretations of external events are seen in black or white terms. Things cannot or couldn't be interpreted differently because things "are just this way."

Stage 3

Personal constructs are still extremely rigid, but the person's construal of external events now includes some references to himself. His talk is not confined solely to external situations but may involve the effects external situations have had on him and he may detail his response to these external situations.

Indications

1. The client may appear to be justifying his position. He seems to be defending his perception of his environment and his reactions to it. To do this he may try to enlist the aid of the therapist, e.g., by asking the therapist to confirm his perception of his experience.
2. The client may appear to be clinging to his constructs "for dear life." The quality of his verbalization is such as to suggest that the client is saying, in effect, "this (the way I see things) has just got to be correct," but at some, as yet unacknowledged and unaccepted but implicitly evident level, he seems to doubt this.
3. The client may attempt to justify his present position (construct system) by describing external situations, other people's attitudes, behavior, etc., which are like his own. He is in effect saying to the therapist, "You see, they do it too, and if other people's behavior is like mine then mine must be O.K." The client enlists this external behavior in support of his interpretations of experience, without regard for the context of his present situation and the ways in which it might consequently differ from his descriptions of other's behavior. In short he force-fits other situations and behavior into his own

construct system to provide support for his interpretations of his experience.

Stage 4

Personal constructs are rigid but at times the client will indicate verbally, or in his approach to his experience, that he recognizes the possibility that his perception may not be, or was not, correct.

Occasionally he may verbally, or in his approach to understanding his experience, question the validity of a construct. The form taken of the questioning is more likely to be a recognition of *possible* "errors" in interpretation of experience rather than suggesting that a different approach could have been taken.

Indications

1. As the client recounts his behavior he conveys the impression that he is beginning to see how he construed his experience through his own eyes, rather than with a blind acceptance of events and situations as external facts having no relation to himself.
2. Here the verbalizations have more of the flavor of "explanations" for behavior. He is not so much trying to *justify* his behavior as he is seeking to help himself and the therapist *understand* how he saw or sees things.
3. There is a general feeling of unhappiness about his interpretations of experience.
4. He may identify characteristic ways of behaving in different situations, e.g., "I must punish myself," or "I was always the pacifier." The above ways of behaving are global and undifferentiated, but differ from stage 2 behavior in that they are constructs about the *self, not externals.*

Stage 5

There is a beginning loosening of personal constructs. With some frequency it is discovered that experience has been construed as having a certain meaning but that this meaning is not inherent, absolute, nor externally valid at all times. There is a questioning of the validity of some present constructs, organizations of experience, and meanings and feelings.

Indications

1. Increasingly there is a discussion of specific, self constructs rather than global ones as found in stages 2 and 3, e.g., within the global construct "I must punish myself," the client details specific behavior

and specific ways he saw things, and he begins to ask himself why he saw things the way he did.

2. The client's verbalization suggests that he is quite aware of the way he has construed his experience. The significant feature is his awareness of the inappropriateness of his approach to his experience, i.e., his questioning of the validity of his interpretation of the events which compose experience.

3. This stage may be characterized as one in which the client reinterprets his experience but doesn't reformulate it. He expresses his awareness that he saw things in a certain way and he is aware that his experience could have been interpreted differently, but he's not at all sure of just how. He is in the process of dropping old constructs, but he has not as yet substituted different, more appropriate ones.

Stage 6

There is a more or less continuous loosening of constructs as the client realizes that many constructs which have seemed to be solid guides are only ways of construing a moment of experiencing. The difference between this stage and stage 5 is that in addition to continued loosening of constructs there is tentative "commitment" to new constructs. The client recognizes these new ways of construing experience are more appropriate, realistic, etc., ways of construing himself and events.

Indications

1. Here the client is often clearly able to contrast his past constructs with his new and different ways of interpreting his experience. He seems to have discovered that he doesn't *have* to behave in a certain way, that there are alternative interpretations for experience and he is sharply aware of the difference between past and present constructs. Further, he is able to describe the alternatives. He not only questions validity but also makes "recommendations" for change. He perceives clearly *how* and *what* he could or can do differently.

2. The new constructs are tentative, as if he is afraid to give up completely the old ways of construing his experience. The flavor is sort of "it could be this way, if I let it."

3. Often the dissolving of old constructs will have an impelling immediacy about it. The client might say something like, "My God, all my life I've behaved like this, and it wasn't necessary." The quality is one of immediate fresh discovery coupled with the feeling that this is experience which means something—it's the *right* way to see things.

Stage 7

Experience is tentatively construed as having a certain meaning but this meaning is always held loosely and is checked and rechecked against further experiencing.

Indications

1. The client seems to realize that even these new constructs, right as they seem to be, can be held loosely and are subject to constant reinterpretation in accord with different experience. He can predict his own behavior only by knowing the events which compose the situation in which the behavior occurs.
2. The client will explore at length the meaning of his new constructs, making changes when appropriate and making minor, fresh discoveries within the framework of the new construct. These minor discoveries may be about past experiences reinterpreted in light of new constructs or they may be amendments to the new constructs in light of present experience.
3. The quickness of change of constructs (minor) indicates the looseness of the present major construct. It is open to constant reinterpretation and amendment.

Appendix C.3. A Scale for Rating the Manner of Problem Expression

Ferdinand van der Veen and T. M. Tomlinson

This is a scale that describes the way a person specifically talks about his problems. It is not a sickness-health scale. Healthy persons can be at any stage on the scale, depending upon what they say about their problems.

Different stages on the scale refer to distinctly different ways of verbalizing or talking about problems. There are two criteria, one positive (Y) and one negative (N), for each stage except the first and last which have only one. The negative criterion in one stage becomes the positive criterion for the next stage, so that successive stages are mutually exclusive.

The total scale uses six objective indices for the criteria. These are: talking (not talking) about a problem (A); talking (not talking) about own direct involvement (B); talking (not talking) about own reactions (C); talking (not talking) about own contribution (D); talking (not talking) about own understanding of self (E); and talking (not talking) about actual resolution (F). The client is given the highest rating that most accurately fits the particular selection, taking the whole selection into account. The scale is intended to be cumulative so a selection should not be rated at a certain stage unless the positive criteria for the stages below it are at least implicitly present in the segment.[1]

Definitions

1. "Direct involvement" (in B): The client includes himself in the problem situation as he describes the problem. This means being a part of a situation in a specific manner as opposed to a general state of affairs that has no specific effect on the actions of the individual. The latter would suggest either *no* involvement or *indirect* involvement.

2. "Own reaction" (in C): The client talks about his own feelings or behavior in reaction to the problem.

1. A *Rater's Guide to the Problem Expression Scale* has been prepared by H. Kenneth Bobele, Graduate School of Business Administration, University of California, Los Angeles.

3. "Contribution" (in D): Refers to the part played by the individual in making the problem.

4. "Understanding" (in E): Refers to the client's talking about his comprehension of the meaning of his own feelings, reactions, and behavior. The client may indicate that he understands them a little or a great deal, but it doesn't matter how much. What is important is that he is talking about his understanding of himself.

5. "Actual" (in F): Means that the client talks about a resolution that, for him, has really occurred or is occurring.

Stages

Stage 1

AN   The individual *does not talk about* problems, i.e., wrongs, difficulties, confusions, conflicts, complaints, etc.

Stage 2

AY   The individual *talks about* problems or problem situations.
and
BN   The individual *does not talk about* his direct involvement in a problem situation or event.

Stage 3

BY   The individual *talks about* his direct involvement in a problem situation or event.
and
CN   The individual *does not talk about* his own reactions in or to the problem situation.

Stage 4

CY   The individual *talks about* his own reaction in or to the problem situation.
and
DN   The individual *does not talk about* the contribution of his own reactions to the problem.

Stage 5

DY   The individual *talks about* the contribution of his own reactions to the problem.
and
EN   The individual *does not talk about* his own understanding of his feelings, experiences, or attitudes.

Stage 6

EY   The individual *talks about* his own understanding of his feelings, experiences, or attitudes.

and

FN   The individual *does not talk about* an actual resolution of the problem situation in terms of changes in his feelings, experiences, or attitudes.

Stage 7

FY   The individual *talks about* an actual resolution of the problem situation in terms of changes in his feelings, experiences, or attitudes.

Rating Outline

If	Score
AN	1
AY and BN	2
BY and CN	3
CY and DN	4
DY and EN	5
EY and FN	6
FY	7

Score	Only if
1.5	Sample fits 1, except for a slight amount of AY
2.5	" " 2, " " " " " BY
3.5	" " 3, " " " " " CY
4.5	" " 4, " " " " " DY
5.5	" " 5, " " " " " EY
6.5	" " 6, " " " " " FY

Appendix C.4. A Scale for Rating the Manner of Relating[1]

Eugene T. Gendlin

Definitions

1. "Relationship quality" refers to explicit signs that the speaker considers at least one of the following to be the case:
   a. The relationship is *meaningful, important;* or it is desirable that the relationship be, or become, meaningful and important.
   b. It is appropriate to communicate *intimately* and *personally;* or it is desirable that it be, or become, appropriate to so communicate.
   c. There is *personal caring* in the relationship; or it is desirable that there be, or come to be, personal caring.
   d. The *intention* of the speaker is *a–c* above, and/or he assumes that intention in the other speaker.
2. "Expressed" relationship quality occurs when the speaker explicitly states something that amounts to *a–d* above.
3. "Assumed" relationship quality occurs when the speaker explicitly states something which does not itself amount to *a–d* above, but which would be inappropriate, meaningless, or absurd if he did not assume the relationship to be *a–d* above.
Note: Both expressed and assumed relationship quality refer to definite explicit signs. The rater must be able to point to such signs.
4. "Non-parallel" relationship quality occurs when one person expresses a widely different relationship quality than the other.

Stages

Stage 1: Refusal of a Relationship

There are definite indications that the individual *refuses* a relationship, and refuses or does not perceive the *likelihood or desirability* of a close personal relationship.

Indications

1. The individual may overtly argue against the desirability or usefulness of a therapy relationship or of "talking," or of "meeting," or of

1. Half-stage ratings may not be used in this scale.

603

"next time." He may indicate clearly that he wishes to leave, to come no more times, to be left alone.

2. He may make explicit an attitude of, "O.K., so you force me to be here. I'll just sit," or "I have nothing to talk about."

3. He may indicate clearly that he fears a relationship, that he is not trusting the therapist enough to talk genuinely to him, or that he suspects him of something. If this occurs, it must be clear (in stage 1) that he has no intention of sharing his real feelings concerning his fear or mistrust. He shows them, perhaps he says as much, but not in a confiding way, and he does not continue to expand them.

4. He may discuss "psychotherapy" for himself in the distant sense of its general nature and its general applicability to people like himself —that is to say, he quite definitely avoids engaging the therapist directly, or sharing with him any actual feelings concerning himself and his troubles or the present interview. He may discuss those who sent him to psychotherapy (the doctors, his wife, boss, dean, etc.) and whether they are right or wrong. If so, he does not discuss these things in terms of his own troubled feelings or the events of his life, but in terms of the general nature of people who need psychotherapy, and of his arguments with others.

5. Silences are preceded or followed by cues that indicate that during the silence the individual has *not* been exploring himself or been thinking about how to approach the therapist or the interview. Rather, the cues indicate that he has kept silent to demonstrate that he has nothing to say and wants to say nothing, and that this is his clearest expression of what he feels about the possibility of a relationship: it is not possible or not desirable.

General instructions for rating stage 1.—For stage 1 there must be *definite indications* of the individual's refusal of a relationship (or his lack of a sense of the desirability of one). To rate stage 1 you must be able to point to some phrases or behavior which, in your opinion, definitely indicate this.

In stage 1 the individual has no perspective on his refusal of a relationship. He does not work it through or share it. He acts it out or states it summarily.

Stage 2: Physical Acceptance of a Relationship without Overt Acceptance

The individual in stage 2 does not reject the relationship overtly, but he also gives *no sign* that he accepts its desirability or possible intimacy.

Indications

1. The individual does not respond to corroborate the therapist's relationship quality. This may happen if the therapist responds in ways that *state* or *assume* a desirable relationship. (For example, the therapist may speak so as to respond to the individual's deeper or more personal feelings in a way that assumes that the individual *intends* to share these. Or, the therapist may offer his personal response to the individual or to something he has said—thus assuming that there is a relationship in which personal responses are appropriate or desirable. The therapist may express care or concern. The therapist may state the commitment he feels to the relationship or that he will continue to see the individual as long as needed, etc. The therapist may express a desire to get to know the individual better—or may state some impression or question about him which assumes a wanting to get to know him better, or a desire to understand better what he just then said or felt, or the therapist may assume this desire to be appropriate and simply ask the individual to make it clearer.)

Note that these different therapist behaviors all either *state* or *assume* that there is a relationship of personal interest, intimacy, and sharing—or at least that such a relationship is desirable. Both stated and assumed (see Definition 3) relationship qualities must refer to specific behavior to which you can point.

In response to any of these therapist behaviors, the individual *never* corroborates the stated or assumed *relationship quality* (Definition 1. *a–d*, p. 603) He does not specifically and overtly reject or fight it, but he does not corroborate it. He either continues as if it had not happened, or keeps silent, or states something which indicates that he has misunderstood, avoided, or ignored it, or treated it as something casual.

Such non-corroboration is noticeable in the "non-parallel" nature of the interchanges. The therapist statements are left hanging with his stated or assumed relationship of sharing while the individual's response each time is casual or avoidant or oblivious. One is embarrassed for the therapist as one listens. In stage 2, whenever the therapist response states or assumes the existence or desirability of a sharing and personally meaningful relationship, this non-parallel responding appears.

Stage 2 behavior can be different than described above when the therapist does not behave so as to state or definitely assume such a relationship quality. Therefore, the following indications are also included in stage 2:

2. Whereas some therapists frequently attempt to state or assume meaningful relationship quality, other therapists do so only rarely, spending most of the time going along with trivial communication, like polite social listeners. Even such therapists, however, do occasionally attempt a deeper, more personal or more personally understanding response. While during the long stretches of trivial talk the two individuals may sound "parallel," the "non-parallel" quality will be noticeable whenever the therapist does attempt a more personal response. Thus, this usually trivial and parallel communication is rated stage 2 provided the touchstone for stage 2 fits. The touchstone still is the same: non-parallel interchange whenever anything of a relationship quality does appear.

3. At stage 2 the individual is not using the relationship (or its desirability and possibility) to project himself directly into it. The individual may ignore the therapist (except for trivial therapist statements). He may also employ behaviors which engage the therapist's role as only authority, without thereby engaging the therapist. For example, the following behaviors, if they constitute most of a segment, and if they are not personally charged and meaningful fit stage 2:

    a) asking the therapist for the answer, the standard;

    b) asking the therapist to ask questions so that individuals will know what to talk about;

    c) expecting the therapist to indicate how the individual should behave in the interview;

    d) asking the therapist to explain what therapy is.

When these behaviors are a meaningful vehicle, a higher stage interaction can be occurring. Usually, however, they indicate that the individual is not relating himself to the therapist's person, but only to the therapist's authority role.

4. Silences will be accompanied before and after by verbalization indicating that the silence is neither a stubborn "There is nothing I want or need to say," nor an exploration of self or approaches to the situation. Rather, the cues will indicate that the silence was simply a lapse, a "nothing" (when asked what he was thinking, the response would be something like "nothing"). Although we do not believe that silences contain "nothing," that is all that is explicitly indicated. Or, the silences will turn out to have been about trivialities ("I was listening to the noises outside."). Or, the topic discussed before silence, and the topic in the post-silence statement may relate (or divert) in such a way that it is clear that no exploration needs to have happened in between.

General instructions for rating stage 2.—The individual does not overtly reject, fight, or devalue the relationship or its desirability. There is evidence, however, that he does not put himself into relationship either. At stage 2 a therapist might comment after the meeting, "At least he comes to the hour," or "The fact that he comes at all seems to have some real meaning to him." This will be said in the sense that, except for this he is not visibly putting himself into the relationship.

Whenever the therapist tries to make the relationship into something established, or tries to give it a more sharing or concerned character, or assumes these, the individual's lack of corroboration for these therapist meanings will be obvious (non-parallel). At other times there will be trivial parallel interchange.

Example, Stage 2

C: What the heck is a guy supposed to talk about at these meetings, these hours, ah — not me, ah er —

T: Seems to me for a while there — you were thinking of — some things that are important to you — maybe couldn't say or —

C: *What?* [*loudly*]

T: Something like that.

C: I was thinking of things?

T: I don't know. I was sitting here guessing what you were thinking but, it felt to me like you were more — things or feeling or something that — maybe it was just that I was wondering what you *were* feeling.

C: Oh, I don't know. There isn't much to talk about.

T: Seems to me the things that are important are hard to talk about.

C: Oh, they ain't hard, to, ain't nothing hard to talk about.

T: Feel hard to talk about —

C: *What?* [*loudly*]

T: Hard to talk about something. Can't yet — to me anyway.

Stage 3: Partial Acceptance of Relationship Quality or Intermittent Parallel Relationship Quality

At stage 3 there are indications *both* of corroboration of relationship quality, *and* of non-parallel or non-corroborating responses. That is, stage 3 is always characterized by indications—in the one brief sample to be rated—that sometimes and on some level, relationship quality *is* occurring and being corroborated, while, however, other moments or other signs indicate the opposite.

Indications

1. Even in one brief segment there are both parallel and non-parallel interchanges. The individual, at least once, clearly corroborates that,

yes, there is a relationship, or that the therapist's statement is important to him, or importantly true, or that the time spent does have much meaning, or that the question of talking deeply to the therapist is a meaningful issue, or that some things are difficult to talk about but he might like to, or might not like to. On the other hand, also in the same brief segment, there will be at least one interchange in which a total non-acceptance of these "relationship assumptions" is shown. For instance one of the individuals may deny, hint at the falseness of, or misunderstand the other individual's assumptions of, a relationship quality (Definition 1. *a–d,* p. 603).

The intermittent nature of the interchange is striking and consistent. One has just about decided that these two people understand each other very deeply when some remark will completely offset that impression and seem to indicate that — "Why — these two people do not understand each other *at all* — they can't have been talking about the same things in the same sense."

2. The individual does put himself into the relationship and interacts with stated or assumed relationship quality, but the therapist does not receive or corroborate the relationship quality. Here it is the therapist who is non-parallel, avoidant, casual, oblivious, or misunderstanding. This condition may persist throughout a segment, or it may be intermittent. It is never resolved or clarified.

3. The individual puts himself into the relationship and interacts with stated or assumed relationship quality, but the two persons misunderstand each other (intermittently or consistently) without resolution or clarification of the misunderstandings. A "mixed up" quality occurs, which may persist, or be left hanging without resolution.

4. Stage 3 may also be rated if there is only "qualified" acceptance of the relationship as a context in which the individual expresses himself. By "qualified" acceptance is meant that, while self-reporting may be smooth and while there may be no non-parallel responses, the individual holds himself back and out of the relationship, does not, of his own accord, express his real meanings, is hesitant, with one foot in and one foot out of relationship quality.

To rate on this indication, there must be definite indications of *some* relationship quality, and there must also be definite indications of the *lack* of an established relationship context for self-expression.

General instructions for rating stage 3.—At stage 3 there are definite indications of relationship quality on the part of the individual, yet there are definite indications *also,* that relationship quality between the two individuals is not established. This may happen in four ways (cues of stage 3):

intermittency
therapist non-parallelism
unresolved misunderstandings
qualified acceptance of relationship quality.

Stage 4: Parallel and Together, the Relationship as a Context of Therapy

The two persons are quite together in what they are doing, what they assume is happening, the importance and value of the meetings and interchanges, and the implicit purpose of each moment's interaction. When there are non-parallel interchanges, both persons assume that these are momentary unclarities which will be straightened out in the next moment. There are none of the persistent events which do occur in stage 3, that one has been entirely mistaken and these two people do not "get" each other at all. Instead there is the sense of an ongoing togetherness in basic assumptions of meaning, intent, and desirable intimacy, from moment to moment.

Rating instructions for stage 4.—The two individuals now share the same stated and assumed relationship quality. There may still be occasional silences rather than corroborations, but there are none of the intermittent or constant non-parallel or "mix-up" events in which one person denies, avoids, or does not receive the other person's meaningful communications.

This smooth parallel together quality, of course, concerns some communications of some meaning, intimacy, personal quality, or shared self (otherwise it is stage 2) but so long as some degree of meaning exists, the content depth is not to be evaluated by the rater.

In stage 4 the individual does live in the relationship and relates his personal expressiveness directly to the therapist. His relationship is the context in which he behaves as he does. Whatever the therapist may do or not do, the individual himself now acts and moves the relationship continuously.

Stage 5: The Relationship as Specific Therapy, Rather Than Only as General Context for Therapy

At stage 5 specific relationship events indicate a greater use of relationship than 4. The individual employs the relationship *both* as in stage 4, *and* in new ways. Stage 5 must fit stage 4 in that both individuals explicitly show that they assume the relationship to be one of sharing, intimacy, personal and self-focused or other's self-focused communication. Even when the relationship is disturbed and troubled, when there are conflicts, etc., these are "worked on" or shared, and both persons perceive them as significant and possibly valuable. Thus, stage

5 is *at least* 4, *and* the following:

Indications

1. Specific indications that the therapist's presence or participation affects not only the given momentary events, but also the global manner of the individual's experiencing. Such statements as "Only here . . ." or, "Only with you . . ." *followed by descriptions of some inward state or process* are examples. The individual explicitly says, or makes quite clear, that the therapist's presence in the relationship is not only the overall context for his expressions, or that a particular response clarifies or vivifies something, but also that the therapist's presence affects the very nature of his self, or inward process.

2. Specific behaviors in which the individual seeks the therapist out personally and engages him in the workings of his therapeutic process —these being events of the interaction, and their significance for the therapeutic process is recognized by the individual, or their importance to him is explicit.

3. Battles or conflicts can be included if they do not shake the sense that each knows what the other means (or soon comes to know), i.e., that both communicate within a "parallel" or "together" context of personal interaction (*otherwise it is stage 3 or below*) and if it is not an argument (verbal, intellectual content, difference of opinion or interpretation) which, even if meaningful and personal, and "parallel" and "together" would be rated stage 4. Thus, only those battles and conflicts which involve stage 5 as it has been described, i.e., events of interaction (rather than argument) *perceived by the individual as significant* are rated stage 5.

4. Silence, at stage 5, would be preceded or followed by explicit statements that during the silence some inward process has occurred which is personally vital to the individual and could not happen except with the therapist's presence.

General instructions for rating stage 5.—Stage 5 includes the "parallel" or "together" relationship quality of stage 4 but adds to that, specific interactional events which the individual indicates as significant to him in his personal processes of therapy.

Stage 6: The Relationship Is Ready to Be a Permanent Reality and Therefore Could Be Approaching Termination

At stage 6 the individual is still in therapy (the scale applies to therapy behavior). Nevertheless, the relationship has become such that it need not be "worked through" further. If there are "working through" explorations specifically concerning the relationship (that is to say, aspects of the relationship which are unresolved) then they concern termination. However, since termination discussions can occur at any stage, the following cues determine stage 6.

Indications

1. Strong positive feelings for the therapist now are *not* explosively needful or conflict-raising. Neither person expresses a need to better understand, eliminate, alter, explore, or suspect these feelings before successful termination is possible. There are no inappropriate feelings, that is, whatever his feelings are, the individual holds them in a way that requires no inappropriate or impossible behavior, and termination would have no disruptive consequences for him.

   Feelings toward the therapist are of the kind which the individual can well take with him into life without therapy.

   (The above two cues mean that there is definitely not a single indication to the contrary, to which you can point. If there is, then the individual must be rated at stages 5, 4, etc., since issues of this kind arise at many stages).

2. The relationship is person to person. Although the professional role of the therapist may be implicit, it does not inhibit the personal feeling between the two individuals. (No definite signs that it does.)

3. The person to person quality is not worked for. It simply is there, without the strain of self-examining surprise that might attend person-to-person feelings in stage 5.

4. The individual's self which he may express in words shows definite indications that stages 4 and 5 have been gone through. Such definite indications might be:

   a) explicit statements concerning earlier therapy events,

   b) private vocabulary between *T* and *C* which they both know and which definitely concerns stage 5 events,

   c) statements concerning the relationship indicative explicitly of therapist was essential at one time to the new self, but is not now.

General instructions for rating stage 6.—You cannot and should not guess when therapy will be successfully over. Stage 6 is a stage of therapy and could continue for a long time. Do not be concerned with therapeutic content, since this is a relationship scale.

At least one of the above must be definitely indicated (you must be able to point to at least a phrase or interaction that indicates it) and none of the above indications can be contradicted by any sign.

INDEX

Index

DATE DUE